God of Sense
Traditions of Non

God of Sense and Traditions of Non-Sense

Sigve K. Tonstad

WIPF & STOCK · Eugene, Oregon

GOD OF SENSE AND TRADITIONS OF NON-SENSE

Copyright © 2016 Sigve K. Tonstad. All rights reserved. Except for brief quotations in critical publications or reviews, no part of this book may be reproduced in any manner without prior written permission from the publisher. Write: Permissions. Wipf and Stock Publishers, 199 W. 8th Ave., Suite 3, Eugene, OR 97401.

Wipf & Stock
An Imprint of Wipf and Stock Publishers
199 W. 8th Ave., Suite 3
Eugene, OR 97401

www.wipfandstock.com

PAPERBACK ISBN: 978-1-4982-3313-2
HARDCOVER ISBN: 978-1-4982-3315-6

Manufactured in the U.S.A. 01/18/2016

Permissions

Scripture quotations are from the New Revised Standard Version Bible, copyright © 1989 National Council of the Churches of Christ in the United States of America. Used by permission. All rights reserved. Unless otherwise noted, all scriptural quotations are from the NRSV.

"Written in Pencil in the Sealed Railway Car" in Pagis, Dan, *The Selected Poetry of Dan Pagis*. © 1989 by the Regents of the University of California. Published by the University of California Press. Used by permission.

"Shema" in Levi, Primo, *Collected Poems* © 1992 by Faber & Faber. Used by permission.

Cover illustration: William Blake (1757–1827), "Job Rebuked by His Friends." Property of The Morgan Library & Museum, 225 Madison Avenue, NY 10016. Used by permission.

Illustrations

Chapter 6

Paradise by Lucas Cranach the Elder (1472–1553) Copyright Kunshistorisches Museum, Wien. Used by permission.

Chapter 7

The Body of Abel Found by Adam and Eve by William Blake. Copyright Tate Gallery, London. Used by permission.

Chapter 14

Elihu Speaking to Job and His Friends by William Blake. Copyright Virginia Museum of Fine Arts. Used by permission.

Chapter 17

Apostle Paul by Rembrandt Harmensz van Rijn (1606–69). Copyright Kunshistorisches Museum, Wien. Used by permission.

Chapter 21

First trumpet in Revelation: thunder, lightning hail, fire, and blood, burning grass and trees (sent down by six devils in a cloud). MS 49, The Apocalypse. Wellcome Library, London. Used by permission.

To the Memory of
William H. Hardt Jr.

Contents

Part III
The Sense of the Ending

Acknowledgments

This book has many mothers and fathers and—I am happy to say—quite a few friends. For the rough contours of the book, I owe the most to the late A. Graham Maxwell who preceded me at Loma Linda University and whose teaching left a lasting influence on more than one generation of students and professionals. Before him are earlier influences in my life, especially the late Jens K. Jensen and Carsten A. Johnsen, and my first teacher in biblical languages, J. Bjørnar Storfjell. From the time I got immersed in earnest in biblical scholarship, I am most indebted to John Jones at La Sierra University, Richard B. Hays at Duke University, and to Bruce W. Longenecker and Richard J. Bauckham at the University of St. Andrews. They have in various ways taught me the value of careful exegesis and of listening to textual whispers that hurried readings are likely to miss. As to people I have only met through books, I owe the most to the many writers who experienced the Holocaust of the twentieth century and lived to tell about it. I have read their works with the deepest respect, and this book bears the imprint of their voices.

I am also indebted to the many students I have met at Loma Linda University for their interest and for feedback that has helped me hone the material in important ways. These students cannot all be named, but I owe special gratitude to Kyle Morawski, Aaron Branch, Matthew Perkins, Monica Ball, David Jasperse, Kelsey and Cody Ryan, David Huber, Nathan King, Jonathan Mayhew, Michael Wozny, Barry Howe, Marlen Pajini, Lynette Emerson, Hayley Hunt, Kindra Landrith, Leanna Marderian Wise, Kevin Kim, Ziphecinhe Ncube, Chelsi Green, Jessica Beatty, Jonathan Burden, and Samuel Hitz. These students are mentioned for their interest and contributions—and some for actually agreeing with me. Many of them have or will have their careers in medicine, and I can only vaguely imagine all the good that they are doing and will do. The students not named here must know that they are not forgotten.

Lately, friends have come forward with substantive material support in the form of means and editorial help. The value of this to someone teaching at an institution where a heavy teaching load and limited resources are a given cannot be expressed. I wish to thank Bud Racine for what he has done by way of financial support, Olivia Seheult for organizing it, and my friend and colleague Bernard Taylor for editorial help. The assistance of a seasoned editor who is a world expert in biblical languages has been of inestimable value.

Of people who have offered advice and encouragement along the way, special thanks go to my wife Serena, to Yaroslav Paliy in Moscow (Russia), to Dragutin Matak in Croatia, to Anthony MacPherson in Australia, and to Jon Paulien, Dave Larson, Henry Lamberton, and the late Roy Branson at my institution. Roy's sudden death happened just as I was reaching the finishing line, and his enthusiasm and joy in the work of others will be deeply missed. Farzaneh Alemozaffar at the Interlibrary Loan service has countless times provided needed material with the utmost grace and speed. I am very grateful to the team at Wipf and Stock for accepting my book for publication and for refining it in the process, with special thanks to Robin Parry, my first contact, and to Matthew Wimer, Brian Palmer, and Calvin Jaffarian.

Fifteen years ago I published the little book *The Scandals of the Bible* in the United Kingdom, a less ambitious attempt to address issues that are here explored in much greater depth. The keenest reader of that book was William H. Hardt Jr, outstanding physician, exceptional human being, and wonderful friend. He had read the *Scandals* at least five times and knew portions by heart even though my little book was only a tiny item in his pilgrimage of ministry and meaning. I had the pain and the privilege of spending precious time with Billy the last two years of his life, discussing many items in *God of Sense* with him until he succumbed to cancer in 2009. I dedicate this book to his memory.

Abbreviations

AB	Anchor Bible Commentary
AJT	*Asia Journal of Theology*
AnBib	Analecta Biblica
ANSE	*Annual of the Society of Christian Ethics*
ANF	*Ante-Nicene Fathers*
ATR	*Anglican Theological Review*
AUSS	*Andrews University Seminary Studies*
BBC	Blackwell Biblical Commentaries
BBR	*Bulletin for Biblical Research*
BDAG	*Greek-English Lexicon of the New Testament and Other Early Christian Literature*, ed. W. Bauer, F. W. Danker, W. F. Arndt, F. W. Gingrich.
BETL	Bibliotheca ephemeridum theologicarum lovaniensum
BI	*Biblical Interpretation*
Bib	*Biblica*
BibSac	*Bibliotheca Sacra*
BK	*Bibel und Kirche*
BKAT	Biblischer Kommentar Altes Testament
BNTC	Black's New Testament Commentary
BR	*Bible Review*
BT	*Bible Translator*
BTB	*Biblical Theology Bulletin*
BZAW	Beihefte zur *Zeitschrift für die alttestamentliche Wissenschaft*
BZNW	Beihefte zur *Zeitschrift für die neutestamentliche Wissenschaft*
CBQ	*Catholic Biblical Quarterly*
CBC	Cambridge Bible Commentary
CC	Continental Commentary
ChrLit	*Christianity and Literature*
ConcC	Concordia Commentary

CSR	*Christian Scholar's Review*
CV	*Communio viatorum*
DCLY	Deuterocanonical and Cognate Literature Yearbook
DRev	*Downside Review*
EKKNT	Evangelisch-katholischer Kommentar zum Neuen Testament
ERT	*Evangelical Review of Theology*
EstBib	*Estudios Biblicos*
ETL	*Ephemerides theologicae lovanienses*
ETR	*Etudes théologiques et religieuses*
ExpTim	*Expository Times*
EQ	*Evangelical Quarterly*
FAT	Forschungen zum Alten Testament
FC	Fathers of the Church
FP	*Faith and Philosophy*
GNB	Good News Bible
HBT	*Horizons in Biblical Theology*
HNT	Handbuch zum Neuen Testament
HTR	*Harvard Theological Review*
HTS	*Hervormde teologiese studies*
HUCA	*Hebrew Union College Annual*
ICC	International Critical Commentary
IJST	*International Journal of Systematic Theology*
Int	*Interpretation*
IRM	*International Review of Mission*
IST	Issues in Systematic Theology
JAAR	*Journal of the American Academy of Religion*
JASP	*Journal of Abnormal and Social Psychology*
JBL	*Journal of Biblical Literature*
JBQ	*Jewish Bible Quarterly*
JECS	*Journal of Early Christian Studies*
JETS	*Journal of the Evangelical Theological Society*
JITC	*Journal of the Interdenominational Theological Center*
JLR	*Journal of Law and Religion*
JPJ	*Journal of Progressive Judaism*
JQR	*Jewish Quarterly Review*
JRE	*Journal of Religious Ethics*
JSNT	*Journal for the Study of the New Testament*
JSJ Sup	Supplements to the Journal for the Study of Judaism

JSNT Sup	Journal for the Study of the New Testament Supplement Series
JSOT Sup	Journal for the Study of the Old Testament Supplement Series
JSOT	*Journal for the Study of the Old Testament*
JSP	*Journal for the Study of the Pseudepigrapha*
JTS	*Journal of Theological Studies*
JTSA	*Journal of Theology for Southern Africa*
KJV	King James Version
LNTS	Library of New Testament Studies
LTE	Library of Theological Ethics
LTJ	*Lutheran Theological Journal*
LW	*Luther's Works*
LXX	Septuagint
MNTC	Moffat New Testament Commentary
Mod Theol	*Modern Theology*
NASB	New American Standard Bible
NCBC	New Century Bible
NICNT	New International Commentary on the New Testament
NIGTC	New International Greek Testament Commentary
NIRV	New International Reader's Version
NIV	New International Version
NJB	New Jerusalem Bible
NKJV	New King James Version
NLT	New Living Translation
NovT	*Novum Testamentum*
NovTSup	Novum Testamentum Supplement
NPNF	Nicene and Post-Nicene Fathers
NRSV	New Revised Standard Version
NSBT	New Studies in Biblical Theology
NSCE	New Studies in Christian Ethics
NTL	New Testament Library
NTM	New Testament Message
NTS	*New Testament Studies*
NTT	New Testament Theology
OBT	Overtures to Biblical Theology
OTS	Old Testament Studies
OWC	Oxford World's Classics
PG	J.-P. Migne, *Patrologia Graeca*
PRS	*Perspectives in Religious Studies*

RB	*Revue biblique*
RevExp	*Review and Expositor*
RHPR	*Revue d'histoire et de philosophie religieuses*
RHR	*Revue de l'histoire des religions*
RSB	*Religious Studies Bulletin*
SBAL	Studies in Biblical Apocalyptic Literature
SBB	Stuttgarter biblische Beiträge
SBL	Society of Biblical Literature
SBLSP	*Society of Biblical Literature Seminar Papers*
SBLDS	Society of Biblical Literature Dissertation Series
SBLMS	Society of Biblical Literature Monograph Series
SBLSP	*Society of Biblical Literature Seminar Papers*
SHBC	Smyth and Helwys Bible Commentary
SJOT	*Scandinavian Journal of the Old Testament*
SJT	*Scottish Journal of Theology*
SNTSMS	Society for New Testament Studies Monograph Series
ST	*Studia Theologica*
TB	*Theologische Blätter*
TDNT	*Theological Dictionary of the New Testament*, ed. G. Kittel and G. Friedrich
TDOT	*Theological Dictionary of the Old Testament*, ed. J. Botterweck, H. Ringgren and H.-J. Fabry
TU	Texte und Untersuchungen
TWOT	*Theological Wordbook of the Old Testament*
TynBul	*Tyndale Bulletin*
TZ	*Theologische Zeitschrift*
VT	*Vetus Testamentum*
VTSup	Vetus Testamentum Supplements
WBC	Word Biblical Commentary
WTJ	*Westminster Theological Journal*
WUNT	Wissenschaftliche Untersuchungen zum Neuen Testament
WW	*Word & World*
ZAW	*Zeitschrift für die alttestamentliche Wissenschaft*
ZK	*Zeitschrift für Kirchengeschichte*
ZNW	*Zeitschrift für die neutestamentliche Wissenschaft*
ZTK	*Zeitschrift für Theologie und Kirche*

Prologue

In the dark of night on November 26, 1942, one hundred taxis lined up on Church Street, one of the main streets of Oslo, the capital of Norway and the country of my birth. Ready, too, were three hundred armed men, three men for each taxi, each group led by a policeman. At about five o'clock in the morning the signal was given to deploy. The taxis fanned out in the city, most of them headed to the city center, every one of them going to apartments and homes inhabited by Jewish individuals or families. The lightning action yielded the prescribed result. Just before three o'clock in the afternoon the same day the German ship Donau left the Oslo harbor, carrying 302 Jewish men, 188 women, and 42 children. The ship arrived at the Polish city Szczecin in the afternoon of November 30 after a difficult passage in rough seas. A train made up of cargo wagons was waiting for them, the men and the women now being separated. The train arrived at Auschwitz—Oswiecim in Polish—late in the evening of December 1, less than one week after its human cargo had left Oslo. The women and the children were forced into the 'little white house' and ordered to undress, from there driven naked and barefoot in sub-zero temperatures into the gas chamber. "Every single child and every woman who were sent with the Donau, were murdered that night," writes Marte Michelet. "188 women and 42 children."[1]

We know there were many more.

The Holocaust is an event of the past, to some belonging to a past that already seems remote, but it remains very much present. First-hand testimonies of that time are still appearing, one of the most riveting ever published during the year of this writing,[2] and several others are still not well known.[3] Only now are we granted access to accounts that are comprehensive in their sweep, and relentless in exposing the forces and factors that made the massacre possible,[4] and only now are we given meticulously-researched biographies of some of the individuals who took the lead in the greatest atrocity on record.[5] We are not likely ever to reach the point where

1. Michelet, *Den største forbrytelsen* [*The Greatest Crime*], 242.
2. Kulka, *Landscapes of the Metropolis of Death* (2014).
3. Hillesum, *An Interrupted Life* (1996); Klemperer, *I Will Bear Witness* (1999).
4. Friedländer, *The Years of Extermination* (2008); Ibid., *The Years of Persecution* (1999).
5. Stagneth, *Eichmann Before Jerusalem* (2014).

attention to the subject will seem redundant or out of touch. The "now" of the Holocaust promises to last indefinitely.

Even more important, the Holocaust is history's most excruciating exhibit of the problem of evil, on the one hand, and God's apparent absence, on the other. For that reason it is also the reality concerning which the quest for *sense* comes up short most acutely. This book treats the Holocaust as an existential and theological problem and not only as a chilling historical event. When I approach the subject under the title *God of Sense and Traditions of Non-Sense*, I am not proposing to make sense of the Holocaust. Evil that is Holocaust-sized shall remain a subject in the face of which we shall swallow uneasily and choose to speak few words. And yet the subject cannot be avoided or be treated dismissively. It must be taken on as a theological obligation; indeed, as the most insistent among theological obligations—and more insistent because it exposes theological sins of commission and many still unacknowledged sins of omission. This book may to some extent be seen as a response to Primo Levi's summons in his post-Holocaust version of the *Shema* (Deut 6:4–9). Levi survived Auschwitz to become one of its keenest low-key chroniclers until, seared by the memory, he ended his life at his own hand in 1987.[6] His poem begins by asking the reader to consider the man who labors in the mud and the woman who is without hair or name or strength to remember. The summons is left for the final stanza.

> Consider that this has been:
> I commend these words to you.
> Engrave them on your hearts
> When you are in your house, when you walk on your way,
> When you go to bed, when you rise.
> Repeat them to your children.
> Or may your house crumble,
> Disease render you powerless,
> Your offspring avert their faces from you.[7]

Thus summoned by a time- and reality-adjusted adaptation of the most hallowed confession of faith in the Old Testament, we are ready to begin. But where do we begin? I begin at the level of description (Chaps. 1 and 2). Description does not equal explanation, but there can be no explanation in the absence of faithful description. Already at this point the Bible comes in. For the task of descriptive adequacy, the Bible in general and the New Testament in particular bring to the table distinctive conceptual and rhetorical resources. What most philosophers and not a few theologians are content to describe as *human* evil, the New Testament will often ascribe to a *demonic* reality without thereby denying human agency. I shall argue—and put

6. Levi, *The Drowned and the Saved* (1989); *If This Is a Man* (1991); *Moments of Reprieve* (1995); *Survival in Auschwitz* (1996).

7. Levi, "Shema" (1992).

forward evidence to support it—that if notions of the demonic are in need of empirical proof, there is no need to dig deep into history to find them. It lies fully exposed on the surface in the twentieth century. Unlike Abel, the first victim of violence in the Bible, the victims of the Holocaust resist burial, and the horror that made them victims spurns the descriptive and explanatory means commonly put to use. To the extent that dismissal of the demonic used to be a sign of sophistication and intellectual maturity, the Holocaust has made it much less so. My assertion on this point will be bolstered by long-neglected insights from the writings of Origen (185–254), the most prolific early Christian apologist (Chap. 3), by New Testament conceptions of human reality (Chap. 4), and by the story of what Jesus *did not do* as that story is told allusively in Paul's letter to the Philippians (Chap. 5). These voices are distinctive for the way they perceive and describe evil as more than a human phenomenon, and they all set up what was and is the great paradox. Celsus, the pagan philosopher and implied target of Origen's apology, above, could not imagine a problem that cannot be solved by force. Origen and the biblical voices have less faith in what force can accomplish because they work from a completely different narrative. Celsus comes out swinging against the Christian outlook in the belief that Christians are simplistic while he is sophisticated and subtle, only to encounter in the soft-spoken Origen an answer that makes Celsus look simplistic and the Christians subtle (Chap. 3).

The first five chapters of the book are intended to be stage-setting. They acknowledge the problem of making sense, identify the relevant ontological elements, outline the plot, trace the threads in the biblical narrative, and, above all, they ponder the most challenging element in the emerging value system. Stated positively—though not necessarily approvingly—that value is freedom. Stated negatively, and still withholding judgment, freedom denotes the repudiation of coercion as a tool in the divine armamentarium. If the stage-setting part of the inquiry will not lead to a *God of Sense* in the sense that the important issues have been resolved, the reason shall not be that those who ask questions are walking a forbidden path (Chap. 1). *Sense*, at this stage at least, does not refer to what a thing means but to the resources we have by which to make meaning.

Section II offers bursts or glimpses of sense, every glimpse a biblical narrative carefully picked for the *sense* it brings to the overall subject. Most of the stories are chosen because they relate to key events or exceptional individuals in the Bible and are by that criterion alone self-selected. With Adam and Eve we have the story of the first choice (Chap. 6), with Cain and Abel the story of the first murder (Chap. 7), with Abraham the story of the first serious discussion with God (Chap. 8). These stories, in that order, shed light on the role of freedom, responsibility, and understanding in the divine economy. The "binding of Isaac" in Abraham's journey to the "Mount of Seeing" defies ordinary conceptions of sense, but it puts new resources and visions at the disposal of the imagination (Chap. 9). In the stories of Moses and Elijah we have more than inklings of a new sense, a movement *away* from a theology of power, shock, and awe to a view of God that has more whisper and less thunder (Chaps. 10 and 12). The new sense matures further by the role Moses and Elijah are given in the New Testament. The Book of Job is a suffering person's quest for sense and, as I intend to show, a quest that is amply rewarded (Chap. 14). When Jesus takes the stage (Chaps. 15 and 16), the sense he offers cannot be understood apart from the Old Testament stories we have looked at so far, especially the story of Adam and Eve in Genesis. Where Old Testament stories point the way to a *God of Sense*, however, the New Testament claims that Jesus brings the divine sense to completion. The last word, as it were, belongs to him. The outliers in this section are the story of the rape of the concubine in the Book of Judges (Chap. 11) and the story of the two prophets in 1 Kings 13 (Chap. 13). The unnamed woman in Judges is arguably the Bible's most alarming example of divine non-intervention and thus a biblical embodiment of the most pressing theological problem after the Holocaust. The two prophets in 1 Kings 13 expose the danger of unquestioning obedience to authority, or, stated differently, the problem of *faith* in the absence of *sense*. All the stories, some more than others, feature elements of divine non-intervention or intervention by means that are very different from what is expected. Absence of divine intervention and intervention by unexpected means are the pieces by which the Bible brings to view what I call a *God of Sense*.

In Section III, attention turns again to voices outside the Bible, first to Ivan Karamazov and his indictment of freedom in the "Poem of the Grand Inquisitor" (Chap. 18). Is it true, as Ivan claims, that freedom and love are incompatible? To Alyosha, Ivan's brother, the 'poem' is not an indictment at all but a tribute to Jesus; and to me, I shall admit, it is the answer to Ivan's creed of anguish. Inching closer to the twenty-first century, we turn to voices that represent *common sense* and *sense uncommon* (Chap. 19). The voices representing common sense are as diverse as Roger Williams and Mark Twain, New World individuals who took issue with traditions that lack compassion. The voice expressing *uncommon* sense is Etty Hillesum. Etty was executed at Auschwitz on November 30, 1943, almost exactly one year after the Jewish children from Oslo met the same fate there. She expresses biblical sentiments from within the Holocaust inferno, herself embodying a response to the problem of suffering that consists in action rather than explanation. Section III then turns to Revelation's vision of divine transparency, a stolen horse, (Chap. 20), and the sense of the ending in the same book (Chap. 21). What that sense is, or whether there is sense, has been a surprise to me as I am certain it will be even to seasoned readers of the last book in the Bible.

Why, then, the need to delineate a contrast? Why, as my title has it, *God of Sense* and *Traditions of Non-Sense*? The decision to pursue the contrast complicates the task, but the aim is to provide clarity and a corrective. For readers of the Bible in the twenty-first century, there is a need to carve out space for urgent questions against a theological tradition that massively denies their legitimacy. It is important to show that we are not only responding to the summons of Primo Levi's revised *Shema*, the summons arising from the ashes of genocide in the twentieth century. We are not forcing upon the Bible unwelcome, illegitimate, and anachronistic questions. On the contrary, we are primarily responding to the summons of the Bible, to questions raised *within* the Bible, and to biblical concerns concerning divine conduct that are as radical as any question brought up in secular literature. As noted already, if it should turn out that the Bible fails to deliver sense that is seen to be that in a way that is humanly meaningful, it does not do it by shutting down questions.

Influential readers of the Bible early on came to the conclusion that God prioritizes *faith* over *sense*. Faith was hailed as the right response to divine inscrutability, and divine inscrutability was a necessary inference from doctrines like election, on the one hand, and eternal torment, on the other. This tradition comes under tremendous pressure by the events that define the twentieth century. The Jewish historian Otto Dov Kulka waited to tell his childhood memory of Auschwitz until very late in life, calling his recollection *Landscapes of the Metropolis of Death*. In one such landscape he recalls how the Nazis maintained a "Family Camp" at Auschwitz, the chosen families inexplicably allowed to carry on semi-normal lives for up to six months. When the six months were up, the residents of the "Family Camp" were exterminated just like other camp inmates. In this corner of the camp, children attended school, played instruments, and performed plays. German officials would attend performances, one attendee of whom was the notorious Dr. Joseph Mengele. In one assignment, each group was assigned to present an imaginary future situation grounded in the Auschwitz reality, says Kulka. "I no longer remember all the shows in detail," he continues, "but I do remember those sarcasms, which both the children and the instructors understood well. Our group presented 'Heavenly Auschwitz—Earthly Auschwitz': as newcomers in Heaven, we discovered to our astonishment that in the world on high there were selections and there were crematoria."[8]

Arbitrary selections and crematoria—the scene imagined and performed by children in the "Family Camp" at Auschwitz—we had not heard that before! Common ground between "Earthly Auschwitz" and "Heavenly Auschwitz"? We shall not easily escape the irony and the anomaly. The heavenly crematoria, as the Christian tradition represents it, does not, like Auschwitz, allow the victim the relief that death brings. In awareness of the fact that this outlook is a key reason why Christian theologians felt duty bound to promote faith while at the same time calling off the quest for sense, the crumbling of this story line opens the gates to questions closed down by the tradition. For this reason the Holocaust is not only a challenge to theology; it could also be a remedy; it is not only an obligation but also an opportunity, the opportunity centering on the need to revisit and revise entrenched elements in the tradition.

My representation of elements in the tradition that are unfriendly to the quest for understanding is selective and does not aspire to be comprehensive. A comprehensive representation of the lives, work, and legacies of people like Augustine, Martin Luther, or Karl Barth would look different from the one given here and in many respects be admiring. Here, it has been my goal only to represent legacies faithfully on points

8. Kulka, *Metropolis of Death*, 20.

that matter to the present inquiry and to show reasons why the tradition in important respects is seriously off course.

Sense is in this book closely related to hope, but there is a reason why I have chosen to highlight the former. When the sense that the Bible brings to bear on human reality comes to light in the Book of Revelation (Chap. 21), the impact is so overwhelming that "there was silence in heaven for about half an hour" (Rev 8:1). That text, and others like it, is the destination of this book's story line. It comes in this Prologue with the advance notice that the silence in heaven signifies how intelligent beings respond to the revelation of a *God of Sense*. Perhaps the scene is not primarily meant to convey that what they have seen makes sense according to a prior measure of "sense." Instead, they have seen what the divine sense is—and thus the silence. Much more must be said before the reader will understand what I mean, and it has been laid out in the following pages. At this early stage of inquiry I shall settle for the modest claim that the Bible has resources with which to capture the experience of suffering from within, and the questions that go with it. Words, and being at a loss for words, are reflective of biblical and human reality alike. We have it here, in the words of Dan Pagis (1930–1986), in a poem "written in pencil in the sealed railway-car." Like Kulka, Pagis was a child of the concentration camps and, unlike the 42 children that came from Oslo to Auschwitz on December 1, 1942, a rare survivor.[9]

> here in this carload
> i am eve
> with abel my son
> if you see my other son
> cain son of man
> tell him that i

The poem comes to us like a postcard thrown from a moving train—many a last-minute postcard were thrown from sealed railroad cars during World War II—the implied author rendered speechless by the first murder and then by many more. Hearing the hushed summons in the card, I push my manuscript to the side, reach for an imaginary postcard, address it "to whom it may concern," and write in wobbly longhand,

> Here in this house
> I have read a card
> among caring friends
> If you see Eve
> and Abel and Cain
> tell them that we

9. Pagis, *Selected Poetry* (1989).

Part I

God and Sense

Chapter One

God of Sense and Traditions of Non-Sense

"Teach us what to say to God; our minds are blank; we have nothing to say. I won't ask to speak to God; why should I give him a chance to destroy me?" the young Elihu says to Job in one of the most startling books in literature (Job 37:19–20, GNB). The warning concludes Elihu's unscheduled speech, his punch line just before God gets the last word in the increasingly-heated exchange. Elihu's intrusion into the conversation, says the narrator, was triggered by the fact that Job's three friends "had found no answer [to Job], though they had declared Job to be in the wrong" (Job 32:3).[1]

After listening to the friends' futile attempt to silence Job, Elihu sets out to do better. While he expresses anger at Job's friends for their ineptitude, he is even angrier at Job. In his eyes Job has his priorities wrong, being more concerned about his own reputation than God's standing (32:2). Elihu's admonition is the final attempt to dissuade the ailing man from his insistence that God owes him an explanation for the calamities that have befallen him.

And Elihu does not mince words. In his closing missive, he cuts off at the feet the merits of Job's complaint, citing human incapacity even when it comes to knowing what to say (37:19). He rebukes Job for insisting on a meeting with God, denying legitimacy to a case that would be irreverent if not for the fact that Elihu has already deemed it incoherent (37:20a; cf. 23:3–6). Incoherence, indeed, could in Elihu's view well be the hallmark of human attempts to address God. "Our minds are blank; we have nothing to say" is a key tenet in the script Elihu places before Job to sign (Job 37:19). He is convinced that Job is so out of bounds that his insolence invites real danger. "Why should I give [God] a chance to destroy me?" he warns, hinting rather unsubtly that if God were to destroy Job it would be self-invited and well deserved (37:20b, GNB). To Elihu, divine transcendence, inscrutability, and sovereignty are the verities against which Job is banging his head. "The Almighty—we cannot find him; he is great in power and justice, and abundant righteousness he will not violate," he counsels (37:23). Job should cease and desist from his demand. "Those who are truly

1. Newsom, *Job*, 200–233 supports the view that Elihu is a later addition to Job, a "first commentary" by a "dissatisfied reader" of the book. Elihu's punch line presents a significant objection to this view by the fact that Job is granted the face-to-face audience with God that his friends and Elihu told him not to expect.

wise," according to Elihu, "know their limitations, and do not expect to be able to argue with God," says David Clines.[2]

Should Job leave it at that? Will he?

Elihu's outburst strikes a posture of newness, but the novelty comes chiefly in the form of bluster and rudeness. By way of content, there is little new in his speech over and above what Job's three friends have argued unsuccessfully throughout three cycles of poetic speeches. Elihu's concluding admonition serves as a summary of the arguments all four have brought to bear on Job, a consensus statement of the view they hold in contrast to Job's minority opinion. What that view is can be stated quite succinctly: Job should concede that his quest for understanding is futile and that he is, even at his best, only capable of speaking nonsense. Given that suffering is the problem for which Job seeks an explanation, this is the specific question concerning which he should retreat into respectful silence. To wring this admission from Job, Elihu and Job's friends are prepared to pay a high price. As we shall see in greater detail (Chap. 14), they are willing to commit to a theology of non-sense, urging Job to do the same (37:19–23).[3] The "nonsense" in question, lest we misunderstand, relates in this context to divine action that does not make sense, or the sense of which lies beyond human comprehension.

Looking at this conversation from the vantage point of history, there can be no doubt that Elihu's admonition has found resonance in the Christian theological tradition. Three examples must suffice for proof, examples that are nevertheless quite decisive because they represent the most influential voices in the history of Christian theology: Augustine, Martin Luther, and Karl Barth.

Augustine (354–430), my first example, echoes Elihu and not Job on the point that takes the basic measure of the divine-human relationship. In a letter to his friend and fellow bishop Simplician written in 397, Augustine says that God "decides who are to be offered mercy by a standard of equity which is most secret and far removed from human powers of understanding."[4] Wherein is the "nonsense" in this statement? Augustine is not claiming that the divine action has no logic but the logic cannot be understood by humans, and there is reason to think that it will never be understood. God's *modus operandi* defies human reason. Human incapacity, in turn, plays out in the context of divine inscrutability. Questioning must necessarily be futile if the questioner is incompetent and the one to whom the question is directed unfathomable! Roughly from that time onwards, Augustine defaults to the position expressed in Elihu's rebuke to Job. "God owes explanations to no one," Paula Fredriksen notes concerning Augustine's mature view on the subject.[5]

Martin Luther (1483–1546) held convictions very similar to Augustine with respect to human capacity and divine inscrutability. Job, we recall, faults God for

2. Clines, *Job 21–37*, 883.

3. See also Job 5:9; 11:7–8.

4. Augustine, *To Simplician*, 398.

5. Fredriksen, *Augustine and the Jews*, 278.

allowing a good man to suffer without giving an explanation. Luther ups the ante, arguing that God arbitrarily consigns humans to damnation and eternal suffering. Like Elihu and Augustine before him, Luther insists that no one should expect an explanation.

> This is the highest degree of faith, to believe him [God] merciful when he saves so few and damns so many, and to believe him righteous when by his own will he makes us necessarily damnable, so that he seems, according to Erasmus, to delight in the torments of the wretched and to be worthy of hatred rather than of love. If, then, I could by any means comprehend how this God can be merciful and just who displays so much wrath and iniquity, there would be no need of faith.[6]

This clip from Luther's debate with Erasmus promises even less by way of explanation for a belief that needs it more. Job looked to death as the remedy for his suffering, and he expressed sorrow that death did not come sooner (Job 3:11, 16). To Luther, by contrast, the perspective is suffering that even death is unable to relieve. He argues that eternal suffering is part of the divine design and that the choice between bliss and damnation is entirely God's prerogative. In order to keep questions at bay in the face of this belief, Luther deploys the twin argument of human incapacity and divine incomprehensibility in much the same way as Elihu. Faith, he says, is the antidote to human incomprehension, and submission the right attitude for anyone who might be tempted to take up a Job-like complaint against God. Human questions must reverentially come to a halt, either because there is no answer or because humans are not meant to know.

In the twentieth century, Karl Barth (1886–1968) relaunched a similar line of thought although his context and reasons were different from that of Augustine and Luther. In the second edition of his hugely influential commentary on Paul's letter to the Romans, Barth responds to critics who allege that there is a "system" in his interpretation that exceeds what Paul is saying in the text. Barth answers that if he has a "system," it is limited to "the 'infinite qualitative distinction' between time and eternity, and to my regarding this as possessing negative as well as positive significance: 'God is in heaven, and thou art on earth.'"[7]

This is not a new thought in light of the Christian tradition. On the contrary, there is broad agreement between Barth and Elihu with respect to human incapacity, on the one hand, and divine inscrutability, on the other. God can speak to human beings; humans can be spoken *to* by God, but humans cannot talk back to God. "God is in heaven, and thou art on earth," says Barth, implying that the first and the last word belongs to heaven (cf. Job 37:19–23). The human measure of reality becomes irrelevant in the presence of such a God. Later in his foreword to the Romans commentary,

6. Luther, *Bondage of the Will*, 62.

7. Barth, *Romans*, 10.

Barth writes that faith "is always a leap into the darkness of the unknown, a flight into empty air." And far from solving the problem of human ignorance of God, Jesus, too, "must be the most complete veiling of His [God's] incomprehensibility."[8]

Where Elihu says that we cannot find the Almighty (Job 37:23), Barth speaks in Romans of God's "complete veiling," "incomprehensibility," and "secret." He fortifies incomprehensibility by describing God as one "made known as the Unknown," speaking in "eternal silence." Getting close to God is out of reach because God "protects himself from every intimate companionship."[9] Barth's dazzling rhetoric has a point because God's revelation in Jesus defies human expectation, but God's purpose was not concealment. Voices all across the New Testament speak of it as a revelation that was seen to be that and was in fact stunningly successful (John 1:14, 18; 2 Cor 4:1–6). Paul calls it a treasure held in an earthen vessel, to be sure, but it could nonetheless be seen to be a treasure (2 Cor 4:7).

In Barth's discussion of Job's suffering in his massive *Church Dogmatics*, the link to Elihu becomes explicit. Like Elihu, Barth offers the advice that Job should serve God "with no claim that His [God's] rule should conform to some picture which he [Job] has formed of it."[10] According to Barth, Job's need for an explanation "is itself a symptom of man's enslavement to moral and logical criteria and norms irrelevant to the conduct of the divinely unique One."[11] God is accountable to no one; comprehension is off the table.[12] Humans can respond to God in faith but not with understanding. In Barth's words, God "does not ask for his [Job's] understanding, agreement or applause. On the contrary, He simply asks that he should be content not to know why and to what end he exists, and does so in this way and not another."[13]

"Be content not to know!"

I have added italics and an exclamation mark to this statement because the admonition to *be content not to know* is an apt summary of the argument that Job's friends throw at him in wave after wave of angry speech. It also works as a summary of the theological tradition that runs in a resilient stream from Augustine in the fifth century to Karl Barth in the twentieth. "Elihu" is in this sense not only a character in the Book of Job; he is a metaphor for a certain point of view; he is a strident proponent for the twin arguments of divine inscrutability and human incomprehension; and he comes across as an unfeeling character who is quite willing to defend what he believes will honor God even if it tramples on human experience. For the latter reason it is important that Elihu is a character in the Book of Job. His original and primary audience is a fellow human being made destitute by loss, a person whose pain is aggravated by the absence

8. Ibid., 98–99.

9. Ibid.

10. Barth, *Church Dogmatics*, IV.3, 431.

11. Schulweis, "Morality and Theodicy," 157.

12. Rodin, *Evil and Theodicy*, 2–3.

13. Barth, *Church Dogmatics* IV.3, 431.

of understanding. In this capacity, Elihu represents the discrepancy between theological dogma and human reality, and also the tension between orthodoxy and empathy.

Already at this early stage, therefore, we need to have the option of taking sides with Job against Elihu. God showers Job with an extensive, personal audience, precisely what Elihu told Job not to request and certainly not to expect (38:1—41:34). After God's speeches, Job concedes that much of what he said about God proved that he did not know (40:3–5; 42:3), and he declares his readiness to be taught (42:4). At no point, however, do we hear him say that he is now *content not to know* or that he understands God to be telling him to settle for not knowing. In the final twist, perplexing to readers through the ages, God says that Job has represented God correctly while the friends have badly misrepresented God (42:7, 8). The need and the right to know are part of Job's view of God. To the extent that God rebukes Job the problem is Job's ignorance and not his desire to know (38:1–3). The message of Job is not that God, having listened to the friends' futile attempt to subdue Job, tries to yank him away from a theology that makes sense, although this is often how the book is understood.

A different view is in order. William Safire (1929–2009) did not write as a biblical scholar, but on important points he was a better reader of Job than Karl Barth and a perceptive critic of the fallacy of traditional readings. As one who had been stung by the abuses of presidential authority in the Watergate scandal, Safire spots Elihu's mistake. The young Elihu, he says, "assumed the role of God's spokesman because he was sure that God was unaccountable and would never respond to the summons of Man."[14] Safire extols Job for pioneering dissent. Dissent, in turn, is a prerequisite for an open society and, as I wish to extrapolate, the precondition for better theology. Job did not challenge God's legitimacy, but he asserted his right to know. In civil society, says Safire, "no need is more urgent."[15]

Is the need to know less urgent in theology? Does the Bible grant that there is a "right to know" to a lesser degree than what we expect from other structures of authority? Could it be the other way around, not that there is a *right* to know but that God *wants* humans to know? Access is not given grudgingly. In the opposite scenario, the problem is not that the human desire to know exceeds God's disclosure policy but that humans take a dim interest in knowing. The latter possibility is more than suggested in the Bible (Isa 65:1; John 16:12). The most serious misconception underlying objections to Job-like questions might be the view that such questions reflect an irreverent and illegitimate urge to "discover what God has concealed from me."[16] In the contrary view, concealment is not God's policy.

Job-like questions and their answers belong loosely to *theodicy*, defined as the "defense of God's goodness and omnipotence in view of the existence of evil."[17] When

14. Safire, *The First Dissident*, 15.

15. Ibid., 199.

16. Berdyaev, *Christian Existentialism*, 41.

17. www.merriam-webster.com/dictionary/theodicy

we turn to the Bible, this definition must be qualified on two points. If God is more eager to let human beings know than humans are interested in knowing, the accent should be on divine revelation and not on the questions humans ask.[18] Job becomes a mediator of revelation because he refuses to be gagged by his friends, but much would be different if the book from beginning to end were read as a case study in divine candor. Carol Newsom says that the primary theme of the Book of Job is "the very meaningfulness of the concept of piety," but she grants, as all readers of the book must, that Job breaks with convention by putting God's action "under the scrutiny of justice."[19] This is the concern of theodicy, and it is precisely in a book of that kind that God appears as a willing revealer.

The second point might seem superfluous, but sometimes the obvious is hardest to see: The biblical texts that address the problem of suffering are not philosophical treatises originating in some ivory tower of abstract thought. Job is the foremost case in point. In this book, and in many others throughout the Bible, the sufferer speaks (cf. Ps 13:1–2; Rev 6:9–10), and the climax comes when God speaks directly to the sufferer.

Why, then, has the theological tradition sided with Elihu? Why Elihu when Job's dissent would seem a better option? The answer to this question is complex, and the most important factor will be left for the end of this chapter. But part of the answer is surely that politics has influenced interpretation more than interpreters care to admit. At a fairly early stage, Christianity was influenced by earthly ideals that were thought to apply in the divine realm. Peter Brown writes that the conversion of Constantine (272–337) in 312 "might not have happened—or, if it had, it would have taken on a totally different meaning—if it had not been preceded, for two generations, by the conversion of Christianity to the culture and ideals of the Roman world."[20] This transformation had a political dimension. Perceptions of the politics of heaven were influenced by the politics of earth. In the earthly system, the final word belonged to the emperor, a "ruler answerable to none."[21] The emperor did not worry about the consent of the governed, and he counted on his subjects to accept that resistance to human political authority was no better than rebellion against God. To the extent that accountability was absent in the imperial system of government, it mirrored the impossibility of divine accountability.

Augustine was not immune to these influences. He "identified God's purposes with Rome's policies," says Fredriksen.[22] This means that he embraced views that would have been unthinkable to an apologist like Origen two hundred years earlier (185–254). Augustine and his comrades-in-arms had been swayed by the way Eusebius

18. Surin ("Theodicy?" 244) writes wisely that theodicy is "an extension of the theology of revelation."

19. Newsom, *Job*, 55, 75.

20. Brown, *Late Antiquity*, 82.

21. Purcell, "The Arts of Government," 163.

22. Fredriksen, *Augustine and the Jews*, 341.

(260–339) interpreted Constantine's conversion.[23] In Eusebius' vision, Constantine's sponsorship of Christianity was part of the divine plan and the ideological blueprint for the Christian state. As S. L. Greenslade puts it, Eusebius "finds correspondence between religion and politics. Polytheism goes with polyarchy and anarchy, monotheism with monarchy. With the Roman Empire monarchy had come to earth as the image of monarchy in heaven."[24]

As Christianity became enmeshed in this constellation of power, the new reality demanded a different set of theological priorities.[25] It is in this regard that Augustine is the innovator. Eric Osborn writes that with the conversion of Constantine theodicy—understood as the quest for insight—"gave way to triumphalism."[26] Augustine began to treat questions that used to be part of the Christian engagement with the world as though they were impertinent and unwarranted. The ideological about-face is striking precisely with regard to questions like human capacity and divine candor. "What earlier apologists celebrate as God's gift to humankind—free will, liberty, autonomy, self-government—Augustine characterizes in surprisingly negative terms," says Elaine Pagels with reference to Augustine's emerging view.[27] In the course of his career as the leading bishop in North Africa, he revised the map of biblical interpretation to fit the new political landscape. Nothing takes the measure of the change better than the fact that he, in the words of Peter Brown, became the first person to write a full justification "of the right of the state to suppress non-Catholics."[28] Coercion, anathema to Christians in pre-Constantinian days, was now legitimate because Augustine had recast basic tenets of the Christian view of God.[29]

In the Christian state, the imperial way of exercising authority continued, empowered by the belief that the exercise of power on earth was patterned upon the way God exercises power in heaven.[30] Dissent could not flourish in the face of such impediments. While Augustine hardly envisioned the implements of the Inquisition, at a distance he was nevertheless its leading theorist.[31] The baby of human rights was

23. Eusebius, *Constantine*, 1890.

24. Greenslade, *Church and State*, 10.

25. See, for instance, Drake, *Constantine and the Bishops*.

26. Osborn, "The Apologist Origen," 58.

27. Pagels, "The Politics of Paradise," 78.

28. Brown, *Augustine of Hippo*, 235. For the primary source, see *The Political Writings of St. Augustine*, 190–240 (excerpts from Letters XCIII and CLXXXV), where Augustine carefully explains the factors that made him change from being opposed to coercion to approving it. See also Vancandard, *The Inquisition*, 13–24.

29. Bowlin ("Justifying Coercion," 49–70) confirms that Augustine became a believer in, and a promoter of, coercion, but he also downplays its significance as though it is no more than what people might condone under certain circumstances today.

30. MacMullen, *Christianizing*, 119. Frend (*The Rise of Christianity*, 505) writes that the ancient world "exchanged the guardianship of one set of divine masters, capricious but generally tolerant, for another that would brook no opposition."

31. Brown, *Augustine of Hippo*, 240.

thrown out with the bathwater of human incapacity. With the help of Augustine's prestigious voice Elihu became a winner in the theological tradition in a way he is not in the Book of Job. The legacy of both, Augustine no less than Elihu, is that the quest for understanding should be held in low esteem

Questions Being Asked

In actual practice, of course, people have asked questions without pausing to check whether there is theological warrant for doing it. In Antiquity, the Greek philosopher Epicurus (341–270 BCE) posed the question that is still considered a succinct formulation of the "problem of evil."[32] Is God willing to prevent evil but *unable* to do so? In that case God is not omnipotent, he said. Is God able to prevent evil but *unwilling* to do so? he asked. If so, God must be malevolent. Is God both willing and able to prevent evil? Why, then, is there evil in the world? Beginning with the single fact of evil, Epicurus's paradigm put the existence of God in doubt. His construct, having gone through many incarnations, is still the linchpin of what is known as the "atheistic problem of evil."

There is much less existential agony in Epicurus's construct than in Job's quest, and he nails down his options in ways that differ from Job by orders of magnitude. And yet it would be a pity if questions arising from within the Bible do not have anything in common with questions arising from without it—or anything to offer questions coming from other quarters. Epicurus's question was revived in the early days of the Age of Reason by the French philosopher Pierre Bayle (1647–1706). Bayle was the son of a Protestant minister living at a time when dissent was still dangerous. He put the reality of human suffering at the center of his massive *Historical and Critical Dictionary* (1697),[33] a widely read series of books in the eighteenth century. To Bayle, ordinary suffering is so rampant that there is no need to justify interest in the subject.

> Man is wicked and miserable. Everybody is aware of this from what goes on within himself, and from the commerce he is obliged to carry on with his neighbor. It suffices to have been alive for five or six years to have been convinced of these two truths. Those who live long and who are much involved in worldly affairs know this still more clearly. Travel gives continual lessons of this. Monuments to human misery and wickedness are found everywhere—prisons, hospitals, gallows, and beggars.[34]

32. Larrimore, *The Problem of Evil*, xviii–xi. Larrimore notes that the question may have originated with the philosopher Carneades (214–129 BCE).

33. Bayle, *Dictionary*. The unabridged version of Bayle's *Dictionary* comprises five volumes in English.

34. Ibid., 146–47.

Bayle did not treat evil as a theoretical problem but was determined to give weight to human experience. This led directly to God and the character of God. In Bayle's *Dictionary*, the question raised by Epicurus returns with renewed force.

> God is either willing to remove evil and cannot, or he can and is unwilling; or he is neither willing nor able to do so; or else he is both willing and able. If he is willing and not able, he must be weak, which cannot be affirmed of God. If he is able and not willing, he must be envious, which is also contrary to the nature of God. If he is neither willing nor able, he must be both envious and weak, and consequently not be God. If he is both willing and able—the only possibility that agrees with the nature of God—then where does evil come from? Or why does he not eliminate it?[35]

There is no rush toward an atheist conclusion in this statement, but there is puzzlement. A God who is "both willing and able"—and still there is evil in the world? Only twelve years after Bayle's publication, in 1709, Gottfried Leibnitz (1646–1716) coined the word *theodicy*. This word had not been part of the vocabulary because, with few exceptions, the theological tradition had for a thousand years effectively shut down such concerns. Leibnitz used the word *theodicy* in the title of his most influential book, taking care to explain its meaning, *Essays on the Goodness of God, the Freedom of Man and the Origin of Evil*.[36] He had been profoundly disturbed by Bayle's *Dictionary*, but in his eyes, as in Bayle's, the problem of evil relates primarily to God's attributes and not to God's existence. In a fastidious argument that is often unfairly caricatured, Leibnitz concluded that our world, for all its horrors, is the best of all possible worlds.

When David Hume (1711–1776) followed suit with his *Dialogues on Natural Religion* in 1776, he revived the atheistic option.[37] The devastating Lisbon Earthquake in 1755 influenced his thinking and, unrelated to the earthquake, the *Dictionary* of Pierre Bayle. In formulating the problem, Hume also turned to Epicurus.

> Epicurus's old questions are yet unanswered. Is he [God] willing to prevent evil, but not able? then is he impotent. Is he able, but not willing? then is he malevolent. Is he both able and willing? whence then is evil?[38]

To Hume, God's power or goodness is not the main concern. By the end of the eighteenth century, the most radical possibility is on the table. Does the reality of evil mean that there is no God?

The thread that runs from Epicurus to Bayle, from Bayle to Hume, and from Hume to contemporary philosophy is striking not for presenting new questions but

35. Ibid., 169.
36. Leibnitz, *Theodicy*.
37. Hume, *Dialogues Concerning Natural Religion*.
38. Ibid., 100.

for bringing up old questions in new contexts. Their secular and philosophical argument differs from the biblical voice of Job on some points that are easy to see. Job is concerned about innocent suffering, but he is not an atheist. Atheism will hardly be the world view of a book that clamors for God to make an appearance and ends with God doing exactly that! From the vantage point of the Book of Job, the arithmetic bent of Epicurus's formula drives the imagination into a corner in a way Job does not.

Evil of the type that befalls Job cannot be accommodated within the Epicurean formula in any of its options. From the very beginning the reader is told that Job's plight will not be ascribed to random forces operating within a materialistic conception of reality. The calamities that strike him in rapid succession are carefully planned and orchestrated. As Philippe Nemo notes, Job's suffering exceeds the explanatory power of impersonal forces.[39] "Evil, in the excess that Job acknowledges, indicates a certain commitment on the part of a certain Intention," says Nemo.[40]

> Job, however, encounters evil that is not neutral. This evil is not satisfied with killing him. Yet it does not desire to kill him either; indeed, it even forbids him to die. It is an evil that tortures him, eternalizes his pain and makes it into a hell. This evil does not reach him in a neutral manner; its madness is not that of chaos. It *looks* for him.[41]

Job is at the receiving end of deliberate intent, careful planning, and meticulous execution. This realization recurs several times in the book, sometimes in direct speech by Job to God, sometimes with Job explaining what God, as he understands the situation, has done to him (Job 10:16–17; 16:12–13). At no point does he entertain the thought that such targeted suffering can be explained in impersonal terms. *His* suffering demands a theological explanation.

> But for Job evil is not Destiny, as Destiny is neutral and blind. . . . It pursues Job, corners him and encircles him in order to get a better look at him. His suffering is machinated and prepared by some mastermind as an aim and a wish. The torture does not take place without a torturer, without cause, without an Intention.[42]

Evil in Job's experience is better understood as some*one* than as some*thing*. Once, fleetingly, before God rolls back the curtain of misperception, Job allows that someone other than God could be involved. "If it is not God [who sends evil], who then is it?" he asks (9:24). This option dominates the frame story (1:6–12; 2:1–7), and it returns at full throttle in the climactic part of God's address to Job (40:15—41:34). Here, indeed, the divine sense that comes to the rescue of a pious man trapped in

39. Nemo, *Excess of Evil*, 112.

40. Ibid., 2.

41. Ibid., 112.

42. Ibid., 113.

existential darkness also blows to smithereens the sclerotic answers of his friends. In the book's last glimpse of Job, we do not see a person who is content not to know but someone who has thrown himself upon God no less for light than for relief (42:1–6). In the end, the terrifying agony is quieted not by a rebuke but by revelation.

Three lines converge in Job with respect to the problem of evil. First, as noted already, Job confers legitimacy on the quest for understanding against a theological tradition that takes the opposite view. Second, Philippe Nemo's notion of an "excess of evil" has relevance for the evil seen in Job as well as for the horrors of the twentieth century. Is not the Holocaust a kindred reality? Must not ideas of randomness, chance, and impersonal accounts yield to story lines that clamor for better conceptual and rhetorical resources? Is not Auschwitz like a bullet to the forehead of Epicurus's mechanistic question? Now, with human civilization still within sight of Auschwitz, the measure of evil again vastly exceeds impersonal accounts. In 1938, at a time when the systematic extermination of the Jews was still in its ideological and practical infancy, the political philosopher Eric Voegelin wrote the following:

> When considering National Socialism from a religious standpoint, one should be able to proceed on the assumption that there is evil in the world and, moreover, that evil is not only a deficient mode of being, a negative element, but also a real substance and force that is effective in the world. Resistance against a satanical substance that is not only morally but also religiously evil can only be derived from an equally strong, religiously good force. One cannot fight a satanical force with morality and humanity alone.[43]

Third, therefore, the theological drama in Job resonates with human reality in the twenty-first century, and human reality resonates with Job. Let me press this point further notwithstanding the risks that will soon be evident.

Obstacles

Rudolf Bultmann (1884–1976), considered by many the most influential interpreter of the New Testament in the twentieth century, lived through the Nazi years as professor of New Testament at the University of Marburg from 1921 until 1951. In oral and written presentations to Lutheran clergy in 1941 and 1942, Bultmann urged on them the necessity of *demythologizing* the New Testament.[44] By this he meant that the gospels and the letters of Paul must be stripped of elements that in his view no longer fit an enlightened view of the world. The New Testament, he claimed, could only speak in a meaningful way to people in the twentieth century when that task had been accomplished. To say that Bultmann was pursuing a message that makes better *sense* is therefore more than a play on words.

43. Voegelin, *Modernity without Restraint*, 24.

44. Bultmann, *Kerygma and Myth*, 323–26.

The list of mythical features that would have to go in Bultmann's project is long, with only a few items reproduced here.

> No one who is old enough to think for himself supposes that God lives in a local heaven.[45]

> An historical fact which involves the resurrection from the dead is utterly inconceivable.[46]

> The mythical view of the world must be accepted or rejected in its entirety.[47]

These assertions deserve to be discussed one by one, but that discussion belongs elsewhere. When Bultmann takes the measure of good and evil, our main concern, he is dismissive toward the view held by believers in the first century.

> Satan may inspire him with evil thoughts. Alternatively, God may inspire his thought and guide his purposes. He may grant him heavenly visions. He may allow him to hear his word of succor or demand. He may give him the supernatural power of his Spirit. History does not follow a smooth unbroken course; it is set in motion and controlled by these supernatural powers. This aeon is held in bondage by Satan, sin, and death (for "powers" is precisely what they are), and hastens towards its end.[48]

Bultmann declared this view to be obsolete. Going to the heart of the matter, he said that "we can no longer believe in *spirits, whether good or evil*,"[49] leaving little room for the supernatural on the side of the good or for the truly demonic on the side of evil. A view of good and evil that made sense to people living in Roman Palestine in the first century had in the twentieth century lost its meaning.

Had it? In light of the atrocities committed against the Jews of Europe during World War II, Bultmann's view of evil could be a colossal failure of perception or, at the very least, an example of terrible timing. His initiative had a context, but that context was not the war or the project to exterminate the Jews.[50] Instead, his call to demythologize the gospels was the late cresting of sentiments that began a century earlier, with David Friedrich Strauss (1808–1874) and others who were convinced that the shelf-life of the New Testament view of reality had expired.[51] Among academics within that discipline, the trend then begun continued into the Holocaust era

45. Bultmann, *Kerygma and Myth*, 4.

46. Ibid., 39.

47. Ibid., 9.

48. Ibid., 1–2.

49. Ibid., 4.

50. Fergusson's book on Bultmann's theology (*Rudolf Bultmann*) is almost completely devoid of references to Bultmann's time, as though a review of the political and historical context of Nazi Germany is irrelevant to an assessment of his theological priorities.

51. Strauss, *Life of Jesus*, 254.

without pausing for a timeout—undeterred by the racial Nuremberg Laws of 1935; by the dismissal of all Jewish university professors the same year; by the *Kristallnacht* of November 9, 1938, when Jewish property was vandalized and synagogues burned to the ground all across Germany; by the decree on September 1, 1941, that all Jews had to wear a yellow star in public; and by the mass deportation of German Jews that began on October 15, 1941.[52] Konrad Hammann, Bultmann's leading biographer to date, says that Bultmann wanted his students "'to continue doing theology' in the direction shown by Karl Barth in 1933, '*as if nothing had happened*.'"[53] A similar logic applied with regard to policies within the Confessing Church. Bultmann argued for equality of Christian believers of Jewish descent *within the church*, but it was thought improper for the church to interfere in regard to what was done to the same people *within the state*. "For although the opponents of applying this legislation [the Aryan laws] to the church stoutly supported the rights of Christians of Jewish descent within the Protestant Church, they did not see it as their task similarly to oppose the increasingly common practice of depriving the Jews of their civil rights," says Hammann.[54] In other words, Bultmann and others were defending the rights of Christians of Jewish descent to serve as elders and deacons in the church while choosing to stay silent about the fact that these people were deprived of dignity, livelihood, and life itself by the state.[55] Saul Friedländer's summary of the situation during the pre-war years is therefore to the point on what was done for the Jews as *Jews*.

> Not one social group, not one religious community, not one scholarly institution or professional association in Germany and throughout Europe declared its solidarity with the Jews (some of the Christian churches declared that converted Jews were part of the flock, up to a point). . . . Thus *Nazi and related anti-Jewish policies could unfold to their most extreme levels without the interference of any major countervailing interests*.[56]

On the whole, Bultmann may have thought that there were benign ways to tame the beast, as evidenced by his attempt to persuade Karl Barth to sign an oath of loyalty to Hitler, as he had done.[57] While he used his influence to oppose the Nazi villainy in respectable ways,[58] the Holocaust context is not easy to spot in his interpretative

52. For these and many more shocking details of ideology, theology, and practice, see *Betrayal*.

53. Hammann, *Rudolf Bultmann*, 283, italics added.

54. Ibid., 296.

55. The large Jewish synagogue on University Street in Marburg, finished in 1897, was, like many other synagogues, burned on November 9, 1938. The damaged walls were blown up with dynamite and the debris hauled off, the expenses charged to the members of the synagogue. The deportation of male members to Buchenwald began shortly thereafter. By 1942 most of the Jews in Marburg had been deported.

56. Friedländer, *The Years of Extermination*, xxi.

57. Barth, *Barth-Bultmann Letters*, 78–79.

58. Hammann (*Rudolf Bultmann*, 267–310) gives Bultmann nothing but praise, his silence notwithstanding.

priorities of the New Testament. These realities did not put evidence on the table that invited conceptions other than the ones he was set on pursuing.

We need mean no insult to those who participated in these discussions if we wonder why it did not occur to them that the near collective spell that fell on Germany could be a case of extraordinary influences inspiring human beings "with evil thoughts" along the lines found in the New Testament. Even if many in that generation of German Bible scholars then alive were unaware of the "Final Solution" that was under way, a proposition that is now impossible to believe,[59] it could do no harm to describe the vilification and murder of the Jews as acts of an aeon "held in bondage by Satan."[60] The shoe of evil was growing larger by the day, meticulously catalogued in Victor Klemperer's bone-chilling diary of the pre-war and early war years in Germany.[61] Could interpreters of the New Testament in such times do no better than to declare that "we can no longer believe in *spirits, whether good or evil*"?[62]

Bultmann's initiative seems oddly detached from its own reality, the detachment all the more striking because of the erudition with which he pursues the project. He puts irony to use in order to drive home the superiority of modernity over Antiquity—how can people who use electric lights and radio "believe in the New Testament's world of spirits and wonders"[63]—but there is more than one way to construct irony. Electricity and radios signify progress and superiority, but the comparison is less beguiling when the electric lights are turned off in the gas chambers at Auschwitz, and when the radio fails to report live from the scene. At that point, the conceptual resources of the ancient world offer a more robust and adequate account of reality. The problem with the demythologized view will not be lack of compassion for the Jews, but defective conceptual and rhetorical means with which to take the measure of evil. Bultmann's attempt to make the message of the New Testament resonate with contemporary reality is challenged by the reality he professed to address. His quest for better sense, if that is what it was, falls well short of the goal.

What, then, of Bultmann's contemporary, Karl Barth? There may have been more teeth in Barth's bite against the Nazi horror,[64] but his view of evil is less forthright than Bultmann's, and it is no better match for the shoe it is supposed to fit.[65] Barth rejected the notion of personified evil that is characteristic of the New Testament. R. Scott Rodin

59. Cf. Gutman, "Character of Nazi Antisemitism," 349–80.

60. Bultmann, *Kerygma and Myth*, 2.

61. Klemperer, *I Will Bear Witness*. More comprehensive and even more chilling is the meticulous account by Friedländer, *Years of Persecution*.

62. Bultmann, *Kerygma and Myth*, 4.

63. Hammann, *Rudolf Bultmann*, 326.

64. Nothing is pretty in the Christian response to the National Socialist movement in Germany. Even the much-touted Barmen Declaration (1934) failed to name the specific *anti-Jewish* project that was in the making; see Baranowski, "The Confessing Church and Anti-Semitism," 90–109.

65. "Much Ado about Nothingness" is the apt title of David Ray Griffin's critique of Barth's view of evil; cf. *God, Power, and Evil*, 150–73.

says that Barth must "be credited for constructing a doctrine of evil devoid of such a concept."[66] As with Bultmann, Barth was at the peak of his powers and influence in the pre-war and war years. In Barth's theology, evil is described in categories of negation. Specifically, evil does not denote a personal or personified reality. The categories of being that matter are God and human beings. Angels, whether good or evil, do not deserve much attention because they "are not independent and autonomous subjects like God and man and Jesus Christ."[67] They "are essentially marginal figures," says Barth.[68]

While Barth recognizes evil as a power,[69] it is difficult to know what he means. Evil is in his conception referred to as *das Nichtige*, literally "*That-Which-Is-Nothing*" or simply "*Nothingness*," but evil is not nothing. It exists "only on the left hand of God, under His No," says Barth, and it exists "only in its own improper way, as inherent contradiction, as impossible possibility."[70] "*Nothingness*," nevertheless, owes its existence to God, and yet it "is that which God does not will."[71] Barth draws a line between what "God positively wills" and "what God does not will and therefore negates and rejects," assigning "*Nothingness*" to the latter category.[72] As with *das Nichtige* ["Nothingness"], the devil and demons "are null and void, but they are not nothing."[73] They belong to a third class because "God has not created them, and therefore they are not creaturely."[74]

Does *Nothingness* thus conceived describe evil in a way that is Holocaust-worthy? Does it fit the reality that comes to light in the Book of Job? Where does this view leave God? Even if we find a way to comprehend how evil exists "only on the left hand of God, under His No," the left hand of God is still God's hand. It is peculiar that the role of the left hand will one day cease, meaning that God must at some point put an end to the use of God's left hand.[75] Evil exists in order to occasion the cross,[76] and yet the cross does not bring an end to evil. Rodin, whose view of Barth's theodicy is generally positive, makes continuing horror his chief objection: "if evil was destroyed on the cross, why is it still amongst us?"[77] Why still the role of what is ultimately, in Barth's terminology, *Nothingness*?

Barth's expressive arsenal is dizzying and holds many readers in awe, but his measure of evil is longer on rhetoric than on content. Nicholas Wolterstorff notes that

66. Rodin, *Evil and Theodicy*, 114.

67. Barth, *Church Dogmatics* III.3 §51, 371.

68. Ibid.

69. Barth, *Church Dogmatics* III.3, §50, 301, 311; Wolterstorff, "Barth on Evil," 586.

70. Ibid, 351–52.

71. Ibid., 352.

72. Ibid., 353.

73. Ibid., 523.

74. Ibid.

75. Rodin, *Evil and Theodicy*, 259.

76. Ford, *Barth and God's Story*, 75.

77. Rodin, *Evil and Theodicy*, 234.

despite Barth's insistence that evil is incomprehensible and inexplicable "there is much about evil that Barth professes to comprehend and explain—more than he should."[78] More to the point, Barth's view, like Bultmann's, seems conspicuously insufficient to its own reality. Aside from the conceptual contortions, Holocaust-size evil is not well described in terms of *Nothingness*, and the decision to address Nazi policy toward the Jews in the domain of the church while bypassing it in the arena of the state remains problematic in the extreme. In 1967, Eberhart Bethge, Dietrich Bonhoeffer's friend and biographer, asked in a letter to Barth, "Was it basically correct that the church, the Confessing Church, mind you—the official church applauded, as is known—was silent about the Nuremberg laws? Was it right, as happened at the time, to say: the granting and denial of civil rights is a matter for the people and the state alone, and does not concern the church? Was it right that in 1938 the persecuted Jews were not at all or hardly prayed for?"[79]

This does not mean that theologians like Bultmann and Barth harbored anti-Semitic sentiments—they did not. It is also imprecise to describe the problem as the fault of any one individual as though he or she made it happen. The problem, rather, centers on their measure of evil, an inadequacy made more conspicuous by the times in which it happened and by the non-deployment of resources still at the disposal of readers of the New Testament. My view, by contrast, implies the need to *remythologize* perceptions of reality, as if to dispatch a rescue crew to the landfill where the enlightened view left Satan to languish, retrieve him, bandage the wounds that contempt inflicted on him, dress him in uniform, and send him forth into battle to be part of the sense the Bible makes of human reality. Like the sufferings of Job, the Holocaust demands a larger foot than the impersonal and negative categories Barth deploys. Conceptually, it is difficult to grasp his measure of evil except to say that his perception seems strangely inert and a far cry from the personal power that evil is made out to be in the New Testament, a far cry, too, from the epic evil Barth tried to counter. Failure at the level of conception will be mirrored in failure at the level of practice.

In a clean break with these sentiments, Gordon Graham writes that when confronted with evil "the naturalistic and humanistic presuppositions of modernity are inadequate to its own purposes."[80] Counting on the cosmic perspective in the Book of Revelation to explain what he means (Rev 12:7–10), Graham says that "the idea of an evil agency external to self-generated human action can actually be made quite plausible in the context of attempting to explain phenomena that are as much a part of our experience as that of the ancient world."[81] This view represents a return to an understanding of evil that Bultmann relegates to obsolete mythology and that Barth

78. Wolterstorff, "Barth on Evil," 598.

79. Brumlik, "Post-Holocaust Theology," 176.

80. Graham, *Evil and Christian Ethics*, xv.

81. Ibid., 63.

deprives of content with the notion of *Nothingness*.[82] It means that evil should be treated neither as a purely human problem nor as though God is the only other being who deserves consideration. In addition to human and divine agency, there is the possibility of demonic agency. This option, turned away at the front door by many in Bultmann's generation of interpreters, has returned via the back door by force of the reality to which they seemed wanly oblivious.

And yet the most deep-seated obstacle to a theology of sense lies deeper in the tradition, aching and unrelieved even if the demonic is restored to the place it holds in the New Testament. More is needed than to say that the devil is in the details with reference to the commission of outright and outrageous evil. For this obstacle to rise to the surface we need to return to Elihu and Job's friends with whom we began. "Will you speak falsely for God, and speak deceitfully for him?" we hear Job say to his friends as the conversation is becoming more heated (Job 13:7, NRSV). Other translations add helpful nuances of wording.

> Why are you lying? Do you think your lies will benefit God? (GNB)
>
> Do you mean to defend God by prevarication and by dishonest argument? (NJB)
>
> Are you defending God with lies? Do you make your dishonest arguments for his sake? (NLT)

Job finds his friends guilty of theological malpractice. "As for you, you whitewash with lies; all of you are worthless physicians," he contends (Job 13:4). The doctrines found to be at fault in their repository are punitive justice and divine inscrutability. These doctrines, we have seen, are to varying degrees verities in the theological tradition that runs from Job's friends and Elihu through Augustine and Luther and all the way to Karl Barth (Barth eschews punitive justice but retains divine inscrutability). Punitive justice, in turn, will in the theological tradition not be finite suffering as in the case of Job, but suffering that exceeds normal suffering in intensity and has no end with respect to duration.

This, more than all of the above, is where the ship of sense founders on the reef of non-sense. Can more suffering be the remedy for the problem of suffering when suffering is the problem? Worse yet, can more suffering, especially in a Holocaust perspective, remain part of the *Christian* answer to the problem of suffering? "Christian theology invincibly confirms this, in that it tells us that the torments of the damned will be eternal and continuous, and as strong at the end of one hundred thousand years as they were the first day," Pierre Bayle wrote in his *Dictionary*, acutely aware

82. Given that Bultmann and Barth were both master dialecticians, it is never easy to pin down exactly what is what in the demythologizing controversy. We can be certain, however, that neither one conceived of angels, whether good or evil, as ontological meaningful beings.

that mainline Christian theology does not promise an end to suffering.[83] Susan Neiman captures the contradiction in the Christian view as it was unsentimentally formulated by Bayle.

> The problem lies, rather, in the internal structure of the Christian solution itself. The torments of the damned, even without the doctrine of predestination, are the block on which reason stumbles. For however bad a sin may be, it has to be finite. An infinite amount of hellfire is therefore simply unjust. To imagine a God who judges many of the forms of life He created to be sinful, then tortures us eternally for our brief participation in them, is hardly to imagine a solution to the problem of evil. Positing a God who may permit infinite and eternal suffering is of little help in stilling doubt about a God who clearly permits finite and temporal suffering.[84]

Just as the Holocaust poses a challenge to conceptions that see evil in purely human terms, it subjects the notion of everlasting torture to a reality check. Scenarios of torture that formerly existed only in the imagination of preachers and on the canvas of artists now have a counterpoint in actual chambers for gassing and real ovens for burning so as to question the belief that "the torments of the damned will be eternal and continuous."[85] For those who look to Christian theology for a remedy to the problem of suffering and to whom the Holocaust is the most acute problem for which relief is sought, this version of Christian theology will not be the solution. In more ways than one, Auschwitz has depleted the notion of everlasting torture as a meaning-making resource in theology.

When Pierre Bayle thought about these questions in the seventeenth century, he was keenly aware of thinkers who had immersed themselves in the subject. With respect to his own Christian background, he admits that it is difficult to escape the criticism that God, on the one hand, is the author of sin,[86] and, on the other hand, that the doctrine of everlasting torment rules out an end to human suffering. Scholars disagree as to Bayle's core convictions, but his advice to those who defend the orthodox position is consistent and clear. In his advice we come full circle, back to the voice of Elihu in the Old Testament, who advised Job to stop bringing up certain questions (Job 37:19–20). "All of this warns us that we should not dispute with the Manicheans[87]

83. Bayle, *Dictionary*, 171.

84. Neiman, *Evil in Modern Thought*, 19.

85. Bayle, *Dictionary*, 171.

86. Ibid., 183.

87. Although Manichaeism has been considered a Christian heresy, it should also be seen as a religion in its own right. Mani, a Persian, taught in the latter part of the third century that there are two co-equal principles in the world, one good and one evil. The evil principle is manifested in and through matter. Augustine was a Manichean before he embraced Catholic Christianity, and some of his most trenchant writings are attempts to refute the Manicheans.

until we have established the doctrine of *the elevation of faith and the abasement of reason*," Bayle counsels.[88]

"What must be done then?" he asks in the same connection. "Man's understanding must be made a captive of faith and must submit to it. He must never dispute about certain things," he answers.[89]

Is this where it ends in the twenty-first century? Does the Christian account entail a scenario so forbidding that the suspension of reason has to be the bottom line for the person of faith? Is the human condition before God faithfully captured by a tradition that shuts down questions by the two-pronged argument of human incapacity and divine inscrutability? Must sense yield to nonsense, "nonsense" now not an epithet meant to disparage a point of view? The non-sense, instead, is a fair and precise term admitted by the proponents for the tradition they pay dearly to defend. A scenario for which no reason can be given will be salvaged by giving up on reason altogether.

Long before the curtain fell on the twentieth century, Franz Kafka wrote of Joseph K. who was arrested one fine morning by warders who will not say who sent them; charged with a crime that he never gets to know what it is; tried before a court he never gets to see; sentenced without a definite hearing and even without knowing for certain whether there has been one; and then executed in the dark of night as if by the force of sheer inevitability. In his last hour, nothing in his predicament is more demeaning than the sense of being cornered by nonsense. "Where was the Judge whom he had never seen?" Joseph K. wonders. "Where was the high Court, to which he had never penetrated?"[90]

If Kafka's depiction captures human life in the grip of modernity, as many believe it does, or human reality without regard for any specific period in history, the predicament is dire. It will not be helped by the Christian tradition because the tradition has made the notion of unaccountable authority the most hallowed characteristic of God: a God beyond comprehension. The irony of finding convergence between perceptions of reality without God and reality with the God of the theological tradition cannot be exaggerated. But this will not be the only reason to start over. The weightiest rationale will be the one found in the Book of Job. In that book Job proves that his friends, well-meaning stalwarts of the theological tradition, are guilty of defending God with lies (Job 13:7).

88. Bayle, *Dictionary*, 177.

89. Ibid., 177.

90. Kafka, *The Trial*, 228. The original German version of *Der Prozess* was first published in 1925 although written in 1914.

Chapter Two

Creed of Anguish

"It's not that I don't accept God, Alyosha, I just most respectfully return him the ticket."[1]

This widely quoted sentence is taken from one of the most influential books in Western literature. The speaker is Ivan Karamazov, the brother of Alyosha. Together they are two of the four sons of Fyodor Pavlovitch Karamazov in *The Brothers Karamazov*, the crowning masterpiece of the Russian novelist Fyodor Dostoevsky. The father Karamazov is "a monster of lust and debauchery,"[2] an unscrupulous pleasure-seeker who neglects his children and takes from them what is theirs. In the course of the story the father is murdered. His son Mitya is arrested, tried, and sentenced for the murder even though the reader, better informed than the jury that passes the guilty verdict, knows that Mitya is innocent. The actual murderer, it turns out, is the despicable Smerdyakov, the illegitimate son of the father, who was raised as a servant in his house. While the murder of Fyodor Karamazov is an important aspect of the book, its fame and influence are in large measure due to the conversation between Ivan and Alyosha, and the sentence quoted above is Ivan's sharpest arrow.

More than anything else in Dostoevsky's authorship, the chapter entitled "Rebellion" and the chapter following it, entitled "The Grand Inquisitor," are the reasons why Dostoevsky is perceived as a thinker who deals head-on with the problem of suffering and the blow that suffering deals to the quest for sense. Today, hardly any discussion of the subject will omit mentioning Ivan Karamazov's protest or be able to shy away from its implications. The book's status has not been diminished by the fact that it was written sixty years before the unimaginable horror of the Holocaust.

The Brothers Karamazov was first published in installments in *The Russian Messenger* from 1879 through most of 1880, each issue of the journal eagerly anticipated by the reading public. The completed work was ready in a two-volume edition in December 1880, shortly before Dostoevsky's death on January 28, 1881, at the age of

1. Dostoevsky, *The Brothers Karamazov*, 245.
2. Simmons, "Historical and Analytic Introduction," 32.

59.[3] In large measure due to this book, Dostoevsky is considered one of the greatest Christian novelists who ever lived and in the eyes of many, Christian or not, one of the greatest writers ever. The impact of *The Brothers Karamazov* is perhaps best gauged by the verdict of readers who did not share Dostoevsky's spiritual aspirations. Sigmund Freud wrote that "*The Brothers Karamazov* is the most magnificent novel ever written."[4] Friedrich Nietzsche confessed that he found in Dostoevsky's work "the most valuable psychological material I know," hastening to add that his own sentiments tended in quite the opposite direction.[5]

Nicholas Berdyaev says that Dostoevsky "was among the most brilliant and keen-minded men of all time," and he calls the Legend of the Grand Inquisitor the high point of his work.[6] Joseph Frank, Dostoevsky's encyclopedic biographer in English, singles out the chapter describing Ivan's 'rebellion' and the Legend of the Grand Inquisitor as "ideological heights for which there are few equals."[7] These tributes are based on the conviction that Dostoevsky was not playing at the fringes of human reality or outside it; indeed, he was not playing at all.

But why should one turn to a fictional account to put evil into perspective? Surely human reality is sufficient to handle this on its own, not needing help from fiction, someone might say. This objection has merit to the extent that there might be fiction that does not intend to portray reality. With regard to the examples of the suffering that Ivan describes with white-hot fury in the chapter entitled "Rebellion," there is nothing fictional. In a letter to N. A. Liubimov, the editor of *The Russian Messenger*, dated May 10, 1879, Dostoevsky writes that "all the anecdotes about children actually happened; they were reported in our newspapers and I can show you where. I've thought up nothing."[8] He proceeds in the same letter to describe two of the stories, saying that "the whole story of the General who set his dogs on a child is a real event; it was published last winter in *Arkiv*, I think, and reprinted in many newspapers."[9] He is equally at pains to preserve the original accounts undoctored, imploring the editor not to alter a specific word used in his source. "There is the fact of the little five-year-old girl who is smeared with *excrement* by those who were bringing her up, because she did not ask to go to the bathroom at night. But I beg you not to eliminate this word. I took this from the recent trial record," he pleads.[10] Literature is not imitating life in

3. Frank, *Dostoevsky*, 760–932. This massive biography is a condensation of the earlier and much larger five-volume biography.

4. Freud, "Dostoevsky and Parricide," 41. Freud's accolade may have to be tempered by the fact that he somewhat opportunistically found support for one of his own cherished theories in the book.

5. Quoted in Frank, *Dostoevsky*, 205, n. 8.

6. Berdyaev, *Dostoevsky*, 34.

7. Frank, *Dostoevsky*, 867.

8. Letter to Liubimov, 3–4.

9. Ibid., 3.

10. Ibid., 3–4.

Ivan's speech in the sense that alien elements are intruding on human reality. On the contrary, the author tries to come to terms with conditions that he has not made up.

Sense Impossible

Even before the conversation between Ivan and Alyosha starts in earnest, Ivan declares his position.

> Yet would you believe it, in the final result I don't accept the world of God's, and, although I know it exists, I don't accept it at all. It's not that I don't accept God, you must understand, it's the world created by Him I don't and cannot accept. . . . That's what's at the root of me, Alyosha, that's my creed.[11]

This declaration marks the point of departure for one of the most focused and hard-hitting attacks on Christian belief in print. Even though Dostoevsky makes it clear that Ivan's position is not his own, so much thought and emotion are poured into the effort that critics "have wondered whether the book as a whole succeeds in overcoming its subversive impact."[12] It is clear, nevertheless, that it was Dostoevsky's intention not to let Ivan's protest stand alone. Thus, in another letter written while he was hard at work on his 'answer' to Ivan, Dostoevsky says that "I have not yet answered all those atheistical propositions and they have to be answered. I am frankly quite worried and upset about this. For I intend to give the answer to all this negative side . . . I tremble for it on this account. Will it be enough of an answer?"[13] This struggle on the part of the writer shows that we must pay heed to the context of Ivan's argument before we hear the evidence on which his anguished creed is based.

It is therefore simplistic to conclude that Ivan Karamazov's rejection of Christian belief because of the suffering of children is the main message of *The Brothers Karamazov* or the position of the author. In 1849, the year that marked the beginning of a ten-year ordeal in Dostoevsky's life, he was sentenced to death by firing squad on the charge of holding subversive political views.[14] At the very last minute the sentence was commuted by Tsar Nicholas. Instead of execution, Dostoevsky was sent to the city of Omsk in Western Siberia for four years of hard labor followed by another four years of health-sapping military service. While he was on his way to the prison, Mrs. Natalya D. Fonvizina, a devout woman who deserves to be remembered by name, handed him a copy of the New Testament.[15] This book would be his only source of reading during

11. Dostoevsky, *The Brothers Karamazov* (Garnett translation), 218–19.

12. Frank, *Dostoevsky*, 869.

13. Letter to Pobedonostsev, in *The Brothers Karamazov and Its Critics*, 6. Dostoevsky's answer to Ivan's 'atheistical propositions' begins in book VI in the chapter entitled "The Russian Monk." He intended it to be "the direct opposite of the view of the world stated earlier [Ivan's view]—but again not presented point by point, but as an artistic picture so to speak."

14. Frank, *Dostoevsky*, 169–242.

15. Williams, *Dostoevsky*, 15; Frank, *Dostoevsky*, 187.

his imprisonment. Dostoevsky fondly kept it under his pillow during the four years in Omsk and read from it often. His copy, soiled and worn, is one of only three books in existence that carry marginalia in the author's own hand.[16]

The imprisonment and his reading of the New Testament had a profound impact on Dostoevsky. In a letter to Mrs. Fonvizina written in 1854, the year of his release from prison, he stated his personal *Credo*, quite different from Ivan's.

> This *Credo* is very simple, here it is: to believe that nothing is more beautiful, profound, sympathetic, reasonable, manly, and more perfect than Christ; and I tell myself with a jealous love not only that there is nothing but that there cannot be anything. Even more, if someone proved to me that Christ is outside the truth, and that *in reality* the truth were outside of Christ, then I should prefer to remain with Christ rather than with the truth.[17]

This statement has been subject to much debate. Did Dostoevsky posit an opposition between Christ and "the truth," opening for the possibility that "the truth" might actually be outside Christ? Must his commitment to Christ, therefore, be seen as willingness to turn his back on "the truth," if indeed it could be established that Christ is outside the truth? What was his idea and picture of Christ?

We do not need to answer these questions in detail in order to say unequivocally that Dostoevsky did not set out to undermine the message of the New Testament or let it appear that Ivan had the resources with which to do it. His aim was quite the opposite. Ivan must state the problem with all the force that can be mustered because only when the problem has been stated in all its horror can the believer or anyone else face reality with honesty. For a person who found his faith sustained by the Gospel of John, as Dostoevsky's marked New Testament shows, Christ can be found outside the truth only when human beings take the wrong measure of "truth." In this Gospel, the relationship between Christ and the truth is contested ground, but John's Gospel does not make Christ the loser. "I am . . . the truth," Jesus says in John, meaning that there is no space between Christ and the truth (John 14:6). In answer to critics who wrote dismissively of Dostoevsky's aim to defend faith in the midst of the horror of suffering, he insisted that he did not affirm faith by closing his eyes to reality. Only a few days before his death he confided to his diary that it is not "as a child that I believe in Christ and profess faith in him, but rather, my *hosanna* has come through the great *crucible of doubt*, as the devil says in that same novel of mine."[18] The novel in question, of course, is *The Brothers Karamazov*. In this light, Dostoevsky's *Credo* is best understood as an emphatic tribute to Christ and not as though he postulates that Christ might be outside the truth.

16. Kjetsaa, *Dostoevsky and His New Testament*, 5.

17. Dostoevsky, *Complete Letters*, 195. I have used Frank's translation (*Dostoevsky*, 220).

18. Williams, *Dostoevsky*, 44; Frank, *Dostoevsky*, 913.

When Ivan brings his logic to bear on Alyosha, the latter does not mount a point by point rebuttal. Ivan has Alyosha on the ropes, so to speak, bloodied, barely whispering, and bowed. In response to Ivan's attempt to disconfirm Christian belief by rational argument and logic, Alyosha's initial refuge is silence and tacit concurrence. Readers may be fooled at this, focusing narrowly on the chapters where Ivan is in the driver's seat. Dostoevsky, however, explained that *the whole book* is an answer to Ivan, in the stories of *all* the brothers.[19] Alyosha's 'answer' does not lie on the level of argument but in his embodiment of love: it does not primarily lie in *what he is saying*. He is a kindly person who loves his conflicted brothers, and he acts compassionately and redemptively toward them. The narrator says of Alyosha that he "was incapable of passive love. If he loved any one, he set to work at once to help."[20] Behind Alyosha stands Zosima, "the Russian monk" and Alyosha's mentor, who in Dostoevsky's plan was meant to be the answer to Ivan's propositions even more than Alyosha. Zosima, too, is not an answer "point by point" but rather presented as an "artistic picture" and "a form of life."[21]

Dostoevsky was aware of the risk of this strategy, and doubts about the adequacy of 'the answer' persisted in his mind. Are the two representations, Ivan finding it impossible to reconcile suffering with faith in God, Alyosha and Zosima embodying a contrary "form of life," ultimately like ships passing each other in the night without reference to one another?

Dostoevsky's character profile of Alyosha compensates somewhat for this impression and counts for more than many readers realize. Bart Ehrman says of Alyosha that "he is deeply religious but still displays some (at times delightful) naïveté," implying that Alyosha is hardly Ivan's equal when it comes to reasoning powers.[22] Nevertheless, with respect to the question of who has murdered their father, the intuition of Alyosha is superior to the logic of Ivan. Alyosha alone has the sensitivity and strength of vision to question evidence that to others seems to point in one direction only. The jury's verdict is reasonable but wrong because the jury, like Ivan, fails to reckon with the complexity of the characters involved. While Alyosha alone possesses redeeming powers that reach out to the brother who is falsely convicted and to Ivan, the brother who shares a measure of responsibility for their father's death even though he is not the murderer, he also surpasses Ivan in the realm of understanding.

The credibility of Ivan's protest is weakened by inconsistencies in his own experience and choices. While he cries out on behalf of the children who are victimized, and while there is no doubt that his protest is genuine and deeply felt, Ivan betrays justice by committing to the notion that "everything is lawful" and by appearing to consent to the murder of his father by the hand of his half-brother. Even though it is in his power

19. Frank, *Dostoevsky*, 880.

20. Dostoevsky, *The Brothers Karamazov* (Garnett translation), 176.

21. Letter to Pobedonostsev, 6.

22. Ehrman, *God's Problem*, 265.

to prevent the murder, he does not lift a finger. The servile half-brother who is the actual murderer is confident that he has Ivan's permission to proceed. Though a self-proclaimed master of reason, Ivan's arithmetic approach is again inadequate for the complexity of human nature, and by extension, the complexity of the world plot. The trajectory of his life is one of descent and disintegration until he finds himself helplessly trying to sort reality from unreality and failing precisely on the point that was the strongest part of his rational system. Ivan seems to be up against truth constructed in such a way that its negation becomes its confirmation along lines envisioned by the apostle Paul. "For we cannot do anything against the truth, but only for the truth" (2 Cor 13:8).

These introductory caveats are necessary so as not to misjudge the context of Ivan's 'rebellion' or misconstrue the author's intention. More than one reader has failed to catch or convey a sense of the whole. When Bart Ehrman makes Ivan Karamazov an important voice in his closing argument in his book on how the Bible fails to answer "our most important question," he offers no context or background that might alert the uninitiated reader to understand that Dostoevsky's errand is different from his.[23] For a scholar whose claim to fame owes to some degree to his skill in exposing people who allegedly were guilty of misquoting Jesus,[24] Ehrman ends up badly misquoting Dostoevsky.

"I No Longer Want to Understand"

In the most hard-driving part of *The Brothers Karamazov*, the analytical and facts-oriented Ivan tries to dissuade Alyosha from entering a clerical vocation.[25] He puts before his brother images of suffering children, arguing that their suffering makes it impossible for him to find meaning. As we have seen already, the point of Ivan's argument is not to deny the existence of God. God may very well exist, but Ivan wants nothing to do with such a Being.

Ivan begins his argument by describing the suffering of children at the hand of Turkish soldiers. "These Turks, among other things, have also taken a delight in torturing children, starting with cutting them out of their mothers' wombs with a dagger, and ending with tossing nursing infants up in the air and catching them on their bayonets before their mothers' eyes. The main delight comes from doing it before their mothers' eyes," says Ivan.[26] This turn in the conversation puts Alyosha on the alert, and he asks apprehensively, "What are you driving at, brother?"[27]

Alyosha does not have to wait long for the answer because Ivan has given a lot of thought to this subject and is well prepared. His next exhibit is Richard, a Swiss

23. Ibid., 265–70.

24. Ehrman, *Misquoting Jesus*, 265–70.

25. Dostoevsky, *The Brothers Karamazov* (Pevear and Volokhonsky translation), 236–45.

26. Ibid., 238.

27. Ibid., 239.

orphan who grew up among the people of Geneva. Little Richard was not allowed to eat from the food that was fed to the animals that he was tending. More than once Dostoyevsky proves that he knows his Bible. Richard is worse off than the prodigal son in the Gospel of Luke, who was at least allowed to alleviate his hunger with food fed to the swine. When, as an adult, Richard kills a person in a drunken brawl, the attitude of the Christian community changes. Until that point they have given him nothing. Now they descend on him in the prison, urging Richard to accept grace before he faces execution. The Christian mindset and priorities in the account are odd. Geneva, one of the most religious and cultured places in Europe, did not do anything for the orphaned boy when he was in dire need as a child. Why do they take such interest in him when he is found guilty of murder? The apparent change of heart lacks depth, the cruelty of the initial stance now giving way to apparent compassion. When Richard repents and accepts Jesus, the citizens still feel duty bound to execute him. Ivan cannot conceal his scorn. "And so, covered with the kisses of his brothers, brother Richard is dragged up onto the scaffold, laid down on the guillotine, and his head is whacked off in brotherly fashion, forasmuch as grace has descended upon him, too."[28]

Ivan's next example is bestial cruelty against a little girl by parents who do not lack education or culture. Bestial cruelty is an understatement because animals do not treat their offspring the way the little girl is treated. For the offense of failing to get up in the middle of the night to go to the bathroom, the five year old girl is beaten, flogged, and kicked black and blue. The parents lock her up in the ice-cold outhouse all night, and the mother smears her face with excrement and forces her to eat it. (We recall how it was important to Dostoevsky to preserve the exact wording of the original account). "Who wants to know this damned good and evil at such a price?" Ivan asks scornfully.[29]

His final example is cruelty toward a little boy by a powerful, wealthy, and educated official. This man, a general in the army, one day discovers that one of his prized dogs is limping. He finds out that the dog was hurt when an eight year old boy accidentally hit one of the dog's paws with a stone during play. The general tracks down the boy, takes him away from his mother, and has him locked up for the night. The next day, with his mother present, the boy is paraded naked in front of the general's retinue of servants, horsemen, and dogs. At the general's command, the boy is forced to run, and then, the next moment, he commands the dogs to hunt the boy down. The dogs know their assignment, tearing the boy to pieces. All this happens in front of the boy's mother. Having thus put his evidence before the shaken Alyosha, Ivan turns to him, shouting, "Well . . .what to do with him [the general]? Shoot him? Shoot him for our moral satisfaction? Speak, Alyoshka!"[30]

28. Ibid., 240.

29. Ibid., 242.

30. Ibid., 243. Note the extra -k in Alyosha's name, added by Ivan for emphasis.

Ivan's question is best understood in light of what he will say subsequently. The problem is not only that something has been done to a child and his mother that breaks the boundaries of sense. It is also that there is no meaningful remedial option.

Alyosha has listened to his brother without saying anything, but now he has been commanded to speak, and he does. "'Shoot him!' Alyosha said softly, looking up at his brother with a sort of pale, twisted smile."[31] This is not what he wants to say or what he is supposed to say in light of his Christian convictions, but what can he say? What can he say except to confirm the absurdity?

Ivan proceeds to the closing argument, beginning with the problem of understanding.

"'I don't understand anything,' Ivan went on as if in delirium, 'and I no longer want to understand anything. I want to stick to the fact. I made up my mind long ago not to understand. If I wanted to understand something, I would immediately have to betray the fact, but I've made up my mind to stick to the fact.'"[32]

What does Ivan mean by saying, "I no longer want to understand anything"? What does he mean when he says, insisting, "I want to stick to the fact"? How are we to interpret his assertion that "if I wanted to understand something, I would immediately have to betray the fact"? He means, of course, that explanations and attempts to understand would devalue the currency of the fact; they would, so to speak, demean and diminish the fact of the children's suffering; the quest for understanding would by its very nature be an insult to the fact. The morality of this position means that the higher moral ground belongs to the person who does not understand and refuses to understand. Stewart Sutherland says that Ivan

> sets aside as hopelessly and wholly inadequate, the response to the sufferings of children which leads to acceptance of, or even worse, debate about, a theory or hypothesis. The theories thus spun, he argues, are only countenanced at the expense of 'the facts,' at the expense of moral blindness, the dulling of moral sense. These theories try to make comprehensible what is incomprehensible, and they do so at the price of "altering the facts."[33]

Ivan's protest, therefore, rests on a moral foundation. The Christian expectation that all will be well one day is to him just as unpalatable as the quest for understanding because it cannot make up for the suffering of children in present human reality. Even if there is final harmony at some future point, Ivan wants no part in it.

> You see, Alyosha, it may well be that if I live until that moment, or rise again or see it, I myself will perhaps cry out with all the rest, looking at the mother embracing her child's tormentor: "Just art thou, O Lord!" but I do not want to cry out with them. While there's still time, I hasten to defend myself against

31. Ibid.

32. Ibid.

33. Sutherland, *Atheism and the Rejection of God*, 29.

> it, and therefore I absolutely renounce all higher harmony. It is not worth one little tear of even that one tormented child who beat her chest with her little fist and prayed to "dear God" in a stinking outhouse with her unredeemed tears! Not worth it, because her tears remained unredeemed. They must be redeemed, otherwise there can be no harmony. But how, how will you redeem them? Is it possible? Can they be redeemed by being avenged? But what do I care if they are avenged, what do I care if the tormentors are in hell, what can hell set right here, if these ones have already been tormented? And where is the harmony, if there is hell?[34]

Ivan's reasoning is too clear to demand further explanation, but two of his points deserve to be highlighted. First, future harmony, as Christians envision it, cannot make up for the torment of the child whose fate he has described, or for the torment of millions of children whose stories have never been told. No amount of future harmony will be sufficient to warrant present suffering, and some imaginary scenes of future harmony are positively offensive. "I hasten to defend myself against it, and therefore I absolutely renounce all higher harmony," he says.[35]

Second, the Christian vision of future harmony is a smokescreen. In actual fact there is no harmony. Will the child's tears be redeemed by having the parents punished in hell? Hell fails as a remedial action because its aim is punishment, and it fails spectacularly with respect to eternal harmony. "What can hell set right," says Ivan, "if these have already been tormented?" Can more torment, now inflicted on the erstwhile tormentors, be the solution? Is eternal torment an element in Christianity's definition of harmony? To Ivan, this exposes the traditional Christian vision as a dream that is self-contradictory at its core.[36] "And where is the harmony, if there is hell?" he asks.[37] If human suffering is the problem in the first place, eternal suffering can only make the problem worse, a sentiment that is quite similar to Susan Neiman's comment on the contradiction in the Christian 'solution' (Chap. 1).[38] The proposed cure is worse than the disease. So far, neither retribution nor the prospect of harmony has succeeded in putting Ivan's mind at ease.

Indeed, putting the mind at ease is precisely *not* what is in progress. On the contrary, Ivan is agitated over the suffering of children, and his agitation is made worse by the proposed remedies that he brings up one after the other. Forgiveness, possibly the strongest card in the Christian arsenal with respect to making right what has gone wrong, will also be weighed and found wanting. On the whole, as he sees it, forgiveness merely cements and aggravates injustice. Let the victim of injustice forgive, but

34. Dostoevsky, *The Brothers Karamazov*, 244–45.

35. Ibid., 244.

36. Sutherland (*Atheism and the Rejection of God*, 31) says perceptively that Ivan accepts and projects the trivialization of God as 'God' is represented in the Christian apology.

37. Dostoevsky, *The Brothers Karamazov*, 245.

38. Neiman, *Evil in Modern Thought*, 19.

let no one take it upon themselves to forgive injustice done to others. The mother should not think it in her right to forgive injustice and cruelty done to her child. She, being the mother, says Ivan, should not forgive even if the child were to forgive the tormentor who had his dogs tear her child to pieces.

> I want to forgive, and I want to embrace, I don't want more suffering. And if the suffering of children goes to make up the sum of suffering needed to buy truth, then I assert beforehand that the whole of truth is not worth such a price. I do not, finally, want the mother to embrace the tormentor who let his dogs tear her son to pieces! She dare not forgive him! Let her forgive him for herself, if she wants to, let her forgive the tormentor her immeasurable maternal suffering; but she has no right to forgive the suffering of her child who was torn to pieces, she dare not forgive the tormentor even if the child himself were to forgive him! And if that is so, if they dare not forgive, then where is the harmony? Is there in the whole world a being who could and would have the right to forgive?[39]

The harmony that fails to materialize when the tormentors are brought to justice in hell also extends to the harmony that forgiveness is supposed to bring about. Ivan is daring the victims not to forgive. Aside from the fact that there cannot be harmony where there is hell, there cannot be harmony where there is no forgiveness, and, to repeat his point, there should not be forgiveness. Retribution and punishment, no less than mercy and forgiveness, all come up short as a viable road to final harmony. The bottom line, however, is not that Ivan wants harmony if only it were to be found.

> I don't want harmony, for love of mankind I don't want it. I want to remain with unrequited suffering. I'd rather remain with my unrequited suffering and my unquenched indignation, *even* if *I am wrong*.[40]

"*Even if I am wrong*"? We do not expect such sentiments from the analytical, Euclidean mind of Ivan, whose mode of operation is to analyze matters, follow the path on which logic guides him, and have the assurance that he has arrived at the correct answer without allowing emotions to dictate the outcome. Professing commitment to a point of view that he will hold even if it is the wrong one is a breach in the armor of rationality. And yet it may be no more than a way to express a commitment where the whole is larger and stronger than the sum of its parts.[41] Curiously, Ivan here echoes the inverse of Dostoevsky's personal creed expressed at an earlier point in his life that "if someone proved to me that Christ is outside the truth, and that *in reality* the truth were outside of Christ, then I should prefer to remain with Christ rather than with

39. Dostoevsky, *The Brothers Karamazov* (Pevear and Volokhonsky translation), 245.

40. Ibid., 245.

41. Sutherland (*Atheism and the Rejection of God*, 35) notes that Ivan rejects "the possibility of *any other* account of belief than that of a 'Euclidean mind.'"

the truth."[42] Ivan, if proven wrong, would not agree to abandon his outrage, outrage representing the moral bottom line of his objection to 'this world of God's.' His most biting scorn is reserved for harmony as such.

> Besides, they have put too high a price on harmony; we can't afford to pay so much for admission. And therefore I hasten to return my ticket. And it is my duty, if only as an honest man, to return it as far ahead of time as possible. Which is what I am doing. It's not that I don't accept God, Alyosha, *I just most respectfully return him the ticket.*[43]

Ivan rejects harmony, choosing solidarity with suffering humanity rather than submission to a divine design that offends his sense of justice. His conviction does not revert to the usual atheistic argument that there is no God, but the world that exists is such a vale of tears that it reduces God's existence to irrelevance. Moreover, Ivan's moral argument for returning the ticket is a more stinging rebuke to God than the 'atheistic problem of evil,' whose adherents take evil to mean that God does not exist. A God who does not exist cannot be blamed for the way things are. To Ivan, however, nothing in the future will be sufficient to make up for present reality; "they have put too high a price on harmony, we can't afford to pay so much for admission," he says.

His sharpest arrow is left for last. We do well to pause in order to put it in context before reading it one last time. Whereas the usual stance in Christian theology is to plead for mercy before the throne of God, the relationship is inverted in Ivan's argument. In the traditional framework, God is axiomatically in the right, and human beings are self-evidently in the wrong. No one has the right to question God's justice. Human need centers on finding mercy in God's eyes. This is the legacy of Christian theology as a whole, and it is even more the legacy of the Protestant Reformation. With this background in mind, we are better prepared to gauge the boldness of Ivan's final arrow.

"It's not that I don't accept God, Alyosha, I just most respectfully return him the ticket."[44]

"'That is rebellion,' Alyosha said softly, dropping his eyes."[45]

After the Storm

Let us suppose that there is forgiveness, some kind of accountability for the perpetrators of evil, and final harmony in the end. Let us even suppose that there is a free ticket, the right of admission to bliss that the human imagination in its present state cannot fathom. All these things are taken for granted in Ivan's argument. It is in awareness of

42. Frank, *Dostoevsky*, 220.

43. Dostoevsky, *The Brothers Karamazov* (Pevear and Volokhonsky translation), 245, emphasis supplied.

44. Ibid., 245.

45. Ibid.

these claims that he proposes to return the ticket and to do so ahead of time without taking the risk that he might be emotionally overwhelmed when harmony arrives. What we see, therefore, is a person who is offered all that a human being yearns to have within the traditional framework of theology, and yet he turns it down. Importantly and not to be missed, Ivan turns it down in the name of morality and justice. This is Ivan's rebellion, defiance inspired by commitment to moral standard that has been violated. Ivan's outrage implies knowledge of what that standard should be and certainty that it has been trampled upon.

When Alyosha says that his brother's final word amounts to rebellion, Ivan hesitates for a moment but refuses to back down. He extracts from Alyosha the concession that if it were up to him, that is, if it were up to Alyosha, he, no more than Ivan, would agree to let the tears of even one little child be among the building blocks for future harmony. "Would you agree to be the architect on such conditions?" Ivan demands to know.[46] "No, I would not agree," Alyosha answers softly.[47]

This is a critical point in the dialogue and a significant admission on the part of Alyosha. If Ivan's stance amounts to rebellion, what is Alyosha's stance? Is he, too, in a state of rebellion, given that he, too, would not "agree to be the architect"? The implied answer is clearly "no," because Alyosha sees Ivan to be in a state of agitation and rebellion in a way that he, Alyosha, is not. What, then, is the difference?

Albert Camus, writing as one of many who found it impossible not to take this conversation seriously, takes his point of departure in Ivan's rebellion.[48] He comments that to Ivan "faith presumes the acceptance of the mystery of evil and resignation to injustice."[49] Is this what Alyosha is doing, his faith rescued by resignation to injustice? Is acceptance of injustice the stance that gets 'faith' off the hook? To Camus, the answer is "yes," because he proceeds to declare that questioning is incompatible with genuine faith. "When a man submits God to moral judgments, he kills him in his own heart," he says.[50] With reference to Alyosha, this could mean that Alyosha has decided to take moral judgments out of the equation of faith and has thereby salvaged his devotion. More seriously, Camus's assertion and the certainty with which he holds it could itself be a profound misperception. He makes it appear that 'God' is a given as though 'God' is above questions of representation and interpretation, the devout crusader and the pious pacifist created of the same cloth as long as they avoid moral judgments. It follows from this that Camus has fallen too easily into the trap set up by a non-questioning theological tradition, and it follows, too, that bringing moral judgment into the equation of faith is not to kill God in one's heart. Abraham, as we shall see, makes moral judgment a cornerstone of faith and is affirmed by God for

46. Ibid.

47. Ibid.

48. Camus, *The Rebel*.

49. Ibid., 56.

50. Ibid., 62.

his stance even if his stance has been bleached by the tradition (Chap. 8). "It is not enough to say that one believes in God," as Terence Fretheim says wisely. "What is important finally is the *kind* of God in whom one believes."[51] But these caveats actually enhance rather than silence the voice of Ivan Karamazov, and they do not negate Camus's concerns. Knowing, as both do, that the Christian tradition does not offer relief from suffering and refusing to eschew moral judgment, Camus says that there "is no possible salvation for the man who feels real compassion."[52]

Sensing that the torrent is over and that Ivan has talked himself empty, Alyosha ventures forth with a thought of his own, speaking as though the thought has been overlooked.

> You asked just now if there is in the whole world a being who could and would have the right to forgive. But there is such a being, and he can forgive everything, forgive all and *for all*, because he himself gave his innocent blood for all and for everything. You've forgotten about him, but it is on him the structure is being built, and it is to him that they will cry out: "Just art thou, O Lord, for thy ways have been revealed!"[53]

Forgiveness, retribution, harmony, and understanding have been weighed and found wanting in Ivan's argument. Now comes the turn to Jesus. "You've forgotten about him, but it is on him the structure is being built!" Alyosha exclaims.[54]

Has Ivan forgotten about *him*? Not at all! "Ah, yes, the 'only sinless One' and his blood!" Ivan responds, at first sounding unimpressed. "No, I have not forgotten about him; on the contrary, I've been wondering all the while why you hadn't brought him up for so long, because in discussions your people usually trot him out the first thing."[55] This sounds dismissive, as though talk of "the only sinless One" will have no more impact than the other elements in the Christian account.

And yet there appears to be a slight hesitation, a subtle change in the emotional and verbal tenor. No, Ivan does not expect his brother to say anything about "the only sinless One" that will make a difference to his view of the suffering of children. He has no illusions that Alyosha will bring out anything game-changing concerning the person "your people usually trot . . .out the first thing." As far as his expectations go on this point, Ivan remains indifferent. Let the Christian add Jesus to his or her apologetic arsenal, in addition to forgiveness and the prospect of final harmony, and it will change nothing.

But the reader cannot fail to notice that Ivan's voice is less combative than earlier in the conversation. His creed of anger, indignation, and protest, as it is usually

51. Fretheim, *The Suffering of God*, 1.

52. Camus, *The Rebel*, 57.

53. Dostoevsky, *The Brothers Karamazov* (Pevear and Volokhonsky translation), 246.

54. Ibid., 246.

55. Ibid.

perceived and represented,[56] is not only red-hot fury. Ivan now sounds mellow and almost bashful, as if to show that his anger might be a mask for pain and that his creed is best understood as a creed of anguish. What should a person feel and how should he or she express himself or herself when coming face to face with the realities Ivan has presented? The emotional tenor of Ivan's outburst is in that sense not a lapse from rationality but rather proof of it. That is to say, absence of emotion would diminish and betray the reasons that are at the heart of the emotion.[57] Moreover, is not absence of emotion one of the things that offends Ivan the most in the believer's stance toward the suffering of children?

"You know, Alyosha—don't laugh!—I composed a poem once, about a year ago," Ivan suddenly confides.[58] The need to tell his brother not to laugh signals Ivan's self-consciousness about his 'poem.' Now that his outrage has been vented, the real analysis that is the staple of Ivan's rational approach can begin in earnest. And he will, somewhat in violation of the genre of rational argument, deliver it as 'poetry.'

The disclosure that Ivan has written a poem creates a renewed sense of suspense. If there is a soft spot in Ivan's argument, a door left slightly ajar, it depends on 'the only sinless One' that makes a belated appearance in the discussion. Moreover, and to our great surprise, if anything truly compelling can be said for 'the only sinless One,' it will be up to Ivan to say it better than in the conventional version. In the remote and unlikely event that there is a theodicy that could satisfy Ivan, we begin to suspect that he knows what it is.

A less tantalizing view has to most readers seemed more plausible. If the poem is a continuation of Ivan's attack on faith, the poem will state his reason with less heat and more light. Ivan will show more fully his ideological commitment but not in the sense that it casts doubt on what he has said to his brother so far. As we shall see (Chap. 18), the poem will pay sustained attention to 'the only sinless One,' and it will frame 'the only sinless One' in such a way that readers have barely been able to tell whether Ivan is defending the value that dominates the poem or whether he is attacking it. To Alyosha, Ivan's one-person audience in *The Brothers Karamazov*, it seems as though his poem is a contrast to his creed of anguish to the point that it answers Ivan's philosophical and moral predicament.

What that contested value might be, however, will at this stage have to wait. First there is other ground to cover, in perspectives that have been lost or overlooked, in stories that have been ignored or misinterpreted, and in events that clamor for a better match between human reality and attempts to find sense.

56. See, for instance, Sutherland, *Atheism and the Rejection of God*, 141–42; McGrath, *Christian Theology*, 205.

57. Sutherland (*Atheism and the Rejection of God*, 64–65) touches on this aspect of Ivan's protest, but seems to make more of the role of emotion on the side of faith.

58. Dostoevsky, *The Brothers Karamazov* (Pevear and Volokhonsky translation), 246.

Chapter Three

God of Sense in the Early Christian Narrative

About the year 175 in the Christian era, perhaps in the year 177, a new book hit the market in the Roman World.[1] The emperor at that time was Marcus Aurelius, notable for his enlightened beliefs, but also for allowing persecution of Christians in many places in the empire. The author of the book was the philosopher Celsus, and the title was *On the True Doctrine*, hardly a title destined to make the book a bestseller.

But the book is remarkable for a number of reasons, the first of which is that it was written at all. Why would a non-Christian author like Celsus, a philosopher of some note, write a book on the Christians and their beliefs? Part of the answer is no doubt that Celsus did not like the teachings of believers in Jesus. But this is not the whole answer. Admitting that we know very little about Celsus, we can be sure that he disliked many things that did not bother him enough to make it the subject of a book.

The other element that helps explain Celsus's book, therefore, is the growing influence of Christianity. The new faith was impacting the Roman world; it could no longer be ignored; its influence was reaching the educated tier of society. Celsus's book set for itself the task of countering the influence of the Christian message. In this sense his book was the first of its kind. It would not, as is well known, be the last.

Celsus is thought to have been a philosopher in the Platonic tradition.[2] When he goes on the attack against Christianity, he writes as an educated person, and he speaks as one who has done his homework reasonably well. For this reason his portrayal of the Christian message offers a rare opportunity to listen in on what Christians were saying in the latter half of the second century.

With respect to tone Celsus is condescending, never missing an opportunity to spite Christians or put down their beliefs. While this may be a feature of polemical literature of that period, Celsus excels at it. We see it in the following example, where he directs his scorn at the belief that he finds most objectionable.

> *Their utter stupidity* [of the Christians] *can be illustrated in any number of ways, but especially with their misreading of the divine enigmas and their insistence*

1. For a more in-depth treatment of this subject, see Tonstad, "Theodicy and the Theme of Cosmic Conflict," 169–202.

2. For an introduction to the thought-world of Middle Platonism, see Dillon, *The Middle Platonists*.

> *that there exists a being opposed to God, whom they know by the name of devil (in Hebrew, Satanas, for they refer to one and the same being by various names).*[3]

In Celsus's eyes, the Christians are not very bright. The teaching that proves their stupidity better than anything else is the notion that *there exists a being opposed to God*. Having immersed himself in the preaching and teaching of the Early Church, Celsus has discovered that Christians operate with *a third category of being*, a being that is neither God nor human. A central tenet in the early Christian account, therefore, is to Celsus the epitome of nonsense.

Christians in the Early Church, we learn, see the earth as the stage of a cosmic conflict that involves God, human beings, and Satan. Satan is a fallen angel. His fall happened before the fall of human beings. After Satan had fallen, he played a crucial role in breaking up the relationship between human beings and God (Gen 3:1). This is the story Christians find in the Bible, and this view is at the core of their belief. Christians who read Celsus's book will disagree with his criticism, but they will not say that Celsus has failed to state what the Christian belief is.

Celsus is mystified by Christians who depart from what he calls the "divine enigmas," the true mystery of God. Thinkers and philosophers have in his view thought long and hard about God and God's ways. The result of the hard work would go to waste for anyone who accepts the Christian teaching. In the eyes of the philosopher, the figure of Satan is unthinkable for what it says about God.

> *But they [the Christians] show how utterly concocted these ideas are when they go on to say that the highest god in heaven, desiring to do such and such—say, confer some great gift on man—cannot fulfil his purpose because he is opposed and thwarted by a god who is his opposite. Does this mean that the Son of God can be beaten by a devil?*[4]

This statement is as clear as it gets in Celsus's book. He writes as a philosopher, but he is not irreligious. Far from it, he is a believer, seeking to defend God against the calumny with which the Christian teaching sullies God's dignity. What is this, we fairly hear him shout, portraying God as though God has an opponent that limits God! What is this but a god who is spineless, a pushover, and a weakling! In Celsus's view and in the view of the best philosophical tradition of the second century, God should be a sovereign god and the undisputed boss. If asked, Celsus would answer that God's defining attribute is power. There should be no power within sight that somehow challenges God.

3. Hoffmann, *Celsus on the True Doctrine*, 98–99.

4. Ibid., 99.

> *It is blasphemy to say that when the greatest God indeed wishes to confer some benefit upon men, He has a power which is opposed to Him, and so is unable to do it.*[5]

Celsus does not reject the notion of Satan because he refuses to believe that there is anything beyond the human sphere. His opposition to the Christian teaching is theological rather than ontological, as scholars might put it. He is offended by the Christian view for what it says about God, not because it posits an unfamiliar category of being. A world-view that includes Satan diminishes God. The Christian teaching puts God's sovereignty at risk, jeopardizing the doctrine that is most sacred to Celsus. They make God seem less than what God ought to be. Celsus feels duty bound to defend God's honor. His outrage is palpable when he comments on Jesus.

> *But the Christian notion that the Son of God accepted the punishments inflicted upon him by a devil is merely ludicrous, especially if we are to think that this is to teach us to endure punishments quietly. In my view the Son of God had a right to punish the devil; he certainly had no reason to threaten with punishment the men he came to save, the very ones who had suffered so much from the devil's abuse.*[6]

The power relation between Jesus and Satan is in the Christian outlook turned on its head. Jesus, who must be strong if he is to do any good at all, seems the weaker party. His apparent weakness means that there cannot be a connection between Jesus and God. No god who takes God's dignity seriously would consent to be treated abusively and be kicked around the way Jesus was. If Jesus were truly representing God, as the Christians claim, he would have put the devil in his place. He would do it by force, the greater the force the better. In the Christian teaching, logic and decency are violated because the bad one is allowed to inflict suffering on the good, and the good and the strong, whether God or Jesus, allow the bad one to get away with it.

To Celsus, this does not make sense. Who can respect anyone who lets himself be treated this way? Who in their right mind would want *God* to be like that?

> *It is mere impiousness, therefore, to suggest that the things that were done to Jesus were done to God. Certain things are simply as a matter of logic impossible to God, namely those things which violate the consistency of his nature: God cannot do less than what it befits God to do, what it is God's nature to do. Even if the prophets had foretold such things about the Son of God, it would have been necessary to say, according to the axiom I have cited, that the prophets were wrong, rather than to believe that God has suffered and died.*[7]

5. *Contra Celsum* (Chadwick translation), 6.42.

6. Hoffmann, *Celsus on the True Doctrine*, 100.

7. Ibid.

Celsus has a fully-developed idea of what God must be like that rules out the Christian view before the Christians get to the starting line. To him, the story of Jesus violates "the consistency of God's nature," taking God to such a low level that the Christian God is good for nothing. "*God cannot do less than what it befits God to do, what it is God's nature to do*!" Celsus exclaims. If the prophets of the Old Testament predicted otherwise, they were not telling the truth, and we should not believe them.

It cannot be clearer than this. Non-Christian thinkers in the second century have found their voice. According to Celsus, the basic tenet of good theology centers on the power and sovereignty of God. There should be no ifs, ands, or buts. The Christian belief makes God into a Being that no thinking person can respect. What the writers of the New Testament praise as *good news*, never tiring of this term, is news that makes Celsus cringe in revulsion. He dismisses Christianity because he considers it an insult to God.

Explaining the Christian Belief

Sadly, the complete text of Celsus's book has been lost. We owe the quotes I have given above to the service of another author. Some seventy years after Celsus's book, probably around 244 CE, a leading Christian thinker was prevailed upon to write a rebuttal. The author of the Christian reply was Origen of Alexandria (185–254 CE), and the title of his book was short and to the point, *Against Celsus*.[8] If we venture to guess why Origen wrote *his* book, the answer will be the exact opposite of Celsus's motivation. Origen believed that Celsus's attack on the Christian message was unjustified. The fact that he wrote a lengthy book, discussing Celsus's arguments point by point, should be taken to mean that Celsus's book might be slowing the influence of Christianity.

Origen, the author of the second book, is remembered as one of the most devout and learned men in the history of the Christian Church. Today he is known somewhat in the Roman Catholic Church and hardly known at all in the Protestant world, but he remains the most influential theologian in the Orthodox Church. Origen is also one of the most prolific authors ever, and, as one historian has said, he "is one of those figures, none too common even in Church history, of whose character we can say that we know nothing but what is good."[9]

Origen does a great service to our knowledge of Celsus because he quotes the work of the deceased philosopher before answering him. We know what Celsus was saying thanks to Origen's rendition. Before he answers, he lets Celsus speak in his own voice. This might give the appearance of a dialogue, an impression that is misleading if it causes the reader to believe that the two writers are actually talking to each other. While Origen is talking to Celsus, Celsus was not addressing Origen. The members of

8. Crouzel (*Origen* [Worrall translation], 47) calls *Contra Celsum* "the most important apologetic work of antiquity" along with Augustine's *The City of God*, written almost two centuries later.

9. Butterworth, *Origen on First Principles*, v.

Celsus's audience were readers in the latter part of the second century, and, to the extent that he had Christian readers in mind, they preceded Origen by at least two generations. It is important to realize that Celsus was not attacking what Origen believed. Through Celsus, we gain access to the beliefs of Christians at a much earlier date. As to style, Origen's work is simple and matter-of-fact, "a work without pretension," it has been said, "where style counts for nothing, thought for everything."[10]

Two things need to be emphasized concerning Origen's book. First, Origen says that Celsus *misunderstands* the Christian teaching, but he does not say that Celsus has *misrepresented* what the Christian teaching is. For instance, when Celsus attacks the Christian belief in Satan, Origen does not say that Christians do not hold this belief. He firmly believes that Celsus is misguided, but he does not try to get Christians off the hook by walking away from the belief that is being attacked. Second, and equally important, the Christian belief in Satan is not invented by Origen in the third century CE. Those who ascribe the Christian view of Satan to Origen have their facts wrong and their timing mixed up by almost a century. When Celsus attacked Christians for believing in Satan, *a being that is opposed to God*, Origen was not yet born. This means that we must read Origen judiciously and, as I seek to do here, give priority to Celsus's perception and critique of the Christian story decades before Origen speaks to the subject. Much in Origen's outlook has its origin in Platonic thought: his cosmology, his dualist anthropology, his antipathy toward the material world, and his belief in the pre-existence of souls. These ideas muddy the water.[11] But when Origen affirms the cosmic conflict perspective that riles Celsus, he is drawing on a uniquely *Christian* belief, and he explains it carefully.

> The name Devil, and Satan, and Wicked one, is mentioned in many places of scripture, and he who bears it is also described as being the enemy of God.[12]

We find this message everywhere in Origen's books, so much so that Origen has been called the greatest diabolist—meaning a person who takes Satan seriously—in the history of the Christian Church. The theme of cosmic conflict constitutes the framework for his understanding of reality, and it bears on the most puzzling elements in God's story. Origen never lets his readers forget it.

> He who was Lucifer and who arose in heaven, he who was without sin from the day of his birth and who was among the cherubim, was able to fall with

10. Crouzel, *Origen*, 57.

11. As Crouzel notes (*Origen*, 217), Origen's idea of the pre-existence of souls proved vulnerable and won few defenders. Origen's thinking on universal salvation is sometimes ambiguous but seems to be confirmed in *First Principles* I.6.1; see also Greggs, "Exclusivist or Universalist?" 315–27; Fredriksen, *Sin*, 100–112. Scott ("Guarding the Mysteries of Salvation," 347–68), sifting through the maze of ambiguities and apparent contradictions in Origen's thought, argues that the drift toward universalism is qualified by pastoral and pedagogical concerns.

12. Origen, *First Principles*, 1.5.2.

> respect to the kindness of the Son of God before he could be bound by chains of love.[13]

This is a comment on a passage in Paul's letter to the Romans (Rom 6:8–10). Many readers will find it strange because the statement cannot be explained on the basis of a specific cue within the text. The reason, rather, is that Origen never strays far from the theme of cosmic conflict. In this particular comment he manages to highlight the most important points in Lucifer's 'biography': He "*was* Lucifer," the splendid "Son of the Morning" (Isa 14:12). He "*arose* in heaven." He "*was* without sin from the day of his birth" (Ezek 28:15). He "*was* among the cherubim" (Ezek 28:14). And yet, despite the exalted origin and high standing, something went wrong. Lucifer "was able to fall with respect to the kindness of the Son of God before he could be bound by the chains of love."[14]

Origen has here touched on the essential hard facts of Lucifer's story as well as on the subtle side that may not be apparent to readers unfamiliar with Origen. The thought that Lucifer was not bound by "the chains of love" is a strange expression because "chains of love" represent a bond that arises from within. It is a counterpoint and contrast to other kinds of chains, such as chains of obligation or force applied from without. To be bound by "the chains of love" means to be bound in freedom.

Origen is not in the slightest shaken by the ridicule Celsus heaps on the Christian story. The Christians in the third century, like the Christians in the first and the second centuries, still *"make a being who is opposed to God"*; they do believe in the reality of Satan. Origen defends this belief. It anchors his view of the world. He finds its source in the Bible. And he takes on Celsus for what he considers flaws in Celsus's view of God and human reality.

The source of the Christian belief, of course, is the Bible, the Old Testament as well as the New. Critics who claim that the Old Testament does not say much about Satan will hear a different story from Origen. To him and to the Christian community preceding him, the scarcity of material about Satan in the Old Testament could also apply to the role of Jesus in the same body of literature. A number of Old Testament texts that in the New Testament are harnessed as prophecies pointing to Jesus were not, in their original context, fully recognized as Messianic.[15] In light of the life of Jesus these texts have found the referent that does justice to their meaning.

The role of Satan in the Old Testament is similar in the sense that texts that on the surface refer to a human power, such as the king of Babylon in Isaiah (Isa 14:12) or the prince of Tyre in Ezekiel (Ezek 28:12), have a meaning that looks beyond the human factor. They project a non-human reality on the screen. This insight is basic to the

13. *ComRom* 5.10.16, books 1–5, 5.10.16 (Scheck translation), 377.

14. *ComRom* 5.10.16.

15. A case in point is Ps 110:1–5, one of the texts quoted most frequently in the New Testament, cf. Matt 22:42–45; Mark 12:35–37; Acts 2:34; 1 Cor 15:25; Eph 1:20–22; Heb 10:12–13.

Christian interpretation of the Old Testament, and Origen defends it vigorously. His discussion of the text describing the prince of Tyre in Ezek 28:12–19 is a case in point.

> Who is there that, hearing such sayings as this, "Thou wast a signet of likeness and a crown of honour in the delights of the paradise of God," or this, "from the time thou wast created with the cherubim, I placed thee in the holy mount of God," could possibly weaken their meaning to such an extent as to suppose them spoken of a human being, even a saint, not to mention the prince of Tyre? Or what "fiery stones" can he think of, "in the midst" of which any man could have lived? Or who could be regarded as "stainless" from the very "day he was created," and yet at some later time could have acts of unrighteousness found in him and be said to be "cast forth into the earth"? This certainly indicated that the prophecy is spoken of one who, not being in the earth, was "cast forth into the earth," whose "holy places" also are said to be "polluted."[16]

The Christian interpretation is to Origen taking stock of what is found in the Old Testament text, adding nothing and taking nothing away. Perfection of the kind envisioned in Ezekiel's poem is not found in the human realm, especially when the one who fell was originally counted among the cherubim. To suggest that a historical prince of Tyre at some point was "the signet of perfection" is to miss the mark entirely. Ezekiel, Origen contends, is concerned about a figure that transcends anything found in the human realm.

So, too, in the Book of Job, argues Origen.

> It is there written that the devil stands near God, and asks for power against Job that he may encompass him with very severe calamities, first by the destruction of all his possessions and his children, and secondly by affecting Job's whole body with a violent attack of the disease called elephantiasis. . . . Moreover, in the last chapters of Job, where the Lord spoke to Job through a whirlwind and the clouds the sayings in the book bearing his name, several passages could be taken which deal with the serpent.[17]

Isaiah's description of the king of Babylon (Isa 14:12–20) is deployed and defended along similar lines.

> Again, we are taught by the prophet Isaiah the following facts about another opposing power. He says: "How hast Lucifer, who arose in the morning, fallen from heaven. He who assailed the nations is broken and dashed to the earth. Thou saidst indeed in thy heart, I will ascend into heaven; above the stars of heaven I will place my throne, I will sit upon lofty mountains which are toward the north, I will ascend above the clouds; I will be like the Most High. But now shalt thou be cast down to the lower world, and to the foundations of the earth. All who see thee shall be amazed over thee and say: This is the man

16. *First Principles* I.5.4; cf. *Contra Celsum* 6.43; 6.44; *Homélies sur Ézékiel*, 411–13.

17. *Contra Celsum* 6.43.

> that affected the whole earth, that moved kings, that made the whole round a desert, that destroyed cities and did not loose those who were in chains.[18]

As with the passage concerning 'the prince of Tyre' in Ezekiel, no person or power in the human realm has feet large enough to fit the shoes of Isaiah's poem. The notion that the Bible has texts that contain a 'surplus of meaning' must in this connection not be taken to mean that the alleged 'surplus' is imported to the text by the reader.[19] If there is a 'surplus' in Isaiah's poem, it refers to an opposing power that has an angelic or demonic referent. The 'surplus,' as noted, is not added to the text by restless and imaginative readers. It is the text itself that has the surplus; it is put there by the author, who aspires to describe evil in ultimate and definitive terms. On this point, at least, Henri Crouzel's depiction of Origen seems well taken. Origen "possesses to a unique degree the gift of the exegete, analogous to that of the inspired author; he knows how to listen to God."[20]

Origen, following the precedent of the New Testament, will argue that Isaiah's poem is a thinly veiled telling of the power that is opposed to God.

> It is most clearly proved by these words that he who formerly was Lucifer and who "arose in the morning" has fallen from heaven. For if, as some suppose, he was a being of darkness, why is he said to have formerly been Lucifer or light-bearer? Or how could he "rise in the morning," who had in him no light at all? Moreover the Saviour teaches us about the devil as follows: "Lo, I see Satan fallen as lightning form heaven." So he was light once.[21]

The foregoing are only a few smatterings of the way Origen mines the Bible for an account of the demonic. In his answer to Celsus and readers in his own time, he recounts the biblical basis for this teaching so as to make it seem above question. Origen is soft-spoken on behalf of his effort, but he does not harbor the slightest doubt that the Bible tells the story of a cosmic conflict or that it traces the footprints of evil back to a non-human point of origin.

> However, although we have boldly and rashly committed these few remarks to writing in this book, perhaps we have said nothing significant. But if anyone with the time to examine the holy scriptures were to collect texts from all the sources and were to give a coherent account of evil, both how it first came to exist and how it is being destroyed, he would see that the meaning of Moses and the prophets with regard to Satan has not even been dreamt of by Celsus

18. *First Principles* I.5.5; cf. *Contra Celsum* 6.43.

19. Cf. Ricoeur, *Interpretation Theory.*

20. Crouzel, *Origen*, 28. von Harnack's verdict (*Der kirchengeschichtliche Ertrag*, part 2, 4), based on a thorough and critical reading of all the available works of Origen, is worth noting: "There has never been a theologian in the Church that so wholeheartedly was and wanted to be an exegete of the Bible as Origen" (translation mine).

21. *First Principles* I.5.5; cf. *Contra Celsum* 6.43.

> or by any of the people who are dragged down by this wicked daemon and are drawn away in their soul from God and the right conception of Him and from His Word.[22]

As explained and defended by Origen, the biblical account is not interested in Satan for Satan's sake only. If the story cannot avoid paying attention to Satan, it is because Satan has distorted the truth about God. This is the all-important subject. Origen maintains an unremitting focus on how Satan has misrepresented God. His statement on the scriptural basis for the role Christians attribute to Satan, quoted above, goes to the heart of the problem. People "are drawn away in their soul from God and the right conception of Him and from His Word."[23]

As Celsus knew well, the pagan world also had myths of cosmic combat and opposition to God, but, he says, *these myths are not like the [Christian] tales which tell of a devil who is a daemon, or (and here they are nearer the truth) which speak of a man who is a sorcerer and proclaims opposing opinions.*[24] On this point Celsus has understood the distinctive of the account almost as well as Origen.

What, as Celsus hears it, are the Christians saying about Satan? They are talking about a figure who "*proclaims opposing opinions.*"[25] It is on the strength of these opinions that people are deceived. Recalling again the story in the Garden of Eden (Gen 3:1–6), the false opinions that Satan is promoting are opinions about God. Celsus, however, cannot respect a God who allows Satan to get away with it. He understands that this is what the Christians are saying, and he repudiates such a God. For God to be a Person in whom Celsus can believe, God must be an undisputed sovereign who will not allow anything to stand in God's way.

The ideological stumbling block in this dispute is freedom. Celsus cannot understand the God of the Christians because the category of freedom is undeveloped or absent in his view of reality. His vision of God is thoroughly imperial. If we imagine Celsus thinking of God in political terms, God is the divine emperor before whom humans have no voice. He might even be the subject who does not *want* to have a say. Or, just as likely, he might be a subject who is happy to make do with less freedom because it means less responsibility. Celsus's mentality resembles that of Seneca, who for a number of years served as something like a chief of staff to the emperor Nero. "Tell me what I have to do," Seneca is reported to have said, "I do not want to learn. I want to obey."[26] This is one reason why it is impossible for Celsus to make sense of Jesus and the apparent power gap between Jesus and Satan; "*the Christian notion that the Son of God accepted the punishments inflicted upon him by a devil is merely ludicrous.*"[27]

22. *Contra Celsum* 6.44.

23. Ibid.

24. Ibid., 6.42.

25. Ibid.

26. Quoted in Miller, "Divine Command and Beyond," 26.

27. *Celsus on the True Doctrine*, 100.

The things that are a stumbling stone to Celsus are to Origen the cornerstone. Crouzel calls Origen "the supreme theologian of free will."[28] René Cadiou wrote that for Origen "liberty became the most general of all the laws of the universe."[29] Evil arose in the context of freedom. There could not be evil if the angels and human beings were not endowed with the gift of freedom. And yet freedom only provides the opportunity and is not the *cause* of evil. Freedom, too, is the value that God will not surrender even in the face of sin.

> For freedom of will shall always remain in rational natures. It was possible even for him who was Lucifer, owing to the splendor of his glory, and who rose in the morning because of the light of knowledge, to be changed from his own glory and become darkness because of the evil which he received. And to him who was without stain from the day of his birth and dwelled with the cherubim and lived in the midst of fiery stones and was clothed with the entire adornment of the virtues in the paradise of God, there was no tree of virtues which could compare. But later, iniquities were found in him and he was cast from heaven to earth.[30]

Unlike the God envisioned by Celsus, the God who is revealed in Jesus values freedom to a degree that will be a stumbling block to many a thinker and many an ideology.

> We certainly do not deny that free will always will remain in rational natures, but we affirm that the power of the cross of Christ and of his death which he undertook at the end of the ages is so great that it suffices for the healing and restoration not only of the present and the future but also of past ages. It suffices not only for our human order, but also for the heavenly powers and orders. For according to the Apostle Paul's own pronouncement: Christ has made peace "through the blood of his cross" not only with "the things on earth" but also with "the things in heaven."[31]

This complex statement is in need of nuancing with regard to Origen's underlying ideology. While, on the one hand, freedom is alien to Celsus's outlook, in the Christian account it is the most precious of all values. Freedom is grounded in the character of God. God is willing to defend freedom at a high cost rather than solve the cosmic conflict by giving up on freedom. At all stages of this argument lies the conviction that God's remedy will not overrule or eclipse freedom.

On the other hand, however, Origen's commitment to freedom comes with a question mark. He sometimes construes the choices of celestial and human beings as though no one can ever make a choice that has irremediable consequences: no

28. Crouzel, *Origen*, 21.

29. Cadiou. *Introduction au système d'Origène*, quoted in Danielou, *Origen*,205–6.

30. *ComRom* 5.10.16, books 1–5, 5.10.16 (Scheck translation), 377.

31. *ComRom* 5.10.16; see also *First Principles* I.6.1.

creature will ever say "no" to God *irreversibly*. Is this view compatible with Origen's otherwise consistent and deeply felt commitment to freedom? Does his construct of creaturely choices that never mean a final "no" to God and never have permanently negative consequences represent an affirmation or a trivializing of freedom?

As noted in the statement above, Origen describes salvation as healing. On this point, too, he strikes a note that fell silent in later Christian theology. Jesus's death on the cross heals in the sense that it disproves the misrepresentation of God for which Satan is responsible (John 12:23–32). Satan made God out to be a Person to be dreaded. Far more than I can show here, Origen sees the message of the Bible as a message of healing. Salvation is to him best understood in medical terms, and healing begins with the way human beings look at God. When we listen to Celsus, on the other hand, prohibition and coercion are among the resources with which he will combat evil. Celsus's god is at his best precisely when he is feared the most. Reviewing some of the statements we have visited earlier, we hear Celsus ask with poorly disguised contempt,

> *Does this mean that the Son of God can be beaten by a devil?*[32]

> *It is blasphemy to say that when the greatest God indeed wishes to confer some benefit upon men, He has a power which is opposed to Him, and so is unable to do it.*[33]

> *In my view the Son of God had a right to punish the devil.*[34]

In these statements God's most characteristic attribute is power. The relationship between God and humans begins with divine sovereignty. Celsus stands at a loss before the Christian story. Why would Jesus submit to abuse by Satan if Jesus had the power of God at his command? Why would God choose *not* to do something that it is in God's power to do? Why would God *not* put Satan in his place and thus bring an end to the indignity of which Satan is the instigator?

Celsus has no compunction about coercion. Indeed, he seems to relish the thought of its deployment, as if convinced that coercion more than any other method would drive home God's honor and glory.

To Origen, coercion is anathema. Not only is use of force incompatible with freedom, but if used, it will compound rather than solve the problem of evil. God allows good and evil to develop and to run their course until each side has declared itself. "It was necessary for God," says Origen, "who knows how to use for a needful end even the consequences of evil, to put those who became evil in this way in a particular part of the universe, and to make a school of virtue to be set up for those who wished to

32. *Celsus on the True Doctrine*, 99.

33. *Contra Celsum* 6.42.

34. *Celsus on the True Doctrine*, 100.

strive lawfully in order to obtain it."[35] God's remedy is revelation and not compulsion, persuasion and not force.

Determinism Old and New

In his argument against the Christian view of reality and the message of Jesus, Celsus is confident that he has an edge because he is a philosopher. Early in his attack he creates the expectation that he will provide a better and more persuasive explanation for the existence of evil than the Christians. After throwing his punches at the Christian story, he is ready to bring forth a superior view.

> *I turn now to consider the existence of evil, which is analogous to matter itself in that there can be no decrease or increase of evils in the world—neither in the past nor in the future. From the beginning of time, the beginning of the universe, there has been just so much evil, and in quantity it has remained the same. It is in the nature of the universe that this be the case, and depends on our understanding of the origins of the universe itself. Certainly someone who has no learning in philosophy will be unaware of the origin of evil; but it is enough that the masses be told that evils are not caused by God; rather, that they are part of the nature of matter and of mankind; that the period of mortal life is the same from beginning to end, and that because all things happens in cycles, what is happening now—evils that is—happened before and will happen again.*[36]

What is this? The passage is hard to read, but it is mostly hard to read because it lacks coherence. "*It is not easy for one who has not read philosophy to know what is the origin of evils*," Celsus says condescendingly.[37] The masses should not expect to understand. For them it is enough "*to be told that evils are not caused by God*."[38] He adds that the masses may also be told that evils "*inhere in matter and dwell among mortals*."[39] The elitist, patronizing stance of Celsus is thus one of its most striking features.

But Celsus appears unconvinced by his own argument. He fails to deliver on the expectation that the philosopher will give an answer that puts the Christian account to shame. Quite unexpectedly he offers a fatalistic and pessimistic outlook, asserting that "*according to the determined cycles the same things always have happened, are now happening, and will happen*."[40] Evil, accordingly, has no beginning and no end. It has always existed in the same amount. It will never cease. But if evil is a necessity, and if

35. *Contra Celsum* 6.44.
36. *Celsus on the True Doctrine*, 100.
37. *Contra Celsum* 4.65.
38. Ibid.
39. Ibid.
40. Ibid.

human beings are trapped in a cycle that no one can escape, does the concept of evil have any meaning?

Origen is not impressed by what Celsus brings to the table, but he answers in a humble tone. Having read philosophy no less than Celsus, he states modestly that "it is not easy even for one who has read philosophy to know the origin of evils, and probably it is impossible even for these men to know it absolutely, unless by inspiration of God it is made clear what are evils, and shown how they came to exist, and understood how they will be removed."[41]

The great difference in *content* between the convictions of Celsus and Origen is matched by their very different *source* and *character*. Celsus argues on the basis of philosophy. Origen, by contrast, relies on a revealed *story*. The logic that underlies his account is the logic of narrative. If we ask why a certain story goes this way and not another, the answer is that we can only tell the story this way because this is what happened. This is the logic of narrative.

So much confusion exists on this point that it deserves a follow-up thought. John Hick (1922–2012), one of the leading thinkers to grapple with the problem of evil in the twentieth century, speaks to this issue in two ways that are of interest. Like Celsus, Hick rejects the role of Satan in the Christian account albeit for a different reason. Hick is convinced that Satan is incompatible with what "most educated inhabitants of the modern world" are prepared to accept.[42] Next, he makes a philosophical objection to the early Christian account that puts the contrast between narrative logic and philosophical logic in bold relief. According to Hick, sin and evil should not logically arise in a flawless world, as the traditional account has it. [43] If the story says that evil arose without a cause, the story must be wrong.

> It is impossible to conceive of wholly good beings in a wholly good world becoming sinful. To say that they do is to postulate the self-creation of evil *ex nihilo*! There must have been some moral flaw in the creature or in his situation to set up the tension of temptation; for creaturely freedom in itself and in the absence of any temptation cannot lead to sin.[44]

The exclamation mark in this passage is Hick's own, intended to expose the fallacy of the original Christian account. A being that is genuinely good should not fall prey to evil. There would have to be a defect somewhere for evil to arise, says Hick.

How does the Christian account respond to this objection, so damning in the eyes of the critic? The answer, of course, is that the Christian account relies on the logic of narrative and not on philosophic logic. With respect to narrative, there is no traction for the argument that what is said to have happened cannot have happened because

41. Ibid.

42. Hick, "An Irenaean Theodicy," 40.

43. Hick, *Philosophy of Religion*, 43; ———, "An Irenaean Theodicy," 43–44.

44. Hick, *Evil and the God of Love*, 250.

it is philosophically impossible. If, from the point of view of the narrative, something happened, it must be recounted the way it happened. Narrative logic is obligated by the narrative. Origen answers Celsus by falling back on the biblical narrative. Philosophy must yield to the story, adjusting its view of what is possible by taking into account what actually happened. Philosophy, in turn, should not consider it an insult to its dignity that it is unable to explain something when that something cannot be explained causally. The Christian account relates what happened not so much as an *explanation* but as a fact. What philosophy characterizes as impossible proves the limitations of philosophy; it does not negate the narrative of how evil came into existence.

Yet another example might be instructive, this one coming from a person who felt the reality of suffering in his bones. Primo Levi, addressing readers' responses to his books about his experience at Auschwitz, makes a keen distinction between *understanding* and *knowing* that bears on the dilemma above. With regard to *understanding*, he hews close to Ivan Karamazov's line that understanding evil is impossible and could well be immoral. "Perhaps one cannot, what is more must not, understand what happened, because to understand is almost to justify," writes Levi.[45] In saying this, he puts his foot in the way of *causal* accounts of evil. What is left to do, then, if understanding is out of reach? Levi describes Nazi hatred as hatred without rationality; "it is a hate that is not in us; it is outside man," as if to concede that human reality features elements that cannot be explained in purely human terms. "If understanding is impossible," however, "*knowing* is imperative," he adds.[46] While *knowing* is the indispensable prerequisite for *understanding*, it could be the one thing left to us where understanding is out of the question.

In the 'discussion' between Celsus and Origen, the Christian account comes with an exclamation mark of its own, proclaiming that something happened that should not have happened. Evil came into being although it does not have a cause. In a sentence that is less strident than the passage quoted above, Hick concedes as much. "For we can never provide a complete causal explanation of a free act; if we could, it would not be a free act," he admits.[47]

The source that informs and obligates Origen's account is found in the Bible. It leads to knowing even as it sequesters evil as a phenomenon that has no cause and no explanation. The biblical story involves God, human beings, and a third order of being. While the story gives rise to many questions, the framework for the questions is given by the story. This thought is alien to Celsus. Origen admits that he tells a story that he knows only "by inspiration of God"; that the Bible makes clear "what are evils"; it tells how evils "came to exist" and "how they will be removed."[48] Narrative towers above philosophy in this account.

45. Levi, *If This Is a Man*, 395.

46. Ibid., 396.

47. Hick, *Philosophy of Religion*, 43.

48. *Contra Celsum* 4.65.

The conflicting accounts lead to very different views of reality. To Celsus, "*all things happen in cycles, what is happening now—evils that is—happened before and will happen again.*"[49] 'Evil' is a constant and a constituent of reality; *there can be no decrease or increase of evils in the world.*[50] This is a fatalistic view, to say the least. It flies in the face of the Christian account and, indirectly, in the face of Celsus's claim that he can give a better and more hopeful explanation. Not only does the Christian story see reality in a linear way; it also promises another ending. On this point Origen is ambiguous, but he repudiates the doctrine of eternal punishment, taking it as an example of what it means to be drawn away from "a right conception" of God.[51]

Origen, as noted, is not well known in large circles of the Christian Church today, and the account of evil that was current in the Early Church has likewise fallen on hard times. When theologians in our time discuss the cosmic conflict perspective in the early Christian account, they consider Augustine (354–430) the best spokesperson, not Origen.[52] This is strange for a number of reasons. Almost two hundred years separate Augustine from Origen. Many of the convictions that are clear and emphatic in Origen's writings have been abandoned by Augustine. While it is true that Augustine retains the notion of a cosmic conflict in his account of evil, the story he tells has been bleached by competing concerns in his own experience and by the changing fortunes of the Church.

The unbleached narrative in Origen's account of the cosmic conflict is in Augustine increasingly a philosophical construct that he deploys according to the demands of the situation.[53] Augustine will argue that freedom made sin a possibility,[54] but his most deeply held convictions lie elsewhere.[55] Divine sovereignty is now the overriding truth, informing and mandating a policy that justifies the use of coercion against dissidents. In this regard Augustine's theology stands in contrast to Origen and is actually closer to the imperial theology of Celsus.

49. *Celsus on the True Doctrine*, 100.

50. Ibid.

51. *Contra Celsum* 6.44.

52. Plantinga, *The Nature of Necessity*, 164–95; ———, *God, Freedom, and Evil*, 29–64; ———, *Warranted Christian Belief*, 459–89. Plantinga takes Augustine as his point of departure for his free will defense, leaving Origen entirely out of the picture. Griffin (*God, Power, and Evil*) begins his review of traditional Christian theodicies with Augustine, as if the latter is the foremost spokesperson for the cosmic conflict story and the Christian defense of free will.

53. Greer, "Augustine's Transformation of the Free Will Defence," 471–86. Greer argues that the contradictions in Augustine's writings ultimately must be resolved in the context of Augustine's experience. He could see no other way to salvation than by God overruling his will, that is, the will of Augustine.

54. Augustine, *On the Problem of Free Choice*, 75.

55. Augustine, *On the Predestination of the Saints,* Chap. 14; see also Fredriksen in *Augustine and the Jews*.

Peter Brown calls this "profound and ominous changes" in Augustine's attitude,[56] a stance all the more radical in view of the convictions of the Early Church. With respect to the latter, theology and policy were also linked, but the biblical message was understood differently. To the Early Church, the cosmic conflict perspective put freedom at the center. In the revised account, the arbitrary will of God counts for more than the choice of created beings, and this belief is the one Augustine can least do without.[57] The ones whom God has predestined to be saved in the Augustinian account cannot refuse God's decision, and, by implication, those whom God has not predestined to be saved do not have the option of choosing it.[58] The argument is polemical, but the trend of the argument magnifies God's sovereign will over the choice of created beings. Even further from Origen, perhaps, is Augustine's conviction that those who are not saved will be consigned to eternal punishment in hell despite the fact that choosing salvation is not an option for them.[59] "For both biblical theologians," says Paula Fredriksen,

> God's two great attributes are justice and mercy. But Origen's god expresses these attributes simultaneously and universally. To each soul he is both just and merciful. Augustine's god expresses these attributes serially and selectively. To each soul, God is *either* just *or* merciful, and those who receive mercy are in the minority. For Augustine, even babies, if unbaptized, go to hell, and the greater part of humanity is justly predestined to damnation.[60]

The notion of divine sovereignty that looms large in Celsus's view of God gets a new lease on life in the theology of Augustine, and it rises to still greater heights in Luther's theology even if divine sovereignty reduces the notion of freedom to nothing. Where Celsus, the neo-Platonic philosopher, faults the beliefs of the Christians in the Early Church because they hold views that violate his notion of divine sovereignty, Luther is similarly concerned. The softer voice of Origen stands between these two points, eclipsed within the Christian tradition precisely with regard to the conviction that once was the most distinctive.

The shift in emphasis is easier to fathom when the dramatic change in context is taken into account. As the Church grew more powerful, it felt less inclined to tell the biblical story of the origin of evil, or, for that matter, to explain anything. In particular, it had less interest in telling a story that put freedom at the center. Adapting to the change of fortune, the Church drifted away from the 'weak' god of the Early Church to the no-nonsense god of Celsus and pagan philosophy. The result was a theology and a policy that had more in common with the ideology of Celsus than with the story

56. Brown, *Augustine of Hippo*, 235; see also Fredriksen, *Augustine and the Jews*, 343.

57. Hick, *Evil and the God of Love*, 64–69; Griffin, *God, Power, and Evil*, 57–69.

58. Stump, "Augustine on Free Will," 134–47.

59. Augustine, *City of God*, Book XXI (964–1021).

60. Fredriksen, *Augustine and the Jews*, 334.

and the theology of the Early Church. The imperial god that sat enthroned on high in Celsus's view of reality retook lost ground, not as a relic of Celsus's religion but as the god of the Christian Church. The spineless god of the Early Church was out. Power was in. For the Church that early in its history made the origin of evil the centerpiece of its narrative and held liberty to be "the most general of all the laws of the universe,"[61] it became necessary to revise and reinterpret the narrative as the Church adapted to a different reality.

This transformation, as we have glimpsed already, represents a process of contraction. The field of vision narrowed from the big story of the rebellion of Lucifer to the smaller story of personal salvation and to doctrines like the trinity and the nature of Christ.[62] I have elsewhere characterized this as a "more detailed picture within a much smaller frame."[63] The values changed, too. One value that went precipitously into decline, as the history of Christianity demonstrates, was freedom.

In his answer to Celsus, Origen says that "[n]o one will be able to know the origin of evils who has not grasped the truth about the so-called devil and his angels, and who he was before he became a devil, and how he became a devil, and what caused his so-called angels to rebel with him."[64] To Origen, his conviction on this point translated into a prescription for conduct and policy. In the story of the cosmic conflict, the first Christians saw uncovered the monstrous foot that fits the monstrous shoe that fits the monstrous footprint of evil in human experience. And here, too, they found the source of misconceptions about the God who permitted it to happen—and the path to a God of sense.[65]

61. Danielou, *Origen*, 205–6.

62. Osborn, "From Theodicy to Christology," 58.

63. Tonstad, "Theodicy and the Theme of Cosmic Conflict," 192.

64. *Contra Celsum* 4.65.

65. Tonstad, "Theodicy and the Theme of Cosmic Conflict," 202.

Chapter Four

The Problem of Making Sense

A STATEMENT MENTIONED BRIEFLY in the previous chapter begs for more attention. Before reading the statement again, it is well to remember that its author, Origen of Alexandria, was an intellectual, a Bible scholar, and an apologist for faith in Jesus at a time when this commitment could be life-threatening. Origen's father suffered martyrdom during the reign of Septimius Severus (193–211), when his son was only seventeen.[1] Origen expected martyrdom himself,[2] and there is evidence that he actively sought it, being held back at one critical point when his mother hid his clothes to prevent him from leaving the house.[3]

Origen's statement concerns the Bible, specifically the relation between the Bible and the reality of evil.

> But if anyone with the time to examine the holy scriptures were to collect texts from all the sources and were to give a coherent account of evil, both how it first came to exist and how it is being destroyed, he would see that the meaning of Moses and the prophets with regard to Satan has not even been dreamt of by Celsus or by any of the people who are dragged down by this wicked daemon and are drawn away in their soul from God and the right conception of Him and from His Word.[4]

This claim is quite immodest. Origen contends that the Bible gives "a coherent account of evil," an account that includes "how it first came to exist and how it is being destroyed."[5] If we were to ask Origen whether the Bible is the go-to source for anyone who takes evil seriously, he would certainly answer in the affirmative. In fact, Origen's argument is on this point a Bible-*only* argument, contending, as we have seen, that "*[n]o one* will be able to know the origin of evils who has not grasped the truth about

1. Trigg, *Origen*, 4–5.
2. Cf. Origen, *Exhortation to Martyrdom*.
3. Crouzel, *Origen*, 6–7.
4. *Contra Celsum* 6.44.
5. Ibid.

the so-called devil and his angels."[6] In this statement Origen claims that the most reliable account of the existence of evil is found in the Bible and nowhere else.

Many voices will be ready to contest this claim. A case in point is an acclaimed book arguing the exact opposite opinion, proclaiming it unsubtly in the title, *God's Problem: How the Bible Fails to Answer Our Most Important Question—Why We Suffer.*[7] We need not doubt that Origen in the third century would disagree with the title of this book. As the statement quoted above suggests, Origen did not think that the Bible fails in the least, and he was particularly confident with respect to what the Bible says about evil. If we were to conjecture the title of the book Origen might have written on the subject, it might go like this, *God's Surprise: How the Bible Answers Our Most Important Question.*

I venture this guess on the basis of Origen's answer to Celsus and statements in many of his books. We find in these sources a low-key but firm confidence in the Bible even though it is well known that believers within its pages hold nothing back with respect to their most important questions.[8] As to which questions should have priority, there might actually be agreement between Origen and Bart D. Ehrman, the author of *God's Problem.* The disagreement begins with the answer and not with the task of sorting out which question to ask. It falls to us to wonder why readers of the Bible reach such different conclusions with respect to its treatment of the reality of evil. Why does Ehrman think that the Bible fails while Origen did not think so?

If my question seems contrived, there are more than superficial similarities between these individuals. Origen was without question the most towering biblical scholar of his generation, an intellectual whose erudition no one will call into doubt. Ehrman does not stand out to quite the same degree in our time, but he is one of rather few New Testament scholars whose reputation in some circles approaches that of a rock star. Few scholars in this field live to see their books published in the numbers Ehrman has done.

Ehrman made his scholarly reputation as an expert on the manuscripts that are the basis for the New Testament, earning his doctoral degree at Princeton University under Bruce Metzger, one of the leading Greek scholars and New Testament textual critics of the twentieth century. But Origen in the third century also knew something about the text of the Bible, being the author of a monumental project of biblical scholarship that has not been rivaled. His *Hexapla,* of necessity written in longhand, consisted of six parallel versions of the entire Old Testament. The first column featured the Hebrew text, the second column a Greek transliteration of the Hebrew text, and the next four columns featured four different translations of the Hebrew text in Greek.

6. *Contra Celsum* 4.65

7. Ehrman, *God's Problem.*

8. Pss 6:3; 74:9–10; 79:5; 80:4; 90:13; 94:3–7; Isa 6:11; Jer 4:21; 23:26; 47:5–6; Hab 1:2–4; Zech 1:12; Dan 8:13; 12:6; Rev 5:9–10.

This was not a task for the fainthearted at a time that knew nothing about typewriters or computers. The sheer magnitude of the project still baffles the imagination.

Sadly, much of the *Hexapla* can be described only in the past tense. A few scattered fragments are known to scholars today, prized pieces eagerly scoured for the light they may shed on the preservation of the text of the Old Testament and its translation into Greek. Just as the task of making the book in the first place was daunting, the labor of copying it was prohibitive. This fact alone could explain why the book has been lost, although it is also possible that the *Hexapla* was among the casualties of the purge that took place during the reign of Justinian (527–565). By that time Origen was out of favor in the Church, and his books were burned or suppressed. Textual critics of Ehrman's caliber would be thrilled to have access to an unabridged version of the *Hexapla*. Being denied that option except for fragments here and there, footnotes to the critical editions of the New Testament in Greek nevertheless teem with references to Origen's writings.

It is therefore legitimate to see more than casual points of contact between Origen in the third century and Ehrman in the twenty-first. Both (have) made a career of working closely with the text of the Bible. While Origen was a Christian apologist and not a textual critic as we understand the discipline today,[9] he certainly knew enough about the text of the books of the Bible to deserve a seat at the table in Ehrman's field of scholarship.

With this background in mind, it is time to repeat the question posed earlier: Why do readers of the Bible reach widely different conclusions with respect to its message? Neither learning nor intellectual capacity explains the difference in the case of Origen and Ehrman. These two scholars have been reading essentially the same text. One comes away saying that the Bible fails while the other scholar, in less flashy and flamboyant terms, will make no concession to failure.

My question does not have a simple answer, but one factor is easily overlooked or under-projected in contemporary criticisms of the Bible. This factor does not concern itself with differences in presuppositions or scholarly method, two areas where the contrast between Origen and Ehrman would be huge. It will not seize upon the possibility that the personal journeys of these two men to some extent read as journeys in opposite directions: for one [Ehrman] a journey *from* a rigid faith in the verbal inspiration of the Bible to a view inclined to treat the Bible as any other ancient text; for the other [Origen] a journey *to* the Bible and a high view of its inspiration. The neglected factor will not focus on personality or psychological dispositions because these areas are fraught with so many unknowns that they are better left alone. Even if someone were to suggest that the populist bent of Ehrman's books compares unfavorably with the subdued earnestness of Origen's writings, this will not be the point of difference that has the greatest explanatory power.

9. Brock, "Origen's aims," 215–18.

Ehrman lets the reader in on how, in the process of studying the Greek manuscripts that are the basis for the current text of the New Testament, he gave up his conviction that the Bible is verbally inspired, a view of inspiration that is not specifically 'Christian' in the first place. But he is also careful to point out that this change of outlook is not what dealt the death blow to his Christian faith. The deal breaker for him was less the Bible than the world. He relates the erosion of his faith with a mixture of frankness and sadness, disclosing the end-stage of the journey early in his book, "I came to a point where I could no longer believe."[10]

If we press him for specifics, Ehrman says that "I could no longer explain how there can be a good and all-powerful God actively involved with this world, *given the state of things*."[11] He reviews the story of Jesus in the New Testament, then asks, "If God had come into the darkness with the advent of the Christ child, bringing salvation to the world, *why is the world in such a state*?"[12] The question betrays the expectation that the world should be a better place because of the advent of Jesus; indeed, he hints the world *was* in a better state for a fleeting moment, thus warranting the next damning question, "Where is this God now?"[13] Ehrman tells of an experience sitting in church at a Christmas service with his wife, wishing to connect with his lost faith and reset his frame of mind to the state it once enjoyed, and yet finding himself unable to do so. "But I couldn't," Ehrman writes. "The darkness is too deep, the suffering too intense, the divine absence too palpable."[14]

Obviously, *how* a person reads the Bible will affect a reader's conclusions. R. C. P. Hanson has said of Origen that he "plods through the Bible, blind to its merits, deaf to its music, like a scientist trying to distil chemical formulae from Shakespeare."[15] This uncharitable characterization is inspired by Origen's tendency to read biblical texts as allegories for spiritual formation instead of prioritizing the literal meaning of the text. Hanson's scathing put-down proves that Origen has not been without his critics, but it does not fairly represent Origen's view of the Bible.[16] Someone might just as easily say—with more justification—that Ehrman's approach to the Bible is mechanical and insensitive to situational and rhetorical factors, faulting *him* for plodding through the Bible 'like a scientist trying to distil chemical formulae from Shakespeare.' Method matters in the sense that readers' conclusions depend as much on *how* they read as on *what* they read. This, nevertheless, is in my view not the most important difference.

10. Ehrman, *God's Problem*, 3.

11. Ibid.; italics added.

12. Ibid., 5, italics added.

13. Ibid.

14. Ibid., 6.

15. Hanson, "*Origène*," 279.

16. For an in-depth view of Origen's approach to the Bible, see Torjesen, *Hermeneutical Procedure and Theological Method*; ———, "Influence of Rhetoric on Origen's Old Testament Homilies," 13–25; ———, "The Rhetoric of the Literal Sense," 633–44.

Expectations

Perhaps the most important contrast between these two readings of the Bible is found at the level of expectations. "If God had come into the darkness with the advent of the Christ child, bringing salvation to the world, why is the world in such a state?" Ehrman asks.[17] At that stage in his book, he finds an intolerable discrepancy between what is and what ought to be, or, more specifically, a discrepancy between what is expected and what has actually happened. In light of the claims made in the New Testament, the world by now ought to be a better place.

Turning to Origen, we see a striking difference in expectations. Writing some two hundred years after the time of Jesus, should not Origen also be shaken by the failure of Jesus to transform the world? Noting that Ehrman finds the promised coming of the kingdom of God intolerably delayed,[18] should not Origen in the third century be sufficiently vexed at the apparent delay for this to generate doubts?

This is not happening. Origen does not seem to find conditions in the world an obstacle to faith. To our surprise, he seems to take the state of the world as confirmation of his convictions. With regard to the apparent delay of the kingdom of God, the two thousand years between Jesus and the twenty-first century are a much longer period of time than the two hundred years between Jesus and Origen, but two hundred years should be enough of a 'delay' to weaken a person's faith and more than enough for the eroding power of time to be felt. Nevertheless, we do not see this happening. With the memory of the martyrdom of his father Leonides never distant, Origen had additional reasons to backpedal on his commitment. Once again, the exact opposite happens. The reality of persecution, too, fit his expectations. When the hammer of adversity came down on Origen's father, Leonides had the opportunity to renege on his Christian commitment and a host of reasons to do so, concern for his family being one of them. But the son will say nothing to weaken his father's resolve. In a letter from Origen to his father, one precious fragment preserved of the many letters that have been lost, Origen writes, "Be careful not to change your mind because of us."[19] Translating this amazing statement from a son to his father in terms that are easily understandable, the son is saying that the father must under no circumstances compromise his faith.

Disappointed expectations are scarce in Origen's writings. This cannot be explained by assuming that he lived in a better world, somehow shielded from the reality of evil and suffering. The breaking point, rather, owes to different expectations.

The question of expectations becomes even more critical when we turn to the New Testament. The apostle Paul, in a letter written within twenty-five years of the death of Jesus, reminds believers in Asia Minor of the one "who gave himself for our

17. Ehrman, *God's Problem*, 5.

18. Ibid., 259–60.

19. Crouzel, *Origen*, 6.

sins to set us free from the present evil age, according to the will of our God and Father" (Gal 1:4). In ways that a reader today is able to appreciate only with great difficulty, Paul refers to human reality as "the present *evil* age" (Gal 1:4). According to this scenario, evil is not a troubling fact that puts believers fatally on the defensive. The reality of evil is firmly a part of the believer's view of the world. When Paul speaks of "the present evil age," he sees an age held captive to supernatural, non-human, demonic powers.[20]

Other New Testament texts sound the same theme. In a text sometimes referred to as the Synoptic Apocalypse, Jesus tells his followers not to allow deteriorating conditions in the world to weaken their faith.

> And you will hear of wars and rumors of wars; see that you are not alarmed; for this must take place, but the end is not yet (Matt 24:6).

Four remarkable things are suggested in this brief statement. First, Jesus depicts a world in increasing turmoil, a world "of wars and rumors of wars." He is not predicting better times, at least not initially. Second, he counsels them not to construe these conditions as a threat to their faith but rather as a reality that is assumed by their faith. "See that you are not alarmed," he says. Third, Jesus introduces the notion of necessity, saying, strangely, that "this *must* take place." This is a challenging idea. Wherein is the *necessity*? Similar puzzling ideas are found in the letters of Paul (2 Thess 2:1–12) and the Book of Revelation (Rev 20:1–3), suggesting a stable and widely-shared outlook in the New Testament.[21] In all these instances, a revelation or *exposé* is implied. If evil is posing as something other than what it is, the truth will come to light only when evil is made to show its hand. If, too, the divine intent is to make manifest the self-destructive character of evil, this happens only by letting evil stage its own defeat, as happens in Revelation (20:1–10).[22]

Fourth, Jesus warns his followers not to foreclose on the meaning of the world's trouble in the sense of thinking that everything will soon be over. "The end will come," he says (Matt 24:14), but he is equally concerned to point out that "the end is not yet" (Matt 24:6; cf. 24:8, 13, 37–39). Overall, the not-yet-ness of the end is a conspicuous feature in the speech. Although Ehrman brings up texts in the New Testament that emphasize imminence with the intent of showing that the expectation of imminent fulfillment has been defeated by the passage of time,[23] the emphasis in the Synoptic Apocalypse is less on imminence than on perseverance and endurance in the face of a reality that is different than expected and "not yet."[24]

20. Cf. Beker, *Paul the Apostle*, 188.

21. See Tonstad, "The Restrainer Removed," 133–51.

22. Murdock, "History and Revelation in Jewish Apocalypticism," 167–87.

23. Ehrman, *God's Problem*, 218–19; 242–44; 259–60.

24. Nelson Jr., "'This Generation' in Matt 24:34," 383.

Although many texts in the New Testament envision a triumphant ending, they do not promise a world that will be dramatically improving.

> And because of the increase of lawlessness, the love of many will grow cold (Matt 24:12).
>
> Then he said to them, "Nation will rise against nation, and kingdom against kingdom; there will be great earthquakes, and in various places famines and plagues; and there will be dreadful portents and great signs from heaven" (Luke 21:10, 11).
>
> There will be signs in the sun, the moon, and the stars, and on the earth distress among nations confused by the roaring of the sea and the waves. People will faint from fear and foreboding of what is coming upon the world, for the powers of the heavens will be shaken (Luke 21:25, 26).

What are these descriptions but an inventory of human history, written with conflict and suffering front and center? What is this but a sketch suggesting a worsening and deteriorating reality? "Increase of lawlessness," "dreadful portents," "distress among nations," "fear and foreboding": this is the New Testament take on the world in disclosures that are meant to be representative and comprehensive. Contrary to the view that Jesus had in mind a local and imminent reality, he predicted uprisings on a global scale, nation rising against nation, and "kingdom against kingdom" with famines and plagues "in various places."

The 'blood-dimmed tide' that in William Butler Yeats' twentieth century poem threatens the structure of faith from outside is in the New Testament flowing *within* its story. In the last book of the New Testament history is just that, a blood-dimmed tide, described in so many words.

> When he opened the second seal, I heard the second living creature call out, "Come!" And out came another horse, bright red; its rider was permitted to take peace from the earth, so that people would slaughter one another; and he was given a great sword (Rev 6:3, 4).
>
> The second angel blew his trumpet, and something like a great mountain, burning with fire, was thrown into the sea. A third of the sea became blood, a third of the living creatures in the sea died, and a third of the ships were destroyed (Rev 8:8–9).
>
> The second angel poured his bowl into the sea, and it became like the blood of a corpse, and every living thing in the sea died (Rev 16:3).

These glimpses from the seals, the trumpets, and the bowls in Revelation picture the earth as the location of strife and bloodshed. The pattern of Revelation's narration defies the expectation of progress. We do not see things going from bad to better. Instead, at least with regard to matters that are important to the narrator of the story, history seems to go from bad to worse. Divine restraint on the powers of evil is loosened (Rev 7:1–3; 9:14, 15). Within this scenario, we read in connection with the second trumpet that "a third of the sea became blood, *a third* of the living creatures in the sea died" (Rev 8:9). In the bowl sequence, all restraint is off; the sea "became like the blood of a corpse, and *every* living thing in the sea died" (16:3). In the end, it is as though evil has the entire field to itself.

Revelation is even clearer than Paul as to the identity of the forces of destruction. Where Paul perceives a demonic reality enmeshed in the affairs of "the present evil age" (Gal 1:4), Revelation gives a more complete account, revealing in pointed terms what is behind the suffering in the world.[25] "I saw a star that had fallen from heaven to earth," says John (Rev 9:1; cf. Isa 14:12–14). This fallen star unlocks the netherworld: "from the shaft [of the bottomless pit] rose smoke like the smoke of a great furnace, and the sun and the air were darkened with the smoke" (Rev 9:2). This is a picture of darkness, described in imagery that would seem wildly overwrought if not for the fact that it is meant to convey a demonic reality. Revelation's imagery is more bizarre than other depictions of evil in the Bible, but its view of reality comes off the same apocalyptic page as "the present evil age" in Paul's writings. Revelation says that the forces of destruction "have as king over them the angel of the bottomless pit; his name in Hebrew is Abaddon, and in Greek he is called Apollyon" (Rev 9:11). There are plenty of clues in these scenes of horror to decide 'whodunnit.' In verse after verse and panorama after panorama, it is as if John finds the passport, the credit card, the finger prints, and copious amounts of DNA of the destroying agent. 'Abbadon,' the name of the perpetrator in Hebrew, and 'Apollyon,' the name in Greek, means 'Destroyer.' Nowhere in the New Testament is there a clearer and more emphatic message that a demonic reality is at work in the world. In Revelation, human history is the arena where the demonic reality at last will implode.[26]

Understanding the New Testament concept of "the present evil age" (Gal 1:4) constitutes the most important background with respect to shaping expectations. This question is discussed broadly and from a host of angles in the New Testament. It might come as a surprise, too, to discover that the discrepancy between expectations and reality did not take a break during the time of Jesus. John the Baptist, the forerunner of Jesus and the first person to declare publicly in his favor (Matt 3:3, 11; John 1:34) at one point showed that Jesus failed to meet *his* expectations. John's disappointment had to do with the fact that he was arrested and put on death row by king Herod for criticizing the king's illicit marriage to his brother's wife (Matt 14:3–5), but it was also directly related to the less-than-expected impact of Jesus. From his prison cell John sent two of his disciples to Jesus on a mission of inquiry. In the Gospel of

25. See Tonstad, *Saving God's Reputation*, 108–43.

26. Tonstad, *Saving God's Reputation*, 144–55.

Matthew, John's commission to his disciples and their execution of the commission are carefully reported.

> When John heard in prison what the Messiah was doing, he sent word by his disciples and said to him, "Are you the one who is to come, or are we to wait for another?" (Mat 11:2–3)

John's question exposes an existential crisis on his part, a crisis of faith. The man who fearlessly had proclaimed that Jesus was "the one who is to come," the promised deliverer (Matt 3:11; John 1:27–34), suddenly finds himself gripped by second thoughts. Even this man, who was not only a forerunner and foreshadower of Jesus but also a model disciple, concerned neither with what to wear nor what to eat (Matt 3:4; 6:25–33) nor with storing up treasures on earth (Matt 6:19–21), is shaken.[27] As the noose of hardship tightens around his neck, Jesus no longer fits the billing set for him by John's earlier expectations. Jesus's answer to John, therefore, is more a corrective to John's expectations than a message meant to reassure him that his expectations will be met (Matt 11:4–6). "John's uncertainty signifies that in moments of crisis and unfulfilled expectations, one may question an earlier confession of faith," Lisa Bowens says in a sympathetic comment.[28]

The faith of John the Baptist is not rescued because Jesus gets him out of trouble. Nothing happens to alter John's imprisoned state.[29] At a banquet thrown by Herod (Mark 6:17–30; Matt 14:3–12), his daughter by his brother's wife, at that time most likely between nine and nineteen years of age, performed a dance that scholars believe had a sexual connotation to the point of eliciting incestuous pleasure on the part of the king.[30] Thus aroused, Herod "promised on oath to give her whatever she might ask" (Matt 14:7). It is quite possible that the séance had been staged in advance with her mother as an active participant. Given that she had been the wife of Herod's brother before the latter's murder, she was even more resentful toward John the Baptist than the king. Consulting her first, the daughter stormed back into the banqueting hall "immediately and with haste" with her request, "Give me the head of John the Baptist here on a platter" (Matt 14:8).

And so it was. "The head was brought on a platter and given to the girl, who brought it to her mother," the platter serving to underline the cannibalistic flavor of the event (Matt 14:11; Mark 6:28).[31] So it was, we must repeat, the beheading of Jesus's forerunner and first disciple taking place during the earthly life of Jesus and with Jesus fully aware of John's plight.[32]

27. Bowens, "John the Baptist," 312.
28. Ibid., 315–16.
29. Ibid., 317.
30. Collins, *Mark*, 308; cf. Glancy, "Unveiling Masculinity," 34–50.
31. Marcus, *Mark 1–8*, 403.
32. According to the Gospel of John, John the Baptist is the first to declare faith in Jesus (John

More disappointed expectations are to come. Luke treats the subject in connection with one of the post-resurrection appearances of Jesus. This account features two of Jesus's lesser known disciples walking to the town of Emmaus the very day that Jesus allegedly rose from the dead (Luke 24:13–34). While in sad but animated conversation with each other, Jesus discreetly joins them on the road. Crucial to the plot is the fact that they did not know that Jesus had risen from the dead, and they did not recognize him. Jesus slips into the conversation as a person who has missed out on the events that are so upsetting to the two men. The punch line, spoken from the point of view of disappointed expectations, runs like this: "But we had hoped that he was the one to redeem Israel" (Luke 24:21).

Disappointment runs thick in this sentence, revealing an acute discrepancy between expectation and perceived reality. Even when we factor in the rest of the conversation, where at last "their eyes were opened and they recognized him" (Luke 24:31), the bottom line is not their discovery that Jesus has risen and that their expectations therefore have been met. The hope they lost is rekindled, but it is no longer anchored at the point where they lost hope. Instead, the hope is restored within the framework of changed expectations.

Among the Gospels, John goes even further down this road than the Synoptic accounts. This Gospel features individuals who were first-hand witnesses to the works of Jesus and his teachings, yet refused to be swayed by what they saw and heard (John 5:38–47; 6:64; 9:18–41). For them, the discrepancy between expectation and reality is turned on its head. The reality revealed in Jesus exceeds and trumps expectations, not in the usual sense within which people must deal with disappointed hopes but in the sense that the framework of earlier beliefs is shattered. Rather than adjusting expectation to *this* reality, however, Jesus's critics dig in their heels, unwilling to be persuaded.

In what may well be the most compelling story of this kind, Jesus is reported to have healed a man who was born blind (John 9:1–7). Immediately, and contrary to reader expectations, the man is subjected to hostile interrogation, giving the story the flavor of a lawsuit.[33] Where the interrogation of the man is meant to disestablish that a miracle has taken place (9:8–15, 18–23), and, failing that, to impugn the character of Jesus (9:16–17; 24–34), the aggressive questioning backfires. The account establishes the identity of the man and his blindness (9:9, 20), the fact of his healing (9:13, 21), and, eventually, the identity of the healer (9:17, 25, 30–33). None of this helps, however, because the belief system of the opponents is immune to evidence. "Well, here is an amazing thing, that you do not know where He is from, and *yet* He opened my eyes," the formerly blind man says to his interrogators in a frantic last attempt to persuade them (John 9:30, 34 NASB). The 'amazing thing' in *this* story, therefore, "is not faith, but unbelief!" exclaims George Beasley-Murray.[34] To the extent that we see human

1:29–34).

33. Asiedu-Peprah, *Johannine Sabbath Conflicts*, 8–9, 13–38.

34. Beasley-Murray, *John*, 158.

suffering as a stumbling block to faith, we expect faith to ensue when the stumbling block is removed. This does not happen in John. "Although he had performed so many signs in their presence, they did not believe in him," says the narrator in this Gospel (John 12:37).

By now it is evident that the Bible does not draw straight lines with respect to the problem of evil, breaking it down to neat, predictable equations. On the one hand, the first disciples of Jesus saw their expectations disappointed, but they did not react by giving up completely. Instead, their faith was redirected so as to include suffering and the apparent defeat of that in which they had believed. On the other hand, opponents of Jesus in the Gospels appear to have vested interests that were not overcome when the sick were healed or Lazarus was raised from the dead, taking these stories at face value (John 5:16; 9:16; 11:47–48). Both kinds of responses are found within the New Testament. It is not as though the difficult questions only arise later, at a time when there is no Jesus, or even a John or a Paul, who might be able to address them. In fact, the New Testament finds a complexity in human reality and in human responses to Jesus even to the point of challenging the idea that suffering is our most important question.

Where does this leave *us*, meaning those who, in time and place, live at a distance from the events in the New Testament? The answer must be that it leaves us in a hopeful situation. After taking away the assumed advantage of those who were eyewitnesses to the ministry of Jesus, the Gospel of John proceeds to take away the assumed *disadvantage* of those who will only hear of Jesus second hand. The fact that seeing does not always lead to believing is in John followed by the tantalizing prospect that believing can happen without seeing first hand. To Thomas, who insisted that "unless I see . . . , I will not believe" (John 20:25), Jesus gave preference to those who will believe the testimony of those who did see firsthand. "Have you believed because you have seen me? Blessed are those who have not seen and yet have come to believe," Jesus says to Thomas (John 20:29). To our surprise, the Gospel of John does not consider the one who has not seen to be at a disadvantage. On the terms of John, seeing firsthand is not a prerequisite for believing.

"How will it be when none more saith, 'I saw'?" Robert Browning asks in his nineteenth century poem *A Death in the Desert*, a meditation on the death of the author of the Fourth Gospel.[35] How will it be when the firsthand witness is gone? Browning's answer is anticipated partly in the lack of a predictable connection between seeing and believing and the connection between *not* seeing and believing in John's Gospel (20:29). If seeing of itself does not lead to believing, and if believing is possible in the absence of seeing, the passage of time is not a threat to the possibility of faith. Seeing is not done away with: someone did see firsthand. But the second hand testimony is not inferior to the eyewitness account. Many who saw the story first hand did not believe, and many who have only seen second hand have believed with no loss of authenticity. The genius of Browning's poem is to suggest that the passage of time does not change

35. Browning, *A Death in the Desert*, 7.

anything. "To me, *that story—ay, that Life and Death* Of which I wrote 'it was'—*to me, it is*," says the dying person in the poem.[36] To him, Jesus is present reality and not only a historical memory. The story *is*, meaning that it not a story about the past only. Every generation faces the same challenge and the same opportunity. John's Gospel thus "emphasizes the continuity of the church of his own time with Jesus and his disciples."[37]

Where does this leave us with respect to belief and the reality of suffering? Much of what we have considered in this chapter will be well known to Ehrman, who concludes that the Bible fails. His book shows awareness of the apocalyptic world view of the New Testament, and he describes the character of the resurrection faith of the New Testament better than Origen could have done.[38] But it is all for naught because, to him, "*that story—ay, that Life and Death*" of which the Beloved Disciple wrote, "It was," wasn't after all.

As his book winds down, Ehrman strikes a more pugnacious tone, resorting to sweeping assertions in an attempt to nail down his case. "I have to admit that the apocalyptic view is based on mythological ideas that I simply cannot accept," says Ehrman.[39] The New Testament cannot help us, he claims, because "there is no God up there, just above the sky, waiting to come 'down' here or to take us 'up' there."[40] This is less subtle and elegant than Bultmann's critical assertions, but it amounts to the same. The future hope is in doubt because "the fervent expectation that we must be living at the end time has proved time after time—every time—to be wrong."[41] In a closing word of censure, Ehrman claims that the Christian hope is not only factually untenable but morally corrupting.[42] When he ends the book with a call to action, however, billed as a counterweight to the complacency that he blames to faith,[43] his call comes across as a dutiful and limp afterthought compared to the vigor he has poured into his attempt to demonstrate how the Bible fails.

Toward the end of Ehrman's book there are echoes of Ivan Karamazov's anger, or, more to the point, of the voice of Juror Number Three in the movie *Twelve Angry Men*, picking up the story just before this juror changes his vote to 'not guilty.'[44] If you do not remember the movie and its plot, it features twelve male jurors who are sequestered in a hot and humid room in order to discuss the evidence against a seventeen year old

36. Ibid., 10.

37. Barrett, *Gospel According to St. John*, 573.

38. Ehrman, (*God's Problem*, 238–42) shows correctly that Paul expected a resurrection of the body, thinking of the resurrection as a material reality. Origen, being heavily influenced by the dualism of Plato, is much less clear on this point and less biblical.

39. Ibid., 259.

40. Ibid.

41. Ibid.

42. Ibid.

43. Ibid., 278.

44. I am discussing the 1957 movie directed by the late Sidney Lumet, screenplay by Reginald Rose.

defendant who, if found guilty, will go to the electric chair. At first eleven of the jurors vote for a guilty verdict, with only one arguing that he will not vote with the rest before having a thorough review of the evidence. In the course of the discussion, evidence that initially seems to point in one direction opens up to other interpretations. At last all but one come down on the side of acquittal. All eyes are now on the hold-out juror.

"We want to hear your arguments," Juror Number Eight tells him.

"I gave you my arguments," Juror Number Three angrily replies.

"We want to hear them again," says Juror Number Eight.

"*Everything*!" exclaims Juror Number Three. "*Every single thing* that took place in that courtroom; I mean *everything*, says that he is guilty! *Every single thing*. . . ." He then proceeds to review all the pieces of evidence that have been discussed by the jury: the knife that was supposed to be one of a kind but wasn't; the old man who hurried from his bed to the top of the stairs where he saw the young man run away, a feat found by the jurors to be physically impossible; the testimony of the lady who claimed to have seen the murder through the windows of a passing train but who could not have seen it because she had taken off her glasses for the night. In the course of the deliberations, each item has become subject to a different interpretation than the one that seemed obvious at the outset, no item supporting the view to which Juror Number Three adamantly clings.

Ehrman's litany of objections to the Bible ends on a similar note, as an argument from *everything* and an objection to *everything*. His personal testimony, sprinkled generously throughout the book, is part of the persuasive strategy. Augustine, to be fair, used the same strategy in his spiritual autobiography *Confessions*, but to the opposite end. By telling the reader how he came to believe that the Bible fails to answer our most important question, Ehrman succeeds to a certain degree in wrapping his conclusions in the garb of inevitability. But the argument from *everything* at the end impairs the aura of objectivity that the book otherwise aspires to convey.

Origen, by contrast, and not only because he was writing at a time when writing conventions were different, keeps himself modestly in the background. If we are persuaded by him, it will not be because he makes his biography part of the argument even though Origen's biography, anchored in the crucible of suffering and persecution, would be no less compelling than Ehrman's.

If there is an all-powerful God and if Jesus came to make right what is wrong in the world, "*why is the world in such a state*?" Ehrman asks.[45] Why, indeed? One response could be to take seriously the New Testament take on the world and the expectations it seeks to instill in characters within its pages and in readers without. Another will be to consider Origen's claim that "[n]o one will be able to know the origin of evils who

45. Ehrman, *God's Problem*, 5, italics added.

has not grasped the truth about the so-called devil and his angels."[46] These are more than polite or tentative recommendations from the writers of the New Testament, all of them certain that the Bible measures human reality with tools equal to the task.[47] What they offer is meant for faith, but it is also meant for sense, and 'our most important question' does not catch them by surprise. The surprise, rather, must be that the Bible brought up and addressed our most important questions before we did.

46. *Contra Celsum* 4.65.

47. Ibid., 6.44.

Chapter Five

What God Did Not Say and Jesus Did Not Do—and Why It Matters

To modern readers of the Book of Hebrews, a peculiar line of thought is likely to raise eyebrows.

> For to which of the angels did God ever say, "You are my Son; today I have begotten you?" (Heb 1:5).
>
> And again, when he brings the firstborn into the world, he says, "Let all God's angels worship him" (1:6).
>
> But to which of the angels has he ever said, "Sit at my right hand until I make your enemies a footstool for your feet?" (1:13).
>
> When he had made purification for sins, he sat down at the right hand of the Majesty on high, having become as much superior to angels as the name he has inherited is more excellent than theirs (2:3–4).
>
> Now God did not subject the coming world, about which we are speaking, to angels (2:5).
>
> You have made them for a little while lower than the angels (2:7).
>
> . . . but we do see Jesus, who for a little while was made lower than the angels (2:9).

I shall begin by taking for granted that the author of these lines was a thoughtful person. I will also assume that he or she was addressing readers of sound mind, intending his or her account to be taken seriously. The language of Hebrews supports these assumptions because it constitutes "the finest Greek" in the New Testament, excelling with respect to vocabulary, structure, and rhetorical force.[1]

1. Lane, *Hebrews 1–8*, xlix.

And yet the author refers to *angels*, not once but many times. My list is incomplete because there are a total of fourteen occurrences of this word in Hebrews, not counting pronominal references such as *they*, *them*, or *theirs*. Hebrews features an argument that gives angels a place of importance. It is noteworthy that the author has no need to explain the term as though angels represent an unfamiliar category of being. The ontological status of angels, *ontology* meaning the things or beings that exist, is not in question.

When we look more closely at the examples I have listed, it is clear that angels are neither divine nor human. The author is at pains to clarify the relationship of Jesus to angels, proving that Jesus is not an angel. God has said things to him that God would never say to an angel. "To which of the angels did God ever say?" repeated twice, sets Jesus apart from angels with respect to status (1:5, 13). When God in these texts calls upon the angels to worship Jesus (1:6), it means that Jesus belongs to the divine side of the ontological divide between God and created beings. Humans are an exalted category of being because they are made "a little lower than the angels" (2:7). But if humans are made "a little *lower* than the angels," what does that say about angels? The statement puts angels in a higher category than humans. At the same time the author infers that something in the human experience might place humans at a higher level than their ontological rank would otherwise suggest. As for Jesus, he was "for a little while . . . made lower than the angels" (2:9), meaning that he occupies both sides of the ontological divide.

To the uninitiated, these are dizzying thoughts. Nonetheless, a 'plain English' reading of Hebrews cannot avoid the conclusion that the author reckons with the existence of angels. He or she draws a line of demarcation between angels and Jesus, on the one hand, and between angels and human beings, on the other. Moreover, the detailed argument that sets Jesus apart from angels gives the statement the tenor of a clarification or corrective. When all is said and done, Jesus is vastly superior to the angels (2:3–4).

But why does the author of Hebrews pay attention to angels at all? Why does he or she issue such a painstaking clarification? And why, in particular, must the author concentrate so much effort into drawing a line of demarcation between Jesus and the angels? These questions are rarely asked because scholars have for generations treated angels dismissively. "The great theologians of the twentieth century had simply forgotten them or were ashamed of them," says Uwe Wolff.[2] Before we address these questions in greater depth, therefore, we need some remedial work.

A quick perusal of the New Testament shows that Hebrews is not the only book to make angels a subject of interest. At the close of Jesus's temptation in the wilderness, the Gospel of Mark says that "the angels waited on him" (Mark 1:13). Mark is sparsely worded, and the glimpse of angels is fleeting. Nevertheless, the text in Mark suggests not only that the angels brought relief to Jesus, but also that they were vigilant and at

2. Wolff, "The Angels' Comeback," 695.

the ready to do so. As in Hebrews, Mark takes for granted that the reader has prior knowledge of angels, making no attempt to make up the difference to those who are not in the know.

In Matthew, an angel visits Joseph with the message not to break his engagement to Mary because of her pregnancy (Matt 1:20). Just as in Mark, "angels came and waited on him" after his ordeal in the wilderness (Matt 4:11). At the end of time "the Son of Man is to come with his angels in the glory of his Father" (Matt 16:27; cf. 24:31).

In the birth narratives in Luke, angels are out in force, with special attention to Gabriel, an angel with a name and a defined identity that highlights his importance. Gabriel appears first to Zechariah with a message concerning the birth of John the Baptist (Luke 1:11–20) and then, six months later, to Mary in Galilee with a message to her about the birth of Jesus (Luke 1:26–38). Luke's mention of Gabriel has particular interest because Gabriel is featured in the Old Testament in Daniel's visions of the end (Dan 8:15–16; 9:21).

In John, Jesus tells one of his first disciples that he "will see heaven opened and the angels of God ascending and descending upon the Son of Man" (John 1:51). This is an allusion to the story of Jacob, who, anxious and alone, saw a ladder reaching from heaven to earth in a dream, and heavenly beings ascending and descending on the ladder (Gen 28:12). At the end of John's Gospel, Mary Magdalene, bending over to look into the tomb on the morning of Jesus's resurrection, "saw two angels in white, sitting where the body of Jesus had been lying, one at the head and the other at the feet" (John 20:12). This scene is choreographed to convey the ultimate revelation of God along lines laid out in the Old Testament, a glimpse of the Most Holy now shining forth in earthly reality (John 1:14; Exod 25:17–20).[3] From the perspective of the Gospels, angels do not represent a new and hitherto unknown category of being whether in the form of Gabriel or unnamed angels.

Angels acting on the side of the good dominate in the texts noted above, but all angels are not good or on the side of good. The role of angels in the New Testament has a dark side. Like the angels themselves, the dark side of the story is so much part of the glasses through which the New Testament sees the world that it is mostly implicit. Modern readers who do not know the story are left to piece it together from snippets scattered throughout the New Testament. In Matthew, for instance, Jesus speaks of the day when "the Son of Man" will separate the sheep from the goats in the final day of reckoning (Matt. 25:31–46). On that day, Jesus will tell "those at his left hand" to depart from him "into the eternal fire prepared for the devil and his angels" (Matt 25:41). Why, here, angels? Why angels, given that Jesus in the body of the parable speaks of human beings and not a word about angels? And why the term "the devil and his

3. Schneiders, ("Touching the Risen Jesus," 165) argues that the two angels in the tomb allude to the cherubim at the golden throne, the mercy seat of the ark of the covenant (Exod 37:6–7, 38:5–8, LXX).

angels"? The answer is that the role of angels is assumed, but this does not reduce their importance. The angels in this text are in cahoots with Satan. Jesus ascribes a primary role to these angels as though their contribution to evil exceeds that of human beings.

The sinister side of the story is corroborated in the letters of Paul. In one of the most eloquent and sweeping passages in Romans, Paul expresses the conviction that "neither death, nor life, nor *angels*, nor rulers, nor things present, nor things to come, nor powers, nor height, nor depth, nor anything else in all creation, will be able to separate us from the love of God in Christ Jesus our Lord" (Rom 8:38–39). We cannot fail to hear the language of conflict and combat in this passage. The stakes are high because "angels" and "powers" are working against God's purpose, sparing no effort to separate believers from God. The plight against which the love of God alone will prevail can be appreciated only within a cosmic framework. No matter how powerful and determined the hostile powers, they will not be able to separate the believer from the love of God.[4]

"Do you not know that we are to judge angels?" Paul asks believers in Corinth, again with the understanding that angels exist and that the angels that will be subject to judgment are evil (1 Cor 6:3). In a follow-up epistle to the same group he explains that the *modus operandi* of evil is not apparent on the surface. "Even Satan disguises himself as an angel of light," he warns (2 Cor 11:14). In Ephesians, Paul avers that "our struggle is not against enemies of blood and flesh, but against the rulers, against the authorities, against the cosmic powers of this present darkness, against the spiritual forces of evil in the heavenly places" (Eph 6:12). In 2 Thessalonians, a letter that has not received the attention it deserves, Paul depicts and explains the end of evil against the background of its beginning, leaving no doubt that a non-human realm and reality are in view (2 Thess 2:1–12).[5]

No book in the Bible gives the angels broader exposure than Revelation. *Angel* (sing.) is mentioned fifty-three times and *angels* (pl.) twenty-three times in this book, outnumbering references to angels in all the other books of the New Testament combined. As in the Gospels and the letters of Paul, angels are good or evil. The language of combat is conspicuous. In the central twelfth chapter, the narrative Ground Zero in the book, the human condition is placed within the framework of a conflict originating in heaven.

> And war broke out in heaven; Michael and his angels had to fight against the dragon. The dragon and his angels fought, but they were defeated, and there was no longer any place for them in heaven. The great dragon was thrown down, that ancient serpent, who is called the Devil and Satan, the deceiver of the whole world—he was thrown down to the earth, and his angels were thrown down with him (Rev 12:7–9, translation mine).

4. Gaventa, "Neither height nor depth," 265–78.

5. Tonstad, "The Restrainer Removed," 133–51.

Like other books in the New Testament, Revelation does not see evil merely as a human problem, or, as in many commentaries, as a Roman imperial problem. Spatially, evil has a cosmic scope. Temporally, evil arose primordially in the non-human realm. Revelation breaks the stereotype of heaven and earth because it does not say that all is well in heaven, portraying it as the calm counterpoint to earthly strife.[6] Quite the contrary, earthly horror is in Revelation set in the context of cosmic turmoil.

What does this survey say about angels? At the very least, it contests the view of Karl Barth, who claimed against a mountain of evidence that angels "are essentially marginal figures."[7] With angels thus in eclipse in contemporary theology, the position of Satan and evil angels is also threatened. Susan Garrett writes that

> for decades mainline theologians and Church leaders have insisted that belief in Satan is not important to authentic Christian faith. Or, if not dismissing Satan and other such powers outright, they have simply ignored those parts of the biblical and theological tradition in which the powers play a role. In turn, thousands of pastors educated in mainline seminaries have done likewise. They never speak of Satan from the pulpit, convinced that he and his demon-servants belong to an obsolete worldview.[8]

The ingrained and selective readings to which Garrett points compromise the message of the New Testament. Hebrews, our first exhibit, pays attention to angels because they belong in the story. Reality dictates their inclusion. Far from being "marginal figures," the angels are central to the plot. While Revelation presents the cosmic perspective in its most complete and developed form, the 'big picture' is not absent from any of the books in the New Testament. All share the same world view and apocalyptic outlook.[9] With respect to Paul, for generations seen as the least apocalyptic voice in the New Testament, J. Christiaan Beker says that his gospel "seems welded to the apocalyptic world view."[10] This means a world inhabited by beings other than God and other than human beings. Loss of the cosmic scope leaves out key characters and elements in the story. "[F]ar from considering the apocalyptic world view a husk or discardable frame, Paul insists that it belongs to the inalienable core of the gospel," says Beker.[11] The message is whole cloth even if this means that it imposes a distinctive world view on non-Jewish believers.[12]

6. For the idea that Revelation contrasts earthly turmoil with heavenly peace, see Charles, *The Revelation of St. John*, I, 102–3; also, Rowland, *The Open Heaven*, 425. For the view that Revelation explains earthly turmoil in light of heavenly conflict, see Tonstad, *Saving God's Reputation*, 108–43.

7. Barth, *Church Dogmatics* III.3 §51, 371.

8. Garrett, *No Ordinary Angel*, 105.

9. Even Galatians, sometimes seen as a non-apocalyptic letter, meets this criterion; cf. Martyn,"Apocalyptic Antinomies," 410–24.

10. Beker, *Paul the Apostle*, 171.

11. Ibid.

12. Ibid.

If we wonder why Hebrews and other voices in the New Testament pay attention to angels, the answer is that they could not leave them out. God said something to Jesus that he did not say to the angels (Heb 1:5), suggesting that the status of Jesus relative to angels was in need of clarification. Modern readers of the New Testament must work to overcome the paralysis of prejudice and unfamiliarity. Instead of wondering why the angels are there, readers will do better by seeking to understand the clarification that is so much the concern of Hebrews. Why, as noted earlier, does this author expend so much effort in drawing a line of demarcation between Jesus and the angels (Heb 1:5–6, 13; 2:3–4, 7)? There would be no need to say what something or someone is *not* unless someone thought that something or someone was *that*. Hebrews seems especially determined to disestablish the notion that Jesus is an angel. He cannot be an angel, we learn, because Jesus belongs to the identity of God in creation (1:2). He is the reflection of God's glory (1:3), and he alone "sat down at the right hand of the Majesty on high" (1:3).

Why, however, would anyone think of Jesus as an angel in the first place?

Hebrews does not quite answer this question. Fortunately, the so-called 'Christological Hymn' in Paul's letter to the Philippians goes a long way toward making up the difference. The hymn ends on a similar note of resounding affirmation with respect to the identity and role of Jesus (Phil 2:5–11). As in Hebrews, Philippians traces the story of Jesus from his pre-existence to his exaltation until, at the end, "every knee should bend, in heaven and on earth and under the earth, and every tongue should confess that Jesus Christ is Lord, to the glory of God the Father" (Phil 2:10–11). This is not hugely different from Hebrews, "And again, when he brings the firstborn into the world, he says, 'Let all God's angels worship him'" (Heb 1:6).

How Philippians gets to that point, however, is unique. To understand this, we must move from what God did not say in Hebrews to what Jesus did not do in Philippians.

What Jesus Did Not Do

Pauline authorship of Philippians is rarely disputed,[13] but there is considerable disagreement as to whether the Christological Hymn should be ascribed to Paul (Phil 2:6–11).[14] This question does not bear significantly on interpretation, although there is no compelling reason to say that Paul did not compose it.[15] Richard J. Bauckham,

13. Hawthorne, *Philippians*, xxvii. Enslin (*Christian Beginnings*, 280) says that "no letter can make a stronger claim to be from Paul." Schenk (*Die Philipperbriefe*) promotes the idea that Philippians in its current form is a composite of several Philippian letters by Paul.

14. Marchal ("Expecting a Hymn," 245–55) argues that the quest to nail down the genre of the "hymn" might compromise grasp of content.

15. Bauckham (*God Crucified*, 27) attributes the "hymn" to Paul. Lohmeyer (*Kyrios Jesus*, 1–7) argued in favor of a pre-Pauline source; for this view, see also Käsemann, "Kritische Analyse," 313–60; Feuillet, "L'hymne christologique, 352–80; Martin, *Carmen Christi*.

who argues for Pauline authorship, draws attention to the hymn's high Christology, "the highest possible Christology" because it proclaims "the inclusion of Jesus in the unique divine identity."[16] There is obvious merit to this assertion, but it is not the whole story. A closer look at the key passage in the hymn reveals the need for more detail work.

> Let the same mind be in you that was in Christ Jesus, who, though he was in the form of God, did not regard equality with God as something to be exploited (Phil 2:5–6, NRSV).

> Let this mind be in you which was also in Christ Jesus, who, being in the form of God, did not consider it robbery to be equal with God (Phil 2:5–6, NKJV).

We read in this text that Jesus "was in the form of God [*en morphē theou huparchōn*]." And we observe that Jesus did not consider it robbery "to be equal with God [*to einai isa theō*]." But how does "the form of God" relate to being "equal with God"?[17] The verbal action is not clear in our translations. The NRSV says that Jesus "did not regard equality with God *as something to be exploited* [*ouk harpagmon hēgēsato*]" while the NKJV says that he "*did not consider it robbery* [*ouk harpagmon hēgēsato*] to be equal with God" (Phil 2:6). Needless to say, the translators have chosen different routes on this point, one saying "exploited" (NRSV) and the other "robbery" (NKJV).[18] Realizing that what Jesus did not consider doing is the premise of the hymn, it will be worth our effort to find out what this might be.

Three main possibilities have crystallized. The first option sees Jesus as the sole reference point for the verbal action. Did Jesus, when considering the options before him, decide against pursuing the alternative to which Paul draws attention? Should we say that when presented with two possible courses of action, he decided to choose one and not the other? He "was in the form of God," but he "did not regard equality with God something to be exploited," as the NRSV has it? In this translation "the form of God" and "equality with God" are virtually synonymous.

The second option also sees Jesus as the sole reference point for the verbal action. Confronted with two possible courses of action, he decided to choose one and not the other. He "was in the form of God," but he did not make that a reason "to be equal with God." In this translation "the form of God" and "equality with God" are linked by a more complex view of Jesus, and the two phrases are not synonymous. Jesus did not "consider it robbery to be equal with God," as the NKJV puts it.

The third alternative is very different. The text still says that there was something *Jesus* did not consider doing, but in this alternative the focus is on the identity of the acting subject. Paul says that *Jesus* did not consider doing "it." Did someone else? In

16. Bauckham, *God Crucified*, 27.

17. The phrases are not simply synonymous; cf. Steenburg, "The Case Against," 77–86.

18. KJV has "robbery" while NASB, NET, NIV, and NJB have "something to be grasped."

this alternative, two subjects are confronted with a choice, but the focus is on someone other than Jesus. Jesus did not consider taking the action that is in view, but the other figure did contemplate such an action and set out to put it to the test. As I wish to show below, the best reading of this text is a combination of alternatives two and three.

In order to give these alternatives undivided attention, other questions in the passage must be settled by way of considered answers. The hymn refers to the pre-existence of Christ.[19] Arguments to the contrary have not been persuasive.[20] It describes a heavenly being who willingly went from the highest position possible to the opposite lowest point, from "the form of God" to "the form of a slave" (2:6–7). Jesus is depicted as a person who belongs to the divine identity. Creation and redemption are held together in the person of Jesus.[21] When the hymn ends with the worship of Jesus (2:9–11), his divine identity is certified.[22]

But the hymn does not take us directly to the worship of Jesus. His exaltation is preceded by a series of steps in the opposite direction, going from a high to a low position. Indeed, the hymn seems intent on showing that even in his pre-existent high position Jesus made himself to be less than he is. Being "in the form of God [*en morphē theou huparchōn*]," here meaning that Jesus belongs to the divine identity, he did not put forth an effort "to be equal with God [*to einai isa theō*]." The one who was "in the form of God" did not struggle to be seen as though he was "equal with God," not because it was obvious to all that he belonged to the divine identity, but because it was not in his disposition to make the claim that was easily his to make: "to be equal with God" (2:5–6). It is fine to say that Jesus gave up the "power and glory" that were the determining elements of his identity in his pre-existent state,[23] but it is necessary to say that Jesus even in his pre-existent state did not have "power and glory" as his calling card. On this point the hymn echoes the idea that "even in the days before Jesus of Nazareth lived on earth, the pre-existent Christ had made God's glory known."[24]

This view of the beginning of the hymn gives momentum to the ending. By the criterion of belonging to the divine identity, there should be worship of Jesus at the beginning just as much as at the end. In fact, worship of Jesus should be a foregone conclusion at any point in his story. But there is a point to the exaltation and worship

19. Lohmeyer, *Kyrios Jesus*, 20; Käsemann, "Kritische Analyse," 317; Barr, "The Word Became Flesh," 22; Martin, *The Epistle of Paul*, 96; Hurst, "Re-enter the Pre-existent Christ?" 449–57; O'Brien, *The Epistle to the Philippians*, 215–16.

20. Talbert ("The Problem of Pre-existence," 141–53) argues the case against pre-existence, unsuccessfully, in my view, on the basis of what he sees as an implied parallel between Adam and the human Jesus. Glasson ("Two Notes on the Philippian Hymn," 133–39) asserts that the case against the traditional position of pre-existence seems ironclad. Bauckham (*God Crucified*, 57) dismisses the case for an Adamic Christology as "a red herring in the study of this passage."

21. Gibbs, "The Relation between Creation and Redemption," 281.

22. Martin, *Philippians*, 105.

23. Müller, "Der Christushymnus Phil 2 6–11," 25.

24. Garrett, "Jesus and the Angels," 165.

of Jesus at the end of the hymn that is lost unless we take the right measure of the beginning. "The plot of the passage requires that the final state of Jesus be higher than the initial state," says Adela Yarbro Collins.[25] Only at the end of the hymn, after Jesus "emptied [*ekenōsen*] himself, taking the form of a slave, being born in human likeness" (2:7); after he "humbled [*etapeinōsen*] himself and became obedient to the point of death—even death on a cross" (2:8), is there exaltation (2:9). Only then is there acknowledgement of Jesus throughout the entire cosmos (2:10)—with a degree of resonance and clarity that projects a more dramatic story than what is apparent to the casual reader (2:11).[26] Jesus cannot be the object of worship unless he belongs to the divine identity, but he is not the object of worship for that reason only. In fact, as we shall explore next, the focus in the hymn is not only on reasons for the exaltation of Jesus, but on the contrast between Jesus and someone else.

This leads into the third alternative: the thought that another person aspired to do what Jesus did not. The crux centers on the verbal action at the beginning of the hymn: Jesus "*did not consider it robbery* [*ouk harpagmon hēgēsato*] to be equal with God" (2:6). What kind of scenario underlies the violence that is implied in this expression, even more violent than what the translation of the NKJV is able to convey? The word translated "robbery," *harpagmos*, occurs only in this verse in the New Testament. The lexical meaning denotes "a violent seizure of property, *robbery*," or "something to which one can claim or assert title by gripping or grasping."[27] The verbal cognate *harpazō* is likewise fraught with violent action; "snatch, seize," in the sense of taking something "suddenly and vehemently," or "to make off with someone's property by attacking or seizing." The action in view, in other words, is robbery by violence. The related adjective *harpax* refers to someone who is rapacious or ravenous.

It has long been realized that Jesus is a poor fit for the verbal action in this verse. Jesus did not do anything that corresponds to the action implied in these terms. While the notion of a violent robbery does not fit any conceivable activity on his part, it works perfectly when we take it as a comparison between the course taken by Jesus and someone else. Ernst Lohmeyer's study *Kyrios Jesus* marked a watershed in the treatment of this passage and is the most promising way of doing justice to the full range of actors and actions in the hymn.[28] His exposition is mindful not only of the violent action that is in view but also of the important negation in the sentence. There was something terrible Jesus did *not* do, and that something needs the contrast to be fully appreciated. Wherein was the violence implied in the expression? Wherein the battle, the violent seizure of something not belonging to the person instigating the action? Jesus cannot be the subject of that action.

25. Collins, "Origins of Christology," 366.

26. Thus Barr ("The Word Became Flesh," 22), who sees the whole sweep of the mystery of the incarnation of Phil 2:5–11 predicated on pre-existence.

27. BDAG, art. ἁρπαγμός.

28. Lohmeyer, *Kyrios Jesus*.

But there was violent action. In order to account for this action, the verbal element is in need of another subject. Who could that be? And what "is the object of this robbery?" as Lohmeyer asks.[29] He answers that there is an implied contrast in the statement, and this contrast comes to its own only when the cosmic and conflict-laden character of the statement is appreciated. The hymn aligns the narrative about Jesus's pre-existence, humiliation, and exaltation with the story of a heavenly being that proved to be differently disposed. To this end, Lohmeyer's interpretation brings to view the angel who said in his heart, "I will ascend to heaven; I will raise my throne above the stars of God; . . . I will make myself like the Most High" (Isa 14:13–14).[30] It will not be missed that this action is one of self-exaltation and ascent while the course taken by Jesus is one of self-emptying and descent. Awareness of the polar opposites in disposition and action makes the course taken by Jesus all the more amazing.

Isaiah's poem depicts how the "shining one," known as Lucifer since Jerome's Vulgate translation, set out to make the leap across the ontological divide between the Creator and created beings (Isa 14:13–15). The most important element in the poem is captured succinctly by Hans Wildberger's Isaiah commentary: "there was war."[31] The reality of fierce conflict is confirmed with the elaboration that the Day Star was "cut down to the ground" (Isa 14:12). This expression, seeing the conflict from the point of view of its outcome, makes discernible that Lucifer "must have been involved in a severe struggle."[32]

This is the background against which we must read the beginning of the Philippian hymn. It is focused precisely on negation of the violent action that forms the background for its portrayal of the pre-existent Christ. This negation, says Ralph P. Martin,

> has suggested to many commentators that there is a latent contrast in the mind of the writer. He has in view not only the spirit which animated the pre-incarnate Christ but, as though to form a backcloth to His exemplary action in not seizing or clinging to "equality with God," the spirit of some person who *did* aspire to this equality as a desirable thing and who *did* from a favourable position reach out after his own glory. The chief point in favour of this search for intended parallels is the negative form in which the sentence is cast.[33]

André Feuillet argues along the same line that the contrast in the hymn in Philippians is not only between two options available to Jesus or a contrast between Jesus and Adam.[34] The proposition to "be like God" does not originate on the human level

29. Ibid., 27.

30. Ibid., 27–8; Stauffer, *Die Theologie des Neuen Testaments*, 47–51; Käsemann, "Kritische Analyse," 317.

31. Wildberger, *Jesaja 13–27*, 550.

32. Ibid., 552–53.

33. Martin, *Carmen Christi*, 154.

34. Feuillet, "L'hymne christologique," 375–76. The relevant passages are Isa 14:12–15, Ezek

but in the non-human realm. In Isaiah's poem, the most splendid of all created beings said in his heart, "I will make myself like the Most High" (Isa 14:14). Accordingly, the allusion in the Philippian hymn refers to the self-exaltation of the figure behind the "king of Babylon" (Isa 14:12–20) and the "prince of Tyre" (Ezek 28:12–19) in the Old Testament.[35] The cosmic sweep and heavenly setting that are implied in the beginning of the hymn become explicit toward the end. There, the hymn returns to the setting of the beginning (Phil 2:9). Intelligent beings "in heaven and on the earth and under the earth" join in acknowledging that "*Jesus Christ* is Lord to the glory of God the Father" (Phil 2:11).[36]

The notion of conflict is not sustained only by the contrast between two acting subjects and violent seizure of something not his on the part of one of the subjects at the beginning of the hymn. The ending of the hymn narrates the resolution of the plot set up at the beginning (2:9–11). Worship of Jesus at the end effectively rules out the possibility that the hymn contrasts Jesus and Adam, a view that appeals to scholars who fail to see the cosmic perspective in the hymn. At the end of the hymn there is clarity with respect to the identity and character of Jesus to an extent that is not the case at the beginning. While Adam, prodded by the serpent in Genesis, reaches for something not his on the fallacious claim that it will make him "like God" (Gen 3:4–6), there is no rivalry between Adam and Jesus. Moreover, Adam's action does not have the violent character that is pictured in Philippians (2:6). Even more implausible for the notion that the hymn features a contrast between Adam and Jesus are the worship and acknowledgement of Jesus at the end of the hymn (2:9–11). When the contrastive slant of the hymn is carried to its logical conclusion, there is acknowledgment of Jesus at the end in a sense that would be inconceivable and meaningless if Adam were the implied 'other' in the contrast. Returning once more to an image we have used before, Adam's foot is too small for the shoe of the other character in the Philippian hymn.

No such difficulty arises if the contrast begins in a primordial, heavenly setting between Jesus and the highest being among the angels (Isa 14:12–20; Ezek 28:12–19).[37] A reading that respects the parameters of contrast and conflict will see, first, a being who tried by a violent thrust "to be equal with God" even though he was *not* "in the form of God," and, second, a being who, although he was "in the form of God," did *not* consider by a violent thrust "to be equal with God." Two movements are in view, both of which crucial to the plot of the hymn. With regard to the subjects of the hymn, Jesus stands in contrast to someone who tried to grasp what was not his. With respect to the action, the one who was "in the form of God" did not make it his calling card "to

---

28:12–19, and Dan 11:36–37. These passages also underlie the description of Antichrist in 2 Thess 2:3–4. See also Grelot, "Deux expressions difficiles," 501; Wanamaker, "Son of God or Adamic Christology?" 179–93; Vollenweider, "Der 'Raub' der Gottgleichheit," 419–21.

35. For a more in-depth discussion of these passages, see Tonstad, *Saving God's Reputation*, 89–102.

36. Gibbs, "Creation and Redemption according to Phil. II.5–11," 270.

37. Fisch, *Ezekiel*, 188; Greenberg, *Ezekiel 21–37*, 588–89.

be equal with God." Both elements are part of the plot that finds its resolution in the worship and acknowledgement of Jesus at the end (2:9–11).

"Jesus Christ is Lord, *to the glory of God the Father*," concludes the hymn (2:11). Even though the hymn has been called 'Christological,' it ends on a resounding *theological* note. The character of God has been put on display in the descent, incarnation, servanthood, and suffering of Jesus.[38] Jesus, who did not strive "to be equal with God" but who was "in the form of God" and who belongs to the divine identity, has in all his manifestations revealed the glory of God the Father. "Only in the Lord, it shall be said of me, are righteousness and strength," explains the text from which the Philippian hymn borrows one of its most important lines, and "all who were incensed against him shall come to him and be ashamed" (Isa 45:24).

This means that the message of the hymn vastly exceeds the tendency to reduce it to a moralizing tale along the lines that 'pride goes before the fall.' As worthy as it is to hold forth Jesus as an example to be emulated, the story told in the hymn is too large for that to be its primary message. Ernst Käsemann's essay on the Philippian hymn restores to it a thrust that is lost when we make its lesson to be that humility goes before exaltation. Jesus is archetype [*Urbild*], not example [*Vorbild*], he says.[39]

"Let the same mind be in you that was in Christ Jesus," we can now read,

> although he was in the form of God,
>   it did not enter his mind
>   to attempt by a violent thrust
>   to attain equality with God
> [in contrast to the action of the highest angel].
>
> But he emptied himself,
>   taking the form of a slave,
>   being born in human likeness.
>
> And being found in human form,
>   he humbled himself
>   and became obedient to the point of death
>   —even death on a cross.
>
> Therefore God also highly exalted *him*
>   and gave *him* the name
>   that is above every name
> [including that of the highest angel],

38. Bauckham (*God Crucified*, 61).writes that "this is not the contrast of two natures, divine and human, but a contrast more powerful for first-century Jewish theology with its controlling image of God as the universal emperor, high on his heavenly throne, inconceivably exalted above all he has created and rules. Can the cross of Jesus Christ actually be included in the identity of this God?"

39. Käsemann, "Kritische Analyse von Phil. 2,5–11," 345. A similar muting of the ethical use of the passage is advocated by Sanders, "Dissenting Deities," 289.

so that at the name of *Jesus*
every knee should bow,
in heaven, and on earth
and under the earth,

and every tongue should confess
that *Jesus Christ* is Lord,
to the glory of God the Father (Phil 2:5–11, my annotations).

Jesus and the Angels

It should now be easier to appreciate that angels are part of the story and essential to the plot. The author of Hebrews is not on a wild goose chase when he or she draws a line of demarcation between Jesus and angels, and the Philippian hymn has not lost its bearings when it goes out of its way to prove that Jesus did not resort to violence in order "to be like God." If the line between angels and Jesus seems blurred, the reason will not be found in the realm of ontology, but in the sphere of character. Ontologically, the pre-existent Jesus was "no ordinary angel."[40] With respect to character, however—and I say this in terms that are self-consciously anthropomorphic—he may have appeared to be one. In this reading, the premise for his exaltation in the Philippian hymn is his disposition and not simply ontology.

Other puzzling features of the representation of Christ in the New Testament are less mystifying when the disposition of the pre-existent Jesus is given its due. Perhaps Jesus does not mind being represented as an angel or even thought of as one? Why would it offend him to be represented as an angel when he is clearly not bothered by being seen as a human being—and actually being one? On this point we do not need to guess because the question is addressed in Hebrews. To be seen as lower in rank than what he is and not consider it shameful—this is fully consonant with the disposition of Jesus. "For the one who sanctifies and those who are sanctified all have one Father. For this reason Jesus is not ashamed to call them brothers and sisters, saying, 'I will proclaim your name to my brothers and sisters, in the midst of the congregation I will praise you'" (Heb 2:11–12). This Jesus is not 'one of us' in name only, but in reality. As James Barr has pointed out, Jesus did not make a cameo appearance as a human being. In light of the Philippian hymn, the exaltation after the Cross "is not a re-metamorphosis into the original divine form; the Incarnation is thus not a temporary stage in the history of the Christ, for it is natural to assume, although and because it is not explicitly stated, that it is the form of man and the form of the servant that is now taken up into glory."[41]

40. Cf. Garrett, *No Ordinary Angel*.

41. Barr, "The Word Became Flesh," 22.

There is no doubt that the risen Christ in Revelation is portrayed in language previously used by Daniel, investing him with angelic characteristics (Rev 1:13–16; Dan 10:5–6).[42] When the risen Jesus in Revelation says of himself, "I was dead, and see, I am alive forever and ever" (1:18), he has angelic or angelomorphic attributes,[43] mingled with features belonging to "the Ancient of Days" (Dan 7:9, NKJV).[44] Adela Yarbro Collins concludes that Revelation "expresses an angelic Christology which is best understood in the context of the Jewish motif of the principal angel."[45]

In Revelation 12, as noted earlier, the cosmic battle pits "Michael and his angels" against "the dragon and his angels," saying that "Michael and his angels had to fight against the dragon" (Rev 12:7, translation mine). The dragon comes up short in this war (Rev 12:8–9). But when the heavenly host celebrates the victory, Michael, who led the fight, is nowhere to be seen. "Now have come the salvation and the power and the kingdom of our God and the authority of his Messiah," proclaims the loud voice in heaven (Rev 12:10). The Messiah, not Michael, is declared the winner. John J. Collins observes that "when the dragon has been defeated the kingdom is awarded, not to Michael and his angels, but to Christ."[46]

What happened to Michael?

Collins answers that the celebration of victory in Rev 12:10 is best understood as an example of "angelic christology" where the role attributed to Michael is allotted to Christ.[47] Jesus is not an angel but he is represented as one and functions as though he is one. Michael does not disappear from the picture but is subsumed in the Messiah. In studies of this subject, Christopher Rowland sees early Christology aided by Jewish angelology.[48] Robert H. Gundry finds Revelation replete with angelomorphic [angel-like] representations of Christ in the sense that Christ assumes the functions of an angel with no apparent offense to his dignity.[49] An identification of Christ with Michael seems almost certain in the *Shepherd of Hermas*, a much beloved non-canonical text in the Early Church.[50] In light of what we have seen in Hebrews and Philippians, the representation of Jesus as an angel should not be seen as a mistake or as the consequence of limited resources for representation. Instead, the representation has basis in reality.

42. Carrell *Jesus and the Angels*, 148–65.

43. Collins, *Cosmology and Eschatology*, 172–73.

44. Carrell, *Jesus and the angels*, 155–56.

45. Collins, *Cosmology and Eschatology*, 159.

46. Collins, "The Son of Man," 65.

47. Ibid.

48. Rowland, "The Vision of the Risen Christ," 1–11; ———, "A Man Clothed in Linen," 99–110.

49. Gundry, "Angelomorphic Christology," 662–78. See also Holtz, *Die Christologie der Apokalypse*, 117–18.

50. *Herm. Sim.* 8.3.3; cf. Daniélou, *Theology of Jewish Christianity*, 124. See also Moxnes, "God and His Angel in the Shepherd of Hermas," 49–56; Osiek, *Shepherd of Hermas*, 204.

The clarifying character of texts that draw lines of demarcation between Jesus and the angels become less puzzling when we keep this background in mind. The exaltation of Jesus in Philippians and Hebrews is justified because Jesus belongs to the divine identity, but this is not the dominant focus of these texts. They expend an immense effort on locating the exaltation, acknowledgement, and worship of Jesus at the end of the story, *after* his humiliation, at the point when Jesus is fully *human*.

> But when He again brings the firstborn into the world, He says: "Let all the angels of God worship Him" (Heb 1:6, NKJV).

> Therefore God also highly exalted him and gave him the name that is above every name, so that at the name of Jesus every knee should bend, in heaven and on earth and under the earth, and every tongue should confess that Jesus Christ is Lord, to the glory of God the Father (Phil 2:9–11, NRSV).

These texts do an excellent job in the service of Christology by showing that Jesus is not an angel. But their effort in this regard is not much ado about nothing. The delineation between Jesus and the angels is not a foregone conclusion in the Bible, not because Jesus's ontological credentials are in doubt but because of his self-emptying disposition. This distinction, in turn, means that these texts serve theology more than they clarify Christology. God, these texts insist, does not want to be worshiped for ontological reasons only; even God does not want to have "power and glory" as the determining elements of the divine identity.[51] Jesus, in his pre-existence and in his human form, has revealed the divine disposition. He was not embarrassed to be seen as an angel in his pre-existent state, and he is not ashamed to be a human being, never to let go of his human identity (Heb 2:11). What he was and is, and what he did and does, have all been "to the glory of God the Father" (Phil 2:11).

It is not easy to find a workable analogy for this construct, but one story may help. I was once a medical student at the university where I am now teaching. Before my time, the university had a legendary professor of anatomy whose name was Samuel Crooks. Anatomy is a foundational subject in medicine, appropriately placed at the head of the curriculum and taught at a time when the students are in the most intimidated state of mind. I was told by reliable sources that professor Crooks, the head of the Department of Anatomy, would start the course every year dressed in blue overalls. He would first meet the students for orientation in the lab where the dissections take place and then face them in the auditorium for the opening lecture.

One year as the new students were getting familiar with cadavers and the smell of formaldehyde in the lab on the first day of school, a student accidentally bumped into a glass jar that contained an anatomical specimen. The specimen fell to the concrete floor, broke, and spilled its content of a human body part and foul-smelling

51. See Müller ("Der Christushymnus," 25) for the idea that power and glory are not the determining elements in the identity of the pre-existent Christ.

formaldehyde. Flustered, the student spotted a man in blue overalls in the lab. Assuming that he must be the janitor, he walked over to him and explained his predicament. Would he be willing to clean up the mess on the floor?

The man in blue overalls nodded in agreement. Fetching a bucket and the appropriate cleaning materials, he cleansed the floor of the formaldehyde and swept up the broken glass. Moments later, when the students assembled in the auditorium for the first lecture, the man in blue overalls, no longer self-evidently the janitor, walked to the lectern. The shock and embarrassment of that student on his first day of school do not need to be explained. Professor Crooks wished to make a statement about the dignity of labor so as to disabuse budding physicians of the idea that janitors in blue overalls are of lesser value than physicians in white coats. In important respects, the Philippian hymn projects a vision of Jesus similarly disposed.

But the analogy fails if it gives the impression that Jesus in his pre-existent state dressed up in 'blue overalls' mostly to set an example of humility. Following the lead of Käsemann's reading of the Philippian hymn, this is precisely *not* the point.[52] What Jesus did is explained by his disposition and not by a lesson he sought to teach. With respect to the cosmic rebellion, we might even say that the disposition revealed in the pre-existent Christ could actually *increase* the risk that a created being could conceive of the idea of being his equal.[53] Would not divine sovereignty and authority be better served by keeping distance? Would not Jesus, who could claim "to be equal with God" by right and not by robbery (Phil 2:6), serve the cause of stability better by making the space between the divine and the created realm as wide as possible? We have surveyed evidence that God did not do this.

Nicolo Machiavelli, advising his prince as to how earthly rulers ought to wield power, said that "it is much safer to be feared than loved, when, of the two, either must be dispensed with."[54] Keeping distance so as to instill the proper measure of fear, he urged, is better, "for love is preserved by the link of obligation which, owing to the baseness of men, is broken at every opportunity for their advantage; but fear preserves you by a dread of punishment which never fails."[55] Allowing for enormous differences between heaven and earth, between pre-sin and post-sin reality, and between the disposition of angels and "the baseness of men," we do not see God keeping distance. I admit the anthropomorphism, but we may wonder whether it occurred to Lucifer to make the leap across the ontological divide between the divine realm and that of angels on the rationale that the lowly disposition of the pre-existent Jesus made the distance appear negotiable.

If the highest angel took the disposition of Jesus to mean that his violent attempt to make himself "like the Most High" would succeed (Isa 14:14), he miscalculated in

52. Käsemann, "Kritische Analyse," 345.

53. See Johnsen, *The Maligned God*, 24–38.

54. Machiavelli, *The Prince*, 63.

55. Ibid.

his estimation of the divine character no less than with respect to the magnitude of the ontological divide. On the terms outlined in these texts, humans were not the first to take the wrong measure of the divine sense. The care with which the New Testament delineates angels from God and from human beings and the precision with which these texts labor to draw a line between angels and Jesus is remarkable. They make angels ontologically important, and they suggest a plot that made it necessary to spell out the contrast between Jesus and the highest angel (Phil 2:5–11). Most of all, these texts set Jesus apart, of whom and to whom God said things that God never said to the angels (Heb 1:5, 13).

Part II

Bursts of Sense

Chapter Six

Paradise Lost: Making Sense of Opposing Senses

The world had ideas about good and evil prior to Christianity, but these views "*are not like the tales which tell of a devil . . . who is a sorcerer and proclaims opposing opinions*," the philosopher Celsus wrote in the second century of the Christian era.[1] We must access the biblical account at the point of its origin in Genesis in order to understand the birth of this notion. In the first two chapters of Genesis we have the story of creation told twice in somewhat different ways. If the first account is largely declarative in character (Gen 1:1—2:3), the second account is strikingly interactive (2:4—3:24).[2] Indeed, if God *declares* how things will be in the first account, in the second account we hear God asking a series of bombshell questions.

"Where are you?" (3:9).

"Who told you that you were naked?" (3:11).

"Have you eaten from the tree of which I commanded you not to eat?" (3:11).

"What is this that you have done?" (3:13)

Why is *Yahweh Elohim* talking like this? Why these questions, each one resonant with horror that will not be diminished by the context that frames the questions? God is speaking, reacting to discoveries that come to light while "walking in the garden at the time of the evening breeze" (3:8). Even though the narrator does not say so explicitly, it is evident that God is shaken by the fact that the expected encounter with human beings this time fails to materialize. As Adam and Eve heard *Yahweh Elohim* approaching, they "hid themselves from the presence of the Lord God among the trees of the garden" (3:8). Thus the question, "Where are you?" Thus the next question, "Who told you that you were naked?" And then the question, "both indignant and incredulous," as Ellen Davis translates it, "From the tree that I commanded you *not to* eat from it—you ate??!!" (Gen 3:11).[3]

1. Origen, *Contra Celsum* 6.42.
2. Welker, *Creation and Reality*, 10.
3. Davis, "Learning Our Place," 114.

They ate. In the immediate aftermath of eating, the human condition changes from carefree un-awareness of the self to uneasy and uptight self-awareness, a precipitous decline in what we today might call a person's self-image (2:25; 3:7). Human intimacy gives way to reproach of the other in a display of calculated self-preservation, meaning that the social fabric is coming apart at the core (2:23; 3:12). Lastly, the keepers of the Garden of Eden are stripped of their privileges, facing loss of place and banishment (2:15; 3:23–24).

Deepest of all is the change in relationship between God and human beings. When they hear God approaching—and here we can hear the narrator speak in hushed tones—"the man and his wife hid themselves from the presence of the LORD God among the trees of the garden" (3:8). Then the question, in what Phyllis Trible calls "a love story gone awry,"[4] "Where are you?" (3:9) And then the answer, bursting at the seams with sudden and inexplicable alienation, "I heard the sound of you in the garden, and I was afraid" (3:10).

Celsus, the non-Christian philosopher, was certainly correct that the pagan world did not have a story like this.[5] They had stories of combat, of opposition to God, and of rebellion against divine authority. But there is nothing in ancient literature that is as subtle and challenging as this story, nothing that puts an opposing *opinion* in the foreground, nothing that makes that opinion the breaking point, and nothing that makes the quest for *sense* so pivotal.

Tangles of Senses

The opposing view took the form of a question, the first in the Bible, a question better described as a *questioning*. "Did God say," the questioner asked, "You shall not eat from any tree in the garden?" (3:1).

Why would a question like that arise in the Garden of Eden? If we regard the statement as a comment more than as question, no reader can fail to notice that this is a comment on something God did *not* say. God had spoken concerning the trees in the Garden (2:16–17), but God had not said anything like *that*. Until the opposing opinion appears like lightning out of the blue, *Yahweh Elohim* comes across as a God who *provides* and not as a God who *prohibits*.

> Out of the ground the LORD God made to grow every tree that is pleasant to the sight and good for food, the tree of life also in the midst of the garden, and the tree of the knowledge of good and evil (2:9).

The two perspectives on creation speak with one voice on this point. In both versions the word "good" is conspicuous. "It was good," the first story says at the close of each stage of creation (1:4, 10, 12, 18, 21, 25); indeed, "it was *very* good" (1:31). The

4. Trible, *God and the Rhetoric of Sexuality*, 72–143.

5. Cf. McKenzie, "The Literary Characteristics," 541–72.

second story is no less effusive: trees appear that are "pleasant to the eyes and good for food" (2:9, 12; 3:6), putting emphasis on the fact that whatever God is bringing into being is *good*. Moreover, what God creates is meant for the good of human beings. "See, I have given you every plant yielding seed that is upon the face of all the earth, and every tree with seed in its fruit; you shall have them for food," God says in the first account (1:19). The second account comes off the same page: it would be meaningless for the narrator to say that *Yahweh Elohim* made trees that were *good for food* unless they were intended to serve that purpose (2:9).

Until the dissenting view intrudes, the message in the creation stories is provision and not prohibition. Why, then, this attempt to portray God's command as a stern and all-encompassing ban? The notion of not being allowed to eat "from *any* tree in the garden" is not the first thought that comes to mind in light of what God has said and done so far in these accounts. An all-out prohibition, moreover, would certainly fail the test of *sense*. Will a lesser prohibition, if that is what we have, do the same?

A tree of life is known in other ancient narratives of origins but not a tree of knowledge. Nahum Sarna says that this tree "has no parallel outside of our biblical Garden of Eden story."[6] Attention in the story is focused on this tree more than on the tree of life, further highlighting its importance in Genesis.[7] I am therefore tempted to add one word concerning this tree, "Out of the ground the LORD God made to grow every tree that is pleasant to the sight and good for food, the tree of life also in the midst of the garden, and *[even]* the tree of the knowledge of good and evil" (2:9). In order to forestall a hohum reading, it may be appropriate to end the sentence with an exclamation mark. Pressing the point that God was creating good things, there is no letting up in this respect. The story envisions ever more spectacular exhibits of "good." According to this logic, the tree of knowledge is good, and it is good that it is there.

Having ascertained that priority and purpose are in view with regard to the tree of knowledge, it is time to hear what God actually said.

> And the LORD God commanded [*tṣāwâ*] the man, "You may freely eat of every tree of the garden; but of the tree of the knowledge of good and evil you shall not eat, for in the day that you eat of it you shall die" (2:16–17).

Where shall we place the emphasis in this statement? Considering the statement as a whole, should the focus be on permission, or on prohibition? Considering the tree of knowledge only, is the prohibition not to eat meant as a restriction? Phrasing the inquiry in open-ended terms, what is the message of this tree?

A reading that puts the weight on quantitative parameters is likely to conclude that God imposes a restriction. In a garden of 3000 trees, choosing this number only for the purpose of illustration, one tree is now forbidden territory. The arithmetic is easy: 2999 trees is one less than 3000. The difference, albeit a small one, signifies a

6. Sarna, *Understanding Genesis*, 26.

7. Ibid.

restriction. In quantitative terms, a person is more restricted who has access to 2999 trees rather than to 3000.

James Barr objects to the story not only because God imposes a restriction, but also because the alleged restriction does not make sense.[8] Barr refers to "the sheer irrationality of the command." Irrationality is aggravated by the threat of death should there be "the slightest deviation from the slightest divine command." Worse yet, the command is "devoid of perceptible ethical basis." Still worse, God "has made an ethically arbitrary prohibition, and backed it up with a threat to kill, which in the event, he does nothing to carry out."[9] Adding up these ingredients, God is the one "who is placed in a rather ambiguous light."[10] This scathing verdict from one of the most astute biblical scholars of his generation cannot be taken lightly: the command, even when we dissociate it from the serpent's exaggeration, fails the test of sense.

This assessment goes beyond a mere quantitative assessment, but one should not miss that the underlying logic is deprivation. Everything may have been "good" until this point, but now the story is chilled by a policy of restriction, and a meaningless restriction at that. "Good" is giving way to "not good." In fact, what has seemed "good" in the story now looks disconcerting. The restriction reveals what God is actually up to, and it is not good.

If, however, our reading takes the qualitative route, the outcome could be quite different. In a qualitative assessment it is not the raw number of trees that matters but their meaning. In this scenario the quality of human existence is not measured only according to material parameters, but in spiritual and political terms. Where the quantitative assessment is forced to register a subtraction, placing the tree of knowledge in the column of loss, the qualitative approach sees in the tree an added quality, recording it in the column of gain.

Ellen Davis admits that at first sight "the presence of that forbidden tree smack in the middle of Eden makes no sense at all."[11] But then, on further reflection, she calls it "the most logical thing in the world."[12] "Indeed," she says, "the forbidden tree points to the logic that undergirds the world."[13] The logic now emerging must be compared to the ideal of taking what we want with no regard for limits. Thus, says Davis, now casting the tree as entirely positive, the tree symbolizes that our place "entails living by the practice of restraint."[14] The nonsense that initially seemed evident now begins to look better.

8. Barr, *Garden of Eden*, 12.

9. Ibid.

10. Ibid.

11. Davis, "Learning Our Place," 115.

12. Ibid.

13. Ibid.

14. Ibid.

"God's words had emphasized freedom—the man could eat of every tree with only one prohibited," says R. W. L. Moberly in an attempt to restore to the command the dignity of making sense.[15] In other words, freedom is the predominant emphasis, restriction the lesser one, but there is nevertheless a restriction. A genuine qualitative reading will go further than this, construing the apparent restriction not as a limitation of freedom, but as its confirmation. "God is good in giving this commandment, for they are free to eat from any tree in the Garden, including the tree of life, with one exception," says Sidney Greidanus.[16] Moreover, only a mean-spirited view will read the prohibition as a limitation. "This one prohibition is also good because God treats man as a free moral agent."[17] There is now an added quality in this tree, the quality of choice. The mind that thinks in terms of quantity sees loss, as we have seen, but the mind attuned to quality sees gain.

Restraint, consent, and choice are in these readings set forth as core elements in God's value system. Where the quantitative interpretation sees less freedom, the qualitative reading sees more. Indeed, the qualitative reading sees freedom itself. Remove the tree of knowledge, the qualitative logic asserts, and what is thus removed is the possibility of choice. We might wish to qualify this view by admitting that the author through the symbolism of the tree "teaches that the human person is free in all respects but one: determining what is right and wrong solely on the basis of human insight."[18] This view has merit, but it should not take away that choice itself could be a primary function of the tree.

Walter Brueggemann sees in this story a triplet denoting *vocation*, *permission*, and *prohibition*, noting, however, that God's will for vocation and freedom has been lost to the effect that God "is chiefly remembered as the one who *prohibits*."[19] This is a correct observation, but it is not worded strongly enough. As a category that is related to permission and provision, it has been suggested that God intended the tree to promote wisdom and discernment on the part of human beings.[20] God was not trying to restrict humans or plotting their downfall. On the contrary, God was putting in place the means by which human beings could grow and develop so as to make good on the high destiny God intended. William Wilder combines the notions of illumination and investiture, the former pointing to the quality of discernment and the latter indicating the high calling held out to humans. "Rather than serving as the means of their downfall," he says, the tree "would have served as the means of their exaltation—to the righteousness, power, and glory God intended them to enjoy."[21] In this scenario, the

15. Moberly, "Did the Serpent Get It Right?" 6.

16. Greidanus, "Preaching Christ," 266.

17. Ibid.

18. Scotchmer, "Lessons from Paradise," 81–82.

19. Brueggemann, *Genesis*, 46.

20. Wilder, "Illumination and Investiture," 51–69.

21. Ibid., 52.

idea that best describes God's purpose is that of *promotion*, yet another notion that is a far cry from the prohibition that is the mantra of the opposing view.

The tree could even be placed in the category of *protection*. "The divine prohibition is for man's own protection," says Jerome Walsh.[22] This may seem like an odd concept because Walsh does not mean protection from an external threat. Humans are tempted to occupy the center, and this temptation, if distilled to its essence, has to do with betrayal of trust. Where ancient myths see the hero braving obstacles in order to attain the center, in the Garden of Eden human beings need not resort to heroics to get it right. To get it right, they merely have to accept that the tree is there for their good; they have to forgo the heroic urge to conquer the center. To get it wrong, as this story tells it, "the grandeur of the heroic achievement is transformed into the sordidness of a sin of disloyalty."[23]

While this view has much to commend it, is protection against overreaching the chief danger God wishes to prevent? Is the most ominous peril within or without the human self? Protection is called for where there is danger; it is not needed where there is none. If there is an external threat to human well-being in the Garden, as a few interpreters are willing to grant, the notion of protection rises much higher on the list of possible meanings. In this scenario it will be necessary to consider the possibility that "evil already lurked amidst the happiness of Eden."[24] On this point the story in Genesis assumes awareness on the part of the initial audience that the modern reader lacks. As Umberto Cassuto notes, key concepts in the story are introduced using the definite article, as though they are familiar to the audience: the tree of life, the tree of knowledge of good and evil, the cherubim, the flaming sword, and the serpent.[25] The story maps a path into the encounter with the opposing opinions that makes it possible to see God's command regarding the tree of knowledge as a calculated measure against a known threat (2:16–17). If the tree is intended as a protective measure, the "sheer irrationality of the command" that James Barr alleges is not the compelling argument that he takes it to be.[26] While awareness of a genuine threat comes to the modern reader as a late discovery, an afterthought, or not at all, it could be an early premise in the story. The serpent, as noted, is one element concerning which no explanation was needed. In a protective scenario the tree is meant as a restriction, but the restriction applies to the threat and only indirectly to human beings. In the Garden they "are provided for and at the same time protected from danger," says Claus Westermann.[27]

The dots that must be connected now run between the opposing view and the one promoting it. On this point the Christian reading of the story stands apart because

22. Walsh, "A Synchronic Approach," 173.

23. Ibid.

24. Skinner, *Genesis*, 71.

25. Cassuto, *Commentary*, 74.

26. Barr, *Garden of Eden*, 12.

27. Westermann, *Genesis 1–11*, 239.

it pinpoints the source of the opinion. The account, as Celsus pointed out, speaks of "*a devil . . .who is a sorcerer.*"[28] The success of the opposing opinion depends on wiliness on the part of its promoter, shrewdly trying to turn the divine sense of giving into a command that takes everything away (3:1). In quantitative terms, it should be noted, the serpent's version of the divine command is not that one tree is off limits, but that all are. An order that speaks of provision, promotion, and even protection, all by divine intent, does not easily collapse into the single notion of prohibition. The story envisions not only a clever opinion but also a devious and determined intent to win acceptance for it.

"*The objective accent falls on WHAT is said, the subjective accent on HOW it is said,*" says Søren Kierkegaard.[29] Just as a qualitative view of the tree differs from a quantitative approach, Kierkegaard's distinction has far-reaching consequences. A person may say the same words with completely different meanings. Was it said sincerely or sarcastically? Was it said as though the answer is already known, the question only meant to bring an unwelcome discovery into the open? Applying this distinction to the serpent's speech in Genesis, the weight of emphasis is not only on the thought, but also on how the thought is expressed.

Contemporary interpreters tend to be dismissive of the Christian reading on this point, faulting it for seeing a demonic power at work. Illustrious scholars of the Old Testament will say that the New Testament and the Early Church made too much of the story in Genesis, failing to recognize that it is only a legend;[30] that the temptation was merely a conversation the woman had with herself;[31] or that it is "an exceedingly marginal text."[32] They will urge that the story is only interested in what is said and not in who is saying it;[33] that there is in the Bible "no Fall before the Fall"[34] and no evil antecedent to human sin. It has been argued that the Old Testament does not have a notion of evil on the order of Satan in the New Testament.[35] The weight of scholarship behind these opinions is formidable.

And yet we should hesitate to accept that the New Testament and the Early Church took the story in Genesis into places where it had no intention of going. To imply that the Christian interpretation imposed itself on Genesis in brazen disregard of what the account meant to convey is too simplistic. While the views of modern scholars on this point threaten to undermine tenets that the New Testament treats with the utmost respect, they also fail to recognize the Old Testament account as it stands.

28. Origen, *Contra Celsum* 6.42.
29. Kierkegaard, *Concluding Unscientific Postscript*, 181.
30. Gunkel, *Genesis*, vii–xi; von Rad, *Genesis*, 30–35.
31. Cassuto, *Genesis*, 141–42.
32. Brueggemann, *Genesis*, 41.
33. Von Rad, *Genesis*, 85.
34. Ansell, "The Call of Wisdom," 36.
35. Tate, "Satan in the Old Testament," 461–74.

More Than Animal Speech

The woman's encounter with the serpent in Genesis begins with the surprise of animal speech. "The *serpent* . . . said to the woman," says the narrator in Genesis (3:1). There is no further comment on, or reaction to, the report of animal speech. The serpent speaks, proclaiming unsettling opinions, but the narrator sees no reason to cue the reader in on how this is possible.

The absence of elaboration leaves the door wide open for interpreters to supply explanations. One such explanation, and a very influential one, is offered by Hermann Gunkel. With confidence that is typical of a scholar at the beginning of the twentieth century, Gunkel alleges that this feature of animal speech fails to elicit the slightest show of surprise on the part of the woman. "It is not remarkable for animals to think and speak like humans in fairy tales, animal fables, and even in legends," he says.[36] Having determined that the genre of the story approximates that of a legend, animal speech poses no reason for surprise. "Therefore the woman was not at all surprised when the serpent suddenly opened its mouth," he says.[37]

How does he know that? This statement is itself proof of failure to grasp one of the most basic features of the Old Testament narratives. "The Hebrew Bible is terse, it does not use three words where two or one or none will do," says Pamela Tamarkin Reis.[38] Recognition of this means that we cannot determine whether the woman was surprised only on the basis of what is explicit in the text. The stories are full of unexpressed thoughts and feelings, tugging and pulling at the reader to unearth what lies under the surface. The stories demand reader participation because the author "rarely tells us what anyone feels or thinks; we must intuit that."[39]

In Gunkel's view, the woman was not surprised at the serpent speaking because he believed that he was reading a primitive tale and because the text does not say that Eve was surprised. But this view loses its appeal if its underlying premise does not hold up. Gunkel draws unwarranted conclusions concerning things that are not stated in the text. Turning his point around, it is surprising that interpreters are not surprised at the fact of animal speech.

Given the view that we are reading legends and fairy tales, the rarity of animal speech in the Old Testament is astonishing. In the entire Old Testament there are only two instances of beastly speech, both happening under extraordinary circumstances (Gen 3:1–5; Num 22:28–31).[40] In the second of these instances, the speech of Balaam's donkey, the narrator is careful to point out that "*the* LORD opened the donkey's mouth" (Num 22:28, NIV), indicating that animal speech on this occasion is unusual

36. Gunkel, *Genesis*, 15.

37. Ibid.

38. Reis, "What Cain Said," 110.

39. Reis, *Reading the Lines*, 10.

40. Savran, "Beastly Speech," 33–55.

and divinely ordained. If, on the terms of the world view of the Bible, it is not strange that an animal is speaking, the reason cannot be that the stories belong to a genre in which animals routinely speak. Animal speech in the Old Testament is an exceptional and extraordinary phenomenon. Surprise in the face of this phenomenon should be expected within the story and on the part of those who read it. Once the exceptional character of animal speech in the Bible is recognized, it is amazing that interpreters are unimpressed. The most likely explanation, far more likely than Gunkel's jaded view, is that the woman was startled in the face of animal speech.

The account in Genesis treats the serpent as an acting subject. In the beginning of the story, the serpent speaks (Gen 3:1–5). Later on, when the man and his wife have eaten of the tree, God speaks directly to the serpent (3:14–15). Sandwiched between these two portions of speech *by* the serpent and speech *to* the serpent, the woman attributes to the serpent a decisive influence on her decision to eat of the tree (3:13). This view is not contested when *Yahweh Elohim* addresses the serpent.

> The Lord God said to the serpent, "Because you have done this, cursed are you among all animals and among all wild creatures; upon your belly you shall go, and dust you shall eat all the days of your life" (3:14).

Four things are evident in God's address to the serpent. First, the serpent is treated as a significant character that is worthy of God's attention. In fact, the serpent comes first in order of priority when God takes stock of the factors that have led to the eating of the tree. Second, there is acknowledgment of influence. God ascribes responsibility to the serpent for what has happened even though it is not the serpent's fault alone. Third, God specifies consequences to the serpent for its role in deceiving the woman. Fourth, God's address to the serpent includes a promise of intervention, a statement that early was seen as a commitment to make right what has gone wrong.[41]

> I will put enmity between you and the woman, and between your offspring and hers; he will strike your head, and you will strike his heel (3:15).

The text includes the serpent in a triangular relationship involving God, the woman's seed, and the serpent. The as-yet-unspecified intervention anticipates that the enmity ultimately will be an enmity between the woman's seed and the serpent. God's address envisions a conflict in which the serpent will come up the loser; it will "bite the dust."[42]

Animal speech is one thing we should *not* expect from the story in Genesis. The two versions of creation are united in drawing a line of demarcation between human beings and animals, treating them as different orders of being. In the first story (1:1—2:3), the ontological divide relates to the roles assigned to human beings with respect to the rest of creation. On this point the thought in the story is fully developed

41. Martin, "The Earliest Messianic Interpretation," 425–27; Campi, "Genesis 1–3," 251–71.

42. Haupt, "The Curse on the Serpent," 155–62.

and explicit. Already at the planning stage it is clear that God is contemplating an order of being that stands apart from, and above, non-human creation.

> Then God said, "Let us make humankind in our image, according to our likeness; and let them have dominion over the fish of the sea, and over the birds of the air, and over the cattle, and over all the wild animals of the earth, *and over every creeping thing that creeps upon the earth*" (1:26).

At the planning stage the creative vision in regard to human beings is sweeping and all-inclusive. Human dominion extends to "*all* the wild animals of the earth," and it is to include "*every* creeping thing that creeps upon the earth" (1:26). It follows that no animal is exempt, not even if that animal claims the distinction as the most illustrious within the animal kingdom (3:1).

Genesis says that God follows through on this plan, being careful to repeat it to the least detail.

> So God created humankind in his image, in the image of God he created them; male and female he created them. God blessed them, and God said to them, "Be fruitful and multiply, and fill the earth and subdue it; and have dominion over the fish of the sea and over the birds of the air *and over every living thing that moves upon the earth*" (1:27–28).

Within this order, humans are a singular kind of being, belonging to an ontological category of their own. Only humans are created in the image of God. Human beings alone are singled out for the task of dominion. Dominion, in turn, is not meant in the sense of predation or exploitation but as a delegated responsibility of care. The beings that are created in the image of God are expected to act toward the rest of creation according to their likeness to God: in the stance of caring and blessing (1:22).

In the second story in Genesis, the description of the human mandate is shorter, but the message runs along the same lines.

> The Lord God took the man and put him in the Garden of Eden to till it and keep it (2:15).

Attention to the human role is again primary, and the vocation assigned to human beings combines dominion and responsibility. Human beings are given the task to till and to serve, or, as Phyllis Trible puts it, the task of "lordship and servanthood."[43] Non-human beings are yet to appear at this stage in the second account, but when they do appear, they are assigned to a different sphere.

> So out of the ground the Lord God formed every animal of the field and every bird of the air, and brought them to the man to see what he would call them; and whatever the man called every living creature, that was its name. The man

43. Trible, *God and the Rhetoric of Sexuality*, 77.

> gave names to all cattle, and to the birds of the air, and to every animal of the field (2:19–20).

Beyond the specified task to till and to keep, the human distinctive in this account focuses on language. The naming of the animals points to an ability that is unique to human beings. While superior human ability is the prerequisite for dominion in a limited sense, it speaks even more of discernment.[44] The assignment of naming the members of non-human creation has a descriptive core that is possible because God has endowed human beings with the intellectual resources with which to succeed. The ontological divide between human beings and animals is undiminished, now residing specifically in the human ability to comprehend and describe the rest of the created order. The image of God and dominion in the first account, the notion of lordship, discernment, and speech in the second, set human beings apart from non-human creation in the most striking and exquisite way. Looking ahead to the tree of knowledge and the serpent that speaks, the reader has been thoroughly primed *not* to expect anything like that.

Again, however, interpreters grasp at the straw that he or she is reading a story that does not "fetter the imagination with logic."[45] This suggestion might have worked except for the fact there is reason and logic aplenty in story, in the form of divine command (Gen 2:16–17), opposing opinions (3:1–5), reflection (3:6), and a host of serious consequences (3:7–19). Has a story that is so aware of itself and so explicit with respect to its own errand suddenly thrown everything overboard? Does the narrator forget that he is messing up his own categories of being when he introduces a serpent that speaks and an animal that is wiser than human beings? On this point interpreters do not need to reach for the desperate view that there is absence of logic. It is far better to join those who, like Martin Emmrich, find other elements in the drama.

> But how then are we to understand the serpent's function in our story? On the one hand, the author wants to convey the idea of an actual snake as one of the animals Yahweh had made. But it is precisely this kind of referentiality that seems to entail some tension: What about the snake's ability to speak? How is it that the snake is not only more shrewd than all the other animals, but also, at least in some sense, more knowledgeable than man?[46]

For the reader who decides not to take the road that he or she is reading stories that are devoid of sense, the answer must be that the story envisions more complex characters and a more complicated plot. Logic will not be absent within a more respectful plot construct. This applies especially to the character of the serpent, on the face of it an animal under human dominion, dumb literally and figuratively, and yet in this story speaking with wisdom and guile surpassing that of human beings. Absence

44. Ramsey, "Name-Giving," 24–35.

45. Trible, *God and the Rhetoric of Sexuality*, 72.

46. Emmrich, "The Temptation Narrative," 10.

of sense is not a workable solution for the story especially when we bring the original readers into the picture.

> It has been claimed that the wisdom of the serpent here is ambiguous in that the reader is not told whether it is good or bad. But even the very first verse in the temptation account seems to militate against such a view, for how would the Israelite audience react to the tempter's questioning God's command, which gives expression to the snake's craftiness? No matter whether we are here dealing with a neutral term or not, a contextual analysis will lead us to the conclusion that the serpent is depicted not only as being rebellious against God, but also as displaying an evil kind of cleverness in engaging the woman.[47]

The story features a triangular drama involving God, human beings, and the serpent, but it is not animal wisdom that is on display. Human beings are not enticed and persuaded by animal wisdom; they are not tagging along under the spell of animal speech. The story has not tangled its ontological categories, forgetting the distinctions between human and non-human creation that have been established. On these grounds, the serpent in the story represents more than itself.

When Genesis says that the serpent "was more crafty than any of the wild animals the Lord God had made" (Gen 3:1), therefore, it is not dismantling its own orders of being. Instead, the story exploits the notion of the serpent as originally a beautiful creature and a vector for evil. For this point there is extra-biblical support to the extent that Gunkel sees a mythological residue in the serpent figure. "Originally the 'serpent' will have been an evil, serpentine demon, hostile toward God and humans," he says.[48] The serpent figure is larger than itself, bringing with it a history. John Skinner echoes this view. "It is more probable that behind the sober description of the serpent as a mere creature of Yahweh, there was an earlier form of the legend in which he figured as a god or a demon."[49]

These are credible observations, and they bring to the subject the non-animal and non-human dimension that helps bridge the gaps created by the omission of explanations with respect to terms like the tree of life, the tree of knowledge of good and evil, and the serpent. When the serpent speaks, therefore, it has not transcended its limitations as an animal but is better seen as an evil personage operating in animal guise.

The figurative meaning, seeing the serpent as a figuration of personified evil, is supported by one of the loftiest prophetic visions in the Old Testament.

> The wolf and the lamb shall feed together, the lion shall eat straw like the ox; but the serpent—its food shall be dust! They shall not hurt or destroy on all my holy mountain, says the Lord (Isa 65:25).

47. Ibid., 12.

48. Gunkel, *Genesis*, 15. Gunkel was the foremost exponent of what is called the "History of Religion school."

49. Skinner, *Genesis*, 71–72.

In this vision, future harmony is envisioned as the restoration of concord that once was lost. Quite unexpectedly, Isaiah calls attention to a creature that will be excluded from the future harmony (Isa 65:25c). To the modern reader, the sudden and gratuitous mention of the serpent will seem mysterious and unwarranted. Why the caveat in the vision, introduced by the carefully aimed "but"? Why the mention of the serpent only to exclude this creature from the harmony?

The answer, of course, lies in the Genesis story of the serpent that is implicit in Isaiah's vision.[50] The creature eating dust is no ordinary serpent, and it does not appear in the prophetic message by accident. Only a fraction of the original story is echoed in Isaiah, but the connection is not to be missed. In Isaiah, indirectly, we hear God pronounce the verdict on the serpent, "Because you have done this, cursed are you among all animals and among all wild creatures; upon your belly you shall go, and dust you shall eat all the days of your life" (Gen 3:14). The severe indictment of the serpent does not arise from nowhere, a point that is easily seen when we line up the statements next to each other:

> "and dust you shall eat all the days of your life" (Gen 3:14)
>
> "but the serpent—its food shall be dust!" (Isa 65:25)

Isaiah does not need to repeat the entire verse in Genesis for the message to emerge in force. In Isaiah as in Genesis, the serpent is a figure larger than itself, a significant figure, fully deserving the prophetic outburst that is at once emphatic and reassuring. The role of the serpent in Genesis belies the opinion of scholars that the stories in this part of the Bible are tales from a primitive age, reflecting a time, "the ancients would tell us, when animals could still speak."[51]

Instead, the foregoing suggests that scholars have badly underestimated the evidence for the New Testament understanding, misjudged the sources, and relied on presuppositions that are contradicted by the text. When the New Testament sees the serpent in Genesis as an external threat to human beings, the best explanation is that the narrator in Genesis put it there because there was such a threat. When the New Testament features a personage called "a liar and the father of lies" (John 8:44), the reason lying most readily at hand is that the opposing opinion expressed in Genesis carries weight throughout the story. If, too, the message of the New Testament is meant to counter and defeat the opposing opinion in Genesis (John 12:20–33; Acts 3:18–21), the best explanation is not that the New Testament got it wrong, but that it represents a keener reading of the ancient story. When the last book of the Bible sets up a showdown between God and "that ancient serpent, who is called the Devil and Satan, the deceiver of the whole world" (Rev 12:9; 20:2), priority should be given to views that take the story in Genesis to be more consequential than scholars have

50. Cf. Blenkinsopp, *Isaiah 56–66*, 287.

51. Gunkel, *Genesis*, 15.

tended to do. Armed with this understanding, we will not want to miss the details in the dialogue between the serpent and the woman in Genesis.

Destroying Reputations

A number of details have been discussed already, but a few salient points remain. The most striking feature, and the most lethal, is that the opposing voice in Genesis sets out to destroy God's reputation and standing. The best translation of the serpent's opening words will convey less a question than "a half-interrogative, half-reflective exclamation."[52] Martin Buber says that the serpent "speaks as though it knew very imprecisely what it obviously knows very precisely."[53] The ploy is to attribute a command to God that is known to be false while concealing the source of the falsehood. "Ay, and so God has said [*'āmar*]," is Skinner's suggested translation. With this statement it is "as if the serpent had brooded long over the paradox, and had been driven to an unwelcome conclusion."[54] He would like to think better of God, as it were, but the sweeping prohibition that is rumored makes a positive view impossible. God's side is similarly put on the defensive in Gunkel's reading; the serpent "takes the position that it has only imprecise information and would like now to be precisely informed by the people themselves."[55] The serpent speaks as though he, too, wants to clear God of the misrepresentation that is circulating, careful not to betray that he is its source. Evil is characterized by exquisite subtlety: it whispers; it does not shout; it entices; it does not command; it promises a greater good. Above all, it does not walk and talk as self-evidently evil.

The cleverness and impact of a misrepresentation that is couched as concern for the truth are spectacular. When the woman tries to defend God against the misrepresentation, she is already underestimating the serpent's evil intent (Gen 3:3). In her eyes, the serpent has not only established himself as a sincere inquirer but also as an honest broker. His credibility is enhanced by the aura of neutrality, seeking to know the facts and then to pass an unbiased verdict on the facts if the anonymous rumor of God's prohibition turns out to be true.

The woman's corrective reveals defenses that are buckling under the force of the misrepresentation. "God said [*'āmar*]," she says, but her corrective contains a misrepresentation of her own, as though God had said, "You shall not eat of the fruit of the tree that is in the middle of the garden, *nor shall you touch it*, or you shall die" (3:3). Try as she might to rescue a less harsh view of God, the conversation has swung in favor of the serpent. The smoke of the prohibition to which she admits, points to the fire of God's arbitrariness. Although she limits the sweep of the prohibition, she is unable to slow the momentum of the serpent's representation. What matters here, says Moberly, "is not

52. Skinner, *Genesis*, 73.

53. Buber, "The Tree of Knowledge," 15.

54. Skinner, *Genesis*, 73.

55. Gunkel, *Genesis*, 16.

that the serpent's words are obviously false, but that they imply that a total prohibition is the sort of unreasonable prohibition that one might expect from God."[56] The woman's, "nor shall you touch it" (3:3), is early proof of a convert in the making.

There is also a subtle shift in the way God's word is represented. Neither the serpent nor the woman refers to God's words as a *command* (3:1–3). In the dialogue between the two, "God's commandment is reduced to a mere saying."[57] The absence of the command levels the playing field. It is easier to put a saying under the magnifying glass and to subject it to criticism than to sit in judgment on the divine command. The authority of God's word is diminished and the urgency obscured.

The subtle shift is accentuated further by the way the dialogue refers to God. *Yahweh Elohim* gives way to *Elohim*. With respect to God, the subject under discussion, intimacy gives place to distance. "God is the remote Potentate, perhaps even arbitrary, and not the immanent covenant God Yahweh," says Emmrich.[58] Paul F. Scotchmer aptly sketches the movement from misrepresentation to alienation along similar lines.

> The conversation was subtle and urbane. For the woman it was intoxicating. Like a couple of sophisticates hobnobbing at a party, the woman and the serpent refer to God as *Elohim* (the Creator-God), rather than *Yahweh-Elohim* (the Covenant-God). In doing so, they intentionally objectify the Almighty, depicting their maker as someone remote and official, rather than close and personal. God is no longer Thou, but It. He is now the object of a new discipline, founded by the woman and the serpent: theology, the study of God.[59]

The damage is done by the time the serpent makes his second statement. The boldness of this statement, a barefaced attack on God's credibility, would be fool's play unless the serpent had a firm sense that the first statement had achieved its purpose.

> But the serpent said to the woman, "You will not die; for God knows that when you eat of it your eyes will be opened, and you will be like God, knowing good and evil" (3:4–5).

While at this point "the world gapes asunder" for the woman,[60] she merely faces the widening of a chasm that had already shattered her outlook: the divine command no longer makes sense, and it no longer obligates. "Truth against truth—God's truth against serpent's truth," Dietrich Bonhoeffer says of the dilemma.[61] And yet we must acknowledge that there would have been no dilemma except for the success of the serpent's first statement. It would never have come to this if not for the serpent's cunning

56. Moberly, "Did the Serpent Get It Right?" 6.
57. Emmrich, "The Temptation Narrative," 12.
58. Ibid., 12–13.
59. Scotchmer, "A Study of Genesis 2:4—3:24," 83.
60. Bonhoeffer, *Creation and Fall*, 71.
61. Ibid.

in transmuting God's provision into a prohibition. Already from the first charge, therefore, as Emmrich notes, "the goodness and generosity of God is seriously damaged."[62]

In Lucas Cranach the Elder's *Paradise*, the most harrowing detail is alienation.
© Kunshistorisches Museum, Wien. Used by permission.

If we grant this text the dignity it has been denied, the conflict of senses in the story is as much political as it is theological. In a political reading, God is the ultimate ruling power, and the dispute centers on the terms of existence in God's domain. What is the character of the divine rule and, by inference, the character of God? In one representation, God gives ability, freedom, and responsibility to human beings. God stands for principles valued in a free society: life: liberty, and the pursuit of happiness. Above all, God's command makes sense, inviting consent and admiration on the part of human beings and not only obedience.

On the other side in the conflict, God is represented as a tyrant who wields authority arbitrarily, exemplified in a savage prohibition and certainly not along lines of provision, promotion, or protection. This God is hostile to the pursuit of happiness, as evidenced by the allegation that the divine economy is an economy of deprivation and lack (3:1). In this representation, the harsh terms must be hurriedly overturned for life to flourish. An important feature in either representation is *absence of demonstrable suffering* at the point when the charges are made. To the serpent, God is at fault not because there is demonstrable suffering, but because there is lack of freedom.

62. Emmrich, "The Temptation Narrative," 13.

Epicurus, and after him Pierre Bayle and David Hume, cast the problem of evil as a deficiency either in God's power or God's love. The narrative in Genesis will not be held hostage to either of these options except, perhaps, in the sense that when the serpent spins the alleged absence of freedom he turns it into a cipher for absence of love. On the whole, however, Genesis sets up a plot very different from the one that has dominated discussions of God and human suffering in ancient and modern philosophy.

Not to be missed in the representation in Genesis is the fact that God allows an opposing power to misrepresent God in the most barefaced manner. God does not curtail false speech by shutting it down. The serpent who blames God for issuing harsh and senseless prohibitions is itself the beneficiary of God's permissive stance. The God who allegedly puts a restriction on the freedom to eat, has not restricted the freedom to talk even when the talk is malicious and untrue.

What now? What now of a problem that seems out of hand because the divine policy of permission has allowed it? Careful readers of Genesis will not be dismissive toward a plot construct that attributes a key role to the serpent, or take lightly that violation of the divine command was preceded by misrepresentation. The implied solution will be analogous to the principle laid down in the First Amendment as this principle was interpreted by Supreme Court Justice Louis D. Brandeis. The constitutional remedy for false speech, said Brandeis, is not suppression but "more speech."[63] With recourse to this analogy, I will suggest that the rest of the Bible can be read as God's version of "more speech," not suppression or retribution, but more speech.

"Have you eaten from the tree of which I commanded you not to eat?" *Yahweh Elohim* asks the man and his wife in the cool of the day in the Garden of Eden (3:11). By then the reader knows that the opposing opinion has accomplished its objective. In fact, God's command has ceased to be a factor in the woman's view of reality. Intimacy, trust, and a sense of a God who provides are now replaced by a God who plays no role at all. "In Gen. 3.6 the woman consciously chooses: she sees, assesses, judges and acts, without a single thought to the prohibiting divine words."[64]

> So when the woman saw that the tree was good for food, and that it was a delight to the eyes, and that the tree was to be desired to make one wise, she took of its fruit and ate; and she also gave some to her husband, who was with her, and he ate (3:6).

Contemporary interpreters find the Christian reading of Genesis fanciful for seeing a demonic power at work, expressing wonder that "so simple a story has been made to bear the sins of the whole world."[65] To this view the New Testament, the Early Church, and careful readers in the twenty-first century respond: It is not so simple a story.

63. Turner, *Figures of Speech*, 126–27.

64. Dragga, "A Story of Liberation," 8.

65. Trible, *God and the Rhetoric of Sexuality*, 72.

Chapter Seven

Sense and Nonsense in the Murder of Abel

The insight that the Hebrew Bible "is terse, it does not use three words where two or one or none will do,"[1] cannot be repeated too often. This feature applies in force to the story of Cain's murder of his brother Abel.

The Bible says that "Abel was a keeper of sheep, and Cain a tiller of the ground" (Gen 4:2). This information may at first sight appear trivial, but the narrator in Genesis has worked hard to show that it is more.[2] The vocations of the two brothers are not elements of accident but embedded in God's purpose for human beings from the beginning.

> There was no one to till (ʿ*ābad*) the ground (2:5).
>
> The Lord God took the man and put him in the garden of Eden to till it (ʿ*ābad*) and keep it (*shāmar*) (2:15).
>
> Therefore the Lord God sent him forth from the garden of Eden, to till (ʿ*ābad*) the ground from which he was taken (3:23).
>
> Now Abel was a keeper (*rāʿâ*) of sheep, and Cain a tiller (ʿ*ābad*) of the ground (4:2).

The dual commission "to till it (ʿ *ābad*) and keep it (*shāmar*)" is the earliest statement of God's purpose for human beings (2:15). Men and women are to have a role with regard to the care of the world. They will "till" (ʿ*ābad*), meaning that they will serve, minister to, and preserve the earth. They will "keep" (*shāmar*), meaning that they will guard, protect, and shield the earth from harm. The narrow occupational connotation of Abel as "a keeper of sheep, and Cain a tiller of the ground" must not be cut off from the broader vocational scope. Cain the tiller and Abel the keeper are not only engaged in useful employment in the work that is most readily at hand. They are fulfilling

1. Reis, "What Cain Said," 110.
2. Swenson, "Care and Keeping," 373–84.

their God-ordained vocation. Just as tilling and keeping in the sense of ministering and protecting belong together, Cain and Abel are *together* entering their vocation.

An inkling of conflict first appears in the area of religious practice in the brothers' life. "In the course of time Cain brought to the Lord an offering of the fruit of the ground, and Abel for his part brought of the firstlings of his flock, their fat portions," says Genesis (4:3–4). In so doing they trigger the chain of reactions that dominate the rest of the story. All through the story, the narrator combines action and reaction, but the *reaction* dominates. We are left to infer the preceding action from the reaction of the characters in the story even when the prior action is not featured in the text.

If we designate the brothers' offering as the initial action, the reactions are bound to startle, with God being the first one to react.

> And the Lord had regard for Abel and his offering, but for Cain and his offering he had no regard (4:4, 5).

God, we see, does not respond in the same way to the offerings. Abel's offering is greeted with approval, Cain's is not. In response to Abel's offering, God "looks." With respect to Cain's offering, God "does not look," or, phrasing the response another way, God "looks away." Why, the reader is left to wonder, does God react so differently?

The next reaction will not be long in waiting. It is Cain's turn to respond to God's reaction. "So Cain was very angry, and his countenance fell" (4:5). This is a rare instance of detail, sparse though it is. Genesis reports on Cain's emotional state, saying that he "burned with anger." The narrator adds that Cain's anger manifested itself in his facial expression. Whatever we conjecture with regard to his state of mind prior to this experience, Cain now comes across as an angry man. The pattern of reactions is striking.

Action	*Reaction*	*Reaction*
Cain brought to the Lord an offering of the fruit of the ground, and Abel . . . brought of the firstlings of his flock (4:3, 4).	And the Lord had regard for Abel and his offering, but for Cain and his offering he had no regard (4:4, 5).	So Cain was very angry, and his countenance fell (4:5).

Some of the most influential interpreters of the Old Testament, assuming lack of discernible sense, give the brothers' offerings the status of being the initial action. They also advise that one should not assume a deficiency in Cain. Hermann Gunkel says that God's reaction serves the brothers notice that God has favorites and preferences not previously known. By responding unequally to the brothers, "the narrative maintains that Yahweh loves the shepherd and animal sacrifice, but wants nothing to do with the farmer and fruit offerings."[3] This view will be no comfort to Cain, of course, incriminating his occupation as well as his offering.

Other scholars do not invoke an interpretation quite this harsh, but they maintain that we must not look for a problem in Cain to explain why God refuses to look at his offering. Absence of sense with regard to God's reaction is promoted as the premise for the story. No less an interpreter than Gerhard von Rad said that we must stop looking for the 'why' behind God's action.

> And now it is further stated that God did not honor both sacrifices, but only Abel's. One has looked diligently for the basis of this preference, but it lies neither in the ritual nor in Cain's attitude. Nothing of that kind is indicated. The only clue one can find in the narrative is that the sacrifice of blood was more pleasing to Yahweh. Obviously the narrator wants to remove the acceptance of the sacrifice from man and place it completely within God's free will. Therefore he is hesitant about representing the decision in favor of Abel as though connected with humanly-reasonable logic.[4]

Non-sense is here hailed not as an incidental feature in the story but as its message. Absence of any problem in Cain also lies at the heart of Claus Westermann's reading. To him, Cain's innocence is the story's premise.

> When it is narrated that God regarded the sacrifice of one brother and not of the other, then it is saying that one experienced commendations from God and the other rejection. When such an experience as the brothers had is traced back to a divine action, then this is a sign that it is something immutable. It is fated by God to be so. God's disregard for Cain's sacrifice does not go back to Cain's attitude nor to a sacrifice that was not right nor to an incorrect way of offering the sacrifice. It is saying something about the immutable; it happens so.[5]

We are advised to desist from making any problem in Cain the reason for God's conduct. God's action is off limits and not subject to review, inscrutable and immutable. Rather than looking for anything in the brothers' disposition or actions, Westermann urges the reader—and Cain—to come to terms with the fact that inequality is built into the warp and woof of human existence.

> Now inequality enters in; it has its origin in the regard of God. It is a misunderstanding of the real meaning to look for the reason for the inequality of God's regard. The narrator wants to say that in the last analysis there is something inexplicable in the origin of this inequality. It does not consist in application, in attitude, or in any circumstance that one can control. When such inequality between equals arises, it rests on a decision that is beyond

3. Gunkel, *Genesis* , 43.

4. von Rad, *Genesis*, 101.

5. Westermann, *Genesis 1–11*, 296.

> human manipulation. The reason why God regards Abel's sacrifice and not Cain's must remain without explanation.[6]

Here, too, non-sense is not incidental or accidental in the story but a signal to Cain and to the reader that sense is out of reach. Walter Brueggemann echoes the same view.

> The trouble comes not from Cain, but from Yahweh, the strange God of Israel. Inexplicably, Yahweh chooses—accepts and rejects. Conventional interpretation is too hard on Cain and too easy on Yahweh. It is Yahweh who transforms a normal report into a life/death story for us and about us. *Essential to the plot is the capricious freedom of Yahweh.* Like the narrator, we must resist every effort to explain it. There is nothing here of Yahweh preferring cowboys to farmers. There is nothing here to disqualify Cain. . . . *The rejection of Cain is not reasoned but is a necessary premise for the story.*[7]

These interpreters stumble over each other in their eagerness to spare Cain any blame, unperturbed if this renders God's conduct inexplicable. We need not hesitate to put these interpretations squarely in the 'non-sense' tradition of Elihu that we explored in Chapter 1. Having removed Cain from the list of possible explanations, Yahweh is left to bear sole responsibility for the slight shown to the older brother. John Byron is surely correct that "God's seeming capriciousness in rejecting one sacrifice over the other creates a theological problem."[8] Although this is perplexing, the interpreters quoted above defend it with gusto.

Other readers of this story have not been as willing to let Cain off the hook. Earlier interpretations have assumed that the text knows more than it says.[9] Byron explores a wide range of options found in the earliest interpretations, from the possibility that there was something wrong with the offering (not the right kind and not the best he had); that it was a problem of timing (he was dragging his feet); that there was a flaw as to the way it was offered (liturgy); or that there was something wrong with Cain's attitude (resentment).[10] None of the earliest interpretations seems inclined to embrace that God's disapproval of Cain is proof of divine capriciousness.

When writers in the New Testament discuss God's disapproval of Cain, they do not subscribe to the belief that God gives Abel preferential treatment for no reason (1 John 3:12; Heb 11:4; Jude 1:10, 11). Intimations of a problem in Cain also find support in the original narrative. Precisely at the moment when Cain gets angry, God speaks to him.

6. Ibid., 297.

7. Brueggemann, *Genesis*, 56, emphasis added.

8. Byron, "Cain's Rejected Offering," 4.

9. Lewis, "The Offering of Abel," 481–96; Kim, "Cain and Abel," 65–84.

10. Byron, "Cain's Rejected Offering," 3–22.

> Why are you angry, and why has your countenance fallen? If you do well, will you not be accepted? And if you do not do well, sin is lurking at the door; its desire is for you, but you must master it (Gen 4:6–7).

While the anger and the change in Cain's facial expression are a reaction to God's disapproval of his offering, God's second question to Cain appears to address a deeper problem than an act of worship gone awry. "If you do well, will you not be accepted?" (4:7). Interpreters that are hung up on the specifics of the offering miss the broader thrust of God's question. The translators of the Hebrew Bible into Greek took the narrow view that Cain was rebuked for adopting "an improper cultic technique."[11] Other ancient interpretations considered Cain to be at fault for not choosing the best offering, in contrast to Abel, who brings "the firstlings of the flock, their fat portions" (4:4).[12] In Philo's view, Cain's careless attitude was compounded by timing because he delayed, bringing his offering "after some days" (4:3).[13]

The preoccupation with Cain's offering that is evident in these interpretations fails to do justice to the broader implications of God's question to Cain, "If you do well, will you not be accepted?" (4:7). This statement implies a broad assessment. The offering is not a sudden and unprecedented lapse, the one feature that makes or breaks the standing of the person bringing it. Already at the point when God "looks" and "does not look" (4:4, 5), the narrator in Genesis allows no space between the person and his offering: "the Lord had regard for Abel *and* his offering, but for Cain *and* his offering he had no regard" (4:4, 5).

A reading along these lines, seeing in the brothers a prior disposition that is expressed in, but not limited to, the offering, opens up other possibilities for the preferential response given to Abel. Why do they bring offerings in the first place? Leon R. Kass is confident that the idea is their own.

> Sacrifice is of human origins. God neither commands nor requests it; we have no reason to believe that He even welcomes it. On the contrary, we have reason to suspect—and will soon give ample evidence to defend this suspicion—that the human impulse to sacrifice is, to say the least, highly problematic, especially from God's point of view.[14]

If the idea is their own, are they sacrificing in order to appease God? Is their motive a sense of obligation even though God has said nothing to create the obligation in the first place? Is the offering meant as a token of gratitude? Does Cain claim a positive response from God as his right, reacting with anger when the equation does not work

11. Byron, "Cain's Rejected Offering," 13. Perry ("Cain's Sin," 258–75) suggests an alternative translation that retains exclusive focus on the offering. "And the Lord had regard for Abel and his offering and for Cain as well, but He had no regard for his *offering*."

12. Ibid., 5–6.

13. Ibid., 8.

14. Kass, "The Story of Cain and Abel," 21.

out as expected? Is his worship grudging, already tinged with anger even before he discovers that God "looks away" from him and his offering? Any of these alternatives might work for the notion that the offering is a human idea.

What is the meaning of the specific kind of offering? Does it merely reflect their choice of occupation, or does the slaughter of an animal set Abel's offering apart from the portion of the harvest brought by Cain? These questions are not answered in the story, but they are touched upon later in the Bible. The writer who said that Abel by faith "offered to God a more acceptable sacrifice than Cain's" (Heb 11:4), implies that Abel's offering is a better signifier of meaning. In the context in which this comment is found the word *typology* should come to mind. Typology means that the type, in this case the offering, points to a reality greater than itself. A typological reading sees gratitude not as a response to favors received, but as a response to favors promised and believed. The typological offering looks to the future, and the typology, in order to be a success, has to convey what the future will bring to light. Understood in this way, the author of Hebrews would not sign on to the notion that the offering is a purely human idea. If Abel offers "a more acceptable sacrifice" in a typological sense, his action will also be seen as a corrective and a rebuke to Cain's failed typology, that is, its failure to convey a reality larger than itself.

The warning to those who "go the way of Cain" in the Book of Jude (Jude 1:11) is less specific, but it might be the reading that is most easily sustained by the text in Genesis. Jude imagines a person who is unwilling to listen and who is consumed by his refusal to take correction when found to be in the wrong. The common denominator in all the biblical comments on the story is that Cain is in the wrong and not that God for no reason decides to "look away" from him and his offering.

Kristin Swenson maintains that "absence of a clear justification for God's action makes the story stronger. God's behavior and speech suggest that what is at issue is not what Cain might have done or not done to deserve God's reaction, but what Cain should do to manage his anger and disappointment in circumstances that seem unfair."[15] To remove the reason why God disapproved of Cain's offering impacts the story, but does it make it stronger? Such a reading certainly intensifies the arbitrariness of God's action. Still less convincing is the assertion that the plot now centers on anger management, anger, by the way, that must not in any way allow itself the luxury of questioning God. Cain has done nothing wrong all the way through his well-intended offering; his problem is his "inability to accept a God who authors these mysterious and inequitable acts of choosing," says Jon Levenson.[16] "What Cain cannot bear," as he sees it, "is a world in which distributive justice is not the highest principle and not every inequity is an iniquity."[17] God-ordained inequality should be accepted

15. Swenson, "Care and Keeping," 379.

16. Levenson, *Death and Resurrection*, 74–75.

17. Ibid., 75.

as a fact, and we are advised to move on to the question of anger management, now said to be the real bite of the story.

Anger management would be a worthy project under ordinary conditions of injustice, but it is less attractive when the one who has caused the injustice is God. To Albert Camus, this would be the "divinity who prefers, without any convincing motive, Abel's sacrifice to Cain's and, by so doing, provokes the first murder."[18] God has "looked away" from Cain for no reason in Cain and for no reason that could be comprehensible to Cain or to the reader of the story. The rest of the story, as 'anger management' readings envision it, catalogues Cain's failure to remain cheerful despite the slight. It will be hard to avoid that Cain's subsequent act of fratricide, "precipitated by God's unexplained rejection of the sacrifice," makes God at least a distant accomplice in the act.[19]

"If you do well, will you not be accepted?" (Gen 4:7) God says to Cain. A broad reading of this question pulls the rug from under interpretations that insist that God's disapproval of Cain has no connection to Cain's attitude or behavior. A reading that finds a problem in Cain prior to his overt anger best fits the import of God's question to him. "Not looking" on the part of God and "not doing well" on the part of Cain are connected. Far from proposing disapproval that is rooted in God's arbitrary action, the text spells out the remedial action that may be taken and thus maps the route to acceptance. God is willing to rescind the disapproval; God is willing to look, as it were, but God is not willing to play games. If Cain will do well, the root of the problem, he will be accepted. "Yhwh's regard and disregard for the oblations is shaped by the attitude of the ones presenting the offerings," says Kenneth M. Craig.[20] God's address to Cain is an indictment of the prior course of action that led God to look away.

This suggests that the brothers' act of worship is not the initial action. At best, it is the initial *re*-action and the one that sets off a train of additional reactions. The initial action belongs to God. Whether we see God's initial action as favor that leads to gratitude, or as a promise that is reflected in a divinely ordained typology, or a call to trust God's ways and to accept the vocation of "tilling" and "keeping" need not be settled with certainty. It will suffice to see God as the one who makes the first move and then to see the offerings as a response to God's prior action. The relationship between action and reaction in the story, the action perceived through the lens of reactions, will have the following shape:

18. Camus, *The Rebel*, 33.

19. Byron, "Cain's Rejected Offering," 4.

20. Craig, "Yahweh, Cain and Their Rhetorical Interchange," 112.

Action	*Reaction*	*Reaction*	*Reaction*
The initial action belongs to God.	Cain brought to the LORD an offering of the fruit of the ground, and Abel . . . brought of the firstlings of his flock (4:3, 4).	And the LORD had regard for Abel and his offering, but for Cain and his offering he had no regard (4:4, 5).	So Cain was very angry, and his countenance fell (4:5).

My Brother's Keeper

A second cycle of action and reactions begins at the point when God speaks to Cain. God's action is now explicit, and the actions that follow are reactions in the sense that they reveal whether God's initial action meets with success.

> Then the Lord said to Cain, "Why are you angry? Why that scowl on your face? If you had done the right thing, you would be smiling; but because you have done evil, sin is crouching at your door. It wants to rule over you, but you must overcome it" (4:6, 7, GNB).

Cain is not smiling, as the Good News Bible translates his body language.[21] It is easier to place the blame for this troubling state of affairs on someone other than oneself, and this is precisely what Cain does. God's address is conciliatory and reflective, but it makes no concession to doubt as to who is at fault. The nihilism of scholars who see no problem in Cain prior to his anger compromises the plot, underestimating the forces that are wreaking havoc in Cain.

In God's warning to Cain, God invokes the word "sin," a word not used before in the Bible. Cain will earn "the distinction of being the first human condemned for an act that is defined as sin. . . . Cain is the first sinner."[22] The etymology of the word "sin" (*ḥaṭṭāʾ*) has the connotation of missing the mark, losing one's way, failing to live up to expectations, or, as the word gains traction in the Old Testament, failing to live up to a known standard.[23] The intriguing distinctive of its use in relation to Cain is that "sin" is put forth as the acting subject. Cain is at risk of being implicated in "sin," but "sin" is personified and externalized, as if acting upon him rather than being the manifestation of Cain's action. The personification of "sin" combines the elements of intent and surprise. "Sin" is plotting Cain's demise, and to this end it has concocted a plan. Part of

21. Kass, "The Story of Cain and Abel," 22.

22. Byron, "Cain's Rejected Offering," 19.

23. Harris, et al., *Theological Wordbook*, entry 638e.

the plan is concealment. "Sin" does not openly announce its nefarious intent. It hides from view, unseen by its victim. God represents "sin" as a predatory animal. The beast is "crouching at the door," ready to fall without warning upon the unsuspecting victim at the opportune time.

Sin is working Cain's demise, not God. There is no mention of a threat to Cain in terms of what God will do to him. If we look backward in the story for clues to what God might do to someone who refuses correction, the best suggestion is that God will "look away," as God did when Cain brought his offering. If, on the other hand, we look downstream from this point in the story, the only threat in sight is what "sin" will do. And "sin" will not treat its victim with kid gloves. The metaphors are symbolic not only in a generic sense, envisioning an ambush from without. They are also symbolic of what might actually happen at some future point in the story. An animal is lying in wait for its victim, ready to pounce upon him when he walks through the door. A victim of "sin," there is now the possibility that he will one day fall upon his unsuspecting brother and kill him.

God, we observe, addresses Cain in friendly terms. When he alerts Cain to the threat that "sin" represents, he casts "sin" as their common enemy. Moreover, God meets Cain with the weapon of persuasion and reason, the interaction suggesting that God is trying to make sense to Cain. Cain, in turn, has time to reflect on his situation and opportunity to change his course.

Unfortunately, the time element in the story has been muddled in the major translations. Worse yet, the reader is presented with one option that does not make sense, and another that tries to remedy the problem by assuming that the text is deficient as it stands.[24] 'Conservative' translations like the King James Version and the New American Standard Bible attempt to render the text literally despite the problems this approach engenders.

> And Cain talked with Abel his brother: and it came to pass, when they were in the field, that Cain rose up against Abel his brother, and slew him (4:8, KJV).

> Cain told Abel his brother. And it came about when they were in the field, that Cain rose up against Abel his brother and killed him (4:8, NASB).

"Cain talked to his brother," we read (KJV). "Cain told his brother" (NASB). What did he say? In this scenario the sentence ends in limbo, and many scholars feel that a portion of the text has been lost.[25] Howard Jacobsen says that "the narrative seems to have a hole in it."[26] The text leads the reader to expect a word or two as to what Cain said, but nothing of the sort is forthcoming.[27] The second difficulty is temporal. How

24. Reis, *Reading the Lines*, 27; cf. Speiser, *Genesis*, 30, n. 8; Hendel, *The Text of Genesis 1–11*, 47.

25. Reis, *Reading the Lines*, 27–31.

26. Jacobson, "Genesis IV 8," 564.

27. The NASB might leave the impression that Cain has told his brother what God told him (4:6,

much time elapses between the moment "Cain talked to his brother" (KJV) and what transpires in the field?

Other English translations have tried to remedy these problems by discounting the Hebrew text, opting for the wording of the Greek translation of the Old Testament.

> Now Cain said to his brother Abel, "Let's go out to the field." And while they were in the field, Cain attacked his brother Abel and killed him (4:8, NIV).

> Cain said to his brother Abel, "Let us go out to the field." And when they were in the field, Cain rose up against his brother Abel, and killed him (4:8, NRSV).

This reading makes good sense. We now know what Cain said or at least what this version of the text makes him say. As to the temporal element, there is no time lapse between Cain talking to his brother and the murder. On the other hand, we do not know whether Cain said, "Let us go out to the field" in order to kill his brother, or whether, having gone out to the field, he happens to kill his brother in a moment of overwhelming rage. That is, we do not know whether the murder is premeditated or a crime of passion. Another unknown is the length of time between Cain's speech to his brother (4:8) and God's address to Cain (4:6, 7).

The problem with this 'solution' is that the Hebrew text does not read this way. So far, translations of the Hebrew text have been saddled with the unattractive option of a reading that does not make sense and the suspicion that the original text has been lost. Allowing the Septuagint to come to the rescue solves the problem of intelligibility, but this 'solution' comes at the price of demoting the original Hebrew text. Confronting these difficulties, scholars have taken a second look at the Hebrew text with surprising results.

Albert Ehrman solves the problem by suggesting that Cain did not say anything.[28] The word translated "said" or "spoke" [*ʾāmar*] may be read as a polaric or bipolar word with the meaning "exalt" at one end of the spectrum, and "despise" at the other. In this context the latter meaning prevails. Cain said nothing, but he thought all the more. "And Cain despised Abel his brother," is the reading we get.[29]

Pamela Tamarkin Reis comes to a similar conclusion. She holds that the 'speech' in question need not be audible or literal. "The use of [*ʾāmar*] in Gen. 4.8 denotes that Cain both spoke against his brother and thought against his brother," she says.[30] This yields a more subtle reading, and it has the advantage of following the Hebrew text as it stands.

---

7), thus alerting Abel to the problem.

28. Ehrman, "What Did Cain Say?" 164–67.

29. Ibid., 167.

30. Reis, "What Cain Said," 109.

> And Cain spoke (thought) against his brother. And it came to pass when they were out in the field Cain rose up against Abel his brother and killed him (4:8).[31]

The emphasis on what Cain was thinking does not exclude actual speaking. He may, for instance, have spoken against his brother to Adam and Eve. In an independent inquiry, Jacobsen also makes Cain's *thinking* the breaking point.

> Cain plotted against his brother. When they were out in the field, etc. (4:8).[32]

Two features are noteworthy in these proposals. First, we do not need to hear what Cain said. The orientation of his speech is internal and inaudible. Cain is nursing a grievance against his brother. Second, the temporal element is conspicuous. Cain's speaking and his act of killing his brother are closely related at the level of intent, but they are separated in time. The sentence breaks after Cain's speech. A new sentence begins. The temporal element is central, and this goes a long way toward settling the question of premeditation.

> And Cain thought against his brother.
>
> (Pause to signify passage of time to let the temporal element become manifest.)
>
> And it came to pass when they were out in the field that Cain rose up against Abel his brother and killed him.

The opening phrase of the second sentence, a single word in Hebrew (*vayehi*), signals distance and a new action, "and it came to pass." The effect of this construct is "to indicate passage of time," implying "an interval of some length between Cain's words and their supposed denouement," says Reis.[33] Cain does not become a murderer overnight.

Passion is not ruled out at the time of the murder by the image of "sin" crouching at the door. Premeditation, however, is ruled in by Cain's nursing a grievance along an extended axis of time. Cain does not make amends when God speaks to him. He digs in his heels, refusing to admit the problem and the end to which it is leading. Reis says perceptively that "Cain's murder of Abel is an object lesson in self-indoctrination. Despite the adversary's innocence and the absence of provocation, a person can become convinced by churning resentment over time that hatred is appropriate and aggression justified."[34] Moreover, the incubator for Cain's future action is found in his

31. Ibid.
32. Jacobson, "Genesis IV 8," 564.
33. Reis, "What Cain Said," 110.
34. Ibid., 107.

thought and speech. The internal process, so remote from the act of murder as to seem ridiculous at the point of its beginning, will with time ripen into the monstrous deed.[35]

Within the framework of action and reaction, Cain's problem is now writ large.

Action	*Reaction*	*Reaction*
The LORD said to Cain, "If you do well, will you not be accepted? And if you do not do well, sin is lurking at the door; its desire is for you, but you must master it" (4:6, 7).	Cain nursed a grievance against his brother (4:8).	And it came to pass when they were out in the field that Cain rose up against Abel his brother and killed him (4:8).

Cain is a hardened man when God speaks to him the second time. Any sense of God's presence is gone, and his conscience no longer offers the resistance that might come from taking the Unseen into consideration. With no human witness he expects to evade accountability. In this calculation Cain turns out to be mistaken. Genesis shows that "in the very next series of verses the killer is promptly apprehended, interrogated, tried, judged, and condemned to exile (4:9–16)."[36]

> Then the LORD said to Cain, "Where is your brother Abel?" (4:9)

God has taken note of the person gone missing. The story is not over, as Cain may have hoped or expected. The fact that God directs his inquiry to Cain suggests that Cain is someone who ought to be in the know. Cain, however, feigns ignorance and innocence.

> He said, "I do not know; am I my brother's keeper?" (4:9).

Both the questions and the answers in this exchange echo the encounter between God and Adam and Eve in the Garden of Eden after eating of the tree of knowledge (3:9–13), only now the distance between the questioner and the one questioned is much greater.[37] In Eden, God's question meets with evasion and blame-shifting (3:11–13). Here, outside Eden, Cain responds with an outright lie, "I do not know" (4:9). In the Garden of Eden, Adam and Eve are on the defensive in their attempt to diminish their sense of responsibility (3:12, 13). Outside Eden, Cain takes the offensive, implying that God is unreasonable in expecting him to know, more unreasonable still for implying that Cain has a failed responsibility on his hands. Because Cain has not admitted to doing anything wrong, the idea may be, "Why did you not stop me from killing your

35. Ibid., 112.

36. Fresch, "Murder, Mystery and *Paradise Lost*," 191.

37. Craig, "Questions outside Eden," 121.

creation?"[38] Cain is pretending not to know and at the same time attempting to shift responsibility from himself to God. "It is up to you to keep track of my brother. You, God, are my brother's keeper. Abel's security is your responsibility, not mine."

The word "keeping" (*shāmar*), primed for major action earlier in Genesis, resounds like peals of thunder in Cain's answer. Cain the tiller takes a narrow view of his role with respect to humanity and the earth. On one level, he will "till" the soil. He has an occupation, but he rejects the vocation to minister, preserve, and protect. On the deepest level, his refusal to be his brother's keeper is a repudiation of the bond of interdependence within which God placed human beings from the beginning. Swenson is too naïve when she allows for the possibility that Cain did not realize that the responsibility of "tilling" and "keeping" goes beyond care for the earth, belatedly waking up to the fact that he is also responsible for the well-being of his brother.[39] This defense might have worked in the context of a lesser oversight, but it does not work when the oversight is murder. She is correct, however, that the story pulls the reader into the text. Cain's, "I do not know," makes the reader want to cry out, "Liar! You know perfectly well."[40] And his question, "Am I my brother's keeper?" makes the reader answer back, "Yes of course you are."[41] Cain's unrepentant evasion of responsibility becomes an aggravating factor in the crime.

The conversation proves that the terms of human existence have not changed outside Eden. God does not take Cain's bait to pick up the slack when Cain refuses to make good on his responsibility. The question of responsibility, in turn, and God's refusal to take over the responsibility that belongs to Cain, are central to the story. Cain's speech signals detachment from humanity, "sober coldness," as Emmanuel Levinas calls it.[42] According to rabbinic thought, moreover, "the evil that took place between Cain and Abel is not a question of God's responsibility, but Cain's."[43] In a further reflection indebted to Levinas, Roger Burggraeve writes that the "pre-original" bond of fraternity rules out the self-centered autonomy implicit in Cain's response.

> Preceding all personal decision from our side, we are already "situated" in an ethical fraternity, whereby we "*are*" responsible for each other, in spite of ourselves. And to this pre-original covenant of fraternity, all inter-human and social relationships refer back, even all commitments and contracts. The reaction of Cain reveals to us, in spite of himself, that we are created in a pre-original ethical relationship of nearness. We are each other's brothers and sisters and that is why we must be each other's keepers. And likewise in reverse:

38. Breitbart, "The Cain and Abel Narrative," 123.
39. Swenson, "Care and Keeping East of Eden," 378.
40. Ibid., 380.
41. Ibid.
42. Katz, "Raising Cain," 216.
43. Ibid., 219.

> if we fulfill the ethical task to be each other's keepers, we become that which we already are: brothers and sisters to each other.[44]

Twice in *The Brothers Karamazov* the question of human responsibility in general and responsibility for the brother in particular echo Cain's answer to God in the aftermath of his murder of Abel. Alyosha, the religious brother, has a premonition of danger to all his brothers. At one point he asks with thinly-veiled concern, "Will my brother Dimitri be back soon?" At the receiving end of this question is his half-brother Smerdyakov, who will murder their father. Smerdyakov's answer is one of supercilious unconcern. "Why should I be informed as to Dimitri Fyodorovich? It's not as I were his keeper."[45]

Not long after the question comes up again, Alyosha now addressing his brother Ivan. "What about Dimitri and father? How will it end between them?" The anxiety on the part of Alyosha is evident, but Ivan does not share his brother's concern. "Don't drag that out again! What have I got to do with it? Am I my brother Dimitri's keeper or something?"[46] The narrator adds that Ivan at this point "snapped irritably, but suddenly smiled somehow bitterly, 'Cain's answer to God about his murdered brother, eh? Maybe that's what you're thinking about at the moment?'"[47] The echo of Cain's response rings loud in these answers, and they speak to the question of human responsibility. Cain in the biblical story, Smerdyakov and Ivan in *The Brothers Karamazov* are determined not to take responsibility for the well-being of the brother. The coldness of Cain toward his brother echoes in the icy detachment of Ivan Karamazov, on that occasion showing indifference to the fate of his fellow human being.[48]

Non-intervention on behalf of Abel raises the question whether God should intervene on behalf of innocent sufferers at any cost. In the case of Cain God tried persuasion to no effect (4:6, 7). What should God do next? Coercion was not attempted, but some form of forceful restraint would have to be the next step. With a known would-be murderer on the prowl, more police in the streets could be the means to keep Abel safe. As to changing Cain's mind, coercion would hardly work, given the possibility that Cain harbored doubts as to the justice of God prior to such intervention. If the prospect of inducing Cain to change his mind by persuasion is out of the question, the only remaining option would be to keep him under constant surveillance, to maim him, or to kill him. Launching a pre-emptive strike against Cain would keep Abel safe, and God could do so on the notion that he knows what is stirring in Cain's heart. Would this course of action be accepted by others? Would Adam and Eve agree to a pre-emptive strike against their first-born son on the suspicion that he is

44. Burggraeve, "Am I My Brother's Keeper?" 357.
45. Dostoevsky, *The Brothers Karamazov* (Pevear and Volokhonsky translation), 226.
46. Ibid., 231.
47. Ibid., 231, 232.
48. Wasiolek, "*The Brothers Karamazov*," 137.

plotting to murder his brother, assuming that this intent is not self-evident? Would a pre-emptive strike stand up in a court of law, applying the standards of our time to the case, including the presumption of innocence until guilt can be demonstrated beyond reasonable doubt? Given Cain's probable state of mind, forceful restraint would only intensify his hatred.

The story shows that the logic of Cain's initial choice is allowed to come to fruition. God does not restrain Cain's hand once he has made up his mind. On the day of the murder God remains silent even though he has served Cain notice that there is danger on the horizon and even though the murder happens in full view of God's all-seeing eye. Abel's hope of survival lies in the hands of his brother. Unless Cain changes his mind, Abel's fate is sealed. To the extent that this story draws up the boundary between human and divine responsibility, God will not be Cain's brother's keeper. The idea that God ought to intervene by force on behalf of Abel and the millions of others who have been tortured and killed through the centuries in the name of religious truth, political ideology, or for reasons of gain, cannot be the lesson of this story.

It might be correct to infer that God's tone of voice changes at this point, shifting "the role from interrogator to that of indignant prosecutor."[49] However, the content of God's speech is more one of describing the consequences of Cain's actions than meting out punishment.

> And the Lord said, "What have you done? Listen; your brother's blood is crying out to me from the ground! And now you are cursed from the ground, which has opened its mouth to receive your brother's blood from your hand. When you till the ground, it will no longer yield to you its strength; you will be a fugitive and a wanderer on the earth" (4:10–12).

Cain, the tiller of the earth, has given the earth blood to drink, expecting the earth to cover up the evidence. But the earth refuses to be an accomplice to the crime. According to the Bible, the sands of time may conceal the evidence, but the facts will not be erased. Years after our story, the prophet Isaiah assures that the victims of injustice are not forgotten. "For the Lord comes out from his place to call the inhabitants of the earth to account for their iniquity; the earth will disclose the blood shed on it, and will no longer cover its slain" (Isa 26:21, translation mine). Similarly, the suffering Job trusts that the eyewitness above and the record preserved in the earth below will not let injustice pass unmarked.

> O earth, do not cover my blood;
> let my outcry find no resting place (Job 16:18).

The eschatological horizon in these passages has already arrived for Cain. While there may be a future day of accountability, there is an immediate reckoning in the present, a disclosure of the bond that has been broken. Cain will be "cursed from the

49. Craig, Jr., "Questions outside Eden," 125.

ground," rejected by the earth that was forced against its will to open "its mouth to receive your brother's blood from your hand" (4:11). "When you till the ground," God tells him, "it will no longer yield to you its strength" (4:12). The curse will not come from above as an arbitrary imposition from God. It will spring from below, from the ground up. Nature itself is against him, demonstrating its outrage by withholding the crops he has come to expect.

> The earth that supports life, now defiled by life's wanton destruction—watered not by rain but by blood, shed by the farmer's hand—becomes an alien place for the murderer. The world is arranged so that murder will not go unnoticed; it will also not go unanswered. The earth shall resist the murderer's plow; nowhere on earth shall he find a comfortable place to settle, both because no one else will welcome him and because his conscience and his fears will give him no rest. A man who has once shed blood knows in his marrow that his own life hangs by a thread, that he lives, as it were, by the grace of God.[50]

Cain "will be a fugitive and a wanderer on the earth" (4:12). He has opted for autonomy and detachment, and the consequence is to be caught in the web of his own making. He will be excluded from the humanity from which he has excluded himself. The one who has refused to be his brother's keeper now has no brother; he will live his life *brotherless*.[51] But this 'punishment' is not imposed on him from above. The sentence is revelatory more than punitive. It is what will be because of what already is.

The priority of revelation over punishment continues despite Cain's protestations in response to the sentence.

> Cain said to the LORD, "My punishment is greater than I can bear! Today you have driven me away from the soil, and I shall be hidden from your face; I shall be a fugitive and a wanderer on the earth, and anyone who meets me may kill me" (4:13, 14).

Assuming, wrongly, that his future fate is arbitrarily imposed on him,[52] Cain makes God the cause of the rootless existence that now awaits him. "*You* have driven me away from the soil" (4:13). This is a gross *mis*-construal of a self-inflicted reality. Ironically, too, the one who has the blood of his brother on his hands does not think himself deserving of the same fate. To the extent that God is imposing consequences on the murderer, we discover to our surprise and perhaps to our dismay that it does not come in the form of *lex talionis*. There is no eye for an eye; the punishment does not fit the crime. Cain fears for his life, and God responds by giving the murderer a mark of protection. Anyone attempting to take the life of Cain will not have God's approval.

50. Kass, "The Story of Cain and Abel," 24.

51. Cf. Wiesel, "Cain and Abel," 20–21.

52. Kass, "The Cain and Abel Story," 24.

> Then the Lord said to him, "Not so! Whoever kills Cain will suffer a sevenfold vengeance." And the Lord put a mark on Cain, so that no one who came upon him would kill him. Then Cain went away from the presence of the Lord, and settled in the land of Nod, east of Eden (4:15, 16).

In this paradigmatic story of crime and punishment in the Old Testament, the notion of 'punishment' in the ordinary sense of jurisprudence has a low priority. Instead, accountability bears down on the guilty in the form of a series of revelations. When the New Testament recalls Cain's murder of Abel, revelation towers even higher over punishment. The most intriguing thought, obscured in most translations, comes at the point when Jesus links the blood of the first murder in the Bible to events in his own life.

> And that is why the Wisdom of God said, "I will send them prophets and apostles; some they will slaughter and persecute, so that this generation will have to answer for every prophet's blood that has been shed since the foundation of the world, from the blood of Abel to the blood of Zechariah, who perished between the altar and the Temple." Yes, I tell you, this generation will have to answer for it all (Luke 11:49–51, NJB).

What "this generation" will have to face, assuming "this generation" to be the people living contemporary to Jesus, will in some way relate to "every prophet's blood that has been shed from the foundation of the world" (Luke 11:50, NJB). Among the prophets, and not only as the name leading the list of victims of injustice in the Bible, Jesus puts Abel's name. To see Abel as a prophetic figure makes him and his action deserving of even closer study. What, however, does Jesus mean when he says that "this generation will have to answer for it all" (Luke 11:51; cf. v. 50)? As it stands, the statement is odd in the extreme. Does he really mean that his own generation will have to answer for crimes committed by others (NJB); that "this generation will be held responsible" (NIV); "that this generation may be charged" (NRSV); or "that the blood of all the prophets which was shed from the foundation of the world may be required of this generation" (NKJV)? This reading is highly problematic. It is far more likely that the word *ekzēteo*, translated "have to answer" (NJB), "hold responsible" (NIV), "be required" (NKJV), or "be charged" (NRSV) in this instance comes with the meaning "to exert considerable effort and care in learning something."[53] It denotes an investigation of facts, a full disclosure, an attempt to get to the bottom of things in regard to things past, adding the thought that the shape of things past will climax and fully come to light in things present. Translators who have put the emphasis on punishment should instead have put the emphasis on revelation.[54] The hard-headed determination to resist truth that was evident in Cain's murder of Abel will come to

53. Louw and Nida, *Greek-English Lexicon of the New Testament*, entry 27.35.

54. Peels ("The Blood," 583–601), while correctly highlighting the notion of accountability, accepts the traditional view that equates accountability with punishment.

a head in his own generation. Jesus stands as the revealer and not as the executioner in this New Testament commentary on the violent death of Abel. The same puzzling logic is evident when God puts a mark of protection on Cain.[55] He will be a fugitive, but he will be protected.

"Listen," God tells Cain, "your brother's blood is crying out to me from the ground!" (Gen 4:10). Little has been heard from Abel in the story, but now, at last, he speaks. Westermann calls this verse "the high point of the narrative," urging the reader not to make the mistake of giving this distinction to the act of murder two verses earlier.[56] At this point, every detail counts.

> This is one of the monumental sentences in the Bible. It needs no explanation and retains its validity through the centuries for each generation. The most important word in the sentence is, "to me." It is no empty sentence that the blood of the victim cries out; there is someone there to whom it cries out. Cain cannot hide his deed. This is but the other side of the situation which he cannot avoid when faced with the question, "What have you done?" The murderer has no escape when faced with this question because there is someone who hears the victim's blood crying out. These words, valid for the whole history of humankind, protect the person as a creature of God from other people. Murder is and remains a possibility; the possibility of its success ('the perfect murder') in the sense of eliminating a human being, is thereby definitively excluded.[57]

Accountability for the murderer is certain and above question. "Cain wanted to be done with Abel. But he is not to be done with; the life that has been stilled cries out."[58] Crimes happen, but there is no crime without a witness and no 'perfect murder.' William Blake's painting of the crime scene, now in the Tate Gallery in London, captures some of the horror. In Blake's view the mother finds her youngest son dead on the ground, embracing him with her arms and wrapping his bruised body with her long hair. Adam's face in the background is that of a bereaved parent, numbed by the double tragedy that Abel has been killed by his brother. Cain is running away in a ball of fire, now a fugitive and an outcast, stunned more by what he has done to himself than by his success. The clouds above are dark, the mountains in the background barren. It is truly a scene from Paradise Lost.

55. Cf. Westermann, *Genesis 1–11*, 311; Breitbart, "The Cain and Abel Narrative," 122.

56. Westermann, *Genesis 1–11*, 304–5.

57. Ibid., 305.

58. Ibid.

The Body of Abel Found by Adam and Eve **by William Blake needs no explanation.**
© Tate Gallery, London. Used by permission.

What Blake's painting does not capture—what no pictorial depiction will be able to capture—is the notion of Abel's blood crying out, and, at the other end, the ear that is listening to his cry. How are we to understand the voice of the blood of Abel and God's listening ear? The fact of accountability for Cain is surely established, taking the form of a series of revelations. But this insight does not exhaust the import of the cry of Abel's blood. It is inadequate to find in God's listening ear mainly an assurance that God will settle the score, acting as Abel's avenger or to believe that Abel's cry will subside when the consequences to Cain come to fruition. How can there be closure for Abel's blood in a retributive sense when God sends the murderer forth in the world with a mark of protection?

The text must have other priorities than expected. On the one hand, the message to Cain includes a commitment on God's part to forestall new cycles of violence. The message to Abel, on the other hand, or rather, the message to those who are concerned about the fate of Abel, entails more than what God will do to Cain. Doing something to Cain, be it protection or capital punishment, does not change the reality of murder for Abel. God's listening ear should be seen as a promise to Abel and as proof that God will make it up to him. God is not finished with Abel. To God's listening ear, neither death nor time brings an end to Abel's voice. The blood that cries out from the ground to God, "to *me*," as Genesis tells it, assures the first innocent victim access to God and God's ongoing attention. Cain moves away from the scene, but the blood on the ground guarantees that the victim will not be forgotten.

Is it possible to trust a God who allows Abel to be killed and who seems to let Cain get away with murder? Is this what makes Jesus register Abel among the prophets? This question turns the story back to its beginning, to Cain the tiller and to Abel the keeper, to their outlook, their view of human reality, and of God. If this question finds expression in their offerings, it will be easier to understand why God "looked at Abel and his offering, but at Cain and his offering he did not look" (4:4, 5). In such a scenario it is too narrow to imagine that Abel, when he took "of the firstlings of his flock, their fat portions" (4:4), is merely expressing human reality before God. He is also expressing the divine reality before human beings. In the *Targum Neophiti*, a text that got its final form in the third or fourth century CE but originated much earlier, we find a reflection on the story of Cain and Abel that covers both of these realities, the human reality before God and the divine reality before human beings. We make the best use of this ancient reflection when we prioritize what this commentary says about the divine reality, that is, the brothers' view of God. Cain and Abel are in conversation, a jury of two, sharing their outlook and connecting it to the question of why God "looked" and "looked away."

"I know the world is not created with mercies," Cain says, thus showing his view of the divine reality. Abel disagrees, saying, "I know the world is created with mercies." This is a crucial difference, but it is only the beginning of their disagreement.

> Cain answered and said to Abel,
> there is no judgment and there is no judge,
> and there is no other world,
> there is no giving good reward to the righteous
> there is no repaying from the wicked.
>
> Abel answered and said to Cain,
> there is judgment and there is a judge,
> there is another world,
> and there is giving good reward to the righteous
> and there is repaying from the wicked in the world to come.[59]

There is more to this ancient reflection than the notion that God arbitrarily "looked at" one and "looked away" from the other, the view that is espoused by many interpreters. Is the world created with mercies? Abel says yes, Cain says no. Is it true that there is no judge? Cain says yes, Abel says no. Is there fairness and equality before the law? Abel says yes, Cain says no. Is God a God of sense? Abel says yes, Cain says no, going forth to translate his perception of nonsense into the senselessness of murder.

59. Chilton, "The Dispute between Cain and Abel," 556.

In the reflection found in *Targum Neophiti*, the most important difference centers on how the brothers see the divine reality. From the point of view of God, the murder of Abel could have been prevented only at the price of negating human responsibility. But prevention by force, protecting Abel at all cost, would deplete the meaning of his faith. The fact that his death is occasioned by his faith does not prove that his confidence has been misplaced. Abel's faith includes trust in a God who allows him to become the victim of murder. "I know that the world is created with mercies," the ancient interpreters heard Abel say.[60]

Something close to this is also the view of the New Testament. Framed by a context that speaks of hope and restitution for the victims of injustice (Heb 11:36–40), the author of Hebrews says that Abel by faith "offered to God a more acceptable sacrifice than Cain's. Through this he received approval as righteous, God himself giving approval to his gifts; he died, but through his faith he still speaks" (Heb 11:4). In the "more acceptable sacrifice," the writer of Hebrews has in mind a quality in God rather than a quality in Abel. A somewhat looser translation could say that 'it was witnessed through [his offering] that Abel had taken the right view of the divine reality, this being the witness of God concerning Abel's gifts' (Heb 11:4, translation mine). Toward that discovery "Abel still speaks, even though he is dead" (Heb 11:4, GNB).

60. Ibid.

Chapter Eight

On Level Ground with the Judge of the All the Earth

Paradise is lost early in the biblical story (Gen 3:1–24). Cain murders his brother (Gen 4:1–16). In the story of Noah, the human race comes close to being eradicated (Gen 6:1—9:29), and the survivors fail to turn the page convincingly for the better (Gen 11:1–25). "Against this background of human sin and failure, so the story goes, God resolved to make a new beginning," says Bernhard W. Anderson.[1] At the point of the new beginning Abraham takes center stage.

Abraham towers above all other characters in the Old Testament. He is present at the creation, so to speak, not at the creation of the world, of course, but present at the beginning of a new nation and a pilgrimage of faith that sees him as the founder and model (Rom 4:16). In fact, while Abraham in the Old Testament gets buried in the rubble of apostasy, wars, and dynastic political aspirations, the New Testament digs him out from beneath the ruins so as to make him an even larger figure in the New Testament than in the Old. Both testaments remember him as "the friend of God" (2 Chr 20:7; Isa 41:8; Jas 2:23). With Abraham, we see "the birth of prophecy,"[2] or better, a man who is a "Seer." His life story is the journey of a man moving from one revelation to the next, a full seven of them, according to Martin Buber.[3] No inquiry about God and sense can afford to bypass Abraham. The last two of the revelations to Abraham, accepting Buber's accounting without discussing its merits, will be the subject of this and the next chapter (Gen 18:16–33; 22:1–19).

Outcry against Sodom

The designation of Abraham as "the friend of God" originates in his plea on behalf of the cities of Sodom and Gomorrah (Gen 18:16–33). These cities are described as places of exceptional notoriety, and their bad name is a crucial premise for the story.

1. Anderson, "Abraham, the Friend of God," 353.

2. Buber, "Abraham the Seer," 43.

3. Ibid., 36. The seven "revelations" are found in (1) Gen 12:1–3; (2) 12:7; (3) 12:14; (4) 15:1; (5) 17:1; (6) 18:1; (7) 22:1.

Genesis locates the cities on the plains in the lower part of the Jordan basin in the area that is now known as the Dead Sea. At some point in the past the region is said to have been the lushest region of the Land of Canaan (13:10).[4]

Our information about the city comes mainly from the story of Abraham and his nephew Lot at the time when they sought a foothold in their new homeland. When the herdsmen of Lot began quarreling with their counterparts among Abraham's household, Abraham sought to calm tempers by proposing that they separate from each other. He generously offered his nephew the first choice of land (13:8–9). Not one to pass up the opportunity, Lot set his eyes on the most fertile and pleasant part of the country. He "looked about him, and saw that the plain of the Jordan was well watered everywhere like the garden of the LORD, like the land of Egypt" (13:10). "So Lot chose for himself all the plain of the Jordan, and Lot journeyed eastward; thus they separated from each other" (13:11).

Lot moved on, at last settling "among the cities of the Plain" and moving "his tent as far as Sodom" (13:12). At this point the narrator weighs in with a piece of background information that gives Lot's choice of location a downside. The city's reputation did not match the favorable surroundings. We are told that "the people of Sodom were wicked, great sinners against the LORD" (13:13).

In other words, if keeping the family out of harm's way should be a priority for a husband and a parent, Lot did not make a good choice. The impression of intolerable conditions in Sodom is heightened when later God shares with Abraham God's concern with respect to Sodom. "How great is the outcry against Sodom and Gomorrah and how very grave their sin!" (18:20).

Something is wrong in these cities, but the traditional interpretation of sexual deviancy is inadequate (19:4–5). Another line points to excessive wealth and indifference to the needs of the poor. "This was the guilt of your sister Sodom," the prophet Ezekiel wrote much later, "she and her daughters had pride, excess of food, and prosperous ease, but did not aid the poor and needy" (Ezek 16:49). Ezekiel's recollection hews close to the passage in Genesis and the reason for the outcry, Ezekiel branding it as a callous form of materialism. There is no mention of sex in his retrospective.

Illicit sex is not the connotation of the concern God expresses to Abraham at the beginning of their conversation about the cities. "How great is the outcry (*zʿākāh*) against Sodom and Gomorrah," God confides to him (Gen 18:20). This statement says more than the unconditioned ear is prone to hear. The notion of an "outcry" appears two more times in the story. In the second instance, God tells Abraham that "I must go down and see whether they have done altogether according to the outcry (*tsʿākāh*, an older form of *zʿākāh*) that has come to me" (18:21). The third appearance of this term happens when heaven-sent visitors tell Lot that God is about to take action against the city "because the outcry (*zʿākāh*) against its people has become great before the LORD" (19:13).

4. Sarna, *Understanding Genesis*, 137–42.

"Outcry against Sodom," repeated three times, has now become a critical element in the story. The "outcry" (*zʿākāh*) in question does not refer to a trivial matter. Nahum Sarna singles out this term as "one of the instances where a Hebrew word cannot be adequately translated into another language."[5] The modern reader stands in need of expert help. The 'outcry' (*zʿākāh*) against Sodom "indicates the anguished cry of the oppressed, the agonized plea of the victim for help in some great injustice," says Sarna.[6] It is grounded in plight inflicted on others, "heinous moral and social corruption, an arrogant disregard for elementary human rights, a cynical insensitivity to the suffering of others."[7] The image that comes to mind through these terms is "the suffering of the poor and the impoverished victim of avaricious exploitation," expressed in terms that are "suffused with poignancy and pathos, with moral outrage and soul-stirring passion."[8]

Gerhard von Rad adds that the word "outcry" "is a technical legal term and designates the cry for help which one who suffers a great injustice screams."[9] The victim, calling out in heaven-rending despair, "appeals for the protection of the legal community."[10] In cases where the outcry is addressed to God, the response is expected to be swift, and the consequences to the offender are thought to be dire, immediate, and unavoidable.[11]

Sodom, then, is portrayed as a community where there is flagrant violation of human rights, exploitation of the poor, and indifference to suffering. As the story unfolds in Genesis, the city appears to be a place that is hostile to visitors and dangerous in or out of doors. When, therefore, the inhabitants of Sodom, "both young and old," show their true colors by laying siege to Lot's house at a critical point in the story, demanding of Lot to bring out the visitors "so that we may know them" (19:4–5), the suggested sexual connotation makes sex a weapon of violence.[12]

The thrice repeated "outcry" originates in other quarters and is not initiated by God. Abraham will plead for justice later in the story, but the original entreaty comes from the victims of oppression. It is not necessary to read the fine print or speculate about the divine intent with respect to taking action against Sodom. If anything, the premise of the outcry is lack of action on God's part. We are thereby advised to approach the subject from the point of view of those who are aggrieved. Sodom's victims find themselves in legal limbo. In the court of human justice, their case falls on deaf

5. Sarna, *Understanding Genesis*, 144.

6. Ibid., 145.

7. Ibid.

8. Sarna, *Commentary on Genesis*, 132.

9. Von Rad, *Genesis*, 206.

10. Ibid.

11. Mafico, "The Crucial Question," 12.

12. Neher, "Ezechiel, redempteur de Sodome," 483–90; cf. also Doyle, "The Sin of Sodom," 84–100; Morschauser, "Hospitality," 461–85. In the last two accounts, critique of the notion that the "sin of Sodom" was primarily sexual perversity is more persuasive than the constructive proposals they offer.

ears. According to Genesis, God pays attention to Sodom because victims of injustice are urging God to do something. They present their plea with a degree of self-evidence and with the kind of passion that expects action from on high.

The fact that the first action in the story comes from the victims and not from God, therefore, is an element in the story that must not be missed. It suggests reluctance on God's part to get involved. "How great is the outcry (*zʿākāh*) against Sodom and Gomorrah," God tells Abraham, placing as much emphasis on the outcry as on the misdeeds giving rise to it (18:20–21). If there is an intervention, it will be grounded in the necessity the outcry has forced upon God.

Investigation before Action

The investigation into conditions in Sodom is represented as the second leg of a two-fold mission. The first part of the mission accomplished—promising an end to Abraham's childlessness (18:1–15)—the visitors get up to leave. Genesis says that "the men set out from there, and they looked toward Sodom; and Abraham went with them to set them on their way" (18:16).

All through the first part of the story Abraham has acted the perfect host, seeing the passers-by from afar, inviting them to his tent, serving them hand and foot, and now accompanying them on their way.[13] Hospitality might explain all of this, but the story quickly moves to a level well beyond hospitality.

Why, at this stage, are the visitors headed for Sodom? Given the reputation of Sodom, why would anyone want to go there? On the whole, this does not look like a good omen for Sodom. The visitors take leave from their host in an atmosphere of suspense, resuming their journey without having addressed crucial concerns relative to their mission. This suspicion is confirmed when the narrator lets the reader in on the silent dialogue that the leading visitor has with himself. "Shall I hide from Abraham what I am about to do, seeing that Abraham shall become a great and mighty nation, and all the nations of the earth shall be blessed in him?" God is reported to be thinking (18:17–18). Most remarkable is the opening question, "Shall I hide from Abraham what I am about to do?" This question carries within itself the answer. "No," reads the answer in the NRSV, "for I have chosen him, that [*lᵉmaʿan*] he may charge his children and his household after him to keep the way of the Lord by doing righteousness and justice; so that the Lord may bring about for Abraham what he has promised him" (18:19).

On this question hinges the character of God's relationship with Abraham. What sort of relationship is it? What kind of relationship can it be when one of the parties to the relationship is God and the other party is a human being? Is it a relationship so unequal in every facet that there can be no common ground, mutuality, or

13. Cohen, "Abraham's Hospitality," 168–72.

understanding? Is the divine sense of such a character that it relates to human sense like ships passing each other in the night?

The phrase that in many Bibles is translated "I have chosen him" (NASB, NIV, NRSV), literally means "I know him" (KJV), or "I have *known* him" (NKJV). This term has a deeply personal undertone. The same word is used when a man knows a woman in intimate sexual union (4:1). If, in the context of Abraham's encounter with God, we prioritize the primary meaning of the word, emphasizing "knowing" above "chosenness," we can distil God's mental deliberation to its essence.

> *Question*: "Shall I hide from Abraham what I am about to do?" (18:17).
>
> *Answer*: "No, for I have known him" (18:19).

The mission cannot be left out, of course, but the answer is adequate as it stands. God will not hide from Abraham what God is about to do because God has "known him." When most translations emphasize chosen-ness and *purpose*, they do it at the cost of obscuring the significance of *knowing* and the *result* that "knowing" brings. If "knowing" is allowed to control the phrase, the emphasis shifts from purpose to result. The legitimacy of making the conjunction *lᵉmaʿan* subservient to the verb so as to say "with the result that" rather than the usual "in order that"" is supported by several authorities.[14]

> *Question*: "Shall I hide from Abraham what I am about to do?" (18:17).
>
> *Answer*: 'No, for I have known him with the *result* [*lᵉmaʿan*] that he may charge his children" (18:19).

"Knowing" is the crucial element in God's mental deliberation. It suggests a relationship of transparency and reciprocity. God is not obligated to keep Abraham posted because Abraham demands it or because it is necessary for his work. If there is an obligation, it is on God's side of the relationship. Greater than Abraham's right to know and greater than his need or demand to know, is God's determination to let him know. God makes the first move, empowering the weaker side in the relationship. The decision to let him know is intrinsic to the kind of relationship God seeks to have with Abraham. While the text explains God's decision not to hide his purpose from Abraham in part with reference to Abraham's mission (18:18–19), "knowing" is not only a prerequisite for carrying out the mission. The mission is as much a consequence of knowing as knowing is the condition for the mission.

It is perfectly legitimate to translate the text, "I have known him as a friend" in order to do full justice to what is transpiring. This wording faithfully conveys the force of "to know" (*yādaʿ*), and it claims no more than what is evident in God's decision to keep Abraham in the know. God's intent does not have the character of a business

14. Leibowitz, *Studies in Bereshit*, 167–69; see also, Pangle, *Political Philosophy*, 160–61.

transaction. As noted already, we might justifiably think that Abraham needs to know in order to carry out his responsibility as a religious instructor to his descendants. But this is not the whole story. What comes to light is not only God's concern to ensure that a certain body of information is passed on to the next generation and beyond. Becoming a "knowing" person denotes a relationship where understanding is crucial. Abraham is taken into God's inner circle of confidence because he is God's friend and not only because God wants him to run his errands. Already at this point we have confirmation that this is the story that won Abraham the characterization as God's friend (2 Chr 20:7; Isa 41:8; Jas 2:23). The key element is the statement, "I have known him" (Gen 18:19).

Before a single word is said between God and Abraham, much is evident. First, God wants to make Abraham his confidante on matters that lie ahead because there is, on God's part, the decision to let Abraham know. Second, the planned disclosures on God's part bring together the twin notions of transparency and accountability. The notion of divine inscrutability that is widely acclaimed in theology finds little support. The God who is determined to let Abraham know is ready to face Abraham's judgment once the disclosure is made. Third, if God does not want to hide from Abraham what he is about to do, it must mean that Abraham at this stage does not know. The extent of Abraham's ignorance with respect to God's intent is not revealed, but the conversation takes as its premise that Abraham does not know. This might be the most important point because Abraham will soon begin questioning God. Anxiety on this point, as though Abraham is probing into matters he had better leave alone, is unwarranted. Abraham, we know already, will be asking questions of a God who wants him to know.

"Then the LORD said, 'How great is the outcry against Sodom and Gomorrah and how very grave their sin!'" (18:20) This view of Sodom cannot be news to Abraham. If there has been an outcry against Sodom because the inhabitants are in violation of basic human rights, the cause of the complaint will not be lost on Abraham. Moreover, the diction of God's opening statement has the character of something that is known. Abraham is expected to nod in agreement.

But what follows from this? What is God planning to do about Sodom's grave sin? To Walter Brueggemann, God has already decided to destroy Sodom.[15] Destroying Sodom must therefore be the action that God will not conceal from Abraham. If we accept this assumption, it has consequences for the rest of the story. On the one hand, the remainder of the dialogue between God and Abraham will be less meaningful because the outcome is already certain, and the exploration of other options will be purely hypothetical. On the other hand, the rest of the dialogue assigns to Abraham the role of pleading on the side of mercy against an assumed verdict that appears harsh. While this might be the case, it should not be treated as a foregone conclusion.

What is explicit in the text relates to a pending investigation and to no more than that. "I must go down and see whether they have done altogether according to the

15. Brueggemann, *Genesis*, 167–73.

outcry that has come to me; and if not, I will know," God says to Abraham (18:21). Taking this text at face value, "Yhwh's words suggest an investigation with no definite decision about Sodom and Gomorrah's guilt or innocence; Yhwh has heard an outcry, and he will investigate the charge before passing judgment," says Nathan MacDonald.[16] While our view of God may regard it as a matter of course that God knows and has no need of an investigation, the narrative does not deal in abstractions and hypothetical constructs. Whatever God knows, the text says that God is planning to conduct an investigation, compare the findings with the complaints against Sodom, and then, in God's own words, "I will know" (18:21). As Claus Westermann points out, there is at this stage no "actual announcement of the destruction of Sodom."[17] Proceeding slowly, meticulously, and methodically, "Yahweh simply informs Abraham that he will verify whether the outcry raised over Sodom is justified."[18]

This means that there will be investigation before action. God is committed to due process for the inhabitants of Sodom. Reading the story as a case study of what God *does* rather than of what God *knows*, there will be no action on God's part with respect to Sodom before the facts are on the table. To Timothy D. Lytton, God is modeling the principle of judicial fairness and due process. This must not be hidden from Abraham. "God wishes to reveal the process of divine decision making, and in doing so, God seeks to model judicial behavior for Abraham," says Lytton.[19]

In the big picture of Abraham's life, the case study may compass more than the state or fate of Sodom. "Shall I hide from Abraham what I am about to do?" as the NRSV translates the text (18:17), applies beyond the immediate situation and God's plans for Sodom. A broader and more general reading is invited by the use of the participle [*ʿoseh*], "that thing which I do" (KJV) or "what I am doing" (NKJV). According to this reading, what will come to light is not only what God will do in this particular situation but also what God is doing generally: *God's way of doing things*. "Shall I hide from Abraham *that which I do* [*asher ani ʿoseh*]—not merely on this occasion, but as a regular practice," is the wording preferred by Lytton. This reading pushes the horizon beyond Sodom.[20] While the full force of this statement has yet to be ascertained, the least we can take away from it includes the notion of due process. Hearsay, rumor, and second-hand reporting are inadmissible as evidence.

16. MacDonald, "Listening," 29.

17. Westermann, *Genesis 12–36*; 285.

18. Ibid.

19. Lytton, "Shall Not the Judge of the Earth Deal Justly?" 35.

20. Ibid.

Who Stands Before Whom

The first round in the conversation is now over. So far Abraham has not said anything, but his silence should not be over-interpreted. The tenor of God's turn of phrase invites concurrence on the part of Abraham.

"So the men turned from there, and went toward Sodom, while Abraham remained standing before the LORD," the narrator continues (18:22). Now the traveling company is reduced from four—three heavenly visitors plus Abraham—to two only. This heightens the intimacy of the exchange. From here on it will be a one-on-one conversation, Abraham and God speaking face to face. Until now they have been walking, a less focused and suspenseful posture for serious conversation. Now they have stopped while the two other visitors in God's company continue on their way. The text implies a moment of silence that could be of some duration, a bit awkward, perhaps apprehensive. Whichever way we read it, the body language betrays a desire to talk. The reader is led to feel a sense of unease as though there is a matter that is too difficult to mention.

The suspense becomes more acute once we take into consideration a variant reading, traces of which remain in the Hebrew Bible. Very likely this text once said, "Yahweh remained standing before Abraham" and not, as now, "Abraham remained standing before Yahweh." This difference inverts the balance of power in the relationship. The one before whom one stands is more in command than the one who stands before that person. If "Yahweh remained standing before Abraham," the power dynamic shifts away from Yahweh.

> As it stands, the text in 18:22 now says, "Abraham stood before the LORD," suggesting the subordination of Abraham to Yahweh. This is what we should expect. But a very early text note (not to be doubted in its authority and authenticity) shows that the text before any translation originally said, "Yahweh stood before Abraham." The picture is one which agrees with our comment about Abraham as Yahweh's theological instructor. It is as though Abraham were presiding over the meeting. But that bold image of Yahweh being accountable to Abraham for this theological idea was judged by the early scribes as irreverent and unacceptable. Therefore, the text was changed to read as we have it. But the earlier version suggests with remarkable candor what a bold posture Abraham assumes and how presumptuous is the issue he raises.[21]

The possibility that we are faced with a scribal correction or emendation (*tiqqûn sôfĕrîm*) cannot be dismissed with regard to this text.[22] Perhaps the mentality that caused the ancient scribes to make the change has explanatory power for one of the most enduring features of the theological tradition. Already here, in one of the deepest layers of Scripture, well-meaning people deemed it necessary to tone down

21. Brueggemann, *Genesis*, 168.

22. MacDonald, "Listening to Abraham," 27.

the notion of divine accountability because they saw it as a risk to God's dignity and reputation. It is contrary to expectations to have Yahweh standing before Abraham. Like Brueggemann, MacDonald notes the rationale. "It was this idea of Yhwh being accountable to Abraham that was so unacceptable to the early scribes, who reversed the subject and the predicate."[23]

But what does it mean to leave Yahweh standing before Abraham, as the original text might have had it? Does Abraham from here on have the leading voice in the dialogue? Is Abraham now "Yahweh's theological teacher" in the story,[24] this relationship rising from the body language of the two characters in the text? Has God relinquished the initiative?

Any version of the story will accommodate the idea that God does not resist being questioned. "Put up or shut up" is not the ideology that comes to mind thus far. Abraham's concerns are not off limits. The thought that a proper respect for God manifests itself in quiet deference to God's inscrutable will is not what we see in the model person of faith. God's unhurried departure is an invitation to let the questions come into the open. Abraham perceives what is stirring in his guest's mind.

Confident that questions are welcome, Abraham asks, "Will you indeed sweep away the righteous with the wicked? Suppose there are fifty righteous within the city; will you then sweep away the place and not forgive it for the fifty righteous who are in it?" (18:23–24)

While this question suggests that God, as Abraham perceives it, has made up his mind before the investigation has been carried out, it could have a different rationale. The other possibility lies in Abraham's knowledge of Sodom and its widely rumored lack of redemptive qualities. On this logic, Abraham's view of Sodom bodes ill for the city on its own terms. The need for some kind of action has not been lost on him.

The moral crisis in Sodom now receives a new dimension. Evil must be called to account, but how? What if the measures lack precision? What if there is "collateral damage," injury to innocent people who will suffer with the guilty? What if the proposed remedy raise questions that would be even more troubling than the ones it seeks to address? The way the story is told makes it look like God comes to the scene of trouble to address complaints about intolerable injustice. In the process of getting to the heart of the matter, Abraham steps forward to become the spokesman for an overlooked concern. His concern changes the focus from the general complaint that God is doing too little to curtail evil to a demand for exquisite care in how to deal with it. "Shall not the judge of all the earth do what is right?" Abraham asks, pressing his case as though God is on trial (18:25).

It is important to note, too, that Abraham is not asking God not to destroy the innocent with the guilty. Quite a different proposition is put on the table: *the guilty should be spared because of the righteous*. While a widely held notion of justice might

23. Ibid.

24. Brueggemann, *Genesis*, 168.

dictate that the innocent be kept from harm, does the idea that the guilty be spared fall within the realm of *justice*? Abraham presses his point in the name of justice even though simple justice is not an adequate framework. "This is no longer a simple appeal to the attribute of justice but a call for divine mercy," Roshwald points out.[25] Mercy and restraint are encroaching on Abraham's notion of justice even though they sail under its banner.

"Suppose there were fifty righteous within the city; would You also destroy the place and not spare *it* for the fifty righteous that were in it?" Abraham asks (18:24, NKJV). He concedes that corrective action is justified, but he insists on reading the fine print. It is as if he is aware that others might want to "send in the Marines" to clean up the city, no questions asked. In his mind justice is not served unless the intervention is carefully specified. He calls for a measured response that tilts heavily toward hope. Life will go on in Sodom if fifty righteous people are found in it. Their influence might be a reason to spare the entire population.

Once Abraham has expressed the thought, its legitimacy forces itself upon him more strongly. He stands ready to argue the point and defend it courageously. "Far be it from you to do such a thing, to slay the righteous with the wicked, so that the righteous fare as the wicked! Far be that from you! Shall not the Judge of all the earth do what is just?" (18:25)

The vehemence in Abraham's appeal now centers on the prospect that the righteous will suffer the same fate as the wicked, but this does not negate the earlier concern that the wicked should be spared because of the righteous. In fact, as noted already, the most important question now centers on the character of God. "Abraham," says Buber, "utters the boldest speech of man in all Scripture, more bold than anything said by Job in his dispute with God, greater than any, because it is the word of an intercessor who is moved by the purpose of his intercession to lose even the awe of God."[26] Abraham speaks as though *his* notion of justice has all the force of self-evidence, and he argues as though his view of God makes God the ultimate bulwark against the action that Abraham's intervention seeks to prevent! The irony is overwhelming and nowhere more acute than in the double admonition,

> "Far be it from you! Far be it from you!" (18:25)

The prospect of indiscriminate destruction is ruled out by the kind of person Abraham believes God to be and by a notion of justice that Abraham takes for granted. "Shall not the Judge of all the earth do what is just?" (18:25) Abraham's argument assumes knowledge on both counts. What, then, is the problem? Is God really contemplating a plan of action that flies in the face of justice and is in violation of God's character? The emotional tenor is striking, suggesting that Sodom's destruction,

25. Roshwald, "Dialogue between Man and God," 133.

26. Buber, "Abraham the Seer," 40.

righteous inhabitants and all, will be averted only by heroic intercession on the part of Abraham. Does it take Abraham to persuade God to act according to God's character?

The leading voice in the exchange, at least for the time being, appears to belong to Abraham. At the very least it cannot be denied that Abraham's opinion matters.

> What strikes us immediately in this encounter is the posture of Abraham. It is not what, with the general theological preconceptions of our and past generations, could be called a humble, self-effacing stand, expected from man facing deity. Abraham, on hearing God's decision to blot out the sinful cities, does not say 'Thy will be done,' 'You know best.' Abraham does not accept the verdict, but reacts to it, appeals against it, argues about it.[27]

It is hard to imagine a more pointed corrective to the Christian theological tradition than the stance of God and Abraham in this story. The corrective will be no less whether we read it with an emphasis on God's commitment to let Abraham know or from the point of view of Abraham's belief that God's notion of justice will be comprehensible. Augustine mobilized the Latin word *occulta* ["hidden"] to describe God's ways, or, as Paula Fredriksen notes, "more frequently, *occultissima*," meaning "*most hidden*." In fact, she says, in Augustine's mature view, "all of God's reasons for making any of his judgments are *occultissimi*."[28] Luther strikes the same note with even greater force and confidence, calling on faith to make up the difference when human reason stumbles before God's inscrutable ways.[29] The quest for understanding must in Luther's view meekly surrender in favor of a higher and hidden idea that may never come to light. Abraham's argument with God over the fate of Sodom takes faith in precisely the opposite direction, beginning with a notion of justice that Abraham is able to understand. Rather than ships passing each other in the night, God tries to convey to Abraham God's sense in broad daylight.

In February of 1944, twenty-four year old Primo Levi arrived at Auschwitz. In an attempt to quench his thirst, the newly arrived prisoner reached his hand through the window of the barrack to get hold of an icicle hanging from the roof outside. He was immediately struck hard by a German guard. "Why?" Levi asked, using what little he knew of the German language. "Here there is no why," the guard answered from outside as he brusquely pushed Levi away from the window.[30] It was the law of the camp that there could be no answers because there were no legitimate questions. The only view that mattered was the view of the person in authority, a person accountable to no one.

Such are not the parameters of this story, and this could well be the most important revelation in the account. Abraham does not surrender to the notion of God's

27. Roshwald, "Dialogue between Man and God," 148.

28. Fredriksen, *Sin*, 146.

29. Luther, *The Bondage of the Will*, 62.

30. Levi, *Survival in Auschwitz*, 29.

inscrutable will. He does not concede that understanding is beyond reach or put his mind to rest by saying that when understanding comes up short, faith will make up the difference. As Sarna observes, "Abraham's struggle to apprehend the nature of God's purposes assumes that God must act according to a principle that man can try to understand." [31] In a wonderful book on political philosophy and the God of Abraham, Thomas Pangle finds support in this story for the principle that "even God—that God above all—must adhere to *intelligible* justice."[32] Roshwald concurs that the entire discussion in Genesis is predicated on the assumption that there can be meaningful communication between God and human beings.

> Yet, the fact that God is believed to be just and man is capable of perceiving right and wrong, facilitates an argument of man with God about issues of morality. God and man are here on common ground, they speak the same language and agree to the same premises, and so a discussion should be both feasible and meaningful.[33]

Where is faith in this discussion? Where is trust? Its contours are sharply drawn. Abraham trusts that God will act according to a notion of justice that is comprehensible to him. To the extent that Abraham is the father of those who trust God, as Paul maintains (Rom 4:16), he exemplifies an ideal that has fallen on hard times in Christian theology. The accent in this story is on understanding and not on faith, and certainly not on blind faith. For Abraham, trust in God means to be certain that God is not a Person who will act against basic notions of justice, thus understood. This assumption, as Roshwald notes, makes the exchange between God and Abraham possible and meaningful.[34]

Abraham's insistence that the Judge of all the earth must do what is right (18:25) takes for granted that there is accountability on the part of the ruling authority. God does not rebuff Abraham on this point or indicate that he is out of line. Lytton, who argues that God models ideal jurisprudence before Abraham, holds that accountability on the part of the ruling power is an indispensable constituent of moral authority. Importantly, Abraham does not impose accountability on God against the latter's will.

> Accountability is a central feature of the judicial role that God models for Abraham. By initiating the conversation, God willingly places Himself in a position to be held accountable. Accountability is a kind of reciprocity between a superior and his subordinates. In the case of judicial accountability, judging subjects the judge to the judgment of others.[35]

31. Sarna, *Genesis*, 133.
32. Pangle, *Political Philosophy*, 155.
33. Roshwald, "Dialogue between Man and God," 150.
34. Ibid.
35. Lytton, "Shall Not the Judge of the Earth Deal Justly?" 46.

Abraham begins his questioning of God's intent by positing fifty as the hypothetical number of righteous people in Sodom. "Suppose there were fifty righteous within the city; would You also destroy the place and not spare *it* for the fifty righteous that were in it?" (18:24, NKJV).

God's reply makes it clear that Abraham's criteria for sparing Sodom meet criteria that are well within the margin necessary for Sodom to escape judgment. "If I find in Sodom fifty righteous within the city, then I will spare all the place for their sakes," God says (18:26, NKJV).

Trouble is, Abraham now realizes, he has overestimated the qualities of people living in Sodom. Abraham is unsettled not because God has been reluctant to accede to his request but because his opening bid has been unrealistically high. A downward adjustment to a much lower figure is necessary.

> Then Abraham answered and said, "Indeed now, I who *am but* dust and ashes have taken it upon myself to speak to the LORD: Suppose there were five less than the fifty righteous; would You destroy all of the city for *lack of* five?" So He said, "If I find there forty-five, I will not destroy *it*." And he spoke to Him yet again and said, "Suppose there should be forty found there?" So He said, "I will not do *it* for the sake of forty." Then he said, "Let not the LORD be angry, and I will speak: Suppose thirty should be found there?" So He said, "I will not do *it* if I find thirty there." And he said, "Indeed now, I have taken it upon myself to speak to the LORD: Suppose twenty should be found there?" So He said, "I will not destroy *it* for the sake of twenty." Then he said, "Let not the LORD be angry, and I will speak but once more: Suppose ten should be found there?" And He said, "I will not destroy *it* for the sake of ten" (Gen 18:27–32, NKJV).

The entire conversation turns into a remarkable calibration of redemptive intent, a probing for limits, and a shared commitment to err on the side of caution. At last the realization settles on Abraham that Sodom does not meet the prerequisites for its life to go on. The cities of the plain have no redeeming features, no element that makes for a realistic hope that conditions will change for the better. The thought that God "remained standing before Abraham," explored above, and that God remains thus standing throughout the conversation as though he is the lesser of the two,[36] is softened by Abraham's deferential and respectful tone. "I who *am but* dust and ashes have taken it upon myself to speak to the LORD. . . . Let not the LORD be angry. . . . I have taken upon myself to speak to the LORD. . . . Let not the LORD be angry, and I will speak but once more" (18: 27, 30–32). Abraham knows who is who in the dialogue, but this is not an adversarial relationship. If God here answers to Abraham, Abraham's posture combines boldness and humility. Honesty need not be rude or forthrightness turn into brazenness, as Abraham shows.

36. Ibid., 38.

Limits

But why does Abraham stop at ten? Why, noting with Nathan MacDonald that "[t]o every bid that Abraham lodges there is only a divine yes and never a no"?[37] MacDonald, who contends—correctly, I believe—that God is the leading voice in the dialogue, interprets this as a failure on the part of Abraham. He should have proceeded beyond ten. Had he done so, God would have continued granting his petition.

> Abraham does not appeal to the mercy of God and ask for full forgiveness; instead, presuming Yhwh to be a harsh judge, he prepares to barter with him. His strategy is undone by Yhwh's persistent acceptance of Yhwh's offer; Yhwh turns out to be far more merciful than Abraham imagines. Drawing the line at ten indicates not only the depth of Sodom's sin but also that Abraham has not plumbed the depths of Yhwh's grace.[38]

If this were the reason, would not God be free to overrule Abraham, sparing Sodom in the absence of a human request to that effect? Is Abraham to blame for the alleged mercy-deficit of the subsequent action, seeing that he failed to ask for it? This seems doubtful.

Roshwald asks similar questions, but his proposal has a different rationale. Neither weakness nor lack of perseverance will explain the fact that Abraham stops at ten. "*The decision is the Lord's, and had Abraham pursued his argument to the logical end, God would have appeared as left with no freedom to reach His own decision.*" [39] According to this logic, Abraham stops at ten in order to leave God room for discretion. Roshwald adds that Abraham must do this because he has taken his point as far as it is legitimate to go. "The intent of the story is to show the moral commitment of Abraham; it is not to present God as the pupil of Abraham."[40]

Sarna offers a third option, what we might call "critical mass." To him, "Abraham has reached the limit of the ability of a righteous individual to outweigh the cumulative evil of the community. Ten is a round and complete number that symbolizes totality. Ten persons thus constitute the minimum effective social entity."[41]

In the end, it could be that Abraham's project comes unglued because, in the course of the bargaining, it dawns on him that there are not ten righteous people in Sodom, not five, not even one.[42] The premise on which his argument rests disintegrates. Abraham could have continued lowering the bar until he had reached the number of the household of his relative Lot, six adults, including Lot's wife, his daughters, and their fiancées. What some interpret as a failure of nerve at the end has in this

37. MacDonald, "Listening to Abraham," 35.

38. Ibid., 40.

39. Roshwald, "Dialogue between Man and God," 155 (emphasis his).

40. Ibid.

41. Sarna, *Genesis*, 134.

42. Turner, *Genesis*, 85–86.

option less to do with his estimate of divine mercy than in wishing to avoid making explicit the moral bankruptcy of Lot's family. At the very end God painstakingly arranges to bring Lot and his family to safety despite evidence that Lot bears the marks of decadence, not unlike the people of the city where he lived (19:1–26, 30–38).

God saves Lot not because Lot is righteous or because God remembered *Lot* but because "God remembered *Abraham*" (19:20). "So it was that, when God destroyed the cities of the Plain, God remembered Abraham, and sent Lot out of the midst of the overthrow, when he overthrew the cities in which Lot had settled" (19:29). Lot and his daughters make it to safety in spite of themselves, and because Lot is the beneficiary of Abraham's relationship with God. In accordance with the logic of Abraham's dialogue with God, Lot is saved because Abraham is righteous.

The Next Day—and Thereafter

At last Sodom and the cities on the Plain are destroyed. We see the result, on the morning after, through the eyes of Abraham.

> Abraham went early in the morning to the place where he had stood before the Lord; and he looked down toward Sodom and Gomorrah and toward all the land of the Plain and saw the smoke of the land going up like the smoke of a furnace (19:27–28).

I imagine the narrator at this point speaking in a subdued voice, noticeable even in a report that is remarkable for sparse wording. The spectacle that greets Abraham is a scene of utter horror, the Bible's Hiroshima, and the story does not attempt to make explicit Abraham's feelings or describe the expression on his face. For that very reason the narrator proves that the less said says it better. Abraham, who the day before was party to discovering God's ways, remains in the same pursuit. He is there, "*early in the morning*," and he is there, in "the place where he had stood before the Lord" (19:27). The scene suggests continuity, a conversation and a work in progress after a sleepless night, as though Abraham is still standing "before the Lord." For Abraham, *the next day* is a day of reflection, inviting the reader to participate. Should we read this story as a precedent and model for divine action, and retribution as the lesson it teaches?

I raise the question because the action against Sodom is generally cited as a precedent-setting example of divine retribution. Indeed, the story is often held to offer a preview to the prospect of vengeance by unquenchable fire at history's end. When "Sodom" appears on the screen, caveats enabling nuanced readings are often missing. What, in our *the-day-after* reflection, shall we make of the "outcry against Sodom," having noted that the outcry originates with the downtrodden and marginalized and not, as is often imagined, as divine action against alleged sexual deviancy? What shall we make of God's apparent reluctance to get involved, action taken only when the "outcry" of the downtrodden can no longer be ignored (18:20)? Where shall we place

God's decision to keep Abraham informed of *God's way of doing things* (18:17), inviting a broader horizon of God's action than Sodom alone? How do we take the measure of God's commitment to due process, protection of the innocent, and a notion of justice that is willing to spare the guilty for the sake of a few people of integrity?

Martin Buber links Abraham and Noah as a twosome in Genesis who are said to be "righteous" [*tsaddik*], "whole" [*tamim*], and "walking with God."[43] They are people of integrity in their generation, individuals in whom there is "agreement between 'within' and 'without,' between 'truth' and 'reality,' between the rightness of a cause and its recognition, between conviction and behavior," says Buber.[44] From the shared possession of these characteristics, Noah and Abraham face the reality of evil (Gen 6:5; 18:20). In the case of Noah, there is divine action in the form of the flood (Gen 7:11–23). In the case of Abraham, fire rains down on the cities of Sodom and Gomorrah, Admah and Zeboiim (Gen 19:24–2; cf. Gen 10:19; Deut 29:23).

But what happens next? We know the answer in the case of Noah. After the ravages of the flood comes the pointed and repetitive pronouncement: *never again*. The statement is repeated three times, "*never again* shall all flesh be cut off by the waters of a flood, and *never again* shall there be a flood to destroy the earth; . . . the waters shall *never again* become a flood to destroy all flesh" (Gen 9:11, 15).

It is not contrived to ask, now with respect to Abraham: What happens next, after the fire? Have we witnessed a precedent, a form of divine retribution from which God will not backtrack? After the Flood, death by drowning is a spent force in the divine armamentarium, marking it off as an exception (Gen 9:11, 15). Is death by fire still a viable option after Sodom? Do Noah and Abraham, the exceptional twosome in Genesis, come off the same page not only with respect to what they have in common *before* and *during* their experiences but also with respect to the *aftermath*?

Support for this possibility is suggested by a prophetic retrospective on the destruction of the cities of the Plain (Gen 10:19; Hos 11:8–9). Reviewing the past and weighing the option of similar action in the present, the prophet Hosea invokes the memory of these cities as an example of what God will *not* do.

> How can I give you up, Ephraim? How can I hand you over, O Israel? How can I make you like Admah? How can I treat you like Zeboiim? My heart recoils within me; my compassion grows warm and tender. I will not execute my fierce anger; I will not again destroy Ephraim; for I am God and no mortal, the Holy One in your midst, and I will not come in wrath (Hos 11:8–9).

Hosea circumscribes the destruction of the cities of the Plain to make it an event that will not be repeated, at least not in the historical context of the prophet even though he seems to be confronting a repugnant spiritual and social reality. The prophetic voice, recalling the destruction of "Sodom and Gomorrah, Admah and

43. Buber, "Abraham the Seer," 31–32.

44. Ibid.

Zeboiim" (Deut 29:23), in this respect strikes the same note as God's message to Noah after the destructive ravages of the Flood.

Sodom is destroyed in Genesis, but the topic lingers in biblical literature. When the disciples of Jesus are turned away in a Samaritan village, inhospitality very much in evidence (Luke 9:52–53), his disciples invoke their understanding of divine action in the past as a prescription for similar action in the present. "Lord, do you want us to command fire to come down from heaven and consume them?" they ask (Luke 9:54). But there is no green light for the proposed action this time around. Instead, they receive pointed reproof for an attitude all too willing to think in terms of punishment and an implicit rejection of the theological rationale sustaining it. "But he turned and rebuked them," says the narrator (Luke 9:54). In the Gospel of Matthew, Jesus compares Sodom favorably to conditions in his own time, saying that "if the deeds of power done in you had been done in Sodom, it would have remained until this day" (Matt 11:23). Even if we allow for possible rhetorical hyperbole, the Sodomites are in this recollection not the poster-children of depravity that they have been made out to be (Matt 11:24; cf. 10:14–15).

In Genesis, the outcry rising from the downtrodden is met by divine action, but it is not divine action without sense or sense that is off limits to humans. What Abraham knows going out, moreover, is more than he knew going in, God making good on his intention not to hide from him God's way of doing things (Gen 18:17). Genesis says that Abraham "rose early in the morning to go to the place where he had stood before the Lord" (19:27), standing, as it were, in the posture of a person who seeks understanding.

Genesis will repeat this sentence one more time, saying of Abraham that "he arose early in the morning," this time saddling his donkey, and taking two of his men with him, and his son Isaac (22:3). Whither now, sense?

Chapter Nine

Singular Sense: Abraham and the Binding of Isaac

All the hard-won gains made with respect to the reasonableness of God's actions in the story of Abraham's pleading for Sodom seem to be demolished by the story that in Jewish tradition is remembered as the *Akedah*, "the binding of Isaac." The account derives its name from the scene when, as Genesis tells it, Abraham "bound his son Isaac, and laid him on the altar, on top of the wood" (Gen 22:9). The scene of the father binding the son in preparation for the son's slaughter etched itself on the imagination of readers.[1] This story is the capstone of the Abraham narratives in the Old Testament and the seventh and climactic revelation in Abraham's journey according to Martin Buber's criteria.[2] It begins like this:

> After these things God tested Abraham. He said to him, "Abraham!" And he said, "Here I am." He said, "Take your son, your only son Isaac, whom you love, and go to the land of Moriah, and offer him there as a burnt offering on one of the mountains that I shall show you" (Gen 22:1, 2).

For a man who had to wait into old age to have a son, how can God now call him to return to childlessness? At the beginning of Abraham's journey, God gave him the promise that "I will make you a great nation" (12:2). The promise was fulfilled only after a long wait. Why, now, must the clock be turned back? "After these things" encompasses the trauma of prolonged childlessness (15:2); the surrogate motherhood of Sarah through her maid Hagar (16:2–10); the hostility of Sarah toward Hagar (16:11–16); the insistence that Abraham's heir would be *Sarah's* son (17:17–19); the repeated promise that Sarah would have a son (18:10); the birth of Isaac (21:1–3); and the expulsion of Ishmael and his mother (21:9–14). What God's command proposes to take away in the story of the binding of Isaac can be appreciated only in light of what God at last had given. As Nahum Sarna points out, the story "is organically connected with the preceding chapter,"[3] and, as Abraham's protracted childlessness shows, it caps

1. The Hebrew stem ʿ-*k*-*d* means "to bind"; cf. Sarna, *Genesis*, 150; see also Spiegel, *The Last Trial*.
2. Buber, "Abraham the Seer," 41.
3. Sarna, *Genesis*, 150.

and recapitulates the chief concern of the entire narrative.[4] The sensitized ear will not miss the emotional tenor of the call to Abraham, the long deferment acutely magnifying the terms of endearment, "your son, your only son Isaac, whom you love" (22:2).

The divine command is clear and to the point but where, now, is reason? Where, now, is sense? Where is understanding, directing the question in both directions: Where is the God who wants Abraham to understand? And where is the man who previously struck such a bold stance on behalf of his right to understand?[5] Has understanding run its course, brutally eclipsed by an unreasonable command to which God expects unquestioning obedience?

Few stories in the Bible have attracted as much attention or raised as many questions as this one. Readers beyond the usual crowd have flocked to the scene, alternately appalled and enthralled by the account. One such reader was the German philosopher Immanuel Kant (1724–1804), surely one of the most influential philosophers of all time. To Kant, God's command to Abraham cannot be universalized and should therefore not be obeyed. He was so offended by the story that he used it as proof of his thesis that human reason must question and reject religious claims that are contrary to the categorical imperative. Arguing that it is difficult to know whether God is speaking to a person at all, Kant asserted that it is possible to be certain of messages that *cannot* have come from God.

> For if God should really speak to man, man could still never know that it was God speaking. It is quite impossible for man to apprehend the infinite by his senses, distinguish it from sensible beings, and *recognize* it as such. But in some cases man can be sure that the voice he hears is *not* God's; for if the voice commands him to do something contrary to the moral law, then no matter how majestic the apparition may be, and no matter how it may seem to surpass the whole of nature, he must consider it an illusion. [6]

A human being, says Kant, can "be sure that the voice he hears is *not* God's" if that voice commands something that is known to be wrong. And human beings can know that when a father is charged with the task of slaughtering his only son the proposed action is wrong. God will not command a person to act contrary to the moral law. Appending it as a footnote to the statement quoted above, Kant turns to Abraham's sacrifice of Isaac for proof of this conviction.

4. Schmid, "Abraham's Sacrifice," 268–76. One does not need to share the author's conjectures with respect to the time of the composition of the story in order to appreciate the view that "Gen 22 presupposes and reflects on the Abraham story in Gen 12–21" (p. 273). Buber's view that the *stories* about Abraham must be seen as one connected story is crucial.

5. Boehm (*The Binding of Isaac*, 20–33) contends that the Abraham of uncompromising protest is still there, claiming on behalf of this opinion that in an original, older version of the story that Abraham actually disobeyed the command.

6. Kant, *Conflict of the Faculties*, 115.

> We can use, as an example, the myth of the sacrifice that Abraham was going to make by butchering and burning his only son at God's command (the poor child, without knowing it, even brought the wood for the fire). Abraham should have replied to this supposed divine voice: "That I ought not to kill my good son is quite certain. But that you, this apparition, are God—of that I am not certain, and never can be, not even if this voice rings down to me from (visible) heaven."[7]

Kant's solution to the enigmatic story in Genesis 22 is simple. God is not behind the idea that Abraham should "butcher and burn" his only son; this is something God could *not* have said. The claim must be rejected as an illusion.[8] On this supposition there is no need to worry that this story might defeat the message of Abraham's plea on behalf of Sodom because, if we accept Kant's objection, the story should not be admitted as evidence.

But Kant's "solution" fails for a number of reasons, one of which is that Abraham is not "man," a generic person who suddenly and out of the blue hears the voice of someone pretending to be God. The story bursts at the seams with prior familiarity. Abraham "walks before God" and is "whole" (*tamim*; Gen 17:1). God shows intimate knowledge of Abraham even in the formulation of the command (22:2). To respond as Kant suggests, therefore, is not an option for Abraham, and it will not get the reader off the hook.

Rather than dismissing the *Akedah* as an offense to faith, Søren Kierkegaard (1813–1855) embraced the divine command to Abraham as a foundational story that explains the meaning of faith. In *Fear and Trembling* he proposed four different scenarios for the struggle in Abraham's mind, each straining to soften the apparent unreasonableness of God's command.[9]

In the first scenario, Abraham tries to make God's command seem sensible, hoping to win Isaac's acceptance for his fate.

> It was early in the morning. Abraham arose betimes, he had the asses saddled, left his tent, and Isaac with him, but Sarah looked out of the window after them until they had passed down the valley and she could see them no more. They rode in silence for three days. On the morning of the fourth day Abraham said never a word, but he lifted up his eyes and saw Mount Moriah afar off. He left the young men behind and went on alone with Isaac beside him up the mountain. But Abraham said to himself, "I will not conceal from Isaac whither this course leads him." He stood still, he laid his hand upon the head of Isaac in benediction, and Isaac bowed to receive the blessing. And Abraham's face was fatherliness, his look was mild, his speech encouraging. But Isaac was unable to understand him, his soul could not be exalted; he embraced Abraham's

7. Ibid.
8. Kant, *Religion within the Limits*, 175.
9. Kierkegaard, *Fear and Trembling* (Lowrie trans.).

> knees, he fell at his feet imploringly; he begged for his young life, for the fair things of his future, he called to mind the joy in Abraham's house, he called to mind the sorrow and loneliness. Then Abraham lifted up the boy, he walked with him by his side, and his talk was full of comfort and exhortation. But Isaac could not understand him. He climbed Mount Moriah, but Isaac understood him not.[10]

Abraham strives to explain to Isaac what he is about to do, but he is rebuffed by Isaac's inability to understand. What is Abraham to do next? Will he sacrifice Isaac against his will? Will he proceed in obedience to the command despite the fact that it is incomprehensible to Isaac? Worse yet, is Isaac's inability to understand only a consequence of Abraham's inability to explain it? And still worse, is Abraham's inability to explain it intrinsic to a command that lies beyond reason; a command, indeed, designed to drive home divine incomprehensibility?

In this desperate bind, Abraham adopts the posture of Kant, only with greater creativity and presence of mind.

> Then for an instant he turned away from him, and when Isaac again saw Abraham's face it was changed, his glance was wild, his form was horror. He seized Isaac by the throat, threw him to the ground, and said, "Stupid boy, dost thou then suppose that I am thy father? I am an idolater. Dost thou suppose that this is God's bidding? No, it is my desire." Then Isaac trembled and cried out in his terror, "O God in heaven, have compassion upon me. God of Abraham, have compassion upon me. If I have no father upon earth, be Thou my father!" But Abraham in a low voice said to himself, "O Lord in heaven, I thank Thee. After all is it better for him to believe that I am a monster rather than that he should lose faith in Thee."[11]

Abraham tries to absolve God of responsibility for the command by pretending that he has come up with the idea himself. He is willing to look bad in the eyes of his son in the interest of salvaging Isaac's faith in God. Isaac's faith will weather the ordeal on the assumption that God did not give the command.

In the second scenario, Abraham carries out the command according to specifications, but it leaves him a broken man.

> It was early in the morning, Abraham arose betimes, he embraced Sarah, the bride of his old age, and Sarah kissed Isaac who had taken away her reproach, who was her pride, her hope for all time. So they rode on in silence along the way, and Abraham's glance was fixed upon the ground until the fourth day when he lifted up his eyes and saw afar off Mount Moriah, but his glance turned again to the ground. Silently he laid the wood in order, he bound Isaac, in silence he drew the knife—then he saw the ram which God had prepared.

10. Ibid., 27.
11. Ibid.

> Then he offered that and returned home. . . . From that time on Abraham became old, he could not forget that God had required this of him. Isaac throve as before, but Abraham's eyes were darkened, and he knew joy no more.[12]

Isaac is a marginal figure in this alternative; it is all about Abraham. He travels slowly, his glance "fixed upon the ground until the *fourth* day when he lifted up his eyes and saw afar off Mount Moriah." This is a way of saying that he is running behind schedule, and the silence reveals a man who has lost the ability to talk. His obedience is blind, numb, and joyless. In the aftermath, "Abraham's eyes were darkened" because the command exceeds what reason can fathom. He obeys, going through the motions, but he ends up embittered and faithless for the remainder of his life.

In the third alternative, Abraham suffers pangs of conscience for being willing to obey the command.

> It was early in the morning, Abraham arose betimes, he kissed Sarah, the young mother, and Sarah kissed Isaac, her delight, her joy at all times. And Abraham rode pensively along the way, he thought of Hagar and of the son whom he drove out into the wilderness [Ishmael], he climbed Mount Moriah, he drew the knife.
>
> It was a quiet evening when Abraham rode out alone, and he rode to Mount Moriah, he threw himself upon his face, he prayed God to forgive him his sin, that he had been willing to offer Isaac, that the father had forgotten his duty toward the son. Often he rode his lonely way, but he found no rest. He could not comprehend that it was a sin to be willing to offer to God the best thing he possessed, that for which he would many times have given his life; and if it was a sin, if he had not loved Isaac as he did, then he could not understand that it might be forgiven. For what sin could be more dreadful?[13]

There are many journeys to Moriah in this set-up. In fact, journeying to Moriah has in Kierkegaard's third reading become a way of life. On the first journey Abraham carries out the command, weighed down with a sense of his many losses. But the first journey to Moriah merely sets the stage for many trips to come: "It was *a quiet evening* when Abraham rode out alone. . . . *Often* he rode his lonely way." Abraham now rides in penitence, having lost faith in himself for being willing to obey the command. He is also confused at the thought that he should be willing "to offer God the best thing he possessed" but cannot do so except at the cost of compromising his fatherly duty toward Isaac.[14] Divine inscrutability has in this construct found a perfect match in human incomprehension.

12. Ibid., 28.

13. Ibid., 28–29.

14. Cf. Simmons, "What About Isaac?" 336.

In the fourth and last alternative, Abraham and Isaac are equally at the center of the action, Isaac's eyes capturing the father's every move and expression.

> It was early in the morning, everything was prepared for the journey in Abraham's house. He bade Sarah farewell, and Eleazar, the faithful servant, followed him along the way, until he turned back. They rode together in harmony, Abraham and Isaac, until they came to Mount Moriah. But Abraham prepared everything for the sacrifice, calmly and quietly; but when he turned and drew the knife, Isaac saw that his left hand was clenched in despair; that a tremor passed through his body—but Abraham drew the knife.
>
> Then they returned again home, and Sarah hastened to meet them, but Isaac had lost his faith. No word of this had ever been spoken in the world, and Isaac never talked to anyone about what he had seen, and Abraham did not suspect that anyone had seen it.[15]

What did Isaac see in that fateful moment? He saw *fear and trembling*, the body language that Kierkegaard chose to be the title of his book. Abraham carried out the command "calmly and quietly," maintaining his composure and doing nothing to arouse suspicion. But then, when he drew the knife, "Isaac saw that his left hand was clenched in despair; that a tremor passed through his body."[16] Abraham meant to obey, but fatherly love could not suppress the quiver of dissent. The hand clenched in despair conveys to Isaac Abraham's resistance to the command. Isaac lost his faith because for one fleeting moment he saw Abraham's revulsion. Life goes on without the terrible secret ever being discussed in the world, the secret that father and son suffered loss of faith because of God's command.

Missing in these meditations upon the story of the binding of Isaac is the ending. Kierkegaard does not say anything about the last minute intervention of God (22:11), the ram caught with its horns in the thicket that Abraham will offer as a sacrifice instead of his son (22:13). Initially, he treats the apparent resolution and the happy ending as though it is of marginal interest, afraid that conventional approaches will reduce the story to ho-hum platitudes and let the reader off with premature and undeserved relief. His mental experiments on the story block the reader's hustle for the easy exit. This is in contrast to the stolid rationality of Kant, who argued that the story should be dismissed for its obvious lack of moral sense. Kierkegaard insists to the contrary that we cannot escape the story or delete it. The remedy in his reading, if there is one, will be faith in the absence of understanding.

15. Kierkegaard, *Fear and Trembling* (Lowrie trans.), 29.

16. Ibid.

Questions

"After these things God tested [*nissá*] Abraham," says the narrator in Genesis (22:1). Neither the concept of testing nor its purpose is explained, but it is important to know that the story is billed as a test. Why, nevertheless, must Abraham be subjected to a test in his old age? Must the journey of faith end like this? If obedience to God's command is the point, is it necessary to resort to something that lies so far beyond ordinary conceptions of duty for obedience to prove its mettle? If God seeks deeper knowledge about Abraham, what happened to the earlier claim, "I have known him"? (18:19).

Clues that this story marks the climax of Abraham's journey are conspicuous. We see markers of continuity in the fact that the call to Abraham to leave his country (12:1) and the call to sacrifice Isaac (22:1, 2) follow the same pattern.[17]

> *Call at the beginning*: "Go forth . . . to the land that I will show you" (12:1).
>
> *Call at the end*: "Go forth . . . to the land of Moriah . . . on one of the heights that I will point out to you" (22:2).

These parallels suggest that the journey that began at Haran, where Abraham was residing at the beginning, nears completion when he receives the second call. The call at the end refers to the last leg of the journey, but the last leg is implicit from the beginning. Buber says that "each one of the revelations [to Abraham] . . . has its particular place in the pattern and could not stand in any other."[18] Nahum Sarna emphasizes the link between the point of origin (Haran) and the destination (Moriah), observing that the Hebrew phrase *lekh lᵉkha*, "go forth" (12:1; 22:2) does not occur again in the Bible.[19] The calls to "go forth" mark the outer edges of the journey, *from* highlighting the point of origin and *to* marking the destination, the latter stated fully only in connection with the final call (22:2). Aligning the two calls, God will be heard saying, "Go forth *from* your country . . . *to* the land of Moriah [*to*] one of the mountains that I will show you" (12:1; 22:1, 2). This linkage is reinforced by the terms of endearment that run on parallel tracks in the two calls, the last one of which is especially forceful.[20]

> *Call at the beginning*: "your land, your homeland, your father's house" (12:1)
>
> *Call at the end*: "your son, your only son, Isaac, whom you love" (22:2)

When the elements of renunciation and loss in these images are given their due, they show that the call to Abraham at the end is not an afterthought. The phrase "I will show you" in connection with the first call (12:1) and the phrase "I will tell you" in the second (22:2) heighten the expectation of a "show and tell" at the point of destination.

17. Sarna, *Genesis*, 150.
18. Buber, "Abraham the Seer," 36.
19. Sarna, *Genesis*, 150.
20. Ibid.

Showing and *seeing* are suggested even by the name of the place to which Abraham is directed.[21] Abraham is called to go to *Moriah* (22.2), and Moriah is best understood as a noun derived from the verb *rāʾā*, to "see." The place to which he will be going, therefore, is a "Place of Seeing."[22]

Something beckons to be seen in this story. At the end of the journey there will be a revelation.

In literal and material terms, the call to Abraham flies in the face of the prior promise. In view of the events up to this point in Abraham's life, "Isaac's death would invalidate all of God's promises," says Gunkel.[23] Brueggemann highlights the stark contrast between the *promise* and the *command*, the promise stating that "through Isaac your descendants will be named" (21:12), the command that Isaac must be killed.[24] He finds it imperative to hold together and to embrace these two extremes, "the *dark command* of God and his *high promise*," urging that the dark command is intended to prove God's sovereignty.[25] While this view fits well with a long-held tradition in Protestant theology, other and better options should be considered. Interpreters who stress the contrast between the promise and the command fail to reckon with Abraham as a mediator of revelation.

> So Abraham rose early in the morning, saddled his donkey, and took two of his young men with him, and his son Isaac; he cut the wood for the burnt offering, and set out and went to the place in the distance that God had shown him (22:3).

Abraham's socioeconomic status is brought into view in this verse. Taking along two young men shows that he is a man of wealth. "An aristocrat travels in this fashion," says Gunkel.[26] Of more importance is the lack of a verbal response on the part of Abraham after the command has been spoken. "He who was so daringly eloquent on behalf of the people of Sodom surrenders in total silence to his own bitter personal destiny," says Sarna.[27] His acquiescence to the command and the swiftness with which he starts to execute it raise more questions. Do we now see a man acting in blind obedience to the divine imperative, knowing that the command is set in stone and that questions are unwelcome? Where he earlier stood before God asking questions, is he now conceding that this command cannot have an explanation and that there are

21. Moberly (*Bible, Theology, and Faith*, 108–18) argues quite convincingly that the place is Jerusalem and the site of the future temple (2 Chr 3:1).

22. Moberly, *Genesis 12–50*, 47.

23. Gunkel, *Genesis*, 234.

24. Brueggemann, *Genesis*, 188.

25. Ibid., 189.

26. Gunkel, *Genesis*, 234.

27. Sarna, *Genesis*, 151.

no questions to be asked? With a view to terms we have used previously, is the divine-human relationship of *sense* now crashing into the wall of *nonsense*?

"Does God really test in this way?" Brueggemann asks. Does God subject the aging Abraham to a *dark* command, a command of "destructive harshness"?[28] "The premise of the story," Brueggemann answers, "is that he does."[29] This view, so widely held, must at the very least be qualified by the reminder that something will be *seen* at the end of the journey.

> On the third day Abraham looked up and saw the place far away. Then Abraham said to his young men, "Stay here with the donkey; the boy and I will go over there; we will worship, and then we will come back to you" (22:4, 5).

How does Abraham know that this is the place? Is there some token of the divine presence not only at the point of origin but also at the point of destination (22:1, 4)?

The obvious reason for leaving the servants behind, as Gunkel notes, is that they "should not witness the horrible scene."[30] What does Abraham expect the outcome to be? When he speaks to the servants, he uses the plural form throughout, "*we* will worship, and then *we* will come back to you" (22:5). So far, the story has intimated that Abraham might return without Isaac. If strictly true to this expectation, Abraham should be saying, "*we* will worship, and then *I* will come back to you" (22:5). Is Abraham protecting the terrible secret with a white lie? Or, hoping against hope, does he say it believing that Isaac will not be left in ashes on the mountain?

> Abraham took the wood of the burnt offering and laid it on his son Isaac, and he himself carried the fire and the knife. So the two of them walked on together (22:6).

Isaac, we now know, is old enough to carry the wood. Given the purpose for which the wood is brought along, it will represent a significant load that would be beyond the ability of a very young person to carry. A boy old and strong enough to carry this load will also be old enough to have reached the age of understanding. Kierkegaard's variant readings, some assuming more participation on the part of Isaac than others, do not overestimate Isaac's age. Moreover, the question of his age means that a degree of consent on Isaac's part is vital. Consent is implied at the outset of the final leg, Isaac carrying the wood, Abraham carrying the fire and the knife, and the two of them walking together. So far this is a joint venture. The narrator is stymied by his subject and can do no better than so say, "So the two of them walked on together" (22:6). "There is perfect rapport between the two, encompassed as they are in mutual solitariness and enveloped in silence. The tension between the unsuspecting

28. Von Rad, *Genesis*, 234.
29. Brueggemann, *Genesis*, 190.
30. Gunkel, *Genesis*, 234–35.

innocence of the son and the unuttered agony of the father does not disturb the harmony," Sarna says of this scene.[31]

When Isaac at last breaks the silence,[32] the dreaded question can no longer be evaded.

> Isaac said to his father Abraham, "Father!" And he said, "Here I am, my son." He said, "The fire and the wood are here, but where is the lamb for a burnt offering?" (22:7).

The evident omission had to come up at some point, and now it has. Gunkel may well call these verses "a masterpiece of psychological depiction."[33] Something is missing with respect to the sacrifice that is the purpose of the trip. Isaac points out what it is. He also leaves out one thing that is *not* missing. "The fire and the wood and the *knife* are here," we can imagine him saying. Isaac does not mention the knife.

When Abraham answers, he does not tell Isaac to his face that God told him that *he*, Isaac, is the sacrifice. The identity of the sacrifice remains unknown or at least unuttered, veiled in an answer that is partly hopeful and partly evasive.

> "God himself will provide the lamb for a burnt offering, my son" (22:8).

This translation is not an error, but the narrator's preoccupation with *seeing* is lost. "God will see to him the lamb," or "God himself will see the lamb" are legitimate alternatives. This is more ambiguous in English than the wording preferred by most translators, but it keeps the theme of *seeing* in the foreground. R. W. L. Moberly notes that "the context seems to require a sense of 'see' other than the usual one."[34] Translators have concurred by resorting to the word "provide" at the cost of eclipsing the idea of *seeing*. It is worth noting that the translators of the Septuagint were not bothered by the apparent awkwardness of the word "see." In any event, Abraham's answer "that God will see" could be read as a partial withholding of the truth, as an answer born of hope, or even as proof that he will not lose Isaac. E. A. Speiser offers a cogent summary of the story up to this point.

> Each successive moment in that seemingly interminable interval of time is charged with drama that is all the more intense for not being spelled out: the saddling of the pack animal; the unarticulated orders to the servants; the splitting of the wood for the sacrificial fire; the long, wordless trip to the spot from which the chosen site can be first seen; the forced matter-of-factness of Abraham's parting instructions to the attendants. As father and son go off by themselves on the last stage of that melancholy pilgrimage—the boy burdened with the wood for his own sacrificial pyre, and the father fidgeting with the

31. Sarna, *Genesis*, 152.

32. Von Rad, *Genesis*, 236.

33. Gunkel, *Genesis*, 235.

34. Moberly, *Bible, Theology, and Faith*, 107.

> flint and the cleaver—the unwary victim asks but a single question. The father's answer is tender but evasive, and the boy must by now have sensed the truth. The short and simple sentence, "And the two of them walked together" (v. 8), covers what is perhaps the most poignant and eloquent silence in all literature.[35]

On the surface Abraham has said nothing to the effect that Isaac is the lamb for the burnt offering, and yet Speiser suggests that "the boy must by now have sensed the truth."[36] If he has, how did he bridge the distance between the hope expressed in Abraham's answer and the terrifying conclusion that he, Isaac, is the sacrifice? For this to be the answer to Isaac's question would surely be the most remote of all conceivable options and the one that Abraham's answer sought to avoid. As noted earlier, consent on the part of Isaac is vital to the mission. How can Abraham win Isaac's consent without saying anything other than what is reported in the text? How can the vast, seismic shifts now taking place come about in the absence of words and with quiet agreement on the part of Isaac? Consent is again implied when the storm of Isaac's question has swept across their common path.[37] In the eyes of the narrator, there is no more distance between the father and the son than there was before the question was asked, "So the two of them walked on together" (22:8).[38]

> When they came to the place that God had shown him, Abraham built an altar there and laid the wood in order. He bound his son Isaac, and laid him on the altar, on top of the wood (22:9).

Of all the statements indicating consent on the part of Isaac, none is more arresting than the sentence, "He bound his son Isaac" (22:9). The readers who secured for this sentence the distinction of giving name to the story made a good choice. In the absence of further talk and without a hint of resistance on Isaac's part, he allows himself to be bound. As Sarna notes, "not a word escapes the father's lips. Isaac, too, is speechless. The intensity of the anguish is beyond the ability of words to express."[39] "We are supposed to listen with [bated] breath," says Gunkel.[40]

> *Then Abraham reached out his hand and took the knife to kill his son* (22:10).

"To kill his son"! At the zenith of the story, the father raises the knife "to kill his son"! The question posed earlier screams once more at the reader: Where, now, is reason? Where, now, is sense? But the story will not be deterred by the questions raised against it. "The execution, right to the very end, deviates not a bit from God's

35. Speiser, *Genesis*, 164–65.
36. Ibid.
37. Wenham, *Genesis 16–50*, 115.
38. Sarna, *Genesis*, 152.
39. Ibid., 153.
40. Gunkel, *Genesis*, 235.

command. God has commanded that the son be sacrificed—Abraham stretches out his hand to kill his son," says Westermann.[41] If this were a nightmare, it would be past the time for waking up. And yet Abraham is not play-acting, and it is more than a bad dream. On the level of intent, the act is all but complete. Abraham appears to have it in him to be willing at God's command to put his son Isaac to death.

> But the angel of the Lord called to him from heaven, and said, "Abraham, Abraham!" And he said, "Here I am" (22:11).

The double "Abraham, Abraham!" expresses urgency, occurring only once in the Bible. It represents a telling contrast to the single "Abraham!" at the beginning (22:1).[42] If the original command to slaughter Isaac was important, the command *not* to do so is doubly urgent. For the third time in the story we hear Abraham saying, "Here I am" (22:1, 7, 11), a response signifying "an attitude of attention and receptivity."[43] In Hebrew, the single word *hinneni* that lies behind this translation is the only word Abraham says to God throughout the entire ordeal (22:1, 11).

> He [the angel of the Lord] said, "Do not lay your hand on the boy or do anything to him; for now I know that you fear God, since you have not withheld your son, your only son, from me" (22:12).

Is the content of *this* command, revoking the previous imperative, sufficient to warrant Westermann's view that the angel "is saying only what was there in God's plan from the beginning: nothing is to happen to the child"?[44] If this assertion is correct—Westermann repeats it—did Abraham know that this was God's intention from the beginning? Did he imagine that the command had some other purpose? Did he know that it was far from God's purpose to allow harm to happen to the child?[45]

On the surface, Abraham has passed the test, and its alleged purpose has been achieved. "Now I know that you fear God," says the angel of the Lord (22:12), hinting that Abraham has proved something that was in doubt until this point. Moreover, Abraham's hope that "God himself will provide the lamb for a burnt offering" has been vindicated (22:8). In the translation of the NRSV, the anguished plot of the story appears to find its resolution when God provides a ram to take Isaac's place. On the surface, at least, the suspense is over.

> And Abraham looked up and saw a ram, caught in a thicket by its horns. Abraham went and took the ram and offered it up as a burnt offering instead of his son. So Abraham called that place "The Lord will provide"; as it is said to this day, "On the mount of the Lord it shall be provided" (22:13, 14).

41. Westermann, *Genesis 12–36*, 360.

42. Ibid., 361.

43. Sarna, *Genesis*, 151.

44. Westermann, *Genesis 12–36*, 361.

45. See Podmore, "The Sacrifice of Silence," 70–90.

A Vision on the Shoulders of Sense

"What is the meaning of this shattering ordeal?" Speiser asks, voicing the question that leaps from the lips of every reader.[46] He answers with word of caution, admitting that "[i]n this infinitely sensitive account the author has left so much unsaid that there is now the danger of one's reading into it too much—or too little."[47] Proceeding to heed his own advice, he is nevertheless confident with regard to what is *not* the take-home message. "Certainly," he says, "the object of the story had to be something other than a protest against human sacrifice in general, or child sacrifice in particular—an explanation that is often advanced."[48] Along the same line, Gunkel dismisses a supposed polemic against child sacrifice as a remote concern.[49] To Gerhard von Rad, the story "concerns something more frightful than child sacrifice," implying, disturbingly, that there could be something more frightful than that.[50] Many readers will agree with Speiser that if the author had intended to expose the barbaric custom of child sacrifice, he could have done it in a different way.[51]

To Gunkel, who reads the story as a legend, the need to come up with a creditable message is not all that important. In his reading, the purpose is to tell yet another story of the heroic exploits of Abraham, and the implied plot resolution is shallow: "God has truly provided himself a sacrifice according to his will. And it was not Isaac!"[52] Beyond this happy discovery, no further thought is required. "Thinking of this," says Gunkel, "Abraham joyfully exclaims, 'Here, at this site, I have learned that God provides for himself what he wants!'" He adds that "Abraham's reward was the fact that he could keep Isaac—a fully sufficient reward for the paternal heart!"[53] All of this is meant to tell the reader that the story has a happy ending, duly highlighted by the use of exclamation marks.

In the most influential interpretations the accent falls on obedience. The means designed to test obedience is the incomprehensible command. This view puts into bold relief the character of God, who is the source of the command, and the quality of Abraham's obedience, who does not question it. These premises feed off each other because the quality of Abraham's obedience rises in proportion to the severity of the command, and the severity of the command—the fact that it defies comprehension—is the necessary prerequisite for obedience to prove itself. Speaking to one side of this issue, Abraham's obedience, von Rad says that the exposition of the story "is much

46. Speiser, *Genesis*, 165.

47. Ibid.

48. Ibid.

49. Gunkel, *Genesis*, 237. This view is also shared by Westermann (*Genesis 12–36*, 355).

50. Von Rad, *Genesis*, 239.

51. Speiser, *Genesis*, 165.

52. Gunkel, *Genesis*, 236.

53. Ibid.

more accurate when it discovers in the narrative above all the idea of a radical test of obedience."[54] Radical obedience is so much the premise of the story that when God "gives a command to one of the patriarchs, it must be carried out without any why or wherefore."[55] This is certainly a straightforward and unsentimental goodbye to *sense*.

As to God's character in the story, Brueggemann discerns a "strange contradiction in the heart of God," exemplified by the contrast between the *dark command* and the *high promise*. He finds support for this view in Lutheran theology, contending that "Luther is correct to say that no human reason or philosophy comprehends these two marks of God." "Faith," he says, "is the readiness to answer to this strange *contradiction in God*. Faith says 'yes' to the promise, which is no small matter. It also says 'yes' to the command which makes the promise only a promise."[56] But this widely held view lays itself open to challenge. Does God need to contradict the promise for the promise to retain its purity? Does the story really make unquestioning obedience the ideal? Have we, at the end of Abraham's journey of faith, come to discover that disclosure on the part of God and understanding on the part of human beings have been overtaken by an incomprehensible command on the part of God and obedience in the absence of understanding on the part of humans?[57]

Arguing on the side of the incomprehensible command, von Rad reveals why he thinks that the story concerns something more frightful than child sacrifice. "It has to do with a road out into Godforsakenness, a road on which Abraham does not know that God is only testing him," he says.[58] The sense of God's absence is acute in this interpretation, the trauma made all the more intense by the apparent contradiction that lies behind the command. It is as though God wants "to remove the salvation begun by himself," taking away with one hand what had been given by the other. This unrelenting contradiction is meant to be there because, in von Rad's emphatic view, "in this way Yahweh tests faith and obedience!"[59]

All readers have not signed on to this interpretation. "Was it, then, the aim of the story to extol obedience to God as a general principle?" Speiser asks.[60] His implied answer is "no." Abraham had already demonstrated obedience by responding to the original call. Unquestioning obedience is precisely *not* what God wants from a human being, says Zoltan Fischer.

> It is my thesis that the test was not whether Abraham would willingly slaughter his son. In my thinking, God would find blind obedience a disappointing

54. Von Rad, *Genesis*, 239.

55. Westermann, *Genesis 12–36*, 358.

56. Brueggemann, *Genesis*, 189, emphasis added.

57. Thus Podmore ("The Sacrifice of Silence," 72), "just what manner of God is revealed in the command to make this sacrifice?"

58. Von Rad, *Genesis*, 239.

59. Ibid.

60. Speiser, *Genesis*, 165.

> performance, far below the potential for making ethical decisions that was the reason for Abraham's selection in the first place. The test was whether the request would open Abraham's thinking to new questions, new possibilities, a re-examination of his mission, and a better understanding of his and our God. Simply put, God did not want Abraham to be all that willing to sacrifice Isaac. God wanted to hear an argument put forth from Abraham's ethical nature, that side of him that had many problems with human sacrifice.[61]

Obedience has not been taken out of the equation in this interpretation, but the obedience happens within the framework of understanding. Rather than keeping the focus exclusively on Abraham, attention shifts to God and to the possibility that the test will lead to "a better understanding of his and our God."[62]

> Abraham started to collect his thoughts and his reasoning may have been as follows: "I must not be understanding the command properly. How can Isaac do all that has been foretold if I slaughter him? God would be contradicting Himself. Would my God act in such an erratic way, one year miraculously giving my wife a child and another year taking him away from us? No, I have trouble believing He is like that."[63]

Needless to say, this is exactly what Abraham should *not* be thinking if the point is to demonstrate obedience that does not ask questions. The questioning that Abraham is denied by many interpreters assumes either that there is no good reason for the command or that the reason is unintelligible. In the contrary view, there is a reason, and the reason is something other than to accept that only an unintelligible command would work for the purpose in view.

Abraham in *Fear and Trembling*

The most influential reading of the *Akedah*, Kierkegaard's meditation in *Fear and Trembling*, sees divine inscrutability and human incomprehension writ large in the story along the lines we have found in the theological tradition and in the interpretation of leading Old Testament scholars. Johannes de Silentio, who speaks for Kierkegaard, is committed to the view that "in the temporal world God and I cannot talk together, we have no language in common."[64] This is but another version of Kierkegaard's contention that there is "an infinite qualitative difference" between divine and human reality,[65] the consequence of which is that human beings should heed the divine command without pausing to question it.

61. Fischer, "Sacrificing Isaac," 174.
62. Ibid.
63. Ibid., 176.
64. Kierkegaard, *Fear and Trembling*, 16.
65. Kierkegaard, *The Sickness Unto Death*, 141–50.

And yet Kierkegaard does not necessarily affirm the tradition. He stands apart if only for arriving at his conclusion with a peculiar sensitivity that is missing in hard-nosed formulations of similar doctrines. Important contextual and biographical features cushion the similarities further. Kierkegaard makes Abraham's sacrifice of Isaac a forceful corrective to Immanuel Kant, who put ethics above faith and made the principle of universalizability the lodestar for human conduct. He found in the story an even greater rebuke to the philosophy of Georg Wilhelm Friedrich Hegel (1770–1831), who held that a citizen's duty boils down to the dictates of the state.[66] Both of these philosophers proposed ethical systems that are independent of theology. As we have seen in the case of Kant, the system became the measuring stick by which to know what theology can and cannot obligate a human being to do.[67] Kierkegaard finds Abraham to be a person who cannot be fitted into a system whether ethical or dogmatic: he is a singular figure through whom God ordains a "teleological [purpose-driven] suspension of the ethical."[68] Moreover, just as the story instils silence in the reader, Abraham must remain silent. He cannot speak because he lacks the conceptual and verbal means by which to make his action intelligible to others. This makes him a weird and lonely figure.[69] "He is unable to speak, he speaks no human language," says Kierkegaard. "Though he himself understood all the tongues of the world, though his loved ones also understood them, he nevertheless cannot speak—he speaks a divine language . . . he 'speaks with tongues.'"[70] Abraham does not keep silent out of ill will, secrecy, egoism, or elitism. "He cannot translate his actions into the language of universality; he cannot make it intelligible that 'he is willing to sacrifice Isaac because it is a trial.'"[71]

The silence that accompanies the deed is precisely the problem of *making sense*. How can a deed of such exceptional import be absolved of the requirement to *explain* it? The silence, not only the deed, poses an ethical dilemma.[72] Jonathan Jay Malesic tries to justify Abraham's silence by invoking the notion of *interiority*.[73] By this he means that all humans have an inner life that is inaccessible and off limits to others. Respectful of a person's *inner* life, religion makes allowance for things that are not *sayable* without thereby creating doubts about a person's moral integrity. This suggestion could go a long way toward solving Abraham's problem if not for the fact that the command he is called to obey involves the slaying of his only son.

66. Grenz, "The Flight from God," 147–59.

67. Kant, *Conflict of the Faculties*, 115.

68. Kierkegaard, *Fear and Trembling*, 28–33; Santurri, "*Fear and Trembling* in Logical Perspective," 225–47.

69. Podmore, "The Sacrifice of Silence," 86.

70. Kierkegaard, *Fear and Trembling*, 66.

71. Kline, "Absolute Action," 517–18.

72. Malesic, "Secrecy and Normativity," 446–68.

73. Ibid., 465–66.

A biographical note reinforces the need to read Kierkegaard's wrestling with Abraham in its own context and not as a tribute to the Protestant tradition that has embraced absence of sense. With regard to local matters in his native Denmark, Kierkegaard used the story to take issue with the complacency of the Lutheran state religion, wishing by his meditation "to transmit an unsettling shiver down the spine of bourgeois modern Christendom."[74] Scholars also recognize in *Fear and Trembling* the autobiographical subtext of Kierkegaard's aborted engagement to Regine Olsen.[75] She was the Isaac of his life, the beloved whose companionship he had to forgo in obedience to his understanding of the divine command to *him*. In contrast to Abraham, however, there will be no happy ending for Kierkegaard. When he realizes that he has misinterpreted the command, it is too late to get Regine back.[76] Faithful obedience, he learns, is not only a matter of willingness but also of timing.[77]

A Vision on the Mountain

We cannot read Kierkegaard's interpretation intelligently without taking these matters into consideration, and yet they do not resolve his claim that the ethical appears to be suspended for a higher purpose in God's command.[78] As to what the purpose might be, the inquiry should begin with the idea that Abraham walks on the path of revelation, mediating to others God's intent not to hide from Abraham "that thing which I do" (KJV) or "what I am doing" (NKJV), that is, *God's way of doing things* (Gen 18:17).[79] Within this construct, Abraham's experience on the way to Mount Moriah does not negate his encounter with God when pleading on behalf of Sodom. The story of the binding of Isaac does not change the *kind* of relationship Abraham has with God. Thomas Pangle shows the requisite circumspection when he says that "[o]nly if we bear that dialogue in mind will we reflect properly on, and appreciate correctly, the import of the fact that in this case, despite the horror of what is commanded, Abraham raises no objections."[80] Instead of conceding that the notion of understanding has been abandoned, we are nudged toward the opposite conclusion: God's revealing purpose is brought to completion in the story of the binding of Isaac. When Abraham has the vision on the mountain, therefore, he is standing on the shoulders of sense.

Second, revelation is further embedded in the material elements of the story, one of which is that Abraham is told to go to a place already known as a "Place of Seeing."

74. Podmore, "The Sacrifice of Silence," 72.

75. Garff, *Søren Aabye Kierkegaard*, 173–91, 226–29, 491–93, 675–77, 680–85.

76. Podmore, "The Sacrifice of Silence," 79.

77. Crocker, "Sacrifice in *Fear and Trembling*," 125–39.

78. Kierkegaard, *Fear and Trembling*, 28–33; Santurri, "*Fear and Trembling* in Logical Perspective," 225–47.

79. Lytton,"Shall Not the Judge of the Earth Deal Justly?" 35.

80. Pangle, *Political Philosophy and the God of Abraham*, 163.

Third, as Claus Westermann notes, the focus should be less on the testing and more on the naming of the mountain in the end. "The narrative as a whole is to be understood with reference to this goal," he says. "One does not grasp the meaning if one sees the goal merely in the words of the angel: 'because now I know that you are a God-fearing man.'"[81] Buber argues likewise for the notion of seeing, saying that "the theme-word 'to see,' which has accompanied us through all the stations of the way of God and man, opens up for us in all its depth and meaningfulness."[82] Abraham's obedience sets the stage for the revelation, but it is the revelation and not the obedience that dominates the story. Toward this end, the narrative "reaches its goal with the naming of the mountain, 'God reveals himself' or 'God sees.'"[83] Translations that emphasize *seeing* over *providing* should therefore be preferred.

> *Ephraim Speiser*:
> And Abraham named that site Yahweh-yireh, hence the present saying, "On Yahweh's mountain there is a vision."[84]
>
> *Claus Westermann*:
> And Abraham gave this place the name, "Yahweh sees," of which one says today: "On the mountain Yahweh makes himself seen."[85]
>
> *Nahum Sarna*:
> And Abraham named that site Adonai-yireh, whence the present saying, "On the mount of the LORD there is a vision."[86]

A vision? A vision on the mountain? A vision at the end of Abraham's wanderings? Having arrived at the "Place of Seeing," what does he see? What is the content of this vision, projecting it on the wide canvas of Abraham's life?

Having thrown the story open to the prospect of *seeing*, Westermann closes it down again by suggesting that the happy moment for Abraham is not "that he has passed the test, but: 'My child is saved; thanks be to God.'"[87] Is this—the return of the son unharmed—what God intended him to see? Can the father and the son now go back to business as usual, relieved that no harm befell Isaac?

Kierkegaard was so wary of this interpretation that he left out the ending in his four variant readings. In his reading, initially at least, Abraham does not really get Isaac back even though Isaac escapes the knife. "Venerable Father Abraham! When you went home from Mount Moriah, you did not need a eulogy to comfort you for

81. Westermann, *Genesis 12–36*, 364.
82. Buber, "Abraham the Seer," 41–42.
83. Westermann, *Genesis 12–36*, 364.
84. Speiser, *Genesis*, 162.
85. Westermann, *Genesis 12–36*, 353.
86. Sarna, *Genesis*, 153–54.
87. Ibid., 365.

what was lost; for you gained everything and kept Isaac—was it not so?" Kierkegaard asks.[88] The implied answer, of course, is negative. "No, it was not so;" it was not back to happy days at Sarah's table and the good old life in the hills of Hebron. The story does not end in a burst of relief at the thought "it was not Isaac!"[89] or with the exclamation, "My child is saved; thanks be to God."[90] While this is how the story ends on the material level, on the level of *seeing* it has not ended at all.

Fourth, the content of the vision must in some way reflect and compass the naming of the mountain: "On the mountain *Yahweh* makes himself seen."[91] When Yahweh is seen on the mountain, however, *the focus is not only the ending of the story*. It has been shown that the story in Genesis 22:1–19 is structured as a chiasm.[92] The center of the chiasm and the most important part of the story, therefore, is the part referred to as "the most poignant and eloquent silence in all literature."[93] Silence frames the dialogue in these verses (22:6, 8): the son breaks the silence and speaks, the father answers, the son speaks again, the father answers, and then, again, there is silence. In verbal terms, the words that matter most are the son's address to his father, the single word *ābi* ('My Father), that I would like to translate "Daddy," and the father's two-word answer, *hinneni bᵉni*, "I am right here, my son" (22:7, translation mine). This conversation is carefully framed by the most compelling visual image in the story, repeated twice, "So the two of them walked together" (22:6, 8). This, above all, is the scene that meets the eye when Yahweh makes himself seen on the mountain (22:14).

To the naked eye, this is a description of Abraham and Isaac, of course, but to the eye sensitized to see a revelation of God on the mountain, the canvas is filling with the actual characters now being revealed. Where readers have diverged between those who stress the (happy) ending and those who stress the silent middle,[94] the best option is to see the excruciating middle absorbed, magnified, and projected by the ending. The vision on the mountain has become a vision of God in the sense that Abraham is walking as the embodiment of "the ways of God." Yahweh is seen on the mountain not only or primarily in Yahweh's person at the end of the story but in the person of Abraham in the crucial middle, in the strange choreography that makes Abraham the mediator of what God is up to. Abraham has in this way experienced the full meaning of God's commitment not to hide from him "that thing which I do" (18:17, KJV).

Fifth, then, there will now be much less reason to think that the God revealed on the mountain is a God of harsh and incomprehensible commands. Abraham's obedience is not an end in itself, and the command cannot be generalized. If God is seen

88. Kierkegaard, *Fear and Trembling*, 22.

89. Gunkel, *Genesis*, 236.

90. Westermann, *Genesis 12–36*, 365.

91. Westermann, *Genesis*, 353; so also Buber, "Abraham the Seer," 42.

92. Doukhan, "The Center of the Aqedah," 17–28.

93. Speiser, *Genesis*, 164–65.

94. Doukhan, "The Center of the Aqedah," 17–18.

in Abraham, as my interpretation suggests, the imperative to Abraham enables God's disposition to come to light. What at face value seems to show a God who takes away becomes the revelation of the God who gives, and Abraham's faith becomes the means by which to project God's faithfulness.

Sixth, though often omitted in translations and comments on the story, Abraham's naming of the mountain and the proverb to which his experience gives rise are unmistakably oriented toward the *future*. Building on translations we have used above and squeezing the text to empty itself fully of its nuances, the following translation preserves the notion of seeing and the idea that seeing is yet future. "So Abraham called that place, 'Yahweh will be seen,' as it is said to this day, 'On the mount of Yahweh he will be seen'" (Gen 22:14, translation mine). Abraham, the text seems to say, has at best provided a preview. A fuller disclosure is yet to come, couched in imagery of revelation and an expectation nurtured and kept alive by proverb in Israel *to this day*, "Yahweh will be seen on the mountain" (Gen 22:14).

The most important echoes of the *Akedah* in the New Testament will not seem so strange to readers who take seriously that Abraham is a mediator of revelation, and make *seeing* the most important element in Genesis 22. Paul's argument in Galatians, otherwise rather strained, now seems less contrived. "Now the promises were made to Abraham and to his offspring (singular); it does not say, 'And to offsprings (plural)' as of many; but it says, 'And to your offspring,' that is, to *one* person, who is Christ," he argues (Gal 3:16). Paul states bluntly—I imagine him pounding the table for emphasis in the hope of putting the Teachers in Galatia in their place—that Abraham's singular *offspring* is not Isaac, but Jesus. According to his reading, the story in Genesis was meant all along to convey a singular reality beyond itself and far more than a father's obedience to a harsh command.[95] The story was meant to mediate revelation, a point that Paul grasps in a way that neither his opponents in Galatia nor modern readers have. "In Galatians, Abraham is distinctly a punctiliar figure rather than a linear one," says J. Louis Martyn, "he is not at all the beginning of a line that can be traced through something properly called history, for he does not have 'seeds,' but rather a 'singular seed.'"[96] Abraham's witness to the singular seed, as Paul sees it, is therefore also a window to singular sense.

Echoing the *Akedah*, Paul asks in Romans, "He who did not withhold his own Son, but gave him up for all of us, will he not with him also give us everything else?" (Rom 8:32; cf. Gen 22:16). In this echo of Genesis, the person "who did not withhold his own son" is not Abraham. The accent in Romans is on God's self-giving, and the alleged harshness of the divine command is nowhere to be found. The promise that all the families and nations of the earth "shall be blessed" through

95. See Tonstad, "Inscribing Abraham," 15–27; Alexander, *Abraham in the Negev*; Hahn, "Covenant, Oath, and the Aqedah," 79–100.

96. Martyn, "Events in Galatia," 173.

Abraham culminates in his encounter with the God who is revealed on the mountain (Gen 12:3; 22:18, NKJV).

The priority of *seeing* over *obeying* also dominates Jesus's comment on Abraham in the Gospel of John. "Your ancestor Abraham rejoiced that he would *see* my day; he *saw* it and was glad," Jesus said to people who resisted the thought that Jesus could be a greater figure than the founding father (John 8:56). *Seeing* is once more the key word: it is all about seeing, and seeing brings a new sense. God does indeed give a command that seems inscrutable, but the command is meant to take *seeing* to a new level, and seeing is the twin brother of sense.[97] The explosive, shattering character of the story in Genesis is evident even without the help of the New Testament. A new sense is rising, not, as interpreters maintain, of a god who assaults an old man with a dark command, but of a God who draws the outline of self-giving to a new scale.

Kierkegaard's exceptional meditation on the binding of Isaac makes too little of revelation.[98] His re-telling turns Abraham into a martyr, his martyrdom not only the aborted sacrifice of Isaac but also the inability to make himself intelligible to others, "the martyrdom of being uncomprehended."[99] His fourth option, when Isaac saw that Abraham's left hand "was clenched in despair; that a tremor passed through his body,"[100] is a fitting description of how Abraham's God has been perceived in the world. The sense of revelation is also missing in Kierkegaard's last written entry in 1855, just before he was hospitalized with the illness that would claim his life at the young age of forty-three.[101] Melancholy and loss dominate, the harsh fate accepted in faith, but the sufferer unable fully to hide the clenched fist.

Abraham's walk with Isaac on the path of revelation strikes a different cord, a cord that has less fear but not less trembling. The singular character of the story goads the reader to discern in it revelation more than obedience, giving more than demanding, God more than Abraham, and, from the vantage point of Genesis, the future more than the past. As the proverb to which the story gave rise put it, "Yahweh will be seen on the mountain" (Gen 22:14). Above all, the singular sense of the story is not synonymous with nonsense. In Genesis, it took the two to make Yahweh seen on the mountain, in silent, unspeakable togetherness, father and son. Behind the *ābi* ("My Father") of Isaac in Genesis we hear Abraham's answer, now speaking not only for himself, "I am right here, my son" (Gen 22:7, translation mine).

97. Barr, "Abba, Father," 179; ———, "'Abba' Isn't 'Daddy,'" 28–47.

98. Pangle, *Political Philosophy and the God of Abraham*, 180–81.

99. Kierkegaard, *Fear and Trembling* (Lowrie trans.), 90.

100. Ibid., 29.

101. Garff, *Søren Aabye Kierkegaard*, 775.

Chapter Ten

Face to Face with the God of Sense

Moses dominates four of the first five books in the Bible. This alone makes it impossible to ignore him, and quantity is matched by quality. In Moses's relationship with God there is intimacy (Exod 33:11), reciprocity (33:12–13), and understanding (Exod 34:5–7; Deut 31:19, 20; 32:4) with few caveats or qualifications. He is singled out as an exceptional mediator of revelation (Exod 3:10, 14). God "made known his ways to Moses," says one of the most substantive Psalms (Ps 103:7). At the point of the initial call he receives a generous mandate to speak for God. Aaron "shall serve as a mouth for you," God tells him, "and you shall serve as God for him" (Exod 4:16). When Moses at the most mature point in his leadership slips up, however, his career comes to an abrupt end. This part of Moses's story—the part less well known—ensures his inclusion here. At the point of his dismissal, Moses gives advance delivery on God's "sense" in such a way that his failure counts toward that end more than his earlier successes (Num 20:12; 27:13–14; Deut 3:24–26). At the end of the books within which Moses is the leading character, the writer concludes that he is without peer despite the slip-up. "Never since has there arisen a prophet in Israel like Moses, whom the Lord knew face to face" (Deut 34:10).

The Man Moses

"When God chose Moses at the burning bush, he chose a man who was unafraid to argue with him," says Pamela Tamarkin Reis.[1] She considers this Moses's most outstanding trait of character: a person who is not only contending with others on God's behalf, but someone who is willing to contend with God concerning God's ways and verdict (Exod 32:32–33; Deut 9:13–20). If this is a correct assessment, we are from the outset invited to see Moses as a *thinking* person and, by extension, a person to whom understanding is not a matter of indifference. And yet he is not brazen or self-important. A charming (and recognizable) side to Moses's humanity is evident when, after hearing God's plans for him, he tells God, "O my Lord, please send someone else" (Exod 4:13). God, however, is not in the mood to search for other candidates, apparently convinced that this is a task for Moses and no one else. Three or four other qualities stand out that

1. Reis, "Seeing Moses Plain," 213.

might explain God's insistence. Moses appears to care about justice despite the fact that he is raised in privilege. His commitments reach beyond his socio-economic group and class. When one day he sees a fellow Jew oppressed by an Egyptian, probably witnessing a case of massive and wanton abuse, he is so incensed that he kills the Egyptian (Exod 2:11–12). His reaction may be attributable to poor impulse control, and perhaps it was, but it could also be proof of a caring person. He injects himself into another dispute the very next day (2:13–14), suggesting a low threshold for getting involved in situations of conflict. Ari Zivotofsky describes Moses as

> an individual who is incapable of standing idly by while an injustice is being perpetrated by one person or group on another person or group. Whatever consequences he may face, he nonetheless feels obligated to act to undo and correct the injustice. He is a *man* in a place where there are no *men*. And he always recognizes such situations. Others may say that they would help if they had recognized the need; Moses was uniquely sensitive to recognize the need.[2]

Forty years will go by between Moses's unsolicited intrusion into the abuse of a fellow Jew and the call to lead the Israelites on a march to freedom; and yet his reaction to oppression in his younger years might linger as a reason for the call. Who can better feel with the oppressed as a matter of vocation than one who has shown himself able to feel with the oppressed—and without being paid to do it?

Moses epitomizes service in leadership. The historical record is littered with leaders of nations and causes who made national interest subservient to the privilege and prosperity of the leader. "*L'état, c'est moi*," Louis XIV (1638–1739) declared at the high point of absolutist rule in France. By this he meant that the state existed for his sake and benefit, and that he had the prerogative to decide on a course of action without having to consult anyone else. Occasional historians remember that he acted accordingly. When the Sun King was busy building the gardens in Versailles, six million French starved to death.[3] There is no such self-serving sentiment in Moses. He comes across as a servant-leader who is truly committed to his people and willing to suffer personal loss in order to promote their well-being. When the Israelites were in a state of mutiny and their future in jeopardy, Moses stood ready to forgo his relationship with God if it would undo the damage. Please forgive their sins, he tells God, "but if not, blot me out of the book that you have written" (Exod 32:32; Deut 9:13–20).

Lack of self-importance goes hand in hand with willingness to put everything on the line for the sake of the people he is called to lead. At a point when a challenge to his leadership is brewing, the narrator reports that "the man Moses was very humble, more so than anyone else on the face of the earth" (Num 12:3). This is unself-importance writ large, an example of leadership that does not mistake the person for the mission. When a member of Moses's most intimate entourage believes that

2. Zivotofsky, "The Leadership Qualities of Moses," 266.

3. Acton, "The History of Freedom in Christianity," 100.

unauthorized people are infringing on the leader's turf, Moses is unperturbed. "Are you jealous for my sake?" he tells the one who wants to silence the unauthorized voice. "Would that all the LORD's people were prophets, and that the LORD would put his spirit on them!" (Num 11:29). In this incident, substance matters more than symbolism and results more than getting the credit. Moses is not a person who is afraid to share authority.[4]

Another characteristic is fortitude. This is remembered in the New Testament. "By faith he left Egypt, unafraid of the kings anger; for he persevered as though he saw him who is invisible," says Hebrews (Heb 11:27). Fortitude of the Mosaic kind combines courage and perseverance. When Moses goes head to head with Pharaoh, the latter accustomed to wielding absolute power, Moses will not be the first one to blink. And when Pharaoh ratchets up the rhetoric in threatening terms, telling Moses, "Get away from me! Take care that you do not see my face again, for on the day you see my face you shall die!" Moses shows no sign of being intimidated. "Just as you say!" he responds, "I will never see your face again" (Exod 10:28–29). We can be sure that no Egyptian heard anyone talk to Absolute Power in such language. 'How dares he!' we can fairly hear people whisper when they see Moses passing in the street. And we read in a knowing comment that Moses earned the respect of his opponents. He "was a man of great importance in the land of Egypt, in the sight of Pharaoh's officials and in the sight of the people" (Exod 11:3).

And yet Moses is above all a spiritual man. If being unafraid to ask questions even of God is one aspect of his spirituality, he is also a person who is aware of his needs and limitations. He is not shy to admit dependence. In the most exquisite scene of intimate communication with God, Moses will have nothing to do with the mission unless he has the assurance that he is not left to himself. "If your presence [lit., "face"] will not go, do not carry us up from here," he tells God (33:14). He cannot go anywhere on the strength of his own resources or even on the strength of his conviction that liberation from slavery is a worthy cause until he has the assurance that everything will happen under God's face.[5] "For how shall it be known that I have found favor in your sight, I and your people, unless you go with us? In this way, we shall be distinct, I and your people, from every people on the face of the earth" (33:15).

The yearning for God's presence may be seen as the nexus that links the private and the public spheres in Moses's life. He leads the people, to be sure, and he admits that he does not dare to lead them on his own (33:14–15). For this reason he retreats to spend time with God. Exodus describes a pattern and a familiar sight to the Israelites, perhaps a little like the philosopher Immanuel Kant who was said to stick to his daily routine so predictably that people could adjust their clocks to the time when, at 7:00 PM, he took his evening walk. This element in the story takes its beginning in the

4. Reis, "Seeing Moses Plain," 225.

5. Thus Jacob (*Theology of the Old Testament*, 78), "The face of God is thus the presence of God without any reservation."

encounter Moses had with God at Mount Sinai for the purpose of receiving the Ten Commandments the second time. When Moses "came down from the mountain with the two tablets of the covenant in his hand, [he] did not know that the skin of his face shone because he had been talking with God," says the narrator (34:29). From that time onwards, the splendor of the initial encounter turns into a routine and habitual sight.

> When Moses had finished speaking with them, he put a veil on his face; but whenever Moses went in before the Lord to speak with him, he would take the veil off, until he came out; and when he came out, and told the Israelites what he had been commanded, the Israelites would see the face of Moses, that the skin of his face was shining; and Moses would put the veil on his face again, until he went in to speak with him (Exod 34:33–35).

The veiling is precisely the opposite of what we might expect. Moses should put on the veil when he goes before God, but that is when he takes it off. Conversely, he should remove the veil when he goes before the people, but that is when he puts it on. We can infer that these visits are work-related, necessitated by Moses's responsibility and mission, but they seem to be more than that. At the juncture between the private and the public sphere in Moses's life, the private sphere is getting the upper hand. Moses spends time with God in order to carry out his mission, but the contact between God and Moses away from the public eye has the body language of endearment. The veil comes off, so to speak, showing directness and intimacy. God becomes as much the reason for the encounters as the mission.

At one point Moses acknowledges the imbalance in the relationship, noting that God's knowledge of him exceeds Moses's knowledge of God. He requests redress of the imbalance, for shrinkage of the distance between heaven and earth. "Yet you have said, 'I know you by name, and you have also found favor in my sight.' Now if I have found favor in your sight, show me your ways, *so that I may know you* and find favor in your sight" (Exod 33:12–13). Here, in so many words, Moses is saying, 'You know me better than I know you. Please, and here the words of the text suffice admirably, "show me your ways, *so that I may know you*"' (33:13). The boldness of this proposition has not escaped comment. "Moses criticizes the imbalance in his relationship with God with some audacity. Yahweh knows the name of his servant Moses, yet Moses does not know the name of the servant whom Yahweh will send, nor does he fully know Yahweh himself," says William Propp.[6]

Yahweh could at this point demur, telling Moses that it is possible for God to know Moses but impossible for Moses to know God. But this is not what we hear. Instead, Yahweh now speaking, "I will do the very thing that you have asked; for you have found favor in my sight, and I know you by name" (33:17). This, of course, can only incentivize Moses further, as he realizes that God is placing the green light before him. "Show me your glory, I pray," Moses says (33:18).

6. Propp, *Exodus 19–40*, 602–3.

Divine Availability

What is now the force driving the account forward? The language suggests that it is no longer Moses's mission despite the responsibility that weighs heavily on him. *God* is the subject of interest, and Moses, unveiled, up close and personal, takes the plunge. But this view, too, must be qualified by the overwhelming sense that God controls the choreography and is drawing him in. Divine availability counts for more than the human quest, the former encapsulated in the initial call to Moses, "Come up to me on the mountain" (24:12).

The initiative remains with God in these encounters, God showing willingness to be known.

> And he said, "I will make all my goodness pass before you, and will proclaim before you the name, 'The Lord'; and I will be gracious to whom I will be gracious, and will show mercy on whom I will show mercy. But," he said, "you cannot see my face; for no one shall see me and live" (Exod 33:19–20).

Readers of this passage cannot avoid noticing the oscillation between seeing and hearing, the request to *see* being met by the promise that something will be *heard*. In fact, Yahweh specifically emphasizes that Moses will hear but he will not see. "Sight is submitted to hearing," says Samuel Terrien. "Man never sees God, but the word is heard. The eye is closed but the ear is opened. Hebraism is a religion not of the eye but of the ear."[7] Hearing, however, is not an inferior mode, in part because the visual representation is more susceptible to subversion than the word, and the word may in important respects convey more than the vision (Exod 20:4–6; Deut 4:15–18).[8] It is for Moses's own good that he cannot see God's face in visual terms.[9] God thus seen, even if Moses were to survive the encounter, moreover, cannot be shared meaningfully with others. Moses will hear the name uttered and explained in one of the most enthralling instances of divine self-disclosure in the Old Testament. As for his request to see, there will be seeing, too, calibrated to the level of human capacity and carefully timed with regard to Yahweh's "passing by.'" The divine hand that will prevent Moses from seeing God's face will be removed just in time to allow him to see God's back.

> And the Lord continued, "See, there is a place by me where you shall stand on the rock; and while my glory passes by I will put you in a cleft of the rock, and I will cover you with my hand until I have passed by; then I will take away my hand, and you shall see my back; but my face shall not be seen" (Exod 33:21–23).

This is quite amazing. Moses is the recipient of revelation in vision and word that is without precedent. "As the revealer of covenant law, Moses stands alone, without

7. Terrien, *Elusive Presence*, 112.

8. Rendtorff, *Canonical Hebrew Bible*, 54.

9. Durham, *Exodus*, 452.

predecessor, associate, or follower. No other revelatory figure in the Old Testament has experiences of revelation like Moses," says John L. McKenzie.[10] "The concept of 'face to face' comes to symbolize the Almighty's relationship with Moses," H. Barzel writes in a literary assessment of the story. "Moses is accorded what is given to no ordinary mortal: he achieves maximum proximity to God."[11] His experience will subsequently be shared, we know, but there are elements in the experience that cannot be imparted to others. Moses will pass on to the Israelites what he has heard, but what he has seen will remain with him to remind all readers that some things in life can only be experienced first-hand.

> The Lord descended in the cloud and stood with him there, and proclaimed the name, "The Lord." The Lord passed before him, and proclaimed, "The Lord, the Lord, a God merciful and gracious, slow to anger, and abounding in steadfast love and faithfulness, keeping steadfast love for the thousandth generation, forgiving iniquity and transgression and sin, yet by no means clearing the guilty, but visiting the iniquity of the parents upon the children and the children's children, to the third and the fourth generation" (Exod 34:5–7).

And so, with Moses hidden in the cleft of the rock, Yahweh "stood with him there," bombarding him with a catalogue of divine attributes that comprises the richest and most far-reaching theological vocabulary in the Old Testament. Missing from the list, some have noted, are the items usually linked to power and majesty: the text "does not depict what one might expect of a full revelation of Yahweh: a beaming, armed, kingly figure, lauded as Creator, Conqueror and Administrator."[12] "Instead of a visual image, we and Moses receive a *verbal* portrait of Yahweh's personality," says Propp.[13] So also Brevard Childs, "the revelation of God is in terms of his attributes rather than his appearance."[14]

What have we seen? In this encounter, God's willingness to disclose smothers the notion that God prefers to stay distant and hidden.[15]

> Moses: "Show me your ways, so that I may know you" (Exod 33:13).
>
> God: "My presence ["face"] will go with you, and I will give you rest" (33:14).
>
> Moses: "If your presence ["face"] will not go, do not carry us up from here" (33:15).

10. McKenzie, *Theology of the Old Testament*, 70–71.
11. Barzel, "Moses: Tragedy and Sublimity," 127.
12. Propp, *Exodus 19–40*, 611.
13. Ibid.
14. Childs, *The Book of Exodus*, 596.
15. Barth, *Romans*, 98–99.

God: "I will do the very thing you have asked" (33:17).

Moses: "Show me your glory, I pray" (33:18).

God: "I will make all my goodness pass before you, and I will proclaim before you the name, 'The LORD.' . . . But you cannot see my face" (33:19, 21).

All this transpires in the eye of the storm of the Sinai theophany, on the inside of a display of majesty and might that to most Israelites signal the need to keep distance. The contrast between the people's reaction and that of Moses is an important feature in the account. "When all the people witnessed the thunder and lightning, the sound of the trumpet, and the mountain smoking, they were afraid and trembled and stood at a distance, and said to Moses, 'You speak to us, and we will listen; but do not let God speak to us, or we will die'" (20:18–19). "Leave the task of intimacy with God to Moses!" they seem to be thinking. "Let him trouble himself with it! Let him know God vicariously on our behalf!" The anxiety is revealing, the people keeping distance while Moses approaches God without a hint of fear (20:21).

Closeness in spatial terms is surpassed only by the torrent of content by way of theological capital. "I will make all my goodness pass before you, and I will proclaim before you the name, 'The LORD'" (33:19). "*All* my goodness" is precisely what the text says: nothing held back, nothing left to ambiguity, nothing of importance hidden. Importantly, too, the noun is "*goodness*"—that word alone and by itself—as though that one word suffices. The divine presence showers goodness on the world, the deluge of goodness washing over Moses in such concentrated bursts that the spoken word could be the reason why he needs to be protected by Yahweh's solicitous hand as much as the visual splendor.

God is supposed to be evenhanded, "mercy" and "justice" sharing the same amount of turf in the divine economy. But it isn't quite like that. The scales tip to the side of mercy, or rather, "justice" and "mercy" are not polar opposites that must be balanced one against the other. Instead, the passage brings to light God's redemptive inclination, "justice" now defined as a commitment to set right what is wrong. In Propp's translation, God is "great in trust and reliability."[16] "Mercy" is the means by which to bring about "justice," defined restoratively. "Wrongs" are in this economy more quickly forgotten than "rights," the latter sending ripples through the fabric of human relations for a thousand generations. Conversely, "wrongs" face a dynamic that runs in their disfavor, a causal construct of damage limitation that has the momentum of "wrongs" expiring within four generations. Human actions do not count for nothing, however. Accountability remains the twin of responsibility.

16. Propp, *Exodus 19–40*, 611.

Commandments as Teaching

The intimate disclosure to Moses in the private sphere runs on parallel tracks with the giving of the law on Sinai in public. Law, for centuries cast as a negative in Protestant theology, is here a teaching moment that can be appreciated correctly only when we recover the notion of the law as gift.[17] The law is best understood as a prescription for security in much the same way as the nation that has established "the rule of law" is thought to be superior to nations that have not. "The rule of law," in turn, contrasts with arbitrary rule—where "might makes right." In the ancient world, the gods were particularly prone to such rule.

The contrast coming to view at Sinai is shattering, for the law thus understood is precisely the means by which to remove unpredictability and fear. "Because of this the fear that constantly haunts the pagan world, the fear of arbitrariness and caprice in the Godhead, is excluded. With this God men know exactly where they stand; *an atmosphere of trust and security* is created," says Walther Eichrodt.[18]

The benign intent of the Ten Commandments is evident throughout (Deut 10:12–13), the fourth commandment ensuring relief to the weakest and most vulnerable members of society. "Six days you shall labor and do all your work. But the seventh day is a sabbath to the LORD your God; you shall not do any work—you, your son or your daughter, your male or female slave, your livestock, or the alien resident in your towns" (Exod 20:8–10). This stipulation, promising a day of rest even to the slave, the resident alien, and *livestock* cannot be construed as other than an intervention of mercy from on high, and mercy that human masters are disinclined to grant. For the liberated slaves coming out of Egypt, no stipulation in the Ten Commandments drives home the contrast between slavery and freedom as forcefully as this one. Equality is also evident when, in the second iteration of the Ten Commandments, the line between the privileged and the less privileged is erased—"so that your male and female slave may rest as well as you" (Deut 5:14).

If, on the first table of the Ten Commandments, there is concern for the honor of God, the second table begins with concern for parents. "Honor your father and your mother, so that your days may be long in the land that the LORD your God is giving you" (Exod 20:12). This commandment comes with a purpose clause that spells out the benefit that will ensue. What nation, Moses argues, will not want to know more about Yahweh and Yahweh's ways, seeing the benefit to those who have adopted Yahweh's law? Noteworthy, too, is the way this text makes closeness to God and knowledge of God go hand in hand.

> You must observe them diligently, for this will show your wisdom and discernment to the peoples, who, when they hear all these statutes, will say, "Surely this great nation is a wise and discerning people!" For what other great nation

17. Stevens, "Obedience of Trust," 133–45.

18. Eichrodt, *Theology of the Old Testament*, I:38; see also Wright, *Old Testament*, 59.

> has a god so near to it as the Lord our God is whenever we call to him? And what other great nation has statutes and ordinances as just as this entire law that I am setting before you today? (Deut 4:6–8)

Such a perception cannot turn law into a burden or the means intended to complicate life. This text makes the law less a divine command than an instance of divine persuasion, the call to obey of one piece with the reason for doing it. Patrick D. Miller captures the call for understanding that is part and parcel of the divine command.

> The presence of divine persuasion indicates that the commandments cannot be reduced to blind obedience. They are not arbitrary or capricious. Nor does God simply set them out to be obeyed. The one who commands also encourages obedience and seeks to draw forth a positive response from those before whom the commands are set. From the side of God, that is, on God's part, it is not assumed that the rightness of the command is self-evident or to be imposed from above. The consent of the commanded people is a true consent of the mind and heart.[19]

What is the most conspicuous feature in this body of law? And what is the most striking contrast to other attempts at legislation in the ancient world? Again and again concern for the most vulnerable stands out, rolled out and repeated over and over in matters large, such as the Sabbatical Year (Exod 23:10–11; Lev 25:2–7) and the Jubilee (Lev 25:8–20), and in matters small, such as in the requirement to pay the day laborer his wage on the same day before sunset (Deut 24:14–15). Mercy thus institutionalized counts on support from the people's experience in captivity and from the kind of person God is said to be. Moses strives to prevent the memory of being oppressed slipping from the people's sense of identity. In Deuteronomy, in particular, this notion plays like a mantra in connection with the many ordinances seeking relief for the poor. "Remember that you were a slave in the land of Egypt, and the Lord your God redeemed you; for this reason I lay this command upon you today" (Deut 15:15; cf. 5:15; 16:12; 24:18, 22).

The entire edifice rests on the kind of person God is. Does God care? Is God attuned to the human predicament, especially to the plight of the poor and the oppressed? We see a narrative overflowing with the sense that nothing in the human experience is lost on God. In Egypt, at the beginning of the Moses story, the Israelites "groaned under their slavery, and cried out. Out of the slavery their cry for help rose up to God. God heard their groaning, and God remembered his covenant with Abraham, Isaac, and Jacob" (Exod 2:23–24). When God gets Moses's attention at the burning bush, the motivating factor for God, again, is the people's suffering. "I have observed the misery of my people who are in Egypt; I have heard their cry on account of their taskmasters. Indeed, I know their sufferings, and I have come down to deliver them from the Egyptians" (3:7–8, 9). In the retrospective in Deuteronomy, the same

19. Miller, "The Divine Command and Beyond," 25–26.

story is recounted, God's sensitivity to suffering given as the reason for the intervention. "When the Egyptians treated us harshly and afflicted us, by imposing hard labor on us, we cried to the Lord, the God of our ancestors; the Lord heard our voice and saw our affliction, our toil, and our oppression" (Deut 26:6–7). God's stance in these scenes denotes presence, not absence, engagement, not detachment, and divine commitment before there will be commandments.

Already at the burning bush Moses asks to know the divine name, "If I come to the Israelites and say to them, 'The God of your ancestors has sent me to you,' and they ask me, 'What is his name?' what shall I say to them?" God said to Moses, "I am who I am." He said further, "Thus you shall say to the Israelites, 'I am has sent me to you'" (Exod 3:13–14).

This sounds circular and enigmatic, almost like someone saying, "I said what I said" without letting on what was said. If we read it this way, God's answer could be construed to mean that God is inscrutable and unknowable. But the answer is not meant to draw Moses into the mist of inscrutability. Instead, it sets Yahweh apart from other gods and, even more, it certifies that the God who sends Moses is "the God of your ancestors" (3:13). It is not illegitimate to read God's answer as a statement about divine self-existence, but the emphasis is more on describing God in terms of God's character and God's prior involvement with human beings. With respect to Moses's request to know God's name, we can say that "God's name identifies his nature, so that a request for his 'name' is equivalent to asking about his character (Exod 3:13; Hos 12:5)."[20] God's answer, "I am who I am" means that the One who *is* first and foremost is the One who *is with you*. As Benno Jacob notes, "it is not the idea of eternity which is primary when the Israelites pronounce the name Yahweh, but that of presence . . . God is he who is *with* someone."[21]

All this is part of the divine name that Moses comes to know in his encounter with God. God is shown to be knowable and keenly attuned to human need. To know "the name," therefore, "was not merely to have the identification tag; it was also to experience the reality of the thing named."[22] Disclosure from God's side must have its corollary in comprehension on the part of Moses. Moses did not see God's face with respect to splendor, but he saw the face of God with respect to character, God speaking to Moses "as one speaks to a friend" (Exod 33:11).

Prophet Moses

Moses's insights, therefore, belong to the highest order. At the time when his leadership is contested, the pretenders are informed that God communicates with Moses in ways God does *not* relate to anyone else. This detail establishes categories for divine

20. Harris et al., *Theological Wordbook*, art. YAHWEH.

21. Jacob, *Theology of the Old Testament*, 52.

22. McKenzie, *Theology of the Old Testament*, 73.

communication that continue to resonate in later texts. There are, as it were, higher and lower levels of communication, with the communication between God and Moses occupying the highest level.

> And he [God] said, "Hear my words: When there are prophets among you, I the LORD make myself known to them in visions; I speak to them in dreams. Not so with my servant Moses; he is entrusted with all my house. With him I speak face to face—clearly, not in riddles; and he beholds the form of the LORD. Why then were you not afraid to speak against my servant Moses?" (Num 12:6–8)

This text, in direct divine speech, is a crash course on the modalities of divine communication in general and a rundown on God's communication to Moses in particular. Of the former, there are visions, dreams, and riddles, communication fraught with symbolism, ambiguity, and obscurity. With regard to Moses, speech is clear, "not in riddles," encounters happening "face to face" to the point that Moses "beholds the form of the LORD" (Num 12:6–8). The privileging of Moses is grounded in exceptional intimacy with God and the communication taking place, the intimacy reflecting Moses's availability and sense of need.

Whatever measure we take of this, Moses is a recipient of revelation. He stands out as an exceptional prophet even though he is rarely recognized as that, a person in tune with God by means not commonly available to ordinary prophets (Deut 34:10). Words and concepts originating in Moses's encounter with God are so vital that they resound throughout the New Testament. When we read in the Prologue of the Gospel of John that "the Word became flesh and lived among us, and we have seen his glory" (John 1:14), we will not miss the echo of Moses's request of God, "Show me your glory" (Exod 33:18). When Jesus in John says that "I do not call you servants any longer, because the servant does not know what the master is doing; but I have called you friends, because I have made known to you everything that I have heard from my Father" (John 15:15), Moses will again come to mind. He was a person to whom God spoke "as one speaks to a friend" (Exod 33:11, 19). Where Jesus says that "the hour is coming when I will no longer speak to you in figures, but will tell you plainly of the Father" (John 16:25), it cannot fail to impress that God spoke to Moses "clearly, not in riddles" (Num 12:8).

Moses also appears thinly veiled in the letters of Paul. Paul tells the Corinthians that "now we see in a mirror, dimly [*en ainigmati*], but then we will see face to face. Now I know only in part; then I will know fully, even as I have been fully known" (1 Cor 13:12–13).[23] Echoes of Moses ring loudly in these verses, too. God did not speak "in riddles [*di' ainigmatōn*]" to Moses. For him the "then" of the future was actualized in speaking with God "face to face" in the present (Num 12:8; Exod 33:10; Deut 34:10). The reciprocal knowing and being known that beckon in Paul's letter is found in God's

23. Hollander, "Seeing God," 395–403.

dialogue with Moses: "I will know fully, even as I have been fully known" (1 Cor 13:13; Exod 33:12–13). When Paul in 2 Corinthians casts about for imagery with which to capture the revelation of God in Jesus, he finds the answer in Moses. "And all of us, with unveiled faces, seeing the glory of the Lord as though reflected in a mirror, are being transformed into the same image from one degree of glory to another" (2 Cor 3:18).

Moses Demoted

All this makes the sudden demotion of Moses a strange and challenging theological milestone. Why did God remove him from office? Why, in light of his exceptional record of service, did God insist on letting him go despite Moses's begging God to the contrary?[24] At the point when he is about to reap the long-awaited fruit of his efforts, his service is abruptly terminated (Num 20:12; 27:12–14; Deut 3:24–26).[25] Another person who cannot match Moses's vision and depth of experience is selected to take his place (Num 27:18–22). The incident is noteworthy as it stands—and more noteworthy because removal from office was hardly the norm in the ancient world. Even today, the demotion of someone having the stature of Moses would fill headlines and stir pundits into action for weeks and months and years on end. Moses's lapse from consistency and his subsequent demotion from power are thus a large element in his legacy.

The crisis precipitating Moses's downfall is told in the Book of Numbers. Thirty-eight years after the exodus from Egypt, we read that the Israelites

> came into the wilderness of Zin in the first month, and the people stayed in Kadesh. Miriam died there, and was buried there. Now there was no water for the congregation; so they gathered together against Moses and against Aaron. The people quarreled with Moses and said, "Would that we had died when our kindred died before the Lord! Why have you brought the assembly of the Lord into this wilderness for us and our livestock to die here? Why have you brought us up out of Egypt, to bring us to this wretched place? It is no place for grain, or figs, or vines, or pomegranates; and there is no water to drink." Then Moses and Aaron went away from the assembly to the entrance of the tent of meeting; they fell on their faces, and the glory of the Lord appeared to them (Num 20:1–6).

On the surface, at least, the discontent in the wilderness of Zin is nothing new: lack of provisions, distrust, discontent, public outcry, and conspicuous amnesia with regard to the hardship the people had known in Egypt (Exod 14:11–12; 15:23–24; 17:1–4). If there is anything new this time, it is discontent expressed with unusual ferocity. The riotous sentiments call for resolute action.

24. See, for instance, Emmrich, "The Case against Moses Reopened," 53–62.

25. Barzel ("Moses: Tragedy and Sublimity," 129) notes Moses's life cut short "just below the peak of his ambition."

> The Lord spoke to Moses, saying: "Take the staff, and assemble the congregation, you and your brother Aaron, and command the rock before their eyes to yield its water. Thus you shall bring water out of the rock for them; thus you shall provide drink for the congregation and their livestock." So Moses took the staff from before the Lord, as he had commanded him (Num 20:7–9).

The staff is a crucial implement in this scene (Num 17:25–26). Shortly after crossing the Red Sea, when the water supply had been a critical issue, a similar scene of complaining had erupted (Exod 17:4). At that time Moses had been instructed to "take in your hand the staff with which you struck the Nile, and go. I will be standing there in front of you on the rock at Horeb. Strike the rock, and water will come out of it, so that the people may drink" (Exod 17:5–6). Moses did exactly as he had been instructed, with salutary results.

Now, in this encore, the staff is again prominent. Moses is to take the staff, but this time he is to "*speak to* the rock" (Num 20:8); he is not supposed to *strike* it.[26] This seems simple enough, but the context bristles with provocation. Moses is surrounded by a sea of people angrily complaining, criticizing, taunting, heaping insults on him and his fellow leaders with abandon.[27] He has born it patiently for thirty-eight years, never losing his composure. We can imagine him at this point surveying the surging mass of people, searching for signs of coolheaded elements and restraint. Instead, he faces a dense, steady roar of distrust and resentment.

What will he do this time? The assignment is to speak and not to strike. "Moses and Aaron gathered the assembly together before the rock, and he said to them, 'Listen, you rebels, shall we bring water for you out of this rock?' Then Moses lifted up his hand and struck the rock twice with his staff; water came out abundantly, and the congregation and their livestock drank" (Num 20:10–11).

There is much to take note of in this passage, details that must be scoured in order to make sense of the consequences to Moses. Tone of voice is rarely described in the Bible, but with all speech there is tone of voice. In this instance, we run no risk in assuming that there is anger in Moses's voice, his face darkened, his eyes flashing, "Listen, you rebels!" (20:10)

Second, there a sense of aggrieved self-referentiality. "Shall *we* bring water for you out of this rock?" (20:10) Moses at that moment implying that he and Aaron are the providers for the people's need. Their representative function is momentarily eclipsed, Moses talking as though he and Aaron independently possess powers far beyond what they actually have.[28]

26. Emmrich, "The Case against Moses Reopened," 61.

27. Kahn, "Moses at the Waters of Meribah," 87.

28. Boorer, "The Place of Numbers 13–14 and 20:2–12," 61; Emmrich, "The Case against Moses Reopened," 61.

Third, as Suzanne Boorer notes, Moses was instructed to speak to *the rock* while, instead, he speaks to *the people*. This, too, hides God from view. The interaction is now primarily between Moses and the people rather than between the people and God.[29]

Fourth, "Moses *lifted up* his hand and struck the rock *twice*" (20:11). The implied body language hardly warrants comment. Above, the text suggests an angry voice, and the body language drives home the anger, the uplifted hand and the rock being struck not once but twice![30] The latter suggests a motion out of control, a man lashing out without restraint, the momentum of the swing so intense that he cannot stop at one strike. He is hitting the rock with all his might, suggesting that he would have liked to bring the rod down on the backs of the people.

We then read that "water came out abundantly, and the congregation and their livestock drank" (20:11). God delivers at God's end of the deal despite Moses's failure to execute according to the script. As for the people, there is no indication that anyone was bothered by the way it was done although this impression may be subject to revision. The subsequent dismissal of Moses does not come about by popular demand, but is entirely of God's making. "But the Lord said to Moses and Aaron, 'Because you did not trust in me, to show my holiness [character] before the eyes of the Israelites, therefore you shall not bring this assembly into the land that I have given them'" (20:12). For this one act, Moses's ministry is terminated by divine decree.

Why? Why the big deal? Philip J. Budd explains that Moses and Aaron "prevented the full power and might of Yahweh from becoming evident to the people, and . . . thus robbed him of the fear and reverence due to him."[31] Pinchas Kahn is more specific, suggesting that Moses's self-referential outburst was a case of idolatry in the making, aborted only by the urgent demotion.[32] This view seems to makes Moses's slip-up worse than it actually was, but the demotion is certainly a fact. William Propp stays at the level of description when he writes that "the sin of Moses is striking the crag with Aaron's rod and addressing the people instead of displaying the rod and commanding the rock to produce water."[33] Few readers will disagree, but many will want to go beyond mere description.

Martin Emmrich captures the paradigm shift that is building in the story—the pointed *non*-use of the staff, indicating that the future belongs to more delicate leadership.

> Yahweh's instructions . . . could be rendered in the following way: "Take the rod (. . . the one you have used countless times before . . .)—but do not use it!" The sign featured a decisive break with respect to the involvement of the "rod of God." It was no longer to be employed in miraculous performances, since

29. Ibid.

30. Wong, "And Moses raised his hand," 397–400.

31. Budd, *Numbers*, 218.

32. Kahn, "Moses at the Waters of Meribah," 89.

33. Propp, "The Rod of Aaron and the Sin of Moses," 26.

> its symbolic significance was temporally limited to the period of the exodus and the wilderness journeys. Now this era was nearing its end, and God was about to open a new chapter in the history of Israel's redemption.[34]

God had made an issue of the manner in which Moses was to proceed, stating that "*in this way* you will bring water out of the rock for the people, for them and their animals to drink" (Num 20:8, GNB). Which would be more impressive, speaking or striking? Which would more effectively subdue the crowd? Which action would drive home most forcefully that God can be trusted? Which, too, would be more reflective of the kind of person God is, speaking to the rock or striking it?[35]

In the dismissal note that God gives to Moses, the accent is less on his disobedience than on the missed opportunity. Moses, God seems to be saying, failed in his *representative* role. He was meant to be a revealer of God's ways, a window through which a transcendent reality could be seen. Moses fails in this role just when conditions seemed ripe for a spectacular moment of clarity. His privileged position—the rare opportunity to put the correct picture before the people—makes the failure more consequential. "Because you did not trust in me, to show my holiness before the eyes of the Israelites, therefore you shall not bring this assembly into the land that I have given them," God tells Moses in the note of sudden dismissal after the incident (Num 20:12). The key word is trust: "you did not *trust* me"—*lo' he'emantem bi*—the indictment against Moses, is also the problem of the people he was appointed to lead. "And how long will they not trust me"—*'ad 'ānāh lo' ya'ᵉminu bi*—the same words in the form of a question, is the problem that needs to be remedied (Num 14:11). How can this problem be fixed when Moses, too, has shown himself to be a person who fails to trust at the critical moment? On a deeper level still, how can *God* be seen as trustworthy, realizing that Moses's lack of trust is indirectly an indictment of God's trustworthiness? Thomas W. Mann takes the correct measure of the calamity when he refers to "the seriousness of Moses' transgression," this view clearly expressed in the retrospective perspective in Deuteronomy (Deut 32:49–51). Mann hears a voice suggesting

> a surprisingly unsympathetic, even hostile attitude toward the figure of Moses, who here seems to incorporate the most negative traits of a recalcitrant people. The resulting opprobrium for one such as Moses is appalling, indicating the boldness of the author and the seriousness of the issue.[36]

What do we make of this? For the present purpose, the notion of a "hostile attitude toward the figure of Moses" is unnecessary, especially if it implies that Moses

34. Emmrich, "The Case against Moses Reopened," 61.

35. Mann ("Theological Reflections," 483) acknowledges ambiguity in the story but finds Moses's transgression to be that he struck the rock instead of speaking to it, "perhaps coupled with his denunciation of the people as 'rebels.'"

36. Mann, "Theological Reflections," 484.

was incapable of the kind of self-criticism that Mann has outsourced to an alleged critical voice that comes much later. Instead, the focus should be on "the seriousness of the issue." To help readers along in this regard, Diana Lipton offers two additional insights. First, she notes Moses's evident rage in the incident, particularly his use of the word "rebels" (Num 20:10), most likely shouted at full decibel. "By this hurled insult, his suggestion that he and Aaron will provide water for the people, and his impatient striking of the rock, Moses implies that he no longer numbers himself among them," she says.[37] This means failure at the level of *representation* because Moses is no longer *with* them, that is, he fails as a representative of the God whose chief attribute is that God is *with* someone.[38] But the distance now said to exist between Moses and the people, expressed verbally and in telling body language, is actually an illusion. Moses may not number himself among the people, but now he is what they are: a rebel. God says as much in Numbers: "you rebelled against my command" (Num 20:24; 27:14).

Second, Lipton builds a case that makes God's verdict and reaction fit the gravity of Moses's failure, no more but also no less. By the specifics in the text,

> we can see not only that he [Moses] is no longer in tune with the people, as evidenced by his insult and impatience, but also that he is no longer in tune with God. His arrogant exclusion of God when promising to bring forth water, and his violent assault on the rock he had been ordered to address, are unmistakable signs that Moses' days as a leader and, more particularly, as an intermediary, are numbered.[39]

Moses's dismissal is by this criterion not excessively severe; it is no more than what we should expect. In fact, it might even be a reaction that the people would understand. In the big picture of things, an opportunity of this kind might not happen again any time soon. This realization could be included in the lament that "never since has there arisen a prophet in Israel like Moses, whom the Lord knew face to face" (Deut 34:10). Conversely, the termination of Moses that at first sight seems excessive will in that case be a remedy for the damage done. Moses fails as a revealer, but his dismissal alerts people to the fact, his dismissal now a reason for reflection as much as a successful representation would have been.

The paradigm shift in the story, *speaking* to the rock instead of *striking* it, is in these texts focused sharply on representing God correctly. Within this line of reasoning, the aim of God's instruction to Moses must lie on the level of revelation and not on the level of results. Perhaps a better representation would have given better results, but that should not be the main concern. Moses failed to act in the theological idiom God intended.

37. Lipton, "Inevitability and Community," 87.

38. Jacob, *Theology of the Old Testament*, 52.

39. Lipton, "Inevitability and Community," 88.

Moses Pleading

Moses's struggle to come to terms with the consequences of failure represents a neglected biographical and theological treasure in the Old Testament. In Deuteronomy, his inner struggle is brought to view to a degree that is not found anywhere else. Why, feeling the sting, must he be kept from seeing the project through to completion? Will not God retract the dismissal if asked—and if made to understand how terrible Moses feels? "O Lord God," Moses is said to have prayed, "you have only begun to show your servant your greatness and your might; what god in heaven or on earth can perform deeds and mighty acts like yours! Let me cross over to see the good land beyond the Jordan, that good hill country and the Lebanon" (Deut 3:24–25).

This plea gets him nowhere. "But the Lord was angry with me on your account and would not heed me. The Lord said to me, 'Enough from you! Never speak to me of this matter again! Go up to the top of Pisgah and look around you to the west, to the north, to the south, and to the east. Look well, for you shall not cross over this Jordan'" (Deut 3:26–27). For a God known for giving second chances, there will be no second chance for Moses. Tone of voice is missing from the dialogue, but it can be inferred. We can be certain that this is an emotional and existentially vexing topic for Moses. The form of the verb for his request suggests not only that Moses pleads but that he pleads *again and again*, increasing the intensity as the time nears (Deut 3:23).[40] And what is God's tone of voice? The texts says that God was "extremely cross" with Moses. This needs a caveat. Rather, we see Moses bringing up the subject over and over until God, finally, tells him to cease and desist in a tone that leaves no doubt that the matter is closed. We are not inferring too much if we believe the subject to be a sensitive one for God, as well, perhaps wishing to grant Moses's request and yet knowing that his legacy will be better served by standing firm. Aaron, God tells Moses, "shall not enter the land that I have given to the Israelites, *because you rebelled against my command* at the waters of Meribah" (Num 20:24). Moses will have the same consequence but with the consolation prize that he will see the land from a distance.

> The Lord said to Moses, "Go up this mountain of the Abarim range, and see the land that I have given to the Israelites. When you have seen it, you also shall be gathered to your people, as your brother Aaron was, *because you rebelled against my word* in the wilderness of Zin when the congregation quarreled with me. You did not show my holiness before their eyes at the waters" (Num 27:12–14).

And, once more, as though unable to stop talking about it, Moses says to the Israelites, "The Lord was angry with me because of you, and he vowed that I should not cross the Jordan and that I should not enter the good land that the Lord your God is giving for your possession" (Deut 4:21). Lest we believe that Moses by now has

40. Christensen (*Deuteronomy 1:1—21:9*, 68) emphasizes the solemnity of Moses's request rather than its repetitiveness.

reached an age at which retirement will be easy to accept, Deuteronomy reports that he has the vitality to continue on. The narrator says that when Moses was buried at an anonymous place at the age of one hundred and twenty years, "his sight was unimpaired and his vigor had not abated" (Deut 34:6–7). Neither illness nor old age can be invoked in the case of Moses's death. For him, death coincides with the demotion.

The Song of Moses

There would be fewer reasons to keep circling this part of Moses's story if not for the fact that it caps the Moses narrative in the Old Testament and then, surprisingly, pivots into the New Testament so as to become part of the capstone there, too. In Deuteronomy, at the point when Moses is depicted handing over the reins of leadership to Joshua, he is commissioned to write a song!

> Now therefore write this song, and teach it to the Israelites; put it in their mouths, in order that this song may be a witness for me against the Israelites. For when I have brought them into the land flowing with milk and honey, which I promised on oath to their ancestors, and they have eaten their fill and grown fat, they will turn to other gods and serve them, despising me and breaking my covenant. And when many terrible troubles come upon them, this song will confront them as a witness, because it will not be lost from the mouths of their descendants. For I know what they are inclined to do even now, before I have brought them into the land that I promised them on oath (Deut 31:19–21).

There is nothing particularly cheerful about this commission, predicated as it is on an adversarial relationship between the Israelites and God. But the pedagogical strategy is impressive. God counts on poetry and song to be a resilient form of communication, a teaching residue that will not be lost, and a presence in times of absence.

"That very day Moses wrote this song and taught it to the Israelites," says Deuteronomy (Deut 31:22). The delivery is speedy, Moses said to be writing the text, composing the music, and arranging choir practice all in the span of one day. As for the quality of the composition, it was good enough to furnish words for the song that the Book of Revelation says will be sung at the very end of the human story.

> And I saw what appeared to be a sea of glass mixed with fire, and those who had conquered the beast and its image and the number of its name, standing beside the sea of glass with harps of God in their hands. And they sing the song of Moses, the servant of God, and the song of the Lamb:
>
> Great and amazing are your deeds,
> Lord God the Almighty!
> Just and true are your ways,
> King of the nations!

Lord, who will not fear and glorify your name?
For you alone are holy.
All nations will come and worship before you,
for your judgments have been revealed.

Rev 15:2–4

As my footnote shows,[41] the song in Revelation is stitched together from a number of Old Testament passages, but the most important element is taken from the Song of Moses in Deuteronomy (Deut 32:4). In fact, the entire hymn is so suffused with Moses that it bears his name, billed as the joint composition of Moses and Jesus![42] Revelation's version is more cheerful than the song in Deuteronomy, joyful through and through, but the Mosaic contribution is liberally acknowledged. In Revelation, the foreboding prospect in Deuteronomy gives way to a relieved and triumphant retrospect, but the convergence is striking. Both versions of the song imply that God's ways have been contrary to expectations, and yet the songs defend the thesis that God's ways will inspire reverence and gratitude once it is understood. Crucially, the bottom line of Moses's story and song is *sense* and understanding, and the conjunction linking Moses and Jesus is explanatory: 'the song of Moses, that is to say, the song of the Lamb.'[43] We must take this to mean that the composition arises from the same ideological point of view, and that the phrases have the figurative sense of "legacy."

This may come as a surprise to many who are accustomed to see Moses as a counterpoint to Jesus and not one who strikes the same note. Moses's contribution to the hymn in Revelation is found in the words,

The Rock, his work is perfect,
and all his ways are just.
A faithful God, without deceit,
just and upright is he (Deut 32:4).

While the hymns celebrate God's *victory*, they are best seen as praise for God's *ways*. Indeed, their preoccupation with God's ways makes the link between Moses and Jesus the most enticing feature in these texts. Remember from where we have come in the story of Moses. He struck the rock instead of speaking to it, in the process assuming an angry and threatening posture. The subsequent dismissal happened because he failed to give the correct representation of God. The New Testament knows of no such failure in the life of Jesus. This should preclude joint authorship, as it were, making it impossible to place Moses at the same level as Jesus. But the claim that the two sing

41. Pss 22:3 (21:4, LXX); 86:9 (85:9, LXX); 111:2 (110:2, LXX); 139:14 (138:14, LXX); Amos 4:13; Deut 32:4; Jer 10:7; see also Tonstad, *Saving God's Reputation*, 149–54.

42. Aune, *Revelation 6–16*, 872–73; Beale, *Revelation*, 793.

43. Ibid., 792.

from the same ideological sheet is resolved if "the song of Moses" is personalized to reflect Moses's experience of God's ways in connection with his dismissal. Speaking to the rock would have been better than striking it; speaking would have brought a preview of God revealed in weakness (2 Cor 13:4; Rev 5:6); it would have been an early audition of "the song of the Lamb" years before Jesus came to sing it without the need for the corrective action that followed in the aftermath of Moses's striking the wrong note. To be credited with joint authorship with Jesus for the last song in the Bible, therefore, is no small vindication for Moses. Either Moses had it in him to give the correct representation of God, suggested by the fact that God gave him instruction that it was in Moses's power to carry out, or Moses took the dismissal to heart, offering proof of that in his song. In the end he accepted the dismissal, declaring God's work to be perfect and all God's ways to be just, including his demotion (Deut 32:4). In this scenario, it is not surprising to find the subject of Moses's dismissal loom large in the story, with Moses leaving office on the very day his song was composed and premiered.

> *On that very day* the LORD addressed Moses as follows: "Ascend this mountain of the Abarim, Mount Nebo, which is in the land of Moab, across from Jericho, and view the land of Canaan, which I am giving to the Israelites for a possession; you shall die there on the mountain that you ascend and shall be gathered to your kin, as your brother Aaron died on Mount Hor and was gathered to his kin; because both of you broke faith with me among the Israelites at the waters of Meribath-kadesh in the wilderness of Zin, by failing to maintain my holiness among the Israelites. Although you may view the land from a distance, you shall not enter it" (Deut 32:48–52).

This is how Moses's story ends in the Old Testament. The New Testament, however, gives him an encore that has as much to do with his defeat as with his faithfulness. Moses stands to the first books of the Bible as Copernicus to our understanding of the solar system or Einstein to physics. Perhaps, too, he is like them a great proponent of *understanding*. Deuteronomy can pay him no greater tribute than to anchor the sense that is yet to come to the standard set by Moses. "I will raise up for them a prophet like you from among their own people; I will put my words in the mouth of the prophet, who shall speak to them everything that I command" (Deut 18:18; cf. John 1:45).

Chapter Eleven

Sense Dismembered: The Rape of the Concubine in Judges

What good will it do to read the story of the gang-rape of the concubine in the Book of Judges? Judging from the evident lack of interest in the story, the answer must be, not much. In her story, the problem of God's apparent absence reaches heaven-rending intensity. Perhaps this is the reason why preachers and expositors rarely go there. Phyllis Trible says in her retelling that "[t]he betrayal, rape, torture, murder, and dismemberment of an unnamed woman is a story we want to forget but are commanded to speak."[1] For many, however, this is not a story we want to forget or a story that we have forgotten but a story we have never heard. Now we will respond to its summons. By any standard, it is "one of the ugliest stories in the Bible,"[2] truly a text of terror, or, somewhat understated, not a "cheerful story."[3]

"In those days when there was no king in Israel, a certain Levite, residing in the remote parts of the hill country of Ephraim, took to himself a concubine from Bethlehem in Judah," says the narrator in Judges (Judg 19:1). In temporal terms "those days" are the time before the monarchy, referring to events before 1000 BCE,[4] but the author is more interested in the characteristics of the age than in a date on the calendar. A few pages earlier, the narrator has told the story of a mercenary priest who set out *from* Bethlehem *to* the hill country of Ephraim (Judg 17:7—18:27). The journey of *this* Levite is reversed. It is not implausible that the two stories are linked. The second Levite could be a descendant of the former Levite or a person of the same kind. If the fact that the man belongs to the priestly vocation leads to raised expectations of his character, the earlier story of the Levite has warned readers not to set our hopes too high (17:7—18:27). At the risk of creating prejudice on the part of the reader, Pamela Tamarkin Reis suggests as much.

1. Trible, *Texts of Terror*, 65.

2. Reis, "The Levite's Concubine," 125.

3. Eynikel, "Judges 19–21," 101.

4. Judges says that "Phinehas son of Eleazar, son of Aaron" was the priest at the tabernacle in Bethel (20:26–28), locating the story in the early years after the exodus from Egypt.

> We immediately distrust . . . a Levite sojourning in Ephraim. Why is he not living in one of the cities allotted to Levites? How does he support himself away from his appropriate milieu? Is he perhaps another such scoundrel as the anonymous itinerant Levite sojourning in Ephraim in the preceding chapter (18:20) whose "heart is glad" to play the priest, for a price, before graven and molten images?[5]

Bethlehem was a little village in those days. In some ways it is little more than a village today, tightly squeezed by the tall separation barrier that now cuts conspicuously across a troubled land. From the hilltops of Bethlehem, directly to the north, one can easily see Jerusalem on a clear day. She probably could, too. If she did, the town in the distance was from her point of view hostile territory, a town she would never visit, just as it is for many inhabitants of Bethlehem today.

But our narrator is more interested in ideology than in chronology, and more concerned about behavior than geography. On more than one occasion we are told that "in those days there was no king in Israel" and that "all the people did what was right in their own eyes" (17:6; cf. also 18:1; 19:1; 21:25). In this way the narrator suggests that before the monarchy there was anarchy. With no system of law enforcement and no central authority, people literally got away with murder. The storyteller appears to operate under the conviction that monarchy will be better, a conviction that is not convincingly demonstrated by subsequent events in Israel.

Nothing is known of the concubine's early years except what we can infer from other sources of rural life in the ancient world. In all likelihood she was one of many children at a time when most men had more than one wife, and when sons had more going for them than daughters. When the time comes to marry, her future is cemented into the pattern established by tradition. The woman's lack of say in the matter is conspicuous in the language that is used. The Levite "*took to himself* a concubine from Bethlehem in Judah" (19:1). There is no mutuality in the relationship, no sweet exchange of vows, only acquiescence on her part.

The match is also a mismatch. As Trible points out, a Levite "has an honored place in society that sets him above many other males; a concubine has an inferior status that places her beneath other females."[6] This creates a power gap in the relationship. "He is subject. She is object. He controls her. How he acquired her we do not know; that he owns her is certain," says Trible.[7]

The unknowns in the story extend to her marriage. Her husband-to-be has a wife already, perhaps several, making her lot that of an associate wife, an inferior role with less security and recognition. In those days such an arrangement was perfectly legal, as it still is in Moslem countries and tribal cultures in Africa. Her contribution to the household is that of a worker and less that of lover. Childbearing and hard labor are

5. Reis, "The Levite's Concubine," 127.

6. Trible, *Texts of Terror*, 66.

7. Ibid.

likely to be the main ingredients in the life that awaits her. Again, the sparse wording of her story proves that our source has other priorities than to discuss matters of background. The moving van interests the author more than the wedding. Before we have a chance to absorb the situation, she is off to live with her new partner "in the remote parts of the hill country of Ephraim" (19:1). The remoteness of her new home suggests isolation, a person cut off from the outside world, perhaps a suggestion of abandonment. *She is now on her own, and there is nobody there for her.*

The Sense of the Text

Although we have barely started the story, and although we do not know how long she stays in the hill country of Ephraim, the narrator moves to fast forward. Having said only the barest minimum about the beginning of the concubine's married life, the narrator skips to the point where trouble arises. This creates problems of a different kind for the reader because Bibles offer very different accounts of what goes wrong in the relationship. As shown below, we are given two main alternatives in the leading English translations.

Alternative I:

> *But his concubine played the harlot against him*, and went away from him to her father's house at Bethlehem in Judah, and was there four whole months (Judges 19:2, NKJV; cf. KJV, NASB).
>
> *But she was unfaithful to him*. She left him and went back to her father's house in Bethlehem, Judah (NIV)

Alternative II:

> *But his concubine became angry with him*, and she went away from him to her father's house at Bethlehem in Judah, and was there some four months (NRSV; cf. RSV).
>
> *In a fit of anger his concubine left him* and went back to her father's house at Bethlehem in Judah, and she stayed there for some time—four months (NJB)
>
> *In a fit of anger she had left him* and had gone to her father's house in Bethlehem (NEB).

Needless to say, these are very different options. In the first alternative, the concubine is sexually unfaithful, suggesting that the trouble in the relationship is her fault. In the second alternative, she becomes angry with him, indicating that the trouble in the relationship is his fault. The Douay-Rheims American Edition (1899) offers a third alternative, seeking to bypass the difficulty by omitting the reason for her decision to return home.

> *And she left him*, and returned to her father's house in Bethlehem, and abode with him four months (19:2; Douay-Rheims American Edition).

This omission, while simple, is of no help because it is better for the plot to have a reason for the unusual turn of events even if the reason poses a problem. Moreover, this alternative should be dismissed because the best texts on which the English translations are based are not mum as to what caused the concubine to return to Bethlehem.

Translations that portray the concubine as a woman who "played the harlot" against the Levite are based on the Hebrew text. Textual critics and translators are by the best standard of the trade obligated by the Hebrew original and will only reluctantly opt for other solutions. And the Hebrew text, using the word *zānâ*, makes it all but impossible to deny that a sexual boundary is violated in the story. Interpreters who take this route along the line of the translations above commit to a reading that will be problematic for the remainder of the story, as we shall see.

Puritan sermons that are based on this translation come down hard on the woman. She is unfaithful and the one at fault. At heart she is insubordinate and lustful. What happens to her in the rest of the story is the wages of her sin. By contrast, they find in the Levite the spirit of generosity and forgiveness, given that he goes after her to woo her back (19:3). If her father has a flaw, it is that he is excessively lenient when he receives her into his home. Had he been a man of principle and not a man overcome by parental affection, he would have told her at the door, "I can be no father to a harlot."[8]

The Puritan reading, however, runs into grave problems precisely with regard to the consequences of her action. If she had "played the harlot *against* him" (KJV, NKJV, NASB), it is unlikely that she would have been welcome home, and it is even more unlikely that the Levite would have tried to win her back. Such a woman, says Victor H. Matthews, "would be stoned at her father's door or would go to live . . . with her lovers" (cf. Deut 22:13–21; Hos 2:5).[9] Translators who stick with this option do so out of loyalty to the Hebrew text even though the translation sets up a plot that runs into major problems in the rest of the story.

A third and quite creative option, as suggested by J. Cheryl Exum, argues that the narrator is not thinking in terms of actual adultery *prior to* the concubine's decision to return to her father's house.[10] The focus should not be on anything she *did* before the separation but on the social meaning of her decision to leave. The notion of adultery is based on the point of view of the narrator. He—and most interpreters think that the

8. Gunn, *Judges*, 250–54. The quotation is taken from a sermon by Thomas Lye (1621–1684).

9. Matthews, *Judges & Ruth*, 181.

10. Exum, "Whose Interests," 65–89.

narrator must be a male—is appalled at the woman's assertion of autonomy. His choice of words is a reflection of his ideology and not of her conduct. According to this reading, the issue "is male ownership of women's bodies, control over women's sexuality. A woman who asserts her sexual autonomy by leaving her husband—and whether or not she remains with him is a sexual issue—is guilty of sexual misconduct."[11]

This is a creative interpretation that respects the primacy of the Hebrew text. It explains the connotation of sexual misconduct as a feature of context and not of conduct. But this view should not persuade everybody. Even if it were possible to see the concubine as a feminist in the making, having no reason to leave the Levite except to assert her sexual autonomy, the suggested construct fits our time better than hers. The specific features in her story get submerged in the agenda of the interpreter. Although the agenda is commendable, and although Exum is right to emphasize the power gap between the men and the woman in the story, this interpretation makes the concubine a type more than the individual that she is in the story.

The second alternative, stating that the concubine "became angry with him" (RSV, NRSV) is based on the Greek translation of the Hebrew text. While most modern translators prefer the Hebrew text, as noted, there are exceptions, and this is one. It is virtually impossible to bridge the gap between the Hebrew text and the Greek 'translation' by looking at the words alone. Preference for the Greek version is therefore predicated on one major advantage: it makes better sense. In the rest of the story the concubine is the victim and the aggrieved party to a degree that makes sense only if we see her as a victim from the beginning. Some translations exaggerate the assumed grievance in the Greek text almost to the point of negating it. If the concubine left "in a fit of anger" (NJB, NEB), it seems that she left on a whim, as if to say that the problem is anger management on her part and not a real grievance. Marriages may fall apart 'in a fit of anger' in the twenty-first century in Europe and the United States, but it is unlikely that a mere 'fit of anger' on the part of a concubine would be sufficient to make her embark on a dangerous journey in an age destitute of respect for women's rights. If anger on her part truly was the reason, it must have been building over time, and the situation must have become intolerable before it would trigger her unusual and desperate move.

Eric Eynikel seeks additional support for the Greek version of the text. He believes that the Hebrew text originally did say that "the concubine became angry with him" but that subsequent copyists and redactors could not stomach this idea. Specifically, "for the redactor or copyist of the Hebrew text it was unthinkable for a woman who had no right of divorce to leave her husband."[12] For this reason the Hebrew text was changed to say that "the concubine played the harlot against him" even though this is not what the text said originally. According to this hypothesis, the wording in the Greek translation is based on the Hebrew text *before* the latter was changed. The

11. Exum, "Whose Interests?" 83.

12. Eynikel, "Rape, Murder, War and Abduction," 104.

problem with this proposal is that there is no manuscript evidence to support it; it is purely speculative, and it assumes a degree of discretion on the part of copyists that is troubling. As noted, however, the Greek version fits the rest of the story well. If the concubine is the aggrieved party, we understand why the father accepted her when she returned home, and we are not at a loss to believe that the Levite would try to win her back.

We cannot proceed except by registering serious misgivings with respect to each of the options reviewed above. The quest for a better translation is not an item of luxury. If the beginning is unclear, the rest of the story is compromised. The notion that the concubine "played the harlot *against* him" fits so poorly with the rest of the story that the characters become unconvincing and the events unintelligible. The idea that the concubine "became angry with him," while posing no threat to the plot, lacks support in the Hebrew original.

The textual issue that has bedeviled and disheartened interpreters may at last have been solved by Pamela Tamarkin Reis. She proposes a translation that does not disregard the Hebrew text or throw the plot into confusion. The alternate reading centers on the meaning of the preposition that goes along with the idea of promiscuity. She "played the harlot," the Hebrew text says, but it is not necessary to say that she "played the harlot *against* him." Equally possible, and far more plausible, is the reading that turns the preposition *'al* in the opposite direction.[13] The concubine did play the harlot, but she didn't do it *against* him. On the contrary, 'she played the harlot *for* him.' In Reis's translation,

> And his concubine whored *for* him and went from him to the house of her father, to Bethlehem in Judah, and was there the days of four months.[14]

This translation clarifies the plot, and it transforms the story in shocking ways. Sexual boundaries are violated, but she does not initiate it. There is illicit sex involving her, but she is the victim. The Levite, his high and holy calling notwithstanding, made her do it! He "was prostituting his wife."[15] In this scenario, the woman who leaves the hill country of Ephraim, braving danger to return home, is not leaving "in a fit of anger" although the Septuagint gets it right despite itself. She is leaving a violated and disgusted woman, seeking refuge in the only place available to her. The initial suspicion that the Levite in the story is a less than noble character is more than confirmed. We now have an intact text and a persuasive plot, reprehensible though it be.

But the Levite is not ready for divorce, and she has no right to get one. Why he waits four months before initiating the next move is hardly a mystery. If a wait that long before attempting reconciliation wins the approval of common sense, it is not

13. Brown et al., *Hebrew and English Lexicon*, section II and 754–55.; see also Reis, "The Levite's Concubine," 129, n. 15.

14. Ibid., emphasis added.

15. Ibid.

a good omen for her. Eynikel points to a number of examples in the Old Testament where "the number four has bad connotations."[16] The circumstances of the Levite's arrival in Bethlehem add to the sense of unease.

> Then her husband set out after her, to speak tenderly to her and bring her back. He had with him his servant and a couple of donkeys. When he reached her father's house, the girl's father saw him and came with joy to meet him (19:3).

Nothing in the story so far suggests that the Levite is motivated by genuine love. The claim that he set out "to speak to her heart" is insufficient to make a change of heart on his part seem credible (19:3).[17] The fact that *he* has to win *her* back corroborates a plot construct that sees her as the aggrieved party. He has to speak to her heart because he has violated her. Indeed, the Hebrew text does not say that the Levite set out "to return *her*" but that he traveled "to speak to her heart and to return *him*," that is, "to take *him* back."[18]

In point of fact, however, reading the text as it stands, there is no evidence that the Levite speaks to her at all. If love is not his motive, money might be. Reis says that he wants "to recover his meal ticket."[19] A similar but less blunt possibility is that he knows the power of customs and contracts. Custom made it unnecessary to seek her consent for the marriage in the first place, and the force of custom makes it unnecessary to seek her consent with respect to taking him back. The Levite has reason to feel confident that she will come back because she has no choice.

While the father's hearty welcome will offend many readers, it does not break the plot that now seems firmly in place. The father should not be happy to see the man who has made his daughter a prostitute, of course. The most likely explanation is that the concubine did not tell him and that he did not know. In a culture of honor and shame certain topics are off limits. Even in our time, the victim of rape or sexual molestation feels shame that makes him or her keep the violation a secret. The shame factor was much greater in the ancient world, and in some cultures the silencing power of shame persists unabated. Another possibility is that even if the father knew, custom dictates that he and his daughter will not make it a topic of conversation. Together, they will keep up appearances and say nothing to each other or to anyone else. In terms of status, the Levite has the upper hand.[20] If he has made his concubine

16. Eynikel, "Rape, Murder, War and Abduction," 105.

17. Trible (*Texts of Terror*, 67), starting with ambiguity as to why the concubine left, is willing to give the Levite the benefit of the doubt, seeing him capable of communicating "reassurance, comfort, loyalty, and love." It will be difficult to maintain this view if he had indeed prostituted his concubine.

18. Reis, "The Levite's Concubine," 128.

19. Ibid., 129.

20. Jones-Warsaw ("Toward a Womanist Hermeneutic," 20) points out that the Levitical priesthood was highly regarded and that the Levite quite likely was a man of some wealth.

do something that seems unimaginable, it is off limits to bring it up. Again, and in a big way, the story registers a win for keeping up appearances.

Sense of Doom

It is thus not strange that the father appears to take the side of the Levite rather than making his daughter's feelings his main concern. Perhaps he, too, has vested interests, fearful that he might have to return the bride-price. Perhaps he is merely realistic on her behalf. Fences are mended quickly. The negotiations, if any were held, give no role to her. Her return to the Levite is a foregone conclusion. Compounding the sense of doom that is building in the story, the issue now is not whether she will have to return with the Levite but that the return is delayed.

> His father-in-law, the girl's father, made him stay, and he remained with him three days; so they ate and drank, and he stayed there. On the fourth day they got up early in the morning, and he prepared to go; but the girl's father said to his son-in-law, "Fortify yourself with a bit of food, and after that you may go." So the two men sat and ate and drank together; and the girl's father said to the man, "Why not spend the night and enjoy yourself?" When the man got up to go, his father-in-law kept urging him until he spent the night there again. On the fifth day he got up early in the morning to leave; and the girl's father said, "Fortify yourself." So they lingered until the day declined, and the two of them ate and drank (19:4–8).

This passage foreshadows trouble. The couple's departure is plagued by delays. The delays loom like storm clouds on the horizon. Three days pass, clearly more than the Levite intended to spend. The tranquility is deceiving in view of the troubled relationship that led to the visit. The Levite has come to reclaim his spouse, not to enjoy an extended vacation. His eagerness to hit the road early in the day is a sign that he knows the dangers of travel. Further delay might unsettle conditions back home. He is likely to have commitments as to the time of his anticipated return and has already exceeded the limit. The timing of the couple's departure grows into a matter of critical concern, a tug-of-war between the father and the Levite. Even though the story is told in a low-key, matter-of-fact manner, the intensity has heightened considerably. Behind the forced socializing the ghost of danger is lurking. Four days of partying go by, and the number four, as noted earlier, is a bad omen. The Levite and her father appear to be dining on the deck of the Titanic while their ship is speeding toward disaster. The delay creates the premonition of an impending calamity.

Aside from the delay itself, two specific elements in the account must be highlighted. As for the first three days, the narrator says that "they ate and drank, and he stayed there" (19:4). Come day four, the Levite intends to leave, but the father of the woman has other plans. "So the two men sat and ate and drank together," and the departure is again delayed (19:6). Even on the fifth day, when departure seems certain, "they lingered until the day declined," and, to come to the point, "the two of them ate and drank" (19:8). The Levite and the woman's father are eating and drinking in a conspicuous fashion, continuing this pattern well into the fifth day. This is no ordinary eating and drinking but rather a description of irresponsible revelry. As Reis points out, "[e]ach of the four occurrences displaying these two linguistic elements [eating and drinking] bears a suggestion of alcoholic excess."[21]

By now the concubine is fully marginalized, at the mercy of the two men in her life, neither of whom pays attention to her. Her implied vulnerability is further emphasized by a second specific feature in the text. The narrator is not content to refer to the father as "the father" only; the phrase is consistently "father of the woman," occurring a full six times within a mere seven verses (19:3–9). This, says Reis, "refers to the father of a woman, who, because she is married, is no longer under his protection and who, furthermore, is vulnerable in a sexual matter."[22] If this is correct, it means that the father has relinquished responsibility for his daughter's well-being to the Levite. The Levite is already on record as to how he interprets this responsibility.

True as it is that "states of mind are rarely communicated in Scripture,"[23] the story is capable of inducing states of mind in the reader. By now the sensitized reader is expected to feel in his and her bones that a journey that begins late in the day is courting disaster. Even on the fifth day, swayed by the manipulating guile of the concubine's father, the Levite "tarries until after the siesta," leaving only "at a peculiar moment in the afternoon, so that he will not be able to reach his home in a one-day march."[24] The day is waning. Night is approaching, and the notion of 'night as danger' can hardly be overstated.[25]

> For the ancient reader the evening/night setting would almost certainly have imbued each narrative from the outset with an aura of foreboding and sinister premonition, of trepidation and anxiety, for night and violence, danger and darkness were inseparably joined. Evening was the time to make for the safety of the private home, where at least some light from a fire or oil lamp or candle was available. Night was the time to remain within the bounds of this safe haven.[26]

By now, too, it is evident that by leaving late in the day the travelers will head straight into the night, as it were. For this reason the meal on the fifth day cannot be a happy occasion. Every word between the Levite and the concubine's father now seems

21. Reis, "The Levite's Concubine," 134.
22. Ibid., 132.
23. Ibid., 131.
24. Fokkelman, "Structural Remarks on Judges 9 and 19," 41.
25. Fields, "The Motif 'Night as Danger,'" 17–32.
26. Ibid., 22.

irresponsible; every second on the clock that ticks away unbearable; every bite of the meal a concession to mortal danger. Under the pretext of hospitality the concubine's father is the chief cause of the delay, and the daughter is caught in the verbal tussle between an insensitive father and an irresolute spouse.

When, at long last, the Levite gets up to leave, the father seeks another delay. "Look," he says, "the day has worn on until it is almost evening. Spend the night. See, the day has drawn to a close. Spend the night here and enjoy yourself. Tomorrow you can get up early in the morning for your journey, and go home" (19:9). On this point the father is right, of course. It is far too late to leave, but it is also far too late for sober-minded reasoning. Even though there is no possibility that they can complete the trip in what remains of the day, the Levite is determined to get on his way. The late departure, says Fields, transforms the journey "into a virtual race against the sun."[27] As for the concubine,

> she is too sunk in desolation and despair to speak. Her father's joyful welcome of the man who demeaned her, and his unpaternal relinquishment of her, dispatch her to misery and justify the biblical author's abhorrence. Now the concubine has nowhere to run. Her father will not safeguard her; he will just return her to her husband, and in this lawless land, a woman under no man's protection would be every man's prey.[28]

Thus the return trip from Bethlehem to the hill country of Ephraim begins under the least favorable circumstances and with the worst possible prospect for success. The Levite, possibly inebriated, "would not spend the night; he got up and departed, and arrived opposite Jebus (that is, Jerusalem). He had with him a couple of saddled donkeys, and his concubine was with him" (19:11). At last they are off, trying to make up for the lost hours and the lack of resolve by hurrying.

They travel through what to us has become familiar country, from Bethlehem to Jerusalem. It is not far. I have personally run the distance on paved roads in less than forty-five minutes. On rugged trails the ancient travelers could cover the distance on foot in less than two hours.[29] For the travelers in Judges, however, the land has yet to be subdued by civilization. It is anything but a unified country. Nightfall is approaching in threatening, hostile surroundings. The voice of reason is speaking when the servant says, "Why don't we stop and spend the night here in this Jebusite city?'" (19:11, GNB)

The servant's reluctance to continue should not be understood only in terms of the lateness of the hour. They depart shortly after noon from Bethlehem. The trip to Jerusalem takes no more than three hours, probably less, because of the hurry created by the late departure. The journey from Jerusalem to Gibeah, the next village, crossing more craggy terrain, might take another two hours. It might be possible to cover the

27. Ibid., 25.

28. Reis, "The Levite's Concubine," 136.

29. Fokkelman, "Structural Remarks on Judges 9 and 19," 41.

distance to Gibeah before dark. For this reason the servant may have thought more about finding the best haven for the night than about time running out.

But the Levite will not listen. The inhabitants of Jerusalem are not Israelites. He shuns contact with them even though his own situation has placed him in a state of need. Unwilling to heed the prudent suggestion, the master says, "We will not turn aside into a city of foreigners, who do not belong to the people of Israel; but we will continue on to Gibeah. Come, let us try to reach one of these places, and spend the night at Gibeah or at Ramah" (19:12–13). Despite the lateness of the hour he decides to press on, expecting a more congenial reception from his own people. This turns out to be "an attractive prejudice that will be put to shame," says Jan P. Fokkelman.[30]

> So they passed on and went their way; and the sun went down on them near Gibeah, which belongs to Benjamin. They turned aside there, to go in and spend the night at Gibeah. He went in and sat down in the open square of the city, but no one took them in to spend the night (19:14–15).

By now the disastrous nature of their mission rises into full view. When the travelers pull into the town square, they are expecting someone to take notice, but the anticipated response is not forthcoming. This treatment is out of character with their expectation and with standards of hospitality in the Middle East. As a student, I once visited a small village in Syria together with a group of fellow students. Our arrival, by coincidence at nightfall, was totally unexpected on the part of the villagers. Nevertheless, they gave us a reception worthy of people whose arrival had been anticipated for weeks. A whole house was vacated and graciously offered to guests whom the villagers had never seen. By contrast, the village in our story has lost its native hospitality. Loss of hospitality is a warning of trouble to come.[31] For strangers, at least, Gibeah is a dangerous place. As suggested earlier, it is not implausible that the servant's preference for overnighting with the foreigners in Jerusalem had to do with his knowledge of the people in the respective towns. If the question, "Where will we spend the night?" has been on the travelers' minds so far, it now hits home mercilessly. At this point they have run out of options and have nowhere to go.

> Then at evening there was an old man coming from his work in the field. The man was from the hill country of Ephraim, and he was residing in Gibeah. (The people of the place were Benjaminites.) When the old man looked up and saw the wayfarer in the open square of the city, he said, "Where are you going and where do you come from?" He answered him, "We are passing from Bethlehem in Judah to the remote parts of the hill country of Ephraim, from which I come. I went to Bethlehem in Judah; and I am going to my home. Nobody has offered to take me in. We your servants have straw and fodder for

30. Ibid., 42.

31. Matthews, "Hospitality and Hostility," 3–11.

> our donkeys, with bread and wine for me and the woman and the young man along with us. We need nothing more" (19:16–19).

It is not unimportant that the person who at last invites the travelers to his house is himself a resident alien. Even though he is an Israelite, he is vulnerable because he does not belong to the local tribe. When he, the alien, extends the hand of hospitality to the Levite, he puts himself at risk because the sojourner should not bypass the wishes of the resident villagers. However, the villagers' inhospitality must be kept in the foreground rather than breaches of the hospitality ritual on the part of the Levite or his host.[32] It is to make up for this problem that the old man says, "Peace be to you. I will care for all your wants; only do not spend the night in the square" (19:20). This is the signal to the travelers to lower their shoulders. Despite the botched planning, things seem to be working out for them. "So he brought him into his house, and fed the donkeys; they washed their feet, and ate and drank" (19:21).

But the trouble is far from over. In fact, it is only now trouble begins in earnest.

> While they were enjoying themselves, the men of the city, a perverse lot, surrounded the house, and started pounding on the door. They said to the old man, the master of the house, "Bring out the man who came into your house, so that we may have intercourse with him" (19:22).

Nothing happens in a Middle Eastern village that is not instantly known throughout the community. Moreover, nothing like the things that happen in this story can take place unless there is a tacit sentiment of approval in the community. The villagers who did not lift a finger to provide shelter for the travelers are more than willing to come out in force to deal with the one who has offered shelter *and* with his visitors. Striving to capture who they are, translators tend away from the literal "sons of Belial" of the *King James Version*, preferring a more descriptive approach: "certain worthless fellows" (NASB), "some of the wicked men" (NIV), "scoundrels" (NJB), "perverted men" (NKJV), or "base fellows" (RSV). In the LXX they are "sons of lawlessness." While the notion of demonic evil may not be intended, the narrator strives to capture a category of evil that is out of the ordinary. These people are not the village thugs but are representative for the village. When the time of reckoning comes, the Levite will claim that "*the lords of Gibeah* rose up against me" (20:5), meaning that leading citizens of the village were involved. Although the Levite may not be the most reliable witness, the whole tribe of Benjamin is later willing to stand in defense of the perpetrators (20:13). The villagers are proposing to commit homosexual rape of the visiting Levite, expecting the host to acquiesce. Small talk aside, the text says that the villagers started beating down the door, and that the knocking grew louder and louder.

32. Matthews (*Judges & Ruth*, 184) argues convincingly that the Levite breaches the hospitality ritual on many points, failing to acknowledge his dependence on the host and, in this situation, the risk to the host.

Sense Dismembered

All of a sudden the safety of the house seems illusory, crumbling under the onslaught of the mob. The notion of *night as danger* has returned in force. While the host can bolt the door, he knows that it will be to no avail against the assailants. Talk is unlikely to dissuade them, but he wants to give it a try. "And the man, the master of the house, went out to them and said to them, 'No, my brothers, do not act so wickedly. Since this man is my guest, do not do this vile thing'" (19:23). The impact of this plea is nil. His method of last resort is a tactic of appeasement. "Here are my virgin daughter and his concubine; let me bring them out now. Ravish them and do whatever you want to them; but against this man do not do such a vile thing" (19:23–24).

The old man's hierarchy of values is clear: he wants to protect his male guest as the first order of business more than protecting the concubine and more even than defending his own daughter. By his standard sacrificing a virgin daughter or the female companion of his guest is the lesser evil. To let the male guest bear the brunt of their attack is unthinkable.

But the man from Ephraim is speaking to deaf ears. The norms of hospitality are suspended, and the appeal to restraint finds no resonance; "the men would not listen to him" (19:25). At this point the Levite springs into action, knowing what it will take to calm the mob and get himself off the hook.

> So the Levite took hold of his concubine and brought her out to them (19:25, NJB).
>
> the man seized his concubine, and put her out to them (19:25, NRSV).

The point of this comparison is to offer more than one version of the action at the point when the concubine's fate is sealed. She will go to other men again, and again she will go against her will. Whether we read that the Levite "took hold of his concubine" or that he seized his concubine," no reader should miss the point. She must be cowering in the corner, having heard the host's proposal to turn her and his virgin daughter over to the villagers, along with his offer on their behalf: "Ravish them and do whatever you want to them" (19:24). She is ready for the worst. And the worst comes at the hands of the Levite, the man who allegedly came to Bethlehem "to speak to her heart" and make her take him back (19:3). Now he seizes her, and she, being the weaker, is no match for him. The text shows him taking her by force, overcoming her active resistance, and putting her out into the night. This Levite is no loving protector, determined to defend his beloved at any cost. From the ashes of what now seems to be a brutal, unfeeling husband, she is thrown into the fire of an inflamed crowd of men.

And it was night.

The text in Judges does not quite say that. It drapes the veil of darkness over a scene of terrible abuse that would be worthy of a Mel Gibson movie.

> And they knew her and abused her all night until morning; and when the day began to break, they let her go (19:25, NKJV).
>
> They had intercourse with her and ill-treated her all night till morning; when dawn was breaking they let her go (19:25, NJB).
>
> They wantonly raped her, and abused her all through the night until the morning. And as the dawn began to break, they let her go (19:25, NRSV).

"They *knew* her," the wording of the NKJV, is literally correct, employing the most endearing term for sexual intimacy in the Old Testament. But the context transforms the word, and there is nothing endearing about this form of intimacy. The idea that "they wantonly raped her" (NRSV) is more to the point. They do not leave it at that. The abuse depicted in the second half of the sentence is repetitive, using a form of the Hebrew verb that suggests a back-and-forth motion, an act happening again and again. The abuse is not over in seconds but continues for minutes and hours. The whole night the villagers of Gibeah come at her, one after the other. We can imagine her resisting, but her resistance only confirms their power over her. She pleads for mercy merely to discover that her pleading makes them more cruel. We should imagine her screaming in pain, but no one cares. If the experts are correct that rape is a crime of aggression rather than of sexuality,[33] her pain simply reinforces the aggressors' sense of superiority. At last she surrenders in resigned compliance, hoping to bring an end to the ordeal. It is no longer a question of whether they will stop, but of survival. Her assailants, bold and shameless in the dark, retreat before the scrutiny of the morning light.

While it is true that the host in Gibeah seems to consider heterosexual rape a lesser crime, we should heed Reis's view that "the male to male rape described in these two stories [Sodom and Gibeah] has nothing to do with homosexuality."[34] It is the Levite as stranger and not as sexual partner that makes him the object of attack. Understanding this, the Levite succeeds in outsourcing his role to his concubine. The attackers, in turn, are perfectly able to perform their act of sexual aggression against a woman. She substitutes for him not only in the role of woman but also in that of stranger. "By hurting and humiliating the woman whose protection is the Levite's responsibility, these Gibeathites dishonor him."[35]

The war of ethnic cleansing in Bosnia during the last decade of the twentieth century provides a context to the crime. Gang rape of Moslem women by Serb soldiers was used on a large and organized scale in order to humiliate and demean the

33. Thus Exum ("Whose Interests?" 84), stating that "rape is a crime of violence, not of passion, and the men of Gibeah want to humiliate the Levite in the most degrading way, by forcing him into a passive role, into the woman's position."

34. Reis, "The Levite's Concubine," 138.

35. Ibid., 139; cf. Eynikel, "Rape, Murder, War and Abduction," 108.

enemy. By acts of sexual violation, the enemy was deprived of their humanity when the aggressor made rape an instrument of power that would force the hated people to submit or, better yet, to leave.

In Gibeah, the attackers retreat at the first glimmer of dawn. At the same time, "[a]s morning appeared, the woman came and fell down at the door of the man's house where her master was, until it was light" (19:26). The assailants have left her lying listless on the ground, naked, shivering in the cold night air. Slowly she manages to put on some clothes; slowly she inches her way toward the house where she found refuge the night before. Each little gain costs effort, demanding that she stops to rest before she stumbles on. At the house, there is no vigil behind the curtains. The husband and the host seem to be sleeping unperturbed inside as she finally reaches for the door.

She is unable to open it from outside. Inside, the husband and his host remain oblivious to her fate. As the sun rises above the horizon, her body language tells the story of the impossible effort. "In the morning her master got up, opened the doors of the house, and when he went out to go on his way, there was his concubine lying at the door of the house, with her hands on the threshold" (19:27). What is the message of the now lifeless body? She is dying not only because the villagers raped and abused her, but because there was no one there to open the door, help her inside, and nurse her back to life. Stuart Lasine says that

> [t]he woman collapses while struggling to reach the safety [!] of the house "where her master was." Yet when the reader recalls that this dramatic gesture is directed toward the same husband and "master" who has just come out of the house "to go on his way," the incongruity between her struggle and his indifference is almost too great for the reader to feel outrage over his callousness.[36]

Likewise, Reis's exquisite reading helps us see that before the concubine collapses and dies,

> she tries to enter the house, perhaps beating on the door, weeping and begging for help and succor. We learn from this detail that her lord and host were not waiting anxiously, keeping watch for any sound of her. They were most likely asleep in a drunken stupor after making their hearts merry (v. 22). And with no aid, no tender nursing, no one to care, and probably no will to live, the concubine dies.[37]

As the day dawns, the Levite does not betray any sense of loss, outrage, or anger. It appears that the events of the night have not disturbed his sleep. He is ready to proceed with his journey as though nothing has happened. "Get up, we are going," he says to her, taking the art of insensitivity to Olympic levels (19:28). "But there was no answer," the narrator continues calmly (19:28). For the concubine the journey is over.

36. Lasine, "Guest and Host," 44–45.

37. Reis, "The Levite's Concubine," 142.

She has reached a state where no one can harm her. "Then he put her on the donkey; and the man set out for his home" (19:28).

At home, as soon as the Levite "had entered his house, he took a knife,[38] and grasping his concubine he cut her into twelve pieces, limb by limb, and sent her throughout all the territory of Israel" (19:29). The man who made his concubine play the harlot until she saw no way out except to leave him; who made her take him back because, again, she had no choice; who showed lack of resolve and poor judgment that exposed her to unnecessary danger; who retreated in cowardly self-interest, ignoring his wife's pleas and struggle to escape, finally throwing her outside by force; who slept through the night when she was being abused and into the late morning while she was making the final effort to reach the door; who made neglect on his part the cause of her death as much as the abuse she suffered at the hands of others; this man is now seeking redemption by blaming everyone but himself for what happened. "Has such a thing ever happened since the day that the Israelites came up from the land of Egypt until this day? Consider it, take counsel, and speak out" is the message that accompanies his exhibit on wheels (19:30). What is conspicuously missing from the account is the merest hint of his role in her demise.

Inspired by moral outrage, the intensity of which is inversely proportional to its shallowness, the nation proceeds to make amends only to impress upon the reader that the remedy perpetuates and aggravates the problem. Three rounds of punitive action end with the death of forty thousand Israelites and the tribe of Benjamin almost extinct, leaving only six hundred male survivors (20:8–48). But the attempt to punish the sins of the Benjaminites leads to a serious case of buyer's remorse (21:1–3). In order to correct the consequences of the first remedial action, the Israelites now have to find wives for the surviving Benjaminites lest the tribe that they just tried to annihilate become extinct. They cannot give their daughters in marriage to the men, having taken a hasty oath not to do so (21:1). Instead, they arrange to kill the inhabitants of a whole village on the pretext of impiety (21:5–11), sparing "four hundred young virgins who had never slept with a man" (21:12). These young women they give to the now rehabilitated men of Benjamin (21:13–14). In order to make up the shortfall of two hundred brides, they organize a random abduction of two hundred of their own daughters, scheming to persuade the hapless fathers affected by the bridal lottery to let the men keep their prey (21:16–23). What is intended to bring closure thus opens new wounds. The concubine, the lone victim at the beginning, is now joined by six hundred virgins who become the brides of unworthy men against their will, the last two-hundred with the consent of their fathers.

38. The Hebrew text says that the Levite "took *the* knife," not that he "took *a* knife." As Trible (*Texts of Terror*, 80) and Reis ("The Levite's Concubine," 143–44) both point out, this act echoes the non-sacrifice of Isaac and Abraham, the only other person in Scripture who "took the knife" (Gen 22:10). But the meaning is reversed; Abraham does not use the knife, and Isaac is spared.

"In those days there was no king in Israel," ends the narrator, futility now thick in the air, "all the people did what was right in their own eyes" (21:25).

Sense of Candor, Pity, and Respect

To Phyllis Trible, the narrator in Judges is a detached male, a misogynist reporting on the deeds of worse misogynists. She sees a woman who is "alone in a world of men" because, in her view, neither the characters in the story nor the narrator "recognizes her humanity."[39] This is a line of thought, by the way, that could also include the way the woman has suffered continued abuse by Christian interpreters.[40] In a related line of thought, the concubine's fate is misappropriated by men who borrow from the dark luster of *her* suffering in order to magnify *theirs*. This tradition begins within the story itself when the Levite, in retelling the story, omits to mention *his* role in *her* suffering while at the same time making it appear that *her* suffering is incidental to *his* (20:4–7). The most famous reader of this story, Jean-Jacques Rousseau, seems to have been drawn to the story for similar self-pitying reasons, using her plight as a magnifying glass for his own.[41]

In her keen hearing of the story, Reis does not perceive the voice of a callous male chauvinist. She finds a woman who is "pitied and respected by the text, who has been silenced by an intolerable predicament."[42] I agree. In the muted telling of the story, there are revealing flashes of emotion, empathy, and moral outrage, as when the narrator depicts the Levite forcing the concubine out to the mob (19:25) and when he or she sees her lying outside the house in the morning "with her hands on the threshold" (19:27). The subdued tone of the narration is the best he or she can do. The raw scenes must not be eclipsed by a show of emotion on the part of the narrator. He or she must stand back, allowing the story to speak for itself. The story must only be told; it must not be performed. The events depicted exceed the ability of language to describe them. The narrator's restraint in this regard leaves room for the reader, mobilizing reader engagement. Despite views to the contrary, the narrator is not siding with the perpetrators, but, as in Kurt Vonnegut's description of the firebombing of Dresden by allied forces during World War II, the voice is defeated by the story it tries to tell.[43] Vonnegut begins to tell the story but ends up circling it, only occasionally handing the reader a picture that permanently sears the imagination just as it has scorched his. Each image of the result of the firebombing is followed by the knowingly inadequate comment, "So it goes."

39. Trible, *Texts of Terror*, 80.

40. For a critique, see Exum, *Fragmented Women*.

41. Kamuf, "Author of a Crime," 187–207; in the same volume, Mieke Bal, "A Body of Writings," 208–30.

42. Reis, "The Levite's Concubine," 136.

43. Vonnegut Jr., *Slaughterhouse Five*.

A residue of victimhood remains for the Levite even though the present retelling from the beginning makes him the chief victimizer. Katharina von Kellenbach assumes an ambiguous beginning of the story, but her point is not fully deflated even with a storyline that is less favorable toward him.[44] When the villagers in Gibeah attack the house, the Levite becomes a victim, too. Kellenbach connects the Levite's dilemma to the Jewish ghetto policeman who faced the 'choiceless choice' of executing Nazi policy toward his own family. Calel Perechodnik, who tells one such story, was forced to load his wife and two-year-old daughter onto a train that transported them to their deaths in Treblinka.[45] Is he, a victim, now also an accomplice to murder? Kellenbach finds the Levite in a similarly impossible situation. "As contemptible as his decision to sacrifice his concubine may have been, it was a choice made *in extremis*—not unlike the inhuman choices forced upon many Jewish men and women during the Holocaust."[46]

Reis says that the story of the concubine is best understood from the point of view of its cause rather than the consequences. The consequences are inhospitality, cruelty to women, and xenophobia, but the cause is loss of the spiritual center. The narrator in Judges has a theme, and "[h]is theme is the wages of sin. He describes a nation that disregards God's laws, tramples social justice, and turns wives into whores. Israelites, like Sodomites, show senseless hatred toward the stranger and try to rape and humiliate him. A husband saves himself by flinging his wife to the rabble."[47]

To hindsight, and to fore-sight, as well, there is linkage of imagery and not only of birth place between the unnamed concubine from Bethlehem and the child that, in the New Testament, was born centuries later to a virgin mother in Bethlehem (Matt 1:18–23; Luke 1:26–35; 2:1–7). We read in the latter story that in Bethlehem, much like in Gibeah, "there was no place for them in the inn" (Luke 2:7). We read of a person who for financial gain looked "for an opportunity to betray him" (Matt 26:16; John 13:21) and that the one who ate his bread lifted his heel against him (John 13:18). We read that "darkness came over the whole land" (Matt 27:45), that "it was night" (John 13:30), and that the night was their hour "and the power of darkness" (Luke 22:53). We see a resident alien, not in Gibeah this time but in nearby Jerusalem, pleading with the mob to show reason and restraint, to cease and desist (John 18:39—19:6). We read of one who "was oppressed, and he was afflicted, yet he did not open his mouth; like a lamb that is led to the slaughter, and like a sheep that before its shearers is silent, so he did not open his mouth" (Isa 53:7). We hear the piercing cry of dereliction (Mark 15:24; Matt 27:46). We read of blood poured out and of a body broken and distributed (Mark 14:22–24; Matt 26:26–28 Luke 22:19). A thousand years go by in the biblical record, and then attention turns again to Bethlehem and its immediate vicinity. There is strange symmetry and unexpected similarity in our discovery that the Bible's most

44. von Kellenbach, "Am I a Murderer?" 176–91.

45. Perechodnik, *Am I a Murderer*.

46. von Kellenbach, "Judges 19–21 as a Parable," 181.

47. Reis, "The Levite's Concubine," 145.

luminous story of hope aligns itself tightly with the Bible's darkest story of horror, not only in terms of location and symbolism, but also in the sense that the threads that weave her garment of horror bear an uncanny resemblance to the threads that will weave the garment of hope.

The story of the concubine is buried in a neglected part of the Bible, but it should not be dismissed as an aberration or as theological no man's land. Its scandalous nature refutes the notion that the Bible avoids unpleasant facts or that it lacks interest in contemporary concerns. Cruelty runs riot without any restraint or occasion for redress. God is conspicuous by his silence. Prayers seem to go unanswered. No voice from heaven interrupts the attackers' assault. The longed-for moment of deliverance does not materialize.

As her body is dismembered, sense is dismembered, too, but the story retains sense that is often missing: the sense of candor, pity, and respect. The abused woman joins a mourning world in the outer darkness of human experience. To find this story in a book that is supposed to tell about God suggests that the Bible presents human reality fairly and unbiased. At face value it is hardly a story to inspire trust in God and reverence for God's ways. On the other hand, the story assures that no attempt has been made to suppress or exclude unpleasant evidence. No shocking incident has been deleted from the record in order to preempt troubling questions from being raised. The Bible does not come across as a cover up in high places or an ancient Watergate scandal where the person in power edits the record to suit his case. There is no eighteen minute gap and no stonewalling and no need to look to Wikileaks for the crime to become known in the public square.[48] Divine accountability, if that is what we will find in the end, begins with full disclosure.

48. "Stonewalling" was a term used about the attempt of President Richard M. Nixon to block the investigation during the Watergate scandal. The "eighteen minute gap" refers to the gap in the secret tapes of conversations in the Oval Office during Watergate.

Chapter Twelve

Moving the Goalposts of Sense

If we were to select the three most prominent characters of the Old Testament, the first two would be Abraham and Moses. Who would be the third? There can hardly be any doubt that the third candidate must be the prophet Elijah. These three top the list not only because of their influence in the Old Testament but also because they are "adopted" and remembered by the New Testament to a greater degree than other Old Testament characters. While Elijah's share of the Old Testament is modest in quantitative terms, he becomes a transformative figure that is larger than life. It is no exaggeration to say that with him, the goalposts of sense are moved. It is also fair to say that many have not noticed.

Setting the Stage

Elijah takes the stage during the reign of Ahab, the king who assumed power in the year 874 BCE, thirty-five years after the death of Jeroboam (Chap. 13). This is at a time in Old Testament history concerning which sources other than the Bible corroborate important features in the biblical story. Much has been found about King Ahab.

Historical and archaeological data suggest that this was a period of prosperity in Israel. In a comment on the battle of Karkar in 855 BCE, the Shalmaneser Monolith says that "Ahab's forces consisted of ten thousand men and two thousand war chariots," making it the largest chariot force of the kingdoms resisting Assyrian domination.[1] Trade flourished. Large building projects were undertaken, the remains of which are still visible in places like Megiddo, Jezreel, Hazor, and Samaria. The extent of these projects is so impressive that Ahab may have been "the greatest of the builder-kings of Israel until the time of Herod."[2] His secular record has earned Ahab the reputation as "one of Israel's most capable rulers."[3]

Other archaeological data pertinent to the Bible have also emerged. The land of Israel was vulnerable to droughts, requiring farmers to take measures to enable

1. Rusak, "The Clash of Cults on Mount Carmel," 34.
2. Stern, *Dor, Ruler of the Seas*, 116.
3. Dever, *What Did the Biblical Writers Know?* 164.

them to get by for at least a year in the event of impending crop failure. Drought is an important subject in the Elijah narrative. It has been confirmed that a serious drought happened during the time of Ahab.[4] With respect to religious practice, there is abundant evidence that worship of Baal was widespread in Israel during this time. Mount Carmel, the mountain that was the locus for the confrontation between Elijah and the king, was actually a shrine for Baal worship.[5] The Bible portrays the reign of Ahab as a period of religious erosion to the point that "Yahwism was in danger of becoming a pagan religion."[6]

There is thus a downside to Ahab's legacy of prosperity, and it is the downside that receives the most attention in the Bible. Ahab brought alien influences to bear on Israel to a greater degree than any of his predecessors. While Jeroboam had sought a religious role in order to consolidate his political power, Ahab embraced the religious ideas of his time far beyond the call of 'political necessity,' if such a term has any meaning. The Bible says that "Ahab son of Omri did evil in the sight of the LORD more than all who were before him" (1 Kgs 16:30).

Ahab and his wife Jezebel did not spend time worrying whether a nation should be ruled by *Rex lex* ('the king is law') or *Lex rex* ('the law is king'). They thought exclusively in terms of the former. Absolute power was in; constitutional power was out. Caprice was in; the rule of law was out. In one revealing example, Ahab found himself coveting a vineyard that bordered his estate, wishing to purchase it from Naboth, the owner (1 Kgs 21:1–2). Unwilling to part with his ancestral inheritance, Naboth turned him down (21:3). At this Ahab became sullen, pouting like a spoiled child, and refusing to eat (21:4). When Jezebel inquired into the cause of his sullen mood, she was taken aback at the king's ineptitude in the art of wielding power. "Is this how you act as king over Israel?" she asked contemptuously. "Get up and eat! Cheer up. I'll get you the vineyard of Naboth the Jezreelite" (1 Kgs 21:7, NIV). This was her way of saying that a king worthy of the title would not take no for an answer from his subjects.

Lest the plan is lost on us, her idea of what it means to "govern" was Machiavellian to the core. Jezebel might be remembered as a textbook example of executive expediency, on the one hand, and scrupulous efficiency, on the other.

> So she wrote letters in Ahab's name and sealed them with his seal; she sent the letters to the elders and the nobles who lived with Naboth in his city. She wrote in the letters, "Proclaim a fast, and seat Naboth at the head of the assembly; seat two scoundrels [lit. "men of the evil one"] opposite him, and have them bring a charge against him, saying, 'You have cursed God and the king.' Then take him out, and stone him to death" (21:8–10).

4. Rusak, "Clash of Cults," 40.

5. Ibid., 40, 45–46.

6. Bright, *History of Israel*, 259.

The script will be familiar to anyone who has studied societies that have contempt for the rule of law. A conspiracy in the halls of power exploits the clout of a compliant bureaucracy. False charges are brought forward by hired witnesses, giving the veneer of due process. The outcome of the 'trial' is never in doubt. A charge of blasphemy or unpatriotic behavior is a reliable weapon in systems where might makes right. In this particular version of the script, Naboth has no chance. The judicial charade runs its course. Naboth is condemned and sentenced to death by stoning. Ahab takes possession of his property as the rightful owner (21:15). No one says anything in protest, fearing that the axe of an unaccountable power might turn on them. No one says anything, I repeat, except for the prophet Elijah. To him, might does not make right.

Try as he might, Ahab never gets away from Elijah. Throughout these narratives, the prophet is either one step just ahead or one step just behind the king, relentless in his rebuke of arbitrary power and untiring in his battle for Israel's spiritual soul. In the story of Naboth's vineyard, Elijah is commissioned to confront Ahab at the very moment when the latter takes possession of the coveted property (21:17–18). All of a sudden the prophet steps out from behind some foliage, reading the king the riot act, "Have you killed, and also taken possession?" (21:19). Ahab answers in a tone of resignation, as though aware that the game is over and that he has more than met his match, "Have you found me, O my enemy?" (21:20)

While Ahab left a large physical footprint in Israel, Elijah's spiritual legacy cannot be overstated. At the point where the Old Testament ends in its current form, the prophet Malachi turns Elijah, the greatest prophet of the past, into a redemptive model for the future (Mal 4:5–6). In the Gospel of Matthew, Elijah is seen as the type for John the Baptist, the forerunner of Jesus (Matt 11:13–14). During the ministry of Jesus, some people think that Jesus is Elijah or a personality like him (Matt 16:14).[7] When Jesus is transfigured on the mountain, Moses and Elijah suddenly appear, talking with Jesus (Matt 17:3). At the point when Jesus cries out just before dying, some bystanders are certain that he is calling for Elijah (Matt 27:46–47).

Such outsized influence can be explained only against the background of an extraordinary experience.[8] This chapter will review the events that earned Elijah his reputation by revisiting two closely linked events in his story. The first relates to Elijah's role in the public square, confronting the cult of Baal on Mount Carmel (1 Kgs 17:1—18:46). The second point is located in the private sphere, in Elijah's encounter with God at Mount Horeb (1 Kgs 19:8–18). These two experiences cannot be separated. Here, then, is the story of a man who began his life as a villager from the remote "Tishbe in Gilead" (1 Kgs 17:1), faced down the combined power of cult and state on Mount Carmel (1 Kgs 18:19–39), and finally was taken alive in a chariot of fire "in a whirlwind into heaven" (2 Kgs 2:1, 11).

7. The notion of Jesus as a prophet like Elijah is even more explicit in Luke; cf. Croatto, "Jesus, Prophet Like Elijah," 451–65.

8. Gese, "Zur Bedeutung Elias," 126–50.

Showdown on Mount Carmel

The account of the showdown on Mount Carmel pictures Elijah engaged in a fierce conflict with the rival cult of Baal. In the early skirmishes of the conflict Elijah is instrumental in bringing a devastating drought on the land because of the unfaithfulness of the House of Ahab (1 Kgs 17:1). Recalcitrant at first, the three-year drought compels the king to reconsider his options. Seeing the land parched and the people suffering under the famine (18:2), the two sides in the conflict agree to a face-to-face meeting (18:17–19).

At Mount Carmel, Elijah calls for an end to the divided loyalties of Israel (18:21). He urges a decisive test to weigh the merits of the competing claims of the two cults (18:22–24), casting the test in terms of the power of the respective objects of devotion. In Elijah's words to his rivals, "Then you call on the name of your god and I will call on the name of the Lord; the god who answers by fire is indeed God" (18:24).

John A. Beck has shown that there is more than meets the eye in this story.[9] Baal was the god of fertility, and, indirectly, the god of rain. Baal's most competitive asset, therefore, was the ability to bring an end to drought. When Elijah proposed to hold the showdown on Mount Carmel, he signaled willingness to meet the opposition where the latter was strongest. As suggested already, Mount Carmel, rising high on the Mediterranean coast south of present-day Haifa, was a site least likely to be affected by drought. Then and now, it was "luxuriant with dense, green foliage," befitting the god said to occupy the site.[10] In other words, Mount Carmel "was no ordinary worship site but an important Baal sanctuary."[11] Baal was 'king of the hill.' The duel with Elijah's God was to take place on Baal's home field.[12]

While water was the chief asset of Baal in agricultural terms, Elijah had the audacity to brandish water on the mountain, and lots of it, too (18:33–35). By contrast, "when the Baal prophets are on center stage, we do not find a drop of water."[13] The prospect of igniting a fire on wet material, as Elijah proposed to do, would not only enhance the subsequent miracle in material terms. Elijah reached into the pocket of Baal, so to speak, using the rival god's main asset to demonstrate the superiority of Israel's God.

Having proposed clear-cut terms for the test, Elijah asked the people to pronounce on its fairness. The people endorsed the terms without reservations. "Well spoken!" they said (18:24).

Elijah let the four hundred prophets of Baal have the first attempt. Working themselves into a frenzy, the hours of the morning go by without the slightest

9. Beck, "Geography as Irony," 291–302.

10. Ibid., 298.

11. Ibid., 299.

12. Ibid.

13. Ibid., 300.

response from Baal (18:26–29). Ridiculing the beliefs of another person is generally inconsiderate and rude, but that is exactly what Elijah starts doing. “Cry aloud! Surely he is a god; either he is meditating, or he has wandered away, or he is on a journey, or perhaps he is asleep and must be awakened,” he taunts the priests (18:27). In fact, his taunt might be worse than the NRSV makes it sound. With respect to the idea that Baal “has wandered away,” Simon DeVries is inclined to go along with Jewish exegetes “in taking this as a racy, sly sarcasm meaning ‘busy at the privy.’”[14] In other words, the fervent prayers of the priests of Baal go unanswered because Baal is on the toilet! As to the notion that Ba‘al “is asleep and must be awakened,” ancient religions “conceived of their gods going to sleep at night—but this is noonday!”[15]

Noise and orgiastic bodily contortions rise to new heights as the priests try to break the impasse. “Then they cried aloud and, as was their custom, they cut themselves with swords and lances until the blood gushed out over them” (18:28). Regrettably, the silence of Baal in the face of the pleas, so terse and magnificent in Hebrew, is but faintly preserved in the English translation: “there was no voice, no answer, and no response” (18:29).

When the turn comes to Elijah, his deliberate and confident demeanor stands in striking contrast to the spectacle of the devotees of Baal. Where his opponents have shouted, he talks in measured tones. Where they have screamed, he fairly whispers. Moreover, while the Baal cult has come up short with a task that would be hard under the most favorable circumstances, Elijah makes the task more difficult. This is where the water comes in, poured three times and in generous amounts over the altar, the wood, and the sacrifice until “the water ran all around the altar, and filled the trench also with water” (18:35). We might call this “quality assurance,” showing, on the one hand, that Elijah is confident that Yahweh will do better, and, on the other hand, that no one will be able to say that he cheated.

Upon Elijah’s prayer, fire comes down from heaven, consuming everything in its path. The outcome is more spectacular by the fact that it happens despite Baal’s home field advantage, using water, the rival’s main asset, to drive home the point (18:36–38). The cult of Baal is shown to lack the assets about which it has been boasting, and Elijah turns those very assets into resources that highlight the superiority of Yahweh.[16] The message is not lost on the people, who exclaim, “The LORD indeed is God; the LORD indeed is God” (18:39). The test results in signal victory for Elijah’s God and in a devastating exposé and humiliation for the royally-sponsored cult (18:30–39).[17] Throughout the proceedings, Elijah has displayed condescension toward the opposition and confidence toward God. Above all, he has seemed fearless.

14. DeVries, *1 Kings*, 229.

15. Ibid.

16. Beck, “Geography as Irony,” 301.

17. Thus Childs (“On Reading the Elijah Narratives,” 132), “[T]he confrontation is between Yahweh, God of Israel, and a sheer delusion.”

Thus far the narrative is straightforward, promising an outcome that should be too decisive for second thoughts to arise.

From Triumph to Dejection

Surprisingly, however, problems emerge in the immediate aftermath of the triumph. Queen Jezebel reacts with fury, vowing revenge (1 Kgs 19:1–2). Elijah, previously confident, fearless, and seemingly untouchable, suddenly appears to panic (19:3). At the very least, the prophet seems overcome by a sense of futility. Elijah "went a day's journey into the wilderness, and came and sat down under a solitary broom tree. He asked that he might die: 'It is enough; now, O Lord, take away my life, for I am no better than my ancestors'" (19:4).

The man who speaks like this has little in common with the hero of Mount Carmel. This Elijah has widely been seen as a man in crisis (19:4).[18] Interpreters struggle to explain his dejected state of mind. Does he flee from Jezebel because he panics? Could some emotion other than fear explain his sudden loss of composure?

Alan J. Hauser, rather harshly, sees the heretofore bold Elijah transformed into "a whimpering defeatist."[19] To Johan Lust, Elijah runs off as a "fugitive fearing Jezebel's anger."[20] Bernard P. Robinson sees an arrogant, self-important man fleeing in panic because Jezebel's threat against his life "has punctured his inflated image of himself."[21] Further accentuating this negative view, Russell Gregory casts the entire narrative as an ironic account that aims to unmask Elijah, expose his vanity, and terminate his service.[22] These views have in common that they place the onus of failure on the shoulders of Elijah, showing little sympathy for him and even less understanding of his situation and mission.

Alternative readings are possible and more plausible. Fear or failure of nerve is not all there is to say about Elijah's reaction when learning of Jezebel's outrage (19:3). Although textual variants of 1 Kgs 19:3 offer the options "and he was afraid" [*wayyira*] or "and he saw" [*wayyar*], most commentators prefer the former on the assumption that it makes better sense.[23] This view sees a man cowering in fear before the rage of Jezebel. The textual evidence for this view is not conclusive, and the context casts doubts on the notion that fear best represents Elijah's state of mind. Jezebel's hostility after the confrontation on Mount Carmel is not a new feature in their relationship. The queen had sought to kill the prophets all along, including Elijah (18:4, 14). Thus, Robert L. Cohn wisely cautions against making fear the overriding emotion, noting that Elijah

18. Hauser and Gregory, *From Carmel to Horeb*.

19. Hauser, *Elijah in Crisis*, 60.

20. Lust, "Elijah and the theophany," 91.

21. Robinson, "Elijah at Horeb," 517.

22. Gregory, *Elijah in Crisis*, 146.

23. See Gray, *I & II Kings*, 361; Cogan, *1 Kings*, 450.

"asks Yahweh for death though he fled Israel to escape it."[24] Peter F. Lockwood may be closer to the truth when he sees Elijah as an "all-or-nothing man" who succumbs to distress because "the victory on Mt. Carmel has not led to the disempowerment of Jezebel."[25] On the whole, it is a stretch to believe that Elijah flees in order to escape death at Jezebel's hand only to flee into the desert to ask God to take his life.[26]

Mental lows may follow in the wake of emotional highs. This has led some interpreters to see Elijah's experience as an ancient example of "burnout."[27] This view is more sympathetic to Elijah even though it attributes to him an exaggerated sense of importance that needs to be remedied before he can continue his mission. An inflated self-image is suggested in Elijah's twice-repeated complaint to God that "I have been very zealous for the Lord, the God of hosts; for the Israelites have forsaken your covenant, thrown down your altars, and killed your prophets with the sword. *I alone am left*, and they are seeking my life, to take it away" (19:10, 14). The dominant sentiment in this outburst, nevertheless, is rather that Elijah is unable to count the spectacular feat at Mount Carmel as the success it was supposed to be.

For this reason it is more logical to understand Elijah's reaction in terms of profound disillusionment and not as a character defect. Looking for objective criteria in the story, Elijah's state of mind is in keeping with the discrepancy between expectations and results. This view has textual support if we make "and he saw" [*wayyar*] the preferred reading with respect to Elijah's state of mind (19:3). According to this logic, the success at Mount Carmel leads Elijah to expect that the fallacy of Baal worship has been exposed and his opponents defeated. When the result falls short of his expectations, as evidenced by Jezebel's unyielding antagonism, Elijah reacts with disappointment. While the display of divine power, on the surface at least, sways the majority of people in favor of Yahweh, Jezebel remains unconvinced and inconvincible.

Where will the disappointed man go? Where will he go when his name is Elijah, looking for a place where he can nurse his mental wounds? Elijah retreats to Horeb, "the mount of God" (19:8). Mount Horeb was the site of Moses's spectacular encounter with God (Exod 3:1; 17:6; Deut 29:1). Recalling the top-three list of personalities in the Old Testament, the third name on the list is now literally traversing the desert and metaphorically the centuries for a "meeting" with Moses, the second name on the list. The notion that he is driven by panic seems exaggerated, and the suspicion of megalomania is too ungenerous. Martin Buber's suggestion that Elijah returns "on Israel's tracks to the mountain of revelation" is more to the point.[28] Elijah may be backtracking to the point where it all began to gain perspective on his faith and experience. If fear is the emotion that starts him off on the long journey to Mount Horeb, it

24. Cohn, "1 Kings 17–19," 342.

25. Lockwood, "The Elijah Syndrome," 53.

26. Epp-Tiessen, "The Renewal of Elijah," 35.

27. Ibid., 37.

28. Buber, *Prophetic Faith*, 77.

is not what motivates him to complete it. We should be friendly to the possibility that Elijah retreats from the scene not primarily because of fear or burnout in ministry, but because of an understandable existential need.

Mount Carmel will be a distant point when he comes to Mount Horeb, but the points are connected and should not be forgotten. 1 Kings says that the journey took "forty days and forty nights" (1 Kgs 19:8). "Forty days and forty nights" matches a period of time associated with Moses (Exod 24:18; 34:28; Deut 9:9). Elijah will not only go to the place where Moses had his encounter with God. He will, as it were, retrace the steps of Moses. He could have gone elsewhere, of course, to a less remote and less storied location. It is hugely important that his journey takes him to scenes hallowed by Moses's encounter with God generations earlier.

Encounter at Horeb

When Elijah arrives at Horeb, there are more allusions to Moses and to the revelation given to Israel at the time of the Exodus (Exod 19:16–18). The story also alludes to Moses on a personal level. Like him, Elijah goes to Horeb, "the mountain of God" (1 Kgs 19:8; Exod 3:1). He, too, enters a cave (1 Kgs 19:9; Exod 33:22). The narrative is at pains to place Elijah in the topographical context where Moses received his great revelation (1 Kgs 19:8–9; Exod 33:18–23). The God who "passes by" in the case of Elijah is the same God who favored Moses by "passing by" at Moses's request (1 Kgs 19:11; Exod 33:18–23; 34:6).[29]

Upon Elijah's arrival at Horeb, however, the setting is stage-managed not only to recall Moses's personal and solitary encounter with God, but also the Sinai experience of Israel.[30] When Moses led Israel to this location, "Mount Sinai was wrapped in smoke, because the LORD had descended upon it in fire; the smoke went up like the smoke of a kiln, while the whole mountain shook violently" (Exod 19:18). As other recollections of this event bear out, the divine presence was manifested in a show of awe-inspiring supernatural power: "all the people perceived the thunder and the lightning flashes and the sound of the trumpet and the mountain smoking; and when the people saw it, they trembled and stood at a distance" (Exod 20:18); "the mountain burned with fire to the very heart of the heavens: darkness, cloud and thick gloom" (Deut 4:11).

Elijah returns to the place where these manifestations took place. What now of past grandeur? Where now the tremor, the lightning flashes, and a mountain literally on fire? Where, now, the divine presence? As the prophet waits, convulsions in nature break loose as if nothing has changed. For Elijah, too, there is thunder, described as a wind "so strong that it was splitting mountains and breaking rocks in pieces before the

29. Jeremias, *Theophanie*, 112; Childs, "Reading the Elijah Narratives,"135; Cohn, "1 Kings 17–19," 342; Robinson, "Elijah at Horeb," 525–27; Cogan, *1 Kings*, 452.

30. Robinson, "Elijah at Horeb," 527.

Lord" (1 Kgs 19:11). Then, "after the wind an earthquake" (19:11). And then, "after the earthquake a fire," just as at the exodus experience at Sinai (1 Kgs 19:12; Exod 19:18; cf. Deut 4:11; 5:22). Yahweh, it seems, "answers Elijah's complaint by displaying the 'theophanic triad' of wind, earthquake and fire, as he did before Moses and the people of Israel (Exod 19:9; 20:18–19; Deut 4:9–10; 5:24–25)."[31] Wind, earthquake, and fire, "the familiar symbols of the theophanic [divine] presence,"[32] at first seem to have lost nothing with regard to their power to show forth the divine identity.

But we must not be fooled. Despite the similarities, it is the contrast that makes the Elijah encounter at Horeb special. Pointed negations dominate this story. "Now there was a great wind, so strong that it was splitting mountains and breaking rocks in pieces before the Lord"—as in the days of Moses, and, at least metaphorically, as in Elijah's recent Mount Carmel performance—"but the Lord was *not* in the wind," reports the narrator (19:11). Then, "after the wind an earthquake"—again, as in the Sinai encounter, and again, metaphorically, as in the 'earthquake' on Mount Carmel—"but the Lord was *not* in the earthquake" (19:11). And then, "after the earthquake a fire"—again, as in the defining Sinai theophany of the Exodus experience, and yet again, metaphorically and literally, as in the spectacular fire on Mount Carmel—"but the Lord was *not* in the fire" (19:12).

Elijah's experience at Horeb stands on the scaffolding of earlier stories. On the one hand, Mount Carmel can be "seen" in the distance, towering high with a fresh and up-to-date message of divine power. The visit to Horeb revives the ancient memory of Moses and Israel as if to suggest that nothing has changed. And yet, on the other hand, blow by deliberate blow, the narrator lays out a series of emphatic negations that take complete command of the account:

> . . . the Lord was *not* in the wind;
>
> . . . the Lord was *not* in the earthquake;
>
> . . . the Lord was *not* in the fire (19:11–12).

Something other than power is nudging itself into the center as the key element in the new sense that has come knocking. After these negations, serving as foil for the message, comes the *qôl dᵉmāma daqqā*, translated as "a still small voice" (KJV), "the sound of a light whisper,"[33] "a gentle little breeze,"[34] or even "sheer silence" (NRSV).[35]

At that point the prophet stands hushed and subdued, his face wrapped in his mantle (19:12–13).

31. Cohn, "1 Kings 17–19," 342.

32. DeVries, *1 Kings*, 236.

33. Burney, *Notes on the Hebrew Text*, 231; Montgomery, *Critical and Exegetical Commentary*, 313–14.

34. DeVries, *1 Kings*, 232.

35. Cogan, *1 Kings*, 453.

There must be a point to this carefully-staged encounter, but what is it? J. J. Stamm claims incredibly that there is no new lesson for Elijah except to continue his ministry as before.[36] Continuity is also the watchword of Eckhard von Nordheim, who casts the Horeb experience narrowly as a contrast to the religions of the ancient Near East, adding little to what was already made manifest on Mount Carmel.[37] Likewise, Ernst Würthwein emphasizes the anti-Canaanite thrust of the Horeb revelation.[38] Cohn, too, thinks that the lesson at Horeb is to draw a contrast between "the silence of Baal and the voice of Yahweh,"[39] even though here it is Yahweh who falls silent. On the apparent assumption that the behavior of the prophets of Baal is the counterpart to the Horeb experience, DeVries reads the story as a rebuke to religious manifestations that "rely on shoutings and flurries of action, while neglecting the way of quiet love, simple piety, and persuasive kindness."[40]

It is not uncharitable to deem these views inadequate. To varying degrees they ignore the contrast between Elijah's experience at Mount Carmel and his encounter with God at Horeb, and they seem equally unmoved by the connection between Elijah and Moses. Elijah's struggle with the Baal cult does not suffice as the grounding for his experience at Horeb. James A. Montgomery aptly takes the lesson of Horeb in a different direction, marveling at the first expression of "the spiritual nature of God and of his self-revelation."[41] This is a bit sermonic, but it prepares for a larger perspective within which the conflict between Yahweh and Baal is no longer the only determinant in the story. Instead, the focus has shifted to become an "internal" matter focusing on Elijah's perception of the Unseen. There is a striking novelty in the traditional revelatory motif in Elijah's Horeb experience,[42] a revision down to bedrock. "In the utter stillness that followed the storm, Elijah heard a voice and YHWH's speaking to him; the intimation seems to be that this is the desired mode of discourse between the prophet and the divine presence," says Mordechai Cogan.[43]

Interpretations of the aftermath of the Horeb encounter follow predictably the lines that interpreters have pursued up to that point. One group sees the end of the line for Elijah's prophetic ministry, either because he resigns his office voluntarily[44] or because he is terminated for reasons of incurable narrow-mindedness.[45] Severe variants within this view portray Elijah as "a figure devoured by egotism," a "*propheta*

36. Stamm, "Elia am Horeb," 334.
37. von Nordheim, "Ein Prophet kündigt sein Amt auf," 153–73.
38. Würthwein, *Die Bücher der Könige*, 230.
39. Cohn, "1 Kings 17–19," 349–50; cf. Robinson, "Elijah at Horeb," 527.
40. DeVries, *1 Kings*, 237.
41. Montgomery, *Kings*, 314.
42. Jeremias, *Theophanie*, 112–13; Robinson, *First Book of Kings*, 221.
43. Cogan, *1 Kings*, 453.
44. von Nordheim, "Ein Prophet kündigt sein Amt auf," 171–73.
45. Hauser, *Elijah in Crisis*, 81; Gregory, *Elijah in Crisis*, 146.

gloriosus" in a pejorative sense,[46] who is no longer fit for service because of pride and "successive acts of non-compliance."[47] These harsh interpretations fail for not having paid sufficient attention to the pointed negations at Horeb and the "still, small voice," and they vastly underestimate God's solicitude for Elijah.

Others take a less harsh view, but they do not see Horeb as a turning point. Rather, they imagine that it is back to business as usual. In this view, Elijah simply resumes his work.[48] God refuses Elijah's resignation papers because there is still a work to be done.[49] As for the view that Elijah's problem was burnout in ministry, the experience at Horeb revives him enough that he is able to return to work.[50]

Much is missing in these interpretations. The view that Elijah is dismissed does not fit subsequent events, and the suggestion that he simply returns to work rejuvenated after his pilgrimage is too trite. We miss the point of Elijah's journey unless we see the encounter at Horeb as a *transformative* experience. At Mount Carmel, the spectacular manifestation of Yahweh reduced Baal to "a sheer illusion,"[51] and yet Elijah is subsequently found in a state of existential despair. For this reason the theophany at Horeb should not be seen primarily as a contrast between Yahweh and Baal. Its true force is best appreciated when it is understood as a deepening—and even a revision—of Elijah's understanding of God.

Moving the Goalposts of Sense

The echoes of Moses link Elijah to his illustrious predecessor. It is not as though Elijah arrives at Horeb only to come to terms with an experience in ministry that yielded smaller results than expected. That, by the way, was also Moses's experience. What awaits Elijah differs from his expectation. Retreating first to the desert thoroughly disillusioned and then to Horeb where it all began, Elijah is still moving about within the paradigm that has let him down. To the extent that Elijah counted on God's power to prevail in the conflict with Baal, having articulated this view in public on Mount Carmel and watched the execution of this premise in a spectacular fashion, he looks for this expectation to be vindicated and to redeem his sense of failure.

What happens at Horeb, however, does not affirm his prior outlook. Instead, the experience shatters the old framework right down to its original Mosaic foundation. The message this time is not for the prophet to show humility in the face of an awesome display of divine majesty and power. It is rather that the reasons for the prophet's

46. Robinson, "Elijah at Horeb," 528, 535.

47. Lockwood, "The Elijah Syndrome," 58.

48. Stamm, "Elia am Horeb," 334.

49. Cohn, "1 Kings 17–19," 342; DeVries, *1 Kings*, 237.

50. Epp-Tiessen, "The Renewal of Elijah," 41.

51. Childs, "Reading the Elijah Narratives," 132.

confidence in God must lie elsewhere, demanding of him a new outlook. God is repudiating before Elijah's very eyes the features on which his prior confidence was built.

If the fury of Jezebel in the aftermath of Carmel impressed on Elijah the limitation of power as a means to induce people to change their minds, Horeb completes the transformation. What begins as a career-ending disappointment becomes the stepping-stone for a different vision of God. The twist brought to bear on the memory of Israel's initial encounter with God takes the lesser question of means to the greater question of essence. God's express *absence* from the carefully-choreographed parade of might and majesty at Horeb is more than a lesson on method. The scene reaches for ultimacy, an unveiling of God's ways tailored to the rare person prepared to absorb it. Whatever the merits of power by other criteria, computed in parallel columns of risks and benefits, the Horeb narrative suggests that ultimately Yahweh's way is not the way of power.

In a computation of what was achieved at Mount Carmel, the net gain approaches zero. Elijah mistakenly thinks that "I alone am left" (19:10) only to be told that a full seven thousand share his outlook, "all the knees that have not bowed to Baal, and every mouth that has not kissed him" (19:18). But these individuals do not repudiate Baal because of what happened at Mount Carmel; they internalized their conviction *before* the confrontation and on the basis of finer points of distinction between Yahweh and Baal than the fire that came down from heaven. This is also part of the insight gained. The narrative implies that the number of the faithful has not increased because of the mind-boggling display. Indeed, the swing in public opinion may not be matched by a genuine change of heart. Jezebel, the chief antagonist, remains unmoved and even energized by what has taken place. These possibilities create a coherent interpretation that does not need the desperate measure of removing the theophany at Horeb from the text in order to make peace with the apparent "business as usual" that follows the Horeb experience.[52] This construct also avoids the resigned interpretation that makes subsequent events override and negate the lesson of the revelation.[53]

The appearance of "business as usual" after the encounter is misleading (19:15–17).[54] New insight on the part of one individual (Elijah) need not translate into new policy toward those who have not shared his experience and are not disposed to appreciate it. Measures of damage control and containment of the old order will continue (19:15–19), but the impact of the experience remains in force in the life of the one to whom it was given. The narrative beckons us, the present readers, to see the

52. The case for this desperate remedy is argued by Würthwein, "Elijah at Horeb," 152–66.

53. Gray (*I & II Kings*, 365) objects to an interpretation that turns the Horeb theophany into a paradigm shift because Elijah is commissioned to anoint Hazael and Jehu (1 Kgs 19:15–17), surely not characters that would implement a new policy of non-violence. Stamm ("Elia am Horeb," 333) is similarly convinced that the future role of these individuals betrays any hypothesis that wishes to turn the Horeb theophany into a higher conception of God.

54. Robinson (*First Book of Kings*, 221–22) notes that "it was Elisha and not Elijah who had contact with Hazael and Jehu," leading him to question whether the command was obeyed and even whether it was ever given.

point. The ultimate next step for Elijah, as if to drive home that he increasingly stands apart as a resident alien in the never-ending, tumultuous conflict, is neither that he is dismissed nor that he is re-commissioned. Instead, he is taken up to heaven in a flaming chariot as the final promotion in his life and the definitive vindication of his ministry (2 Kgs 2:1, 11).

References to Elijah in the New Testament offer enticements for further thought. On the Mount of Transfiguration, Moses and Elijah appear as conversational partners of Jesus in his preparation for death (Matt 17:1–8; Mark 9:2–8; Luke 9:28–36).[55] The joint appearance of Moses and Elijah suggests that they are characters of an exceptional order and two of a kind. To the New Testament writers, Moses and Elijah appear to transmit their legacy on the same wavelength (Matt 17:1–8; see also Rev 11:3–13). This opens up the possibility that Elijah's experience does not revise the prior Exodus narrative as much as my previous assessment has implied. What greets the bewildered prophet as he journeys "on Israel's tracks to the mountain of revelation"[56] is not a revision of Moses's encounter with God, but a correction of his prior misperception of Moses. Moses, too, had met God apart from the trappings of the triad of storm, earthquake, and fire. Long before Elijah, as an exceptional and singular occurrence, "the Lord used to speak to Moses face to face, as one speaks to a friend" (Exod 33:11, cf. Deut 34:10). While Israel might be looking at God from the distance, awed and terrified by God's power, Moses slipped inside the intimidating firewall to know God in ways that did not make God's power the defining feature.

Pausing at a detail that is found only in Luke's story, Moses and Elijah "appeared in glory and were speaking of his departure, which he was about to accomplish at Jerusalem" (Luke 9:31). This might be the most tantalizing element of the transfiguration, because Luke resorts to an allusive term in order to capture the subject of the conversation. Luke says that the three men on the mountain, Jesus, Moses, and Elijah, 'were speaking of his *exodus*' [*elegon tēn exodon autou*].[57] The word "exodus" may refer to someone's death (2 Pet 1:15), but it is widely accepted that the choice of this word in Luke is replete with the *exodus* connotation of Israel (Exod 19:1; 33:38; Ps 104:38, LXX).[58] The entire passage in Luke is embedded in a journey that appears to resemble and recapitulate the exodus story. Specifically, and central to this imagery, there is transfiguration on the mountain and a face-to-face encounter with a divine figure. The human partners in this conversation are the two characters who have been there before, Moses and Elijah.[59]

55. Heil, *The Transfiguration of Jesus*.

56. Buber, *The Prophetic Faith*, 77.

57. Fitzmyer, *The Gospel According to Luke*, 1:793; Moessner, "Luke's Preview," 595; Garrett, "Exodus from Bondage," 657; Nolland, *Luke 9:21—18:34*, 499; Bovon, *A Commentary*, 376.

58. Mánek, "The New Exodus," 8–23; Denaux, "Old Testament Models," 271–305.

59. Ringe, "Luke 9:28–36," 83–99.

To Luke, the implications of this encounter seem to be twofold. First, the transfiguration casts Jesus in the role occupied by God according to the pattern of the prior Old Testament encounters. Jesus is portrayed as though he belongs to the identity of God. Second, and more significant in the present context, Luke's account implies that in Moses and Elijah Jesus meets with a twosome whose prior encounters had prepared them for the subject of the conversation. Jesus will be *going out* as the Israelites did, but he will not *go out* as a figure of power. This thought is made more plausible by the sleepiness and incomprehension of the disciples (Luke 9:32–33): *They* do not understand what is going on, but Moses and Elijah do. To the disciples, the divine sense that has now been internalized by Moses and Elijah is hazy at best. There is continuity with the Horeb experience of Moses and the later Horeb theophany of Elijah on the level of characters and context, but there is also the heralding of an *exodus* that is anticipated by the earlier accounts. Moses and Elijah, the two characters of the Old Testament who had come to understand that God's power does not define divine identity, are distinguished mainly by their readiness to lend support as Jesus goes forth to set things right in other ways than by power.

If, as suggested here, Elijah's experience at Horeb transforms the paradigm of power within which he performed magnificently at Mount Carmel, the Book of Revelation does not only abandon the Carmel paradigm of power—it repudiates it. While Baal and Moloch in the Old Testament have demonic attributes for being complicit in child sacrifice (Lev 18:21; 20:2–5; Ps 106:37–38; Ezek 23:37–39), Baal wilts under pressure at Mount Carmel. Indeed, the job is easy because Baal cannot deliver any of the goods claimed to be his strongest assets. In Revelation's showdown, by contrast, nothing is easy because now the false side is no pushover. The lamb-like false power resorts to a compelling show of muscle in order to prove its divine credentials (Rev 13:14). "It performs great signs," says John, "*even making fire come down from heaven to earth in the sight of all*" (Rev 13:13). This is an unmistakable allusion to the Carmel narrative.[60] Here, in the eschatological drama, fire is again coming down from heaven. By now, however, the revision of the prior paradigm is complete. In the Old Testament account, the true God answers by fire (1 Kgs 18:24). In the revised paradigm of Revelation, the false side makes fire coming down from heaven so as to make it an identity marker for the false side.

Jon Levenson says that "the overwhelming tendency of biblical writers as they confront undeserved evil is not to *explain* it away but to call upon God to *blast* it away."[61] Construing the contest between the cult of Yahweh and the cult of Baal as a conflict between good and evil, Elijah's pre-Horeb mindset belongs in the *blasting* category. God exposes the fallacy of the competing deity in a signal manner, putting the Baal cult to shame and then sending fire that consumed "the burnt offering, the wood, the stones, and even licked up the water that was in the trench" (1 Kgs 18:38). Only

60. Aune, *Revelation 6–16*, 759; Beale, *Revelation*, 709.

61. Levenson, *Creation and the Persistence of Evil*, xvii.

later does it begin to dawn on Elijah that the display of power has limitations that he did not anticipate. It is more than implicit in his post-Carmel experience that use of force may actually energize the opposition rather than persuading it, and if force is persuasive at all it may lead to shallow, short-lived, and often useless convictions.

In theological terms, Elijah's experience at Horeb anticipates Jesus in the New Testament.[62] Resisting the temptation to use the story primarily for this purpose, some implications are nevertheless readily at hand. For Elijah, the retreat from the fiery blast on Mount Carmel to "the still small voice" at Horeb is a journey on the path of revelation. The repeated and insistent comment of the narrator that "the Lord was *not*" in the great wind, the earthquake, and the fire (1 Kgs 19:11–12) means that God will no longer be to Elijah what God was to him in pre-Horeb days. The goalposts of sense are moving. Communication has not ceased, but it transmits on a different wavelength. God now communicates in a hushed voice and by less spectacular means. Unavoidably, the new sense places new demands on the listening ear.

62. Gray (*I & II Kings*, 365) contends that the Horeb theophany anticipates "the divine revelation in Jesus Christ."

Chapter Thirteen

The Man Who Took a Timeout from Sense

It is not difficult to find a person who takes a timeout from sense whether we look within the Bible or to anyone's life journey. But it has taken some thought to find the right title for this chapter, chiefly because the title chosen is the result of hard work on the story itself. As to making the story deserving of our attention, a word from outside will help to show that *sense* as defined in this story is not an item of luxury. Gustav Heinemann, president of the Federal Republic of Germany from 1969 to 1974, once wrote that the Old Testament possesses an openness to the world that has often been embarrassing to Christians.[1] He took as his case in point the subject of this chapter, the story of King Jeroboam and the two prophets in 1 Kings 13. In 1870, a pastor by the name of Paul Geyser wrote a booklet about the story under the title *The Sins of Jeroboam*.[2] Sixty years later, dissenting German Christians reprinted the booklet when it became clear that the official church was willing to subject itself to the dictates of the nationalist-socialist government of Adolf Hitler. They quickly recognized that the government had borrowed a page from the strategy of Jeroboam in Israel: all power in the hands of the state.

The significance of the re-publication of Geyser's booklet was not lost on the millions of Christians who supported Hitler. They felt themselves the target of the book, calling on the secret police to intervene. As a result, the little book was placed on the list of "harmful and unwanted writings." We are thus served notice that this little-known story has unnerved powers to the point of wanting to suppress it. The story, in turn, is critical of concentrations of power and particularly of powers that serve a brew of authority and obedience. Above all, it is the story of a man who, while in the line of duty, took a hazardous timeout from sense.

Of the three main characters in the story, the king is the least interesting, but our bewilderment will be great unless we give him his due. We must therefore begin with him.

1. Heinemann, "Gerhard von Rad zum 70," 11.

2. Paul Geyser, *Die Sünde Jerobeams*, 1911.

Act One: Royal Politics

King Jeroboam enters the biblical narrative at the point when the reign of Solomon, the son of King David by Bathsheba, ends in disappointment. In the historiography of the Old Testament, Solomon brought the nation to its zenith in terms of territorial expansion and wealth (1 Kgs 4:21–24), but it came at an exorbitant cost. Ordinary citizens suffered under the heavy burden of taxation that was required to support royal privilege. In the course of two generations, all of Samuel's earlier warnings against the monarchical system of government proved true (1 Sam 8:10–18). With Solomon's seven hundred wives and three hundred concubines, the figure given in the Bible, the cost of royal privilege mushroomed (1 Kgs 11:3). Samuel had foreseen that one day the king's subjects would complain bitterly, and they did (1 Sam 8:18; 1 Kgs 12:4). Rather than allowing absolutism to continue unchecked, the subjects demanded what might be seen as a nascent version of government by the consent of the governed.

Thus, when Solomon's son and designated successor failed to heed the signals of discontent, ten of the twelve tribes of Israel refused to recognize him. They turned instead to Jeroboam, a talented man who had distinguished himself in the king's service (1 Kgs 11:26–39). Choosing secession, the ten northern tribes anointed Jeroboam their king. Only two tribes remained with Solomon's son (1 Kgs 12:16, 20).

But Jeroboam did not receive an unrestricted mandate. A clause at the time of his accession included a rudimentary version of the rule of law. Between the competing categories of *Rex Lex* ("the king is law") and *Lex Rex* ("the law is king"), the terms set for Jeroboam belonged emphatically to the latter. "If you will listen to all that I command you, walk in my ways, and do what is right in my sight by keeping my statutes and my commandments, . . . I will be with you, and will build you an enduring house," God is said to have told him (1 Kgs 11:38). Describing this type of government in today's terminology, we see a system that envisions the consent of the governed, the rule of law, and, although frequently overlooked even by seasoned readers of biblical texts, the separation of powers.

In fact, under the rubric "separation of powers," the Old Testament is aware of the risk of combining religious and political power, and, expressing it in positive terms, the benefit of separating the religious from the political realm. Jeroboam was entrusted with political power, being specifically denied control of the religious domain.

In his first move, nevertheless, he set out to take control of religious expression. The power calculus of the ancient world made Church and State one.[3] Lord (Sir John) Acton calls this "the *vice* of the classic State," a system of government where there is "only one legislator and one authority."[4] Jeroboam did not consider such a system a vice. He, the king, would be the decider in the realm of religion as much as in the sphere of politics. Fearing that his subjects would return their loyalty to the House

3. Lord Action, "The History of Freedom," 68.

4. Ibid.

of David if they continued the habit of journeying to Jerusalem for the stipulated religious feasts (1 Kgs 12:26–27), he set up two alternative places of worship within his territory (12:28, 30). His second step was to put the priests on his payroll, monopolizing the right to make ecclesial appointments (12:31). His third step was to institute a new religious calendar, beginning with "a festival on the fifteenth day in the eighth month, in the month that he alone had devised" (12:32, 33).

The rapid moves show a purpose-driven man at work. The king tapped into the power of religion in order to make it serve his interest. A system of patronage would make the priesthood subservient to the temporal power. Moreover, the king intended to exercise royal power in an arbitrary way, needing no other rationale than his own will: thus the festival "on the fifteenth day in the eighth month, in the month that *he alone had devised*" (12:33).

We need this background as we try to understand the role of the two prophets that appear in the second and third acts of the escalating drama. Jeroboam's overreaching is more than a curiosity in the Bible. Beyond its impact on the immediate circle of involved parties, the incident provides a representative window on the interaction between religion and politics throughout much of history. We see Jeroboam's scheme—"the vice of the classic State"—in the Roman imperial system, where the emperor held the reins of political and religious power. We see it in the unrelenting power struggle between Church and State in Christendom, where the contested issue between the political and the religious authority centers on who should be the highest authority in both realms, neither authority inclined to think in terms of separation of powers.[5] We see it in the astute political moves of Napoleon, who revived the fortunes of the Roman Catholic Church after the French Revolution as long as the Church stayed firmly under his control. And, as noted in the first paragraph, we see it in the attempt of the Third Reich to make religion subservient to the interests of the state.[6]

Jeroboam did not plan to render religion unimportant but to make it do his bidding. The national shrines, the compliant priesthood, and the new religious calendar were calculated to consolidate his power. The plan appears to have won the consent of the governed. It is reasonable to surmise that his success in this regard was due to his ability to play to patriotic and nationalistic sentiments. With respect to the new shrines our narrator says that "the people went to worship before the one at Bethel and before the other as far as Dan," places that were convenient and close to home (12:30). In summary, the story begins on the assumption that Jeroboam commits a serious offense, inscribing his vision on the body politic of Israel so firmly that subsequent interventions fail to undo it.[7]

5. For an illuminating selection, see Lord Acton, "The History of Freedom," 53–81; Greenslade, *Church & State*; Tierney, *The Crisis of Church and State*.

6. Ericksen and Heschel, *Betrayal*.

7. For evidence of the durability of Jeroboam's scheme, see 1 Kgs 15:34; 16:22; 22:52; 2 Kgs 3:3; 10:29; 13:2, 11; 14:24; 15:9, 18, 24, 28; 17:21–22.

Act Two: A Voice of Protest

The second act begins at the moment when Jeroboam assumes the plenary powers of priest and king. On a day that to us could be equivalent to a presidential inauguration or the Fourth of July, Jeroboam "went up to the altar to offer incense" (12:33). The act, with all due pomp and ceremony, leaves no doubt that executive and religious authority is in the hands of the king. He is acting as priest and ruler in one person. At that very moment, however, the festivities are interrupted by an uninvited visitor.

"While Jeroboam was standing by the altar to offer incense, a man of God came out of Judah by the word of the Lord to Bethel and proclaimed against the altar by the word of the Lord, and said, 'O altar, altar, thus says the Lord: "A son shall be born to the house of David, Josiah by name; and he shall sacrifice on you the priests of the high places who offer incense on you, and human bones shall be burned on you"'" (13:1–2).

The guest seems to appear from nowhere, and he does not have a slot assigned to him in the program. In terms recognizable to us, he might be dismissed and quickly disposed of as an unwelcome heckler. Designating him as "a man of God," however, gives him the credentials of a divinely-appointed messenger. Twice the text says that the man of God came "by the word of the Lord." His mission was not his own idea, and his word, like the word of an ambassador, had the authority of the one who sent him. On this authority he proceeded to condemn the king's project in graphic terms.

For Jeroboam, the timing could not have been worse. If anyone in the audience had misgivings about his attempt to exploit religion in the interest of consolidating his political power, they had their reservations confirmed. For a king determined not to lose face, his options were few. Jeroboam quickly deployed a tested remedy against dissent. Stretching out his hand, he ordered his attendants, "Seize him!" (13:4).

The minor glitch, the king must be thinking, will be quickly fixed by resolute use of force. But then—and to his horror—the hand stretched out against the man of God "withered so that he could not draw it back to himself" (13:4). Adding insult to injury, the altar was torn down by an unseen hand. This, too, happened "according to the sign that the man of God had given by the word of the Lord" (13:5). With this one-two punch, striking the king and the altar, a higher power appears to be putting Jeroboam in his place. Within a matter of minutes, he had suffered profound public humiliation. His physical impairment now placed him in the unaccustomed role of supplicant, pleading with the visitor to pray to God for his arm to be healed (13:6). Despite the king's high-handed ways, the man of God "entreated the Lord; and the king's hand was restored to him, and became as it was before" (13:6).

This was hardly the course of events Jeroboam envisioned at the start of the day. Each move by the man of God placed the king's project in a bad light while at the same time bolstering the credentials of the visiting emissary.[8] The latter had his authority authenticated by the king's withered hand, the healing of his hand, and the destruction

8. Jepsen, "Gottesmann und Prophet," 177.

of the altar. Now on the brink of defeat, Jeroboam had to come up with a different strategy.

At that point he projects a change of heart. Dropping the threatening tone, the king turns to fence-mending, saying to the man of God, "Come home with me and dine, and I will give you a gift" (13:7).

A few minutes earlier Jeroboam intended to put the visitor in chains. Now he wants to host him for dinner! Few readers will see the sudden sweetness as a genuine conversion. Nevertheless, some interpreters see ambiguity with respect to Jeroboam's motive for the invitation.[9] Does he wish to host the man of God for dinner in gratitude for the healing of his arm? This is unlikely, given the fact that his arm was doing just fine until he found himself in violation of his mandate. Does he think that table fellowship would mute the sting of the prophetic rebuke, putting a spin on the day's events that will place his humiliation in a less compromising light? This is a far more likely rationale. What force fails to do a royal banquet might to some extent accomplish. If we look for images that the king might wish to show on the evening newscast, a picture of the king toasting the man of God from Judah at a royal banquet would go a long way toward cushioning the impact of the latter's rebuke. Similarly, the force of the visitor's message would be significantly blunted upon the sight of him seated at table with the king, the king giving a speech in his honor and bestowing a gift, as he promised he would (13:7).

Diplomatic body language is an important part of an emissary's resources. We know that the vocabulary of diplomacy in contemporary practice is precise across a broad range of possibilities. A discussion between two parties in conflict, listed in a descending order of congeniality, might be cordial, constructive, frank, blunt, or angry. Applying this scale to the mission of the man of God, his message belonged distinctly to the blunt category. The diplomatic body language of a royal banquet would by any imaginable criterion compromise the mission. Walter Gross says that the king's motive for the invitation is not explicit in the story,[10] but it is implicit to the point that we can be certain what it was. A figure of power who has orchestrated religious subversion on this scale and staked his reputation on combining the role of king [politics] and priest [religion] is not likely to be suddenly repentant and eager to honor the person who threatens his cherished project. If the prophet of God sits down for dinner with the purpose-driven king, a measure of respectability will be restored to the king.

Whether or not this scenario had been anticipated when the man of Judah set out on his mission, the manner of execution was specified in the original job description. Responding to the king's invitation, "the man of God said to the king, 'If you give me half your kingdom, I will not go in with you; nor will I eat food or drink water in this

9. Gross, "Lying Prophets," 119–20.

10. Ibid., 120.

place. *For thus I was commanded by the word of the LORD: You shall not eat food, or drink water, or return by the way that you came*'" (13:8, 9).

Little is left to chance in this assignment. Now, in the hearing of dignitaries and people assembled for the occasion, the man of God goes on record saying that he was *commanded by the word of the LORD* to deliver the message and to return without stopping to fraternize on the way. The thrust of the formulation goes beyond diplomatic body language of the blunt sort because it includes a biblical way of thinking that requires explanation. Not returning "by the way that you came" is part and parcel of the prophetic sign, a pointed way of signifying "the absoluteness and irrevocability of the verdict."[11] Thus, when the man of God "went another way, and did not return by the way that he had come to Bethel" (13:10), "everyone became aware of the invulnerability of the word of God which he had uttered."[12]

On the authority of his divine commissioner, the man of God has publicly committed himself to a specified course of action with respect to the execution of the mission. As he leaves for home by way of another route than the one by which he came, his footprint in the public square is enormous. A future revocation of the divine command, should such a scenario present itself, is all but ruled out by the terms expressed by the man of God from Judah.[13]

In light of the foregoing, speculation as to the reason for the divine prohibition is unwarranted. Gross, strangely, finds the prohibition as inscrutable as the king's invitation,[14] but the divine instruction is fully congruous with the mission of the man of God. What, we might ask, should the man of God have done if God had not specified how to carry out the assignment? If the manner of delivery is part and parcel of the mission, there would be no need for a command. Interpreters who raise their eyebrows in puzzled incomprehension over the divine command would do better expending their efforts pondering the spectacle of a man of God delivering an uncompromising message only to see him take the sting out of his mission by sitting down at a banquet hosted by the person he came to rebuke. Such a scenario would indicate lack of understanding of the mission and not only disrespect for the divine command. The mission and the manner of its execution are whole cloth.

When act three in the drama is about to begin, the king has behaved badly while the man of God from Judah has acquitted himself well, at least as far as he can be judged from the information that lies on the surface. Enter now a third character, an old prophet living in Bethel (13:11). With respect to his behavior, the ingenuity of the interpreter will be taxed to the limit.

11. Simon, "1 Kings 13," 91.

12. Ibid.

13. Jepsen, "Gottesmann und Prophet," 178.

14. Gross, "Lying Prophets," 120.

Act Three: The Old Prophet

When the prophet living in Bethel enters the fray, the king all but disappears from the story. Although Jeroboam's actions provide the reason for the urgent intervention, the story is more interested in the other two characters: the man of God from Judah and the old prophet living in Bethel.

> Now there lived an old prophet in Bethel. One of his sons came and told him all that the man of God had done that day in Bethel; the words also that he had spoken to the king, they told to their father (13:11).

We do well to ask some questions at this stage in order to be prepared for the challenges that are yet to come.

The man is said to be "an old prophet." In the wider context of 1 Kings, the designation "prophet" does not automatically certify the person as a man of integrity. Later in the same book, one of Israel's kings takes counsel from a host of 'prophets' only to make it apparent that the entire prophetic guild has sold out to other priorities than the service of truth (1 Kgs 22:2–18). The four hundred prophets in the king's service are an assembly of yes-men, parroting the message that the king wants to hear. The king, in turn, eager to embark on an ill-conceived war, gets precisely the slam dunk advice that he needs in order to justify his intention (1 Kgs 22:11–12). We are thus made aware that there can be more than one kind of 'prophet.' While a few prophets in this body of literature are men of integrity, most are not. What kind of person is the old prophet in Bethel? Living in Bethel, why does he not attend the king's ceremony? Old age is hardly the explanation, as the story will show. Was he absent because presence would have signaled tacit endorsement of the king's scheme, approval that he was determined to withhold? What other reasons could there be for him not attending the auspicious event?

Two other features in the later story should also be considered, the first relating to tone of voice, and the other to motive. When the contrarian prophet in the later story is asked to give his advice to the king of his day, he appears to say exactly the same thing as the people-pleasing prophets that precede him (1 Kgs 22:2–18).

> *Advice of the four hundred prophets*: "Go up; for the Lord will give it into the hand of the king" (1 Kgs 22:6).

> *Advice of Micaiah son of Imlah*: "Go up and triumph; the Lord will give it into the hand of the king" (1 Kgs 22:15).

These answers are almost identical, but their meaning is not. Only by inferring tone of voice can we tell the difference. In this case, tone of voice transforms identical words into opposite meanings. The voice of the majority reeks with insincerity and flattery (1 Kgs 22:7). Conversely, the voice that stands against the tide makes the insincerity and flattery more apparent by adding a tincture of sarcasm. The advice of the people-pleasing 'prophets' is exposed for what it is by ridiculing it. Saying the same words but saying it in a different tone gives a completely different meaning (1 Kgs 22:16).

This feature of speech has enormous consequences for interpretation. Meaning is not derived merely from what is said, but also from how it is said. When, for instance, the man of God turns down the invitation from king Jeroboam to be a guest at a banquet in his honor, our reading should not only look at the words as such. We also need to ask *how* he answers the king. Does he respond with conviction? Does he hesitate for a moment or in some other way convey that he would have liked to be the king's guest and to receive the gift he offered him? Would he have done it except for the divine command that stands in the way? What he says is clear enough. "For thus I was commanded by the word of the LORD: You shall not eat food, or drink water, or return by the way that you came'" (13:9). But how does he say it?

The third lesson in the later story in 1 Kings speaks to the question of motive. Micaiah, the dissident prophet later in 1 Kings, explains the message of the false prophets in his day as a God-approved falsehood (1 Kgs 22:19–23). This feature suggests that the false prophets were in some sense also working under inspiration. Theirs was the inspiration of "a lying spirit" (1 Kgs 22:22, 23). The contribution of the 'lying spirit' is chiefly to convince the king to do what he already wants to do while at the same time making clear to the reader that the action in question is contrary to good sense and to God's will. This background might be useful to our view of the old prophet in 1 Kings 13. He, too, will tell a falsehood (1 Kgs 13:18). Does he tell it as a fallen prophet or as a man of integrity? Do we see prophets of different hues telling lies that are approved by God in a given situation? Is the problem in the alleged 'lie' that is told or in the attitude of the messenger from Judah? The emerging plot is certainly not lacking in complexity!

Returning to the story in 1 Kings 13, we recall that one of the sons of the old prophet "came and told him all that the man of God had done that day in Bethel; the words also that he had spoken to the king, they told to their father" (13:11). The plural '*they*' in the last part of this sentence complements the suggestion in the beginning of the sentence that only one of his sons was involved. This detail intimates that the message of the first son is corroborated by the second. The retelling of the day's events has the flavor of two sons speaking to the father in a tone of excitement. How, we ask again, had the man of God spoken? And how did the sons of the old prophet tell their father that the man of God had spoken?

It is safe to assume that the old prophet was eagerly awaiting the sons' return home after the day's events. Being a resident of Bethel, he must have known what the king was up to. In fact, the king's dedication of the local shrine must have been widely known and anticipated. Being a prophet, good or bad, the king's intent would interest him beyond the ordinary. When the great day arrived, he must have known that his sons intended to be present at the event. Given the patriarchal structure of family relations at that time, it is likely that he commissioned them to attend. The fact that they report to him upon their return suggests that the old prophet is awaiting their arrival.

But what is the reason for his interest? Does he hope that the king will succeed in his design, sending his sons as a token of approval? Or does he hope that the king will fail, too upset to attend in person, and yet secretly hoping that something might happen to derail the scheme? Being fully informed of the day's events, the reaction of the father is striking.

> Their father said to them, "Which way did he [the man of God from Judah] go?" And his sons showed him the way that the man of God who came from Judah had gone. Then he said to his sons, "Saddle a donkey for me." So they saddled a donkey for him, and he mounted it. He went after the man of God, and found him sitting under an oak tree. He said to him, "Are you the man of God who came from Judah?" He answered, "I am" (13:12–14).

This is not the action of a person doing something on the spur of the moment. The old prophet's hurried intervention is better explained against a background of someone having an intense interest in the subject. The action is rapid not only in the sense that the old prophet wastes no time upon hearing the report. His decision to go after 'the man of God' is meaningful only if there is a realistic chance of catching up with him. We may therefore hold on to our assumption that the sons have hurried home to tell their father. They give their report within the time frame when it is still possible for the father to intervene. The interaction between father and sons could, from the point of view of the sons, well be that they expect their father to react a certain way. As to age and health, the father is neither too old nor too decrepit to mount the donkey, taking off in hot pursuit of the man of God from Judah. On the whole, these are actions of a man who has a stake in the day's events.

"He went after the man of God, and found him sitting under an oak tree," says the narrator (13:14). Is this scene proof of a chink in the younger man's armor, urgency and vigilance giving way either to fatigue or complacency? Can he safely slacken the pace while still on the enemy's home field without risking that someone may take advantage of his timeout? Will someone yet find him with his guard let down?

From the first moment when the old prophet begins speaking to the man of God from Judah, it is clear that the subject matter centers on the exchange between the emissary and the king earlier in the day. The old man says to him, "Come home with me and eat some food" (13:15). This is almost verbatim a repetition of the king's invitation to the messenger (13:7). The prominence and stability of the theme of sitting down to eat is striking throughout.

> *King to the man of God*:
> "Come home with me and dine" (13:7).

> *Man of God to the king*:
> "I will not go in with you; nor will I eat food or drink water in this place" (13:8).
>
> "For thus I was commanded by the word of the Lord: 'You shall not eat food, or drink water'" (13:9).
>
> *Old prophet to the man of God*:
> "Come home with me and eat some food" (13:15).

The question of sitting down to eat and drink cannot be a trivial matter. Why, we must ask, does the old prophet bring up this subject again? What kind of prophet is he, recalling that of prophets there may be more than one kind?

Allowing for nuances in each category, the two main options are simple: The old prophet could be good, or he could be bad. Many readers will be tempted to consider this question unnecessary in light of what follows next.

> *Man of God to old prophet*:
> I cannot return with you, or go in with you; nor will I eat food or drink water with you in this place; for it was said to me by the word of the Lord: "You shall not eat food or drink water there, or return by the way that you came" (13:16–17).
>
> *Prophet to the man of God*:
> *I also am a prophet as you are, and an angel spoke to me by the word of the Lord*: "Bring him back with you into your house so that he may eat food and drink water" (13:18, italics added).

Based on this information, is the old prophet now a good or a bad person? His message is not in doubt. Despite the high stakes involved in *not* eating or drinking up to this point in the story, the old prophet claims that the original commission has been revoked. Moreover, it has been revoked and replaced with a contrary command that claims the highest authority. First, he says, "I am also a prophet as you are." Second, he claims that "an angel spoke to me." Third, he avers that the angel spoke "by the word of the Lord," aligning the new message with the source of the initial instruction (13:1, 5, 9, 17, 18). Words and events so far in the story highlight the irrevocable character of the commission, and yet here is a voice proposing to revoke the most conspicuous feature.

It is now time to point out that the man of God is on the hook in a way that the reader of the story need not be. After the solemn declaration of the old prophet, alleging revocation of the former instruction, the narrator makes the comment, "But he was lying to him" (13:18, NIV).

Is not this proof that the old prophet must belong to the bad category, of whom, as we have seen, there are many in this book? A bad prophet could be motivated by a desire to embarrass the messenger from Judah, trying to compromise his mission either out of jealousy or because he has the king's interests at heart. Three keen readings of the story lean strongly in this direction. Pamela Tamarkin Reis is convinced that the prophets in the story, including the man of God from Judah, are two of a kind. She detects lack of resolve in the man of God, seeing him as a person who vacillates in the face of the king's invitation, secretly wishing to cross over to the other side. When the old prophet says to him that "I am also a prophet as you are" (13:18), he means it as a signal to a fellow partner in crime: "I am a compromised prophet, and I see that you are, too."

> The old prophet lies, but he can excuse his lie on the rationalization that the man of God is ready to be enticed, desires it, and certainly, by his cupidity, deserves it. Perhaps the old prophet would not have attempted deceit had the man of God shown constancy. And, had the man of God been steadfast, surely he would not have been swayed by a falsehood from a functionary of an idolatrous city. The faltering dedication of the man of God provides the old prophet with his opportunity, his justification, and his success.[15]

Uriel Simon has a different plot construct, but he is similarly convinced that the old prophet is a bad person. He is motivated not so much by his concern for the success of king Jeroboam's project but by his wish to avoid damage to his future grave.[16] Alfred Jepsen sees the old prophet as a fallen messenger and an accomplice with the king, but he does not impute vacillation to the man of God. What stirs the old prophet into action is his intention to succeed where the king failed.[17] In other words, the old prophet has more effective means at his disposal to damage the mission of the messenger, and he is in a hurry to give it a try.

The best argument for seeing the old prophet as a suspect character is in the eyes of many readers the disclosure that "he was lying" (13:18). It will be unnecessary to consider other options after reading this. Given the lying, the thinking goes, he must be a bad man.

But this view cannot stand unchallenged. We have already found evidence in the same book that 'lying' is not an unequivocal criterion by which to judge character (1 Kgs 22:22, 23). At an earlier stage in the Bible, moreover, Abraham is less than forthright with respect to his relationship to Sarah, wishing to hide that she is his wife and thus allowing another man to take her. And yet when God intervenes in the matter, he defends Abraham despite his duplicity, saying that "he is a prophet" (Gen 20:7). An assessment of a person's integrity should therefore not put all its eggs into the basket of this one criterion.

15. Reis, "Vindicating God," 383.
16. Simon, "1 Kings 13," 92.
17. Jepsen, "Gottesmann und Prophet," 178.

Questions regarding the character and intentions of the old prophet are legitimate. If he is truly a supporter of the king, why does he not attend the ceremony earlier in the day? Assuming that he is awaiting his sons' return, what does he expect them to say? It is not likely that he had factored the uninvited man of God from Judah into the proceedings in advance. And what do the sons say that so stirs the old man to make him go after the man of God?

These caveats are sufficient to invite another scenario. In the alternative account, the old prophet does not attend the festivities in the morning because he is opposed to what the king was doing. This explains the charged atmosphere when his sons return home to tell him of the day's events. Reis exaggerates the character flaw in the messenger from Judah,[18] but she deserves credit for suggesting that he did not turn in a persuasive performance. Thus, when the old prophet sets out to confront the messenger, he is doing it in awareness of a weakness in the younger man's armor. Unlike the interpretation of Reis and others, however, his motivation need not be a desire to thwart the mission of the emissary. If we allow ourselves to see the old prophet as a man of integrity and as a person who sides with the mission of the emissary, *the rush into action could be remedial with respect to the latter's mission.* On this logic, the old prophet realizes that the emissary failed to deliver his message in a persuasive way. An echo of this possibility might be heard in the careful narration of the sons' report to their father. The narrator says that "the words also that he had spoken to the king, they told to their father" (13:11), words conveying lack of resolve on the part of the messenger. The old prophet's motive for pursuing the man of God from Judah parallels the mission of the latter toward the king. Just as the messenger from Judah set out to rebuke the king, the old prophet at Bethel goes forth to rebuke the younger man in an attempt to undo the damage caused by his lack of firmness.

Several elements in the remainder of the story fit this construct much better. First, we see that "the man of God went back with him [the old prophet], and ate food and drank water in his house" (1 Kgs 13:19). James K. Mead is certainly correct when he sees this as the turning point in the story, "the disobedient choice the man of God makes when he forsakes the word of Yahweh and returns to Bethel."[19] The phrase relating to *not* eating and drinking that resonates in the account (13: 8, 9, 15) is now reversed to doing precisely what was heretofore ruled out. "Will the man of God go with the prophet?"[20] Mead asks. The answer, we know, is yes; he will go with the old prophet, and he will do exactly what he proclaimed with such fanfare that he would *not* do earlier in the day. This fits the hypothesis that the old prophet saw the emissary as a man betraying an inclination to compromise. Now there is proof of this impression.

18. Reis, "Vindicating God," 377, 382.

19. Mead, "Kings and Prophets," 196.

20. Ibid., 200.

Second, everything in the remainder of the story suggests that the old prophet is firmly on the side of the mission of the man of God from Judah.

> As they were sitting at the table, the word of the Lord came to the prophet who had brought him back; and he proclaimed to the man of God who came from Judah, "Thus says the Lord: Because you have disobeyed the word of the Lord, and have not kept the commandment that the Lord your God commanded you, but have come back and have eaten food and drunk water in the place of which he said to you, 'Eat no food, and drink no water,' your body shall not come to your ancestral tomb" (13:20–22).

On the surface, it seems unreasonable for the old prophet to fault the man of God from Judah for being disobedient when he was the one who contributed to his downfall. But this problem becomes less acute within the line of thought we are presently exploring. If the old prophet went after the emissary in order to confront him for his failure to execute his mission in a convincing way, he has done him no injustice other than to drive the point home. Reis claims that the man of God was ready to be enticed.[21] If this is correct, the old prophet told the lie that the man of God wished to be true and wanted to believe. Mead asks whether the lie told by the old prophet will "excuse the man of God from responsibility?"[22] The implied answer in the story, of course, is 'no.'

Third, if the old prophet wanted the emissary's mission to fail, it is incongruous to see him consciously and confidently acting as though he is executing *his* mission in lockstep with a divinely ordained script. After rebuking the emissary for his apparent disobedience, the old prophet pronounces judgment on him (13:22). He then sends him away astride his own donkey, as if aware that the animal will faithfully perform its part to the point of leaving no doubt that the demise of the man of God from Judah was more than a freak accident.

> After the man of God had eaten food and had drunk, they saddled for him a donkey belonging to the prophet who had brought him back. Then as he went away, a lion met him on the road and killed him. His body was thrown in the road, and the donkey stood beside it; the lion also stood beside the body. People passed by and saw the body thrown in the road, with the lion standing by the body. And they came and told it in the town where the old prophet lived. When the prophet who had brought him back from the way heard of it, he said, "It is the man of God who disobeyed the word of the Lord; therefore the Lord has given him to the lion, which has torn him and killed him according to the word that the Lord spoke to him" (13:23–26).

The behavior of the donkey is a telling image in the story, the donkey and the lion standing side by side next to the corpse of the man of God from Judah. To be party

21. Reis, "Vindicating God," 383.

22. Mead, "Kings and Prophets," 200.

to this choreography would be no mean feat for a man alleged to be a false and fallen prophet!

Fourth, as the story draws to a close, the old prophet comes out in unstinting support for the mission of the fallen man of God.

> Then he said to his sons, "Saddle a donkey for me." So they saddled one, and he went and found the body thrown in the road, with the donkey and the lion standing beside the body. The lion had not eaten the body or attacked the donkey. The prophet took up the body of the man of God, laid it on the donkey, and brought it back to the city, to mourn and to bury him. He laid the body in his own grave; and they mourned over him, saying, "Alas, my brother!" After he had buried him, he said to his sons, "When I die, bury me in the grave in which the man of God is buried; lay my bones beside his bones. For the saying that he proclaimed by the word of the Lord against the altar in Bethel, and against all the houses of the high places that are in the cities of Samaria, shall surely come to pass" (13:27–32).

Here, the narrator points to animal behavior that is contrary to nature. The old prophet finds "the donkey and the lion standing beside the body" of the man of God from Judah. "The lion had not eaten the body or attacked the donkey," we are told (13:28). We do not need further proof that such a scenario would be beyond the ability of the keenest choreographer, keeping the animals in a watchdog position for an extended period of time.

Most remarkable, nevertheless, are the demeanor and words of the old prophet. He mourns over the man of God from Judah, buries him in his own grave, asks to be buried next to him when his turn comes, and finally declares that the emissary's word will come to pass to the smallest detail. While it might be possible to attribute this to a change of heart on the part of the old prophet, it is far more plausible that the prophet is genuinely sorry that the message could only be delivered the hard way.

Prominent interpreters hold that the story makes God out to be "a harsh tyrant,"[23] that the story "violates our sense of justice to the core,"[24] and even that its ethic "approaches the demonic."[25] These damning views should not be accepted out of hand. If the man from Judah fails in the initial delivery of his message and then falls victim to a lie despite being trained to expose falsehoods, the alleged harshness of the story will be less. Those who feel that the judgment is harsh must not overlook that there is vindication for the man of God, too. He is eulogized by the old prophet as a brother in the uphill struggle for truth, and we are assured that his word will stand even though he fell short of being faithful to it (13:30–32). At day's end, the image of the lion, the

23. Robinson, *First Book of Kings*, 162.

24. Schwarzwäller, "Probleme gegenwärtiger Theologie," 491–92.

25. Crenshaw, *Prophetic Conflict*, 48.

donkey, and the corpse dominates the visual field, signifying mission accomplished despite evident and terrible shortcomings.

Dangerous Obedience

While many commentators are puzzled by the story, D. W. van Winkle gives a summary that comes close to a consensus statement as to what the author of 1 Kings 13 intended to impress upon the reader. When all is said and done, says van Winkle, the bottom line is to teach unquestioning obedience to the divine command. Calling it a 'new criterion' for distinguishing between what is true and what is false, he claims that his proposed criterion

> provides a test which would have helped the man of God to recognize the falsehood of the old prophet's assurance that it was all right for him to return and eat. It also provides a test that could have been employed by any Israelite. This criterion is the criterion of obedience to the commandment of Yahweh. The man of God should have recognized the assurance of the old prophet to be false since it encouraged him to violate the commandment of God.[26]

Walter Gross, having expressed bewilderment with respect to the rationale for the divine command and the motive for the king's invitation, draws a similar conclusion.

> When the man of God allows himself to be deceived, it is no longer important if he acts in good faith or not. It is of no importance whether he believed YHWH had rescinded his original prohibition. Decisive alone is that the man of God overstepped YHWH's command. For that he must be punished. YHWH's word may not be ignored, least of all by a man of God. YHWH does punish him but not in spite of his innocence. The text does not present a primitive image of God nor the image of an enigmatic God.[27]

Here, too, the accent falls on obedience. Likewise, Mead makes "the inviolability of Yahweh's word" the lesson of the story.[28] Werner E. Lemke, not mincing words, takes the story to be "a paradigmatic example of the importance of *unquestioning obedience* to the divine will."[29]

Gross claims bravely that it is "of no importance whether he [the man of God from Judah] believed YHWH had rescinded his original prohibition."[30] Such a view is surely too simplistic. For the man of God, the problem is precisely that the revocation of the original command was presented to him as a word spoken to him by an angel,

26. Van Winkle, "1 Kings XIII," 31–43.
27. Gross, "Lying Prophets," 123–24.
28. Mead, "Kings and Prophets," 205.
29. Lemke, "The Way of Obedience," 317, emphasis added.
30. Gross, "Lying Prophet," 123–24.

who, in turn, spoke to him "by the word of the Lord" (13:18). We can fault him for being too ready to believe the claim of the old prophet, but the problem confronting him is not one that is resolved within a paradigm of simple obedience. *We may just as well argue that the weak spot in his armor is obedience*, and, worse yet, that his problem is *unquestioning* obedience. When "the man of God went back with him" (13:19), it is not likely that he acted in conscious and willful disobedience to the divine command. He meant to be obedient, accepting the word of the man claiming to be a prophet like himself. This man spoke as though he had received a command revoking instruction given earlier. In an attempt to distill a bottom line in the story, I suggest the following: *The problem of the man of God from Judah is obedience in the absence of understanding.*

The merit of this conclusion rests on a number of features in the story. How, as suggested earlier, should the man of God have gone about his mission in the absence of a divine command? If we are persuaded that the divine command proposed only what was in character with the mission and its prospect for success, we will not at any point expect the message to be rescinded. When the old prophet appears, his message is at odds with the original instruction given to the man of God *and* with the character of the mission. The man of God turned down the king's invitation in front of the ruling elite and a multitude of onlookers on the strength of God's command. Now, when told that the previous command has been revoked, he can accept this claim only at the risk of making it seem like the original instruction had been given for no good reason. How will he explain this to the people he met earlier in the day? If God's commands are arbitrary and therefore easily revoked, a host of other commands might be in line for annulment, including the commands that Jeroboam had disregarded when he placed religion under the auspices of the state. The most coherent scenario, therefore, is that the man of God had a deficient understanding of God's command, a flawed view of obedience, and an inclination to follow orders uncritically. These proved a lethal combination.

It is possible to see the story akin to a sting operation in which the old prophet acts the part of an undercover agent. Modern governments and law enforcement agencies have employed similar methods in order to expose corruption. Employees with no previous criminal record have been indicted because they accepted bribes from a disguised agent posing as a representative of a conflicting interest. In the ABSCAM scheme that came to light in 1980, FBI officials acting as a fictitious Arab sheik tried to bribe trusted congressmen in return for various favors. Four legislators, including one senator, ended up in jail. Politicians and sports personalities have been arrested for soliciting or accepting sexual services from undercover agents. The ethics of such procedures has been debated, but numerous cases have held up in court because the measures are considered necessary to crack down on corruption, hidden or manifest.

In the case of the man of God from Judah, the line of thought developed above envisions more than a latent flaw in him. His weakness is already out in the open, perceived by the old prophet's sons and reported to him at the point when they return home. For this reason the old prophet sets out to confront and expose in the man of God the same cavalier attitude toward the divine command that the latter had confronted in king Jeroboam.

The relevance of the story to human reality is broad on many counts. At a high point in the history of the medieval papacy, pope Urban II (1088–1099) launched the Crusades, claiming it to be God's will to send armies to the Middle East in order to liberate Jerusalem from Muslim rule. In a carefully choreographed event, the pope talked as if the mission was divinely inspired. Steven Runciman documents that the launch of the Crusades had been rehearsed in advance in order to generate a groundswell of support.[31] Even before the pope had finished his call, the shout "God wills it" erupted from envoys scattered throughout the crowd. Eventually, the refrain swelled into a fervent chorus, "God wills it! God wills it!" The tidal wave of holy resolve generated the momentum the pope had hoped to achieve, and the Christian Holy War was on. There was no one present to express the reservation and contrary point of view, "God does not will it." The Crusades, the most searing event in the history of Christian-Muslim relations, is at its core an example of misguided obedience and willingness to allow a claim to speak for God to go untested.

In 2003, the United States and some of its Western allies launched a war against Iraq based on the assertion that Iraq posed a threat to world peace because it possessed weapons of mass destruction. Colin Powell, then the Secretary of State, went before the UN Security Council in February 2003, arguing forcefully that the United States had incontrovertible intelligence proving stockpiles of chemical and biological weapons in Iraq, the existence of mobile laboratories, and a program to produce nuclear weapons. Hard core evidence was produced in the form of detailed drawings of the mobile laboratories, the most effective aspect of the presentation. Again and again, Secretary Powell repeated the words, "We *know*," emphasizing it with a certainty only slightly short of a divine revelation.

> My colleagues, every statement I make today is backed up by sources, solid sources. These are not assertions. What we're giving you are facts and conclusions based on solid intelligence.
>
> As these drawings based on their description show, we *know* what the fermenters look like, we *know* what the tanks, pumps, compressors and other parts look like. We *know* how they fit together. We *know* how they work. And we *know* a great deal about the platforms on which they are mounted.[32]

Colin Powell's most important source, it turned out later, was an Iraqi refugee in Germany with the code name Curveball.[33] Curveball's testimony, a series of half-

31. Runciman, *The First Crusade*, 188.

32. Powell, Address to the United Nations Security Council.

33. Drogin, *Curveball*.

truths and fantastic fiction, had in the annals of Western intelligence been elevated into hard facts. His status as a source, at no point impressive, suggests that no lie is more persuasive than the one we like to believe, or, at the very least, that things we want to believe lead us to suspend vigilance. The Curveball story is said to be the most colossal intelligence lapse in the history of the United States. How could such a failure happen in an environment dedicated to knowing the 'truth'? Engraved on the foyer of the CIA headquarters, I learned recently, is the statement, "You shall know the truth, and the truth shall make you free" (John 8:32). How could an agency claiming commitment to knowing the truth fail so monumentally?

The stampede of interpreters who turn the story in 1 Kings 13 into a case study of the duty to practice unquestioning obedience is grievous in view of the fact that the story aspires to teach the opposite and more grievous still when we realize that life demands more than unquestioning obedience of humans and prophets. In the aftermath of World War II, C. P. Snow noted that the worst evil in the world has been committed in the name of obedience.

> When you think of the long and gloomy history of man, you will find more hideous crimes have been committed in the name of obedience than have ever been committed in the name of rebellion. . . . The German Officer Corps were brought up in the most rigorous code of obedience . . . in the name of obedience they were party to, and assisted in, the most wicked large scale actions in the history of the world.[34]

Stanley Milgram's study at Yale University the same year offers clinical proof that a person's inclination to submit to authority easily leads to suspending the need to think twice and even to resist authority. Some ten years after the study, Milgram reflected on his findings.

> I set up a simple experiment at Yale University to test how much pain an ordinary citizen would inflict on another person simply because he was ordered to by an experimental scientist. Stark authority was pitted against the subjects' [participants'] strongest moral imperatives against hurting others, and, with the subjects' [participants'] ears ringing with the screams of the victims, authority won more often than not. The extreme willingness of adults to go to almost any lengths on the command of an authority constitutes the chief finding of the study and the fact most urgently demanding explanation.[35]

Milgram was faulted for pushing ethical boundaries with regard to people recruited for the study, but his conclusions have not been seriously challenged.

> Ordinary people, simply doing their jobs, and without any particular hostility on their part, can become agents in a terrible destructive process. Moreover,

34. Snow, "Either-or," 24; cf. Milgram, "Behavioral Study of Obedience," 371.

35. Milgram, "The Perils of Obedience," 62.

> even when the destructive effects of their work become patently clear, and they are asked to carry out actions incompatible with fundamental standards of morality, relatively few people have the resources needed to resist authority.[36]

In the twentieth century, we know, egregious evil was committed in the name of unquestioning obedience.[37] What remedy can be found for this problem if the need to question authority is prescribed by life itself; what remedy is there if questioning a command is not a theoretical exercise; what hope is there if there is no plan B to make up for it where it is lacking?

Immanuel Kant (1724–1804), with whom we had a brief encounter earlier in connection with his criticism of the story of Abraham and Isaac, was possibly the greatest moral philosopher of all time. We owe to him the categorical imperative, stating that our standards of conduct should be such that we will choose a certain course of action only if we would want to give it the status of a universal law. To him, too, we owe the dictum that a human being should be considered an end and never the means to an end. Even the concept of *radical* evil comes from Kant, albeit he was unable to imagine a concept of evil that matches the terrain of reality.[38] But all his painstaking work could be in vain in light of his unremitting commitment to the duty to obey authority.

In one of his clearest statements on the subject, Kant asks, "If the people were to judge that a certain actual legislation will with the utmost probability deprive them of their happiness—what can such a people do? Should they resist?"[39]

Well, should they?

Kant's answer is clear and to the point, "*They can do nothing but obey*."[40]

> Any resistance to the supreme lawmaking power, any incitement of dissatisfied subjects to action, any uprising that bursts into rebellion—that is all the worst, most punishable crime in a community. For it shatters the community's foundations. And this ban is *absolute*, so unconditional that even though that supreme power or its agent, the head of state, may have broken the original contract, even though in the subject's eyes he may have forfeited the right to legislate by empowering the government to rule tyrannically by sheer violence, even then the subject is allowed no resistance, no violent counteraction.[41]

36. Ibid., 75–76.

37. Thus, Laurence Rees, *Auschwitz*; Laustsen and Ugilt, "Eichmann's Kant," 166–80. Obedience to authority was the staple defense in the Nuremberg Process after World War II, and the most revealing feature at the trial of Adolf Eichmann in Jerusalem.

38. Bernstein (*Radical Evil*, 33) gives Kant credit for grappling with the concept of radical evil, but determines that Kant is too optimistic and gullible. "The more we focus on the details of Kant's analysis of radical evil," he says, "the more innocuous the concept seems to be."

39. Kant, *On the Old Saw*, 66.

40. Ibid.

41. Ibid., 67–68; see also Silber, "Kant at Auschwitz," 186; Bernstein, *Radical Evil*, 36.

Kant did not intend duty to negate the categorical imperative; he did not see the categorical imperative as obedience to an external authority; and he would have been horrified that anyone would think the Holocaust compatible with his notion of duty. And yet he pressed the point of obedience to authority to such a degree that it, too, seems an absolute, equal to the categorical imperative itself. "Thus," he says, "it would be ruinous if an officer, receiving an order from his superiors, wanted while on duty to engage openly in subtle reasoning about its appropriateness or utility; he must obey."[42] Careful reasoning about appropriateness, however, is precisely what officers and soldiers had to be willing to do during the Nazi years. They had to think first, and then, having thought, they had to refuse obedience.

Adolf Eichmann invoked Kant at his trial in Jerusalem. Prior to the rise of the Nazi movement, he said, he had tried to live according to Kant's categorical imperative. When that became impossible, he retreated to doing his duty, which, in a twisted application of Kantian ethics, meant that if the state prescribed for him unpalatable tasks, he had no right to refuse. In the name of duty he was no longer responsible for his actions.[43] Kant, says John Silber, subordinated "the individual's determination of law to the law of the state."[44] Not the law only, but the interpretation of the law, was the state's prerogative. For this reason, "Kant's insistence on the ultimate authority of the sovereign and the duty of the subject to obey would appear to support Eichmann's position."[45] This is troubling and enormously consequential, of course, but it is less troubling than to believe that unquestioning obedience is the biblical ideal.

The story in 1 Kings 13 deserves a place in a work exploring the parameters of *sense* because unquestioning obedience has been the substrate for the most monumentally abusive periods in human history. Truth has often been subverted by grand designs and by fiction posing as fact. People of faith have again and again given their support to power grabs along the lines envisioned by Jeroboam. Beyond the many examples of falsehood masquerading as truth in history, we cannot forget that the human story in the Bible begins with conflicting claims as to what is true and who tells the truth (Gen 3:1–5). Falsehood—whether in Genesis 3 or in 1 Kings 13—knows how to bedazzle. The divine command is in both stories made to look arbitrary and can therefore be easily rescinded. Obedience morphs into its opposite when it is obedience without sense. Humans, we are reminded, often fall victim to false claims in spectacular ways, and it is not easy to set things right where falsehood has been spoken and believed.

Speaking to graduates at Harvard University in 1978 on the subject of Harvard's motto *Veritas* [truth], Alexander Solzhenitsyn began his address by saying, "Many of you have already found out and others will find out in the course of their lives that truth

42. Kant, *Practical Philosophy*, 18–19; Bernstein, *Radical Evil*, 37.

43. Arendt, *Eichmann in Jerusalem*, 135–37; Laustsen and Ugilt, "Eichmann's Kant," 169–70.

44. Silber, "Kant at Auschwitz," 190.

45. Ibid., 192.

eludes us as soon as our concentration begins to flag, all the while leaving the illusion that we are continuing to pursue it."[46] The man of God in 1 Kings 13 could be a case in point. He took a timeout from sense at great loss; his timeout now stands as a monumental teaching moment. Solzhenitsyn was right to point out that the pursuit of truth demands vigilance and, as in this story, more than unquestioning obedience. When put under pressure, the man of God lacked sense equal to the need—and to his calling.

46. Solzhenitsyn, *A World Split Apart*, 1.

Chapter Fourteen

The Sense of the Voice from the Whirlwind

There is more than meets the ear in the Book of Job, arguably the most trenchant book ever written on the problem of suffering—and, even more, on the problem of *sense*. One of the items in the "more" or "missed" category relates to the difficulty of translating the poetic portion of the book. When, for instance, we hear Elihu say, "I won't ask to speak to God; why should I give him a chance to destroy me?" (Job 37:20, GNB), we understand that he does not share Job's eagerness for a direct encounter with God, but the words on the page do not supply the tone of voice in which these sentiments were expressed. On this point the narrator comes to the rescue by saying no less than four times that Elihu was angry (32:2, 3, 5). He was angry at Job "because he justified himself rather than God" (32:2) and angry at Job's three friends "because they had found no answer though they had declared Job to be in the wrong" (32:3). Mindful of Elihu's anger, one can assume that there is a threatening tone in his voice, as though he means to embody and express the anger of a God presumed to be angry.[1]

1. Gutiérrez, *On Job*, 22.

William Blake's depiction of *Elihu speaking to Job and his friends* captures the speaker's self-assurance and lack of compassion. © Virginia Museum of Fine Arts. Used by permission.

Communication is more than words, and it is also more than tone of voice. Body language, facial expression, hints and gestures communicate, too. Job has plenty to offer in this regard, as William Blake's compelling pictorial account of the book imagines it.[2] And yet the most important aspect of Elihu's speech is largely lost in translation because it relates neither to body language nor tone of voice. Robert Alter says that the three main interlocutors in the poetic portion of Job—counting Elihu and Job's friends as one—"exhibit three purposefully developed levels of poetry."[3]

That is to say, the conversation in Job and its impact on the original reader depend on the idiom in which they say it. In Alter's stratification of the three levels, Elihu and

2. Blake, *Illustrations*; http://www.tate.org.uk/art/artworks/blake-job-rebuked-by-his-friends-a00021.

3. Alter, *Wisdom Books*, 6.

Job's three friends occupy the lowest level. "In keeping with the conventional moral views which they complacently defend, the poetry they speak abounds in familiar formulations" to the point that "much of their poetry verges on cliché."[4] In addition to anger, Alter helps us understand that the speeches of Job's friends are characterized by the inauthenticity of formulaic speech.

"Think now, who that was innocent ever perished? Or where were the upright cut off?" Eliphaz declares with dogmatic certainty (4:7). "Surely the light of the wicked is put out, and the flame of their fire does not shine," echoes Bildad (18:5). "Do you not know this from of old, ever since mortals were placed on earth, that the exulting of the wicked is short, and the joy of the godless is but for a moment?" parrots Zophar (20:4–5). The truth concerning which they all agree is not in doubt in these statements. While one version of the doctrine holds that sin meets with punishment, it can also be the other way around: "see a man suffering and you can be sure he has deserved it," as David Clines puts it in his massive commentary on Job.[5] Job's misery, therefore, "is by the book."[6]

The monotony of the friends' view is aggravated by sclerosis in the language they use.[7] This feature compromises their argument beyond what translations are able to convey.

Job's poetry occupies the second level. Alter says that "the stubborn authenticity of Job's perception of moral reality is firmly manifested in the power of the poetry he speaks, which clearly transcends the poetry of his reprovers."[8] His speeches are not fixed in place; they have development of perspective, and there are no formulae.[9] Where the views of his friends resonate with tradition and second-hand convictions, nothing is second-hand in Job's speeches. "Job's cosmic poetry, unlike that of the Friends, has a certain energy of vision, as though it proceeded from some immediate perception of the great things it reports."[10]

The third and highest level of poetry belongs to God.

> If the poetry of Job—at least when its often problematic text is fully intelligible—looms above all other biblical poetry in virtuosity and sheer expressive power, the culminating poem that God speaks out of the storm soars beyond everything that has preceded it in the book, the poet having wrought a poetic idiom even richer and more awesome than the one he gave Job.[11]

4. Alter, *Job*, 6.
5. Clines, *Job 1–20*, xl.
6. Ibid.
7. See also Gutiérrez, *On Job*, 29.
8. Alter, *Job*, 7.
9. Clines, *Job 1–20*, xlii.
10. Alter, *Biblical Poetry*, 111.
11. Ibid., 107.

In God's speech, says Alter, there is "a sublimity of expression, a plasticity of description . . . and even an originality of metaphoric inventiveness, that surpasses all the poetry, great as it is, that Job has spoken."[12] The difference is even greater when God's poetry is held up to the speeches of Job's friends, revealing the inadequacy of cliché in the face of new challenges.[13]

What shall we call this? What shall we call it when Elihu and Job's three friends combine anger and cliché in their communicative arsenal? What shall we call the mixture of consternation of voice and predictability of argument?

Before I offer my answer to this question, I will highlight three additional excerpts from the speeches of Job's friends.

> *Eliphaz*:
> Now a word came stealing to me, my ear received the whisper of it. Amid thoughts from *visions of the night*, when deep sleep falls on mortals, dread came upon me, and trembling, which made all my bones shake. A spirit glided past my face; the hair of my flesh bristled. It stood still, but I could not discern its appearance. A form was before my eyes; there was silence, then I heard a voice (4:12–16).

> *Bildad*:
> For inquire now of *bygone generations*, and consider what their ancestors have found; for we are but of yesterday, and we know nothing, for our days on earth are but a shadow. Will they not teach you and tell you and utter words out of their understanding? (8:8)

> *Zophar*:
> So my thoughts give me a rejoinder, by dint of *my inner sense*. I have heard the reproof to my shame, and a spirit from my mind lets me answer.[14] [NRSV, "a spirit beyond my understanding answers me"] (20:2, 3).

These excerpts relate to the source and not to the content of the friends' argument. Each claims a different source, signified by the phrase I have italicized above. Eliphaz claims special revelation; Bildad invokes tradition; Zophar reason.[15] Nevertheless, despite the wide epistemological range, they all come together in the same view. So what shall we call it, the combination of vehement emotion and formulaic argument? When Job makes eye contact with his friend Eliphaz, he sees authority veiling the familiar face. When he looks into the face of Bildad, the endearing face is blurred by the intrusion of dogma. The beloved face of Zophar has also lost much of its humanity, now expressing the unfeeling demeanor of a rigid belief. In sum, the

12. Alter, *Job*, 10.
13. Alter, *Biblical Poetry*, 109.
14. Alter, *Job*, 85.
15. Carmy, "God is Distant," 54.

three friends and the young Elihu make the force of revelation, tradition, and reason bear down on Job and the recalcitrant particularity of his experience.

In this barrage of verbal punches and counterpunches, as they empty their fury on him, Job is unbowed (32:1). His defense is powerful, but the friends are also silenced by the weakness and increasing weariness of their own view, especially when it is heard in playback. How Job tears it to shreds in his final speech might have escaped notice except for the vigilance of scholars who pay attention to *the way* a point of view is expressed. "Most perplexingly," says Carol Newsom of Job's final speech, Job "uses the friends' arguments as though they were a refutation of what the friends had just said."[16] It is difficult to exaggerate the significance of this observation. Job, we gather, is not swayed by his friends' arguments, but in the closing round he does not argue overtly *against* them. Instead, he repeats *their* arguments in a tone of voice that accentuates the inauthenticity. "One can imagine the friends whispering together in confusion: 'That's what *we* said. But he can't mean what it sounds like he's saying. He can't mean what we meant. What does he mean by saying that?'" Newsom comments astutely.[17] In other words, Job "does not mean the same thing the friends do, even if he speaks just like them."[18] In the end, he silences his friends by accenting the formulaic character of their argument.

The friends' commitment to the doctrine of retribution falls on hard times in Job, failing the test of reality. As Clines notes,

> the book of Job is for the most part strongly opposed to the doctrine of retribution. Strict retribution is the position from which both Job and his friends start out, but, though the friends never deviate from the orthodox line, he himself soon comes to believe that his suffering is no punishment for wrongdoing but an unjust assault upon an innocent man. The causal nexus of the retributive principle has been unalterably broken for Job—and for all those of his readers who side with him in his battle against heaven, which means almost every single one.[19]

Why, then, does Job suffer when the book meticulously shatters the link between sin and punishment? Early on we are served notice that Job's innocence is not self-attested. In the frame story that precedes the poetic part of the book, God bears witness to Job's character, corroborating Job's subsequent assertion in the poetic portion (9:15). In fact, the narrator and God invest Job's claims with objective standing.

16. Newsom, *Job*, 164.

17. Newsom, *Job*, 166.

18. Ibid.

19. Clines, "Job's Fifth Friend," 247.

> *Narrator*:
> There was once a man in the land of Uz whose name was Job. That man was blameless [*tām*] and upright [*yāshār*], one who feared God and turned away from evil (1:1).
>
> *God*:
> "Have you considered my servant Job? There is no one like him on the earth, a blameless [*tām*] and upright [*yāshār*] man who fears God and turns away from evil" (1:8; cf. 2:3).

The narrator and God are on the same page in their assessment, lending credibility to Job's claims in the dialogues. Job's spirituality, in turn, is said to be robust and well-rounded. *Tām* means "blameless . . . with the connotation of personal integrity, of something finished, complete, perfect, and therefore exemplary."[20] *Yāshār* is complementary, describing what Gustavo Gutiérrez calls "the internal coherence of his personality."[21] Personal integrity and concern for the poor are in view when Job takes inventory of his life after his friends' attempt to tar his reputation (31:5–34).

The verdict on Job's character by the narrator and God at the beginning of the book is a crucial premise for the entire story, and the interdependence between the prose account at the beginning and the poetic section is a corrective to interpreters who wish to separate the two.[22] Other features will support that the book should be read as an integrated and interdependent whole. The idea that one and the same author could not have written the prose section (1:1—2:13; 42:1–17) and the poetic dialogues (3:1—41:34) is not persuasive. Diversity of expression does not prove multiple authors. "It is not only the style but the whole cast of sentiments and ideas which normally change when the voice or the pen abandons one mode to take up another," says Édouard Dhorme in his highly-regarded commentary on Job.[23] Stylistic variation gives integrity to the characters.

When, in desperation, Job's friends rev up the doctrine of retributive justice to mean that suffering is incontrovertible proof of sin, their innuendo fairly screams at the reader. Job gives an impressive, point-by-point rebuttal (31:5–34), but the definitive refutation is anchored in the frame story (1:1, 8; 2:3). Eliphaz, who at first landed soft blows at Job, will in the end say bluntly,

> There is no end to your iniquities. For you have exacted pledges from your family for no reason, and stripped the naked of their clothing. You have given no water to the weary to drink, and you have withheld bread from the hungry (22:5–7).

20. Gutiérrez, *On Job*, 4.
21. Ibid.
22. See, for instance, Fohrer, *Das Buch Hiob*, 29–42; Pope, *Job*, xxi–xxviii; Habel, *Job*, 5–8.
23. Dhorme, *Job*, lxv.

Anyone reading this while keeping in mind God's assessment of Job in the frame story can only smile at the futility of Eliphaz's position, and wonder at the degree to which he is willing to misrepresent Job in order to salvage his doctrine. Likewise, and even worse because Zophar is rude toward Job at his first chance, we marvel when we hear him say, "Know then that God exacts of you less than your guilt deserves!" (11:5–6). Zophar, of course, does not know that God has spoken about Job in the frame story, saying the exact opposite. But the reader knows the secret. Even in the eyes of the reader, however, Job's case would be precarious if not for God declaring him to be a "blameless [*tām*] and upright [*yāshār*] man" in the frame story (1:8; 2:3).

When Eliphaz turns to belittling human beings in general and Job's piety in particular, he seems at first sight to have an impressive argument.

> Can a mortal be of use to God? Can even the wisest be of service to him? Is it any pleasure to the Almighty if you are righteous, or is it gain to him if you make your ways blameless? (22:2–3)

Who can defend himself or herself against the charge of being self-important that Eliphaz now levels against Job? Having argued that God keeps a watchful eye on human behavior and is quick to punish sin, Eliphaz suddenly pivots to the view that God has no use for humans. Human beings, good or bad, are insignificant. They bring neither joy nor sorrow to God.

Elihu, showing common ground with Job's three friends in this regard, drives the point home with consummate disrespect.

> If you have sinned, what do you accomplish against him? And if your transgressions are multiplied, what do you do to him? If you are righteous, what do you give to him; or what does he receive from your hand? Your wickedness affects others like you, and your righteousness, other human beings (35:6–8).

As in Eliphaz's final speech, the force of this argument lies in the implicit conceit of Job's position. Job is at fault for claiming to be innocent of wrong, but he is also guilty of undue self-importance. In his response, Elihu pushes divine transcendence and human finitude to their outer extremes. Echoing Eliphaz, sin and righteousness are equally irrelevant in the divine reckoning. God is not hurt by the one or gladdened by the other. Job's conduct, virtuous or vile, is only of concern with regard to other human beings.

Job does not mount a rebuttal to this view, and he does not really need to. With recourse to the frame story, readers will again be inclined to smile at the naiveté of Eliphaz, Elihu, and the other two who hammer home these convictions. How can these theologians speak so ignorantly of God when God, in the prose chapters at the beginning, has drawn attention to Job's character precisely because it matters to God? Twice we hear God say to the Adversary in the story, "Have you considered my servant Job? There is no one like him on the earth, a blameless and upright man who fears

God and turns away from evil" (1:8; cf. 2:3). Clearly, Job is not too small for God to take notice, and Job's conduct is not a matter of indifference to God.

With a measure of prestige restored to the frame story, it is time to take a closer look at its characters and plot, especially the dynamics between God and the Adversary. In my view, all is not well in the heavenly council even before the subject of Job comes up. "One day the heavenly beings came to present themselves before the LORD," says the narrator, "and Satan also came among them" (1:6). The notion of a conflict may seem slight at this stage, and yet there are hints of dissonance.

First, with regard to the identity and character of Satan in the story, scholars have either been dismissive of Satan or too eager to cast him as a benign figure. Newsom claims that "God and *haśśāṭān* ["the satan"] are not dualistic opposites, nor is *haśśāṭān* yet the Satan-with-a-capital-S of later Jewish and Christian literature. Rather, *haśśāṭān* is the heavenly being charged with keeping an eye on the world and spotting disloyalty and falsity."[24] This often-repeated view lacks nuance, and it is expressed with too much confidence. Compositional theories for the Book of Job are numerous, complex, and tentative, seeking to account for archaic terms originating in the distant past to a host of Aramaic word endings that suggest influences from the fifth century BCE or later. Interpreters of Job in the twenty-first century cannot be sure that readers of Job in the fourth century took the references to *haśśāṭān* in the frame story to mean a benign figure even if they are certain that this term once upon a time had a benign connotation. Meanings of words are not static and fixed. As James Barr has pointed out, it is the sentence—and by extrapolation the context—that determines the meaning of a word and not chiefly the word that commands the meaning of the sentence.[25]

In reality, the notion of a cosmic rebellion is old enough to accommodate proposed dates for the composition of Job and the frame story to cast Satan as an unambiguous adversarial figure.[26] While the narrator in Job calls this figure "the satan" [*haśśāṭān*], a title rather than a name, the term is descriptive of his character, and the title does not weaken the adversarial connotation. Alter does well by translating the term "*the Adversary*." Scholars who see the Adversary, *alias* Satan, as one who is merely carrying out his God-appointed task, fail to pursue features in the text that

24. Newsom, *Job*, 55. Balentine (*Job*, 51–53) defends the same view.

25. Barr, *Semantics*, 107–60.

26. With regard to the notion of a cosmic rebellion, Gunkel (*Schöpfung und Chaos*, 30–114) shows this theme to be widely diffused in the Old Testament. He explores various combat metaphors such as Rahab (Isa 30:7; 51:9–10; Pss 40:4; 87:4; 89:10–15; Job 9:13; 26:12–13); Leviathan (Pss 74:12–19; 104:25–26; Isa 27:1; Job 3:8; 40:25—41:26); dragon in the sea (Job 7:12; Pss 2:28–34; 44:20; Jer 51:34–40.; Ezek 29:3–6; 32:2–8); serpent (Amos 9:2–3); variants (Ps 104:5–9; Job 38:8–11; Prov 8:22–23; Jer 5:22; 31:35; Pss 33:6–8; 65:7–8). Job is richly represented in Gunkel's selection. Morgenstern ("Mythological Background," 29–126) discusses the myth of the fall of godlike beings in Psalm 82, cross-linked to Isa 14:12–14, with Ezek 28:11–28 and Rev 12:7–9 as reflections of the same story. Page Jr. (*Cosmic Rebellion*, 110–205) concentrates attention on Gen 6:1–4; Isa 14:4–20; Ezek 28:1–19; Ps 82; Job 38:1–38; Dan 11:21, 36–39, 45; 12:1–3).

support the opposite view.[27] That view, to be clear, is that Satan is God's opponent in the story, and also the enemy of Job. Alter wisely spots "an element of jealousy . . . and cynical mean-spiritedness" on the part of the Adversary.[28]

Disruption and dissonance are suggested by the statement that when the heavenly beings assembled before God "Satan *also* came" (1:6; cf. 2:1). The separate mention of Satan could mean no more than an observation of fact, but this is unlikely in light of what follows. With respect to the "also" in the text, Robert Fyall argues that Satan stands at a distance from the council and is someone who is at odds with the rest.[29] He still has access, but he is no longer "one of them."

The sense of disruption and distance is reinforced by the initial dialogue between God and Satan.

> The Lord said to Satan, "Where have you come from?" Satan answered the Lord, "From going to and fro on the earth, and from walking up and down on it" (1:7; cf. 2:2).

This should not be treated as a piece of trivia,[30] or as though Satan has been roaming the earth as a divinely-appointed prosecuting attorney.[31] A better option is to see Satan's roaming "to and fro on the earth" and "walking up and down on it" as proof that he is an outcast who harbors malicious intent.[32] In such a view, Satan will be a 'lost soul' and a menace. An analogy to the former is found in Amos, where people are warned of the day when they will "wander from sea to sea, and from north to east; they shall run to and fro, seeking the word of the Lord, but they shall not find it" (Amos 8:12). Even more suggestive is the convergence between the fallen cherub in Ezekiel and Satan's answer to God in Job.

> *Ezekiel*:
> Thou wast the far-covering cherub; and I set thee, so that thou wast upon the holy mountain of God; *thou hast walked up and down* [*hithhalāktā*] in the midst of stones of fire (Ezek 28:14).[33]

> *Job*:
> The Lord said to Satan, "Where have you come from?" Satan answered the Lord, "From going to and fro on the earth, and from *walking up and down* [*hithhalēk*] on it" (Job 1:7; cf. 2:2).

27. Dhorme (*Job*, 6–7) prefers Satan with capital S and without the article.
28. Alter, *Job*, 12.
29. Fyall, *My Eyes Have Seen You*, 36.
30. Gordis, *Book of Job*, 15.
31. Newsom, *Job*, 55; cf. Habel, *Job*, 17; Fohrer, *Das Buch Hiob*, 82.
32. Pope (*Job*, 11) suggests this possibility without fully committing to it.
33. Fisch, *Ezekiel*, 192, emphasis supplied.

In these texts the subject is in both instances *walking up and down*, a back-and-forth or up-and-down depiction of walking captured in Hebrew in one single word for which there is no English equivalent.[34] But the contrast is as striking as the convergence. In Ezekiel, the cherub is 'walking back and forth *in the midst of the stones of fire*' (Ezek 28:14). He is a being who is at home and at ease in the heavenly realm. Walking "back and forth" under such circumstances is an expression of belonging, confidence, and purpose. In Job, Satan is no longer a regular in heaven. He has been "going to and fro *on the earth*" (Job 1:7). Moreover, the double "*going to and fro*" and "*walking up and down*" has the connotation of futility, on the one hand, and malicious intent, on the other. It pictures the walk of an outcast, a person whose identity and intent cannot be better described than as "the Adversary." The convergence in these texts does not prove conclusively that Job's Satan is the outcast, but Isaiah (14:12–20) and Ezekiel (28:12–19) show that the notion of a heavenly outcast is not a late idea.

When God takes the initiative in the conversation, the topic suggests a discussion long in progress. It is as though God and Satan are picking up where they last left off, on a subject about which they disagree. "Have you considered my servant Job?" Yahweh says to Satan. "There is no one like him on the earth, a blameless and upright man who fears God and turns away from evil" (1:8). If Satan were the vigilant prosecuting attorney that some take him to be—or just a legal clerk in the employ of the heavenly council—he should be the one to bring charges against Job. Instead, he appears to be on the defensive. *When God brings Job to Satan's attention, therefore, it has the connotation of evidence that Satan would like to ignore. In the conflict that is in view, Satan is not the watchful fact-finder that undeservedly dignifies his résumé.*

God's reference to Job's integrity forces Satan to show his hand. He will do it by proposing a test that is meant to give him the edge in the argument with God.

> Then Satan answered the Lord, "Does Job fear God for nothing? Have you not put a fence around him and his house and all that he has, on every side? You have blessed the work of his hands, and his possessions have increased in the land. But stretch out your hand now, and touch all that he has, and he will curse you to your face" (1:9–11).

Here, the Adversary launches a frontal assault on the integrity of the divine-human relationship.[35] The attack on Job also impugns God. "You," Satan intimates, "have bought Job's loyalty. His piety is the devotion of patronage and self-interest. For both of you it is a mercenary relationship." All this, we are called to imagine, Satan is saying in the hearing of the heavenly council. Is it true? Does it matter whether it is demonstrated not to be true?

34. The Hebrew verb has a complexity and multi-functionality that is not found in English. Here, the verb *hālak* ["walk"] appears in the hithpaʿel form, denoting a reflexive-reciprocal action, in Ezek 28:14 as a hithpaʿel perfect, 2nd pers. sing., in Job 1:7 and 2:2 as the infinitive construct of the same verb.

35. Kamp, "With or Without a Cause," 11–12.

Gustavo Gutiérrez notes that Satan does not deny that Job is a devout person.

> What he questions is rather the disinterestedness of Job's service to God, his lack of concern for a reward. The satan objects not to Job's works but to their motivation: Job's behavior, he says, is not "for nothing" (in Hebrew: *hinnām*). In the satan's view, a religious attitude can be explained only by expectation of a reward: we will shortly learn that this is also the view of Job's friends. If, however, Job be regarded as a truly just man, then, even though there be no other like him in the land, the lie is given to this view of religion.[36]

Satan, we realize, claims that Job has selfish reasons for his conduct. Piety and devotion are wise investments in the interest of bringing a bountiful material return. The equation is simple and is, in fact, only another facet of the law of retribution. Piety is rewarded; sin is punished. This is one step closer to realizing how important the frame story is to the rest of the book and how prose and poetry are mutually reinforcing with regard to the theology of Job. Again, in the words of Gutiérrez,

> the central question of Job is raised at the outset: the role that reward or disinterestedness plays in faith in God and in its consistent implementation. God believes that Job's uprightness is disinterested, and he therefore accepts the challenge. The author is telling us in this way that a utilitarian religion lacks depth and authenticity; in addition, it has something satanic about it.[37]

Gutiérrez takes the frame story seriously, and yet something is lacking in these insightful comments. To be sure, Satan attacks the integrity of Job, claiming that his motive is self-interest and that his devotion will evaporate at the first whiff of adversity. Satan's ire against God, however, escapes notice. The sordid bargain to which Job is a partner is of God's making. God, no less than Job, is motivated by self-interest. Job is a special case in the world, an exception, because God has showered him with privileges above and beyond the norm. In Satan's view, God does not have many devotees for reasons that are intrinsic to the divine character. The one person he claims as a faithful follower—Job—will quickly turn away if God rescinds the lavish patronage (1:11).

The adversarial texture to this charge is blatant and explosive. Satan is in effect arguing that selflessness, whether in the divine or the human realm, does not exist. God and Job are in his view in a contractual relationship based on mutual self-interest. In return for gifts received, God earns Job's devotion. Conversely, in return for devotion, God showers Job with rewards. Does it matter whether this charge is shown to be untrue?

36. Gutiérrez, *On Job*, 4.

37. Ibid., 3–4.

Although Job's character is at stake in the book the truth about God is the most controverted subject. God, as Robert Fyall notes, is the implied target in the frame story.[38] We hear this better when we run the satanic response in slow motion:

> "Does Job fear *God* for nothing?"
>
> "Have *you* not put a fence around him and his house and all that he has, on every side?"
>
> "*You* have blessed the work of his hands, and his possessions have increased in the land."
>
> "But stretch out *your* hand now . . . and he will curse *you* to your face" (1:9–11).

God's character, integrity, and reputation are at the heart of the conversation in the frame story as much as the character of Job. As we soon shall see, this is also the recurrent theme in the speeches of Job's friends. Final confirmation that the truth about God is the main concern comes in the prose section at the end. While the friends have misrepresented Job badly, they have done worse in their representation of God. This, God will say, goes to the heart of the matter.

> After the Lord had spoken these words to Job, the Lord said to Eliphaz the Temanite: "My wrath is kindled against you and against your two friends; for you have not spoken of me what is right, as my servant Job has. Now therefore take seven bulls and seven rams, and go to my servant Job, and offer up for yourselves a burnt offering; and my servant Job shall pray for you, for I will accept his prayer not to deal with you according to your folly; for you have not spoken of me what is right, as my servant Job has done" (42:7–8).

There are many surprises in the Book of Job, but this one tops them all. After what most readers take as a no-nonsense rebuke by the voice from the whirlwind directed exclusively at Job (38:1—41:34), God turns around with a tribute to Job! Readers who have imagined God speaking in an angry voice to Job may have gotten it wrong. At the end, God admits to being angry, but the anger is directed at Job's friends! To drive the point home beyond doubt, God authorizes Job to intercede on behalf of the friends that have treated him badly. Crucially, penance is due not for what they have said about Job but for their misrepresentation of God! Job, on the other hand, gets more than a passing grade. Despite the evident shortcomings of his utterances in the poetic section, God's verdict at the end suggests that Job said nothing that was truly offensive. On the contrary, God declares that Job has said of him what is right (42:7–8). We will soon set out to retrace our steps in the poetic section to detect the reasons for this verdict. Such a re-reading, now guided and informed by the ending of Job, will take care not to miss that the book has representations of God as its chief concern.

38. Fyall, *Now My Eyes Have Seen You*, 36–37.

We are now in a position to contest the thought that the plot in the frame story is flimsy and that God, in particular, fails the test of morality. "God's quick acquiescence in the Adversary's perverse proposal is hard to justify in terms of any serious monotheistic theology," says Alter.[39] This would be true within Alter's conception of what constitutes 'monotheistic theology,' where only one will and one point of view count. His verdict is much less compelling if Satan's charges are placed in the context of a cosmic conflict. David Clines seconds Alter's criticism with even greater force. "I blame the book of Job," writes Clines,

> for so naturalizing this outrageous divine behaviour that commentators, almost to a man, see no sign of an ethical problem. Some indeed find the Satan's assaults fiendish, some feel it necessary to affirm that the real responsibility for Job's suffering lies at God's door, and a few raise the question of God's justice—though only to dismiss it immediately.[40]

The offending point is the 'wager' between God and Satan that subjects Job to a test that is unfair without letting him in on what is going on. In this view, heaven is playing games with Job, causing his ruin with regard to possessions, family, and health. "What is truly amazing about the book is that for the most part its readers do not even notice that there are any ethical problems," Clines objects.

> Whole volumes devoted to the book of Job rhapsodize about its theological depth and its grand vision of the governance of the universe without a glance at the act of gross divine injustice against Job that is the springboard of the whole drama—the unprovoked and unjustifiable assault of heaven upon Job's person and property. And that is just one of the several ethical problems the book raises.[41]

If, however, Satan is not the bland court clerk that Clines and others take him to be, and if we take seriously Satan's charge that selflessness does not exist, holding forth on this topic in the heavenly council, the events that follow are less mysterious. God sees in Job a person who is committed to God for reasons other than selfish gain, and God does not bless Job because God is obligated by Job's piety or because God buys Job's piety for a price. Satan makes a false accusation at the beginning that is weighty and consequential for all the parties involved. Would Job, if he knew, be happy to let Satan's indictment of his integrity stand? Is God morally at fault for allowing Satan to put Job to the test? Can one imagine a scenario within which the axis of reward and retribution, a point that is assumed equally by Satan and Job's friends, must be broken for the truth to be known?

39. Alter, *Job*, 5.

40. Clines, "Job's Fifth Friend," 234–35.

41. Ibid., 248.

Does Job get to benefit from the cosmic perspective in the frame story? The answer to this question is complex, but it begins with Job's expressed outlook. In a moment of a darkly pessimistic mood (9:16, 19), Job complains that God "crushes me with a tempest, and multiplies my wounds without cause" (9:17), the entire scheme either morally indifferent or intentionally cruel (9:22, 23).[42] To Job, God is the acting subject in these outpourings except for one momentary caveat. "The earth is given into the hand of the wicked; he covers the eyes of its judges, if it is not he [who sends evil], who then is it?" (9:24)

At that point readers, and certainly this reader, would like to break in with a shout. Barred from the sickroom and from direct contact with Job by a soundproof window, this reader sees himself jumping up and down, gesticulating wildly, nodding one moment and shaking his head the next, eagerly trying to point Job in a different direction. "Job," screams the reader who is informed by the frame story, "you are on the right track; you just asked the right question; you just opened the door to other possibilities. It isn't God, Job! There is someone else!"

The problem, of course, is not that Job is suffering; the problem is suffering that shatters the explanatory framework. Here, in this question (9.24), Job hints ever so slightly at the possibility that someone other than God might be involved, "If it is not *He*, who then is it?"[43] I agree with Fyall that in this question, "the key to unlock the dark prison lies tantalizingly close to Job's hand, indeed his fingers brush against it."[44]

In the end, God gives Job the direct encounter that Elihu warned him not to pursue (37:20; 38:1), and Job declares himself content with the divine manifestation (40:3–5; 42:1–6). But before we get to that point, however, we need to listen to the speeches of Job's friends (42:7) and to God's speeches from the whirlwind (38:1—39:30; 40:6—41:34). What in the speeches of Job's friends stirs God's anger? What does God say to Job that brings closure to his quest for an answer? And, as noted above, do these speeches put Job closer to the insights that the readers get from the frame story?

Cruel Sense

The venom against Job in the speeches of his friends is a case study in cruelty shown to a suffering person. To Bildad, the death of Job's children is proof of their criminality—not exactly a comforting thought for the bereaved parent (8:4). In the eyes of Zophar, Job's personal suffering substantiates his guilt (11:6). Eliphaz, who at first strikes a

42. Morally indifferent: "It is all one; therefore I say, he destroys both the blameless and the wicked" (9:22). Cruel: "When disaster brings sudden death, he mocks at the calamity of the innocent" (9.23).

43. Dhorme (*Job*, 140) notes that this line is shorter than the others, a "broken off sentence, and consequently all the more striking."

44. Fyall, *My Eyes Have Seen You*, 39. He suggests that Job 9:24 might be the most significant verse in the book (p. 163).

kinder note, will in the end bear down on Job for exacting "pledges from your family for no reason" and for stripping the naked of their clothing (22:6), a feat of exceptional cruelty if the naked were exposed in the first place. Their retributive formula works in both directions, from sin to punishment and from punishment to sin.[45] As we have seen, the speeches reek with misrepresentations of Job, all the while betraying the fallacy of the underlying formula.

But what do the friends say about God? This element in the speeches has been allowed to fly under the radar even though, at the end, this is the main concern in the book (42:7–8).

> *Eliphaz*:
> Can mortals be righteous before God? Can human beings be pure before their Maker? Even in his servants he puts no trust, and his angels he charges with error; how much more those who live in houses of clay, whose foundation is in the dust, who are crushed like a moth (4:17–19).

This missive is found in Eliphaz's first speech. In his perception, God is exacting and impossible to please. How can Job, a poor earthling, aspire to be right when God finds fault with heavenly beings? Here, as Samuel Terrien notes, the leading voice among Job's friends deploys a doctrine of radical divine remoteness, 'wholly otherness,' and impassibility, fortifying it with the thought that finitude equals moral corruption.[46] Even if Job is innocent to a point, the divine standard is so rigorous that ordinary conceptions of goodness will not do.

In his second speech, Eliphaz charges Job with gross impiety for questioning his fate, expressing a view that no pious person should dare to entertain. "If you had your way, no one would fear God; no one would pray to him," says Eliphaz (15:4, GNB). Indeed, he tells Job, you are so out of bounds that "your iniquity teaches your mouth, and you choose the tongue of the crafty [*'arûmim*]" (15:5), a term quite possibly intending to align Job's speech with that of the serpent in Genesis (Gen 3:1).[47] If this connection is in the mind of the author, the irony is extreme because Eliphaz's representation of God is as severe as that of the serpent and certainly no corrective to it. He then proceeds to take the theme of divine exactitude a notch higher, moving the moral goalposts beyond the reach of pretenders like Job.

> What are mortals, that they can be clean? Or those born of woman, that they can be righteous? God puts no trust even in his holy ones, and the heavens are not clean in his sight; how much less one who is abominable and corrupt, one who drinks iniquity like water! (15:14–16)

45. Van Hecke, "I would converse with the Almighty," 19.

46. Terrien, *Job*, 75.

47. Clines, *Job 1–20*, 348.

Job is a subject of this speech, but now we are primarily interested in Eliphaz's representation of God. With respect to human existence, creatureliness and sinfulness are said to be two sides of the same coin. With respect to God, nothing is good enough. God does not trust "his holy ones" and "the heavens are not clean in his sight." While God and human beings do not have a common language with respect to right and wrong, Eliphaz's main contribution is to portray God as a person who views created reality with ungenerous, fault-finding eyes.

When Bildad picks up Eliphaz's line in his final speech, repetitiveness has muted its force, but the sense that he is presenting a consensus view of God is building.

> How then can a mortal be righteous before God? How can one born of woman be pure? If even the moon is not bright and the stars are not pure in his sight, how much less a mortal, who is a maggot, and a human being, who is a worm! (25:4–6)

In theological terms, two things are happening in these representations. First, Job's friends set up an extreme ontological distinction between God and created reality, pushing to the outermost the contrast between divine transcendence and human finitude.[48] Second, the friends reinforce the ontological distinction by an extremist moral view, positing demands on humans (and angels) that no one can hope to meet. The fallout is remarkable. On the one hand, they cast God as a person who is remote and detached and to whom human existence and conduct are matters of indifference. On the other hand, as the most stable refrain, they depict God as relentlessly harsh and exacting. While nothing in these speeches is flattering to Job, their mantra is unremittingly unflattering to God.

> If God and man remain external to one another—if man is nothing more than a worm, and God a distant, unmoved and unmovable Being, an Absolute which is detached from the giving and the seeking of love—there is no hope, not even in repentance, or in good deeds of behavior or piety. Prayer is just as irrelevant as blasphemy.[49]

This comment by Samuel Terrien is to the point. Job is doomed if he does [it isn't good enough] and damned if he doesn't [it isn't important]. If the friends are right, human life unfolds under the gaze of a God who is alternately demanding and detached, and this will be so even if Job shuts his mouth. Under the pressure of Job's outbursts, the friends have come forward with a view of God that purports to defend God and yet forces the reader to exclaim that if these are God's friends God has no need of enemies. "In spite of their lip service to the holiness of God, their theism has

48. As Carmy ("God is Distant," 56–57) notes, Zophar pushes hardest for a view of "overwhelming divine transcendence" and a God who is "utterly hidden and incomprehensible." Such a view, he says, "usually claims to be more devout than a theology for which divine morality and responsiveness to the human quest play a central role."

49. Terrien, *Job*, 98.

become a form of idolatry," says Terrien. "Self-appointed speakers for God (15:11), they carry him in their breast-pockets (12:6). They could not understand Job, for they did not truly love God, hence did not truly love their friend."[50]

Does our harsh indictment of Job's friends have merit? Job will answer in the affirmative, accusing his friends of defending God with lies (13:4, 7, 12; 21:34) and of lack of compassion (6:14; 19:21). The two are linked because the friends who revere the exacting God turn out to be unfeeling and cruel toward the sufferer.

Let me take breathing pause to make an assertion, recalling that Job's friends do not believe that humans have the right to ask certain questions of God, or that God is disposed to answer them. What comes from the mouth of Eliphaz, Bildad, and Zophar, and even more crudely from the mouth of Elihu, flows like the Amazon River in the theological tradition, especially from Augustine in the fifth century to Luther in the sixteenth century and from Luther all the way to Karl Barth in the twentieth century. To varying degrees they promote a theology of radical divine transcendence, retributive justice, divine incomprehensibility, and, like Job's friends, they conflate human finitude and sin. God, we heard Augustine say in the first chapter, "decides who are to be offered mercy by a standard of equity which is most secret and far removed from human powers of understanding."[51] This means that God and humans have no shared standard by which humans can understand what God is doing and why.

Martin Luther, seeing it his duty to defend a God who elects some humans to be saved and many more to be damned, seems as convinced as Job's friends that there is nothing wrong with this conception of God even though, to be fair to Job's friends, they are content to defend the justice of finite suffering and not eternal torment. The problem, Luther insists, lies with the person who gets upset with such a picture of God and who thinks that God owes him or her an explanation. To such an impertinent person, Luther will answer like Augustine. "If, then, I could by any means comprehend how this God can be merciful and just who displays so much wrath and iniquity, there would be no need of faith."[52]

When the turn comes to Karl Barth, he, too, takes the side of Job's friends against Job. To Barth, as we have seen, God "does not ask for his [Job's] understanding, agreement or applause. On the contrary, He simply asks that he should be content not to know why and to what end he exists, and does so in this way and not another."[53]

Retribution is muted in Barth's theology, but the booming voices of Augustine, Luther, and Calvin resound like peals of thunder: radical divine transcendence, human finitude, and, above all, divine incomprehensibility. Job's supreme fault, other than his claim of being innocent of wrong, is his insistence on the need to understand.

50. Ibid., 98–99.

51. Augustine, *Earlier Writings*, 398.

52. Luther, *Bondage of the Will*, 62. The same view echoes in John Calvin, as in *Sermons on Job* (31–45; 136–65).

53. Barth, *Church Dogmatics* IV.3, 431.

His friends respond by deploying the doctrine of divine transcendence and its corollary, incomprehensibility.

In the frame story, *the view expressed by Job's friends is carried by Satan.* There, Satan contends that the relationship between God and human beings is best understood within the framework of retribution and reward (1:9–11; 2:4–5). In the poetic section, Satan may seem to be absent, but the viewpoint expressed in the frame story is not. It has gone undercover, so to speak, now finding expression in the theology of Job's friends. While Satan in the frame story stresses the connection between piety and reward, Job's friends tend to emphasize its flip side, the link between impiety and retribution. The topic of conversation has not changed even though the interlocutors are different. And yet, stressing that the representations of God matter more than who is doing what, the poetic section intimates the reality of cosmic conflict in language befitting the poetic idiom.

Who or what, exactly, does Eliphaz claim to be the source of his insight at the outset of the friends' rebuttal? The answer, we have seen, is special revelation. To him, there is no doubt that God is the source of his revelation. Here, again, we have his recollection.

> Now a word came stealing to me, my ear received the whisper of it. Amid thoughts from visions of the night, when deep sleep falls on mortals, dread came upon me, and trembling, which made all my bones shake. A spirit glided past my face; the hair of my flesh bristled. It stood still, but I could not discern its appearance. A form was before my eyes; there was silence, then I heard a voice (4:12–16).

Skeptics in the twenty-first century may counter that Eliphaz never had such an experience, that he made it up, or that he was hallucinating. None of these explanations fits the world of Job. To Eliphaz, the experience is real and defining, and it grounds his theology. Given that he is the lead voice in the friends' answer to Job, content and source are in view not only for his view but for the entire theological edifice. Bildad, Zophar, and Elihu add emphasis and points of nuance, but they do not change the basic framework. Putting the two together, the spirit that glided past his face and the viewpoint expressed by the spirit, we are inching closer to a reading of the poetic section of Job that is rarely entertained.

> Can mortals be righteous before God? Can human beings be pure before their Maker? Even in his servants he puts no trust, and his angels he charges with error; how much more those who live in houses of clay, whose foundation is in the dust, who are crushed like a moth (4:17–19).

Eliphaz, as noted, takes God to be the source of this conviction, thinking that God is his ally against Job. But this claim looks preposterous in light of God's verdict on Job in the frame story (1:8; 2:3), and its absurdity is not lessened when God at the end expresses anger specifically toward Eliphaz, holding him most to blame for the way they have represented God (42:7–8). But if God does not agree with Eliphaz's point of view, a view that claims God as its source, who could be the source? Poetry is deliberately understated and imaginative, calling on the reader to connect the dots. In the frame story, Satan argues that selflessness does not exist. In the poetic section, Job's friends pay lip service to the goodness of God, but their default position is a God who makes extreme demands on his creatures. Assuming that Eliphaz's experience was real, from whom was the vision in the night that made all his bones shake? If it were *not* from God, from whom was it? If the Book of Job repudiates the view, it also casts doubt on its source. Eliphaz and Job become two of a kind, but travelling in opposite directions. To Eliphaz, God is the source of his theology although God isn't, a conclusion about which the book leaves no doubt (42:7–8). To Job, God is the cause of his calamity even though someone other than God is involved (1:12; 2:7). Job will at least entertain the possibility of another explanation. "If it is not he, who then is it?" (9:24) To Eliphaz, there appears to be no other source than God even though his own testimony will lead readers to conclude that Eliphaz has been deceived.

In the frame story God gives permission for Satan to afflict Job, but the intent and its cruel execution originate with the Adversary (1:12–19; 2:4–7). Clues that someone other than God is playing a role in Job's plight, therefore, are clearly attested in the frame story, and it is put forward at least as a hypothetical option by Job in the poetic section (9:24). We cannot compute the evidence of the poetic section in this respect, however, before we have listened to God's speeches to Job.

The Sense of the Voice from the Whirlwind

The encounter with God that Job seeks and against which Elihu warns is no ordinary rendezvous. In its most pointed formulation, Job asks for legal redress. He files a lawsuit against God!

The first suggestion of this intent is tentative and ridden with anxiety. Job entertains the thought, but he is pessimistic of the outcome. "If one wished to contend with him [in court], one could not answer him once in a thousand," he says at first (9:3). "If I summoned him and he answered me, I do not believe that he would listen to my voice" (9:16). There is here, as Newsom notes, "something of the nature of a quest in Job's speeches."[54]

> He is tunneling, overturning obstacles, sinking shafts in the search for something that is not only more precious than gold but beyond all other values. What he seeks, though he may not employ the term *ḥokmāh* [wisdom] for it, is a point of coherency, a vantage point from which God, the world, and his own experience make sense. For Job to be vindicated by God presumes

54. Newsom, *Job*, 177.

> the existence of a set of transcendent values continuous between God and humankind, that serves as the ground by which the distortions of the world can be put right.[55]

Job's lawsuit, and even the idea of a lawsuit, has meaning only if there is overlap between the values of God and humanity. In the absence of common ground, the two cannot meet. This is the premise of Abraham's intervention on behalf of Sodom (Gen 18:25), and this requirement is no less important in Job. But Job despairs of making headway. "If it is a contest of strength, he is the strong one!" he concedes (Job 9:19). "If it is a matter of justice, who can summon him?" he frets (9:19). A strict legal case may not fare better than a match-up of strength because God might decline the summons. In the remote case that God would appear, Job imagines that he, Job, is likely to suffer failure of nerve. "Though I am innocent, my own mouth would condemn me; though I am blameless, he would prove me perverse," he worries (9:20).

But the thought of suing God, once it has been imagined and expressed, gains momentum. Perhaps it is fueled by the sense that he has no other option. Perhaps, too, the friends' unreasonable arguments and their increasingly hostile tone make him think that a direct encounter with God gives him a better chance. Before we are halfway through the poetic section of Job, he has made up his mind. "But I could speak to the Almighty, and I desire to argue my case with God," he says (13:3).

After this there is no turning back. What at first seemed like a risky proposition is now his only hope. Indeed, the odds, initially so forbidding, now glow with promise.

> Oh, that I knew where I might find him, that I might come even to his dwelling! I would lay my case before him, and fill my mouth with arguments. I would learn what he would answer me, and understand what he would say to me. Would he contend with me [in court] in the greatness of his power? No; but he would give heed to me. There an upright person could reason with him, and I should be acquitted forever by my judge (23:3–7).

The reservations expressed at the outset are completely gone. To Job, an encounter with God offers hope even though dialogue with God's self-appointed defenders proved hopeless. The power discrepancy between the divine and the human is no deterrent. God, Job believes, will listen to him and see the point. When Job speaks for the last time in dialogues that ostensibly take place between him and his friends, they have all but vanished from the picture. His mind is set on a meeting with God. He has prepared the legal brief, figuratively speaking, reviewed the evidence, and concluded that he has a strong case.

> Oh, that I had one to hear me! (Here is my signature! let the Almighty answer me!) Oh, that I had the indictment written by my adversary! Surely I would

55. Ibid.

> carry it on my shoulder; I would bind it on me like a crown; I would give him an account of all my steps; like a prince I would approach him (31:35–37).

Job, as Clines notes, pushes ahead with the one option that is available to him.

> Job can only defend himself verbally by creating a scenario where both he and God are obliged to speak, each in his own defense. In short, Job summons God to a lawsuit! He challenges God to give an account of himself—to explain what Job has done wrong to deserve such suffering. But of course since Job believes he has done nothing wrong, implicitly he challenges God to confess that he and not Job is the criminal.[56]

"The words of Job are ended," the narrator reports almost immediately after Job has expressed his final wish for an encounter with God (31:40). His determination in this regard is the punch line of his closing argument. Elihu now steps into the picture, attacking Job in more brazen terms than his friends have done (32:2—37:24). When Elihu makes *his* closing argument, however, he pushes back hard against Job's final wish. "Shall it be told him that I would speak? Did a man ever wish that he would be swallowed up?" he counters (37:20, ESV).

Elihu's protestations are reduced to an asterisk because they do not generate a response from Job and because Job gets what Elihu denies him: God appears. And God speaks as one who has been listening all along.

> Then the Lord answered Job out of the whirlwind: "Who is this that darkens counsel by words without knowledge? Gird up your loins like a man, I will question you, and you shall declare to me. Where were you when I laid the foundation of the earth? Tell me, if you have understanding. Who determined its measurements—surely you know!" (38:1–5)

Is God's arrival a short-lived and mostly Pyrrhic victory for Job in his contest with his friends, as some interpreters hear God's speech? Job gets his encounter, to be sure, but he also gets a rebuke so resounding that his case seems to disintegrate. Except for the fact that God makes an appearance, on first impression God's response confirms the friends' ideas more than they support Job's. Divine transcendence towers forbiddingly over human finitude; omniscience runs circles around one who does not know much (38:1, 4, 21). Who, indeed, "is this that darkens counsel by words without knowledge?" (38:2). God rains question upon question on Job,[57] many more than we can reproduce here.

> Where were you when I laid the foundation of the earth? (38:4)

> Have the gates of death been revealed to you, or have you seen the gates of deep darkness? (38:17)

56. Clines, *Job 1–20*, xliii.

57. Clines, (Ibid., xlv) notes the predominance of questions in God's response.

> Have you comprehended the expanse of the earth? (38:18)
>
> Can you bind the chains of the Pleiades, or loose the cords of Orion? (38:31)
>
> Who provides for the raven its prey, when its young ones cry to God, and wander about for lack of food? (38:41)
>
> Is it at your command that the eagle mounts up and makes its nest on high? (39:27)

God's speeches are stupendous disclosures of complexity and beauty, of order and design, of unfathomable grandeur and, in contrast to Job's death-wish at the beginning (3:1–26), a resounding paean to life.[58] Human life is de-centered by the introduction of other creatures that have their own rhythms, yearnings, and idiosyncrasies (39:1–30). In the first speech, God does not counter Job's claim of being innocent of wrong, but he never directly addresses it, preferring instead to shower him with a meteoric display of life and light.

And somehow, strangely, the voice from the whirlwind succeeds in stilling the storm of Job's quest on its first try.

> Then Job answered the Lord: "See, I am of small account; what shall I answer you? I lay my hand on my mouth. I have spoken once, and I will not answer; twice, but will proceed no further" (40:2–5; cf. 42:1–6).

Some readers have found this response disappointing, accusing Job of folding in the face of 'cosmic bullying.'[59] The better view, I believe, is to hear God speaking to Job in a voice that is not that of a bully. Instead, it is the answer of someone who has listened well and who offers a perspective that has explanatory power. This, as Pierre van Hecke notes, begins with the encounter as such.

> After Job's relentless and determined requests, the fact that God finally agrees to enter into the discussion comes as a relief. As a matter of fact, the formulaic introductions of God's answers (38.1; 40.1,6) make clear that God is the first one really to answer Job. Whereas the replies of the friends are invariably and stereotypically introduced with the phrase "X answered and said," God's answers explicitly mention the name of his interlocutor: "God answered *Job* and said." Job's desire for conversing with God is thus granted.[60]

58. Alter, *Biblical Poetry*, 120–32.

59. Alter (*Job*, 10), while using the term "cosmic bullying," does not think that God is guilty of that. William Safire (*The First Dissident*, 29) finds Job's response "dramatically inconsistent and philosophically jarring," also citing similar sentiments by Elie Wiesel from a course on Job that Wiesel taught on French television.

60. van Hecke, "I would converse with the Almighty," 24–25.

And God is not done speaking. In the second speech, God goes beyond the bounds of necessity, ignoring that Job has declared himself content after the first speech. Having taken Job on a tour of the earth and the cosmos that included astronomy, meteorology, and zoology, God narrows the focus until it rests resolutely on the mysterious Leviathan.

"Can you," God asks Job,

> draw out Leviathan with a fishhook, or press down its tongue with a cord? Will it make many supplications to you? Will it speak soft words to you? Will it make a covenant with you to be taken as your servant forever? Any hope of capturing it will be disappointed; were not even the gods overwhelmed at the sight of it? No one is so fierce as to dare to stir it up. Who can stand before it? *Who can confront it and be safe?—under the whole heaven, who?* From its mouth go flaming torches; sparks of fire leap out. Out of its nostrils comes smoke, as from a boiling pot and burning rushes. Its breath kindles coals, and a flame comes out of its mouth. Its heart is as hard as stone, as hard as the lower millstone. When it raises itself up the gods are afraid; at the crashing they are beside themselves. On earth it has no equal, a creature without fear. It surveys everything that is lofty; it is king over all that are proud (excerpts from 41:1–34).

The poetic idiom is baffling. Here, in God's description of Leviathan, it pulls out all the stops.[61] What, or who, is Leviathan? As we move toward the conclusion of this chapter, I will suggest three answers to this question. First, agreeing with Carol Newsom, we see that at the end of the divine speeches "three characters dominate the scene: Job, God, and Leviathan."[62] This makes Leviathan an important figure, by far the most important of all the creatures that are featured in God's speeches.

Second, I believe that Matitiahu Tsevat is profoundly correct when he says that God's speeches have content and that the content, at least indirectly, resonates with the rest of the book. By way of reminder, Job's quest in the dialogues is understanding. "Is it conceivable," Tsevat asks, "that the author invested this stupendous intellectual energy in the question only to seek, receive, and transmit the solution on a nonintellectual level?"[63]

> Not only is the intellectual element characteristically present in their communion with God, the communion involves: usually the understanding of, often the approval of, sometimes an active sharing in His plan. Job's communion

61. Ozick ("Impious Impatience," 63) describes it as "an artistry so far beyond the grasp of mind and tongue that one can hardly think of their origin. We think of the Greek plays; we think of Shakespeare; and still that is not marvel enough."

62. Newsom, *Job*, 252.

63. Tsevat, "The Meaning of the Book of Job," 82.

> with God is not bought with an intellectual sacrifice, at the cost of renouncing his wish to understand the constitution of the world.[64]

If we take this view seriously, it means that God is not silencing Job with shock and awe. God is not practicing "education through overwhelming" by reason of "that inscrutable business, the government of the world."[65] Others, including great readers like Alter and Robert Gordis, incline to the view that God compensates Job for the injustice of his suffering with a vision of the world's beauty. Tsevat rejects this view, asking how anyone can accept that "the demands of justice are met by the administering of an anesthesia to the victim of an unjust sentence?"[66] These criticisms seem justified and compelling.

But then, failing to give God's description of Leviathan adequate billing, Tsevat drops the ball. God gives an answer to Job, he says, and the answer is that divine justice "is not an element of reality."[67] By 'de-moralizing' the world, Job is prepared "for a pious and moral life uncluttered by false hopes and unfounded claims."[68]

This necessitates a response that goes directly to the identity of Leviathan. Here, if not before, is proof of a cosmos in turmoil. Adversarial powers play a role in human and cosmic reality, an insight that is projected most forcefully in God's second speech to Job.[69] At the end of the book, the Adversary in the frame story reappears, but he is now disguised as Leviathan. In his poetic incarnation he is no colorless figure that keeps himself busy doing God's unpalatable bidding. The poetic idiom bewilders interpreters, but the bewilderment is unwarranted and self-inflicted. Job eschews the axis of retribution and reward, but the book does not throw the idea of justice and discernible sense overboard. Justice, however, is not found in retribution. It consists in making right what is wrong, which is precisely what God is doing in the cosmic struggle with Leviathan.

Leviathan cannot be talked into submission because he does not speak "soft words" (41:3). Deceitful words and destructive action go hand in hand; "from its mouth go flaming torches; sparks of fire leap out. Out of its nostrils comes smoke, as from a boiling pot and burning rushes. Its breath kindles coals, and a flame comes out of its mouth" (41:19–21).

"Its heart is as hard as stone," God tells Job (41:24), meaning that Leviathan has the power to intimidate and crush anything and anyone that stand in its way (41:25, 33, 34). "Who," therefore, "can confront it and be safe?" God asks Job in what is the most poignant of all God's questions, adding, in a tone of rising intensity, "*under the whole heaven, who*?" (41:11)

64. Ibid., 92.
65. Ibid., 93.
66. Ibid., 94.
67. Ibid., 100.
68. Ibid., 104.
69. I am in debt to my friend Anthony MacPherson for this view, who credits Robert Fyall.

Who, indeed? And who can stand up to an adversary whose chief weapon is its *mouth*, as Samuel Balentine perceptively notes.

> At the center of God's portrait is a description of Leviathan's mouth (vv. 18–21). If we read this section alongside the previous description of Leviathan's mouth (41:3–4), then two contrasting images emerge: one that emphasizes *what does not come forth* from its mouth; the other, that which *does*. What does not come from this creature's mouth are "soft words." In the unlikely event anyone should ever successfully capture it and force it into service, even then it would not conform to any "covenantal" relationship that required it to do or say only what its master permitted. Instead, when it opens its mouth it instinctively speaks like a god. The rhetoric emphasizes fire and light, smoke and flames. . . . Like a god, Leviathan announces its presence with an awesome fierceness that commands attention and defies coercion.[70]

Misrepresentations of God abound in Job, beginning with Satan's question in the frame story (1:9–11; 2:4–5), continuing undercover in the theology of Job's friends (15:14–16; 25:4–6), and climaxing in God's speech about the wiliness and fury of Leviathan (41:1–34). God is under attack even more than is Job.

On the other side we have Job. The view that "God challenges Job in order to silence, overpower, and shame him," is common, but must be rejected as widely off target.[71] Equally preposterous is the idea that "God shows the Divine Self to be the more Macho One who outtalks Job the talker," cornering him with "a kind of intergalactic, pyrotechnical, and zoological rhetoric that falls upon Job like an asteroid from outer space. He is squashed. Splat!"[72]

To this we must say, Not at all!

But what did Job say that met God's approval (42:7–8), realizing that much of what Job said was broken sense (38:2; 40:4–5; 42:2–6)? Did God mostly approve of his challenge to theological convention and authority? Was Job's repudiation of the logic of retribution to the point? Or was it Job's maturing conviction that God would give him a hearing and an explanation—and then that God did just that when God spoke to him from the whirlwind? Must we not conclude that God showers Job with the same sense that readers get from the frame story, first-hand and in person? The voice from the whirlwind repairs the broken sense of Job's outlook in the same breath that it repudiates the cruel sense of his friends. We have it from no less an authority than God that Leviathan is on the loose in the world. God alone can defeat Leviathan, and God does it by dealing a blow to the fiery propositions that are coming from Leviathan's mouth.

70. Balentine, *Job*, 689.

71. O'Connor, "Job in the Whirlwind," 48.

72. Ibid.

The Book of Job does not end with God's speech to Job or with Job's concession speech. It ends with God's address to Eliphaz and Job's humbled friends. Something serious was wrong in their pitiless view, and something important was right in Job's incomplete and broken outlook. Job, God says in so many words, has "spoken of me what is right" (42:7, 8).

Chapter Fifteen

Going Head to Head with Bogus Sense

The Synoptic Gospels, meaning Mark, Matthew, and Luke, differ on some points, but they all agree on what came first when Jesus moved into the public eye. Immediately after his baptism, says Mark, the Spirit "drove him into the wilderness. He was in the wilderness forty days, tempted by Satan; and he was with the wild beasts; and the angels waited on him" (Mark 1:12–13).

Matthew begins his account this way, "Then Jesus was led up by the Spirit into the wilderness to be tempted by the devil" (Matt 4:1). In Luke's version, Jesus "was led by the Spirit in the wilderness, where for forty days he was tempted by the devil" (Luke 4:1–2). All three accounts agree that Jesus, under the influence of the Spirit, went into the wilderness. All three say that he spent forty days there. And all three say that he was tempted by Satan during that period; indeed, that he went there for the express purpose of being "tempted by the devil" (Matt 4:1). All agree that Jesus did not stray into the wilderness haphazardly or by accident. He went there deliberately, and he went there as his very first move. The stories signal awareness on the part of the narrators of a task prescribed for Jesus by the human predicament as it is laid out in the Old Testament. From the very first, Jesus's mission is set within a cosmic framework, one critical element of which recalls and recapitulates the encounter between Adam, Eve, and the serpent in Genesis (Gen 3:1–6). While the propositions put forward during the encounter find expressions that seem novel and enticing (Matt 4:1–11), they are familiar and worn—and yet extremely confusing. It is a premise of these stories that Jesus alone has what it takes to untangle the swirling senses that are brought to bear on him. He alone has the disposition to take on the risk; he alone has the vigilance to discern the reality behind the mask; he alone knows how to call out the contradictions; he alone has the serenity to hang on until the underlying malice is forced into the open. At the risk of appearing to prejudge the encounter and its outcome, we shall see the sense of Jesus go head to head with demonic sense, billed in the Synoptic accounts as the D-day in the world plot—with Jesus as the winner.

Into the Wilderness

The three Synoptic accounts differ somewhat with respect to how they tell the story. Mark's account is much shorter than the others,[1] but it is by far the most vivid.

> *Mark*: And the Spirit immediately throws him out into the wilderness (1:12, my translation).
>
> *Matthew*: Then Jesus was led up by the Spirit into the wilderness (4:1, NRSV).

Already in the opening sentence, five differences are worth noting between Mark and Matthew. First, Mark's account has the verb in the active voice while Matthew puts the verbal action in the passive. Dynamism and buoyancy are better conveyed by the active voice, and this instance is no exception. Second, in Mark's version Jesus is not the acting subject. He is the recipient of an action that is executed by the Spirit. He is, as it were, not in the driver's seat, and his name is not even mentioned.[2] Matthew also has the Spirit in the leading role, but the passive voice subdues the action upon Jesus. Third, the verbs are different. Mark uses the forceful and rather coarse *ekballō*, to "*throw out*," while Matthew and Luke have variants of *agō*, to "*lead*." The difference is dramatic. *ekballō* in Mark has the connotation of a "forceful ejection," an uncompromising and almost coerced action,[3] while *agō* in Matthew better preserves the dignity of Jesus. If we were to choose a modern word for *ekballō* in Mark, we could say that the Spirit *catapults* him into the wilderness (Mark 1:12).

Fourth, Mark uses the historical present to report an event that took place in the past. This is characteristic of Mark's narrative style. Here, as in other instances of its use, the historical present creates a sense of immediacy almost to the point of making the reader an eyewitness to the action. Matthew, by contrast, uses a verbal tense that is more neutral [aorist], a summary statement with reference to an event in the past. Fifth, where Mark has the characteristic and abrupt *euthus*, "*immediately*," Matthew opts for the more sedentary *tote*, "*then*," a substitution often made when the former word is encountered in Mark. These five differences contribute to a terse, vivid, and urgent action in Mark. This is not to say that Matthew or Luke thought that less was at stake, but we owe a debt to Mark for using language intended to put the reader in a state of high alert. The distinctives of his account, says Susan R. Garrett, "are like blinking red lights, warning us not to fly through this section of the story."[4]

Three other features in Mark are worthy of note on their own terms and not as items of comparison. Despite the brevity of his narrative, Mark mentions the wilderness twice; Jesus was led "into the wilderness" (1:12), and then, somewhat redundantly,

1. Taylor (*St. Mark*, 162) calls it "brief and bare" while Anderson (*Gospel of Mark*, 80) describes it as "bald and even cryptic."

2. Dormandy, "Jesus' Temptations," 183.

3. Marcus, *Mark*, 167. Mann (*Mark*, 202) has "drove" or "impelled."

4. Garrett, *The Temptations*, 59.

"he was in the wilderness" (1:13). The location is significant for more than one reason, but one factor is surely that the desert was thought of as the domain of Satan.[5] On this reading, Jesus is sent into the lion's den, so to speak, willingly and deliberately entering enemy territory.

The second observation is closely related to the first, this one returning to Mark's choice of verb. Why does Mark say that the Spirit "*throws*" Jesus into the wilderness, using a word that suggests "strong, if not violent, propulsion"?[6] We cannot overlook that of the seventeen times that the word *ekballō* ["*throw out*"] is used in Mark, eleven of them have to do with exorcism.[7] Exorcism, in turn, means to drive out evil forces or influences. When we keep this in mind, we will not primarily see Jesus as the one who is *thrown out*. The Spirit's action upon Jesus anticipates Jesus's action upon Satan. Jesus is *thrown out* into the wilderness in order to *throw out* Satan. While the Spirit takes the lead,[8] the goal of the action is to incapacitate Satan, and the showdown that is in the making is sought more by the One who sent Jesus than by Satan. God is in Jesus invading the territory of Satan in order to liberate it.

This view is supported by a third observation. Mark says of Jesus that "he was with the wild beasts" (Mark 1:13). This detail signifies the success of Jesus's liberating mission. Mark's simple phrase "indicates Jesus' peaceable presence with the animals," says Richard Bauckham.[9] Robert Guelich goes so far as to say that this phrase "holds the key to his temptation narrative."[10] We are likely to miss the messianic and eschatological connotation of this image unless we strain to hear the Old Testament echoes. To Mark, Jesus is the shoot that is to come from "the stump of Jesse" (Isa 11:1) under whose influence recalcitrant hostilities will come to an end (Isa 11:1–10). In that day, says Isaiah, "the wolf shall live with the lamb, the leopard shall lie down with the kid, the calf and the lion and the fatling together" (Isa 11:6). Mark's depiction of Jesus in close and friendly association with the wild beasts is proof that the messianic deliverer has arrived.[11] While Jesus does not universally restore the paradisiac state at that point in time, "he sets the messianic precedent for it."[12]

At the moment of triumph, "the angels waited on him," says Mark (1:13). Bauckham points out that the angels "are the natural friends of the righteous person,"[13] but this insight does not capture the whole picture. In Mark's cosmic drama, the angels

5. Marcus, *Mark 1–8*, 168.

6. Taylor, *Mark*, 163.

7. Marcus, *Mark 1–8*, 168.

8. Jesus went into the wilderness "under divine direction," says Jeffrey B. Gibson; cf. "Jesus' Wilderness Temptation according to Mark," 18.

9. Bauckham, *The Bible and Ecology*, 127.

10. Guelich, *Mark 1–8:26*, 38.

11. Isa 11:6–9; 65:25; Gen 3:14. See also Marcus, *Mark 1–8*, 168; Pokorny, "The Temptation Stories," 121.

12. Bauckham, "Jesus and the Wild Animals," 19.

13. Bauckham, *The Bible and Ecology*, 127.

have an enormous stake in Jesus's success. While "the angels waited on him [*diēkonoun autō*]" in the sense that they were at the ready to meet Jesus's needs after the ordeal,[14] the statement indicating angelic service to Jesus also accommodates the thought that "the angels *worshiped* him" (1:13).[15] Only when this option is included have we done justice to the scope of Mark's story. Despite its brevity and breathlessness, Mark's account heralds closure of the cosmic conflict.

"The Tempter Came" (Matt 4:3)

In his exceptional commentary on Mark, Joel Marcus says that while the forty day period in the wilderness echoes the experience of Moses and Elijah (Exod 24:18; 34:28; 1 Kgs 19:5–8), "the primary biblical model for our passage's portrait of Jesus is not Elijah but Adam."[16] This is a crucial judgment. Even though Mark's temptation account differs from the stories we find in Matthew and Luke, the relationship between Adam and Jesus is not irrelevant to the other two gospels. Ninety percent of Mark is reproduced in Matthew, by and large preserving Mark's sequence and wording.[17] All the elements of Mark's temptation story have been preserved in Matthew with the exception of the wild beasts. The changes otherwise are congruent with the trend that Matthew reads like a sanitized version of Mark, or, as Graham Stanton has suggested, as "a much expanded and revised second edition of Mark."[18] One feature that enlarges the girth of Matthew is this Gospel's extensive references and allusions to the Old Testament.[19] This feature is on display in the temptation story.

It has been suggested that the temptation story in Matthew proceeds on the strength of what is said and not what is done. "Since the three temptations get along with a minimum of narrative requisites, the emphasis falls on the central scripture quotations," says Ulrich Luz.[20] This assessment is valid only if the reader allows the quantitative parameters to dominate interpretation. It cannot be denied that Scripture quotations occupy the lion's share of Matthew's temptation story measured by quantity (Matt 4:1–11), but the quotations are responses to questions and temptations posed to Jesus by Satan. The tendency of interpreters to let the Scripture quotations control interpretation has therefore had unfortunate results. Insufficient attention

14. Thus, "angels took care of him" (NIRV) or "looked after him" (NJB).

15. Marcus, *Mark 1–8*, 168–69.

16. Marcus, *Mark 1–8*, 169. Moses was on the mountain "with the Lord forty days and forty nights; he neither ate bread nor drank water" (Exod 34:28), not to tell us that he was tempted, but that he was sustained. Elijah was fed by an angel before he went "forty days and forty nights to Horeb the mount of God," again with the point of showing that he was able to do it "in the strength of that food" which God had provided (1 Kgs 19:48). Hunger is not a concern in either story.

17. Burridge, *Four Gospels, One Jesus?* 65.

18. Stanton, *Gospels and Jesus*, 63.

19. Stanton, "Matthew," 205.

20. Luz, *Matthew 1–7*, 147.

has been paid to the temptations themselves. In the second temptation, Satan quotes Scripture, too, but he is merely trying to embellish, camouflage, and proof-text an idea that is genuinely his own (4:6). While Matthew's account may be dominated by what is said and not by what is done, the accent should not fall one-sidedly on the Scripture quotations. A keen reading will pay attention to what Satan is saying. This, in turn, will strengthen the connection between Jesus in the wilderness and Adam and Eve in the Garden of Eden.

Moreover, while much is said in Matthew's temptation story, it is not as though nothing is done. Jesus "was led up by the Spirit into the wilderness to be tempted by the devil" (4:1). This is the defining action in Matthew as much as in Mark. "The Spirit's role is thus prior to that of the devil," as Donald Hagner notes.[21] Next, he "fasted forty days and forty nights, and afterwards he was famished" (4:2). Then, but not until then, "the tempter came" (4:3). Much has been done before the first temptation begins. Setting, timing, characters, and the condition of Jesus are all important. And more will be done before the confrontation is over. After the first temptation, "the devil took him to the holy city and placed him on the pinnacle of the temple" (4:5), and, finally, "the devil took him to a very high mountain and showed him all the kingdoms of the world and their splendor" (4:8). These are dizzying actions, going from the wilderness to the pinnacle of the temple, and, lastly, "to a very high mountain" (4:8): It is not as though action is absent in the story; it is not as though nothing is *done*.

In a highly influential interpretation of Matthew's account, Birger Gerhardsson proposed to read it as an example of an early Christian *haggadic Midrash*.[22] This term refers to compositions by creative Jewish rabbis attempting to make Old Testament texts speak to new issues or questions. The practice was Torah-centric, focused on a narrow selection of scripture passages, and had a dialogue akin to that found in rabbinic disputations. As to result, it created a revised story with new implications by means of minor alterations. According to Gerhardsson, Matthew's temptation account is meant to prove that Jesus is the *obedient* Son of God in contrast to Israel, the *disobedient* 'son of God' (Deut 6—8). Jesus's sonship is the contested issue, and "the term *Son of God* is *the key term* in the narrative."[23] Assuming that Jesus is the covenant Son of God, the story implies "*a testing of the partner in the covenant to see whether he is keeping his side of the agreement*," says Gerhardsson.[24] For Jesus, being hungry after the forty days' fast, the issue in the first temptation thus becomes whether he is able to trust God's providence and his provisions. Like Israel in the wilderness, "*hunger and its satisfying*," as Gerhardsson put it, lie at the heart of the test. [25] Jesus cannot prove

21. Hagner, *Matthew 1–13*, 64.

22. Gerhardsson, *Testing of God's Son*, 11.

23. Ibid., 20.

24. Ibid., 26.

25. Ibid., 45.

his sonship by performing a miracle. If the test is "to reveal what lies in his heart,"[26] the character of his sonship must manifest itself in an attitude of submission and trust, that is, in traits opposite the discontent and doubt of the Israelites during their wilderness wandering. Crucially, with respect to Jesus no less than with Israel, God is the one carrying out the test.

Gerhardsson's reading has won praise and cannot be ignored,[27] but it suffers from serious flaws. W. D. Davies and Dale C. Allison concede that it is "certainly brilliant" but object that it is speculative.[28] As to plot structure and narrative elements, Luz points out that "the devil's demand that Jesus perform miracles has no parallels in Jewish texts."[29] While there are intriguing parallels for the first temptation, the Israel typology hardly holds the key to the other two. At best, it provides weak scaffolding for the second temptation and even less for the third. "[O]ne can find no type of the third temptation in Israel's history," says Luz.[30]

Three other problems are more serious. The first one, already mentioned, is to allow the Scripture quotations to dominate at the expense of what is said by Satan. In Gerhardsson's reading, the fixed points in Matthew's account are Jesus's answers from Scripture. He assumes a construct that runs from the answers to the questions and not the other way. In the *Midrash* that he takes this text to be the questions have been crafted to fit the answers.

Gerhardsson also believed that the temptation narrative "was formed within a strongly monist world of thought."[31] On this logic, the devil in the story should be seen as God's agent of testing and not as an enemy. It follows from this that the test is important but Satan is not. Echoing this view, Ulrich Luck says that "the theme of the temptation story is the temptation but not the devil."[32] Satan, this view holds, is not locked in combat with Jesus in a high stakes conflict that pits them against one another. He plays a secondary role to the actual content of the test and could easily be dispensed with altogether.

On what basis are competent interpreters making this claim? Exegesis cannot be the answer; it must owe to presuppositions. But why does this presupposition intrude on the interpretation in such a highhanded way? Two factors are likely to play a role, explored to some extent in chapters 4 and 5. On the one hand, indifference to Satan reflects Satan's precarious status in New Testament theology. D. F. Strauss (1808–74) led the way on this point in the nineteenth century. "If Christ has come in order to

26. Ibid., 51.

27. Stegner's exposition ("The Use of Scripture," 98–105) is largely a summary and expansion of Gerhardsson's key points.

28. Davies and Allison, *The Gospel*, I:353.

29. Luz, *Matthew 1–7*, 148.

30. Ibid., 150.

31. Gerhardsson, *Testing of the Son of God*, 41.

32. Luck, *Das Evangelium nach Matthäus*, 42.

destroy the work of the devil, then there was no need for him to come since there is no devil," said Strauss.[33] A few years later, commenting on the temptation story in Matthew, he elaborated that "the personal appearance of the devil is the great stumbling-block in the present narrative. . . . It is with the existence of the devil as with that of angels—even the believers in revelation are perplexed by it."[34] It goes without saying that interpreters will be reluctant to invest in a character that in their view does not exist. Gerhardsson's interpretation is a case in point in this regard.

Strauss, reading the temptation story as whole cloth, at least sought to give the two protagonists in the temptation story equal treatment. "[I]f there is a devil, but only as the personification of the principle of evil, fine; then it is also sufficient to hold Christ as an impersonal idea," he said.[35] Interpreters will not be as blunt today, but neither will they expend prestige in the unenviable task of restoring to Satan the importance that previous generations took away. There was always less eagerness to reduce Jesus to an impersonal idea; *his* status has not been challenged to the degree envisioned by Strauss.

On the other hand, we have here a reminder that many scholars of Gerhardsson's generation failed to appreciate the apocalyptic grounding of the New Testament. Ernst Käsemann raised many eyebrows when he contended in 1960 that "apocalyptic was the mother of Christian theology."[36] Ten years later, Klaus Koch set off more waves with a book completely dedicated to the subject of apocalyptic. The title of his book was not *The Rediscovery of Apocalyptic*, as in the English translation, but *Ratlos vor der Apokalyptik*, meaning, '*Bewildered in the Face of Apocalyptic*.'[37] Who was bewildered? The bewildered ones were chiefly scholars, who did not know what to do with apocalyptic because it was not part of the Protestant tradition.

To apocalyptic belong obvious elements like angelic messengers (Matt 1:18–25; 18:10; 28:1–7), cosmic conflict (4:1–11; 12:24–28; 25:41; 26:53), upheaval in the cosmic order (27:45–54; 24:29), and the coming of the Son of Man at the end of the age (24:30; 26:64) along with subtler and less widely recognized features.[38] Resurrection is a constituent of apocalyptic (27:52–53), but so is the unprecedented ideals and unheard-of possibilities proclaimed by Jesus in the Sermon on the Mount (5:17–48).[39] Miraculous signs and wonders meant to deceive are part of apocalyptic eschatology (24:23–25),[40] but so is Jesus's statement, echoing Daniel, that "to you it has

33. Strauss, *Die christliche Glaubenslehre*, II, 15.

34. Strauss, *The Life of Jesus Critically Examined*, 253–54.

35. Strauss, *Die christliche Glaubenslehre*, II, 15.

36. Käsemann, "Die Anfänge christlicher Theologie," 102.

37. Koch, *Rediscovery of Apocalyptic*.

38. Sabourin, ("Apocalyptic Traits," 19–36) surveys thirty-one texts or text units that have an apocalyptic tenor and that frequently echo Daniel. See also, Hagner, "Apocalyptic Motifs," 53–82.

39. Garlington, "The 'better righteousness,'" 479–502.

40. Sim's monograph of Matthew's eschatology (*Apocalyptic Eschatology*) teems with dubious presuppositions, but it does not compromise the cosmic dualism of Matthew.

been given to know the secrets of the kingdom of heaven, but to them it has not been given" (13:11; cf. Dan 2:28–29).[41] Judgment and accountability are familiar themes of apocalyptic (Matt 25:19–30; 31–49);[42] less familiar is the thought that apocalyptic encompasses "our Father" and the entire Lord's Prayer (6:9–13)[43] and even Matthew's concern for children and for the poor (18:2–6; 11:5; 19:21).[44] Global mission is a feature of apocalyptic (28:18–20),[45] anchored in the revealed insight that the Son of Man is "the Messiah, the Son of the living God" (16:14,17). Leopold Sabourin declares that Matthew "is the most apocalyptic of the evangelists."[46] What J. Christiaan Beker claimed for Paul can also be said of Matthew. His Gospel, no less than Paul's, "does seem welded to the apocalyptic world view."[47] This world view, moreover, is not "a husk or discardable frame; . . . it belongs to the inalienable core of the gospel."[48]

When we add that these accounts are driven not by philosophical logic but by the logic of narrative, we know why the story is the way it is. To these sources this is how reality is constituted: this is what happened. The belief that Matthew's temptation account originated within "a strongly monist world of thought" is not tenable.[49]

This leads directly to a third point that needs to be reconsidered. Gerhardsson wrote that "the acts of JHWH can never be questioned, his way of fulfilling his covenant 'obligations' is in the end above human criticism; man simply has to accept his division of good and evil in trust and obedience knowing that God is 'righteous' and does not forsake 'the righteous man.'"[50] Is this view valid, looking at the biblical narrative as a whole? Is it valid looking at human reality from an apocalyptic perspective, as Matthew does? Questioning the ordinances of God is precisely the hallmark of the temptation in Genesis (Gen 3:1). Questioning the provisions of God is also the most prominent feature in Matthew's temptation story (Matt 4:3). In fact, *the strength of the temptations in Genesis and in Matthew's temptation account derives precisely from the insinuation that God is at fault in what he commands or amiss in what he provides.* To see the temptations merely as a test of *Jesus* is too simplistic. Running as a deeper current below the surface, there is a common theme to the story of the fall of Adam, the wilderness experience of Israel, and "the testing of the Son of God" in the New Testament. That theme is not that questioning God is disallowed, but that it is mali-

41. Sabourin, "Apocalyptic Traits," 23.

42. Cope, "To the close of the age," 113–24.

43. Trudinger, "The 'Our Father,'" 49–54.

44. Rowland, "Apocalyptic," 504–18.

45. Sabourin ("Apocalyptic Traits," 32) demonstrates the close correlation between Matthew's gospel commission and the establishment of the everlasting kingdom in Dan 7:14. See also Wielenga, "Mission and the apocalyptic," 111–19.

46. Sabourin, "Apocalyptic Traits," 19; cf. Hagner, "Apocalyptic Motifs," 53, 74.

47. Beker, *Paul the Apostle*, 171.

48. Ibid.

49. Gerhardsson, *Testing of the Son of God*, 41.

50. Ibid., 31.

cious and unjustified. This will be apparent in Matthew's account when we turn from the fact that "the tempter came" to what he said.

"The Tempter . . . Said to Him" (Matt 4:3)

At the point when Jesus was weakened and vulnerable by prolonged fasting (4:2), the tempter "came and said to him, 'If you are the Son of God, command these stones to become loaves of bread'" (4:3). What should interest us when reading this text, as our very first order of business, is the implied premise of the temptation. In the tempter's voice, we should hear a tone of concern and not obvious malice. Malice is nevertheless there, in the disconnection between the tone of voice [care] and the actual words. Has God deliberately placed the presumptive 'Son of God' in a state of ruthless and cruel deprivation? What must be said about a God who subjects his beloved son to such treatment? What can we say, other than that God must be harsh and exacting when it does not seem to concern him that Jesus is on the brink of starving to death? The desert setting, the prolonged fast, and the pointed mention of Jesus's hunger even suggests that Jesus could be the *abandoned* Son of God.

In the story of the temptation in the Garden of Eden, there is a similar mix of solicitude and concealed malice when the serpent intones, "Has God really said, 'You shall not eat from any tree in the garden? (Gen 3:1; cf. Chap. 6). As in the Garden of Eden, the temptation in the wilderness has to do with food and eating, but these parallels are helpful only if they bring us to awareness of the shared premise of the temptations. According to the serpent, God placed human beings within a framework heavy with prohibition—"*you shall not eat from any tree*" (Gen 3:1). Satan strikes the same note in the wilderness. God has placed Jesus in circumstances that are weighted toward deprivation. The alleged unreasonable command is the pivot point of the temptation.[51]

Does Jesus have an answer for this? He does. And his answer, we shall see, reinforces the need to focus on the premise of the temptation and not exclusively on his refusal to perform a miracle. "It is written, 'One does not live by bread alone, but by every word that comes from the mouth of God'" (Mat 4:4; Deut 8:3). This answer centers on the quality of the divine command. Jesus rebuts the suggestion that words and commandments have come from the mouth of God that are to the detriment of those who observe them. Not an occasional word but '*every word* that comes from the mouth of God' is good. The slanderer meant to prove the pettiness of God. Jesus rejects the malevolent premise.

Was a fast of forty days really necessary for Jesus to prove himself steadfast? Would not a shorter fast be sufficient? Was it necessary for him to abstain from food virtually *unto death*? The imperfect answer to this question is found in the need to

51. "The testing takes place in conjunction with fasting, which is to be understood as commanded by God," says Hagner (*Matthew 1–13*, 64).

defeat the implied premise.[52] Jesus was subjected to an exaggerated test in order to push back against the satanic charge that God is the source of unreasonable and life-denying commands. *Even if Jesus were to die of hunger, he will not concede to the premise of Satan's innuendo against the divine character*! It need not be necessary to fast for forty days in order to demonstrate obedience, but it was necessary in order to expose the malice of the satanic smear campaign. Were Jesus to have acceded to the temptation, he would have given credence to the satanic premise.

This means that the temptations in Matthew speak to a *theological* concern and not only to matters of Christology. At face value, the tempter taps into Jesus's *ability*. Pierre Bonnard suggests that the devil's opening statement, "if you are the son of God," should be translated "*since* (Fr. *Puisque*) you are the Son of God," rather than "if."[53] Luz and others concur. "When he says 'if you are the Son of God,' the devil is not questioning Jesus' divine sonship, he is presupposing it and putting it to the test," says Luz.[54] Jesus, as we have seen, refused to take the bait. Had he taken it, it would have scored a point for Christology, superficially speaking, but it would have lost the battle for theology. Already in the first temptation, therefore, the chief concern does not revolve around the ability of Jesus or even his identity. It centers on the character of God.

The second temptation offers an opportunity to test the merits of my reading up to this point.

> Then the devil took him to the holy city and placed him on the pinnacle of the temple, saying to him, "If you are the Son of God, throw yourself down; for it is written, 'He will command his angels concerning you,' and 'On their hands they will bear you up, so that you will not dash your foot against a stone.'" (4:5–6)

In the second temptation, there is a change of setting and tactic. The 'sacred' setting wraps the Son of God—a notion Satan has conceded—in the security of God's presence. In the holy city in general and in the temple in particular, God was thought to reveal himself in a special way. "What could be a more appropriate setting for tempting the Son to misuse God's promise of protection?" asks Gerhardsson.[55] Another possibility, less certain, is that the temple setting moves Jesus into the public eye. "And why is Jesus taken from the desert to the temple, if not to gain an audience?" Davies and Allison suggest.[56]

The change of tactic, however, is more important. In the first temptation, Satan urged Jesus to distrust God. Now he is urging Jesus to trust God with abandon. The idea of being under God's special care is highlighted by Satan's proposal that the Son

52. The Israel typology does not eliminate the legitimacy of this question.

53. Bonnard, *L'Évangile*, 44; Hagner, *Matthew 1–13*, 65.

54. Luz, *Matthew 1–7*, 151. Cf. BDAG, 277.

55. Gerhardsson, *Testing of God's Son*, 59.

56. Davies and Allison, *Matthew*, I: 367.

of God should take Scripture at its word, invoking verses that speak of God's promise to protect and deliver his people from danger (Ps 91:11–12). While in the first temptation Satan was asking Jesus to step *outside* the framework of God's word, he now shifts to urging Jesus to spread his wings, figuratively speaking, *within* that framework. "Here he uses Jesus' own weapons against him and also quotes the Bible," says Luz.[57]

If we try to compute the change in tactic more precisely in theological terms, the shift is mind-boggling. In the first temptation, the premise is divine *prohibition*. Now, the premise is divine *provision* with no strings attached. If, in the first temptation, Satan faults God for not being generous, in the second temptation he presses the point of God's promise and generosity. The tempter who questioned whether God can be trusted now feigns to be converted to Jesus's point of view. God *can* be trusted, he insists, Bible in hand, and Jesus should take the Bible at its word. Moreover, since Jesus is the beloved Son of God, the divine promise applies with special force to him.

Another clarification of terms might be helpful at this point. Above, in connection with the first temptation, I outlined the boundaries between theology and Christology. I claimed priority for theology over Christology in the sense that the first temptation is a veiled attack on the character of God and not only a question about the identity and powers of Jesus. In the first temptation, too, but more clearly in the second, theology is deeply intertwined with *anthropology*. Thus, in the first temptation, the divine prohibition [theology] is closely linked to human freedom [anthropology]. The alleged prohibition curtails freedom while, on the other hand, freedom is possible only when the prohibition is broken.

In the second temptation, there is no prohibition. All of a sudden Satan floods the room with promise, provision, and protection. How does this theological premise, so radically different from the first temptation, impact anthropology? The answer is quite obvious. Satan is still pitting theology against anthropology but in a different guise. Divine provision is now meant to negate human responsibility. Only when human responsibility counts for nothing can the Son of God throw himself from the pinnacle of the temple, relying on God's promise to keep him from harm.

Hear it again, "If you are the Son of God, throw yourself down!" (4:6). What is this but human choice without consequences? What is this but a complete negation of human reason and responsibility? And what is this negation but an attack, ultimately, on human dignity? The inverse relationship between theology and anthropology persists. If, in the first temptation, Satan aims to make God look petty with the intent of carving out more space for human freedom, he is, in the second temptation, making human beings inconsequential on the theological premise that God's provision is the only thing that counts. In actual fact he is making mockery of freedom by holding forth that choices do not have consequences.

At the point when the Son's trust in God has been amply confirmed, Satan urges Jesus to work out the implications of that sonship. Confidence is pressed into

57. Luz, *Matthew 1–7*, 152.

overconfidence; trust becomes presumption; a relationship of divine provision [first temptation] *and* human responsibility [second temptation] is made to be a caricature of both. It is as if the devil is saying, "I see that you really trust God. Now here is a promise specifically given to someone who trusts the Almighty. Are you ready to claim that promise?" In the satanic proposal trust is set forth as a substitute for responsibility. Davies and Allison ask, "How should Jesus exercise his powers as the Son of God? The answer given is, In obedience to God."[58] To him, "any peril he must face—and he will face the cross—and any miracle he is to do—and he will do plenty—must arise solely from obedient service to God's purpose."[59]

Echoes from the serpent's second assertion in the Garden of Eden are not difficult to hear in the second temptation in Matthew. In Genesis, "the serpent said to the woman, 'You will not die'" (Gen 3:4). At the pinnacle of the temple, Satan in much the same way entices Jesus with a life-denying proposition that is framed as though God has constituted reality so as to make a life-destroying choice impossible (Matt 4:5–6). Jesus will no more be party to the second equation than to the first. "Again it is written," he tells Satan, "Do not put the Lord your God to the test" (Matt 4:7).

The second temptation makes human choice trivial on the proposition that lack of consequences magnifies divine mercy. Jesus does not take the bait that 'mercy' cancels out responsibility.

In the third temptation Satan pulls out all the stops.

> Again, the devil took him to a very high mountain and showed him all the kingdoms of the world and their splendor; and he said to him, "All these I will give you, if you will fall down and worship me" (Matt 4:8–9).

In the parallel version in Luke, Satan makes the astounding claim, "To you I will give their glory and all this authority; *for it has been given over to me*, and I give it to anyone I please" (Luke 4:6). This claim should be understood with reference to Adam's forfeiture of the stewardship committed to human beings in the Garden of Eden (Gen 1:28). Satan claims this dominion as his without providing any details as to how the dominion was wrested from Adam.

None of this, however, cushions the jarring quality of the third temptation. Recalling that there is "no type of the third temptation in Israel's history,"[60] can anything overcome the dissonance? In Matthew's temptation narrative, there is quite literally a rising trajectory, from the desert to the pinnacle of the temple, and from the pinnacle of the temple to a very high mountain (4:1, 5, 8). The curve intimates that the stakes are raised ever higher toward a definitive climax. At the peak, however, we hear Satan propose to Jesus the distasteful bargain, "All these I will give you, if you will fall down

58. Davies and Allison, *Matthew*, I:367.

59. Ibid.

60. Luz, *Matthew 1–7*, 150.

and worship me" (Matt 4:9). Is this the best he can do? Does he really think that Jesus will *worship* him?

The first two temptations have been about the relationship between God and Jesus. Satan has said things intended to undermine the relationship, but he has kept himself in the background. In fact, he has been careful not to say anything about himself. Now, however, the temptation is about Jesus and *Satan*. We hear Satan talking in terms of 'you' and 'me'—"if *you* will worship *me*" (4:10). Bonnard takes the *proskunesis* [worship] language here to be important, stating that "it is not only a mark of respect, but of *adoration*; v. 10 even shows that Jesus was faced with the choice between adoration of God and adoration of the devil."[61]

On the face of it, this would seem like a ridiculous proposition. Jesus's answer confirms as much. "Away with you, Satan!" (NRSV), "Go, Satan!" (NASB), or "Get out of here, Satan!" (NLT; Matt 4:10), whichever way we read it, suggests an emphatic rebuke to the idea and not only a vehement refusal to go along. What is meant to be Satan's crowning temptation turns out to be a dismal failure, its defeat a foregone conclusion even more than with any of the other temptations. At this point in Matthew's account, therefore, the progression suggests that Satan is not really leading Jesus deeper into his territory. While it is his intent to entangle Jesus one last time, the momentum has shifted in Jesus's favor. He was led into the wilderness to confront Satan, and now Jesus is drawing out Satan to reveal himself. Just as in Genesis each temptation accepted created the conditions for the next one to succeed, each temptation resisted by Jesus makes the next one *less* likely to succeed. In terms of topography, the final temptation in Matthew is the high point in the narrative, but in actual terms it is anticlimactic. It is climactic only to the extent that we are able to appreciate the binary character of the temptations: they are just as much revelatory of the character and intent of Satan as of Jesus. While Satan appears to be in command of the physical framework, he is increasingly running out of options. In the third temptation, he throws a Hail Mary pass that is spectacular for what it reveals about him but quite pathetic as to its chance of success with respect to Jesus.

For the last temptation to make sense, it is necessary to go beyond the testing of Israel in the wilderness and even beyond the serpent's deception in the Garden of Eden.[62] Satan's call to Jesus—his wretched deal—echoes the primordial phase of the cosmic conflict.

> How you are fallen from heaven,
>   O Day Star, son of Dawn!
> How you are cut down
>   to the ground,
> you who laid the nations low!

61. Bonnard, *Matthieu*, 46.

62. The temptation story in Genesis is a lesser echo with respect to the third temptation in Matthew although it, too, holds out the prospect to "be like God" (Gen 3:5).

You said in your heart,
"I will ascend to heaven;
I will raise my throne
  above the stars of God;
I will sit on the mount of assembly
  on the heights of Zaphon;
I will ascend
  to the tops of the clouds,
I will make myself
  like the Most High" (Isa 14:13–14).

In Gerhardsson's construct, the third temptation, like the others, is grounded in lessons from Deuteronomy, and the third lesson has to do with the lure of "riches and idolatry" (Deut 6:10–14).[63] But this moralistic construct is woefully inadequate for the singular, apocalyptic reality than flashes forth on the "very high mountain" in Matthew (Matt 4:8). Let it be that Jesus, unlike Israel, rejects the allure of riches and idolatry.[64] Let it be, too, that Jesus in all the temptations proves himself obedient to God in ways that are relevant to everyday human experience.[65] These applications do not match the highly personal character of the final confrontation. We should not hesitate to state that the Israel typology about riches and idolatry is far too trite to capture the ultimate act. At that point Jesus is not representing humanity in a general sense, and Satan is not playing the generic card of idolatry. With respect to the identity of Jesus, the two previous temptations have been remarkable precisely for Satan's willingness to concede that Jesus is the unique and beloved Son of God (4:3, 6).

More than obedience is at stake. Ethics—and obedience within an ethical framework—cannot do justice to the apocalyptic texture of the temptation story in the Gospels. When Jesus goes forth under the guidance of the Spirit, it is his mission to defeat Satan. By the time we get to the third temptation, it is evident that ethics [how to behave] is secondary to the underlying plot, or better, ethics is an element within the larger story. The fact that Jesus will and must *obey* must not be allowed to obscure what he will and must *defeat*. In his mission in the wilderness, the gospel accounts depict him as one sent to deal with the core issues in the cosmic conflict.

Unless these parameters are taken into consideration, the temptation story will be less than what it is. With the help of Isaiah's poem, the mountain of temptation becomes the mountain of revelation. "Not until the third [temptation] does Satan

63. Gerhardsson, *Testing of God's Son*, 62.

64. Thus Stegner ("Use of Scripture," 103), "Three times in this narrative the devil tempts Jesus to be disobedient to God. Three times Jesus turns aside the temptation with a quotation from Deuteronomy. These three quotations have the same theme—the temptations of Israel in the desert. The situation of Jesus is like that of Israel. So parallel are the situations that Jesus may be said to be reliving the temptations of his ancestors."

65. Cf. Hagner, *Matthew 1–13*, 69. Luz (*Matthew 1–7*, 155) argues against a simple "everyday experience" application in favor of temptations that reveal fundamental principles.

drop his disguise and demand to be worshipped," says Eduard Schweizer.[66] The two protagonists in the conflict face off on very unequal terms in human history, and yet Jesus pulls it off. On Matthew's mountain, the "*I*" who speaks relentlessly in the first person about his aspiration is drawn out to reveal his intent (Isa 14:12–15). More than idolatry is at stake. It is the one who said in his heart, "I will make myself like the Most High," who on the mountain calls on Jesus to fall down and worship him (Isa 14:13–14; Matt 4:8–9).

It should now be apparent why there is little space between the temptation accounts in Mark and Matthew. Mark lays the groundwork by throwing Jesus, under the agency of the Spirit, into the wilderness on a mission of exorcism (Mark 1:12–13). Matthew transmits his message on the same apocalyptic wavelength. The high point comes when Jesus, in the third temptation, commands the tempter, "Away with you, Satan!" (Matt 4:10). The exorcism—and Jesus's language in Matthew belongs to the vocabulary of exorcism—is complete. The brazen self-promoter on the mountain is exposed and rejected in favor of an option more worthy. For "it is written, 'Worship the Lord your God, and serve only him,'" Jesus insists (4:10).

All of this assumes that there is a genuine temptation, a notion that has been contested in various ways throughout history.[67] And yet obedience walks hand in hand with revelation. What good would it do, hypothetically speaking, if Jesus demonstrates unquestioning obedience to an unreasonable command? It would prove his obedience, to be sure, but it would not defeat the demonic premise. What good would it do if Jesus, armed with quotations from Deuteronomy, fends off the tempter with another line from Scripture? It would prove his command of the sacred text, but even Satan can do that (4:6; cf. Jas 2:19). In the second temptation, Satan deploys the equivalent of a slogan often heard in circles of faith in order to disconnect Jesus from reason and responsibility: 'God said it, I believe it, that settles it.' What distinguishes Jesus's reading of Scripture is that he will not divorce text from context, letter from spirit, and obedience from understanding. In the temptation story, Satan's effort to subvert the meaning and intent of the divine command comes to grief. The obedience of Jesus springs from his belief that God has no unreasonable commands, arbitrary expectations, or failed provisions. The corollary to the faithfulness of the Son of God is the love and trustworthiness of God.

"If You Are the Son of God"

We read this sentence three times in Matthew's Gospel, twice in the temptation account (4:3, 6) and once in relation to the crucifixion of Jesus (27:40). The wording is

66. Schweizer, *The Good News*, 58.

67. In a review of the history of interpretation, Luz (*Matthew 1–7*, 153) says that the monophysites in Early Christianity could not take the temptation story seriously because the notion that Jesus could succumb to sin was theologically preposterous and materially impossible within their Christology.

identical in all three instances, "If you are the son of God." In order to appreciate the last instance, we need to read it in context.

> Those who passed by derided him, shaking their heads and saying, "You who would destroy the temple and build it in three days, save yourself! *If you are the Son of God*, come down from the cross." In the same way the chief priests also, along with the scribes and elders, were mocking him, saying, "He saved others; he cannot save himself. He is the King of Israel; let him come down from the cross now, and we will believe in him. He trusts in God; let God deliver him now, if he wants to; for he said, 'I am God's Son'" (Matt 27:39–43).

We might well consider this the final temptation of Jesus, numbering it as the fourth. It connects to the others by repeating Satan's words in the wilderness and at the pinnacle of the temple (4:3, 6). "*If you are the Son of God*" is laid out in such a way that it practically serves as bookends to Matthew's presentation of the public life of Jesus. In the closing instance, the speakers are not Satan but acknowledged experts on theology. This connection could be significant, too, suggesting that a viewpoint originating with Satan has won undeserved acceptance in theology. Like Satan in the second temptation, the mockers at the cross put their rich repository of scriptural knowledge to use (Ps 22:8).

Should we not admit that this time the mockers have reason and good sense on their side, ignoring for a moment the cruelty that energizes their taunts? The person on the cross cannot be the Son of God or in any way be representative of God. Remember the objection of Celsus in the second century:

> *It is mere impiousness, therefore, to suggest that the things that were done to Jesus were done to God. Certain things are simply as a matter of logic impossible to God, namely those things which violate the consistency of his nature: God cannot do less than what it befits God to do, what it is God's nature to do. Even if the prophets had foretold such things about the Son of God, it would have been necessary to say, according to the axiom I have cited, that the prophets were wrong, rather than to believe that God has suffered and died.*[68]

Jesus on the cross is a person of weakness, contemptible, condemned, rejected, and abandoned. Abandoned, indeed!

> From noon on, darkness came over the whole land until three in the afternoon. And about three o'clock Jesus cried with a loud voice, "Eli, Eli, lema sabachthani?" that is, "My God, my God, why have you *abandoned* me?" (Matt 27:45–46, translation mine).

The apocalyptic tenor of this scene is intense. We are privy to an event that in Matthew's eyes has cosmic and revelatory significance. Is it any wonder that those

68. *Celsus on the True Doctrine*, 100.

who witnessed this scene first hand, and especially those who had theological training, considered it ludicrous that Jesus could be the beloved Son of God?

I will desist from pursuing this line of thought further except to say that if the sense of being abandoned by God represents the most acute dilemma for theodicy, Jesus's cry of dereliction reveals that abandonment has been experienced and absorbed *within* the relationship between God and the beloved Son of God. Instead, however, as this chapter draws to a close, I wish to highlight two other aspects from the scene. Both come to expression in the taunts that rain mercilessly on the crucified Jesus, coming from all sides, from the casual passer-by, the passionately engaged, and even from those who were crucified with him (27:39–44). This is what we hear some of them say,

> "Save yourself, if you are the Son of God" (27:40, translation mine).
>
> "He saved others; he cannot save himself" (27:42).

Blocking out the evident scorn of those who say this, the ideological clarity of the statements is astounding. The mockers are appealing to an ideology of self-preservation and self-interest, pitting that ideology against a stance of self-giving. Whether by accident or intent, they associate God with the ideology of self-interest, implying that such a god would be one in whom they could believe. The mockers acknowledge, even if contemptuously, that Jesus has committed to the opposite ideology, "He saved others; he cannot save himself" (27:42). The irony of this disclosure is heightened by its affinity to the demonic that we have noted already (4:3, 6; 27:40). In Matthew's view, the mockers are on the wrong side of the ideological divide, but they are precise and to the point with respect to drawing the lines. And the line they draw applies to God and not only to the crucified Jesus. If Jesus reveals what God is like, God belongs to the self-giving side of the great divide.

Speaking half in second person directly to Jesus and half in third person *about* Jesus, the mockers profess readiness to strike a bargain. We can mark this off as the second point worthy of note before we let go of the temptations of Jesus in the Synoptic Gospels. To our surprise, the mockers are proposing terms, if met, that would suffice to change their minds. The second sentence below is especially notable.

> "If you are the Son of God, come down from the cross" (27:40).
>
> "Let him come down from the cross now, *and we will believe in him*" (27:42).

Echoes of the temptation story in the desert ring loudly in these statements.[69] While we may struggle to grasp why turning stones into bread would compromise Jesus or why coming down from the cross was out of the question for him, we sense at the very least that his calling card must be something other than power. Jesus will

69. Davies and Allison (*Matthew* III: 618–19) point out that the three mockeries summon the memory of the three temptations.

prove himself to be the Son of God some other way, and those who believe in him will believe for other reasons than that he agreed to meet the condition put forward, whether by Satan in the wilderness or by those who mock him at the cross.

In a quest for perspective on the temptations of Jesus in the Synoptic witness, slander against God is central to the plot. Jesus goes forth to confront the claim that human existence under God is constrained by lack of freedom (Matt 4:1–4; cf. Gen 3:1;) and then, having made his case with regard to the first temptation, that the human condition under God offers release from responsibility (Matt 4:5–7; cf. Gen 3:4–5). In the final temptation, Satan throws what he believes is an ace on the table, certain that Jesus will be enticed by self-interest as much as Satan is consumed by it, only to discover that what was meant as the crowning temptation turned out to be his own moment of truth (Matt 4:8–11). The mission in the wilderness, described with unbridled force in Mark and with delicate thoughtfulness in Matthew, shows Jesus unmasking Satan to the bedrock of the original innuendo.

The surprising turns in this story are matched by unexpected responses and outcomes toward the end of Matthew. Some people, perhaps those least expected to do so, are in fact won over. At the point of Jesus's death, "when the centurion and those with him, who were keeping watch over Jesus, saw the earthquake and what took place, they were terrified and said, 'Truly this man was the Son of God!'" (27:54) What did this man see in Jesus that convinced him to drop the "if" and embrace the affirmation? What persuaded him even to the point of exclamation?

The theme of the third temptation recurs as Matthew concludes his gospel. Satan, we recall, said to Jesus, "All these *I* will give you," thinking it his prerogative to set the terms (4:9). In the parting scene in Matthew, however, we hear Jesus say, "All authority in heaven and on earth *has been given* to me" (28:18).[70] The prerogative to wield *all* power are here in hands careful about its use; indeed, in hands whose non-use of power is contrary to expectations, challenging to the imagination, and yet defining for the person's identity and character. Jesus has not made any concession to the one who claimed that the power was his (4:10). Augustine Stock comments that "after Jesus, as the obedient Son, had forgone the divine manifestation of power, had suffered, and had died on the cross, there finally comes, again on a mountain (28:16), the proclamation of his authority not only over the kingdom of the world, but over heaven and earth" (28:18).[71] The cosmic parameters are as conspicuous at the end of the gospel as at the beginning, but the conflicting senses have been sorted out, readers now in a better position to tell which is the divine and which the bogus sense.

70. This formulation, yet again, rings with echoes of apocalyptic in general, and of the dominion given to "one like a son of man" in Daniel (Dan 7:13–14); cf. Davies and Allison, *Matthew* III: 682–83; France, *Matthew*, 1112–13. It can also be heard as a rebuttal of the claim set forth by Satan in Luke's temptation story, "To you I will give their glory and all this authority; for it has been given over to me, and I give it to anyone I please" (Luke 4:6); cf. Gundry, *Matthew*, 595.

71. Stock, *Method and Message*, 54.

Chapter Sixteen

Ambushed by the Sense of Abundance

The Gospel of John speaks in a distinctive idiom, and it pursues a story line that leaves out the temptation account entirely. But the cosmic perspective that we find in the Synoptic Gospels is not allowed to fade. John's cosmic canvas is large, and a conspicuous clearing is set apart at the center. This clearing is devoted to the death of Jesus. Threads leading to the dominant center are paths by which the narrator nudges the reader to travel, never allowing the arresting sights and sounds on the way to slow the march.

The telling of John's center-bound story begins right away. Jesus is said to be present with his disciples at a wedding in Cana of Galilee, going there as a person who is not meant to be at the center of the event (John 2:1–2). But—to the embarrassment of the host—in the course of the festivities "the wine gave out" (2:3). When this comes to the attention of Jesus's mother, she tells Jesus, "They have no wine" (2:3).[1] Jesus's answer has been the subject of much debate, but there is agreement that it is "suggestive of diversity of opinion or interest."[2] "Woman, what concern is that to you and to me?" he responds (2:4).[3]

And then, on what is virtually day one in the greater narrative of John's Gospel, he adds, "*My hour has not yet come*" (2:4).

What most interpreters hear as a 'no' must have been a 'yes,' however, conveyed either by the tone of voice or body language because his mother instructs the servants, "Do whatever he tells you" (2:5). Action quickly follows. We read that there is suddenly an abundance of wine at the wedding, upwards of one hundred and fifty gallons (2:6–8). The master of ceremonies certifies the wine to be of the finest quality (2:10). And, as so often in this Gospel, there is irony because the readers know more than the

1. Toussaint ("Significance of the First Sign," 46) suggests, not implausibly, that Jesus's entourage of disciples was unexpected, given that they had joined him just days earlier and that their presence may have contributed to the shortage of wine!

2. Bernard, *Critical and Exegetical Commentary*, 1:75.

3. Arthur H. Maynard ("TI EMOI KAI ΣΟΙ," 582) says that "it is the intent of the writer to have Jesus indicate a complete separation between himself and his mother." Keener (*The Gospel of John*, 505) concurs, adding that she "approached him not as her son but as a miracle worker; he replies not as her son but as her Lord."

various participants within the story.[4] The master of ceremonies is one individual not in the know. Ignorant of the source of the new wine and its quantity (2:9), he voices surprise to the host over his breach of etiquette. "Everyone serves the good wine first, and then the inferior wine after the guests have become drunk. But you have kept the good wine until now," he says (2:10). Better informed of the goings-on behind the scenes, the reader can only chuckle at the man's naïveté, knowing that there has been a bigger surprise than breach of banquet protocol (2:6–9).

Some readers have taken offense at the story for other reasons than the master of ceremonies in John. In the nineteenth century, it became fashionable to use this miracle as the poster example of something the historical Jesus would *not* have done. The miracle in Cana was held up as a test case of inadmissibility not only because miracles are suspect, but even more because this *kind* of miracle would be out of character with Jesus. David Friedrich Strauss placed the miracle in the inadmissible category on the logic that "Jesus did not, as was usual with him, relieve any want, any real need, but only furnished an additional incitement to pleasure; showed himself not so much helpful as courteous; rather, so to speak, performed a miracle of luxury, than of true beneficence."[5] According to this moralizing reasoning, the miracle in Cana faces double jeopardy, failing because there should not be miracles to begin with and failing again because there should not be a frivolous miracle like this one. In the end, mixing theology, utilitarian concerns, and a general disbelief in miracles, readers like Strauss took interest in the story only to demonstrate that it should be deleted from the record of Jesus's life and work.

Deleting it, however, will not be an easy task. The story is almost tamper proof, being attached by hooks and tentacles to the theme of the Gospel and to the most conspicuous event in the storyline. "My hour has not yet come" is a statement that signals awareness and perspective on the part of Jesus (2:4), a thread leads from the periphery resolutely to the center. The first sign becomes in this respect the occasion by which to announce what will come and thus give advance billing of the rest of the story.

We note, first, that there is a point called 'my hour' in John, brought to our attention at the very beginning (2:4). That point has not yet arrived so as to make it clear that other points in the story, even conspicuous and exceptional ones, must not be taken to be the decisive 'hour' (7:30; 8:20). Jesus knows not only that his 'hour' will come, but also what is and what is not the 'hour' (2:4; 12:23; 13:31–32; 17:1). Awareness on this point means that Jesus will proceed toward his 'hour' according to a script that is of his own making. The 'hour' itself and the commitment to go there are not imposed on him by forces beyond his control (10:17–18; 18:11). The 'hour,' moreover, signifies where the journey is headed and where it will end. In this sense Jesus knows the end from the beginning, serving notice to that effect. "The beginning and ending

4. Duke, *Irony in the Fourth Gospel*, 83–84.

5. Strauss, *The Life of Jesus*, 521.

are both in view in the Cana miracle," Gail R. O'Day aptly observes.[6] We will be able to extricate this story from the Gospel of John only at the cost of making the entire structure fall apart.

The narrator in John kept count, saying that the miracle at the wedding was "the *first* of his signs" (2:11). The score-keeping and the emphasis on Jesus's hour suggest priority and intentionality (2:11). Intentionality, in turn, is very much in character with the behavior of Jesus throughout the Gospel (5:19; 7:2–6; 13:1), and it is evident in Jesus's answer to his mother at the wedding (2:4). The miracle is part and parcel of this Gospel's pattern of intentionality and the means by which to elicit awareness of the whole story from the very beginning.

For Jesus, the 'hour' means the cross.[7] But Jesus, as noted, is not a pawn in a script of someone else's making. Our working hypothesis should be that the first sign is emblematic of what follows and not an exception. Jesus does not launch a contrast between the wedding and the cross, the first an occasion of joy and the second a time of sorrow. From the beginning, this Gospel sets us up not for one surprise but for two, the first a sign said to be out of character with Jesus, and the second an understanding of his death on the cross that to all appearances seems out of character with the cross.

To Fyodor Dostoevsky, the Gospel of John was his most treasured reading while serving time in Siberia. He found nothing in the story of the wedding in Cana that needed to be dismissed or deleted, taking it, instead, as a story that upends and overthrows conventional ideas about Jesus. The overlooked message, as expressed by Father Zosima in *The Brothers Karamazov* and recalled by Alyosha on the occasion of his mentor's death, was this, "*Not grief, but men's joy Christ visited when he worked his first miracle, he helped men's joy. . . . 'He who loves men, loves their joy. . . .'* The dead man used to repeat it all the time, it was one of his main thoughts."[8] Strauss makes lack and grief the best way to take the measure of Jesus. Dostoevsky's Zosima, by contrast, puts Christ resolutely in the service of fullness and joy.

Father Zosima's teaching throws open the door to a different interpretation of the Gospel of John and to a 'new' theology. It is not contrived to suggest that Jesus made it "one of his leading ideas" to help human joy; it is not ridiculous to imagine that this was "one of his main thoughts," now speaking of Jesus and not of Zosima. Strauss was to the point when he said that the "disproportionate quantity of wine with which Jesus supplies the guests, must excite astonishment."[9] However, the surprise should concentrate on the meaning of the sign and not on having it deleted from the record.

6. O'Day, "The Love of God Incarnate," 162.

7. Thus, Schnelle ("Cross and Resurrection," 135), "The ὥρα of Jesus is the 'hour' of the passion of the pre-existent Son of God."

8. Dostoevsky, *The Brothers Karamazov*, 361 (Pevear and Volokhonsky translation), emphasis added.

9. Strauss, *The Life of Jesus*, 522.

Navigating the Web of Context

"Jesus did this, the first of his signs, in Cana of Galilee, and revealed his glory; and his disciples believed in him," says the narrator in John after the wedding (2:11). If the notion of Jesus's 'hour' [*hōra*] is the first thread that weaves the miracle tightly into the web of context, 'glory' [*doxa*] is the second. These notions create a cascade of surprises in John: a miracle thought to be out of character with Jesus; a beginning that heralds the ending even though the beginning is a wedding and the ending the cross; and 'glory' that is manifested at the wedding and at the cross (2:11; 12:27–28). Of these two, 'glory' is the more difficult to master. We can see 'glory,' of sorts, at the wedding in Cana (although Strauss could only see redundancy), but who can see glory at the cross? It is easy to agree with John Ashton that the theology of John is "singular and strange" in the sense that the word 'glory' seems out of place with reference to the latter.[10]

But 'glory' is an important word in John, pointing to the identity and character of Jesus. Already in the Prologue, this word is launched as something akin to a summary of the entire book. "And the Word became flesh and lived among us, and we have seen his glory [*doxa*], the glory as of a father's only son, full of grace [*charis*] and truth [*alētheia*]" (1:14). Here, 'glory' is the key word. The narrator in John, speaking in the first person, claimed to have seen it firsthand. Moreover, the 'glory' that he saw in Jesus is the unique glory of the Father: it enabled him to know what God is like. Crucially, too, what he saw had to be qualified by the words 'grace' and 'truth' so as not to limit the message. 'Grace,' the first of these words, has suffered under its technical use so as to obscure meaning that is important in John. We need the full range of possibilities from the best available lexicon to get the idea: *charis* means "a winning quality that invites a favorable reaction;" it denotes "*graciousness, attractiveness, charm, winsomeness*;" it depicts "a beneficent disposition toward someone, *favor, grace, goodwill*." Very simply it can also means "*favor, gift, benefaction*."[11]

'Glory' thus construed is bursting at the seams with goodwill, generosity, and a giving disposition. This impression is reinforced just two verses later when John adds, "From his fullness we have all received, grace upon grace [*charin anti charitos*]" (1:16). If we translate *charis* with the simple and perfectly legitimate word "gift," the statement will read, "From his fullness we have all received, gift upon gift" (1:16). Already in the Prologue, therefore, John hits the chord on his grand piano that is heard in a fuller tone in the miracle at the wedding. Abundance and joy are in view.

The word 'truth' [*alētheia*] is no less important. Against 'truth' stands its counterpart, falsehood, even 'the lie' (8:44). Truth is the corrective to falsehood and the only viable remedy where falsehood has gained the upper hand. In John, the remedy has been found. When we follow his lead, combining the words 'gift' and 'truth' (1:14), they become mutually reinforcing against the backdrop of attempts to subvert them.

10. Ashton, *Understanding the Fourth Gospel*, 494.

11. Danker, *Greek-English Lexicon*, §7895.

John's Gospel bears witness to a reality that has giving and joy as its hallmark, projecting that reality against a concerted attempt to deny that it is so.

It is therefore no surprise that the theme of glory recurs in force at the point of the cross. "The hour has come for the Son of Man to be *glorified*," Jesus says when informed that Greeks are taking an interest in him (12:23). Likewise, in his parting prayer, the 'hour' and 'glory' are inseparable. "Father, the *hour* has come; *glorify* your Son so that the Son may *glorify* you" (17:1). The stakes are high because there is more 'glory' to be revealed, more 'gift' and more 'truth.' All of this supports the thesis that the cross is the climax and completion of the story that began at the wedding.

Gail R. O'Day argues this view crisply. She says that "John's shaping theological question is not about the meaning of the death of Jesus; it is about the meaning of the life of Jesus."[12] Perhaps this formulates the options too sharply, implying contrasts that are greater than strictly necessary. Nevertheless, her view is a timely corrective to the tendency to break asunder what belongs together, giving the death of Jesus a meaning and a standing that is separate from, or different from, his life. The Gospel of John must be read as whole cloth. In this sense O'Day is profoundly correct when she writes that in John "the defining theological category is and remains the incarnation."[13] She offers the miracle at the wedding as proof of her thesis. "Here, in the opening act of his ministry, Jesus does what will also later be said of his hour: he reveals his glory."[14] Again, using the wedding in Cana as the primary piece of evidence, "Jesus's life and death are of a piece."[15]

We have already seen that the 'hour' and 'glory' belong together in this Gospel (2:4, 11; 12:23; 17:1). When Jesus's 'hour' comes, no one is left in doubt that it has arrived and that we have reached the clearing at the center of John's canvas.

> Now among those who went up to worship at the festival were some Greeks. They came to Philip, who was from Bethsaida in Galilee, and said to him, "Sir, we wish to see Jesus." Philip went and told Andrew; then Andrew and Philip went and told Jesus. Jesus answered them, "The hour has come for the Son of Man to be glorified" (12:20–23).

This passage abounds in tantalizing details—the identity and intent of the Greeks, the identification of Philip and Andrew by name, the name of Philip's home town, the dynamic between Andrew and Philip—suggesting intimate knowledge of people and places on the part of the narrator.[16] In particular, the incident has the texture of a new

12. O'Day, "Love of God Incarnate," 158.

13. Ibid., 159; cf. O'Day and Hylen, *John*, 27.

14. O'Day, "Love of God Incarnate," 160.

15. Ibid.

16. During the past several decades, scholars have upgraded the status of the Gospel of John as a reliable witness to Jesus. Books and essays indicative of this trend are, Robinson, *Priority of John*; Bauckham, *Jesus and the Eyewitnesses*; von Wahlde, "Archaeology and John's Gospel," in Charlesworth, *Jesus and Archaeology*, 523–86; Paul N. Anderson, "Historicity in the Gospel of John," in *Jesus and*

beginning—and yet a beginning that recapitulates the first encounter between Jesus and the same named individuals (1:40–44). But the main focus is the 'hour,' its arrival disclosed by Jesus, "*The hour has come*" (12:23).

As we have seen up to this point in the story, John points out what is *not* the 'hour' (2:4; 7:30; 8:20). Now he locates precisely what it is (12:23, 27, 31). In the latter category, there is more than one statement.

> Now before the festival of the Passover, Jesus knew that *his hour had come* to depart from this world and go to the Father (13:1).

> After Jesus had spoken these words, he looked up to heaven and said, "Father, *the hour has come*; glorify your Son so that the Son may glorify you" (17:1).

Statements pinpointing the 'hour' converge at the point where Jesus is getting ready to die. Awareness of this does not begin when soldiers come to arrest him (18:1–11). It has been part of the script from the beginning, as evidenced by Jesus's answer to his mother at the wedding in Cana (2:4). "By virtue of performing the sign at Cana, his 'hour' begins; Jesus embarks on his journey to the cross," says Jo-Ann Brant.[17]

Expelling "the Ruler of This World"

If, by itself, the 'hour' encapsulates what is most important in the story of Jesus, and if, within that 'hour,' Jesus will die, what is the meaning John gives to Jesus's death? John Ashton answers—correctly, I believe—by connecting the dots between the wedding in Cana and the death of Jesus on the cross. "So Jesus performs a miracle—more than a miracle, a sign—and it is in this miracle, symbolically foreshadowing something strange, new, marvelous, that Jesus's glory is seen for the first time. Had it not been seen, there would have been no glory; δόξα [*doxa*] is a relationship word—it implies *revelation*."[18]

This is emphatically the case. Often overlooked, however, is the fact that the revelation happens in the context of conflict. In the most pointed statement on the subject, Jesus says, "Now my soul is troubled. And what should I say—'Father, save me from this *hour*'? No, it is for this reason that I have come to this *hour*" (12:27). Here the '*hour*' is mentioned twice. We can almost hear the footsteps of the detachment that is approaching to arrest Jesus (18:1–11). We learn that Jesus is in a state of distress: "my soul is troubled," or "my soul quakes," as Brant translates it.[19] More than one scenario is possible with respect to his distress, one of which is to say, "Father, save me from this hour." *That* alternative is weighed in the Synoptic Gospels only to be rejected (Mark

Archaeology, 587–618.

17. Brant, *John*, 57.

18. Ashton, *Understanding the Fourth Gospel*, 499.

19. Brant, *John*, 193.

14:32–42; Matt 26:36–46; Luke 22:39–46). In John, the idea of backing away from the 'hour' is entertained only on the hypothetical level. To say, "Father, save me from this hour" is precisely what Jesus will *not* do (John 12:27). We are forcefully reminded of the underlying reason, "No, it is for this reason that I have come to this hour" (12:27), or, as the *Good News Bible* puts it, "that is why I came."

In other words, Jesus knows what the hour is about, not only as to timing but as to purpose. He knows why he came (12:27). We could read this only as though Jesus knows what is to happen, having rehearsed it in his mind a thousand times. Knowledge of certain facts, however, is not the same as knowledge of purpose. The person who knows *what* knows the facts, but the person who knows *why* knows the purpose. Jesus knows the purpose, and knowledge of purpose is at the heart of his answer to his mother at the wedding in Cana (2:4). Events are unfolding according to a plan that Jesus is intent on carrying out and carrying to completion.

Thus, when they come to arrest him, Simon Peter, ignorant of the script and far less convinced of its merit, strikes out with his sword at the detachment of armed men. Details are again eye-catching. He "struck the high priest's slave, and cut off his right ear," says John, noting that it was the *right* ear, and then, gratuitously, saying that "the slave's name was Malchus" (18:10). These tidbits have an eyewitness quality, again reflecting intimate knowledge.[20] But more important in the present context is Jesus's corrective to Peter. "Put your sword back into its sheath. Am I not to drink the cup that the Father has given me?" (18:11) In saying this, Jesus does not cast himself as a victim of fate or circumstances. Power relations at the time of his arrest run contrary to expectations, but Jesus behaves as though he is in control of the proceedings (18:1–11). The soldiers and attendants appear to operate at his discretion despite the fact that they have come there "with lanterns and torches and weapons" in order to lead him away (18:3).

Three times in the most telling passage in John (12:20–33) Jesus mentions the 'hour' (vv. 23, 27). And three times within the span of the same verses, the notion of the 'hour' is intensified further by the adverbial '*now*,' reinforcing the sense that we are at the high point of the story.

> Now [*nūn*] my soul is troubled. And what should I say—'Father, save me from this hour'? No, it is for this reason that I have come to this hour (12:27).

> Now [*nūn*] is the judgment of this world; now [*nūn*] the ruler of this world will be driven out (12:31).

20. Bauckham (*Jesus and the Eyewitnesses*, 39–92) argues that names early on become a casualty of memory and that preservation of names therefore should be seen as proof of the (eyewitness) quality of the testimony in John.

The 'hour' is a point in time, but it is most of all *decisive* and *significant* time. 'Now' is also a point in time, even more sharply focused than the 'hour.' It, too, aims to depict a moment of immeasurable significance. Brant's translation captures it well,

> Now is the critical moment of this world, now the ruler of this world will be expelled [*ekblēthēsetai*] (12:31).[21]

This is a surprising statement, rendered in an excellent translation of the Greek text. Exploring the statement in small steps, Jesus says, first, that we are at "the *critical moment* [*krisis*] of this world" (12:31). *Krisis* is a judicial term, but it does not in this instance give us a picture of a court scene or put us in the presence of a judge who is about to issue a verdict. Instead, *krisis* prepares us for an event that will turn the case one way or the other. Judgment is in this sense revelatory and not judicial, as Jacques Ellul says about a similar passage. The judgment in view alters and enables "comprehension of the divine reality."[22]

Second, Jesus's death will happen in the context of battle between two warring parties, one of which is called "the ruler of this world" (12:31). This designation poses a problem because, as we have observed on several occasions, modern readers do not take the world view of the New Testament seriously. Interpreters who identify "the ruler of this world" with Roman political powers press this term into service for which it was not intended.[23] Susan Garrett, quoted earlier (Chap. 5), is quite right to point out that "mainline theologians and Church leaders have insisted that belief in Satan is not important to authentic Christian faith."[24] Here, Jesus is engaged in a cosmic conflict, his opponent a non-human figure.

As David Aune notes, "the ruler of this world" and his aliases "Satan" and "Devil" designate a personal being.[25] Likewise, Craig R. Koester says that "Jesus has come to cast out 'the ruler of this world,' *who is not the Roman emperor but Satan* (12:31)."[26] Judith L. Kovacs takes the same view, placing "the ruler of this world" at the center of the passion story.[27] In John, therefore, the combat theme constitutes the background against which the Gospel interprets the death of Jesus, fully justifying the notion of a cosmic canvas. "The story this Gospel has to tell concerns the battle between God and Satan," says Kovacs, "a battle acted out in the sphere of human history."[28] John 12:31, announcing that "the ruler of this world will be expelled," together with the closely related passages in John 14:30–31 and 16:8–11, "suggest that the Fourth Evangelist

21. Brant, *John*, 193.
22. Ellul, *Apocalypse*, 172.
23. For a discussion of the cosmic dualism in John, see Tonstad, "The Father of Lies," 193–208.
24. Garrett, *No Ordinary Angel*, 105.
25. Aune, "Dualism in the Fourth Gospel," 287.
26. Koester, *The Word of Life*, 96, emphasis added.
27. Kovacs, "Jesus' Death as Cosmic Battle," 227–47.
28. Ibid., 233.

sees the death, resurrection, and ascent of Jesus as the turning point in the conflict between God and the forces of evil."[29]

Third, Jesus speaks as though he has a battle plan. Koester's suggestion that "Jesus possesses superior battlefield intelligence" is succinct and to the point.[30] Now he is about to make his final and decisive move, making an announcement to that effect (12:27, 31). His impending death marks "the critical moment of this world."

Fourth, at that critical moment "the ruler of this world" will be defeated (12:31; 16:11). This is the most surprising feature because, as all readers of the Gospels know, the battle ends with the death of Jesus on the cross. How can his death be a victory, as Jesus says? How can the apparent loser be the winner?

"John does not provide enough material to construct a complete picture of evil, its origins, or its cosmology," says Jo-Ann Brant.[31] Few will want to disagree with this statement if we take it at face value. John does not present "a *complete* picture," but this admission is not to say that there is no picture at all. I will say to the contrary that John provides enough material to construct a *representative* picture of evil, its origins, and its cosmic reality with no need to claim that it is *complete*. John's Gospel represents evil in personified terms; it identifies the main protagonists; and, although it is rarely recognized, it spells out the issue at the heart of the conflict.

Already in the Prologue, John describes a struggle between light and darkness (1:4–5, 7–9), developing this theme with consistency in the narrative portion of the book. The light is personified in Jesus and has no reality apart from him (3:19–21; 8:12; 9:5; 11:9–10; 12:35–36, 46).

But darkness, too, is personified.

John writes that at the last meal before Jesus's death, the devil had "put it into the heart of Judas son of Simon Iscariot to betray him" (13:2). In the course of the meal, Jesus "dipped the piece of bread, he gave it to Judas son of Simon Iscariot," thereby identifying the betrayer to the readers of the Gospel (13:26). "After he received the piece of bread, Satan entered into him," says John. At that point Jesus tells Judas, "Do quickly what you are going to do" (13:27). This should not be taken to mean that Judas has been handed his part of the script and will dutifully perform the paragraphs assigned to him (13:30). Neither will be helpful if we make it a case study in demon possession. Rather, the account serves to personify the struggle between light and darkness, revealing how things work on the dark side of the divide. Judas is in the crosshairs of darkness that has a demonic promoter. "So, after receiving the piece of bread, he immediately went out," says John (13:30). Then, intending it less as a piece of information regarding the hour of day or night than as a statement about the character of the occasion, he adds, "And it was night" (13:30). This close-up of the

29. Ibid., 231.

30. Koester, "The Death of Jesus and the Human Condition," 149.

31. Brant, *John*, 183.

connection between darkness and the demonic is chilling. It means that the darkness that increasingly envelops Judas cannot be understood in impersonal terms.

John gives the adversarial power a name, 'the ruler of this world,' 'Satan,' and 'Devil.' These are designations for the same being, a second feature in John's picture of evil. If this were all we had, however, we would be left with a still frame without a plot, and it would be necessary to concede that John does not provide enough material to construct a coherent picture of evil.[32] Specifically, we would not know enough to determine what is at issue in the conflict between light and darkness. Ignorance on this point would leave us at an intolerable disadvantage with respect to understanding how Jesus defeats Satan in the Gospel of John.

But this is not all we have. "The ruler of this world" has yet another name, "the father of lies" (8:44). This adds a third element to the emerging picture. With this element John deploys a pivotal story from the Old Testament, culled from Jesus's most heated discussion with Jewish religious leaders.

> You are of your father the devil and want to do the wishes of your father. That one was a manslayer [*anthrōpoktonos*] from the beginning and has not stood in the truth, because there isn't truth in him. Whenever he speaks as he is wont, he speaks the lie [*to pseudos*], for he is a liar and the father of the lie (8.44).[33]

This statement has sometimes been read as a wholesale indictment of ethnic Jews, but it should be read as a criticism leveled by one Jew [Jesus] against fellow Jews, removing the ethnic element. The Jewish opponents not only have a different opinion than Jesus but are also, on the terms of John's Gospel, conspiring against Jesus in order to kill him (8:37; cf. 5:18; 7:19–25). Moreover, the problem addressed in the text is *views* and not *Jews*; that is, the problem is not how the parties in the discussion are constituted as human beings, whether Jesus or his opponents.[34] The problem centers on the views they hold and the consequences of these views when carried to their conclusion. Just as Jesus again and again in the Gospel ascribes his works and words to the Father (5:19–20; 8:39–40; 15:15), he assigns blame to Satan for the views of his opponents and for deeds that are in the making (8:41, 44). The drama is further inflamed by the fact that his opponents charge him with a demonic pedigree (8:20; 8:48, 52; 10:20). The merits of the respective claims and counterclaims are not fully resolved on the part of the participants *within* the text of John's Gospel, but they are spectacularly evident to the reader of the text. One side in the conflict is working to heal and restore while the other side is plotting to kill the Restorer (10:32). Significantly, John places the accent on the paternity of the conflict, giving credit to the Father for the deeds of Jesus, on the one hand, and putting blame on "the father of lies," on the other (8:44).

32. Brant, *John*, 183.

33. Ibid., slightly modified.

34. Tonstad, "Father of Lies," 206–8.

Jesus's indictment of his cosmic opponent, now known as "the ruler of this world" (12:31) *and* as "the father of the lie" (8:44), is enormously helpful to interpretation. This allusion to the Old Testament sets up a story line that is better appreciated when it is broken up into its constituent pieces, as below.[35]

> You are from your father the devil
> and want to do the wishes of your father.
> That one was a manslayer from the beginning
> and has not stood in the truth [*tē alētheia*],
> because there isn't truth [*alētheia*] in him.
> Whenever he speaks as he is wont,
> he speaks the lie [*to pseudos*],
> for he is a liar [*pseustēs*]
> and the father of the lie [lit. '*of it*'] (8:44).

What is the point to which Jesus has anchored his understanding of evil in John? The first chapters of Genesis fairly shout the answer at the reader. This is no surprise because the Gospel of John begins with the very same words as Genesis (Gen 1:1; John 1:1).[36] John is focused on the beginning. Jesus, the true light in his account, was there at the beginning as the Creator of all things (John 1:1–3). But his opponent, the protagonist of darkness, also played a role "from the beginning" (8:44). The notion that he "was a manslayer *from the beginning*" might be partly explainable by the story of Cain's murder of Abel, but it could also point to murderous intent on the part of "the father of lies" that initially was concealed. If we take this to be the meaning, Jesus's statement is intended to expose an opponent who feigned to have a benign intent but who, known only to God, "was a murderer from the beginning" (8:44).

While murder is part of Jesus's indictment of his opponent, the main concern centers on his opponent's relationship to the truth. The *words* of "the father of lies" are projected in larger letters than his *deeds*: what he says commands attention. Jesus does not let up with respect to this characteristic. His adversary "has not stood in the truth; there isn't truth in him;" the only thing on his mind and the only thing that comes easy to him is to speak the lie; "he is a liar and the father of the lie" (8:44).

All of this is anchored in the Genesis story of the beginning, and—to make that option untenable—it cannot be explained with reference to the Roman Empire or a human power. Telling the truth was not the strong suit of the Roman imperial power, but it would be undeserving of the designation, "the father of the lie." Just as the identity of this figure must be determined within the boundaries of the biblical narrative, so must his problem with respect to telling the truth.

35. I am following Brant's translation (*John*, 146), slightly tweaked.

36. Bultmann (*Gospel of John*, 20) says that "it would be hard for the Evangelist to begin his work with ἐν ἀρχῇ, without thinking of the בְּרֵאשִׁית of Gen 1:1." See also Reim, *Studien zum alttestamentlichen Hintergrund*, 99.

Brant's literal translation of John 8:44 preserves the definite and specific character of the falsehood that is in view; "he speaks *the* lie; he is the father of *the* lie" (8:44).[37] Does anything in the Genesis story qualify as *the* lie? And—with reference to John's quest for the bedrock of beginnings—is it possible to determine not only the identity of the one who failed to tell the truth but also the content of the truth he failed to tell? Do we get access to the subject matter of the lie? Can the opening gambit be established?

These questions can all be answered in the affirmative. The opening ploy in Genesis was the question, "Did God say, 'You shall not eat from any tree in the garden'?" (Gen 3:1; see Chap. 6). The tenor and intent of this question sought to make human beings take a negative view of God and the divine command. What, indeed, was 'the lie' other than a spectacular subversion, turning what was meant as a gift into an all-encompassing prohibition? Putting this in more abstract terms, what is 'the lie' if not the attempt to portray God as harsh when, in fact, God meant to be generous?

She "took of its fruit and ate; and she also gave some to her husband, who was with her, and he ate," says Genesis (Gen 3:6). 'The lie' achieved its purpose. After eating of the tree, says the narrator, Adam and Eve "heard the sound of the Lord God walking in the garden at the time of the evening breeze, and the man and his wife hid themselves from the presence of the Lord God among the trees of the garden" (Gen 3:8). The lie led to misperception of God. Misperception gave rise to distrust. Distrust ripened into the need to keep distance. Finally, once the new reality had taken hold, there was fear (Gen 3:1–10).

In the preceding, I have submitted to the features in the text that speak of 'the lie' as a defined and singular phenomenon (8:44). This exercise has rewards because it draws attention to the opening maneuver of the serpent in the Garden of Eden. Much as Jesus specifies the lie as if it boils down to one single act of not telling the truth, however, he also generalizes. Taking a sweeping view of the opponent, he says that he "has not stood in the truth because there isn't truth in him" (8:44). When we apply the generalizing character to the encounter between the deceiver and human beings in the Garden, it becomes clear that we cannot confine this text to one single lie even though Jesus's statement has a focus (Gen 3:1–5). "You will not die," the serpent said to the woman (Gen 3:4). Was that true? Finally, as a third assertion, the serpent held out the prospect that "your eyes will be opened, and you will be like God, knowing good and evil" (Gen 3:5).

From the sweeping indictment in the Gospel of John, now read with reference to the claims that were set forth at the beginning (John 8:44; Gen 3:1–5), the answer must be that 'the father of the lie' was dealing in lies retail and wholesale. In the words of Jesus, now repeated with emphasis, 'there isn't one iota of truth in him' (John 8:44).

37. The Greek says "*the* lie" only once, *otan lalē to pseudos* [the lie], *ek tōn idiōn lalei, hoti pseustēs estin kai ho pater autou* [of "*it*," i.e., the lie], but the pronoun at the end obviously has reference to "the lie" mentioned initially.

This is not a *complete* picture of evil, but it is an illuminating picture that contributes greatly to our understanding of the 'hour' of Jesus in John. When we recognize that the texts with which we have composed the picture address an audience that shared John's world view, the picture will seem less incomplete. If, too, we look beyond the Gospel of John to other New Testament writings attributed to John or the Johannine circle,[38] we might even have something that approaches a complete picture, confirming the claim that the Bible offers "a coherent account of evil, both how it first came to exist and how it is being destroyed."[39]

"Now the ruler of this world will be expelled [*ekblēthēsetai*]," Jesus says at the point of entry to his 'hour' (12:31). By now it is evident that Jesus does not announce the *death* of "the father of the lie" but his *unmasking*. The enemy has ruled the world on the strength of 'the lie,' and now, in the 'hour' and the 'now' of John's story, 'the lie' will be refuted.

"*Ekblēthēsetai* can also mean 'be exposed,'"[40] and this should probably be the preferred translation (12:31). "The *critical moment* of this world" is best understood as the moment when God produces evidence that settles the disputed case in God's favor (12:31). In the judgment false claims and pretenses are exposed. In a conflict where the other side has wielded influence by telling 'the lie,' God prevails by revealing the truth. "The ruler of this world will be exposed" because the lies through which he has held sway are refuted. God has countered the problem of falsehood with the remedy of truth, fully in line with Justice Brandeis's view that the remedy for false speech is "more speech."[41] In the case of Jesus, "more speech" is the death of Jesus on the cross. This sets the stage for his claim and promise, "And I, when I am lifted up from the earth, will draw all people to myself" (12:32).

John weaves a tapestry using threads of complementary colors that contribute to making Jesus's 'hour' the riveting focal point. At the wedding in Cana, as his first thread in the loom, Jesus serves wine in abundance to "help men's joy."[42] This thought has tremendous force by itself, and it is amplified a thousand times by the cosmic conflict that comes to a head in John. Indeed, the miracle of the wine might be treated as an anomaly except for the way it blends with Jesus's mission to defeat 'the lie' (8:44). Why wine, a product that is well outside the norms of necessity? Why perform his first sign at a wedding, an occasion not seriously afflicted by grief even if the wine runs out? And why lavish the choice beverage on the celebrants in such amounts and to such excess? Is this any way to build a case against 'the lie'?

38. This would include the Book of Revelation, the most extensive cosmic conflict text in the New Testament. While common authorship of John and Revelation is disputed, a number of scholars hold common authorship to be the most coherent interpretation of the evidence; cf. Johnson, *The Writings of the New Testament*, 512–15; Pate, *Writings of John*, 17–21, 338–39.

39. Origen, *Contra Celsum* 6.44.

40. Brant, *John*, 194.

41. Turner, *Figures of Speech*, 126–27.

42. Dostoevsky, *The Brothers Karamazov*, 361 (Pevear and Volokhonsky translation).

We shall acknowledge that it is that and more. In the Garden of Eden, deprivation and lack were said to be the hallmark of the divine economy. God was represented as saying, "You shall not eat from any tree in the garden" (Gen 3:1). Through this onslaught, God lost his good name.

In John's Gospel, Jesus performs his first sign at the wedding in Cana (John 2:11). If we place this sign and the six hundred liters of choice wine in the context of 'the lie,' what is the message? Is Jesus a person who provides or one who deprives? Does he give, or does he withhold? Is the divine economy one of lack or one of plenitude? Does the brief account from the wedding in a Galilean village suggest a person capable of saying, "You shall not eat of *any* tree in the garden"? (Gen 3:1)

As the wedding winds down, the narrator explains the meaning and computes the result, saying that "Jesus did this, his first sign, in Cana of Galilee, and he revealed his glory" (John 2:11). The beginning of a continuum is established. When his 'hour' comes at the cross, it will also declare his 'glory' (12:23, 28).

The recurrence of 'glory' is striking in these passages. First, Jesus announces that "the hour has come for the Son of Man to be glorified" (12:23). Then, in a strange dialogical sequence between earth and heaven, he exclaims, "Father, glorify your name" (12:28). This exclamation does not fall on deaf ears because a voice responds from heaven, "I have glorified it, and I will glorify it again" (12:28). When Judas later leaves the table heading into the night (13:30), Jesus elaborates further, saying, "Now the Son of Man has been glorified, and God has been glorified in him. If God has been glorified in him, God will also glorify him in himself and will glorify him at once" (13:31–32).[43] John's distinctive idiom piles it on in these verses. Finally, Jesus prays, "Father, the hour has come; glorify your Son so that the Son may glorify you" (17:1).

These expansive excursions are not aberrations in John's Gospel, as we have seen (1:14, 16; 2:11). Further help is available because the 'glory' statements echo critical passages from the Servant Songs in Isaiah, greatly amplifying their impact in John.

> I am the Lord, that is my name; my *glory* [Hebr. *kabod*, Gr. *doxa*] I give to no other, nor my praise to idols (Isa 42:8).

> And he said to me, "You are my servant, Israel, in whom I will be *glorified*" (Isa 49:3).

"Glory," we must admit, is a word from religious discourse. We rarely use it in everyday speech. It would sound awkward if I were to say, speaking to another person, "I have glorified your name today." And yet I have done it, and we all do it from time to time. To "glorify" someone's name is to speak well of a person, to praise him or her, to affirm them, to highlight to others that person's qualities.

43. Caird ("The Glory of God", 271, 276) argues on behalf of an intransitive passive meaning, "God has revealed his glory in him." This reading is best appreciated when it is recognized that the author is writing "translation Greek."

In John, the question of 'glory' occurs in the context of controversy. When the serpent in Genesis asked, "Did God say, 'You shall not eat from any tree in the garden'?" (Gen 3:1) he did not intend to glorify God's name. The converse of glorifying someone's name is to slander that person's character and reputation. When we keep this perspective in mind, we realize that the 'glory' passages in John do not primarily capture the movement from a good name to a better name. Jesus is acting on behalf of someone who has lost his good name. "Father, glorify your name" should therefore be read as a petition to God to take back his good name. John's interest in the theme of God's glory comes off the same page as his awareness of 'the lie' (8:44). Through 'the lie' God lost God's good name and reputation (8:44; Gen 3:1). Now, at the 'hour' that has come, Jesus steps forward to reclaim God's good name (12:23, 28).

This view coheres with the high and demanding Christology in John. Many read this Gospel as though its main concern is to prove that Jesus belongs to divine identity, but John's horizon rises higher than that. The identity and status of Jesus are not an end in itself. Claims made with respect to the identity of Jesus certify him as the only one who can reliably explain God to the world.[44]

> *Prologue*: No one has ever seen God. It is God the only Son, who is close to the Father's heart, who has made him known (1:18).
>
> *At the zenith of controversy*: If I am not doing the works of my Father, do not believe me. But if I do [them], even though you do not believe me, believe the works, with the result that you may know and understand that the Father is in me and I am in the Father (10:37–38).
>
> *At the 'hour' of Jesus*: Then Jesus cried aloud: "Whoever believes in me believes not in me but in him who sent me. And whoever sees me sees him who sent me" (12:44–45).
>
> *During the farewell address*: Jesus said to him, "Have I been with you all this time, Philip, and you still do not know me? Whoever has seen me has seen the Father. How can you say, 'Show us the Father'?" (14:9)

These statements are all committed to a high Christology. And yet their main concern is not Christology but *theology*. For Jesus, the point is not to see him but to see the Father. When Philip tells Jesus, "Show us the Father, and it suffices for us" (14:8), Jesus does not disagree that seeing the Father is enough (14:9). In John, therefore, salvation is best understood as revelation.[45]

John's greatest paradox comes to light most fully in the vision of being "*lifted up*" (12:32). Two statements to the same effect are found earlier in John. Jesus says to

44. Tonstad, "The Priority of Theology in John."

45. Forestell, *Word of the Cross*, 72.

Nicodemus that "just as Moses *lifted up* the serpent in the wilderness, so must the Son of Man be *lifted up*" (3:14). Then, in the context of the most heated exchange in the Gospel, he predicts a moment of undimmed clarity, "When you have *lifted up* the Son of Man, then you will realize that I am [he]" (8:28).[46]

I have foreclosed somewhat on the meaning of these statements by claiming that they refer to the 'lifting up' of Jesus on the cross, and I am not aware of good arguments against this view. Strictly speaking, however, Jesus does not mention the cross. He only talks about being 'lifted up.' To be 'lifted up,' leaving the cross out of the picture, suggests upward mobility. The person who is 'lifted up' comes into a position of honor. By itself, this verbal element implies exaltation and not humiliation. It takes a helping hand from the narrator to establish that the subject is the cross, "But he was saying this to signify the sort of death he was about to die," says the narrator (12:33).[47]

How can being 'lifted up' on the cross be exaltation? Is John at this stage playing games with the reader, investing his terms with meaning that is so far from the usual as to leave us dizzy and bewildered? We might be tempted to think so unless the Old Testament had come to our rescue. 'Lifted up' is a term from Isaiah, taken from the fourth and last vision of the Suffering Servant.

> See, my servant shall prosper; he shall be *exalted and lifted up*, and shall be very high [LXX: *hupsōthēsetai kai doxasthēsetai sfodra*]. Just as there were many who were astonished at him—so marred was his appearance, beyond human semblance, and his form beyond that of mortals—so he shall startle many nations; kings shall shut their mouths because of him; for that which had not been told them they shall see, and that which they had not heard they shall contemplate (Isa 52:13–15).

In this text, the puzzling mix of metaphors is already at an advanced stage. Exaltation and suffering go hand in hand even though they would normally be mutually exclusive. The Servant "shall be exalted [figuratively] and lifted up [literally], and shall be very high [figuratively and literally]." The prophet's representation confounds reason (52:14). He says that the Servant is marred "beyond human semblance" (52:14), and yet it is precisely his marred state that constitutes the scaffolding for his exaltation. This spectacle will at first confuse, but it will ultimately clarify. "When you have lifted up the Son of Man, then you will realize that *I am*," says Jesus (8:28).

It is not incorrect to say, as does Gail O'Day, that Jesus's 'hour' refers to "the interrelated moments of Jesus's death, resurrection, and ascension" or that "[t]his constellation of moments will reveal God's glory."[48] Likewise, it is not incorrect to say with Udo Schnelle that the revelation of Jesus's glory [*doxa*] (2:11) "includes miracles, passion,

46. The Greek text says "then you will know that I am." Leaving out 'he' is necessary for the force of Jesus's claim to be appreciated; cf. Brant, *John*, 144.

47. Brant, *John*, 194.

48. O'Day, "The Love of God Incarnate," 162.

and resurrection" or that Jesus 'hour' places his ministry in the perspective of the cross and the resurrection.[49]

Nevertheless, these assessments fall short because they do not make the essential distinction, failing to highlight the element that should not under normal circumstances belong to the constellation of glory. Resurrection and ascension conform to notions of glory that offend no one. Crucifixion belongs in a different category. All things are not equal. It is the cross, not the resurrection and ascension that defeats 'the lie.' At the very least, what defeats 'the lie' in the cosmic conflict is the cross more than the resurrection and ascension. When Isaiah combines being *lifted up* with suffering (Isa 52:13–15), he makes crucifixion the riveting focal image. Craig Koester has the correct priority when he says that "the crucifixion defines what glory is."[50] John Ashton is on the same page. "John's theology of glory is first and foremost a theology of *revelation*."[51] Revelation, in turn, especially in a book like John, is to see something that exceeds and defies expectations.

What can we say to this, attempting to discern the pattern and harmony in these threads? In relation to God, Jesus gives proof of his divine credentials in the currency of self-giving. Power is a divine attribute, but it is not the *defining* divine attribute. The defining attribute, Jesus says, will only be evident "when you have *lifted up* the Son of Man" (8:28). Only then "will you know that *I am he*" (8:28). Jesus manifests his divine identity not by outward splendor but by an inward disposition that admits no counterfeit. On this point the Synoptic Gospels and John are in complete harmony. And when the Prologue in John says that "we have seen his glory" (1:14), the image outshining all others is the cross.

Symmetry of Abundance

Everything in John, then, contributes to refuting 'the lie' (8:44; 12:31). Toward this end, the Gospel constructs a symmetry of abundance. God's glory is revealed so as to disprove the proposition that God's economy is one of lack and deprivation (Gen 3:1). Giving in abundance at the wedding at Cana reveals God's glory (John 2:11), and abundance is written in even larger letters when God's glory is revealed in the 'hour' of Jesus (12:23, 28). This connection means that the cross is not a contrast to Jesus's first sign at the wedding but its continuation and climax. At the wedding, Jesus plays softly, in *pianissimo*, the melody that will be played in *fortissimo* at the cross. Strange though it seems and contrary to ingrained readings, the cross is not a melody played in a minor key, in a state of disconsolate grief. The cross in John is a melody played in a major key, as triumph and the antidote to grief.[52]

49. Schnelle, "Cross and Resurrection," 135, 145.

50. Koester, "The Death of Jesus," 153; ———, *The Word of Life*, 122.

51. Ashton, *Understanding the Fourth Gospel*, 497.

52. Schnelle, "Cross and Resurrection," 135.

Seeing Jesus on the cross is not to see a loser or a victim. Brant is profoundly perceptive when she says that the dying Jesus is not a sight from which we need to avert our eyes. Even though the punishment of crucifixion "was not just the pain itself, but the infliction of pain upon a body rendered completely helpless," she writes, "John makes it possible to gaze upon Jesus's body upon the cross without feeling his humiliation or needing to look away."[53] The dying Jesus is a winner in the war against 'the ruler of this world,' and his cry at the very end is the cry of the winner, "It is finished [*tetelestai*]!" (19:30).

In John's symmetry of wedding and cross, the mother of Jesus appears on these two occasions only. At the wedding, Jesus provides in abundance at his mother's request (2:3–8). At his crucifixion, John reports that "standing near the cross of Jesus were his mother, and his mother's sister, Mary the wife of Clopas, and Mary Magdalene" (19:25). Again, under more trying circumstances, Jesus takes notice of his mother. John says that "[w]hen Jesus saw his mother and the disciple whom he loved standing beside her, he said to his mother, 'Woman, here is your son'" (19:25). We cannot read this as anything other than an exquisite picture of a great provider, who, even in his hour of need, has the good of others on his mind (19:26).

Images of abundance line up in rapid succession in connection with the cross. When soldiers are sent to either hasten the death of the men condemned to die or to verify their death, they discover that unlike the other two, Jesus is dead already (19:31–33). This detail corroborates that Jesus retained control of the script to the very end. "No one takes it [my life] from me, but I lay it down of my own accord," he had said earlier (10:18). Here is the proof. At that point, says John, "one of the soldiers pierced his side with a spear, and at once blood and water came out" (19:34). To the naked eye, this is hard core evidence that Jesus's death is for real, but we are expected to see more than that. 'Blood' and 'water' have been primed in John as symbols of life and plenitude (6:35, 53–57; 4:10; 7:37–38). To John's idiosyncratic and singular perception, the blood and water at the cross are not symbols of death but of life-giving and abundance. The action of the soldiers may have been routine and disengaged, but in the context of John, the soldiers, too, are adding their part to the script of abundance.

Once it is clear that Jesus is dead, Joseph of Arimathea and Nicodemus come to claim the body in order to give it an honorable burial (19:38–42). Nicodemus, we recall, was the first one to hear that Jesus must be *lifted up* "just as Moses *lifted up* the serpent in the wilderness" (3:14–15). Speaking of Nicodemus, "who had at first come to Jesus by night," John says the he "also came, bringing a mixture of myrrh and aloes, *weighing about a hundred pounds*" (19:39). This is perfumed balm in abundance, to put it mildly, just as there was wine in abundance at the wedding. Wittingly or unwittingly, Nicodemus has executed a script that has abundance as its theme. He, too, has added his voice to defeating the lie. There will be grief, of course, but grief in John wears a thin shroud. It cannot hide the life and the triumph that are hidden underneath. The

53. Brant, *John*, 257.

joy to come is imperfectly concealed in images of abundance (19:40–42).[54] All this, of course, is of one piece with Jesus's declaration half way through the Gospel of John, reading it now with awareness of the cosmic ramifications of John's story. "The thief comes only to steal and kill and destroy. I came that they may have life, and have it abundantly" (10:10).

In John, Jesus orchestrates a cascade of surprises from the beginning to the end of the story. At the wedding in Cana, the master of ceremonies knows much less than there is to know, but he knows enough to be ambushed by the sense of abundance (2:9–10). The woman at the well in Samaria moves from one ambush to another (4:10, 12, 19), ending up springing a big surprise on her fellow villagers (4:29). In the same story—but for a different reason—Jesus's disciples are at a loss for words when they see him serving the woman at what can only be described as a table of abundance (4:27, 31–34). In Jerusalem, those who listen to Jesus are taken by surprise at his teaching (7:15), and not less so when, on "the last day of the festival, the great day, while Jesus was standing there, he cried out, 'Let anyone who is thirsty come to me, and let the one who believes in me drink. As the scripture has said, 'Out of the believer's heart shall flow rivers of living water'" (7:37–38). At that point those who are sent to arrest him return empty-handed, exclaiming in a voice of astonishment, "Never has anyone spoken like this!" (7:45–46)

Greater than all ambushes, however, is the surprise that comes at the *lifting up* of Jesus on the cross. "See, my servant shall succeed," exclaimed Isaiah in the passage that John's Gospel makes its own (Isa 52:13, translation mine). Klaus Baltzer explains that the setting within which success is predicted "is set in a court of law, where a dispute about the view to be taken of a certain person is under consideration. Those present are: the judge, the person in question, witnesses brought by the disputing parties, and listeners."[55]

In this setting, we are told, the Revealer "shall be exalted and lifted up, and shall be very high" (Isa 52:13). All at once, in John's appropriation of Isaiah, the vision blending crucifixion and exaltation is suddenly a scene in a court of law.

> Just as there were many who were astonished at him—so marred was his appearance, beyond human semblance, and his form beyond that of mortals—so he shall startle many nations; kings shall shut their mouths because of him; for that which had not been told them they shall see, and that which they had not heard they shall contemplate (Isa 52:14–15; cf. John 12:31–32).

Recalling that "[t]he scene is set in a court of law, where a dispute about the view to be taken of a certain person is under consideration,"[56] what will the verdict be? Has the Revealer in John helped the cause of the Person that is under consideration

54. Schnelle, "Cross and Resurrection," 141.

55. Baltzer, *Deutero-Isaiah*, 398.

56. Ibid.

(Isa 52:13; John 12:31)? Can the One who lost his good name win it back? Completing the cascade of surprises in this book, readers are supposed to know that the one who "helped men's joy" at the wedding in Cana is the Person who set up the divine economy at the beginning (Gen 1:1; 2:16–17; John 1:1; 2:1–11). There has been no change in the economy of abundance except for the fact that no one had known its actual measure. They had rarely thought of it in terms of six huge stone jars of the finest wine—and never in terms of blood and water (John 2:6–7; 19:34).

Chapter Seventeen

Lost Sense in the Letters of Paul

All the gospels tell of a messenger who is *sent*, a notion that has complete command of the story line in John.[1] When the person sent is led by the hand of the Spirit into the wilderness, as in Matthew and Luke, or catapulted into the wilderness by the Spirit, as in Mark (Mark 1:12; Matt 4:1; Luke 4:1), the reason for which he is sent is sharply focused. When the heaven-sent person in John goes to the cross, saying "that is why I came" (John 12:27, GNB), we are there, too, at a point in the story where the purpose of the one who sent Jesus and the understanding of him who is sent merge into a seamless whole (John 12:27–30).

In the letters of Paul, especially in the two most influential letters, Galatians and Romans, Jesus is also presented as one who is *sent* (Gal 4:4, 6; Rom 8:3). This is important because Paul's letters are older than the gospels, this view all but a settled matter. The first and oldest letter is 1 Thessalonians, written within eighteen years of the death of Jesus to believers in what is now the city of Thessaloniki in the northern part of Greece.[2] This reflects the early and rapid spread of the message about Jesus and the status which Paul's letters quickly achieved. It is nothing short of remarkable that these occasional and highly situational letters have been preserved for posterity so well that their authenticity is rarely questioned.[3] Simplistically speaking, the gospels contain the story of Jesus and the letters of Paul the interpretation of that story, but Paul's interpretation is so dominant that it controls interpretation even of the message in the gospels. Moreover, at the time when the letters were written Paul could not interpret the story without first telling it. This means that he must have been telling the story himself, outside and beyond what we find in the letters. The quest to recapture lost sense in the letters of Paul, if this is what we shall find, therefore begins with the story

1. The notion that Jesus is a person who is 'sent' is shared by all the gospels, but this emphasis never lets up in the Gospel of John; cf. Matt 10:40; 21:37; Mark 9:37; 12:6; Luke 4:18, 43; 10:16; 13:34; 20:13; John 3:17, 34; 4:34; 5:23–24, 30, 36-38; 6:29, 38–39, 44, 57; 7:28–29, 33; 8:16, 26, 29, 42; 9:4; 10:36, 11:42; 12:44–45, 49; 13:16, 20; 14:24; 15:21; 16:5; 17:3, 8, 18, 21, 23, 25; 20:21.

2. Murphy-O'Connor (*Paul: A Critical Life*, 102) makes A.D. 49/50 the most likely year for the composition of *1 Thessalonians*, a view shared by Schnelle (*Apostle Paul*, 172).

3. For the situational character of Paul's letters, see Beker, *Paul the Apostle*, 25.

he told in person.[4] Scholars are now urging the need to read this story in a 'widescreen edition' if we want to recover the *story* he was telling.[5] The cosmic, widescreen projection of Paul's message will unearth sense that has been lost even in very competent readings of Paul.[6] Here, then, at the door of entry into Paul's message, I will state the short version why Jesus was sent according to the letters of Paul: Jesus was sent in order to overcome human misperception of God—and with it the alienation and fear arising in the wake of such misperception (Gal 4:1-6; Rom 8:1-4, 15).[7]

Paul told a story, readers are rediscovering,[8] even though Paul's leading interpreters in the past did not think so. Martin Luther, Paul's most influential interpreter, did not read these letters in order to find the *story*. His view of Scripture prioritized *doctrine* over *story*, making *doctrine* the chief concern, and he constituted the Bible primarily as *doctrine*. In the law-gospel polarity that dominated Luther's view the Bible is either law or gospel. Luther would certify only the interpreter who masters this distinction. In his *Lectures on Galatians*, Luther says that "whoever knows well how to distinguish the Gospel from the Law should give thanks to God and know that he is a real theologian."[9] Gospel and Law are to be, respectively, "like the light and the day, and the other like the darkness and the night."[10] Mixing or conflating these terms put both at risk. "If we could only put an even greater distance between them!" Luther exclaims.[11] In his construct, the story is barely discernible and mostly a foil for the doctrine that the Bible seeks to inculcate, a doctrine that is meant to lead to faith in Christ.

This view straitjackets the story aspect of the Bible, and it truncates Paul's message. As argued by Richard B. Hays,[12] Paul's letters are not meant as an independent statement, complete in itself. Prior knowledge of the message is assumed because Paul was writing to established churches, most of which he founded himself. His train of thought becomes much clearer if we recognize the narrative elements and the allusive character of the text. For instance, Paul writes to the Galatians that "when the fullness of time had come, *God sent his Son*, born of a woman, born under the law" (Gal. 4:4). As in the Synoptic Gospels and the Gospel of John, Paul pictures Jesus as one

4. Hays, *The Faith of Jesus Christ*, 33–117; see also ———, "Is Paul's Gospel Narratable?" 221; Longenecker, *Narrative Dynamics in Paul*.

5. Gaventa, "The Cosmic Power of Sin," 229–40; ———, "Interpreting the Death of Jesus Apocalyptically," 125–45.

6. Largely left out even in N. T. Wright's cogent and massive attempt at retrieving an authentic Paul (*Paul and the Faithfulness of God*) is Paul's exposé of the *apocalypse* and implosion of evil in *2 Thessalonians*, to be explored below.

7. I have developed this perspective in greater depth in: Tonstad, *Letter to the Romans: Paul among the Ecologists*.

8. See, for instance, Grieb, *The Story of Romans*.

9. Luther, *Lectures on Galatians, 1535, Chapters 1–4*, 115.

10. Ibid., 342.

11. Ibid.

12. Hays, *The Faith of Jesus Christ*, 33–117.

who is *sent*. The sentence above bursts with narrative, each element adding up to the panorama that had been told and elaborated on a previous occasion.[13] Jesus's mission accomplished, in Galatians as well as in Romans, spells an end to the fear that torments human existence (Gal 4:1-6; Rom 8:15).

Paul's extensive use of the Old Testament is a key element in reclaiming this story.[14] The novelty on this point is not that Paul counts on Scripture to corroborate his testimony, a feature no reader of Paul will deny.[15] It is rather that when Paul reads the Old Testament, he is more sensitive to the original context than scholars have been willing to grant.[16] Paul's voice interprets and amplifies the Old Testament, but the Old Testament voice is not sublimated.[17] It fills in the broad narrative framework of the letter, that is, the voices of the Old Testament blend with Paul's preached message in person and with his written word of the letter. As Hays argues regarding Paul's use of the Old Testament in Romans, "once the conversation begins, the addressees recede curiously into the background, and Paul finds himself engaged with an older and more compelling partner."[18]

Now aware of the narrative scaffolding of Paul's letters and of his use of the Old Testament, we are ready to explore two exhibits of lost sense in the letters. I will call the first *the apocalypse of God's faithfulness.*[19]

The Apocalypse of God's Faithfulness

In Romans, Paul turns to the prophet Habakkuk for scriptural proof for his message. He is not ashamed of the gospel, he says, because

> in it the righteousness of God [*dikaiosynē theou*]
> is revealed [*apokalyptetai*]
> through faith for faith [*ek pisteōs eis pistin*];
> as it is written,
> "The one who is righteous will live by faith" (Rom 1:17, NRSV).

This is what Paul is reported to be saying in one highly regarded translation (NRSV). Is this what he actually said, however? How might this hugely important text be heard if we think of Paul's message as *a story that is illuminated by the Old*

13. According to Murphy-O'Connor (*Paul: A Critical Life*, 24), Paul arrived in Galatia in September 46 CE. He spent two winters there (46–48 CE), allowing him ample time to cover the story of Jesus and its interpretation in depth.

14. Hays, *Echoes of Scripture in the Letters of Paul*; ———, *The Conversion of the Imagination.*

15. See Evans and Sanders, *Paul and the Scriptures of Israel.*

16. Sanday and Headlam (*A Critical and Exegetical Commentary*, 289) claimed that Paul's use of the Old Testament was proverbial only, not intended to make the O.T. the basis for his argument.

17. Hays, *Echoes of Scripture*, 36–42.

18. Ibid., 35.

19. For a review of the subject, see Tonstad, "*Pistis Christou*," 37–59.

Testament? The Old Testament prophet from which Paul's key text is taken, looks in horror at a world where injustice runs rampant. This leads him to despair at the fact of God's apparent non-intervention.

> O LORD, how long shall I cry for help,
> and you will not listen?
> Or cry to you 'Violence!'
> and you will not save?
> Why do you make me see wrongdoing
> and look at trouble?
> Destruction and violence are before me;
> strife and contention arise.
> So the law becomes slack
> and justice never prevails.
>
> (Hab. 1:2–4)

In its native Old Testament context, Habakkuk's plea is "the passionate prayer of a desperate man" who sounds the note of "moral outrage and perplexity."[20] The source of the perplexity is God's apparent *un*-faithfulness. Habakkuk confronts a moral order that seems to be disintegrating for lack of the expected action on God's part. When the prophet takes up his position at his watch post, eagerly awaiting what God "will say to me, and what he will answer concerning my complaint" (Hab. 2:1), there can be little doubt that the backdrop is God's seeming failure to keep things on course in the world.

The question in Habakkuk, therefore, is first of all a theodicy question, a question that finds human reality so disconcerting that God's reliability is on the line.[21] This is where the reference to Habakkuk in Romans comes in, by way of the context from which Paul's text is taken. To state the options clearly, God's answer to the prophet's complaint could either be to urge him to continue believing, come what may, or it could be a promise to address the reason for his complaint. As we shall see, God's answer falls into the second category. The expectation in Habakkuk, in the response to his question, is to wait for something to happen.

> Then the LORD answered me and said:
> Write the *vision* [Hebr. *ḥazon*, Gr. *horasis*];
> make *it* [the vision] plain on tablets,
> so that a runner may read *it* [the vision].
> For there is still a *vision* for the appointed time;
> *it* [the vision] speaks of the end,

20. Andersen, *Habakkuk*, 123, 125.

21. "Righteousness" and "faithfulness" are synonymous and mutually reinforcing in several key texts in the Old Testament; cf. Richards, "Martin Luther's Legacy," 198. The featured texts in his argument are Isa 11:5 and Ps 143:1.

and [*it*] does not lie.
If *it* [the vision] seems to tarry,
wait for *it* [the vision];
it [the vision] will surely come,
it [the vision] will not delay.

(Hab 2:2–3)

I have italicized the key word 'vision' in the text and all the impersonal pronouns referring to this word, emending the NRSV in one place only where 'it' is warranted as much as in all the other instances of its use. God's answer to the man standing at his watch post uses the word 'vision' [*ḥazon*] twice in these two verses, and it refers to the 'vision' pronominally eight times, creating the effect of a virtual drumbeat.

But what is the vision? What is the texture of the 'it' that will surely come at "the appointed time"? The "it" that seems to tarry cannot be construed as anything other than God's intervention. Something will happen in history. "*It*" refers to the in-breaking of a singular and singularly important event. While the facts on the ground are profoundly unsettling to faith, God promises to do things that will give proof of God's faithfulness.

The punch line in God's answer to the man standing "on the ramparts" (NIV), whether we read it in Hebrew or in Greek, projects the word "faithfulness" in bold letters on the screen.

Translation of Hebrew text:	'the righteous one (adj. masc. sing.) by *his* faithfulness (third pers. masc. sing.) shall live' (Hab 2:4, BHS)
Translation of Greek text:	'but the righteous one (adj. masc. sing.) by *my* faithfulness (first pers. sing.) shall live' (Hab 2:4, LXX)

Neither the Hebrew original nor the Septuagint supports the translation "the righteous live by their faith" (Hab 2:4, NRSV) or the wording of other mainstream Bible translations into English.[22] Indeed, the choice of wording in most translations can best be understood by the translators' desire to put words in Habakkuk's mouth that will fit what the same translators assume Paul to be saying when he quotes Habakkuk in Romans. Rather than allowing the Old Testament prophet to influence our understanding of Paul, we have the Paul of Protestant orthodoxy retroactively influencing translations of Habakkuk. To ears attuned to the wording given to Paul in Romans,

22. Thus, "the just shall live by his faith" (KJV); "the righteous will live by his faith" (NASB); "the righteous will live by his faith" (NIV); "the upright will live through faithfulness" (NJB); "the just shall live by his faith" (NKJV).

the Hebrew text of Habakkuk is disconcerting: it seems to endorse righteousness by works, "the righteous shall live by his faithfulness" (Hab 2:4, BHS). This problem is eliminated if we recognize the messianic connotation of Habakkuk's prediction. The text will now say, "The Righteous One shall live by his faithfulness."[23] A Christologic reading excludes righteousness by works.

The Greek translation of Habakkuk, probably the text with which Paul was most familiar, poses different problems. How did these pioneer translators get from "*his* faithfulness" [*emunatō*] in the Hebrew text to "*my* faithfulness" [*pistis mou*] in the Greek translation? One possibility is evident. In the unpointed Hebrew text, the difference is slight, either *emunatō* with a ו [waw] suffix or *emunati* with a י [yod] suffix. It is not necessary to know Hebrew to be able to tell that these two letters are very similar. We do not know whether the translators' text read ו or י, but we know the result whichever way it was. The person whose faithfulness is in view in God's answer to Habakkuk must be the faithfulness of the Person who is speaking to him in answer to his concern, that is, it must refer to the faithfulness of God.

By way of summary, the *problem* for Habakkuk is the apparent absence of God's faithfulness. The *promise* to Habakkuk is that something is to happen that will address his question and put God's faithfulness on a firm footing. The *summons* to Habakkuk, in a non-Messianic translation of the LXX, is that "the righteous will live by my faithfulness."

Reading Romans 1:17 under the influence of Habakkuk's question leads to different results than the view that has been in vogue since Luther. 'The righteousness of God' in this text is precisely the attribute of God that seems to be in doubt, viewing human reality through the eyes of Habakkuk. Moreover, the remainder of the text has the character of a story outlined by the movement from *problem* to *promise* to *summons* in Habakkuk.

> For the righteousness of God [*dikaiosynē theou*]
> is revealed [*apokalyptetai*] in it
> *from* faithfulness *for* faithfulness [*ek pisteōs eis pistin*]
> as it is written,
> The righteous shall live by [my] faithfulness.[24]

To Luther, God's righteousness was so much a foregone conclusion that he did not consider it legitimate to question it. His discovery was that grace, not retribution, was the message revealed in "the righteousness of God."[25] In a construct that is influenced by Habakkuk, however, the righteousness of God is not above question. For the Old Testament prophet, the vexing question was not the assumed terror of divine

23. Hays, "The Righteous One," 191–215; Heliso, *Pistis and the Righteous One*. Other OT texts that are relevant for this question are Pss 2:7; 89:3, 20; Isa 53:11; Heb 10:38.

24. A Messianic implication would read, "the Righteous One shall live by faithfulness."

25. *Preface to the Complete Edition of Luther's Latin Writings* [1545], 335–37.

retribution but *absence* of action on God's part. This view of God's righteousness is not resolved until the promised critical point in the story, and *this* revelation operates on the level of real events in the world. In Habakkuk, the problem is not simply "a righteousness that originates from or is mediated by faith but is hidden *from the minds* of the unbelieving Jews and Gentiles."[26]

When echoes of Habakkuk are allowed to influence our understanding of *ek pisteōs eis pistin*, the range of this phrase will not be "through faith for faith" (NSRV) or "by faith from first to last" (NIV). This might have worked if Paul were only speaking of the importance of having faith. When, however, he carries forward Habbakuk's concern, *from* and *to* delineating the outer boundaries of *pistis*, the former denoting source—*God's faithfulness*—and the latter highlighting the result—*faithfulness* in the human realm.[27] The boundary, therefore, will not be 'faith' but 'faithfulness' (Rom 10:2–4).[28]

With respect to the influence of Habakkuk on Romans, Hays asserts that "parties on all sides of the debate have been surprisingly content to assume that Paul employs the passage as a prooftext for his doctrine of justification by faith with complete disregard for its original setting in Habakkuk's prophecy."[29] Instead, he says,

> when Paul quotes Hab. 2:4, we cannot help hearing the echoes—unless we are tone-deaf—of Habakkuk's theodicy question. By showcasing this text—virtually as an epigraph—at the beginning of the letter to the Romans, Paul links his gospel to the Old Testament prophetic affirmation of God's justice and righteousness.[30]

Paul's argument on behalf of God's faithfulness is more easily perceived when we acknowledge the *apocalyptic* character of the message. Here, the notion of *apokalypsis* is barely conveyed by the word "revelation." "Now before *'pistis' came*, we were imprisoned and guarded under the law until *'pistis'* would *be revealed* [*eis tēn mellousan pistin apokalyphtēnai*]," Paul writes in Galatians (Gal 3:23). He proceeds to press the point that *'pistis'* now "*has come*" (3:25, italics mine). But *'pistis'* does not make 'faith' the innovation that has burst upon the scene. *Pistis* has become shorthand for an event and not for the stance of the believer. Translations that convey Paul's intent might be 'before the message came,' 'before Christ came,' or even, grasping that *pistis* is shorthand for a larger story, 'before [God's] faithfulness was demonstrated' (3:23).

Seeking to pin down the force of Paul's use of *apokalyptō* in this passage, J. Louis Martyn describes a motion and not a still picture.

26. Heliso, *Pistis and the Righteous One*, 89.

27. Richards, "Romans 1:16–17 Revisited," 198.

28. The movement "*from* faithfulness *to* faithfulness" in the faith-construct of Romans persists toward the end of the letter (Rom 15:4–5, 8, 12, 18).

29. Hays, *Echoes of Scripture*, 39.

30. Ibid., 40.

> Here we see that, in Paul's mouth, the verb *apokalyphthēnai*, "to be apocalypsed" means more than its literal equivalent, "to be unveiled." It is not as though faith and Christ had been all along standing behind a curtain, the curtain then being at one point drawn aside, so as to make visible what had been hidden. To explicate the verb *apokalyphthēnai*, Paul uses as a synonym the verb *erchomai*, "to come on the scene." And the result is startling, for it shows that Paul's apocalyptic theology—especially in Galatians—is focused on the motif of invasive movement from beyond.[31]

This insight pushes the accent of *pistis* firmly from the traditional emphasis on *faith* toward the *faithfulness* that is at the center in these passages (Rom 1:17; 3:21, 22, 25; Gal 3:23, 25). The subject of the revealing action, 'the faithfulness of Christ,' points to the subject of the revealing intent, 'the righteousness of God" (Rom 3:21, 22, 25). In another break with precedent, Hans Dieter Betz notes that *pistis* in Galatians 3:23 and 3:25 "describes the occurrence of a historical phenomenon, not the act of believing of an individual."[32] Carried by narrative and framed by apocalyptic, *the faithfulness of Christ* [*pistis Christou*] is the most riveting picture in the story. Within the apocalyptic framework, God's right-making intervention happens within a *cosmic-universal drama*. In the words of Martyn, now referring to Galatians, "the subject Paul addresses is that of God's *making right what has gone wrong*."[33]

Paul speaks more in depth about 'the right-making of God' in Romans (3:21–26).[34] He deploys a series of action-oriented verbs so as to make *demonstration* the basis for the conviction that God has been shown to do right. Recalling that God's righteousness is revealed *ek pisteōs eis pistin* (1:17), the words denoting revelation in Romans 3:21–26 hardly thinks of something that is "by faith from first to last" (NIV).

> 1:17 the righteousness of God *is revealed* [*apokalyptetai*]
>
> 3:21 the righteousness of God *has been disclosed* [*pefanerōtai*]
>
> 3:25 *to show* his righteousness [*eis endeiksin dikaiosunē autou*][35]

How is God's righteousness revealed? Paul answers that it has been disclosed *by the faithfulness of Jesus Christ* [*dia pisteōs Iēsou Christou*] (3:22). This is consistent with

31. Martyn, "The Apocalyptic Gospel in Galatians," 254.

32. Betz, *Galatians*, 176, n. 120.

33. Martyn, *Galatians*, 250. In Romans 3:21–26, the *locus classicus* for the traditional interpretation of "justification by faith," Jewett (*Romans:A Commentary*, 268–94) eschews the term "justifies" in favor of the less technical "set right" (3:22) and "makes righteous" (3:26).

34. Campbell, "Romans 1:17, 265–85; ———, "The Faithfulness of Jesus Christ in Romans 3:22," 57–71.

35. The entry for *endeiksis* in the *UBS Greek Dictionary* has "to demonstrate, to show;" "the means by which one knows that something is a fact;" "proof, evidence, verification, indication."

a story line that has not forgotten the concern of Habakkuk.[36] As Douglas Campbell points out, the conventional reading cannot explain "a 'faith' that discloses or reveals the 'righteousness of God' in instrumental terms."[37] 'Faith' alone is at best only a short-lived remedy if the root problem centers on someone whose reliability is in doubt. The need for faith has not subsided, but it is secondary to the revelation upon which faith will rest. It is in this sense that Jesus is not only the object of *pistis* but its subject. As subject, he is the one who has revealed "the righteousness of God."

Romans 3:21–22 may thus be translated as follows:

> But now apart from law
> the righteousness of God
>   has been disclosed,
>   witnessed by the law and by the prophets,
> the righteousness of God
>   through the faithfulness of Jesus Christ
>   to all who trust in him.

Habakkuk, we recall, was assured that something would happen (Hab 2:3). Toward the end of Romans, we hear another Old Testament voice saying much the same thing, but this voice does not leave "it" anonymous. "And again Isaiah says," '*The root of Jesse* shall come . . . in him the Gentiles shall hope'" (Rom 15:12; cf. Isa 11:1–10). This settles the actual identity of Habakkuk's mysterious "it," now personified and embodied so as to leave no doubt what Paul takes to be the solution to the prophet's acute concern. The minor voice of Habakkuk at the beginning of Romans is emboldened by the major voice of Isaiah.[38] Like bookends in Romans, these Old Testament voices throw their weight behind the revelation of the faithfulness of God in Jesus. In Galatians as much as in Romans, 'the faithfulness of Jesus Christ' is shorthand for the apocalypse of God's faithfulness.

36. Bultmann (art. *pistis*, *TDNT* 6:174–82) demonstrates that *pistis* in classical Greek carries the meaning "reliability," "trustworthiness," and even as "proof" and the "means of proof," as well as the stance toward one whose trustworthiness is above question, that is, "confidence" or "trust." According to Ian G. Wallis (*The faith of Jesus Christ*, 1–23), lexical evidence for pre-New Testament use of *pistis* in the Septuagint and in Hellenistic Jewish Literature favors the notion "faithfulness" rather than "faith."

37. Campbell, "The Faithfulness of Jesus Christ in Romans 3:2," 69.

38. Romans 15 has a catena of echoes to Isaiah, some whispers and some louder than that; cf. Rom 15:5 and Isa 65:16; Rom 15:12 and Isa 11:1, 10; Rom 15:21 and Isa 52:15. Suffice it to say here that in Isaiah "the righteousness of God" and "the faithfulness of God" are virtually interchangeable (Isa 11:5); God's action in the world is described as a comprehensive right-making action and not mainly a legal project (Isa 42:1–9; 49:1–9); the emphasis on revelation is unrelenting, construing revelation as something God will do in the world (Isa 40:5; 53:1; 56:1); the content of revelation is so shocking it leaves the recipients speechless (cf. Isa 52:13–15; 53:1–3).

The Apocalypse of Evil

The foregoing outline of the apocalypse of God's faithfulness is increasingly how many scholars think that Paul's message should be understood. And yet something is missing, in part because of scholarly disdain for the demonic, in part because the story Paul tells has been eclipsed by the tendency to make him an expositor of doctrine, and in part because his legacy is largely determined by Galatians and Romans to the exclusion of other letters. To retrieve the apocalypse of evil in Paul's letters, I now turn to 2 Thessalonians, an epistle that is often relegated to the margin of the Pauline corpus.[39] Here, a missing part of Paul's apocalyptic vision is laid out and explicated; and here, too, Habakkuk's concern about divine justice reasserts itself.

Second Thessalonians is occasioned by persecution of believers (2 Thess 1:3–10) and by misconceptions with regard to "the day of the Lord" on the part of members in the fellowship (2:1–2).[40] From Paul's point of view, what must be urgently corrected is the misconception "that the day of the Lord is already here" (2:2). Believers are mistaken about events yet to take place, and they are also in error about time. To make matters worse, somebody has been trying to affix Paul's signature to the mistaken belief that Paul sets out to correct in his letter. We can tell this by the fact that Paul now urges the Thessalonians "not to be quickly shaken in mind or alarmed, either by spirit or by word or by letter, *as though from us*" (2:2). Thus, he more than hints that there are letters in circulation falsely claiming to be from Paul.

Despite this striking and troubling feature, a number of scholars argue that the letter from Paul that says explicitly that there are letters in circulation falsely claiming to be from Paul is itself a false letter! This fact says more about biblical scholarship than about Paul's letters. How can a letter that certifies its own authenticity by explicitly setting itself apart from letters that falsely claim to come from Paul itself be inauthentic? This possibility would be audacious in the extreme. Pseudonymity means loss of prestige, and attempts to downplay the implications have not been successful.[41] While claims of pseudonymous authorship make it possible to exonerate Paul for views deemed unworthy of him,[42] it also gives the scholar an outsize role in determining the range of Paul's message. 'Tricks' used by the writer to win acceptance

39. See Tonstad, "The Restrainer Removed," 133–51.

40. Malherbe, *Thessalonians*, 351.

41. Menken (2 *Thessalonians*, 40) takes the view that pseudonymity must not be equated with forgery. But pseudonymity in this case does not mean anonymity and is in fact an implicit admission that the material itself is *not* sufficient to carry its own weight without the added prestige of the recognized author.

42. Trilling's influential work on the authorship of 2 Thessalonians (*Untersuchungen*, 106) is ambivalent on the question of pseudonymity. On the one hand, he takes the line that the criterion for authenticity (*Echtheit*) is doctrinal and disciplinary content, allowing that 2 Thessalonians passes this test. On the other hand, Trilling uses the alleged pseudonymity of 2 Thessalonians to exonerate Paul from statements thought not to befit him (cf. *Der zweite Brief*, 157–58). A. Strobel (*Untersuchungen*, 110–11), recognizing the apocalyptic texture in Paul's letters, argues for authenticity.

for the letter certainly leave the composition open to the charge of outright deception and forgery. William Wrede is therefore justified in his contention that if the concept of forgery is to have any meaning, it must apply to 2 Thessalonians, unless, of course, the letter is taken to be authentic.[43]

When Abraham J. Malherbe applies the logic of a situational need to 2 Thessalonians, changes in the affairs of the church serve to authenticate the letter fully. This makes 2 Thessalonians a priceless source for understanding of Paul's communication with the churches.[44] Pauline authorship also enlarges the range of what constitutes genuine 'Pauline theology.' If, as the letter claims, Paul had *spoken* to the Thessalonians about the subject in 2 Thessalonians before *writing* and sending the letter by way of reminder (2:5), his prior oral communication was unsolicited and not the consequence of a particular situation. This lifts the status of the letter in general and the prestige of the *subject matter* of the letter in particular. Paul's view of the apocalypse of evil was not a subject relevant only to this particular group of believers. That said, it does not resolve the difficulties in the latter.[45]

Paul makes much of the fact that he had spoken about the subject in-depth to the members of the church on prior occasions. In the midst of the passage that describes the appearing of "the lawless one" (2:8), he pointedly asks, "Do you not remember that I told you these things when I was still with you?" (2:5). Part of the author's corrective consists of reminding his readers of the instruction embedded in the previous narrative. The most critical passage in 2 Thessalonians has at least ten concepts concerning which some degree of prior understanding must have existed between the author and the Thessalonian believers, here listed in the order of their occurrence (2:3–12):

'the falling away' [*hē apostasia*] (2:3)

'the figure of lawlessness' [*ho anthrōpos tēs anomias*] (2:3)

'the son of destruction' [*ho huios tēs apōleias*] (2:3)

'the restraining element' [*to katechon*] (2:6)

'the mystery of lawlessness' [*to mystērion tēs anomias*] (2:7)

'the restrainer' [*ho katechōn*] (2:7)

43. Wrede (*Die Echtheit*, 86), while accepting that there are examples of 'legitimate' or innocent use of pseudonymity in the first century, concludes that if the concept of deceit is to have any meaning, it must apply to 2 Thessalonians.

44. Malherbe, *Thessalonians*, 349–53. Scholars arguing for the authenticity of 2 Thessalonians are Rigaux, *Saint Paul*, 112–52; Best, *A Commentary*, 37–59; Jewett, *The Thessalonian Correspondence*, 3–18; Marshall, *1 and 2 Thessalonians*, 28–45; Wanamaker, *Epistles to the Thessalonians*, 17–44; and Murphy-O'Connor, *Paul*, 110–11.

45. Jewett (*The Thessalonian Correspondence*, 18), defending the authenticity of 2 Thessalonians, claims that "modern Pauline scholarship has in fact discovered . . . that Paul's style and vocabulary are brilliantly situational; the variations are comprehensible when one takes the unique circumstances of each letter into account."

'the lawless one' [*ho anomos*] (2:8)

'the love of the truth' [*hē agapē tēs alētheias*] (2:10)

'the lie' [*to pseudos*] (2:11)

'the truth' [*hē alētheia*] (2:12)

All the nouns and participles on the list have the definite article in one form or another in the context of their occurrence. This favors the view that the author is invoking a known concept or entity.[46]

Rembrandt's depiction of Paul has the light shining equally on Paul's eyes and his text. The accompanying caption highlights Paul as a seer, his vision—remarkably—said to be the apocalypse of "the man of sin" and "the removal of the Restrainer" in 2 Thessalonians that only rarely gets the attention of interpreters. © Kunshistorisches Museum, Wien. Used by permission.

46. Cf. Wallace, *Greek Grammar Beyond the Basics*, 217–18; 222–25). Whether the article should be seen as anaphoric, referring to Paul's prior introduction of the term while with them in person, or as pointing out a subject or character that is 'in a class by itself,' 'one of a kind,' or 'well known,' the assumption of familiarity remains.

As noted above, the author had spoken to them about this subject on a previous occasion (2:5). The liberal use of terms that are at one and the same time complex and specific strengthens the impression that Paul's terms are grounded in historically-shared knowledge. While most of the terms suggest a narrow and specific application, such specificity may in this letter apply even to the terms that have a familiar ring, like 'the lie' [*to pseudos*] (2:11) and 'the truth' [*hē alētheia*] (2:12), terms that might otherwise invite broad definitions. Nevertheless, it cannot be denied that the concepts in the passage represent a formidable challenge.

And yet significant pointers do exist, beginning with the apocalyptic worldview of the New Testament and the author's use of the Old Testament. N. T. Wright contends that "to ignore worldviews, either our own or those of the culture we are studying, would result in extraordinary shallowness."[47] The worldview of 2 Thessalonians is apocalyptic, one element of which envisions a cosmic conflict between good and evil.[48] While the letter aspires to portray the climax and ending of the conflict culminating in the *parousia* of Jesus (2:8), it is profoundly aware of the *modus operandi* of the opposing power (2:7).[49]

This speaks directly to Paul's determination to correct the misconception "that the day of the Lord is already here" (2:2). He insists that "the day of the Lord" is still future, and he explains the apparent delay of the "Parousia" of Jesus by invoking "the falling away" or "the rebellion" that must come first (2:3). When this "falling away" happens, it will reveal "the figure of lawlessness, the son of destruction" (2:3). As noted, the use of the definite article with these metaphors indicates that they are familiar to the audience. But even where familiarity cannot be assumed, the terms have the connotation of ultimacy. What is described is not a peripheral, occasional, or local manifestation of evil. Later in the passage, the author describes "the figure of lawlessness" that is to be revealed as "the lawless one," that is to say, "*the* lawless one" and therefore the source and epitome of lawlessness and chaos (2:8).[50]

The terms used suggest a comprehensive narrative. Paul's ability to outline the final exposé and undoing of evil indicates awareness of who is who in the story and even of the 'origin of evil.' The logic of the ending is informed by the shape of the problem at the point of origin. To that end "the man of lawlessness," *alias* "*the* lawless one," is appropriately called "the son of destruction" (2:3). This expression is not to be construed as though "the son of destruction" is merely the progeny of evil, as the modern ear might hear it. The phenomenon in view is not only to be destroyed but is

47. Wright, *The New Testament and the People of God*, 124.

48. Beker, *Paul's Apocalyptic Gospel*, 14–15.

49. Thus Bilde (*2 Cor.* 4,4: The View of Satan," 31), "the surviving epistles of Paul actually represent only a few fragmentary expressions—of the general religious thinking which we may assume as lying behind his actual writing. Therefore, I regard Paul's letters as relatively accidental expressions of his overall religious thinking."

50. Menken (*2 Thessalonians*, 102) is no doubt correct that the definite article in "*the* apostasy" and "*the* man of lawlessness" shows that "the addressees are supposed to be familiar with both entities."

also the foremost agent of destruction. This yields the curious result that "the *son* of destruction" is intimately related to the author and father of destruction. The NRSV is factually correct in translating *ho huious tēs apōleias* as "the one destined for destruction," but it must not be missed that these telling nominatives seek to capture the cause as much as the final result (2:3).[51]

Three subtle verbal elements support this logic. First, Paul writes that "the mystery of lawlessness is already at work" (2:7), indicating a phenomenon that is mysterious as to its character and secretive as to its mode of operation. This phenomenon is not to come from nowhere at some future point; it is "already at work" (2:7).

Second, Paul explains that the lawless entity "opposes and exalts himself above every so-called god or object of worship, so that he takes his seat in the temple of God, declaring himself to be God" (2:4). Here he is bringing together texts taken from the Old Testament story of cosmic rebellion, featuring the most audacious examples of overreaching (cf. Isa 14:13–14; Ezek 28:2, 12–19; Dan 11:36).[52] Of particular interest is the poem in Isaiah since this poem catches the primordial origin of the rebellion.[53] In this poem "the shining one" is overheard saying to himself,

> I will ascend to heaven;
> I will raise my throne above the stars of God;
> I will sit on the mount of assembly on the heights of Zaphon;
> I will ascend to the tops of the clouds,
> I will make myself like the Most High.
>
> (Isa 14:12–14)

In 2 Thessalonians, the author is not featuring Old Testament passages merely in a metaphorical or typological sense. The evil power traces its roots to a primordial point of origin and to a non-human 'person' as to cause. We have before us in 2 Thessalonians the story of cosmic rebellion, highlighted with particular force and poignancy in the poem about "the shining one" quoted above (Isa 14:12–20) and in the closely related poem about "the anointed cherub who covers" in Ezekiel 28:12–19.[54] Second Thessalonians harnesses this story in order to explain the delay of the *parousia*

51. Menken identifies these genitive constructions as Semitisms, emphasizing that they point to a quality (*2 Thessalonians*, 103–4). He prefers the word "perdition," but "destruction" is equally correct and pertinent.

52. Aus, "God's Plan," 541–42.

53. The wide and early diffusion in the Old Testament of this story is well attested, as is the fact that these texts became the quarry for the modified dualism of good and evil in the New Testament, as noted in chapter 14.

54. Cf. Menken, *2 Thessalonians*, 106. That these text have been quarried for the background of personal evil in the New Testament account, as in Luke 10:18, in the hymn in Phil 2:5–11, in Rev 12:7–9, and now here, suggests a pattern and not mere serendipity.

and the end-time unveiling of evil, understood as a process that will afflict the church from within.[55]

Third, the unveiling is described in a series of the passive form *apokalyphtein*, "to be revealed," or, as in Louw-Nida, "to uncover," "to take out of hiding," "to make fully known."[56]

> "and the lawless one is *revealed*" [*kai apokalyphthē ho anthrōpos tēs anomias*] (2:3)
>
> "so that he may be *revealed*" [*eis to apokalyphthēnai auton*] (2:6)
>
> "then the lawless one will be *revealed*" [*tote apokalyphthēsetai ho anomos*] (2:8).

The verb charged with the task of making evil emerge from hiding into broad daylight is *apokalyptō*, the very same verb that has the disclosure of God's faithfulness in its portfolio. Paul's exposition is nothing if not a confident, pointed, in-the-know account of the unveiling of evil, even to the point of implying a certain progression in time until the moment of final disclosure. If *apokalypsis* retains the meaning of "showing a thing up for what it is,"[57] it confirms that the phenomenon thus described has concealed its true character and owes its success to some kind of disguise or false pretense. It is therefore not only the *appearing* of the "man of lawlessness" that is awaited but the *exposure* of his real nature.

These soundings prepare for "the restrainer," generally considered to be the crux of the riddle.

> And you know
> what is now restraining [*to katechon*] him,
> so that he may be revealed
> when his time comes.
> For the mystery of lawlessness
> is already at work,
> but only until the one
> who now restrains [*ho katechōn*] it
> is removed (2:6–7).

The overall message so far may be compacted into the following summary:[58]

1. "the day of the Lord" points to a future event (2:2)

55. There is little doubt that 2 Thessalonians envisions the manifestation of "the man of sin" as a threat arising *within* the church; cf. Malherbe, *Thessalonians*, 431.

56. *Louw-Nida Greek English Lexicon of the New Testament*, art. ἀποκαλύπτω.

57. Whiteley, "The Threat to Faith," 168.

58. Peerbolte, "KATÉXON/KATÉΩN," 140.

2. "the figure of lawlessness," *alias* "the son of destruction" and "the lawless one," has not been revealed.

3. "the figure of lawlessness" has not yet been revealed because something is holding him back.

As noted, Paul is addressing a familiar topic and therefore has no need to explain his terms.[59] This includes terms that have proved most resistant to interpreters' advances, first among which is the author's use of the neuter participle "that which restrains" [*to katechon*] in v. 6 and the switch to the masculine participle 'the restainer' [*ho katechōn*] in v. 7. The second difficulty is the expression "disappear from the middle" [*ek mesou genētai*] in v. 7, an expression so dense that the NRSV simply ignores it. A resolution of these difficulties, if achievable, holds the key to understanding the passage.

Who or what is 'the restrainer'? This is the biggest enigma. If resolved, it promises to yield insights not only into the workings of evil but even more into the ways of God. Some options that have been suggested through the years may be dismissed. Colin Nicholl argues that it cannot be the Roman Empire or a Roman emperor because the removal of such a restrainer has insufficient explanatory power.[60] Paul must also be dismissed since it is unlikely that he would refer to himself in such cryptic terms or fit the shoe attributed to "the restrainer." Satan must also be excluded, given that "the rebel's parousia is 'by the working of Satan'" (vv. 9–10a).[61]

Who is left? Some proposed Old Testament antecedents are too trite.[62] The most persuasive view is the one proposed by August Strobel and subsequently adopted and developed by Wolfgang Trilling and Maarten J. J. Menken.[63] On theological rather than strict verbal grounds Strobel finds the key to the Restrainer in Habakkuk's vision of the delay (Hab 2:3), the text we have looked at earlier as a key passage in Paul's description of the revelation of God's faithfulness. Habakkuk's concern reappears in 2 Thessalonians, now directed at the eschaton. On the basis of this text, Strobel adopts a theocentric interpretation of this letter. The generative textual concept relates to a word that means "to delay," "tarry" or "defer," and may be seen as analogous to the restrainer [*katechōn*]. This text achieved a key role outside the New Testament with

59. Thus Nicholl, "Michael, the Restrainer Removed," 27.

60. The main objection to seeing the Roman Empire as the restrainer relates to the well-attested fact of emperor worship in the imperial cult. How, the question goes, could the emperor stand in the way of a practice of which he was himself guilty? On textual grounds the most important reservation with respect to the Roman application is that the restrainer is to be removed *ek mesou*; see below.

61. Nicholl, "Michael, the Restrainer Removed," 31–32.

62. For Aus ("Isaiah 66 and the Restraining Factors," 544–47), the main reason for the delay is to allow the preaching of the Gospel (p. 540). Stephen G. Brown agrees with Aus that Isaiah 66 is basic to the interpretation of 2 Thessalonians, but not as to how Isaiah affects the latter. In his view Isa 66:17 is the key text, and it applies to a local phenomenon in Thessalonica; cf. Evans and Sanders "The Intertextuality of Isaiah 66.17 and 2 Thessalonians 2.7, 254–75.

63. Strobel, *Untersuchungen*, 79–106; Trilling, *Der zweite Brief an die Thessalonicher*, 89–93; Menken, *2 Thessalonians*, 108–112.

respect to explaining the timing of God's purpose. The appearance of a delay is only that—an appearance—because there is no real delay that has not already been factored into God's plan. It follows that the restraining factor is God's will, and the actual restrainer is God![64] This interpretation finds support in the Qumran commentary on Habakkuk, where believers also looked to Habakkuk 2:3 for an explanation for *their* perception of a delay.[65] In this understanding of the 'delay,' everything falls within God's deliberate plan and purpose. To Paul, therefore, there is less distinction between *what* restrains [God's plan] and *who* restrains [God] than most interpreters make of the switch from the neuter to the masculine participle of *katechein*.[66]

The standard objection is easily anticipated. God, the objection holds, cannot be the Restrainer because God cannot be "removed."[67] But this difficulty is theological more than textual, and the textual reservations disappear in Menken's translation.

> And now you know what restrains him,
> so that he will be revealed at his own time.
> For the mystery of lawlessness is already at work,
> only until the one who restrains now *will have disappeared*.[68]

Is *God* the Restrainer? Will God *disappear*, as the text now appears to suggest? This view has so scandalized interpreters that they feel the need to define the actual restrainer in terms of delegated agency. The proposed solution is to see the Restrainer [*ho katechōn*] as an angel, ostensibly Michael, who exercises delegated authority according to God's plan.[69] Such an explanation is compatible with biblical concepts,[70] but "Michael" will only be a little better than candidates such as the Roman Empire, Paul, or Satan. The focus must remain on the rationale intrinsic to God's plan and, no matter how alarming the thought, on the object of worship that is left once the Restrainer has "disappeared." And the text keeps the focus on God because the Restrainer is to

64. Strobel, *Untersuchungen*, 103.

65. Harris's paraphrase (*The Qumran Commentary*, 39) of the comment on Hab 2:3 reads, "Here is a reference to the fact that the Last Days may be delayed beyond any expectation of the prophets, for God fulfils his purposes according to his own timetable. Then again there are the Men of Truth—those who fulfil the law, who never grow weary of serving the Truth never mind how long drawn out the Last Day may be. Nevertheless, all the times God has appointed will reach their final consummation, for the very reason that he has determined in his infinite wisdom."

66. Trilling (*Der zweite Brief*, 92) writes that "the restraining element is a primary, formal concept that embodies the extension of the end time in the face of the breaking in of the eschatological evil." For this reason the shift from neuter to masculine is of no concern.

67. The KJV and the NKJV have the wording, "taken out of the way."

68. Menken, *2 Thessalonians*, 6; see also M. Barnouin, "Les Problèmes de traduction," 498.

69. Menken, *2 Thessalonians*, 112–13. Nicholl ("Michael, the Restrainer Removed," 33–49) works out the rationale for seeing this angel as Michael.

70. Michael has a mediating role in Dan 10:13, 21; 12:1, and angels are seen to exercise a restraining influence in Rev 9:13–15.

disappear "*from the middle*" [*ek mesou*] (2:7). As will be shown below, this expression keeps God at the center.

The notion that something or someone is to be removed "*from the middle*" [*ek mesou genētai*] has an allusive quality (2:7), that is, more must be seen than what is said. Indeed, the expression is so challenging that many translators simply—and regrettably—leave it out.[71] This cannot be our 'solution.' Stephen G. Brown finds the background for the middle in mythic imagery, a location that should be seen as "an archetypal symbol referring to a sacred center, a place where earth and heaven met originally."[72] This 'middle' is actually the "garden of God" (Ezek 28:13), or even the "mountain of God" (Ezek 28:14). The adversarial power that we have noted on many occasions is in view. According to Ezekiel, "the anointed cherub who covers" (NKJV) or the "great shielding cherub"[73] was once "on the holy mountain of God," walking back and forth '*in the middle* of the stones of fire' [*en mesō lithōn purinōn*] (28:14). From this state of exaltation and innocence, when "iniquity was found in you" (28:15), the adversary was made to leave the mountain of God. "I banished you, shielding cherub," '*from the middle* of the stones of fire' [*ek mesou lithōn purinōn*] 28:16).[74] The *middle* is a recurring theme in this passage, as a telling and specific concept. It warrants the conclusion that "Paul's reference to a 'middle' was neither nebulous nor obscure but was familiar to his audience, either by its widespread currency in the ancient world or by Paul's previous instruction."[75] With the Old Testament antecedent in mind, the expression 'from the middle' [*ek mesou*] belongs in the category of things Paul told the Thessalonian believers when he was still with them (2 Thess 2:5). The cosmic perspective in Paul's letter excludes that the topic only had local interest to people in Thessalonica.[76]

The foregoing suggests that the unmasking of "the man of lawlessness" is set against a primordial and cosmic background.[77] Drawing on the allusive qualities of his terms, Paul grounds his portrayal of "the lawless one" in Old Testament imagery. He forges a symmetry of beginning and ending in his account of evil. Important Old Testament metaphors are concretized and personified in "the man of lawlessness." In ways that are sure to disturb, Paul writes that the Restrainer will vanish from the "middle" and from his vigilant watch over the adversary. Other candidates weighed and found wanting, God is now the most promising candidate for who the Restrainer might be. When, as 2 Thessalonians suggests, the Restrainer disappears *from the*

71. Malherbe (*Thessalonians*) omits any discussion of this phrase, as do most commentators.

72. Brown, "Intertextuality," 263.

73. Greenberg, *Ezekiel 21–37*, 579, 584.

74. Ibid., 579.

75. Brown, "Intertextuality," 264.

76. LaRondelle, "Paul's Prophetic Outline," 63.

77. This interpretation of the "middle" constitutes a substantial textual and exegetical argument against the widely held view that the restrainer is the Roman Empire.

middle (2:7), the divine vanishing act allows "the lawless one" to take the coveted place—in the 'middle.' This scenario, so shocking and unimaginable on first mention, only repeats what has been said about the apostasy and its agent already, "He opposes and exalts himself above every so-called god or object of worship, so that he takes his seat in the temple of God, declaring himself to be God" (2:4).[78] Moreover, and very much to the point, it recalls and exposes the objective of the cosmic rebel,

> I will ascend
> to heaven;
> I will raise my throne
> above the stars of God;
> I will sit on the mount of assembly
> on the heights of Zaphon;
> I will ascend
> to the tops of the clouds,
> I will make myself
> like the Most High (Isa 14:13–14).

Just as the passage in 2 Thessalonians does not strive to differentiate between the restraining principle and the Restrainer, it also leaves a very delicate line of demarcation between "the mystery of lawlessness" (2:7), "the lawless one" (2:8), and Satan (2:9).[79] If "the man of lawlessness" is a surrogate for the evil one,[80] he is thinly veiled, and the transparent guise reveals more than it conceals. "The lawless one" will have a 'coming' that precedes and parallels the 'coming' of Jesus (2:8–9). The end-point is the unveiling of "the lawless one" (2:8), who, when other candidates have been considered, can be none other than Satan.

The passage ends by pairing the familiar words "the lie" (2:11) and "the truth" (2:12). Crucially, the author speaks of both with the definite article, "*the* lie" and "*the* truth." While it is possible that this expression points to the immediate context, referring to the one who claims to be God but is not (2:4), a wider connotation is unavoidable. Paul writes elsewhere that "the serpent deceived Eve by its cunning" (2 Cor 11:3), adding that even now "Satan disguises himself as an angel of light" (2 Cor 11:14). In Romans, the unbelievers "exchanged the truth of God for the lie" (Rom 1:25). In an exceptionally important statement, Paul explains to the Corinthians that "the god of this world[81] has blinded the minds of the unbelievers, to keep them from seeing the light of the gospel of the glory of Christ, who is the image of God" (2 Cor 4:4). This

78. Here "the temple of God" (2:4) reflects an understanding that sees the temple as the conduit between heaven and earth.

79. "Just as Christ 'came' by the power of God, so the man of lawlessness will 'come' *by the activity of Satan*;" cf. Whiteley, *Thessalonians*, 102.

80. An analogous conception is found in the book of Revelation (Rev 13:2, 12; 16:13).

81. Paul designates the agency behind the continued sway of the deception as ὁ θεὸς τοῦ αἰῶνος τούτου (2 Cor 4:4).

light brings "the light of the knowledge of the glory of God in the face of Jesus Christ" (2 Cor 4:6).[82]

In the view of 2 Thessalonians, truth alone is insufficient to hold the ground against the mystery that is at work. In fact, the character of the mystery suggests a compelling rationale for the calibration of restraint gradually loosened, as sketched by the author in the following English rendition, drawn from insights noted above.

> And you know what is now restraining [him]
> so that he may be fully exposed
> when his time comes.
> For already the mystery of lawlessness
> is hard at work,
> only [awaiting the moment]
> when the One who now restrains
> [has disappeared] from the middle (2:6–7).

In this complex plot, it is in everyone's interest that the truth be known. The concealment of "the lawless one" will at last unravel, culminating in the alarming prospect that the god revered in the "middle" will be "the lawless one" (2:10).[83] In Paul's account, all hell literally breaks loose, but believers must not lose heart because the exposé happens by the will and design of the Restrainer.

Lost Sense in the Letters of Paul

What now of the claim that there is lost sense in the letters of Paul—other than to confirm that it is sense that bears profoundly on the problem of God's apparent absence in the world? Two huge, unexpected, and singular moves appear on the apocalyptic horizon in his letters, one in the message of the trustworthiness of God through "the faithfulness of Jesus Christ" (Rom 3:22), the other in the message of the Restrainer who disappears "from the middle" (2 Thess 2:6–7). The latter of these moves is still a residual black hole in the canvas of Paul's outlook and legacy. When we add to this the story of what Christ Jesus did not do in Paul's letter to the Philippians (Phil 2:5–7), discussed in Chapter 5, it is evident that Paul's sense is organically and not accidentally set in the context of the cosmic conflict.[84]

But this also means that the sense on behalf of which Paul is spokesperson rests on an independent footing: it is not sense measured by a prior conception. To the

82. Bultmann (art. ἀλήθεια, *TDNT*, 238) shows that the most common antonym of ἀλήθεια is ψεῦδος. The etymological root of ἀλήθεια carries a meaning similar to ἀποκάλυψις, both signifying non-concealment.

83. The translation here is that of Menken, *2 Thessalonians*, 6.

84. The cosmic perspective in Colossians and Ephesians is further evidence that this is a core theme and not a situational aspect in Paul's outlook (Col 2:8–15; Eph 6:12).

Corinthians, for instance, Paul does not cavort with a known standard for what constitutes sense.

> For the message about the cross is foolishness to those who are perishing, but to us who are being saved it is the power of God. For it is written, "I will destroy the wisdom of the wise, and the discernment of the discerning I will thwart." Where is the one who is wise? Where is the scribe? Where is the debater of this age? Has not God made foolish the wisdom of the world? For since, in the wisdom of God, the world did not know God through wisdom, God decided, through the foolishness of our proclamation, to save those who believe. For Jews demand signs and Greeks desire wisdom, but we proclaim Christ crucified, a stumbling block to Jews and foolishness to Gentiles, but to those who are the called, both Jews and Greeks, Christ the power of God and the wisdom of God. For God's foolishness is wiser than human wisdom, and God's weakness is stronger than human strength . . . God chose what is foolish in the world to shame the wise; God chose what is weak in the world to shame the strong; God chose what is low and despised in the world, things that are not, to reduce to nothing things that are, so that no one might boast in the presence of God (1 Cor 1:18–29).

This all-out, unqualified prioritization of the story of God in Christ crucified shows Paul's determination to make the story take command of the subject from A to Z. It is also a good place to consider E. P. Sanders's suggestion that Paul's reasoning runs from solution to plight and not the other way around.[85] To Sanders, Paul is so transfixed by Christ that his theology runs backwards, from Christ as the solution to the problem so as to make the problem less well defined than the solution and also less important. The traditional, formulaic reading that begins with sin as the problem to which Christ is the solution does not capture Paul's actual emphasis. And yet Sanders, too, underestimates the cosmic conflict within which the *apokalypsis* in Paul's letters is set. 'Solution' will still tower above 'plight' so as to remain the dominant image on the canvas. However, the solution is not measured according to the scale of human sin but to the reality of cosmic crisis. On behalf of such a measure, Paul claims that there is sense aplenty, driving the point home precisely in his discussion of sense and nonsense in 1 Corinthians.

> But we speak God's wisdom [*sense*], secret and hidden, which God decreed before the ages for our glory. None of the rulers of this age understood this; for if they had, they would not have crucified the Lord of glory (1 Cor 2:7–8).

Here, 'solution' matches 'plight' to the T, God outsmarting and outmaneuvering "the rulers of this age" to leave them defeated and discomfited on the cosmic battle field. Love laid a trap, as it were, deploying humility and unselfishness against power

85. Sanders, *Paul and Palestinian Judaism*, 443.

and pride and hubris, a mismatch so stupendous that the outcome seemed a foregone conclusion until "the rulers of this age" woke up to see their scheme disintegrate.[86]

A person could not move sure-footedly through this vast subject the way Paul does in his hymn about the mind of Christ in Philippians, in his view of the faithfulness of Christ in Romans and Galatians, and in his exposé of the *parousia* of "the man of sin" in 2 Thessalonians unless the subject was important to him and the story line reasonably clear. And the sense in it, at least in the train of thought that runs from Habakkuk to Paul, relates especially to the problem of suffering. Let Habakkuk stand as a post-Holocaust voice heard in pre-Holocaust times, scanning the horizon for evidence that God has not abandoned the world and left the agents of chaos free to run riot. "If it seem slow, wait for it; it will surely come, it will not delay," Habakkuk was admonished (Hab 2:3).

According to the New Testament "it" did come. Paul says that God's way of being righteous—and God's way of setting things right—is revealed in the gospel, apart from law, "although the law and the prophets bear witness to it, the righteousness of God by the faithfulness of Jesus Christ" (Rom 3:21, 22, translation mine).

86. Girard, *I See Satan Fall Like Lightning*, 149–51.

Part III

The Sense of the Ending

Chapter Eighteen

The Grand Inquisitor and the Sense of Jesus

When we took a break from Ivan Karamazov's fury earlier in this book (Chap. 2), Ivan was about to share a 'poem' with his brother Alyosha. At the same time there is a lull in the conversation, coinciding somewhat with a transition from emotion to reason or from passionate outburst to ideological clarity. The subject of Ivan's 'poem' is Jesus. Few attempts to pinpoint the sense that comes to light in the life of Jesus match Dostoevsky's work in *The Brothers Karamazov*, and fewer still succeed. We have seen that Ivan's indictment of God goes deeper than atheism. God may well exist, but who can relate to a God who permits the suffering of children? Who can relate to a God who allows a five year old girl to have her face smeared by excrement by her mother or who lets an eight year old boy be mauled to death by the dogs belonging to a revered general at the general's command? Ivan's review of the options in the Christian repository of answers finds each proposed remedy inadequate. Neither retribution nor forgiveness nor the prospect of final harmony will make up the difference. Jesus, too, is weighed and found wanting, at least in the version of his life that is current among Christians.

But next to Jesus's name there is an asterisk, a question mark, a marginal note to suggest that his story can be told in more than one way. Whether a different telling of the story will help or harm the case for faith is not obvious when Ivan tells Alyosha that he has written a 'poem.'

"You wrote a poem?" Alyosha asks surprised.[1] He does not expect the analytical and facts-oriented Ivan to be the kind of person who writes poetry. But Ivan is quick to retreat. No, he has not really written a poem; in fact, he has not written anything. He has just allowed himself to imagine certain things, and his 'poem' is an unfinished project of his imagination.

And yet we should not discount the importance of calling the story a 'poem.' Poetry is usually a labor of inspiration and love. There is a soft side to Ivan, and in his poem he is allowing his brother to see it. The 'soft' side might quite possibly be a different approach to the problem of suffering than the one Ivan has brandished with vehemence so far in the conversation.

1. Dostoevsky, *The Brothers Karamazov*, 246.

"My poem is called 'The Grand Inquisitor'—an absurd thing, but I want you to hear it."[2] After a long introduction that includes mention of Dante and Victor Hugo, Ivan gets to the point. The action of the story "is set in Spain, in Seville, in the most horrible time of the Inquisition, when fires blazed every day to the glory of God."[3] Into this situation Jesus suddenly appears, fifteen hundred years after his earthly sojourn.

> He appeared quietly, inconspicuously, but, strange to say, everyone recognized him. This could be one of the best passages in the poem, I mean, why it is exactly that they recognize him. People are drawn to him by an invincible force, they flock to him, surround him, follow him. He passes silently among them with a quiet smile of infinite compassion. The sun of love shines in his heart, rays of Light, Enlightenment, and Power stream from his eyes and, pouring over the people, shake their hearts with responding love.[4]

Ivan's 'poem' is a work in progress. Having made up his mind that people will immediately recognize that the person in their midst is Jesus, Ivan tries to describe what enables them to identify him. Besides the serene demeanor, Jesus heals the sick and raises the dead, just as he did in the gospel stories. The impact now is as impressive as it was then.

But everyone is not thrilled by the sudden return of Jesus. In the midst of the cries and the weeping, the Grand Inquisitor crosses the square in front of the cathedral. "He is an old man, almost ninety, tall and straight, with a gaunt face and sunken eyes, from which a glitter still shines like a fiery spark," says Ivan.[5] This man "has seen everything, seen the coffin set down at his feet, seen the girl rise, and his face darkens. He scowls with his thick, gray eyebrows, and his eyes shine with sinister fire."[6]

Why does the Grand Inquisitor suddenly appear? Why is he unhappy to see a dead girl restored to life? Why do his eyes "shine with sinister fire"? The unhappiness of the Grand Inquisitor means that Ivan's poem pits the Church against Jesus. What little doubt there may be on this point disappears when the old man proceeds to order Jesus's arrest. "He stretches forth his finger and orders the guard to take him."[7]

Will the people resist this action by the leading man of the Church, a man charged with the task of keeping the Church and its teachings true? Will they turn on the Grand Inquisitor in anger, refusing to go along? The thought that the Church will arrest Jesus and put him in jail is preposterous: we expect the people to remonstrate; we expect them to stand up for Jesus.

2. Ibid., 246.
3. Ibid., 248.
4. Ibid., 249.
5. Ibid.
6. Ibid.
7. Ibid.

But the Grand Inquisitor has the upper hand. There is no protest, only acquiescence on the part of the people. The one who was crucified in his earthly life is again led away.

> And such is his power, so tamed, submissive, and tremblingly obedient to his will are the people, that the crowd immediately parts before the guard, and they, amidst the deathly silence that has suddenly fallen, lay their hands on him and lead him away. As one man the crowd immediately bows to the ground before the aged Inquisitor, who silently blesses the people and moves on.[8]

The power gap between Jesus and the Grand Inquisitor with respect to the people is striking. While the people one moment have been in awe of Jesus, rejoicing at his presence and works, they are unable to stand up to the institutional authority of the Church. It is tempting to dismiss the submissiveness of the people as a trivial feature in Ivan's poem, but similar scenes have been repeated so often in history that it must be more than that. Why is there no dissent, if only as a meek voice here and there raised in protest? Why, in the twentieth century, has there been so little resistance to leaders and movements that have built momentum by projecting authority and glory while explicitly pursuing the goal of genocide?[9]

Ivan's poem makes two important value judgments right from the start. On the one hand, he operates on the conviction that the priorities of the Church and the values of Jesus are at opposite poles. On the other hand, Jesus and the Grand Inquisitor are both people of authority, but they wield authority in completely different ways. On the surface—at least short term—the authority of the Grand Inquisitor easily overwhelms the authority of Jesus.

As darkness settles on Seville, the door of the prison where Jesus is kept opens. The Grand Inquisitor has come to pay his prisoner a visit. He is not happy to see Jesus, and he lets it be known that his decision to confront the latter's interference is an unpalatable task.

> "Why, then, have you come to interfere with us? For you have come to interfere with us and you know it yourself. But do you know what will happen tomorrow? I do not know who you are, but tomorrow I shall condemn you and burn you at the stake as the most evil of heretics, and the very people who today kissed your feet, tomorrow, at a nod from me, will rush to heap the coals up around your stake, do you know that?"[10]

The Grand Inquisitor is confident that nothing will be able to stand in his way even as he admits that the Church will have to eclipse Jesus in order to do its work. Reconciliation is not an option in the clash of visions. If anyone deserves to be branded

8. Ibid., 249–50.

9. To Friedländer (*The Years of Extermination*, 657), this has been the all-important question after World War II.

10. Dostoevsky, *The Brothers Karamazov*, 250.

a heretic in this clash of interests, it will be Jesus. Just as they did the first time, the Grand Inquisitor counts on the people to approve.

Throughout the entire encounter the Grand Inquisitor is the only one speaking. Jesus does not say a word. Behind the voice of the Grand Inquisitor, however, echoes the voice of Ivan Karamazov. He, too, is speaking to Jesus, telling him how he understands his message.

> "Was it not you who so often said then: 'I want to make you free'? . . . For fifteen hundred years we have been at pains over this freedom, but now it is finished, and well finished. You do not believe that it is well finished? . . . Know, then, that now, precisely now, these people are more certain than ever before that they are completely free, and at the same time they themselves have brought us their freedom and obediently laid it at our feet. It is our doing, but is it what you wanted? This sort of freedom?"[11]

The contested word, situated at the center of the poem and of history, is 'freedom.' The Grand Inquisitor says that Jesus came offering freedom. The Church, too, claims to offer 'freedom.' But the 'freedoms' are not the same. Jesus empowers individual choice, freedom of conscience, and personal responsibility. The Church, as Ivan's poem envisions it, offers humans the freedom not to decide for oneself. In a curious sense, the Church offers to take away from the individual precisely the freedom that Jesus extends to each person. This has been the trouble raging across the centuries. The Church found Jesus's idea to be utopian. When the Grand Inquisitor says that "now it is finished, and well finished," he means that the Church is close to putting Jesus's notion of freedom under lock and key for good. In its stead the Church offers to hold human conscience in a blind trust, absolving individuals of the trouble to make agonizing decisions.

The old man will mention Jesus's death on the cross at a later point, but his most important example is the temptation story in the Synoptic Gospels. In that story, as we have seen, Satan comes to Jesus when the latter is weakened after fasting for forty days. Satan asks him to perform a miracle. "If you are the Son of God, command these stones to become loaves of bread" (Matt 4:3). Jesus, however, refuses to be party to the challenge. In biblical terms, Satan insinuates that God is withholding good from human beings to the point of leaving his beloved son on the brink of death. In the thought world of the Grand Inquisitor the plot is simpler but related. Will Jesus authenticate himself by a show of power? Will he agree to Satan's demand for material proof?

We know that the answer will be 'no.' Jesus refuses to prove his identity by turning the stones into bread, in part because he does not seek a conviction based on material proof, and even more because he does not want to lend credence to the premise of Satan's temptation. And so he answers, "It is written, 'One does not live by bread alone, but by every word that comes from the mouth of God'" (Matt 4:4).

11. Ibid., 251.

There is no physical miracle in the temptation story. And yet the Grand Inquisitor and Ivan know that there is a miracle. "And at the same time, if ever a real, thundering miracle was performed on earth, it was on that day, the day of those three temptations."[12] The "real, thundering miracle" is the absence of proof. A person who has the power and the means to produce amazing proof refuses to do so. There is more to the temptation story than Ivan has appreciated in his 'poem,' but his grasp of this point is remarkable.

Will not people rather live by bread than by every word that proceeds from the mouth of God? Must not food come before freedom? Will not people be persuaded by spectacular proof, especially if the proof puts bread on the table? According to the Grand Inquisitor, by refusing to offer proof Jesus has adopted a course that cannot succeed.

> "You objected that man does not live by bread alone, but do you know that in the name of this very earthly bread, the spirit of the earth will rise against you and fight with you and defeat you, and everyone will follow him exclaiming, 'Who can compare to this beast, for he has given us fire from heaven!'"[13]

Dostoevsky knows his Bible. Here he enlivens his metaphors by mixing two images, the image of fire from heaven at Mount Carmel, and the image of bread from heaven in Israel's wilderness experience. It is fire from heaven that people want; its persuasive impact is certain; and there will be fire from heaven (Rev 13:13).

Jesus came with a message of freedom, demonstrating in every encounter that he comes to human beings in the mode of persuasion and not in the mode of coercion. We know that the Gospel of John was Dostoevsky's favorite book in the Bible. No portrait of Jesus in the New Testament is more careful to show him tiptoeing at the boundary of human choice. In John, Jesus will illuminate, convince, and convict, but he will not coerce. For John's Jesus, like Jesus in Ivan's poem, compulsion is a page from the playbook of the enemy.

But freedom thus conceived also means responsibility and personal accountability. While freedom is a precious gift, it comes with a price. Don't you understand, the Inquisitor tells Jesus, that the price is too high for most people? It is unkind to hold humanity to such a high standard. Someone has to relieve mankind of the burden. If he, Jesus, will not do it, the Church will step up to the plate.

> "No, the weak, too, are dear to us. They are depraved and rebels, but in the end it is they who will become obedient. They will marvel at us, and look upon us as gods, because we, standing at their head, have agreed to suffer freedom and to rule over them—so terrible will it become for them in the end to be free!

12. Ibid., 252.

13. Ibid., 252–53.

> But we shall say that we are obedient to you and rule in your name. . . . This deceit will constitute our suffering, for we shall have to lie."[14]

"The aristocratism of Christ's religion disturbs the Grand Inquisitor," says Nicholas Berdyaev, one of the keenest readers of Dostoevsky.[15] To the Grand Inquisitor, Jesus espouses an elitist ethic that seems to lack compassion. Love and freedom are in his mind ideals in conflict: freedom suggests absence of love. Where there is true love, he insists, there will be curtailment of freedom. Suppression of freedom, at least suppression of certain types of freedom, is necessary for the sake of a higher good. Submission, conformity, obedience—rather these things than freedom or, better yet, the Church markets these things to mute the meaning of freedom. The Grand Inquisitor knows that this compromises the values of Jesus, but he is doing it for the good of the people. On the whole, the average person is not suitable material for the freedom Jesus envisions. Jesus has aimed too high. It is all there in the Temptation Story in the gospels, says the Grand Inquisitor.

> "This is what that first question in the wilderness meant, and this is what you rejected in the name of freedom, which you placed above everything. And yet this question contains the great mystery of this world."[16]

What is he saying here? What does 'the first question in the wilderness' mean? How, indeed, can he say that Jesus rejected the temptation 'in the name of *freedom*'? How, too, are we to understand that 'this question contains *the great mystery of the world*'?

Not everything the Grand Inquisitor says is equally lucid, but some things are clear. Human beings are drawn to the material and are susceptible to the indisputable proof. Ivan's earlier reference to "fire from heaven" confirms the persuasive power of the miraculous, but the miraculous carries the risk that the name on the signature line can be forged. What if displays of power lead to mistaken ideas about God, as Elijah discovered after the spectacular triumph on Mount Carmel? What if "fire from heaven" can have another source than God, as in the Book of Revelation (Rev 13:13)? Can displays of power even be a form of coercion, as the Grand Inquisitor hints when he says that Jesus rejected use of miraculous power "*in the name of freedom*"? Freedom of the kind God offers may be lonely and run against the tide, especially when God refuses to make power serve as the divine calling card. If freedom is at the heart of the divine ideology, as Ivan's poem makes it out to be, the Grand Inquisitor represents a religion that seeks to curtail freedom and relieve people of the responsibility that goes with it.

And what of the Grand Inquisitor's contention that "this question contains *the great mystery of the world*"? Is the contest over freedom at the heart of the cosmic

14. Ibid., 253.

15. Berdyaev, *Dostoevsky*, 192.

16. Dostoevsky, *The Brothers Karamazov*, 253–54.

drama? Are the battle lines drawn over this one value, one side contending that love and freedom are indissolubly linked, while the other pits love against freedom? The Grand Inquisitor finds fault with God for practicing freedom to excess before turning to speak condescendingly about human beings for wanting to get rid of freedom at the first possible opportunity.

> "There is no more ceaseless or tormenting care for man, as long as he remains free, than to find someone to bow down to as soon as possible. But man seeks to bow down before that which is indisputable, so indisputable that all men at once would agree to the universal worship of it."[17]

In Ivan's poem, indisputable proof is inimical to freedom. Proof gives a person no way of retreat. Faced with the incontrovertible proof, the person who is in his or her right mind will have to surrender even if yielding happens against his or her will. Jesus offers evidence but not proof, in part because the indisputable proof can be a form of compulsion. In God's economy, it is possible to say no without seeming to be out of one's mind. Assent must be freely given, and it must be given in response to manifestations that are not coercive.

> "You knew, you could not but know, this essential mystery of human nature, but you rejected the absolute banner, which was offered to you to make all men bow down to you indisputably—the banner of earthly bread; and you rejected it in the name of freedom and heavenly bread. Now see what you did next. And all again in the name of freedom!"[18]

Ivan's poem sees freedom everywhere, the ideology written all over the message of Jesus. The gift that Jesus offers is not only love or life: it is freedom. To the Grand Inquisitor, as noted, freedom is certain proof of absence of love. To Jesus, freedom is love's premise. His message is freedom writ large. "Instead of taking over men's freedom, you increased it still more for them!" the Grand Inquisitor says indignantly.[19] "Instead of taking over men's freedom, you increased it and forever burdened the kingdom of the human soul with its torments."[20]

By now it is clear that the Grand Inquisitor, speaking on the strength of the accumulated wisdom of Christian theology, is no fan of freedom. From the point of view of the Church, conformity is more important than freedom, and freedom is often a menace to the 'truth.' The old man knows exactly where the difference lies. He is a practical man who knows what works and what does not work.

> "There are three powers, only three powers on earth, capable of conquering and holding captive forever the conscience of these feeble rebels, for their own

17. Ibid., 254.
18. Ibid.
19. Ibid.
20. Ibid., 255.

> happiness—*these powers are miracle, mystery, and authority*. You rejected the first, the second, and the third, and gave yourself as an example of that."[21]

The Church's threefold corrective to the sense of Jesus are now on the table. 'Miracle' is the enticer. 'Mystery' could be the doctrine of divine inscrutability in its many versions, although here it probably refers to the Church's power to grant or withhold access to the Eucharist. 'Authority' is the last member of the triad, referring to the determination of the Church to subdue dissent by violent means if necessary.

Having spent most of his time expounding on the meaning of Jesus's triple 'no' in the Temptation Story, the Grand Inquisitor is convinced that Jesus made the same point at the cross.

> "You did not come down from the cross when they shouted to you, mocking and reviling you: 'Come down from the cross and we will believe that it is you.' You did not come down because, again, you did not want to enslave man by a miracle and thirsted for faith that is free, not miraculous. You thirsted for the love that is free, and not for the servile raptures of a slave before a power that has left him permanently terrified."[22]

It would have been impressive, would it not, if Jesus had come down from the cross? It would have removed lingering doubts as to his identity, would it not, if he had loosened himself from the nails and tossed away the crown of thorns? It would have settled matters, would it not, if he had uprooted the cross and hurled it away before everyone's astonished eyes? Celsus, the early critic of the Christian God, would certainly have approved. Might it not, as the Grand Inquisitor suggests, have left people permanently terrified? Metaphorically speaking, such a turn in the story would surely have been equivalent to fire from heaven. But Jesus, we know, did not come down from the cross.

What are we to do with this? After all, the tale about the Grand Inquisitor does not report an event that really happened. And yet his view of God comes close to being the truth at the level of representation even as he abhors it at the level of principle and policy. In this scenario, the tirade of the Grand Inquisitor is morally meaningful, and his dress-down of Jesus has merit because the ideology of freedom has created the chaos that the Grand Inquisitor seeks to remedy. In such a reading, Ivan's poem is ideologically of one piece with his earlier indictment of God and the world God has created, and the poetic idiom is an even more effective formulation of the indictment. In this sense there has been forward movement from indignation to real analysis.

21. Ibid., emphasis added.

22. Ibid., 256.

The Status of Freedom in Christendom

We do not at this point need to fully commit as to whether the Grand Inquisitor's accusation is correct, justified, or sincere with respect to the divine ideology. There can be little doubt, however, that when Ivan makes the Church the foe of freedom, he is not grasping at straws. Already in the writings of Gregory of Nyssa (ca. 334–ca. 394), very early in the Constantinian era, a dimmer view of freedom began to emerge. As a case in point, Gregory casts the tree of knowledge of good and evil in the Garden of Eden in negative terms, disputing its centrality in the Garden as a first step toward stripping the tree of ideological prestige. Quite simply, Gregory will argue, it is impossible to have *two* trees at the center.

> But if another center is set alongside the center, the circle must necessarily be shifted along with its center, with the result that the former center is no longer the midst. Since, then, the Garden in that place is one, why does the text say that each of the trees is to be treated as something separate, and that both of them are at the center, when the account which tells us that the works of God are "very good" teaches that the killer-tree is no part of God's planting?[23]

Gregory subjects the two trees to geometrical arbitration, finding in favor of the tree of life. His need to clarify this matter is intriguing, and the rhetorical about-face is remarkable. Designating the tree of knowledge as 'the killer-tree' stigmatizes it as a negative, with Gregory following through by saying that this tree "is no part of God's planting."[24]

Gregory's nod to the tree of life is prescient. Those who argue on behalf of coercion within his lifetime will claim 'life' as their banner and choose 'life' over 'freedom.' Augustine's exposition of the 'freedom-texts' in the Bible changes in step with the improving political fortune of the Christian community.[25] The trend, says Elizabeth Clark, "made effective in the West the flourishing of a Christian theology whose central concerns were human sinfulness, not human potentiality; divine determination, not human freedom and responsibility; God's mystery, not God's justice."[26] In the days of the Protestant Reformation, the early Luther spoke forcefully about freedom,[27] as we have seen, but he ended up condoning coercion, and he encouraged his contemporaries to practice coercion of the most blood-curdling kind against the Jews.[28] His contemporary Ulrich Zwingli preached free grace in Zürich, but he voted with the city council to drown the Anabaptist Felix Manz for committing the sin of advocating believer's baptism. Manz

23. Gregory of Nyssa, *Hom. in Cant., praef.* 220.

24. Ibid.

25. Augustine's preoccupation with Genesis is legendary and is not limited to his major works on the subject; cf. *The Literal Meaning of Genesis*; *On Genesis*.

26. Clark, *The Origenist Controversy*, 250.

27. Luther, "Temporal Authority," 80–128.

28. ———, "On the Jews and Their Lies," 135–305.

was drowned in the Limmat River on a cold January day in 1527 by being immersed three times in the ice cold water in the name of the Father, the Son, and the Holy Spirit. At the third immersion, he was kept underwater until he expired.[29] We are expected to accept that this decision was made in the name of love even as it is spectacularly evident that it could not have been made under the banner of freedom.

John Calvin taught divine grace in Geneva, but he cast his vote with the city council of Geneva in favor of burning the physician and lay theologian Michael Servetus at the stake for the crime of advocating unorthodox Christology.[30] The historiography of this event is fascinating because Calvin's defenders tend to make the victim responsible for his death. John T. McNeill claims that Servetus was drawn to Geneva by "a fatal fascination . . . like a moth to the candle flame," so as to suggest that Servetus brought the calamity on himself.[31] T. H. L. Parker is even less sympathetic, accusing Servetus of "twenty years of play-acting" and describing his final and fatal visit to Geneva as "an incredibly foolish thing," as if it is the victim's responsibility to avoid a cruel and unjust fate.[32] Sincerity on the part of the victim is all but ruled out in these depictions. The tendency of these writers to smear Servetus as an opportunistic personality is contradicted by the fact that he was willing to die for his convictions, maintaining sufficient composure in the face of the flames to hold firm to his disagreement with the Nicene Creed till the end. Servetus is said to have prayed, "Jesus, Son of the Eternal God, have mercy on me," not "Eternal Son of God."[33]

All of these people, from Augustine to Calvin, condoned coercion, and all of them, like the Grand Inquisitor, did it in the name of love. Just as Gregory of Nyssa sought to de-center the tree of knowledge so as not to allow competition with the tree of life, the leading voices in the Christian tradition made access to the tree of life the all-consuming priority. Augustine, "the first theorist of the Inquisition,"[34] would have decried the methods of the Spanish Inquisition, but he was the first to articulate the redemptive motive that all subsequent inquisitors would put to effective use.[35]

These glimpses prove that Ivan's poem does not misrepresent the historical record of the Christian Church with regard to freedom. Beyond the horizon of the

29. Estep, *The Anabaptist Story*, 43–48.

30. See Bainton, *Hunted Heretic*.

31. McNeill, *History and Character of Calvinism*, 174.

32. Parker, *John Calvin*, 121.

33. Bainton, *Hunted Heretic*, 212. In a letter to Mandell Creighton dated April 5, 1887 (*Essays on Freedom and Power*, 333), Lord Acton wrote that "Calvin was one of the greatest writers, many think him the best religious teacher, in the world. But that affair of Servetus outweighs the nine folios, and settles, by itself, the reputation he deserves. So with the medieval Inquisition and the Popes that founded it and worked it. That is the breaking point, the article of their system by which they stand or fall."

34. Brown, *Augustine of Hippo*, 240.

35. Murphy (*God's Jury*) succeeds admirably in showing the stability of inquisitorial and coercive ideology across the centuries and across religious and secular contexts.

Grand Inquisitor and probably unknown to Dostoevsky, Roger Williams (1603–1683) staked out an ideal that had not been heard in the Old World for more than a thousand years. "An enforced uniformity of religion throughout a nation or civil state, confounds the civil and religious, denies the principle of Christianity and civility, and that Jesus Christ is come in the flesh," Williams wrote in 1644 in answer to people who were no less zealous on behalf of the true faith than Calvin.[36]

Servetus was burned at the stake for holding a heterodox view of the Trinity, a capital crime ever since the days of Justinian in the sixth century. Roger Williams, by contrast, made coercion to be the ultimate negation of the message of the New Testament, the capital crime of the spirit, and the denial "that Jesus Christ is come in the flesh." "Forced worship stinks in God's nostrils," he wrote in a letter to a friend in 1670.[37] The Grand Inquisitor's portrait of Jesus in Ivan's poem comes off the same page, but it is also a Jesus he rejects on the logic that Jesus's commitment to freedom exposes a love deficit that better institutions than Jesus have to remedy.

"We Have Corrected Your Deed"

We can now return to the poem, still at the point where the Grand Inquisitor marvels at the fact that Jesus did not turn stones into bread and did not come down from the cross. In the face of the mystery of the divine action, says the Grand Inquisitor, the Church has countered with a mystery of its own.

> "And if it is a mystery, then we, too, had the right to preach mystery and to teach them that it is not the free choice of the heart that matters, and not love, but the mystery, which they must blindly obey, even setting aside their own conscience. And so we did. We corrected your deed and based it on *miracle*, *mystery*, and *authority*. And mankind rejoiced that they were once more led like sheep, and that at last such a terrible gift, which had brought them so much suffering, had been taken from their hearts. Tell me, were we right in teaching and doing so?"[38]

There is more than one version of the twin doctrines of divine inscrutability and human incapacity that we have looked at earlier, but this is one trenchant version, and the Grand Inquisitor is not shy about it. Does God put before human beings a mystery "which they must *blindly obey*"? If this is the ideal, it must be the ideal of the Church and not the ideal we find in the Bible. "Were we right in teaching and doing so," asks the Grand Inquisitor, knowing full well the answer. "No," the answer must be, "you were not right in teaching and doing so." Try as he might, the Grand Inquisitor's version of divine inscrutability and human finitude struggles to find a receptive audience

36. Williams, *The Bloudy Tenent of Persecution*, 2.

37. Roger Williams to Major John Mason, 336.

38. Dostoevsky, *The Brothers Karamazov*, 257.

in Jesus. He maintains his silence, leaving the answer to the Grand Inquisitor's question at the level of self-evidence. To the Grand Inquisitor the silence is unbearable.

> "Why have you come to interfere with us now? And why are you looking at me so silently and understandingly with your meek eyes? Be angry! I do not want your love, for I do not love you."[39]

The Grand Inquisitor has thought this through carefully. He does not believe in God or in an afterlife any more, and no, he does not love Jesus, but he still claims the mantle of altruism. He, not Jesus, is the one who truly loves humanity because he, not Jesus, is the one who has understood that human beings are not suitable material for freedom.

> "Oh, we shall convince them that they will only become free when they resign their freedom to us, and submit to us. Will we be right, do you think, or will we be lying?"[40]

Remember where we have been, or rather, where Ivan has been. In his earlier outburst at his brother Alyosha, he has torn to shreds the Christian belief, insisting that he wants to return his ticket because neither forgiveness nor retribution nor final harmony nor understanding nor even 'the crucified One,' as commonly understood, hold up in the face of the suffering of children. But what is Ivan saying now? The poem has singled out freedom as the disputed value. The Grand Inquisitor blames freedom for the ills of the human situation, committing himself to the task of curtailing it. Extrapolating to cosmic reality, the importance and meaning for freedom will not be less and will not go away. Ivan's poem has in a remarkable manner found freedom to loom large in the divine ideology and, likewise, to find the Church antagonistic to freedom.

But where does Ivan really stand, now that his grasp of the issue seems clear? Does he side *with* Jesus and freedom, or is his loyalty on the side of the Grand Inquisitor *against* Jesus? There is also a question of context. Is Dostoevsky at this point making Ivan's poem less a critique of coercive tendencies in the Christian tradition and more a prophecy of the totalitarian tenets in the secular revolutionary forces rolling across Europe and Russia in the nineteenth century?[41] That is to say, is Dostoevsky here turning Ivan's poem from a review of the past to a prediction of what the future holds? The plausibility of the latter is enhanced by the Grand Inquisitor's admission that he no longer believes in an afterlife and by the seething revolutionary rhetoric at this point in Ivan's poem.[42]

The conversation between the Grand Inquisitor and Jesus must end before we can start adding things up. It ends strangely.

39. Ibid.

40. Ibid., 258.

41. This possibility is argued plausibly by Wood ("Dostoevsky on Evil," 331–48).

42. Dostoevsky, *The Brothers Karamazov*, 258–59.

> "Know that I am not afraid of you. Know that I, too, was in the wilderness, and I, too, ate locusts and roots; that I, too, blessed freedom, with which you have blessed mankind, and I, too, was preparing to enter the number of your chosen ones, the number of the strong and mighty, with a thirst 'that the number be complete.' But I awoke and did not want to serve madness. I returned and joined the host of those who have *corrected your deed.* I left the proud and returned to the humble, for the happiness of the humble."[43]

Here the Grand Inquisitor admits that he, too, in his youth, was enamored with Jesus and freedom. Like John the Baptist, he was a spiritual superman, eating "locusts and roots." But human reality woke him up. The ethic of John the Baptist as forerunner of Jesus or of Jesus as the Revealer could not be sustained. He "did not want to serve madness," meaning Jesus and his freedom agenda. The deed had to be corrected, and so the Grand Inquisitor gave up on the youthful illusion to join forces with "those who have *corrected your deed.*" He construes his decision in this regard as high-minded, leading him to leave "the strong and the mighty" in favor of the humble.

The corrective on this point is so profound and far-reaching that the Grand Inquisitor says bluntly to Jesus, "We are not with Thee, but with *him*—that is our mystery"[44]—with no need to disclose the identity of *him*. The Church of the Grand Inquisitor became the promoter of the ideology of *him*, specifying coercive power as the decisive point of difference between the divine and the demonic. While this self-declared apostasy at first sight reflects negatively on the Church, we need to keep in mind the altruistic motive. Coercion is not meant to be cruel or vindictive but an expression of love. If, indeed, as the Grand Inquisitor suggests, the Church has taken its stand "with *him*," it is because the Church has found *him* to be more genuinely invested in human well-being than God or Jesus. Here, too, the poem oscillates between coercion in the age of faith and the atheistic totalitarian ideologies that were in a fledgling state in Russia at that time. In either version, however, coercion is made to be the calling card of the demonic.

"We corrected your deed," says the Grand Inquisitor in Ivan's poem. The deed that needed correcting, we now understand, was freedom. To Berdyaev, Dostoevsky's perceptive interpreter, freedom is precisely to decide on a course, good or bad, that will not and must not be overruled from without.

> The fires of the Inquisition were the horrifying evidence of this tragedy of freedom and the difficulty found in its resolution even by a conscience enlightened by the light of Christ. Denial of the first liberty, to believe or not to believe, to accept truth or to reject it, leads inevitably to the doctrine of

43. Ibid., 260.

44. Ibid., 257.

> the predestinarians. That truth attracts to itself without the intervention of freedom is a dangerous illusion.[45]

Berdyaev matches the eloquence of Ivan in his attempt to explain the ideology of Jesus.

> He used no coercion to make us believe in him as in God, he had not the might and majesty of the sovereigns of this world, the kingdom that he preached was not here. Therein lies the radical secret of Jesus Christ, the secret of freedom. It needed an extraordinary freedom of spirit, a prodigy of free faith, a spontaneous recognition of "things not seen" to see God beneath the appearance of a bondsman, and when Simon Peter said to Jesus, "Thou art the Christ, the Son of the living God," he made an act of freedom. These words have echoed through man's consciousness. . . . They hold the whole dignity of Christianity.[46]

Moreover, while Jesus presented freedom as the first principle, he was not "a Professor of Freedom." Rather, Jesus was himself the guarantor of freedom, its foremost champion, and the embodiment of what it means to respect the boundaries of another person's will. "There lies the whole secret of Christianity," says Berdyaev, "and every time in history that man has tried to turn crucified Truth into coercive truth he has betrayed the fundamental principle of Christ."[47]

The Parting Kiss

There is one more surprise, one last enigma in the chapter about the Grand Inquisitor. Alyosha is completely at a loss for words, to say the least. His brother, who trampled all over him and who made it seem that nothing could be said about or for Jesus that would be of any help, has now produced the most amazing account of Jesus. "But . . . that's absurd!" he cried, blushing. "Your poem praises Jesus, it does not revile him . . . as you meant it to do."[48]

Has Ivan praised Jesus without intending to, as Alyosha implies? Has he written his 'poem' as a tribute to Jesus, in rapt admiration? We may not be able to answer this question with respect to Ivan, but we can answer it with regard to Dostoevsky. To Joseph Frank, Dostoevsky's principal biographer in English, there is no doubt that "Alyosha's interpretation may be taken as Dostoevsky's own."[49] That is to say, just as Alyosha has heard the poem as a tribute to Jesus and his ideology, so it is. But even Ivan, who seemed determined to return the ticket, seems to vacillate. If there could be a reason *not* to return the ticket, a framework within which the story of Richard, and the little girl who was forced by her mother to eat her excrements, or of the little

45. Berdyaev, *Dostoevsky*, 70.
46. Ibid., 79.
47. Ibid., 197–98.
48. Dostoevsky, *The Brothers Karamazov*, 260.
49. Frank, *Dostoevsky*, 877.

boy who was required to run naked before the dogs tore him to pieces; if there could be a framework within which these stories might *not* be a reason to 'return the ticket,' could the framework of freedom in Ivan's 'poem' be the answer? Ivan's mastery of the ideology of freedom that he attributes to Jesus is so focused and exceptional that it is hard to believe that he has been unaffected by it.

But the 'poem' has not ended completely. Ivan has one last surprise.

> "I was going to end it like this: when the Inquisitor fell silent, he waited some time for his prisoner to reply. His silence weighed on him. He has seen how the captive listened to him all the while intently and calmly, looking him straight in the eye, and apparently not wishing to contradict anything. The old man would have liked him to say something, even something bitter, terrible. But suddenly he approaches the old man in silence and gently kisses him on his bloodless, ninety-year-old lips. That is the whole answer. The old man shudders. Something stirs at the corners of his mouth; he walks to the door, opens it, and says to him: 'Go and do not come again . . . do not come at all . . . never, never!' And he lets him out into the 'dark squares of the city.' The prisoner goes away."[50]

What is the meaning of the kiss, the only active response from Jesus to the Grand Inquisitor? Is it the kiss of compassion, one last attempt to change the heart of the Grand Inquisitor? Is it the kiss of forgiveness? Kisses of that kind can clearly be imagined. Or is it a kiss like the kiss mentioned in the Passion Story, the kiss of Judas, and thus the kiss of betrayal? (Luke 22:48) Has Jesus, in Ivan Karamazov's story and almost to Ivan's disappointment, become Judas? Does he kiss the Grand Inquisitor on the lips as a token of approval and surrender? Has Jesus, who almost seems to have Ivan persuaded to keep his ticket, betrayed himself? Has freedom lost its most compelling champion?

The latter is a tantalizing possibility, but the answer must be 'no.' Jesus has not given Ivan the kiss of Judas, but has acted toward the Grand Inquisitor and indirectly toward Ivan the way he responded to Judas in the Gospels. Ivan seems to say as much: "the kiss burns in his heart, but the old man adheres to his former idea."[51] In that case Ivan, in the guise of the Grand Inquisitor, is Judas, and Jesus is true to himself. Ultimately, the meaning of the kiss is that Jesus's response to Ivan, thinly disguised as the Grand Inquisitor, will not come in the realm of words. The road to redemption for Ivan does not lie in the path of argument but in yielding to the stirrings that tug at his heart.

Eyeing an opportunity, Alyosha tries to make the poem an occasion for Ivan to break away from his nihilism. But Ivan cannot rise to the occasion even when the occasion is created by the options he has presented in the poem. He responds to Alyosha's invite by disowning the poem, calling it little more than "the muddled poem of a muddled

50. Dostoevsky, *The Brothers Karamazov*, 262.

51. Ibid.

student who never wrote two lines of verse. Why are you taking it so seriously?" he asks self-consciously.[52] Ivan, like the Grand Inquisitor, "adheres to his idea," but he will neither join forces with the Jesuits in order to correct the deed of freedom nor commit to Jesus as a believer in the ideology he has attributed to Jesus in the poem. Rather, in an anticlimactic turn, Ivan's intellectual force is not matched by his moral commitments. His plan, he tells Alyosha, is simply to do his own thing until he crashes.

Alyosha does not defeat his brother in the arena of logic and argument. But he loves him intensely and redemptively. If we are still struggling to figure out what Jesus meant to say when he kissed the Grand Inquisitor on his bloodless lips, Alyosha will offer an embodiment of what he, Alyosha, thinks Jesus had in mind. "Alyosha stood up, went over to him in silence, and gently kissed him on the lips."[53]

Ivan knows that Alyosha's kiss is authentic even though he tries to brush it off. "You stole that from my poem!" he quips dismissively.[54] But he ends up thanking his brother. He knows that he can count on Alyosha not to renounce him despite the stridency of his God-denying ideology and the shallowness of his moral commitments. When Ivan leaves, only the most loving eye is able to see the other person's vulnerability with the eye of compassion the way Alyosha sees his brother. "For some reason he suddenly noticed that his brother Ivan somehow swayed as he walked, and that his right shoulder, seen from behind, appeared lower than his left. He had never noticed it before."[55] This is the stance of a person who appears to have been overrun by his brother's argument, but who sees the vulnerability of the brother despite the furor of his protestations.

Ivan's demise has begun although it is apparent only to Alyosha. Later in the book, Dostoevsky returns to Ivan when the devil makes an appearance to him. Now in a state of 'brain fever,' Ivan is no longer able to distinguish between what is real and what is imaginary, once the hallmark of his analytic genius. He has been the leading voice in two of the fieriest chapters in literature, posing questions and proposing options that continue to resonate in our time. Neither logic nor argument finds Ivan wanting, but he falls under the weight of his detached unconcern for the well-being of others. This is precisely what he led Alyosha and us, the readers, to think was his foremost concern. Ivan, of all people, is found not to have the qualities that he claimed were lacking in God.

In this respect Ivan's demise mirrors the plot in the Bible. Satan, we recall, faults God for curtailing freedom (Gen 3:1; Matt 4:1–3) and yet, as Ivan's poem interprets the Bible, hostility to freedom is the ideological DNA of the demonic.

I close this chapter by asking whether Ivan's poem has interpreted the divine ideology correctly. Does he make too much of freedom in his understanding of God

52. Ibid., 262.

53. Ibid., 263.

54. Ibid.

55. Ibid., 264.

and human reality? Is the Grand Inquisitor on target when he makes freedom the focus of his criticism?

Readers of *The Brothers Karamazov* generally agree that Dostoevsky made Alyosha the counterpoint to Ivan.[56] The author's strategy is less to provide an answer to Ivan than to cast Alyosha as an alternative. Where Ivan speaks dismissively of miracle, mystery, and authority, Alyosha represents religious commitments that defy Ivan's stereotype. As a figure of redemption, Alyosha is compelling.

Dostoevsky, however, gave the most important lines to Ivan. The reception history of *The Brothers Karamazov* proves that these are the chapters that earned the book its reputation. Ivan may be inconsistent, but he gives suffering a representation that resonates even in an age that has to factor the Holocaust into the equation of human horror, and he turns the ideological spotlight to the role of freedom with such intensity that it is impossible to duck the question. In the poem of the Grand Inquisitor, freedom and love are made to be mutually exclusive, a deed said to be in need of correction. At the level of practice, the hand of coercion will therefore be the most loving hand. Seen in this light, the answer to Ivan's poem is not found in the alternative that Alyosha represents, but in the choices framed by the poem. In cosmic and human terms, love is not the counterpoint to freedom. Freedom is rather, as Alyosha hears his brother's poem, the premise and expression of love. Conversely, freedom and coercion are opposite and representative ideological poles, one expressing the divine sense and the other the demonic. René Girard makes explicit what in Dostoevsky is slightly submerged or implicit.

> Christianity expands the range of freedom, which individuals and communities make use of as they please, sometimes in a good way, but often in a bad way. A bad use of freedom contradicts, of course, what Jesus intended for humanity. But if God did not respect the freedom of human beings, if he imposed his will on them by force or even by his prestige, which would mean by mimetic contagion [God imitating Satan], then he would not be different from Satan.[57]

When the Grand Inquisitor tells Jesus that he knowingly made a choice not to be with Jesus "but with *him*" over the question of freedom, the secret is out.[58] Even if we allow for Dostoevsky's ambiguity, we owe a debt to him and to Ivan's poem for bringing out more clearly the sense of Jesus.

56. Woods, "Dostoevsky on Evil," 344–48.

57. René Girard, *I See Satan Fall Like Lightning*, 185.

58. Dostoevsky, *The Brothers Karamazov*, 257.

Chapter Nineteen

Common Sense—and Sense Uncommon

On July 8, 1635, Roger Williams was put on trial before the General Court in Boston, Massachusetts, "for diverse dangerous opinions."[1] The first of his two most incriminating views was his insistence that the British monarch had no right to take land belonging to the Indians and distribute it to immigrants without compensation to the owners. For this conviction Williams was merely applying in America a view that had matured in British common law. The second charge was his belief that the state should not interfere in matters of conscience. This conviction was profoundly theological, and it struck his opponents as a dangerous novelty.

Both issues agitated the New World community greatly. Under the influence of the Puritan preacher John Cotton sentiments in Boston ran lopsidedly against Williams. In October, the General Court voted to banish him from their jurisdiction. The verdict was to be put into effect within six weeks. Williams was ill at the time, but friends prevailed upon the magistrates to let him stay in his home until spring. When the Bostonians suspected that he was in violation of the terms of his sentence by allowing people to assemble at his house, however, a contingent was dispatched to arrest him. By then it was January, and New England was in the grip of winter. Williams escaped three days before the band arrived. In the fierce winter cold he found refuge among the Indians, whose trust and friendship he had won from the very beginning of his move to New England.

But the memory of his expulsion would not be easily erased. John Barry writes that people "who had been his fellows, his colleagues, his friends had cast him out. For the rest of his life he could never comprehend their stolid coldness."[2] In *The Bloudy Tenent of Persecution for Cause of Conscience*, published in London less than ten years later, Williams faults John Cotton and his supporters as much for their inhumanity as for their beliefs.

> I desire it may be seriously reviewed by himself and them, and all men, whether the Lord Jesus be well pleased that one, beloved in him, should, for no other cause than shall presently appear, be denied the common air to breathe in, and

1. Barry, *Roger Williams*, 196.
2. Ibid., 214.

> a civil cohabitation upon the same common earth; yea, and also without mercy and compassion, be exposed to winter miseries in a howling wilderness?[3]

Williams files his objection chiefly in the court of common sense. He counts on self-evidence to make the case, confident that there is common ground between common sense and the Bible. The coldness that is evident on the part of believers in New England fails the test of common-sense morality and common-sense interpretation of the Bible. With respect to the latter, however, the harm done to him was presented as a necessity claiming biblical support. Williams, we should note, does not fault his antagonists in Massachusetts only for misdirected coldness, but for the arguments they make in defense of their stance. As noted in the previous chapter, he indicts their reading of the Bible lock, stock, and barrel, writing that "an enforced uniformity of religion throughout a nation or civil state, confounds the civil and religious, denies the principles of Christianity and civility, and that Jesus Christ is come in the flesh" (cf. 1 John 4:2–3).[4]

According to this standard, doctrinal error is a less serious concern than the adoption of wrong methods in the promotion of certain beliefs. Specifically, Williams proscribes coercion as if to say that use of force in defense of the faith is in itself a denial of *Christian* faith, indeed, a denial "that Jesus Christ is come in the flesh." John Barry's depiction of Williams as the most important birth father of what he calls "the American soul" is to the point, but it does not follow that America rolled out the red carpet to Williams and his ideas in his lifetime or subsequently. On page after tedious page in the *Bloody Tenents* and its sequel, *The Bloody Tenents yet More Bloody*,[5] Williams denies ideological cover to the coldness shown by the New England Christians. Where in the Gospel account of the life of Jesus is there evidence of coldness, whether toward friends or enemies? In the Sermon on the Mount, Jesus tells his audience to love "your enemies and pray for those who persecute you" on the logic that God "makes his sun rise on the evil and on the good, and sends rain on the righteous and on the unrighteous" (Matt 5:44–45). Can such texts give warrant for banishing a person from the community simply because he holds disagreeable opinions? The hero in Jesus's most famous story, the Parable of the Good Samaritan, is a person who shows intuitive pity toward a fellow human being when the priest and the Levite fail to rise to the occasion (Luke 10:29–37). Compassion is unshackled from belief structures so as to give it standing all by itself. Moreover, the story counts on common sense to demolish whatever justification the priest and the Levite may have had for not rushing to the aid of the wounded man. A Samaritan who is loathsome for his beliefs becomes the role model to those who see themselves theologically orthodox and seek to put

3. Williams, *The Bloudy Tenent of Persecution*, 370.

4. Ibid., 2.

5. Williams, *The Bloody Tenent yet More Bloody*.

Jesus in his place (Luke 10:36–37). How can Christians justify coldness with such a story in their arsenal?

Williams's manifesto repudiates the ideology of the New England Christians, the tradition that has nourished it, and the coldness to which it leads. In his reading, Christianity and civility are not in conflict. Even if notions of civility rest on common sense alone, it is sufficient to certify the rightness of his course of action and the wrongness of theirs. "The doctrine of persecution for cause of conscience is proved guilty of all the blood of the souls crying for vengeance under the altar," he writes, his own experience included in the indictment (see Rev 6:9–11).[6] Addressing John Cotton's campaign to secure his banishment, Williams invokes another image from the Book of Revelation. "But if by banishing myself he intend the act of civil banishment from their common earth and air, I then observe with grief the language of the dragon in a lamb's lip" (cf. Rev 13:11).[7] Here, the "lamb's lip" suggests a demonic doctrine laying claim to being Christian. In the realm of human relations coldness toward another person catches evil close to its source. In the biblical narrative it is the crime of Cain (Gen 4:9).

Seeds of Coldness

Consider now a statement that would have cheered those who voted to banish Roger Williams, a statement that for more than a thousand years would assuage the conscience of inquisitors and steel the resolve of executioners.

> The mass of men keep their heart in their eyes, not in their heart. If blood comes spurting out of the flesh of a mortal man, anyone who sees it is disgusted; but if souls lopped off from the peace of Christ die in this sacrilege of schism or heresy . . .a death that is more terrifying and more tragic, indeed, I say plainly, a more true death than any other—it is laughed at, out of force of habit.[8]

The author of this statement finds fault with the "mass of men" for having misplaced empathy, laughing when they shouldn't, and failing to grieve when they should. Fearing that humans might be moved to compassion by the sight of suffering, he invokes the notion of the higher good in order to justify the activity he is describing. That activity, in a detail we cannot afford to miss, is coercion. On the sincerely-held logic that a person who persists in an erroneous belief will forfeit eternal life, the author attempts to win acceptance for the use of coercive means, whatever they may be. Inclinations toward pity must be overcome. "Some little severity of discipline," he writes a few years later, hardly more than "medicinal inconvenience," must be accepted as a legitimate Christian remedy toward dissidents who are not brought into line by persuasion.

6. Williams, *The Bloudy Tenent of Persecution*, 1.

7. Ibid., 376.

8. Augustine, *Contra Epistulam Parmeniani* I, viii, 15–16, 232.

The absence of red lines in this statement is remarkable. Noting the possibility of "blood . . . spurting out of the flesh," the author puts his stamp of approval on coercive measures that go beyond confiscation of property or banishment. Actual physical torture is not to be left out of the repository of therapeutic remedies. Acts of torture are allowed to escalate until the objective is achieved. The torturer, in turn, is invested with the prestige of belonging to the healing profession.

These sentiments from the pen of Augustine in the late fourth and early fifth century have not received the attention they deserve. The statement quoted above preceded by some ten years a more elaborate defense of the duty to salvage unity of belief even if it can only be done by inflicting physical harm on recalcitrant dissidents. Augustine's more complete statement is confident in tone, broad in reasoning, and salted with arresting phrases that give proof of his mastery of persuasion. Once he has identified who is good and who is bad from his point of view, the good occupies the high ground even when they use the same means as the bad: the bad are persecutors while the good administer discipline; the former are cruel while the latter show moderation; the former are impelled by lust while the latter act only "under the constraint of love."[9] The argument is a spectacular attempt at co-optation, Augustine claiming the high ground of principle for a policy of coercion.

In a letter written in the year 416 to Boniface, an official in North Africa, Augustine defends the use of coercion at a point when it is already established practice. One of his arguments is the conversion of the apostle Paul, who, in Augustine's view, was at the receiving end of strong-armed measures at God's hand.

> And yet, after calling Peter and the other apostles by His words alone, when He came to summon Paul, who was before called Saul, subsequently the powerful builder of His Church, but originally its cruel persecutor, He not only constrained him with His voice, but even dashed him to the earth with His power; and that He might forcibly bring one who was raging amid the darkness of infidelity to desire the light of the heart, He first struck him with physical blindness of the eyes.[10]

Whether coercion is good or evil depends in Augustine's mind on its purpose. Nebuchadnezzar was wrong when he subjected Daniel and his friends to torture, but Augustine gives him high marks for his subsequent willingness to deploy coercion in the service of Daniel's God (Dan 3:29).[11] He admits that he was originally of the opinion that "we must act only by words, fight only by arguments, and prevail by force of reason, lest we should have those whom we knew as avowed heretics feigning themselves to be Catholics."[12] This reservation, of course, is purely utilitarian and

9. Letter to Vicentius; *Political Writings*, 197.

10. Augustine, *Letter* 185.6.22, 216.

11. Ibid., 199; see also 202–3.

12. Ibid., 203.

not a principled stance toward torture as such. Later, Augustine changed his mind because he came to believe that his fear of insincere conversions was unwarranted. What turned him into a believer in the merits of coercion was neither ideology nor theology. He claims to have been won over by seeing the results.

In the letter to Vicentius from which I am quoting, Augustine turns almost rhapsodic. Dissidents who were formerly at the receiving end of coercion are the ones who, in Augustine's univocal account, speak elatedly for it, all of them lining up to return gratitude. "Thanks be to God," says one, "who has given us occasion for doing it [giving up the erroneous belief] at once, and has cut off the hesitancy of procrastination!" "Thanks be to the Lord," says another, "who has by the stimulus of fear startled us from our negligence!" "Thanks be to the Lord," intones a third, "who by His scourge took away our timid hesitation."[13]

Who can argue against this? Who can contest the use of torture when Augustine has the victims of torture testifying with gratitude in its favor? Who can question the legitimacy of coercion if God is the chief sponsor? "Nay verily," Augustine says at a point when he seems to believe that his reasons approach self-evidence, "let the kings of the earth serve Christ by making laws for Him and for His cause."[14] Lest there be any more hand-wringing over coercion, "let the lions now be turned to break in pieces the bones of the calumniators!"[15]

In the less strident letter to Boniface Augustine argues that the Donatists have no reason for complaint because "they were themselves the first to do what they censure in us."[16] He concedes that it is better to be guided by love than by fear, but "those are certainly more numerous who are corrected by fear."[17] Fear, therefore, cannot be taken off the table except at the risk of great numerical loss. Given that Paul in Augustine's view was forcibly converted, the Church, "in trying to compel the Donatists, is following the example of her Lord."[18] The civil laws mandating the use of torture against the Donatists are expressions of the mercy of God, loving measures for stubborn hearts that cannot be subdued any other way.

Who, again, will want to argue against methods that are said to be approved in the Bible and applauded by those who have been forcibly corrected? If we wonder whether such people existed in real life or whether they were inventions, the answer is most likely that Augustine was not making them up. But this does not remove the possibility that ulterior motives may have played a role in the testimonies he introduces into his argument with great effect. Augustine avoids murky matters like motives. Throughout, he sanitizes the use of torture by beguiling euphemisms, claims dubious

13. Ibid., 205.

14. Ibid., 206–7.

15. Ibid., 207.

16. Letter to Boniface; *Political Writings*, 211.

17. Ibid., 214.

18. Ibid., 218.

biblical support, and adopts a patronizing tone toward his opponents that seems devoid of doubt or self-criticism. Was Paul really forcibly converted on the Damascus road, as Augustine avers? Is the Church following the example of Jesus when it resorts to torture? Were all the victims as rapturous as the voices Augustine enlists?

A policy of coercion was already in place by his time, but the theological justification was not. Augustine's enduring contribution is to provide the missing validation. What matters most in the present context, therefore, is the theology. Otherwise the rhetoric follows a script that by now is familiar. The side administering coercion is above reproach and virtually infallible; the recipient of coercion is misguided and wrong-headed; and the coercive endeavor is delicately couched in medical language. If there is a distinctive in Augustine's argument, it would be that his lineup of grateful testimonials exceeds what generally happens when coercion and torture are used against dissidents.

The mainline Protestant reformers took issue with Roman Catholic belief and practice on many points, but they did not retreat with regard to coercion.[19] Hardly anyone in Christian literature justified coldness for the sake of principle as starkly as did John Calvin in his defense of believers' duty to kill alleged heretics.

> Whoever shall now contend that it is unjust to put heretics and blasphemers to death will knowingly and willingly incur their very guilt. This is not laid down on human authority; it is God who speaks and prescribes a perpetual rule for his Church. It is not in vain that he banishes all those human affections which soften our hearts; that he commands paternal love and all the benevolent feelings between brothers, relations, and friends to cease; in a word, that he almost deprives men of their nature in order that nothing may hinder their holy zeal. Why is so implacable a severity exacted but that we may know that God is defrauded of his honor, unless the piety that is due to him be preferred to all human duties, and that when his glory is to be asserted, humanity must be almost obliterated from our memories?[20]

Calvin's statement is not lacking in sincerity or clarity, but its prescription was running out of momentum in its own time, proving that some of the greatest characters in history were themselves travelers on a journey and not the destination. Augustine in many respects comes across as a more honest witness to the human predicament than his opponents. In the Donatist controversy, he is the better theologian and pastor, less willing than his opponents to stake his case on the purported virtues of monks and priests,[21] and far more kindly disposed toward the Jews than many of

19. Acton ("The Protestant Theory of Persecution," 113–40) describes how the Protestant rationale differed from Roman Catholic theory but the implementation did not. Acton's essay was originally published in 1862.

20. Calvin on the condemnation of Servetus, 462–63.

21. Kaufmann, "Augustine, Evil, and Donatism, 115–26.

his contemporaries.[22] Calvin's view of Michael Servetus and other people deemed to be heretical was no doubt sincerely held, and his desire to honor God should not be doubted. But the wrong method in the service of the right cause can easily turn the good cause into a bad one.[23] "The arc of the moral universe is long but it bends toward justice," a saying generally attributed to Martin Luther King Jr.,[24] needs a similar saying to stand alongside it and given equal standing: *The arc of divine revelation is long, but it bends toward freedom.* That is to say, the arc bends toward freedom and not toward coercion; it bends toward the sovereignty of a person's conscience and not only toward the sovereignty of God, as Calvin imagined it. Indeed, the arc of revelation must in this conception be seen to bend back on itself to the roots of the story, God allowing God's reputation to be slandered without shutting down the slanderer (Gen 3:1–15). And then, as we have seen in a number of chapters in this book, God calls Abraham, Moses, Elijah to walk in the path of discovery, giving them a part in the task of bending the arc in the right direction until the arrival of Jesus. Coercion must be banned when the arc of revelation is allowed to bend to its end, if only to make it evident that when "we resort to force against others, evil attacks us from behind and makes us evil ourselves."[25] On this logic, methods matter. If, as in the case of Augustine and Calvin, the policy of coercion does not conform to the arc of revelation, the tenets used to sustain the policy also come under scrutiny.

Christian apologists urged the need to rein in instincts of mercy on the rationale that church unity and theological purity demand it. The eclipse of compassion happened so early and with such apparent lack of awareness that we may wonder whether the people who led the way felt the tenor of their own sentiments. The hardening stance is evident already in the writings of the apologist Tertullian (c. 160–225).

> However there are other spectacles—that last eternal Day of Judgment, ignored by nations, derided by them, when the accumulation of the years and all the many things which they produced will be burned in a single fire. What a broad spectacle then appears! How I will be lost in admiration! How I will laugh! How I will rejoice! I will be full of exaltation then as I see so many great kings who by public report were accepted into heaven groaning in the deepest darkness with Jove himself and alongside those very men who testified on their behalf![26]

22. Fredriksen, "Augustine and Israel," 119–35.

23. See, for instance, the exchange of views in the correspondence between Creighton and Acton, two of the greatest church historians in the nineteenth century, Lord Acton insisting that coercion is "the breaking point, the article of their [the Reformers] system by which they stand or fall;" cf. *Essays in Freedom and Power*, 328–29.

24. Closing words of the Baccalaureate Sermon delivered by Dr. Martin Luther King Jr. at Wesleyan University, Middletown, CT, in June, 1964. The original source for the saying may have been Theodore Parker in a series of sermons published in 1853.

25. Gollwitzer, "Predigt über Offenbarung," 128.

26. Nietzsche, *Genealogy of Morals*, 33.

Christians were not in a position to use coercion at the time of this outburst, but what, nevertheless, is the gist of Tertullian's sentiment? Is it not coldness in the face of suffering, even outright delight? The spectacle that triggers his glee is the Day of Judgment, when erstwhile oppressors will be called to account. "How I will be lost in admiration! How I will laugh! How I will rejoice!" Tertullian exults.

It bears on the subject that I have taken the statement from Friedrich Nietzsche (1844–1900), from his book *The Genealogy of Morals*, published in 1887. Nietzsche was himself a character not unlike Ivan Karamazov, an outspoken contrarian in the European house of ideas. He quotes Tertullian for proof of his thesis that Christianity is a religion of *resentment*. For this view he is not in want of evidence. At the point when he turns to Tertullian, his rhetoric reeks with scorn.

> Or if we wish to hear a stronger tone, a word from the mouth of a triumphant father of the Church, who warned his disciples against the cruel ecstasies of the public spectacles—but why? Faith offers us much more—says he—something much stronger; thanks to the redemption, joys of quite another kind stand at our disposal; instead of athletes we have our martyrs; we wish for blood, well, we have the blood of Christ—but what then awaits us on the day of his return, of his triumph?[27]

Nietzsche finds in Tertullian a spectacular example of hypocrisy and contradiction. On the one hand, the Christian father wishes to spare his fellow believers the cruelty of the Roman games, but it turns out that his objection to cruelty runs only skin deep when, on the other hand, the prospect of God-ordained torture is the source of his subsequent delight. Tertullian advertises the Day of Judgment as a much better show than the one playing in the Roman Theater, conjuring up images of poets and actors who will give the performance of their lives when God burns them in the flames. Suffering is no longer a problem to him when it happens for a good reason, and there is in his eyes reason enough.

Preceding his reference to Tertullian, Nietzsche features two other Christian voices on the subject, Thomas Aquinas (1225–1274), the greatest moral theologian in the Roman Catholic tradition, and Dante (1265–1321), the foremost writer of the Italian Renaissance.

> For what is the blessedness of that Paradise? Possibly we could quickly surmise it; but it is better that it should be explicitly attested by an authority who in such matters is not to be disparaged, Thomas of Aquinas, the great teacher and saint. "Blissful, in the kingdom of heaven, they will see the sufferings of the damned so that their bliss should be more delightful to them."[28]

27. Ibid.

28. Ibid., 33; Nussbaum translation, 68.

It should not be difficult to imagine Paradise; can it be anything other than freedom from suffering? Nietzsche asks. But if this is the intuition of the lay person, it hits widely off the mark. Correction by expert opinion is needed, Nietzsche says sarcastically. Like Tertullian, Thomas Aquinas holds that the suffering of the damned enhances the joy of the redeemed. Coldness is in this scenario a state of mind in the world to come. Nietzsche hears the same sentiment in Dante, taken from the latter's journey into hell.

> Dante, as it seems to me, made a crass mistake when with awe-inspiring ingenuity he placed that inscription over the gate of his hell, "Me too made eternal love": at any rate the following inscription would have a much better right to stand over the gate of the Christian Paradise and its "eternal blessedness"—"Me too made eternal hate"—granted of course that a truth may rightly stand over the gate to a lie![29]

Which is better theology, Dante's attempt to make hell an expression of the love of God, or Nietzsche's outrage? Nietzsche calls Dante's attempt a case of "awe-inspiring ingenuity," thinking it self-evident that an everlasting hell cannot conceivably have any relation to love. In his view, Dante's eternal hell must be the concoction of eternal hatred, and the prospect of eternal suffering is easily the foremost reason for Nietzsche's belief that Christianity is a religion of resentment. The same sentiment undergirds the view that there "is no possible salvation for the man who feels real compassion."[30]

Nietzsche's intent and rhetoric befuddle readers. Was he really a person who hated Christianity "on account of its enfeebling solicitude for the weak, the outcast, the infirm, and the diseased," as one scholar claims?[31] If he were, the statements above prove that there is more to it than that. What Nietzsche finds at fault in the Christian account in these statements is not solicitude for the weak but cruelty taken to a level that is not imaginable or attainable in this world. The sting of his critique will not be significantly muted even if we make him into a pathetic character[32] or point out that his writings bristle with resentment just where he makes resentment the cardinal sin of Christianity.[33] Perhaps Nietzsche's scorn is less for Christianity than for Christian self-contradiction. If we take seriously his criticism of human suffering in the world to come, his ridicule may not be driven by the fact that the Christian tradition teaches pity, but that it often doesn't.

Nietzsche's mental collapse in Turin in 1889 might thus be illuminating in a symbolic sense. On a January morning that year he witnessed a cabman furiously beating his horse at the cab rank at one of the piazzas in Turin. The spectacle was so revolting

29. Nietzsche, *Genealogy of Morals*, 33.
30. Camus, *The Rebel*, 57.
31. Hart, *Atheist Delusions*, 6.
32. Hollingdale, "The Hero as Outsider," 79–89.
33. Solomon, "Nietzsche *ad hominem*, 180–222.

that the ailing philosopher could not stand it. "With a cry he flung himself across the square and threw his arms about the animal's neck," says R. J. Hollingdale.[34] Historians struggle to make sense of this incident. For our purpose, whatever the meaning of hugging the tormented horse, it does not look like coldness. Nietzsche is by wide agreement alleged to hold pity in low esteem in his writings, but on that occasion, at least, he was unable to resist its summons.

Contrast this to Augustine, who, as we have seen, deployed his eminently sane powers to justify coercion and who resolutely put the prospect of hell before the minds of his readers. In his *magnum opus*, *The City of God*, Augustine argues that the difference between eternal life and eternal death relates only to quality and not to duration of existence.

> For if the soul lives in eternal punishments, by which also those unclean spirits shall be tormented, that is rather eternal death than eternal life. For there is no greater or worse death than when death never dies. But because the soul from its very nature, being created immortal, cannot be without some kind of life, its utmost death is alienation from the life of God in an eternity of punishment.[35]

Humans are in this scenario not given the option not to exist. All will spend eternity in one of two places, heaven or hell. For those who go to hell, bodily pain is made possible when the soul is joined again to the body, as Augustine explains.

> And since this does not happen before the soul is so joined to its body that they cannot be separated at all, it may be matter of wonder how the body can be said to be killed by that death in which it is not forsaken by the soul, but, being animated and rendered sensitive by it, is tormented. For in that penal and everlasting punishment, . . . the soul is justly said to die, because it does not live in connection with God; but how can we say that the body is dead, seeing that it lives by the soul? For it could not otherwise feel the bodily torments which are to follow the resurrection.[36]

Precision and detachment walk hand in hand in this depiction. When the soul and the body are reunited at the resurrection, the human capacity to feel pain is restored. The body will not be able to die again because the immortal soul animates it eternally, keeping it from flaming out in the fire, so to speak. Suffering is eternalized. In the Augustinian tradition, torture without end "falls on unbaptized babies, noble princes and brutal gangsters alike—and its author is the Creator we are bound to revere," says Susan Neiman.[37]

34. Hollingdale, *Nietzsche*, 237. See also, despite the hagiographic tendency, Lesley Chamberlain, *Nietzsche in Turin*, 208–9.

35. Augustine, *City of God*, trans. Marcus Dods, 257.

36. Ibid., 522.

37. Neiman, *Evil in Modern Thought*, 20.

What does this mean? It certainly means that if suffering is the existential problem for which we seek relief, the remedy cannot be the traditional version of Christian theology, as noted at the beginning of this book. Christian theology in this tradition does not teach that suffering will end. Instead, suffering will intensify in the world to come and continue forever. It is also evident that this outlook has influenced practice. Augustine's complaint that "[t]he mass of men keep their heart in their eyes" for being squeamish about suffering is a case in point. His corrective to pity draws inspiration from the prospect of eternal torment, meaning that kindness is the actual reason for coldness. Coercion becomes an act of mercy because it seeks to save a person from "a death that is more terrifying," says Augustine, "a more true death than any other."[38]

Once more, Nietzsche will raise his voice, now in a post-Holocaust rewrite of Nietzsche by Giorgio Agamben.

> Let us imagine repeating the experiment that Nietzsche, under the heading "The Heaviest Weight," proposes in *The Gay Science*. "One day and one night, a demon glides beside a survivor and asks, 'Do you want Auschwitz to return again and again, innumerable times, do you want every instant, every single detail of the camp to repeat itself for eternity, returning eternally in all the same precise sequence in which they took place? Do you want this to happen again, again and again for eternity? This simple reformulation of the experiment suffices to refute it beyond all doubt, excluding the possibility of its even being proposed.[39]

Nietzsche's view in general and Agamben's rewrite of Nietzsche in particular are arguments counting on the power of common sense to wipe the slate clean of ideologies and sentiments that have empowered coldness. In a book asking whether the Holocaust could mark the beginning of a new era, Irving Greenberg has proposed a test by which to determine which doctrines can remain. "Let us offer, then, as a working principle the following: No statement, theological or otherwise, should be made that would not be credible in the presence of the burning children."[40]

What would Augustine teach if he had lived after the Holocaust? Would he be less sanguine about the use of coercion and the coldness necessary for its implementation? Would he be more reluctant to give inquisitors and executioners the dignity of belonging to the healing profession? Would the burning of children at Auschwitz give him second thoughts about the doctrine of eternal torment and the god alleged to orchestrate it? Or would he stand his ground, appealing more tenaciously than ever to the notion of divine inscrutability? When my younger daughter and I some years ago met the bishop of Hippo almost exactly on the spot where Augustine served as church leader sixteen centuries ago, standing with the bishop on a Sunday morning on the

38. Brown, *Augustine of Hippo*, 232.

39. Agamben, *Remnants of Auschwitz*, 99; Neiman, *Evil in Modern Thought*, 264.

40. Greenberg, "Cloud of Smoke, Pillar of Fire," 23.

steps of the cathedral in what is now the city of Annaba in Algeria, the bishop stressed the centrality of love in Augustine's thought. Augustine's mild-mannered apostolic successor could easily have convinced us that his predecessor would have walked back some of the ideas that mar his résumé.[41]

The Third Reich had at its disposal the harvest of the seeds of coldness that had been sown and re-sown centuries earlier. Hitler's cause has no parallel and no ideological antecedent, but the conceptual and rhetorical resources did not need to be invented from scratch. Hitler and his associates approached the 'Jewish Problem' by the logic of what Saul Friedländer calls "redemptive Anti-Semitism,"[42] the task of rescuing the human race from the life-threatening malady of Jewish blood and influence. Hitler was well aware of the history of Jewish-Christian history to the point of telling representatives of the church that he was proposing to do what the church on many occasions had wanted to do but failed to accomplish. For the demonic project to succeed, coldness had to be taken to a new level, all under the umbrella of the redemptive intent. As Hannah Arendt notes, like other people charged with the task of inflicting physical harm on another human being, the instigators of the 'Final Solution' had to "overcome . . . the animal pity with which all normal men are affected in the presence of physical suffering."[43] Nazi leaders and ideologues instilled coldness by "turning these instincts [of pity] around, as it were, in directing them toward the self. So that instead of saying: What horrible things I did to people! the murderers would be able to say: What horrible things I had to watch in pursuance of my duties, how heavily the task weighed upon my shoulders!"[44] While this happened in a cause and on a scale that has no precedent, ideologically-inspired coldness was not a novelty.

"At Auschwitz the devil showed the face that earlier literature merely suspected," writes Susan Neiman.[45] She is right: it was the devil that showed his face. Our glimpse of the devil's face has been helpful to theology for bringing the devil's face to a place where one could see it and for making it possible to see the devil's face where it was previously hidden. Dante's claim that eternal love created hell can in the light of the Holocaust be called for the mislabeling that it is, and doctrines that make suffering a central tenet of God's sense are similarly in need of rethinking and relabeling. The twentieth century did not restore the demonic to the place it has in the New Testament, but the faculties of perception are still convulsing. Dietrich Bonhoeffer (1906–1945), executed by the Nazis shortly before the end of World War II, approaches New

41. In *Augustine and the Jews*, Paula Fredriksen demonstrates that Augustine did not buy into or empower the growing anti-Jewish sentiments among Christians.

42. Friedländer, *The Years of Persecution*, 73–112.

43. Arendt, *Eichmann in Jerusalem*, 106.

44. Ibid. A case in point is Rudolf Höss, the commandant at Auschwitz who admitted to overseeing the murder of at least one and a half million Jews on the logic of carrying out an unpalatable duty; cf. Harding, *Hanns and Rudolf*, 136–37, 255.

45. Neiman, *Evil in Modern Thought*, 280.

Testament ideas in his attempt to achieve descriptive verisimilitude for the reality he witnessed firsthand.

> Instead of the uniform grayness of the rainy day we now have the black storm-cloud and the brilliant lightning-flash. The outlines stand out with exaggerated sharpness. Reality lies itself bare. Shakespeare's characters walk in our midst. . . . They emerge from primeval depths and by their appearance they tear open the infernal or the divine abyss from which they come and enable us to see for a moment into mysteries of which we had never dreamed.[46]

When perceptive thinkers downstream from the Holocaust came to the conclusion that "evil is not only a deficient mode of being, a negative element, but also a real substance and force that is effective in the world,"[47] they are close to reconnecting with biblical notions, sentiments, too, that include the realization that "one cannot fight a satanical force with morality and humanity alone," as Eric Voegelin argued.[48]

Demonic Evil and Human Responsibility

With what means can a satanical force be fought if morality and humanity find themselves overmatched and outmaneuvered on the battlefield of reality? The implied answer, above, is to revive New Testament conceptions that were abandoned because they were thought to be incompatible with an 'enlightened' view of reality.[49] Auschwitz has redrawn the map of reality and redefined the meaning of being enlightened. In the new light, even Kant, the most important writer on ethics since Aristotle,[50] comes up short. He is trumped by Auschwitz because, conceptually, "he could not even conceive of the possibility of the demonic,"[51] and he is complicit in Auschwitz, practically, for his well-nigh unqualified endorsement of the citizen's duty to obey state authority.[52] The evil facing us in Auschwitz, says John Silber, is evil "that far transcends the conceptual limits of Kant's theory."[53]

Marilyn McCord Adams is one contemporary philosopher-theologian who takes an Auschwitz-worthy measure of reality. "For in my effort to make vivid how bad horrors are, I have stressed their disproportion to human agency—how our power to produce them exceeds our capacity to shoulder responsibility for them," she writes.[54] By

46. Bonhoeffer, *Ethics*, 358–59.

47. Voegelin, *Modernity without Restraint*, 24.

48. Ibid.

49. Thus Hick ("An Irenaean Thedodicy," 40), who deems the demonic incompatible with what "educated inhabitants of the modern world" will accept.

50. Silber, "Kant at Auschwitz," 180.

51. Ibid., 194; ———, "The Ethical Significance of Kant's *Religion*," xciv–cxxvii.

52. Silber, "Kant at Auschwitz," 183–94; see also chapter 13.

53. Ibid., 200.

54. Adams, *Horrendous Evils*, 191; see also, ———, "Horrors in theological context," 468–79.

way of the shoe metaphor used earlier, the shoe of evil is in this construct much too large for a mere human foot. But Adams's Auschwitz-worthy perception diminishes from there on to the point of vanishing altogether. She studiously averts her eyes from notions of the demonic, and she reduces human agency to "incompetent incapacity" so as to leave human responsibility in limbo. In her view, the mismatch between human agency and the magnitude of horrors must be made up by God because God is the only one who stands "between created agents and the horrendous consequences of their actions."[55] No remedy is in sight in this life because "incompetent incapacity" in the present can be rectified by "competent capacity" only in the life to come. While the circumstances of human existence are bound to produce horrendous evils, these evils can be overcome only when God one day provides better circumstances.[56] Adams is aware that this takes a toll on responsibility, but she is undaunted. "If this should mean God's causally determining some things to prevent everlasting ruin, I see this as no more an insult to our dignity than a mother's changing a baby's diaper is to the baby."[57]

By disallowing the demonic and by trivializing human agency, Adams diminishes the revisionary impact of Auschwitz. A divine reset in the world to come may not fix the problem of 'incompetent incapacity' as easily as she suggests. Reservations in this regard apply with particular force to the most winsome aspect in Adams's writings, her view of the transforming power of God's identification with horrors. Christ as victim endows horrors with a good aspect, she says, because "divine identification makes the victim's experience of horrors so meaningful that one would not retrospectively wish it away."[58] Horrors are in this way redeemed, washed away in the suffering of Jesus. Adams is not worried about God violating human freedom, staking her hope on a divine rehabilitation project with "new environments and therapeutic exercises."[59]

In a solicited response to Simon Wiesenthal's excruciating account on the limits and possibilities of forgiveness,[60] Abraham Joshua Heschel tells a story about the rabbi of Brisk, probably Rabbi Chaim Soloveitchik from Brest-Litovsk in modern day Belarus. Some time before his death in 1918, the rabbi boarded a train in Warsaw to return to his home town. On the train he ended up in the company of travelling salesmen. They had a jolly time playing cards, but they were increasingly annoyed at the rabbi

55. Adams, "Horrors in theological context," 471.

56. Thus, Adams (Ibid., 473) asserts that "so long as horrors and vulnerability to horrors persist, God's work is not yet done."

57. ———, *Horrendous Evils*, 157. A central tenet in Adams's outlook is the 'size gap' between the divine and the human in general and between divine and human agency in particular. Adams's view of radical transcendence is not unlike that of Job's friends (and Elihu) in the Book of Job. Like them, she appears to conflate finitude and sin.

58. Adams, *Horrendous Evils*, 166–67. Hefling ("Christ and Evils," 872) objects that God's identification with the sufferer in Jesus is "a restatement of the question rather than a 'resource' for answering it."

59. Adams, *Horrendous Evils*, 166–67.

60. Wiesenthal, *The Sunflower*.

for not participating. Finally, one of the salesmen told him either to join their game of cards or to leave the compartment. Moments later, his patience at an end in the face of the rabbi's refusal, he took the rabbi by his collar, pushing him out in the corridor. For the remainder of the long trip on the rickety train, the rabbi had to stand on his feet.

When the train arrived at Brisk, the rabbi was welcomed by a crowd of admirers. "Who is this man?" asked the salesman, surprised. "The famous rabbi of Brisk," he was told. The salesman was taken aback at this, suddenly realizing that he had offended an important person. He hurried to the rabbi to ask forgiveness, but the rabbi declined his request. The salesman, now quite agitated, could not find peace so he sought out the rabbi at his home. Again, the rabbi turned him down. The salesman now went to the synagogue, where he found the members puzzled at the stance of their normally genteel rabbi. They directed him to the rabbi's son in the hope that he might be able to intercede on his behalf. But again, the answer was negative. "I cannot forgive him," the rabbi said to his son. "He did not know who I was. He offended a common man. Let the salesman go to him and ask for forgiveness."[61]

Heschel's story does not place a limit on forgiveness, but it implies that opportunities to redo certain actions are limited. His account is a realistic comment on the difficulty of making up wrongs done to insignificant people. Adams's view of divine action in the future, already carrying a back-breaking load, becomes acutely difficult with regard to the revelation of God in Christ. How does a person accept the revelation of God in Christ when Christ is no longer an insignificant person?

The Holocaust splits open the cosmos to a view of the demonic, but it does not thereby cancel out human responsibility. It was a staple of the Nuremberg trials for the defendants to claim that they were innocent of wrong because they had merely obeyed orders, and equally a staple of the court to reject this line of defense. The problem that came to a head at Auschwitz was coldness toward another human being, says Immanuel Levinas (1906–1995). "For an ethical sensibility—confirming itself, in the inhumanity of our time, against this inhumanity—the justification of the neighbor's pain is certainly the source of all immorality," he writes.[62] This is surely a principled indictment against all attempts to justify torture, Christian and otherwise, written from the vantage point of the twentieth century. Against the backdrop of horrendous evil, Levinas calls on readers to acknowledge "my responsibility for the other person, without concern for reciprocity, in my call to help him gratuitously, in the asymmetry of the relation *one* to the *other*."[63]

Hans Jonas (1903–1993), who was forced to leave the University of Marburg when the Nazi legislative machine turned up the heat, has a more religious view of human reality than Levinas, but his take-home message is the same. "Without a new ethic of responsibility, a new ethic for the future, the very possibility of the continued

61. Heschel in *The Sunflower*, 130–31.

62. Levinas, "Useless Suffering," 163; Bernstein, *Radical Evil*, 172.

63. Levinas; "Useless Suffering," 165; Bernstein, *Radical Evil*, 182.

existence of those others for whom we are responsible is itself threatened," he urges.[64] We have already sampled a thought from Hannah Arendt to the same effect. These Jewish philosophers believed that "one of the most important challenges of Auschwitz—perhaps the most important philosophical challenge—was to rethink the meaning of responsibility," says Richard J. Bernstein.[65]

Sense Uncommon

And then there is Etty Hillesum (1914–1943). She speaks in the writings of Hans Jonas, but she is increasingly heard in her own voice through the diaries that came to light after the war. These intimate disclosures are in some ways influenced by Augustine's *Confessions*, and they are as deserving of attention as the diary of Anne Frank.[66] Etty begins her diary in 1941, her last entry a mere two years later, just weeks before her death at Auschwitz at the young age of twenty-nine. In her life the ethic of responsibility finds embodiment, and it is nurtured by a theology that obliterates coldness. As unspeakable horror unfolds in front of her eyes, she does not retreat into fear, despair, or disillusionment. If part of the content of this chapter belongs under the rubric of common sense, in Etty's writings uncommon sense breaks to the surface.

> *Entry dated July 3, 1942, a Friday evening*:
> I must admit a new insight into my life and find a place for it: what is at stake is our impending destruction and annihilation, we can have no more illusions about that. They are out to destroy us completely, we must accept that and go on from there. Today I was filled with terrible despair, and I shall have to come to terms with that as well. Even if we are consigned to hell, let us go there as gracefully as we can.[67]

One of the secrets behind her transformation, a young woman initially unfocused and confused, is prayer. As the outer life contracts, the inner life expands.

> *Entry on a Sunday morning in 1941*:
> Last night, shortly before going to bed, I suddenly went down on my knees in the middle of this large room, between the steel chairs and the matting. Almost automatically. Forced to the ground by something stronger than myself. Some time ago I said to myself, "I am a kneeler in training." I was still embarrassed by this act, as intimate as gestures of love that cannot be put into words, except by a poet.[68]

64. Jonas, *Imperative of Responsibility*, 127; Bernstein, *Radical Evil*, 194.

65. Ibid., 221.

66. Hillesum, *An Interrupted Life*; ———, *Letters from Westerbork*; see also Woodhouse, *Etty Hillesum*.

67. Hillesum, *A Life Interrupted*, 153.

68. Ibid., 74.

Entry dated May 18, 1942:
The threat grows ever greater, and terror increases from day to day. I draw prayer around me like a dark protective wall, withdraw inside it as one might into a convent cell and then step outside again, calmer and stronger and more collected again. I can imagine times to come when I shall stay on my knees for days on end waiting until the protective walls are strong enough to prevent my going to pieces altogether, my being lost and utterly devastated.[69]

Entry dated July 11, 1942:
What a strange story it really is, my story: the girl who could not kneel. Or its variation: the girl who learned to pray. That is my most intimate gesture, more intimate even than being with a man.[70]

Most remarkably, Etty will not blame God. In her diaries are recorded stirring prayers, a cry for succor to find the strength to help fellow human beings in the name of God; a commitment to help God because God cannot possibly make up for human dereliction of duty and shouldn't; indeed, a plea to help God if only to preserve in oneself a residue of the image of God.

Entry dated Monday morning, probably June 29, 1942:
God is not accountable to us, but we are to Him. I know what may lie in wait for us. . . . The latest news is that all Jews will be transported out of Holland through Drenthe Province and then on to Poland. And the English radio has reported that 700,000 Jews perished last year alone, in Germany and the occupied territories. And even if we stay alive, we shall carry the wounds with us throughout our lives. And yet I don't think life is meaningless. And God is not accountable to us for the senseless harm we cause one another. We are accountable to Him! I have already died a thousand deaths in a thousand concentration camps. I know about everything and am no longer appalled by the latest reports. In one way or another I know it all.[71]

Entry dated July 11, 1942:
And if God does not help me to go on, then I shall have to help God. The surface of the earth is gradually turning into one great prison camp, and soon there will be nobody left outside . . . I don't fool myself about the real state of affairs, and I have even dropped the pretense that I'm out to help others. I shall merely try to help God as best I can, and if I succeed in doing that, then I shall be of use to others as well.[72]

69. Ibid., 133–34.
70. Ibid., 228–29.
71. Ibid., 150.
72. Ibid., 173–74.

> *Sunday morning prayer, July 12, 1942*:
> I shall promise you one thing, God, just one very small thing: I shall never burden my today with cares about my tomorrow, although that takes some practice. Each day is sufficient unto itself. I shall try to help You, God, to stop my strength ebbing away, though I cannot vouch for it in advance. But one thing is becoming increasingly clear to me: that You cannot help us, that we must help You to help ourselves. And that is all we can manage these days and also all that really matters: that we safeguard that little piece of You, God, in ourselves. . . . Alas, there doesn't seem to be much You Yourself can do about our circumstances, about our lives. Neither do I hold You responsible. You cannot help us, but we must help You and defend Your dwelling place inside us to the last.[73]

Extraordinary evil becomes to her a call to extraordinary action; the epic coldness all around her stirs her not to anger but to compassion and warmth. As for the problem of theodicy, it, too, has found a solution because she does not see the atrocities as a reality for which God is accountable. Absent, too, are the formulaic conceptions of Augustine or Calvin with their attendant mandate for coldness, Etty instead sustained by the most edifying sections of Augustine's *Confessions*. Here, indeed, is a person who knows by first-hand experience that one "cannot fight a satanical force with morality and humanity alone."[74]

> *Entry dated July 11, 1942*:
> I shall always be able to stand on my own two feet even when they are planted on the hardest soil of the harshest reality. And my acceptance is not indifference or helplessness. I feel deep moral indignation at a regime that treats human beings in such a way. But events have become too overwhelming and too demonic to be stemmed with personal resentment and bitterness. These responses strike me as being utterly childish and unequal to the fateful course of events.[75]

The last trace of Etty's writings is a card postmarked September 15, 1943, thrown from the train on its way toward Auschwitz one week earlier. "In the end, the departure came without warning," she writes. "On sudden special order from The Hague. We left the camp singing."[76] It is documented that Etty Hillesum was killed by the Nazis at Auschwitz on November 30, 1943. In her glows the antidote to coldness in word and deed, the beauty of uncommon sense. Few, within or without the Bible, have given a more poignant corrective to the question that begins the story of human coldness, "Am I my brother's keeper?" (Gen 4:9).

73. Ibid., 178.
74. Voegelin, *Modernity without Restraint*, 24.
75. Hillesum, *A Life Interrupted*, 176.
76. Hillesum, *Letters from Westerbork*, 360.

Common Sense against Cruel Sense

I want to end this chapter by going back to where it began, to America, this time not to Roger Williams but to Mark Twain and the quintessential American novel, *The Adventures of Huckleberry Finn*.[77] (If we were to read only one American novel, determined to read the most important, this would be it.)

In this book, as though to epitomize the perils and promise of the New World, Huck Finn is on his own. He has run away from his father and later from his adoptive family, and he is complicit in helping Jim, his African-American companion, escape slavery when Jim fears that his owner is about to sell him off to a plantation in the south. But then, in a moment of reflection, Huck Finn is seized by remorse for doing something illegal. He thinks that it might be his duty to return Jim to the owner while wondering how she will treat him and what they will say about him, Huck Finn, who helped Jim escape.

Conscience is eating away at him, primed for action by the sense taught in Sunday school.

> And at last, when it hit me all of a sudden that here was the plain hand of Providence slapping me in the face and letting me know my wickedness was being watched all the time from up there in heaven, whilst I was stealing a poor old woman's nigger that hadn't ever done me no harm, and now was showing me there's One that's always on the lookout, and ain't a-going to allow no such miserable doings to go only just so fur and no further, I most dropped in my tracks I was so scared. Well, I tried the best I could to kinder soften it up somehow for myself by saying I was brung up wicked, and so I warn't so much to blame; but something inside of me kept saying, "There was the Sunday-school, you could a gone to it; and if you'd adone it they'd a learnt you there that people that acts as I'd been acting about that nigger goes to everlasting fire."[78]

In such a bind, what is he to do? Duty seems to dictate that he should return Jim to his owner. What is there to do but pray?

> So I kneeled down. But the words wouldn't come. Why wouldn't they? It warn't no use to try and hide it from Him. Nor from ME, neither. I knowed very well why they wouldn't come. It was because my heart warn't right; it was because I warn't square; it was because I was playing double. I was letting ON to give up sin, but away inside of me I was holding on to the biggest one of all. I was trying to make my mouth SAY I would do the right thing and the clean thing, and go and write to that nigger's owner and tell where he was; but deep down in me I knowed it was a lie, and He knowed it. You can't pray a lie—I found that out.[79]

77. Twain, *Huckleberry Finn*.

78. Twain, *Huckleberry Finn*, 281.

79. Ibid.

The predicament is excruciating. Shall he do what is right, yielding in obedience to convention and authority and to the theology that sustains them, or shall he follow his heart and show compassion for Jim?

> So I was full of trouble, full as I could be; and didn't know what to do. At last I had an idea; and I says, I'll go and write the letter—and then see if I can pray.[80]

This is as practical and pragmatic a test as can be, and the result is salutary.

> Why, it was astonishing, the way I felt as light as a feather right straight off, and my troubles all gone. So I got a piece of paper and a pencil, all glad and excited, and set down and wrote: Miss Watson, your runaway nigger Jim is down here two mile below Pikesville, and Mr. Phelps has got him and he will give him up for the reward if you send.[81]

That should be the end of the predicament. Conscience, now relieved by Huck Finn's decision to do what is right, is at peace. But it isn't the end. In Huck Finn's words,

> I felt good and all washed clean of sin for the first time I had ever felt so in my life, and I knowed I could pray now. But I didn't do it straight off, but laid the paper down and set there thinking—thinking how good it was all this happened so, and how near I come to being lost and going to hell. And went on thinking. And got to thinking over our trip down the river; and I see Jim before me all the time: in the day and in the night-time, sometimes moonlight, sometimes storms, and we a-floating along, talking and singing and laughing. But somehow I couldn't seem to strike no places to harden me against him, but only the other kind. I'd see him standing my watch on top of his'n, 'stead of calling me, so I could go on sleeping; and see him how glad he was when I come back out of the fog; and when I come to him again in the swamp, up there where the feud was; and such-like times; and would always call me honey, and pet me and do everything he could think of for me, and how good he always was; and at last I struck the time I saved him by telling the men we had small-pox aboard, and he was so grateful, and said I was the best friend old Jim ever had in the world, and the ONLY one he's got now; and then I happened to look around and see that paper.[82]

What will Huck Finn do now? On one side, there is convention, legal constraints, and a theology that teaches obedience to authority, disobedience to which puts a person at risk of going to hell. On the other side, there is the slave's enjoyment of freedom, the bond of friendship, and the urging of the heart to resist an ideology that is cruel with regard to content and likewise with respect to method. Formidable forces are aligned to constrain Huck Finn's inclination toward compassion. Conventional sense

80. Ibid.

81. Ibid.

82. Ibid., 281–82.

confronts common sense. We wonder what Mark Twain is up to. Is he about to let Huck Finn go to hell, or will he tell hell and coldness to go there?

> It was a close place. I took it up, and held it in my hand. I was a-trembling, because I'd got to decide, forever, two things, and I knowed it. I studied a minute, sort of holding my breath, and then says to myself: "All right, then, I'll GO to hell"—and tore it up.
>
> It was awful thoughts and awful words, but they was said. And I let them stay said; and never thought no more about reforming. I shoved the whole thing out of my head, and said I would take up wickedness again, which was in my line, being brung up to it, and the other warn't. And for a starter I would go to work and steal Jim out of slavery again; and if I could think up anything worse, I would do that, too; because as long as I was in, and in for good, I might as well go the whole hog.[83]

Huck Finn is on an inner quest for sense, his Good Samaritan intuition of right and wrong unable to yield to custom. So with others we have encountered in this chapter, some sincerely conflicted, some armed with common sense in their battle against coldness in the Christian tradition, and some with the hand of common sense stretched forth to touch the hem of sense uncommon.

83. Ibid., 282.

Chapter Twenty

Divine Transparency—and the Stolen Horse

In the two remaining chapters we shall consider the notion of divine transparency and 'the sense of the ending' in the Bible. Our text is the Book of Revelation, a book described as "a work of immense learning, astonishingly meticulous literary artistry, remarkable creative imagination, radical political critique, and profound theology."[1] This tribute marks a dramatic turnaround in the appraisal of this book,[2] and the compliment is especially noteworthy for perceiving the political message. This message is even more radical than the statement above is able to convey because it includes a vision of heavenly politics that has no peer anywhere. Characters we have met earlier in the Bible re-emerge in Revelation to speak one last time directly or indirectly. If the theo-political vision of Revelation is given its due, it will be evident that God is committed to transparent authority, due process, and accountability, as fully as in God's encounter with Abraham (Chap. 8). In Revelation, "the song of Moses" comes off the same page as "the song of the Lamb" (Rev 15:3) so as to make the singular experience of Moses in the Old Testament and the experience of Jesus in the New Testament testify to the same divine reality. The goalposts of sense that are moved implicitly in the course of Elijah's journey from Mount Carmel to Horeb are moved explicitly in Revelation. Here, with stunning persuasive impact, it is the false side that makes "fire come down from heaven to earth in the sight of all" (13:13).

While Revelation depicts a world replete with suffering and barbarity, going over the same burnt-over ground again and again in sequences of seals, trumpets, and bowls, it never loses sight of the demonic reality that works horror in the world. The determined exposé is carried forward by selective and suggestive allusions to the Old Testament. What begins as a crisis in heaven over God's 'sense' amidst earthly terror, a sense initially so upsetting that it triggers a crisis of confidence in the heavenly council (5:1–4), moves by calibrated increments and sometimes by huge leaps to bring the misperceived sense into view. No book in the Bible is more determined to make sense even though the sense it makes is best understood as a spectacular feat of divine persuasion.

1. Bauckham, *The Climax of Prophecy*, ix.

2. Luther (*Prefaces to the New Testament*, 35:398) virtually denied canonicity to Revelation, claiming that "Christ is neither taught nor known in it."

At the most important transition point in Revelation, John is invited to witness proceedings in the heavenly council first hand.

> After this I looked, and there in heaven a door stood open! And the first voice, which I had heard speaking to me like a trumpet, said, "Come up here, and I will show you what must take place after this." At once I was in the spirit, and there in heaven stood a throne, with one seated on the throne! (4:1–2)

Twice in these two verses the NRSV has supplied an exclamation mark that is not found in the Greek text, but the translators have not meant to embellish the original. If ever an exclamation mark was warranted in the Bible, this must be the place. This text alone, with no need for comment, bears on the question of how God exercises power. What is the open door to heaven but a signifier of access? What is the open door but proof of an authority that is committed to transparency?[3] What is the open door but a signal that the heavenly authority grants what earthly authorities often deny, even authorities that profess commitment to openness and accountability? And what is this text but a stinging rebuke to a theological tradition that claims God's ways to be off limits to scrutiny? What comes to view in this scene is not humans encroaching on forbidden territory, but heaven's policy of candor. For this reason, too, translators are justified to put an exclamation mark.

The opening word of Revelation is *apokalypsis* (1:1), a much misunderstood term that in the popular imagination has come to be associated with doom and catastrophe. Such connotations are far removed from the original meaning of the word. What should come to mind, instead, is a message of disclosure and transparency. *Apokalypsis* describes what the book is up to,[4] conveying the book's character.

Apo-kalypsis means *un*-covering, a removal of the lid in order to bring a hidden item into full view.[5] The word pictures the opposite of concealment and is actually the reversal of concealment. In Revelation, the uncovering happens in the context of conflict. The revealing action aims to expose what the opposing party seeks to hide. *Apokalypsis* confronts *kalypsis*. Uncovering stands against cover-up. In Revelation,

3. See also Rev 1:19, a text announcing complete disclosure. Van Unnik ("A Formula Describing Prophecy," 88) argues that Rev 1:19 refers to "the totality of existence in its three aspects of past, present and future." Likewise, Michaels ("Revelation 1.19," 619) finds in this text the claim that Revelation deals with *reality*. "It is not merely a record of what someone saw, but an account of what *is* or what is *true*."

4. John Collins and others (*Apocalypse*, 9) define an *apocalypse* "as a genre of revelatory literature with a narrative framework, in which a revelation is mediated by an otherworldly being to a human recipient, disclosing a transcendent reality which is both temporal, insofar as it envisages eschatological salvation, and spatial insofar as it involves another, supernatural world." See also Linton, "Reading the Apocalypse as Apocalypse," 9–42. Rowland (*The Open Heaven*, 20) says that the essential character of apocalyptic is "the disclosure of the divine secrets through direct revelation." This view is exemplified in the scene when John finds that "a door stood open in heaven!" (4:1) Koch (*The Rediscovery of Apocalyptic*, 94) says that the destruction of Satan in the final battle is the central idea of apocalyptic. Revelation does not take exception to this claim.

5. The contrasting movements are both in view in Matt 10:26.

the attempted concealment is exposed and reversed. When *apokalypsis* retains the meaning of "showing a thing up for what it is,"[6] as it should, this is precisely what is happening. What we find, then, as announced in the very first word of the book, is the ideology of transparency.

Images of transparency abound in the scene that greets John as he is transported into the heavenly council.

> And the one seated there [on the throne] looks like jasper and carnelian, and around the throne is a rainbow that looks like an emerald. Around the throne are twenty-four thrones, and seated on the thrones are twenty-four elders, dressed in white robes, with golden crowns on their heads. . . . And in front of the throne there is something like a sea of glass, like crystal. Around the throne, and on each side of the throne, are four living creatures, full of eyes in front and behind. . . . And the four living creatures, each of them with six wings, are full of eyes all around and inside (4:3, 4, 6, 8).

While this imagery suggests grandeur and beauty, the rainbow, the precious stones, and the sea of glass, are apt symbols of transparency and not at all, as some interpreters suggest, "a reminder of the separation between God and his creation."[7] Striking, too, is the eye-catching throne in the middle that is flanked by twenty-four thrones (4:4). The number is a lesser concern than what this arrangement suggests with respect to the exercise of authority. If the throne in the middle denotes a seat of authority, what meaning shall we give to the other thrones? The anatomy of the heavenly council suggests participation and power-sharing. Reinforcing this idea, the four living creatures are not located "around the throne, and on each side of the throne," as the NRSV mistakenly says (4:6). Translating the text literally, these strange beings are located "*in the middle of the throne* and around the throne" (4:6b).[8] This arrangement is awkward and well-nigh impossible to visualize, but it emphatically obliterates the distance between God and created beings.[9] These beings, like God, seem to be "in the middle of the throne" and not only around it (4:6b). We are unquestionably in a council where high-level participation is in view. Interpreters who refer to this scene mostly for proof that real authority resides in heaven and not in the Roman emperor miss that the exercise of authority in heaven is conceived along lines that are strikingly at odds with earthly imperial practice.[10]

Do created beings possess abilities that are equal to the trust invested in them? Must not the divine government in the end be a take-it-or-leave-it proposition that cannot be subject to second-guessing, consent, or approval? In John's vision of the

6. Whiteley, "The Threat to Faith," 168 (review).

7. Brighton, *Revelation*, 121. Swete (*The Apocalypse of St. John*, 70) calls it a "vast distance."

8. For further discussion, see Tonstad, *Saving God's Reputation*, 119–21; Aune, *Revelation*, I:297.

9. Blount, *Revelation*, 92.

10. Aune, "The Influence of Roman Imperial Court," 5–26; Reddish, *Revelation*, 92–93.

heavenly council, the eyes are the most conspicuous anatomic feature of the four living creatures. These beings, says John, are "full of eyes in front and behind," and their wings, too, are "full of eyes all around and inside" (4:6, 8). Eyes are a symbol of intelligence, wisdom, and discernment.[11] The profusion of eyes means not only that these attributes are present in abundance; it means that they are the most characteristic feature. The text goes out of its way to emphasize that the four living creatures are *seeing* beings. Created reality is not depicted in a state of incapacity. On the one hand, therefore, we have a God who is committed to transparency. On the other hand, we see creatures endowed with the ability to understand.

In order to participate meaningfully in Revelation's disclosure, the reader must come to terms with the most important prerequisite for understanding this book: It is not sufficient to be a one-time reader. This book extends hospitality only to the *re-reader*, meaning the person who comes back for a second or third reading. We must take seriously J. P. M. Sweet's observation that "the scenes and events . . . are repetitive and jump back and forth in time."[12] Coherence will elude the one-time reader. The seven seals, the seven trumpets, and the seven bowls all seem to tell or recapitulate the same reality from slightly different angles,[13] and yet meanings declare themselves only at the end. Only a re-reader will have awareness of the whole that is necessary for understanding the parts. As noted by H. J. Flowers, "many of the difficulties that scholars have seen in this particular vision would have vanished, if they had once tried to draw the picture which the seer saw."[14]

Scholars have long been aware that the story line in Revelation does not flow from beginning to end, but actually *fans out from the middle of the book*.[15] The importance of paying attention to this compositional distinctive cannot be overstated. Re-reader competency places the reader closer to the vantage point of the writer, who composes his work with awareness of the whole story. Similarly, re-reader expertise makes it easier to follow the lead of an author who waits to tell the beginning of the story until the middle of the book. Even though the war in heaven is described explicitly only at the half-way mark (12:7–12), the reality of the cosmic conflict is assumed from first to last in the book.

11. To Blount (*Revelation*, 93), the profusion of eyes means that these creatures are all-seeing, and their plentiful wings symbolize virtual omnipresence.

12. Sweet, *Revelation*, 58.

13. Bornkamm, "Die Komposition der apokalyptischen Visionen, 132–49. Yarbro Collins (*The Combat Myth*, 13) says that the recapitulation scheme outlined by Bornkamm is actually "far more extensive than Bornkamm's theory shows."

14. Flowers, "The Vision," 526.

15. The central role of Revelation 12 is supported by the position assigned to this chapter in various outlines and by the number of studies devoted to it; cf. Gunkel, *Schöpfung und Chaos*, 172–398; Lohmeyer, "Das zwölfte Kapitel, 285–92; Prigent, *Apocalypse 12*; Gollinger, "Das 'grosse Zeichen,'" 401–16; ———, *Das "grosse Zeichen" von Apocalypse 12*; Collins, *The Combat Myth*, 101–42.

The advantages to the re-reader are reinforced by Revelation's many allusions to the Old Testament. In fact, Revelation reads as a review and summary of the entire Bible.[16] Bauckham says appropriately that John was writing "the climax of prophetic revelation, which gathered up the prophetic meaning of the Old Testament scriptures and disclosed the way in which it was being and was to be fulfilled in the last days."[17] This leads to the strange but necessary conclusion that when a reader of Revelation agrees to become a re-reader, he or she becomes a re-reader of the entire Bible!

Crisis in the Heavenly Council

The heavenly council is not doing business as usual at the session that dominates Revelation's story.

> Then I saw in the right hand of the one seated on the throne a scroll written on the inside and on the back, sealed with seven seals; and I saw a mighty angel proclaiming with a loud voice, "Who has what it takes to open the scroll and break its seals?" And no one in heaven or on earth or under the earth was able to open the scroll or to look into it. And I wept and wept bitterly because no one was found to have what it takes to open the scroll or to look into it (5:1–4, translation mine).

Adela Yarbro Collins says concerning this passage that "[t]he first four verses of chapter 5 imply that the heavenly council is faced with a serious problem."[18] This is very well said. Indeed, the ambience of crisis might be apparent even to the first-time reader (5:3–4). But a problem in heaven? And a *serious* problem? How can this be when heaven is supposed to hold the solution to the problems facing humans on earth? What good can heaven do if heaven turns out to be the source of the problems afflicting earth and not simply the remedy? For us, the late readers of Revelation, many questions will be due at this discovery.

What is the problem represented by the scroll that is written "on the inside and on the back"? What, in the context of a book teeming with symbols, does it mean to 'open' a scroll that is 'sealed'? Why is it so hard to find anyone who has what it takes to open it? What purpose is served by letting us know that "no one in heaven or on earth or under the earth was able to open the scroll or to look into it" (5:3)? Why, and I am imagining this, is everyone staring at the floor when the mighty angel calls for someone to step up to the plate? Why isn't anyone saying something? Paul J. Achtemeier

16. Kermode, *Sense of an Ending*, 6–7.

17. Bauckham, *The Climax of Prophecy*, xi. Farrer (*The Revelation*, 4) calls John's work the result of an exceptionally "intense and systematic meditation on the whole prophetic tradition."

18. Yarbro Collins, *Apocalypse*, 39.

observes that the summons for one who is worthy "is greeted with silence—unaccustomed silence."[19]

These questions will be addressed one by one. I will begin by expressing wholehearted agreement with Adela Yarbro Collins, who, as noted above, says that "the heavenly council is faced with a serious problem."[20] She elaborates that "[i]n the context of the Apocalypse as a whole it is clear that the problem facing the heavenly council is the rebellion of Satan which is paralleled by rebellion on earth."[21]

This viewpoint brings re-reader awareness to bear on the scene in the heavenly council. Up to this point in the story, as noted, Revelation has said little or nothing about the rebellion of Satan. The heavenly war is not described until later in the book (12:7–9; cf. 9:1–11), but there would be no crisis in the heavenly council except for this. A linear reading of Revelation, as though John starts his story where it begins on a temporal axis, can now be seen to fail quite dismally. John's entry into the heavenly council happens at the point where the council is casting about for a solution to the rebellion of Satan. This fact is assumed by the participants in the heavenly council, and must also be assumed by the reader of the book.

It follows from this that the transition into heaven is not meant to give John reprieve from problems on earth, as some outstanding interpreters mistakenly suggest.[22] Rather than placing him in the embrace of "an atmosphere of perfect assurance and peace" and a setting where "an infinite harmony of righteousness and power prevails," as R. H. Charles intimated,[23] quite the opposite view is necessary. John moves from the ashes of earthly strife into the fire of heavenly discord. Heaven, too, is awash in problems! Heaven, and heaven in particular, is at a loss what to do! John's response to the presentation of the scroll confirms as much. "I wept and wept bitterly because no one was found worthy to open the scroll or to look into it," he says (5:4, translation mine). This is not the reaction of a person who has found the solution to the problems facing earth. Rather, it describes the response of a man who has been brought face to face with the cause and the source of the problem—and a cause that makes mockery of solutions! The notion that heaven is a place of perpetual calm misses Revelation's story line badly. Heaven is Ground Zero in this drama, beginning with the being who said in his heart, "I will raise my throne above the stars of God; . . . I will make myself like the Most High" (Isa 14:13–14).

When we take our point of departure in Revelation's depiction of cosmic rebellion (Rev 12:7–9), it will be evident that this theme anchors the story line in the book.

19. Achtemeier, "Revelation 5:1–14," 284.

20. Yarbro Collins, *Apocalypse*, 39.

21. Ibid.

22. Charles, *Revelation*, I:102–3. Rowland (*Open Heaven*, 425) describes the contrast between the earthly and the heavenly reality in more prosaic terms than Charles, but the basic affirmation has the same ring to it.

23. Charles, *Revelation* I, 102–3.

If we take a step back from the story for a moment, we will also see the huge difference between the cosmic combat theme in Revelation and pagan myths of cosmic conflict. In ways that defy comparison, the pagan myths have a plot structure that is simplistic, and they describe a problem that is easily fixed. For instance, scholars argue that *Hêlēl ben Shaḥar*, or 'Lucifer,'[24] the fallen star in the cosmic conflict, corresponds to Phaeton in Greek mythology. They find equivalence between *Hêlēl* and Phaeton, both words meaning "shining."[25] In the Greek myth Phaeton prevails on his father Zeus to let him drive his solar chariot. This turns out to be a bad idea because Phaeton wreaks havoc high and low, being unable to control the powerful solar horses. Order is restored when Zeus strikes him with a thunderbolt.[26]

Other scholars look to Ugaritic mythology for the background of the cosmic conflict theme in Isaiah and Revelation (Isa 14:12–20; Rev 12:7–9), assuming that Lucifer is identical to Athtar, the morning star.[27] Again, little or no attention is paid to the plot in the Ugaritic myth. Athtar is a bland figure who is elevated to the throne by El in Baʿal's absence. Rebellion is not in view, and Athtar does not proclaim "*opposing opinions*," the telltale sign of evil in the biblical account.[28] Athtar steps into Baʿal's role, to be sure, but it quickly turns out that he is unable to fill the seat of the virile Baʿal.[29] The Ugaritic story describes Athtar's inadequacy in graphic terms,

> his feet did not reach the stool
> his head did not reach its top.[30]

This myth does not suggest that Athtar attempts to take Baʿal's throne by stealth or force or that he resists stepping down. The problem is fixed without struggle once the pusillanimity of Athtar is manifest. Despite the identification of Athtar with the morning star, the plot in the Ugaritic myth could hardly differ more from the aspiration and action of Lucifer in the Bible. Not to be ignored is the fact that fitness to govern is in the Ugaritic myths based on proof of sexual virility, an element that is nowhere to be found in the Old Testament stories.[31]

These myths have virtually no relation to the biblical story of cosmic rebellion on the level of plot construct, and even less with respect to plot resolution. There is, however, common ground among the pagan myths, a shared value system that sets up

24. Here, *Hêlēl ben Shaḥar* is written with capital letters because it is best seen as name rather than as a descriptive designation.

25. Grelot ("Isaïe XIV 12–15," 18–48) and Blenkinsopp (*Isaiah 1–39*, 288) favor derivation from the Phaeton myth for the story in Isaiah 14:12–20.

26. Ovid, *Metamorphoses* II, 23–36.

27. Craigie, "Helel, Athtar and Phaeton," 223–25; Clements, *Isaiah 1–39*, 182; Bost, "Le chant sur la chute," 13; Page Jr., *The Myth of Cosmic Rebellion*, 110–205.

28. *Contra Celsum* 6.42.

29. Driver, *Canaanite Myths and Legends*, 21.

30. KTU 1.6 I 59–61, translation by Page, *Cosmic Rebellion*, 66.

31. Pope, *El in the Ugaritic Texts*, 37–39; Page, *Cosmic Rebellion*, 72.

a contrast between these myths and the Bible: their divinities give proof of their credentials in the currency of power. This view fits precisely the view of Celsus in the second century that "*God cannot do less than what it befits God to do, what it is God's nature to do*,"[32] the most important element in pagan scorn for the Christian view of God. A thunderbolt puts the straying Phaeton in his place in the Greek myth. In the Ugaritic myth, it takes even less to ensure Athtar's exit from the too-big throne. The gods in these myths do not have serious problems because there is no challenge that rises to the level of serious, and there is no problem that cannot be solved by force. Zeus's zapping of Phaeton and the runaway solar chariot serves as a case in point. In Revelation, by contrast, the problem confronting the heavenly council is not frivolous, and the rebel is not subdued by force. What, then, is the problem in the cosmic conflict in Revelation? And what is the solution? Why is it taking so long to make things right in the biblical story, recalling that in the pagan myths the problem is fixed in an instant?

Below, in answer to the 'what-is-the-problem' question, I will feature a collage of images from Revelation, each describing traits or activities of the opposing side in the cosmic conflict.

> *Exhibit 1*
> The great dragon was thrown down, that ancient serpent, who is called the *Devil* [*Mudslinger*] and Satan [*Antagonist*], *the deceiver of the whole world*—he was thrown down to the earth, and his angels were thrown down with him (12:9, translation mine).

> *Exhibit 2*
> For the power of the horses *is in their mouths and in their tails; their tails are like serpents, having heads; and with them they inflict harm* (9:19, see also vv. 17–18).

> *Exhibit 3*
> The beast was given *a mouth speaking haughtily and slanderously*, and it was allowed to exercise authority for forty-two months. It *opened its mouth to slander God*, slandering his name and his dwelling, that is, those who dwell in heaven (13:5–6, translation mine).

> *Exhibit 4*
> Then I saw another beast that rose out of the earth; it had two horns like a lamb and *it spoke like a serpent* (13:11, translation mine)

> *Exhibit 5*

32. *Celsus on the True Doctrine*, 100.

The sixth angel poured his bowl on the great river Euphrates, and its water was dried up in order to prepare the way for the kings from the east. And I saw three foul spirits like frogs *coming from the mouth of the dragon, from the mouth of the beast, and from the mouth of the false prophet.* These are demonic spirits, performing signs, who go abroad to the kings of the whole world, to assemble them for battle on the great day of God the Almighty. . . . And they assembled them at the place that in Hebrew is called Harmagedon (16:12–14, 16).

Exhibit 6

He [the angel] seized the dragon, that ancient serpent, who is the Devil and Satan, and bound him for a thousand years, and threw him into the pit, and locked and sealed it over him, *so that he would deceive the nations no more*, until the thousand years were ended. After that he must be let out for a little while. . . . When the thousand years are ended, Satan will be released from his prison and *will come out to deceive the nations* at the four corners of the earth, Gog and Magog, in order to gather them for battle; they are as numerous as the sands of the sea (20:2–3, 7–8).

In these texts featuring the character and activities of the opposing side at various points in the cosmic conflict, the commanding anatomic feature is not hard to discern. John spells it out again and again, almost as if shouting to the reader. Satan, in person or in the guise of surrogate powers,[33] is defined by his *mouth* (9:17–19; 13:5–6; 16:12–14).[34] The verbal activity coming from this mouth is monotonously and notoriously *slanderous* (12:9; 13:5–6, 11; 20:2, 7). When Revelation takes the measure of the mouth and the words coming from it, it finds no better name for it than *Deceiver* (12:9; 16:12–14; 20:2, 7). From its beginning in primordial time in heaven to its conclusion on earth in the eschaton, Satan is portrayed as a hugely successful deceiver. The success of his aspiration is based on posing as something other than what he is and, even more, by misrepresenting God so as to make God seem to be something other than what God is (13:5–6, 11). Toward this malicious end, the mouth is Satan's most prominent anatomic attribute, speech is his chief weapon, and slander his trademark. There is nothing remotely equivalent to this in the pagan myths. On this point, moreover, there is common ground between Revelation and the Gospel of John because "the father of the lie" in John is in Revelation "the deceiver of the whole world" (John 8:44; Rev 12:9; 20:2).

Before we look at the scroll in greater detail, it is evident that the heavenly council is indeed "faced with a serious problem."[35] Revelation has complicated the plot

33. Roloff (*The Revelation of John*, 156) writes that the beast "that rises from the deep is, to a certain extent, the dragon's mirror image."

34. Tonstad, "Appraising the Myth of *Nero Redivivus*, 175–99; see also Schlier, "Vom Antichrist," 117; Roloff, *Revelation*, 157.

35. Yarbro Collins, *The Apocalypse*, 39.

of human reality to the level of its actual complexity before it turns to the task of illuminating and clarifying.

The Sealed Scroll as a Representation of the Problem

In a careful study of heavenly books in Jewish and Christian apocalyptic literature, Leslie Baynes identifies four categories of such books.[36] The first three categories are the *book of life*, containing the names of those who are found worthy; next, the *book of deeds*, containing the record of human deeds; and third, the *book of fates*, the latter of which is rarely found in the Hebrew Scriptures.[37] The scroll that is sealed with seven seals does not fit any of these categories. For this book, Baynes suggests it is best to place it in a separate fourth category, and describe it as the *book of action*.[38] While asserting that "Revelation says absolutely nothing about the alleged written content of the book,"[39] a claim that is contestable, Baynes writes that

> the one thing we do know about its content is that when the Lamb opens each seal, bad things begin to happen: first the arrival of four horsemen who bring slaughter, famine, pestilence, and death (6:1–8), then a vision of martyrdom (6:9–11), and then an earthquake and the dissolution of the heavens "like a scroll rolling itself up" (6:12–16), all eschatological events of momentous portent.[40]

She further holds that the heavenly scroll in Revelation resembles the flying scroll in Zechariah, because the scrolls are written on both sides, and both function to destroy, in Zechariah cutting off those who steal and those who swear falsely (Zech 5:1–4). Thus, Baynes argues, the scroll in Revelation and the flying scroll in Zechariah "effect destruction on the unrighteous."[41] She concludes that the sealed scroll "emerges as a slayer itself, amassing catastrophic destruction as the Lamb opens its seals one by one, emitting slaughter, famine, pestilence, wild animal attack, and the very dissolution of the heavens and the earth."[42]

Who is unleashing these calamities? Baynes's view, shared by a majority of scholars, makes God the acting subject and the reason why "bad things begin to happen." It also suggests that the scroll calls to account people who are morally culpable, effecting "destruction on the unrighteous," even "catastrophic destruction." This representation of Revelation's message is not by any means unique, but it misses the book's errand badly.

36. Baynes, *The Heavenly Book Motif*.

37. Ibid., 7–8, 18; cf. Aune, *Revelation*, I:224.

38. Baynes, *The Heavenly Book Motif*, 8, 18, 150–55.

39. Ibid., 151.

40. Ibid., 152.

41. Ibid., 153.

42. Ibid., 154–55.

If we read Revelation as *apokalypsis*, an *exposé* where *uncovering* confronts *cover-up* and lies and pretense are exposed for what they are, we will reach the exact opposite view. God, acting in the person of the slaughtered Lamb, is the *revealing* agent of the actions that are in view, but the *acting* subject is the opposing side in the cosmic conflict. As Anton Vögtle says, God "is not the only one who is at work in this world—as the Apocalypse makes so abundantly clear."[43]

Two verbal elements recur over and over in Revelation to delineate the logic guiding the exposé. We read over and over in this book: "it *was permitted*" [*edothē*] and "it *must* take place" [*dei*]. With respect to the first of these expressions, God permits the calamities that are happening in the world, but God is not the one inflicting them. Revelation confirms that God allows it, using the verb "it was permitted" [*edothē*] or "it was given" to express divine permission:[44]

> and to the one upon [the red horse] was given [*edothē*] to take peace from the earth (6:4, translation mine)
>
> and was given [*edothē*] to them power over one fourth of the earth to kill by sword (6:8, translation mine).

In both of these examples, one from the second seal and the other from the fourth, we have the verbal action described in the passive voice. The passive voice anonymizes the acting subject, leaving to the reader to infer the agent. If, in the instances noted above, we convert the sentence into the active voice, we can find no stronger role for divine agency than permission. God *permitted* the rider on the red horse "to take peace from the earth" (6:4) and, in the next sentence, God *permitted* them to have "power over one fourth of the earth and to kill by sword" (6:8). Divine permission, however, is not the same as divine agency, and divine permission does not equal divine intent.[45]

This leads to the second verbal element, appreciation for which is crucial to the book's theology. Hand in hand with permission goes the notion of *necessity*.[46] God does not give the evil power permission to commit evil for frivolous reasons. Permission is given only for reasons of necessity. One factor defining the necessity is evident already: a reality that has lies and deceit as its *modus operandi* cannot be seen for what it is except by being allowed to show it. How are we to know the truth about the op-

43. Vögtle,"Der Gott der Apocalypse," 383.

44. The word *edothē* occurs twenty-one times in Revelation (6:2, 4 (x2), 8, 11; 7:2; 8:3; 9:1, 3, 5; 11:1, 2; 13:5 (x2), 7 (x2), 14, 15; 16:8; 19:8; 20:4). It is most often used in a permissive sense, even though scholars often read it as a 'divine passive,' that is, an expression referring to divine action without naming the acting subject; see Black, "Some Greek Words with 'Hebrew' Meanings,", 145–46; Thompson, *The Apocalypse and Semitic Syntax*, 14.

45. Aune, *Revelation 1–5*, 394–95; ———, *Revelation 6–16*, 525–527, 743, 760–761. Aune's comments are helpful but insufficiently attuned to demonic agency.

46. Texts invoking *dei* and the logic of necessity are: Rev 1:1; 4:1; 11:5; 17:10; 20:3; 22:6.

posing side in the cosmic conflict unless Satan is permitted to reveal his true colors? A version of due process is in view. If Satan is guilty of evil, his actions will prove it. And so we read, again and again, that Revelation brings to light

> what *must* [*dei*] soon take place (1:1)
>
> what *must* [*dei*] take place after this (4:1)
>
> what *must* [*dei*] soon take place (22:6)

Revelation never separates permission from necessity. Necessity, in turn, centers on the character of the opposing side in the cosmic conflict. The story in this book begins and ends on the note that something *must* take place (1:1; 22:6). The necessity that is in view concentrates like a laser beam on Satan. There would be no necessity for these things to happen except for the cosmic conflict. In this regard, the biggest challenge to human reason and moral sensibility comes at the end of the book when Revelation describes a course of events that no one would normally assign to the category of necessity. In a sequence of profuse visual imagery and strong action verbs, Satan is "seized," "bound," and "thrown" into the pit, which in turn is "locked and sealed" (20:2). Few readers will raise any objections to having Satan put away. The problem comes when, after the thousand years, Revelation says that Satan "*must be released* for a little while" (20:3).

Why *must* Satan be released? Why does John present this wholly unexpected twist in the story as a matter of *necessity*? The strange ending is a rebuke to interpretations that have paid little attention to Satan as a significant character in Revelation,[47] but it also challenges the imagination of readers who take John's depiction of evil seriously. Even the keenest re-reader of the book might feel the need to run through the story one more time in order to come to grips with the odd ending. Given the likelihood that the ending is intimately linked to the beginning, it is prudent to inquire once more what the problem might be that warrants such an unexpected conclusion. What is the logic or value that makes the release of Satan *a matter of necessity*?

The twin logic of permission and necessity is easier to fathom in connection with earlier portrayals in Revelation.

> And the fifth angel blew his trumpet, and I saw a star that had fallen from heaven to earth, and he was given [*edothē*] the key to the shaft of the bottomless pit; he opened the shaft of the bottomless pit, and from the shaft rose smoke like the smoke of a great furnace, and the sun and the air were darkened with the smoke from the shaft. Then from the smoke came locusts on the earth, and they were given [*edothē*] authority like the authority of scorpions of the earth (9:1–3).

47. Tonstad, *Saving God's Reputation*, 41–54.

If "bad things begin to happen" in connection with the seven seals,[48] worse things happen in the trumpet sequence. The trumpet imagery is charged with bizarre representations that are not found in nature (9:4–10). Here, therefore, the purpose is not only to disclose what is happening, but even more to expose the acting subject behind the horrendous realities. When the angel blows the fifth trumpet, as noted above, John sees "a star that had fallen from heaven to earth" (9:1).[49] The Old Testament background for this allusion is the poem of the fall of the "Shining One" in Isaiah, both texts picturing the fall of a glorious star from heaven to earth, and then from the earth to the abyss (Isa 14:12–20; Rev 9:2–11). The exposé marshals evidence of the same kind we find in the Gospel of John. In John's Gospel, Satan is exposed as a liar and a murderer (John 8:44). In Revelation, the horrors of earthly reality are attributable to the star "who had fallen from heaven to earth" (Rev 9:1). This distinctive figure has the name "Abbadon" in Hebrew, "in Greek he is called Apollyon," and, in English, *Destroyer* (9:11). Permission grounded in necessity opens the floodgates to terrifying events, exposing a perpetrator that thrives on concealment. The cover-up unravels when the perpetrator is exposed as the *Destroyer* (9:11). Two names now attach to Satan in Revelation, *Deceiver* and *Destroyer* (12:9; 20:2, 7; 9:11; 11:18). On this point, again, the message is similar to the Gospel of John because the *Deceiver* in Revelation is identical to the "father of the lie" in John (John 8:44), and the *Destroyer* in Revelation is every bit the murderer that he is found to be in John's Gospel. A simplistic but apt version of the plot in Revelation will sense that it is precisely Satan's success as *Deceiver* that necessitates permission to unmask him as *Destroyer*.

It is now evident that the "bad things" that come to view in Revelation cannot be ascribed to divine agency. Under the fifth seal, martyrs who have been "slaughtered for the word of God and for the testimony they had in their possession"[50] cry out, "How long, holy and true Lord, will it be before you act justly and vindicate us for our blood [shed] by those who dwell on the earth?" (6:9–10, translation mine). Their loud complaint is predicated on the *absence* of divine action. It is not what God is doing that bothers them but the fact that God does not seem to do anything! Indeed, what bothers them is the fact that God is not curtailing the deceit and atrocities of the other side. For this reason—and yet with indebtedness to Baynes' work—I propose a modified view of the sealed scroll. It can still be seen as the *book of action*. As a *book of action*, however, the sealed scroll is primarily a catalogue of *demonic* activity. Moreover, if the book is a depiction of demonic action, the entire scroll magnifies and accentuates the problem of divine *inaction* that is articulated by the slain martyrs, the very problem that precipitates the crisis in the heavenly council. What Revelation rolls

48. Baynes, *The Heavenly Book Motif*, 152.

49. Boring (*Revelation*, 136–37) sees a connection between the "Luminous" in Isa 14:12 and the fallen star in Revelation's trumpet sequence, but treats it mostly as mythological background noise; cf. also Caird, *Revelation*, 114–15; Sweet, *Revelation*, 163; Beale, *Revelation*, 479.

50. For this translation, see Trites, *The New Testament Concept of Witness*, 157.

out under the logic of permission and necessity is deeply troubling to the heavenly council. In the view of the heavenly councilors, we might say, there is no necessity for these realities to take place, and there should be no permission. To them, the scroll is sealed at the level of understanding.

This view takes a path that differs markedly from conventional interpretations, most of which ascribe the calamities in Revelation to divine agency, and to divine agency with a punitive intent.[51] Telling details regarding the scroll, however, do not support the simple view of divine action. This scroll, we have noticed, is "sealed with seven seals" (Rev 5:1). Scrolls are sealed in other instances in the Bible, too, not in the sense of secret content but in the sense of deficient understanding (Isa 29:10, 11, 18; Dan 12:9–10).[52] When such a scroll is 'unsealed,' the benefit does not come primarily at the level of information. Instead, known facts are the cause of perplexity, and 'unsealing' happens at the level of understanding. The person who unseals the scroll makes it intelligible. The essential problem relates not to *what* is seen but to *how* it is seen. This prospect is further enhanced when we keep in mind that the other side in the conflict works by deceit and misrepresentation. Here, the deceiver is unmasked, and the cover-up unravels in open court!

This interpretation gains momentum when the seals are broken. As George B. Caird contends, the process of the breaking of the seals is meaningless unless the accompanying events are related to the contents of the book.[53] The four living creatures, "full of eyes in front and behind" on their bodies and "full of eyes all around and inside" on their wings (4:6,8), seem to know what is written in the scroll, as though they have rehearsed for this moment with eager anticipation.

> I heard one of the four living creatures call out, as with a voice of thunder, "Come!" (6:1)
>
> I heard the second living creature call out, "Come!" (6:3)
>
> I heard the third living creature call out, "Come!" (6:5)
>
> I heard the voice of the fourth living creature call out, "Come!" (6:7)

51. There is astonishing agreement among scholars that the cycles of seven in Revelation describe God's judgments on human disobedience. With respect to the trumpet sequence, Boring (*Revelation*, 134–35) is convinced that "all the plagues come from heaven," are not caused by independent powers, and proceed ultimately "from the sovereign hand of the one God." To Aune (*Revelation 6–16*, 545), the purpose of the trumpet plagues specifically "is not to elicit repentance but to exact punishment." Beale (*Revelation*, 467) writes that "the trumpets must ultimately be understood as punishments that further harden the majority of people."

52. As Stefanovic has shown ("The Sealing of the Scroll in Revelation," 367–68), this understanding of the sealed scroll in Isa 29:10–11 was held by the Qumran sectarians.

53. Caird, *The Revelation of Saint John*, 71.

The choreography is precise, with close coordination between the one who breaks the seals and the commanding voices calling out to the horsemen. Revelatory action by the one who breaks the seals is timed to coincide with revelatory exclamations on the part of the four living creatures. Recalling that these are seeing creatures (6:6, 8), they know what is in the scroll. Only now, on the merits of the one who can break the seals, will it be possible to understand it. In this sense the thunderous "Come! [*erchou*]," hearing it as a loud and four-times repeated imperative, is a call for a reality to reveal itself.[54] Almost in a literal sense, it is time for Satan to show his colors.

Even the first horse, white in color, cannot dispel the impression that these horses are not up to anything good (6:1–2). The horses and their riders come on stage as a group, configured as representations of the same reality. The image of the four horses is taken from Zechariah, and one of Zechariah's horses is white (Zech 1:7–11; 6:1–8). Baynes has shown that white equine imagery was prolific in the world of John for its imperial, heroic, and 'savior god' connotation.[55] To a first century audience, white would be the color of virtue and victory. Domitian, the likely emperor of John's time, was pictured riding on a white horse. Neither the Bible nor Roman imagery contemporary to the author makes the white horse a self-evident symbol of Christ.

What else could be in view if the first horse and its rider do not represent Christ? Louis Vos, comparing Revelation and the Synoptic Apocalypse, answers that the white horse is best seen as a symbol of false Messiahs and false prophecy.[56] To Mathias Rissi, likewise, "the rider on the white horse appears as a part of a group that acts as demonic agents of destruction."[57] This rider is akin to the figure of Gog, the apocalyptic last enemy whose characteristic weapon is the bow (Ezek 39:3, 9). In a similar vein, Allen Kerkeslager takes the white horse to signify deceptive activity on the part of its rider to the point that "the failure of modern interpreters to see the nature of counterfeit in the rider of the white horse displays the success (of, sic) the author's literary device."[58] In another thoughtful study, Pieter G. R. De Villiers concludes that the rider on the white horse "is one of the most important enemies in the book. It tells of a time in which false prophets will be so powerful that they will mislead the world and even the church."[59]

This understanding fits well with the emphasis on false Messiahs and false prophets that dominate Jesus's discourse on the last things in the Synoptic Gospels.

54. As Martyn has shown ("The Apocalyptic Gospel in Galatians," 254), the verb *apokalyphthēnai*, "to be apocalypsed," is virtually synonymous with the verb *erchomai*, "to come on the scene" (Gal 3:23). The imperative form of the latter word is used for all the first four seals in Revelation, indicating a *revealing* action and not merely horsemen riding forth.

55. Baynes, "Horses of Heaven."

56. Vos, *Synoptic Traditions*, 181–92.

57. Rissi, "The Rider on the White Horse," 414–16.

58. Kerkeslager, "Apollo, Greco-Roman Prophecy," 121.

59. De Villiers, "The role of composition," 148.

> *Question by the disciples to Jesus*:
> "Tell us, when will this be, and what will be the sign of your coming and of the end of the age?" (Matt 24:3).
>
> *Answer by Jesus to the disciples*:
> "Beware that no one leads you astray. For many will come in my name, saying, 'I am the Messiah!' and they will lead many astray" (Matt 24:4–5).
>
> And many false prophets will arise and lead many astray (Matt 24:11).
>
> For false messiahs and false prophets will appear and produce great signs and omens, to lead astray, if possible, even the elect. Take note, I have told you beforehand. So, if they say to you, "Look! He is in the wilderness," do not go out. If they say, "Look! He is in the inner rooms," do not believe it (Matt 24:24–26).

There is war, famine, persecution, and cosmic dissolution in the Synoptic Apocalypse, too (Matt 24:6–10), but the most striking feature is the warning against deception. Deceit, even more than destruction, takes priority in the Synoptic exposé of evil. Jesus is, as it were, warning his followers that the opposing side prefers to ride on a white horse and that he is hell-bent on winning followers by posing as someone other than who he is. Is this perspective missing from Revelation 6, otherwise thought to replicate the Synoptic Apocalypse with respect to content and sequence? The 'rider on the white horse' in the Synoptic Apocalypse, in a slightly twisted version of the image, is precisely *not* Jesus. This leads to the strong possibility that in both places someone has stolen his horse!

Concealment and identity-theft are key elements in the strategy of the demonic elsewhere in Revelation. The rider on the white horse strikes the posture of a winner, having a crown on his head and going forth "conquering and to conquer" (6:2). When the dragon goes off to make war with the remnant of the woman's seed in the run-up to the end (12:17), his first move is to put together a duo of winners (13:1–18). The beast from the sea looks like a winner and has victories to show for itself (13:1–10). True to his character, Satan sets out to win by posing as something other than what he is (6:2; 13:7).

To the person who expects new realities to come into view, the disclosures of the book that is sealed with seven seals are anticlimactic. "Then on to the stage of history come only four horsemen representing disasters as old as the human race," says Caird.[60] The reality that comes to view speaks of distressingly familiar scenes of war (6:3–4), famine (6:5–6), death (6:7–8), and persecution (6:9–10). To the question, 'What is new at the breaking of the first four seals?' the answer could be, in qualitative terms, 'Not much.' The novelty, and there is at least one, lies less in the character of the events than in their representation and meaning. The Lamb is in the business of

60. Caird, *Revelation*, 82.

exposing and *explaining*. History, for so long withholding meaning, is now compelled to show its hand. As Michael Wilcock notes, "[w]e do not need Christ to tell us that the world is full of troubles. But we do need his explanation of history if its troubles are not to be meaningless."[61]

This view needs to be qualified by at least two observations in order not to run afoul of Revelation's priorities. While the sealed scroll in important ways portrays a known reality,[62] it is future-oriented, its face turned toward the eschaton. Each of the main cycles climaxes in a revelatory and cataclysmic end, intensified and magnified with each retelling.[63] "The trumpets are worse than the seals, the bowls are worse than the trumpets," as Jan Lambrecht notes.[64] Elisabeth Schüssler Fiorenza describes the pattern as "a cyclic form of repetition with a continuous forward movement,"[65] reading the forward movement to mean that Revelation is "end-oriented rather than cyclic or encyclopedic."[66] Meaning in the present is laid out "with an understanding of the present from the horizon of the future, that is, from the coming of the kingdom of God."[67] Caird may be correct in claiming that the reality that comes to light holds little that is new, but the known reality is not running in place. It has forward movement; it has a pattern; like the four horses it is galloping toward an end.

Even more important, the sealed scroll is itself what the entire Book of Revelation purports to be: an uncovering, a removal of the lid, and a strike against the cover-up that clouds human existence. In the first verse of Revelation, God gave the *apokalypsis* to Jesus Christ, for him to pass it on (1:1). Here, in full view of the heavenly council, God gives the sealed scroll to the only one who is able to open it and explain its content (5:7). In this capacity, referring to the revelatory meaning, the import of the sealed scroll lies more on the level of understanding than on information. For this reason the scroll itself should be considered the *book of revelation*, the *apokalypsis* within the *Apokalypsis*, an enactment and embodiment of Revelation's disclosure. The scroll may also be called the *book of reality*, a succinct representation of the crisis that confronts the heavenly council.

Given that John's allusions to the Old Testament are "meant to recall the Old Testament context,"[68] there is a similar scroll in the Old Testament (Ezek 2:9–10). The setting in the heavenly council in Revelation is reminiscent of Ezekiel's vision of the

61. Wilcock, *I Saw Heaven Opened*, 69.

62. For a discussion of Rev 4:1—8:1 in somewhat greater depth, see Tonstad, *Saving God's Reputation*, 108–55.

63. Without denying some merit to Aune's view (*Revelation 1–5*, xciii), it is surely exaggerated to assert that "no form of the recapitulation theory is valid for the present text of Revelation."

64. Lambrecht, "A Structuration of Revelation 4,1—22,5," 103.

65. Fiorenza, *Revelation: Vision of a Just World*, 33.

66. Ibid.

67. ———, *The Book of Revelation*, 50; Khiok-Khng, "Christ the End of History, 308–34.

68. Bauckham, *Climax of Prophecy*, xi.

throne room (1:4–28), and so is the scroll (2:9–10).[69] In Revelation, the scroll is written "on the inside and on the back" (Rev 5:1). Ezekiel's scroll is described in almost identical terms.

> I looked, and a hand was stretched out to me, and a written scroll was in it. He spread it before me; it had writing on the front and on the back, and written on it were words of lamentation and mourning and woe (Ezek 2:9–10).

Ezekiel's scroll is like the scroll in Revelation; "its front and back were covered with writing,"[70] but its content is no secret. Densely written on both sides, the message is profoundly reflective of human reality, a litany of "lamentation and mourning and woe" (Ezek 2:10). Arthur S. Peake has charmingly said that "the book is so crowded with writing that not only is the inside of it full but the writing had to be continued upon the back."[71] Whatever the meaning of the writing, it is spilling over; it is filling the page; there is hardly room enough for it all.

The scenes that come to light do not immediately reassure that God has everything under control, and that there is no reason to worry. As the crucial fifth seal is broken, the victims of violence say as much.[72] "How long, holy and true Lord, will it be before you act justly and vindicate us for our blood [shed] by those who dwell on the earth?" (6:9–10, translation mine).

How is this cry heard in the heavenly council? Has God failed to act justly? Is there in human experience, especially from the point of view of faith, a discrepancy between expectations and reality? If there is, will not this discrepancy echo at a piercing decibel in the heavenly council? Straight from the scroll that is sealed with seven seals, with the heavenly council in rapt attention, runs the white horse of deception, the red horse of war, the black horse of famine, and the ashen horse of death, only to be followed by the cry of the slain martyrs for redress (6:3–11). Terrors are on the loose in the world. Conditions are going from bad to worse and not from bad to better. What is God doing about it?

Let the rebellion of Satan be the problem facing the heavenly council, as Adela Yarbro Collins wisely suggests,[73] but now mainly in the sense that Satan's rebellion *is less the problem than God's response to the rebellion.* For its considerable merit, her ontological investment in the heavenly world is too stingy to make this connection, fatally compromising the plot at its most critical point.

"How long?" we hear victims scream [*ekraxan*] in a loud voice [*fonē megalē*] (6:10), gathering into itself the many Old Testament voices echoing the same

69. Cf. Aune, *Revelation 1–5*, 339; Beale, *Revelation*, 337.

70. Greenberg, *Ezekiel 1–20*, 60.

71. Peake, *The Revelation of John*, 259.

72. The pivotal function of the fifth seal is widely recognized; cf. Heil, "The Fifth Seal," 220–43; Lambrecht, "The Opening of the Seals," 198–220. Biguzzi ("John on Patmos," 212) says that the cry of the martyrs "is the genetic nucleus of the whole narrative cycle of the scroll" (4:1—8:1).

73. Yarbro Collins, *The Apocalypse*, 39.

sentiment.[74] The echo in Revelation is louder than the original voices (6:9–10), and it is located and expressed at a point that takes possession of the story line in the book. "Moral outrage and perplexity" capture well the sentiments of the slain martyrs and all who have given expression to the same plight.[75] In the heavenly council, there is acute discomfort and embarrassment, not because the fact of injustice is unknown but because it defies comprehension (5:3). Surely God could bring an end to the rebellion of Satan some other way! Surely, if God did bring an end to the rebellion some other way, God would have the support and approval of the slain martyrs and the heavenly council! Beings in heaven seem no less perplexed than human beings on earth (5:3). Surely, in the face of such a reality, there is need for someone who can take the scroll and break the seals! Sense is conspicuous by its absence! Non-sense and anarchy seem to have the upper hand in heaven, on earth, and under the earth (5:3). Surely, as the members of the heavenly council sit in stony-faced silence while John weeps and weeps (5:3, 4), there is need for a Revealer!

74. Pss 6:3; 74:9–10; 79:5; 80:4; 90:13; 94:3–7; Isa 6:11; Jer 4:21; 23:26; 47:5–6; Hab 1:2–4; Zech 1:12; Dan 8:13; 12:6.

75. Andersen, *Habakkuk*, 123, 125.

Chapter Twenty-One

The Sense of the Ending

'It ends well.' Will not this thought suffice, breaking the stalemate in the heavenly council with which we ended the previous chapter (Rev 5:1–6)? Can we not say with Shakespeare, "All's well that ends well"? If it ends well, will not all the existential perplexities of human existence vanish with that one stroke?

As far as visions of happy endings go, Revelation is not easily outdone.

> Then I saw a new heaven and a new earth; for the first heaven and the first earth had passed away, and the sea was no more. . . . And I heard a loud voice from the throne saying, "See, the home of God is among mortals. He will dwell with them; they will be his peoples, and God himself will be with them; he will wipe every tear from their eyes. Death will be no more; mourning and crying and pain will be no more, for the first things have passed away" (Rev 21:1, 3–4).

> Then the angel showed me the river of the water of life, bright as crystal, flowing from the throne of God and of the Lamb through the middle of the street of the city. On either side of the river is the tree of life with its twelve kinds of fruit, producing its fruit each month; and the leaves of the tree are for the healing of the nations. Nothing accursed will be found there any more. But the throne of God and of the Lamb will be in it, and his servants will worship him; they will see his face, and his name will be on their foreheads (22:1–4).

Who needs to ask for more? Many don't, but some do, the leading example of which is the heavenly council in Revelation (5:1–6). To Ivan Karamazov, one of our earthly voices, a happy ending is not enough. In fact, it is precisely the notion of a happy ending that makes present suffering intolerable, compelling his decision to "return the ticket." For reasons of moral integrity we hear him say, "I absolutely renounce all higher harmony. It is not worth one little tear of even that one tormented child who beat her chest with her little fist and prayed to 'dear God' in a stinking outhouse with her unredeemed tears!"[1] Gordon Graham uses different words, but he is similarly con-

1. Dostoevsky, *The Brothers Karamazov*, 244–45.

vinced that a happy ending will not silence questions. Even if a happy ending is in view, "what we want to know is not what God is going to do about these things now that they have happened, but why they were ever permitted in the first place. Accordingly, as a theodicy, the appeal to compensatory bliss fails—and manifestly I should say."[2]

Moreover, the happy endings conveyed in the texts above (21:1–4; cf. 22:1–4) have not by themselves nullified the theological tradition that there will be suffering in the life to come. Despite the allure of these texts, it is precisely Revelation that has served as the ultimate proof that the Christian account does not promise an end to suffering (cf. Rev 14:9–11). Hell could be the sharpest arrow in Ivan Karamazov's scorn and his bottom line for deciding to walk away, "Where is the harmony, if there is hell?"[3] Ivan takes seriously the contention that "Christian theology invincibly confirms this, in that it tells us that the torments of the damned will be eternal and continuous, and as strong at the end of one hundred thousand years as they were the first day."[4] Pierre Bayle's representation of the Christian outlook cannot be made to say that things end well unless we adopt a notion of 'ending well' that includes never-ending suffering. To help us visualize what this could mean, we have Otto Dov Kulka's childhood recollection from Auschwitz, the memory that the earthly Auschwitz was imagined to have a heavenly counterpart complete with selections and crematoria.[5]

Against this background, I have set three goals for the final chapter. First, I will assert that the last book of the Bible unequivocally envisions an end to suffering. Second, Revelation maps a route to evil's demise that highlights the self-destructive character of evil. Third, Revelation does not call itself a book of *revelation* simply for predicting a happy ending. We are left to ponder the idea that the ending and the sense of the ending are not the same.

The End of Suffering

While it is true that the texts quoted above and their vision of a happy ending have not silenced a theological tradition committed to keep notions of eternal suffering alive, they should have. We read of "a new heaven and a new earth" (21:1), a cosmic and comprehensive vision where the emphasis is less on "new" versus "old" and more on "whole" versus "broken."[6] God sends the old order into oblivion but not the earth. The new world is characterized by pointed negations of the most distressing features of the old order.[7]

2. Graham, *Evil & Christian Ethics*, 167.
3. Dostoevsky, *The Brothers Karamazov*, 244–45.
4. Bayle, *Dictionary*, 171.
5. Kulka, *Metropolis of Death*, 20.
6. Thompson (*The Book of Revelation*, 85) translates *kainos* as "renewal."
7. Russell, *"New Heavens and New Earth,"* 208; Rossing, "For the Healing of the World," 170.

they will hunger no more,
  and thirst no more (7:16)

the sea was no more (21:1)[8]

death will be no more;
  mourning and crying and pain will be no more (21:4).

there will be no night (21:25; 22:5)

nothing accursed will be found there any more (22:3).

The earth that has passed away is the broken earth of the present, and the new earth now an earth renewed.[9] 'Newness' and healing are everywhere in the air. The depiction takes as its point of reference the state of creation in Genesis, counting on allusions to the past ("nothing accursed") to convey complete reversal and restoration (Rev 22:3; Gen 3:14, 17). Indeed, there is more than mere reversal because, in the world to come, "there will be no night" (Rev 21:25; 22:5; Gen 1:5, 14, 16), and, to an extent spelled out more fully in Revelation than in Genesis,

the home of God is among mortals.
He will dwell with them;
they will be his peoples,
and God himself will be with them (21:4).

Revelation pictures God relocating from heaven to earth, distance and separation made unthinkable now that God and humans share the same address. If misperception and fear capture best the broken state when things went awry in Genesis (Gen 3:8–10), the contrasting image in Revelation is face to face contact without fear or the need to keep distance: "they will see his face, and his name will be on their foreheads" (Rev 22:4).[10] Light and life and healing flow like a river "from the throne of God and of the Lamb" (22:1), light and life strangely but necessarily blended in "the river of the water of life" that is "bright as crystal" (22:1). The healing that takes place downstream in and along this river harnesses imagery of universal healing in the Old Testament, fruitfulness and plenitude taking hold where there was previously barrenness and want (Rev 22:2; Ezek 47:1–12).[11]

8. Lee (*The New Jerusalem*, 269) points to the relationship between the "sea" and evil powers in Revelation. On this logic, "no more sea" means the vanishing of the evil power.

9. Rossing, "For the Healing of the World," 170.

10. Aune (*Revelation 17–22*, 1179–81) reviews key Old and New Testament perspectives with respect to the meaning of seeing God's face. 'Seeing' God's power and glory is less the point than 'seeing' God's character and understanding God's ways. A Johannine, revelatory perspective is most persuasive. "No one has ever seen God. It is God the only Son, who is close to the Father's heart, who has made him known" (John 1:18). In the context of Revelation, too, Jesus has revealed what God is like to the extent of enabling the seeing of God's face, that is, seeing God fully (Rev 22:4).

11. Fishbane, "The Well of Living Water," 3–16.

I will therefore repeat that the texts describing newness, restoration, and healing in Revelation should be sufficient to silence a tradition committed to keeping alive notions of eternal suffering. These visions of the ending are mutually exclusive spatially, conceptually, psychologically, and theologically; spatially, because newness and restoration lay claim to all the space (Rev 21:1); conceptually, because "no more pain" will not co-exist with suffering except to be defeated by it (21:4); psychologically, because mourning cannot end in the presence of intense and ongoing suffering unless we assume that the redeemed have been psychologically reconstituted so as to be unaffected by the suffering of another human being (21:4); theologically, because Revelation's vision takes God's presence to mean the triumph of life and the end of death and pain (21:1–4; 22:1–4). I press the point a step further with regard to the psychological and theological implications. Psychologically, a scenario of eternal suffering must reckon with Camus's contention that there "is no possible salvation for the man who feels real compassion."[12] In ways words cannot describe, such a scenario also fails Irving Greenberg's minimum demand that no statement be made "that would not be credible in the presence of the burning children."[13]

Theologically, this is the culmination of the theme of alleged divine severity in the Bible, beginning with the serpent's misrepresentation of God in Genesis (Gen 3:1; Rev 12:9; 20:2). Revelation's distinctive contribution to this theme comes in the attention it pays to the mouth of the dragon and the dragon's collaborators (9:9; 13:5–6, 11; 16:12–16). All along, therefore, the activity of the opposite side in the cosmic conflict is best described as misrepresentation and mudslinging (12:9; 20:3, 7). The notion of the 'stolen' white horse in the sequence of the seven seals is part of this constellation (6:1–2), signifying that misrepresentation of God gains a foothold precisely through venues thought to be God's reliable channels. For a predicament of this nature there is no tamper-proof measure in verbal terms. Revelation's disclosures are for this reason addressed to "anyone who has an ear" (2:7, 11, 17, 29; 3:6, 13, 22; 13:9). Like other books in the Bible, this book is in the business of "aural circumcision."[14] Responsibility for getting it right rests on the recipient of the revelation and not only on the source, meaning determined not only by what is said but also by what is heard. The importance of taking the right view on this question cannot be exaggerated, given that the prospect of eternal suffering is the main reason why the theological tradition quite early came to the conclusion that sense is out of reach.

The End of Evil

In Revelation, the demise of evil precedes the visions of healing. In the heavenly council, John discovers common ground between heaven and earth. Deceit, war, scarcity,

12. Camus, *The Rebel*, 57.

13. Greenberg, "Cloud of Smoke," 23.

14. Kermode, *The Genesis of Secrecy*, 3.

death, and injustice defy comprehension there and here, above and below, then and now (Rev 6:1–11). In both realms, intelligent beings wonder why God has allowed evil such a long leash (5:3; 6:9–11), heaven holding an advantage in its knowledge of the opposing side in the conflict. Why, however, even in heaven's view, cannot the carnage be stopped? Why doesn't the end come sooner? Why, in Revelation's telling, does the story go on and on, from seven seals (6:1—8:1) to seven trumpets (8:2—11:19), from seven trumpets to seven bowls (15:1—16:21), and even then the end is deferred?

When the seals are opened in the heavenly council (6:1–11), "bad things begin to happen."[15] In the trumpet sequence, worse things happen, an inferno of misery arising in the wake of the star "that had fallen from heaven to earth" (9:1–11).[16] In the bowl sequence (16:1–21), the terrors reach yet another level of intensity. All three cycles show a demonic power to be at work in the world. This insight is crucial for how Revelation depicts the world, and it is decisive for the transition from the trumpets to the bowl sequence in Revelation. The sixth element in these sequences punctures the notion that the bowls show God inflicting terrors on the world with a punitive intent.

> *Sixth Trumpet*
> Then the sixth angel blew his trumpet, and I heard a voice from the four horns of the golden altar before God, saying to the sixth angel who had the trumpet, "Release the four angels who are bound at the great river Euphrates." So the four angels were released, who had been held ready for the hour, the day, the month, and the year, to kill a third of humankind. The number of the troops of cavalry was two hundred million; I heard their number (9:13–16).

> *Sixth Bowl*
> The sixth angel poured his bowl on the great river Euphrates, and its water was dried up in order to prepare the way for the kings from the east. And I saw three foul spirits like frogs coming from the mouth of the dragon, from the mouth of the beast, and from the mouth of the false prophet. These are demonic spirits, performing signs, who go abroad to the kings of the whole world, to assemble them for battle on the great day of God the Almighty. . . . And they assembled them at the place that in Hebrew is called Harmagedon (16:12–16).

15. Baynes, *The Heavenly Book Motif*, 152.

16. Fourteen times in all, or thirteen times plus one (8:12), the trumpets herald the destruction of a *third* by forces that strike earth and sky on a cosmic scale (8:7–12; 9:15, 18). The profusion of thirds in the trumpet sequence refers to the handiwork of Satan (see especially 8:10 and 9:1; 12:3–4a), putting on the table forensic evidence the equivalent of fingerprints, name, passport, driver's license, and copious amounts of DNA by which to identify the perpetrator.

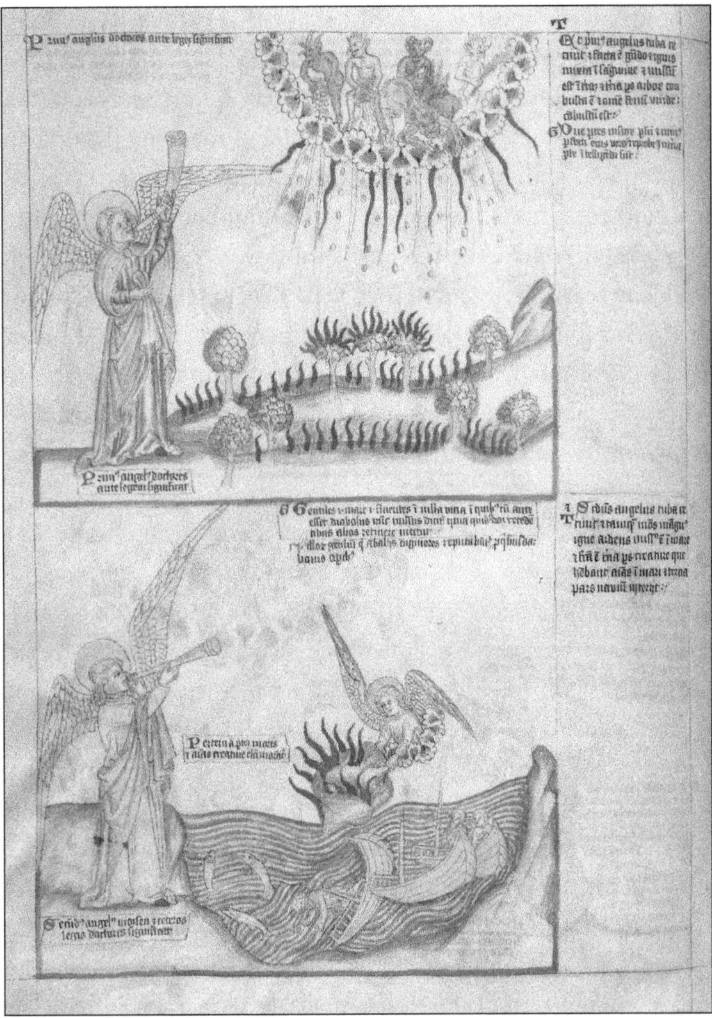

The anonymous artist does for the first trumpet in Revelation what most interpreters fail to see—spot the demonic reality underlying the calamities that are depicted. MS 49, The Apocalypse. Welcome Library, London. Used by permission.

The trumpets and the bowls feature "the great river Euphrates" as the sixth element in the respective sequence (9:14; 16:12).[17] In the trumpet sequence, the forces of destruction mobilize for one last blaze (9:14). The sixth element reverberates with intention, determination, and finality: a process counting down to "the hour, the day, the month, and the year" in the trumpet sequence (9:15) and to "the great day of God the Almighty" in the bowls (16:14). All stops are pulled, suggested by cavalry to the tune of two hundred million horses in the trumpet sequence (9:16), a number wildly exceeding anything that would fit a simple first-century scenario. Revelation spares

17. Tonstad, *Saving God's Reputation*, 108–9; Beale, *Revelation*, 808–10.

no effort to show that the war has a cosmic scope that cannot be contained within a human framework alone. Now, at last, the end is in sight.[18]

In the sixth bowl, Revelation abandons the passive voice so as to make it easier to determine the identity of the acting subject. "*They*," meaning the dragon, the beast, and the false prophet, "gathered them in a place that in Hebrew is called Harmagedon," says John (16:16). This triumvirate is Revelation's counterfeit trinity, marshaling the nations for what appears to be the final showdown. Two of the three members of the triumvirate have earlier presented themselves as imitations of Jesus, one carrying the *stigmata* of Jesus in the form of being slaughtered (13:1–3) and the other posing as a lamb (13:11).[19] Although we are at a very late stage in the story, the demonic side has not given up the ghost. In the plainest English possible, *the sixth bowl describes demonic horror and not divine terror*, as most interpretations of this passage tend to read it.

What does this mean? It means that the bowl sequence, too, carries a *revelatory* message similar to the seven seals and the seven trumpets. *Harmagedon*, the final gathering place in the bowl sequence (16:16), is a strange 'place,' to be sure, but we are not left clueless. Many studies have shown that a strict etymological reading will not solve the riddle. The composite word, *Har magedon*, does not lead to a geographical location because the word was never conceived with an eye to earthly geography. *Har* means that a mountain is in view, but the rest of the word resists translation. Revelation takes the reader to the climax of a process and not to an earthly battle field. Only now and only here, at the figurative mountain called *Har-magedon*, will Satan give a full account of his intent. With help from the beast and the false prophet, the battle promises to be the enactment of the deceiver's purpose from the beginning.[20] Revelation's perception of the ending plays out in the same strange territory Paul describes in his account of the removal of the Restrainer in 2 Thessalonians, restraint removed from 'the lawless one' so as to expose his actual intent (Chap. 17).

18. See *Saving God's Reputation*, 144–46. The concept of the divine 'wrath' working itself out in history comes from Hanson (*The Wrath of the Lamb*, 160–65). This is also the place to put to the test Jacques Ellul's thesis (*Apocalypse: The Book of Revelation*, 65) that it is "the action of these Satanic powers that in every circumstance provokes death in the Apocalypse, and not at all, never directly, the action of God upon men."

19. Tonstad, "Appraising the Myth of *Nero Redivivus*," 175–99.

20. Torrey, "Armageddon," 237–48. Day ("The Origin of Armageddon," 315–26) is not persuaded by the connection to Isaiah, but his own argument for the connection between Rev 16:16 and Zech 12:11 preserves the sense of finality. Oberweis ("Erwägungen zur apokalyptischen Ortsbezeichnung 'Harmagedon,'" 305–24), seeking a referent equal to the billing, argues for the names Nod and Gomorrah spelled backwards and pointing to the demise of Cain, the first murderer and city builder. Jauhiainen ("The OT Background to *Armageddon*, 381–93) pursues an etymological reading based on Hebrew that could refer to "the mountain of gathering troops together," "the marauding mountain," or "the mountain of the cut down," the latter referring to the cutting down of the cosmic rebel in Isa 14:12–13. He finds the third alternative most plausible.

Intent at the Beginning	*Reality at the End*
I will sit in the mount of assembly [*har mō'edh*] . . . I will make myself like the Most High (Isa 14:13)	And they assembled them at the place that in Hebrew is called Harmagedon [*har magedon*] (Rev 16:16).

The seals, trumpets, and bowls represent mind-numbing exposés of demonic activity, but even they do not compass the end of evil. Indeed, the strangest turn is yet to come.

> Then I saw an angel coming down from heaven, holding in his hand the key to the bottomless pit and a great chain. He seized the dragon, that ancient serpent, who is the Devil and Satan, and bound him for a thousand years, and threw him into the pit, and locked and sealed it over him, so that he would deceive the nations no more, until the thousand years were ended. After that he must [*dei*] be let out for a little while (Rev 20:1–3).

At last Satan is captured and contained, says Revelation. Many wonder why he wasn't detained earlier. Still more baffling is the predicted release of Satan at the end of the thousand years, as almost all interpreters admit.[21] Why must Satan be *released*? Why, too, is Satan's release said to be a matter of *necessity*? (20:3, 7)[22]

After the thousand years,

> Satan will be released from his prison and will come out to deceive the nations at the four corners of the earth, Gog and Magog, in order to gather them for battle; they are as numerous as the sands of the sea. They marched up over the breadth of the earth and surrounded the camp of the saints and *the beloved city* (20:8–9).

These texts certainly provide an occasion for trying to "draw the picture which the seer saw," a mere verbal representation unintelligible.[23] We will need to draw the picture in slow motion to get things right with regard to place and time but mostly to get the 'sense' of it. How, precisely, does evil come to an end in this book? And what does Revelation's account of the ending tell us of the kind of person God is?

First, Revelation says that a battle is going to take place in the immediate vicinity of *the beloved city* (20:9). We need re-reader mastery in order to draw this feature in the picture. John does not describe the descent of the New Jerusalem, *the beloved city*, until the very end (20:7–10; 21:1–2).

21. For a survey of interpretations and proposed solutions on this point, see Tonstad, *Saving God's Reputation*, 41–54.

22. Mealy (*After the Thousand Years*) gives an exposition of Revelation 20 that is respectful of the narrative with a constructive interpretation.

23. Flowers, "The Vision of Revelation IV–V," 526.

Second, the New Jerusalem comes down "out of heaven from God, prepared as a bride adorned for her husband" (21:2). This is also strange because the city that comes down from heaven is a city full of people.[24] Readers of the Bible are more accustomed to the idea that the redeemed go *to* heaven. Here, however, with the New Jerusalem, they come down *from* heaven. This detail is unique to Revelation, but we should not therefore conclude that this book is all mixed up.

Third, consequently, the 'heaven part' in Revelation's view must be the same as the rest of the New Testament.[25] At the second coming of Jesus, as we can ascertain from a host of texts, the redeemed go to heaven, never again to be separated from Jesus.

> *Gospel of John*:
> I am going there to prepare a place for you. And if I go and prepare a place for you, I will come back and take you to be with me that you also may be where I am (John 14:2–3, NIV).

> *Paul*:
> For the Lord himself, with a cry of command, with the archangel's call and with the sound of God's trumpet, will descend from heaven, and the dead in Christ will rise first. Then we who are alive, who are left, will be caught up in the clouds together with them to meet the Lord in the air; and so we will be with the Lord forever (1 Thess 4:16–17; see also 1 Cor 15:51–52).

These texts show movement from earth to heaven. The redeemed go from where humans are customarily, to where God is. The Gospel of John and the letters of Paul are in agreement showing the redeemed going to heaven, a view that for centuries has been dear to believers. In Paul's depiction, the resurrection and the ascension to heaven of the redeemed happen at the second coming of Jesus. Revelation does not dissent from this view, placing the resurrection of believers at the beginning of the "thousand years."

> I also saw the souls of those who had been beheaded for their testimony to Jesus and for the word of God. . . . They came to life and reigned with Christ a thousand years. (The rest of the dead did not come to life until the thousand years were ended.) This is the first resurrection. Blessed and holy are those who share in the first resurrection. Over these the second death has no power, but they will be priests of God and of Christ, and they will reign with him a thousand years (Rev 20:4–6).

24. Gundry ("The New Jerusalem, 254–64) rightly pursues the notion of the city as people, but to excess, denying that it is a place for people.

25. Rissi ("Die Erscheinung Christi," 81, 88) argues persuasively that the rider on the white horse in Rev 19:11–19 describes the second coming of Jesus.

Revelation's depiction of the end adds a detail to the picture that is sketched by other books in the New Testament, but it does not take away the idea that the redeemed go to heaven. If the redeemed in the end come down from heaven to earth (21:2), they must at some point have gone to heaven. What is new in Revelation, alone among the books in the New Testament, is that heaven is only a temporary residence. After the thousand years, the New Jerusalem, as a city of people, comes down to earth where the redeemed will have their permanent home in an earth that has been reclaimed and healed (21:1–2; 22:1–3). The remarkable and distinctive feature in Revelation is not that human beings go to heaven. Instead, we have the novelty that God relocates to earth (21:3–7)! Christianity's heaven-centered view of the end is corrected by Revelation's earth-bound view, a fact that is still only vaguely appreciated by readers of the Bible.[26]

Fourth, a wedding and a war are in the making (cf. Matt 25:1–10; John 3:29; Eph 5:25–27). John says that "the marriage of the Lamb has come, and his bride has made herself ready" (Rev 19:7–8).[27] Nuptial imagery runs on parallel tracks with images of war. Satan will march on the city just as the great eschatological wedding is about to be consummated! Wedding and war happen simultaneously, each reflective of the logic that drives the warring parties. This should be treated as more than a curiosity because the wedding image is in itself a fatal blow to Satan's misrepresentation of God. The wedding is not arranged or coerced; it is a dream come true for the bridegroom as well as for the bride. The bride that "has made herself ready" are people who count it as the highest privilege to be the chosen one of the bridegroom, and the bridegroom has made no secret of his intentions, wooing the bride over a long period of time. Triumph and defeat are both writ large in the reality of the wedding in the sense that Satan made God out to be a Person to be avoided and shunned, thinking to bring about a permanent separation. Now the satanic premise is utterly in shambles. What happens here, at "the marriage of the Lamb," is the opposite of shunning. Through the figure of the Lamb God is seen to be loving and loveable, and the union now in the making exceeds the relationship that was broken at the beginning of the story. Instead of a permanent separation, the imagination is invited to contemplate intimate union, suggested by the announcement that the bride "has made herself ready" (19:7). Desire and worthiness are a two-way street in this representation, the parties to the union each finding his and her desire and longing fulfilled in the other.

Fifth, still trying to "draw the picture which the seer saw,"[28] we need to nuance the notion of Satan's capture and imprisonment (20:1–3). If the first resurrection is a resurrection of the redeemed only, as Revelation avers (20:4–6); and if the redeemed go to heaven in Revelation just as in other scenarios in the New Testament (Rev 14:14–16; cf. 1 Thess 4:16–17; 1 Cor 15:51–52); and if the unredeemed are resurrected only

26. Thompson, *Apocalypse and Empire*, 85; Russell, *New Heavens and New Earth*, 208; Rossing, "For the Healing of the World," 170.

27. Miller, "The Nuptial Eschatology," 301–18.

28. Flowers, "The Vision of Revelation IV–V," 526.

after the thousand years, as Revelation explicitly says (Rev 20:5); and if the redeemed return to earth with the New Jerusalem only after the thousand years (21:1–2), the binding of Satan during the thousand years is symbolic and much less spectacular than Revelation's action-packed wording initially led us to believe (20:1–3). Satan will be bound by circumstances and not by coercive forces.

Sixth, upon his release from confinement, Satan commits to one last round of warfare, his designated target now described as "the beloved city" (20:8–9). Here, in the most literal sense, the devil is in the details. If the hand that draws the picture of what the Seer saw gets this part right, it will transform many readings of this book. Revelation portrays the end of evil as self-destruction to an extent that most readings ignore or overlook.

Note that John already has expended great effort to refute the idea that God is the destroyer in the cosmic conflict, drawing upon Old Testament imagery to the same effect. In the trumpet sequence, for instance, the star "that had fallen from heaven to earth" is the certified Destroyer in that part of the story (Rev 9:1, 11). In Isaiah, the text that lies behind the fallen star, the "Shining One" commits to a course of shocking *self*-destruction, by his own activity destroying the land and the people he claims as his (Isa 14:15–20).[29] In Ezekiel's poem about "the covering cherub" (Ezek 28:14), another key background image for the cosmic conflict in Revelation, the cherub comes to an end by fire, but the fire does not strike from without. "I made fire come out from within you, *it* consumed you," God says to the fallen cherub (Ezek 28:18). This is a telling detail that is almost always overlooked or trivialized. It is not fire from without that brings an end to the evil power but evil in her midst that "reduces her to a heap of burnt ruins," says S. Fisch.[30] In his exceptionally-fine work on Ezekiel, Moshe Greenberg writes likewise that the "fire from your midst" signifies "*evil causing its own destruction*."[31] It is impossible to exaggerate the importance of these observations. Will the hand that draws the picture do justice to these finely-tuned elements in Revelation and the Old Testament background texts?

There is more to complete the picture of self-destruction now emerging. As a seventh element, Satan now goes forth to "deceive the nations at the four corners of the earth, Gog and Magog" (Rev 20:8). In the background text for this image, self-destruction is strikingly at work. "I will summon the sword against Gog in all my mountains, says the Lord God; *the swords of all will be against their comrades*" (Ezek 38:21).[32] What is this but self-destruction at work, the project coming unglued as the participants turn on each other? Satan comes to grief by a momentum working from within rather than from without. We see less that evil is destroyed than that it implodes.

29. Holladay, "Text, Structure, and Irony, 633–43.

30. Fisch, *Ezekiel*, 193.

31. Greenberg, *Ezekiel 21–37*, 587, emphasis added.

32. Bøe, *Gog and Magog*, 115.

References to a terrifying battle outside 'the city' is scattered in a number of places in Revelation. Lining up these verses in the opposite order of their occurrence in Revelation clarifies the puzzle.

> And I saw *the holy city*, the New Jerusalem, coming down out of heaven from God, prepared as a bride adorned for her husband (Rev 21:2).
>
> They [Satan and the unredeemed] marched up over the breadth of the earth and surrounded the camp of the saints and *the beloved city* (20:9).
>
> And the wine press was trodden *outside the city*, and blood flowed from the wine press, as high as the bridles of the horses, for a distance of about two hundred miles (14:20, translation mine).

Here, as an eighth element in Revelation's composite picture of the end, the bloodbath *outside the city* is the making of the demonic. Self-destruction is at work. Neither place nor time nor battle nor blood is as important as the *theology* in view. This might disappoint many who are convinced that the texts speak of punitive action that is alleged to be necessary for justice to be served. To those who miss the notion of judgment in the traditional sense, there is the corrective that judgment *is* taking place. "The judgment at this moment is then: to be what one has actually wished to be, but seeing in the light of God what it was," as Jacques Ellul has written with exceptional perspicuity.[33]

In the wider context of apocalyptic depictions of the end, there are strands of evidence to complete and confirm the picture now emerging. One such strand is so close to Revelation that it deserves to be counted as a ninth element in the picture. In *1 Enoch*, a text older than Revelation,[34] there are horses, blood almost like the "shoreless sea of blood" in Revelation,[35] and there is emphatic self-destruction.

> In those days, the father will be beaten together with his sons, in one place; and brothers shall fall together with their friends, in death, until a stream shall flow with their blood. For a man shall not be able to withhold his hands from his sons nor from (his) sons' sons in order to kill them. Nor is it possible for the sinner to withhold his hands from his honoured brother. From dawn until the sun sets, they shall slay each other. The horse shall walk through the blood of sinners up to his chest; and the chariot shall sink down up to its top (*1 Enoch* 100:3).[36]

33. Ellul, *Apocalypse*, 176.

34. Bauckham (*Climax of Prophecy*, 38–48) shows that this *topos* was widely diffused. Its occurrence in Revelation does not necessarily mean derivation in a straight line from *1 Enoch*.

35. Kiddle, *The Revelation of St. John*, 286.

36. Charlesworth, *The Old Testament Pseudepigrapha*.

The parallel to Revelation's scene of horses sinking in a sea of blood is remarkable. *1 Enoch* is noteworthy for the way it details dissolution in the ranks of the losing side, the most intimate and tender relations rendered worthless when the father turns on his son and even on his grandson. The imagery corroborates the view that self-destruction is at work "outside the city" (Rev 14:20) so as to make the notion of self-destruction stand front and center in Revelation's depiction of the end. Fire may still come from above (Rev 20:10), but the fire is a moot point. When it comes, the pictorial construct has already projected the attacking side in a state of utter ruin. The hint of relish for this course of events in *1 Enoch* is absent in Revelation. In the latter book, destruction is rife, too, but the driving force is through and through demonic.

Attention to the theme of cosmic conflict enables and compels a different interpretation of texts that Christians for centuries have taken as certain proof that God will subject those who reject God to everlasting torture. When Revelation says that those who worship the beast and its image will "drink the wine of God's wrath, poured unmixed into the cup of his anger and . . . be tormented with fire and sulfur in the presence of the holy angels and in the presence of the Lamb" (14:9–10), we are again witnessing the scene taking place outside the New Jerusalem. If the devil is in the details, where in the picture is he?

We shall number this as the tenth element in the picture, and this is what we see. Inside the city, a wedding is in the making (19:6–8; 21:2). The Lamb is about to consummate the long-awaited marriage, the redeemed recipients of the promise that they will be "a pillar in the temple of my God" and never to "go out of it" (3:12). Outside the city, there is war, and the attackers are "as numerous as the sands of the sea" (20:7–8). The body language of the attackers exude confidence, *striding* conveying their posture better than *marching*, but marching is what armies do, so we can settle for *marching*. "They marched up over the breadth of the earth and surrounded the camp of the saints" (20:9).

And now what? If we ignore that Revelation transmits is message pictorially and not only verbally, we shall miss entirely the carefully stitched picture of self-destruction. That is, if we read on without pause or nuance, "And fire came down from heaven and consumed them" (20:9), all the images of self-destruction will be for naught, and our theology of the end of evil will be terribly compromised.

With regard to the horrors transpiring "outside the city" (14:20), Jesus and the redeemed participate only as spectators bereft of the means to dissuade the combatants to reverse course (cf. Luke 19:41–44). Satan is the acting subject on the outside (20:7–9), "the holy angels and the Lamb" witnessing a scene that is the creation and culmination of demonic activity.[37] In John's panoramic vision, the logic of self-destruction is working itself out all the way to the end.[38]

37. Tonstad, *The Lost Meaning of the Seventh Day*, 482–91.

38. Cf. Tonstad, "Blood 'as High as a Horse's Bridle,'" paper presented at the Society of Biblical Literature Annual Meeting in Washington, DC, November 5, 2006.

G. B. Caird said that if we "cannot accommodate our minds to the idea of eternal torment, the answer is that neither could John."[39] The background text for John's imagery of everlasting fire is Edom, one of the ancient enemies of Israel. Isaiah describes Edom's downfall as a fire that "shall not be quenched; its smoke shall go up forever" (Isa 34:10; Rev 14:11). Both scenes are symbolic of an irrevocable reality and not of everlasting torture, Revelation's depiction no more than Isaiah's. The ending conforms in every minutia to the logic that guides the story in Revelation. By this logic deceit, war, famine, and death are in the world (6:1–8; cf. 9:1–11). Injustice and sentiments of hopelessness abound (6:9–10). And then, within the same logic—shockingly—Satan must be released after his thousand year confinement (20:3, 7).

Revelation knows why. In the Garden of Eden, Satan insinuated lack of freedom as the defect in the divine government (Gen 3:1). Prohibition was said to be the defining trait of God and the sharpest barb of 'the lie' (Gen 3:1; cf. John 8:44; Rev 12:9; 20:2). Satan's release at the end of the thousand years happens under the auspices of a God who was falsely said to be hostile to freedom. Freedom, not its lack, is in view in these scenes. Freedom is here love's costliest creation, and love is a language that is spoken only in freedom's domain. In Revelation, it is the logic of freedom that leads to Satan's release. Within the logic of freedom, precisely the value said to be lacking in God, Satan proceeds to work his own demise (20:7–9).[40]

Don't Weep

"I wept and wept [*eklaion*] because no one was found to have what it takes to open the scroll or to look into it," John says in response to the crisis to which he is witness in the heavenly council (5:4, translation mine).

Then, at the peak of his distress, one of the twenty-four elders says to him,

> "Do not weep! Look! The Lion of the tribe of Judah, the Root of David, has won the war [*enikēsen*] and has what it takes to open the scroll and its seven seals." And I saw in the middle of the throne and [in the middle of] the four living creatures and in the middle of the elders a Lamb standing as if it had been violently killed, having seven horns and seven eyes, which are the seven spirits of God sent out into all the earth. He went [*ēlthen*]—and he has taken [*eilēfen*] (!)—the scroll from the right hand of the one who was seated on the throne (Rev 5:5–7, translation mine).

My translation differs slightly from what is found in current English versions, but it is not less precise, and it conveys better the immediacy, the excitement, and the need for exquisite tonality when the passage is read. As to points of distinction, my wording is respectful of the shift in verbal tenses in the passage, adding an exclamation

39. Caird, *Revelation*, 186.

40. Tonstad, *Saving God's Reputation*, 155.

mark for emphasis in the text that would otherwise be lost (5:7).[41] More importantly, I have chosen wording that gives a boost to the reality of cosmic conflict that is often lost in interpretations. While the NRSV says that "the Root of David has conquered [*enikēsen*]," the NASB that "the Root of David has overcome," the NIV that "the Root of David has triumphed," and the NKJV that "the Root of David has prevailed," the underlying battle metaphor comes closer to the tenor of Revelation when we say that "the Root of David has won the *war*" (5:5). Leaving the verb without an object is permissible on formal grounds, but an object is implied, and it is necessary to make it explicit. "The Root of David" has not 'overcome' only in a pietistic sense, where the subject of 'overcoming' relates to personal vice or virtue. He has fought and won a war against an external enemy (12:7; 11:7; 13:7; cf. 6:2). Revelation will address believers as those who 'overcome' and 'conquer' [*tō nikōnti*], urging them to persevere, but it is implied that they, too, are engaged in battle with an enemy without.[42] That the battle has an external enemy moves beyond doubt when Revelation says that "they have overcome *him* [*enikōsan auton*]" (12:11; cf. 15:2; 17:14). Here, at the most riveting session, triumph in the cosmic conflict is announced and celebrated (5:5, 9, cf. 12:7–10).

If we set out to identify the assets that enable "the Root of David" to accomplish what no one else is able to do, three features command attention. First, "the Root of David" has "seven horns and seven eyes" (5:6). A horn is a Semitic symbol of power. *Seven* horns refer to perfect power, even infinite power. In the context of Revelation, it is also meaningful to characterize it as *legitimate* power. The ontological implication of power thus described cannot be anything less than *divine* power. "The Root of David" belongs to the divine identity and possesses the power and authority of the Creator.[43] Revelation does not make any concession to Epicurus's suggestion that God's power is defective.

The figure in Revelation is also endowed with "seven eyes" (5:6). Eyes are a symbol of knowledge, wisdom, and discernment. *Seven* eyes do not only mean an abundance of these abilities but that such abilities are present to the full.[44] Just as "the Root of David" is found to have infinite power, the seven eyes mean that he has infinite wisdom. This, again, resounds with the connotation of *divine* wisdom. On the latter point, the text goes out of its way to prove that "the Root of David" is well informed, specifying that the seven eyes "are the seven spirits of God sent out into all the earth" (5:6).

The identification of Jesus with God in the presence of the heavenly council is not a complete surprise because Jesus has earlier referred to himself as "the first and the last" (1:17). In the Epilogue, likewise, he will be "the Alpha and the Omega, the first and the last, the beginning and the end" (22:13). Who can legitimately claim such

41. Matheson, "Verbal Aspect, 58–77.

42. See also Rev 2:7, 11, 17. Rev 2:26; 3:5, 12, 21 and 21:7 have the participle *ho nikōv*.

43. Heim, "The (God-)Forsaken King of Psalm 89," 296–322.

44. Charles, "An Apocalyptic Tribute," *JETS* 34 (1991), 468.

distinctions other than God? And who other than God lays claim to these characteristics in Revelation?

> "I am the Alpha and the Omega," says the Lord God, who is and who was and who is to come, the Almighty (1:8).
>
> Then he said to me, "It is done! I am the Alpha and the Omega, the beginning and the end" (21:6).

Revelation knowingly and intentionally conflates the identities of God and Jesus. What God says of God Jesus can say of himself (1:8, 17; 2:8; 21:6; 22:13).[45] Moreover, the terminology that puts Jesus within the divine identity resists corrosion because it echoes the most emphatic monotheistic affirmations in the Old Testament (Isa 41:4; 44:6; 48:12; cf. 43:10).

Insignia of divine identity mix with proof of genuine humanity. The figure appearing before the heavenly council is described as "the Lion of the tribe of Judah, the Root of David" (5:5). This makes him a real human being, although distinguished among humans by his royal lineage.[46] The allusion to "the Root of David" brings to view the promised Restorer in Isaiah, now raised to universal dominion (Isa 11:1–10). For this reason he is a figure less beholden to David than to Adam. The scope of his mission compasses all of humanity and all creation.

These features add up to much. The one who is able to open the scroll is represented as a being who belongs to the divine identity, and yet he is also human. The gap between the divine and the human realm has been bridged. Divine reality can be conveyed to human reality and *vice versa* by one who knows both realities from within (1:1; 5:1, 6, 7). The Davidic King comes on stage as a Revealer, confirmed by the statement that when his work is done, the earth "will be full of the knowledge of the LORD as the waters cover the sea" (Isa 11:9). Method and results go hand in hand (Isa 11:1–9): the messianic figure exercises exceptional discernment (Isa 11:3); he looks out for the victims of oppression (Isa 11:4); his truthful word is his weapon (Isa 11:4); righteousness is "the belt around his waist, and faithfulness the belt around his loins" (Isa 11:5). Where his influence takes hold, threatening and adversarial relations will be at an end: "the wolf shall live with the lamb" (Isa 11:6). The weakest and most vulnerable has nothing to fear from the strongest and most powerful as witnessed by the fact that the nursing child will be playing "over the hole of the asp, and the weaned child shall put its hand on the adder's den" (Isa 11:8). No one will hurt or destroy on God's holy mountain because the Revealer has filled the earth with "the knowledge of the LORD" (Isa 11:9).

The third descriptive feature of "the Root of David" poses the greatest challenge. For this feature all prior attempts to instill correct expectations will prove inadequate.

45. Bauckham, *God Crucified: Monotheism and Christology*, 53–54.

46. Brighton, *Revelation*, 136.

> And I saw in the middle of the throne and [in the middle of] the four living creatures and in the middle of the elders a Lamb [*arnion*] standing as if it had been violently killed (Rev 5:6, translation mine).

Could anyone imagine *this* to be the solution to the cosmic conflict? Eugene Boring calls it "one of the most mind-wrenching and theologically pregnant transformations of imagery in literature."[47] He adds that "the announced Lion turns out to be a Lamb—slaughtered at that."[48] A figure of power is expected, not a symbol of powerlessness. Majesty is supposed to take the stage, not lowliness. The blend of the divine and the human is strange beyond computation, but when the human is a royal figure the calculus must nevertheless be exaltation. Can one who has been violently killed be the solution when violence is the problem (6:9–10)?

Like other terms in Revelation, the 'lamb' [*arnion*] is a symbolic representation.[49] Loren L. Johns says aptly that the lamb signifies vulnerability. Vulnerability manifests itself in victimhood. John writes that the Lamb looked as if it had been 'slaughtered,' or better, 'as though it had been violently killed' [*hōs esfagmenon*] (5:6). Revelation uses the verb *sfazō*, the same term that is used in a New Testament recollection of Cain's murder of Abel (1 John 3:12; cf. Gen 4:5). If *slaughter* is the connotation of this word, it is mainly in the sense of killing someone with violence.[50] The members of the heavenly council highlight this feature in their tribute to Jesus. "For you were slaughtered" [*hoti esfagēs*]," they say (5:9), again with the odd implication that his ability to open the scroll relates to the fact that he was killed with violence.[51] Battle and martyrdom are the images that come to mind.[52] The combination of *arnion* ["lamb"] and *sfazō* ["kill with violence"] is in Revelation so consistent that we should not think of the one without seeing the other. The fact of having been slaughtered, says Johns, is an essential part of the Lamb's identity (5:6, 9, 12; 13:8).[53] This sets up a defining contrast between the protagonists in the cosmic conflict. As A. T. Hanson notes, "Christ and the saints conquer by dying; Satan and the powers of evil by physical force."[54]

Noting again that the seven eyes and the seven horns are signifiers of divine identity, the imagery makes it "absolutely clear that what Christ does, God does."[55] Why will the heavenly council acknowledge this figure? Why does not this all-wise and all-powerful figure deploy force in order to defeat the opponent? Instead of the

47. Boring, "Narrative Christology," 708.

48. Ibid.

49. Johns, "The Lamb in the Rhetorical Program," 770–71.

50. Cf. *BDAG* 7192.

51. The causal connotation of *hoti* is evident; cf. *BDAG* 5414.

52. Ford, *Revelation*, 90.

53. Johns, "The Lamb," 780. *Sfazō* is in Revelation consistently associated with murder and violence; cf. Rev 6:4, 9; 13:3; 18:24.

54. Hanson, *The Wrath of the Lamb*, 165.

55. Bauckham, *Revelation*, 63.

expected power equation, force is unleashed *against* him rather than being deployed *by* him. The Lamb in Revelation is declared the winner in the cosmic conflict *as a victim of violence*; it is in *that* capacity he is seen as one who has what it takes to unravel the riddle of reality. Non-use of force on the part of the most powerful side in the conflict is the ideological stumbling block—more so because ruthless violence is the characteristic feature of the other side. God's *character*, far more than God's *strategy*, is on display before the heavenly council.

Richard Bauckham says that "when the slaughtered Lamb is seen 'in the midst of' the divine throne in heaven (5:6; cf. 7:17), the meaning is that Christ's sacrificial death *belongs to the way God rules the world*."[56] This statement corroborates the argument I have pursued above, but it must be qualified by the context in Revelation. The parade of deception, war, famine, death, and injustice (6:1–11) is less a statement of "the way God rules the world" than images showing how God conducts the war against the opposing side. Revelation deploys all its powers to the task of showing that God does not conduct the war so as to win it by any means imaginable.

This point cannot be emphasized too strongly. There is war, we have noted, but what is the problem over which the war is fought? Why, in this war, does not the side that possesses superior power simply blast the opposing side away? The Bible has in bits and pieces suggested the answer to this question in stories we have explored in this book. In Revelation, the slaughtered Lamb is God's response to the slander heard in the Garden of Eden (12:7–9; 13:5, 6, 11), taking the battle to "the ancient serpent" deep into enemy territory (12:9; 20:2). Just as deceit ['the lie'] is shattered by the Revealer in the Gospel of John (John 8:44; 12:31), the testimony of "the faithful and true witness" defeats the deceiver in Revelation (Rev 3:14; 12:9; 20:2). Slander is not silenced by force, but by revelation; *mis*representation is countered by *re*presentation (3:14). The slaughtered Lamb wins the war because the Lamb represents the truth about God's character, the subject over which the war is fought.

And yet this view, despite its merit, fails to do justice to the drama in Revelation on at least two levels. Our interpretation falls short if we conclude that this book proves that God is not as bad as we thought, or that God is somewhat better than we thought, or that God is as good as we think God ought to be. In the heavenly council, no one has what it takes to open the book because there is a vast difference between the divine outlook and the view of even the wisest and best informed of created beings (5:3, 4). When the truth is out, the heavenly council will not conclude that God has passed the test by meeting the expectations of the councilors. The council and the entire created order join in praising God (5:9–14), but the God they praise is not the God they knew or the God they thought they knew or even the God they wished for. After the *apokalypsis* of Jesus Christ, they praise God for reasons that differ from prior conceptions. God's revelation in Jesus has taken those who are recipients of the revelation to where they had no inkling of going.

56. Bauckham, *Revelation*, 64.

In my doctoral dissertation on Revelation, I described the problem of the sealed scroll in a series of negative propositions. In the heavenly council, I said,

> the main concern is not whether God in his sovereign will makes certain events happen, or whether God is able to foretell a future yet unknown, or whether Christ is invested with the authority to execute God's will. When Revelation says that "no one in heaven or on earth or under the earth was able to open the scroll or to look into it" (5:3), it . . . means that *absolutely no one else would have solved the cosmic conflict this way.*[57]

I still believe this to be a correct representation of the message of Revelation. And yet there is another and more important level to the heavenly scene. God earns praise not only for the way God has solved the cosmic conflict but for the kind of person God is. The one who sits on the throne and the Lamb win the heavenly council over to a point of view the members of the council did not previously hold. They have come to know God in a new way. As noted above, God's victory is more than a triumph at the level of strategy.

The Sense of the Ending

We can assert without risk that the ending of Revelation brings to view the destruction of Satan and the restoration of creation,[58] but what is the *sense* of the ending in the book? The sense of the ending, sense now understood not as premonition but as understanding, has come to rest on the importance of freedom in God's economy. This is the sense of the ending in this book as I propose to read it, a sense foreshadowed in other stories we have explored in this book. The clinching argument for this view is the ideologically fraught release of Satan at the end of the thousand years (Rev 20:1–9).

Revelation grapples with the question of divine non-intervention more earnestly than any thinker has done, but with better resources at its disposal. The answer that appears 'in the middle' in the heavenly council (5:6) erases whatever distinction we wish to postulate between the character of God and the means God uses in the struggle with evil. To say that commitment to freedom anchors the divine ideology to a degree that is not shared "in heaven, on earth, or under the earth" (5:3), finds staggering expressions in human society. We have in the course of this book seen freedom early on become dispensable in the Christian imperial state. We have seen how Augustine defended the use of coercion, claiming that the apostle Paul was converted coercively. Lack of regard for freedom and individual conscience endangered the life of Roger Williams in the New World, at the hands of the most pious colonists. In secular

57. Tonstad, *Saving God's Reputation*, 141.

58. Koch (*The Rediscovery of Apocalyptic*, 94), again, emphasizing that the destruction of Satan in the final battle is the central idea of apocalyptic.

society, the dispensability of freedom has emerged as a conspicuous characteristic of the modern security state. If, returning to the ideological parameters of Revelation, the crisis in the heavenly council is triggered by a divine commitment to freedom that intelligent beings "in heaven, on earth, and under the earth" do not share (5:3), the prioritizing of conformity over freedom in the history of Christianity and of security over freedom in the modern state serve as confirmation of Revelation's depiction that acceptance for the divine priority is a hard sell.

And yet there is reason to be hopeful. The Bible presents a God of sense, even a God who succeeds in revealing the divine sense persuasively to beings in heaven and on earth.

> And I saw what appeared to be a sea of glass mixed with fire, and those who had conquered the beast and its image and the number of its name, standing beside the sea of glass with harps of God in their hands. And they sing the song of Moses, the servant of God, and the song of the Lamb: "Great and amazing are your deeds, LORD God the Almighty! Just and true are your ways, King of the nations! LORD, who will not fear and glorify your name? For you alone are holy. All nations will come and worship before you, for your judgments have been revealed" (15:2–4).

If absence of sense is the problem in the heavenly council, this scene shows the triumph of sense. Over and over in this book, intelligent beings line up to applaud God's ways, their applause all the more telling when we see it in contrast to the crisis of confidence that gripped the heavenly council at the beginning of the book (5:1–4).

> And I heard the angel of the waters say, "You are just, O Holy One, who are and were, for you have judged these things. . . . And I heard the altar respond, "Yes, O LORD God, the Almighty, your judgments are true and just!" (16:5, 7)

> After this I heard what seemed to be the loud voice of a great multitude in heaven, saying, "Hallelujah! Salvation and glory and power to our God, for his judgments are true and just; he has judged the great whore who corrupted the earth with her fornication, and he has vindicated the blood of his servants [shed] by her hand" (19:1–2, translation mine).

Notions of divine inscrutability and human incapacity come in for criticism at many junctures in the Bible. In light of Revelation, these doctrines fail to capture the message of the book, and the relationship between God and human beings. The last book of the Bible reveals a God of sense and a God whose ways are seen to make sense.

For we read, in one of the strangest statements in the Bible, that "[w]hen the Lamb opened the seventh seal, there was silence in heaven for about half an hour" (8:1). Why the sudden, prolonged hush? What did the Lamb do when he opened the seventh seal so as to bring about a state of protracted silence? As the text stands, no action accompanies the breaking of this seal other than that the Lamb broke it. If there is an action, it is the action of *revelation*.

Silence is not the only response in the heavenly council, as we have seen (5:9–14; 15:3–4). On the whole, Revelation depicts heaven as a noisy place.[59] But silence is itself a distinctive category of response, the most spontaneous and intuitive form of reacting to the unexpected and the most trustworthy measure of the magnitude of the surprise. "Revelation is not comprehended completely in the beginning, but at the end of the revealing history," the young Wolfhart Pannenberg wrote in bold letters at the beginning of his career.[60] This is still true, but Revelation provides advance delivery on comprehension. In narratival terms, the ending of Revelation is the end of Satan (20:1–10) and then a new heaven and a new earth (21:1–4; 22:1–3), but in revelatory terms the end of Revelation centers on the seventh seal. When we make the end of Revelation refer to its purpose and allow that its purpose is to reveal God's solution to a reality that generates weeping on earth and silence in heaven (5:1–4), we will have read this book correctly. God's revelation will be understood only at the end of the revealing history, but we have been told in advance how comprehension plays out to those who experience it.[61]

> My servant will succeed in his task; he will be highly honored. Many people were shocked when they saw him; he was so disfigured that he hardly looked human. But now many nations will marvel at him, and kings will be speechless with amazement. They will see and understand something they had never known (Isa 52:13–15, GNB; cf. Isa 49:7; Rev 8:1).

When we allow this background text to explain the meaning of the silence in heaven, the seventh seal comprises the end as well as the sense of the ending.[62] God has in the context of conflict revealed the divine reality in the person of the slaughtered Lamb. To our surprise, surely, it is the Lamb in the middle—in the middle of the throne and in the middle of history—and not the events at the end that makes the difference. The seals are broken not by what they are in themselves, but by what they are in the hands of the Revealer. Revelation is a different kind of book because the ending and the sense of the ending diverge, the sense of the ending found not in the ending but in the spatial and metaphorical middle. Against tradition, theological and philosophical alike, and against death and doubt, we witness silence induced by understanding—understanding expressing itself in being at a loss for words. In the last book of the Bible, it is the impact on the recipients and the triumph of sense that matters most. "When the Lamb broke the seventh seal," says Revelation, "there was silence in heaven for about half an hour" (Rev 8:1).

59. See (or hear) Rev 5:2; 7:2, 10; 11:12, 15; 12:10; 14:2, 15, 18; 16:1; 19:1; 21:3.

60. Pannenberg, "Dogmatic Theses on the Doctrine of Revelation," 133. 'Revelation' is not here to be understood as the Book of Revelation but as the totality of divine revelation.

61. Beet, "Silence in Heaven," 76.

62. Tonstad, *Saving God's Reputation*, 138–39.

Bibliography

Achtemeier, Paul J. "Revelation 5:1-14." *Int* 40 (1986) 283–88.

Acton, Lord (Sir John). *Essays in Freedom and Power*. Edited by Gertrude Himmelfarb. Gloucester, MA: Peter Smith, 1972.

Adams, Marilyn McCord. *Horrendous Evils and the Goodness of God*. Ithaca: Cornell University Press, 1999.

———. "Horrors in theological context." *SJT* 55 (2002) 468–79.

Agamben, Giorgio. *Remnants of Auschwitz: The Witness and the Archive*. Translated by Daniel Heller-Roazen. New York: Zone, 2002.

Alexander, T. Desmond. *Abraham in the Negev: A Source-Critical Investigation of Genesis 20:1–22:19*. Carlisle: Paternoster, 1997.

Alter, Robert. *The Art of Biblical Poetry*. Revised ed. New York: Basic, 2011.

———. *The Wisdom Books: Job, Proverbs, and Ecclesiastes. A Translation with Commentary*. New York: W. W. Norton, 2010.

Andersen, Francis I. *Habakkuk. A New Translation with Introduction and Commentary*. Anchor Bible 25. New York: Doubleday, 2001.

Anderson, Bernhard W. "Abraham, the Friend of God." *Int* 42 (1988) 353–66.

Anderson, Hugh. *The Gospel of Mark*. New Century Bible. London: Oliphants, 1976.

Anderson, Paul N. "Aspects of Historicity in the Gospel of John: Implications for Investigations of Jesus and Archaeology." In *Jesus and Archaeology*, edited by James H. Charlesworth, 587–618. Grand Rapids: Eerdmans, 2006.

Ansell, Nicholas John. "The Call of Wisdom/the Voice of the Serpent: A Canonical Approach to the Tree of Knowledge." *Christian Scholar's Review* 31 (2001) 31–57.

Arendt, Hannah. *Eichmann in Jerusalem: A Report on the Banality of Evil*. New York: Penguin, 1977.

Asiedu-Peprah, Martin. *Johannine Sabbath Conflicts as Juridical Controversy*. Wissenschaftliche Untersuchungen zum Neuen Testament 132. Tübingen: Mohr Siebeck, 2001.

Auerbach, Erich. *Mimesis: The Representation of Reality in Western Literature*. Translated by Willard R. Trask. Princeton: Princeton University Press, 1953.

Augustine. *City of God*. Translated by Henry Bettenson. London: Pelican, 1972. Reprinted Penguin, 1984.

———. *On Genesis*. Translated by Edmund Hill. New York: New City Press, 2002.

———. *The Literal Meaning of Genesis*. Translated by John Hammond Taylor. New York: Newman, 1982.

———. *On the Problem of Free Choice*. Translated by Dom Mark Pontifex. New York: Newman, 1955.

———. *The Political Writings of St. Augustine*. Edited by Henry Paolucci. Washington, DC: Regnery, 1996.

———. *To Simplician—On Various Questions* in *Augustine: Earlier Writings*. Translated by J. H. S. Burleigh. Library of Christian Classics. Philadelphia: Westminster, 1953.

Aune, David E. "Dualism in the Fourth Gospel and the Dead Sea Scrolls: A Reassessment of the Problem." In *Neotestamentica et Philonica: Studies in Honor of Peder Borgen*, edited by David Aune et al., 281–303. Leiden: Brill, 2003.

———. "The Influence of Roman Imperial Court Ceremonial on the Apocalypse of John." *BR* 28 (1983) 5–26.

———. *Revelation*. 3 vols. Word Biblical Commentary. Dallas: Word, 2002.

Aus, Roger D. "God's Plan and God's Power: Isaiah 66 and the Restraining Factors of 2 Thess 2:6–7." *JBL* 96 (1977) 537–53.

Bainton, Roland H. *Hunted Heretic: The Life and Death of Michael Servetus, 1511–1553*. Boston: Beacon, 1953.

Bal, Mieke. "A Body of Writings: Judges 19." In *Feminist Companion to Judges*, edited by Athalya Brenner, 208–30. Sheffield: JSOT Press, 1993.

Balentine, Samuel. *Job*. Macon, GA: Smyth & Helwys, 2006.

Baltzer, Klaus. *Deutero-Isaiah: A Commentary on Isaiah 40–55*. Hermeneia. Minneapolis: Fortress, 2001.

Baranowski, Shelley. "The Confessing Church and Anti-Semitism: Protestant Identity, German Nationhood, and the Exclusion of the Jews." In *Betrayal: German Churches and the Holocaust*, edited by Robert P. Ericksen and Susannah Heschel, 90–109. Minneapolis: Fortress, 1999.

Barnouin, M. "Les Problèmes de traduction concernant II Thess. II.6–7." *NTS* 23 (1977) 482–98.

Barr, David. *Tales of the End. A Narrative Commentary on the Book of Revelation*. Santa Rosa: Poleridge, 1998.

Barr, James. "'Abba, Father' and the Familiarity of Jesus Speech." *Theology* 91 (1988) 173–79.

———. "'Abba' Isn't 'Daddy.'" *JTS* 39 (1988) 28–47.

———. *The Garden of Eden and the Hope of Immortality*. London: SCM, 1992.

———. *The Semantics of Biblical Language*. London: Oxford University Press, 1961.

———. "The Word Became Flesh: The Incarnation in the New Testament." *Int* 10 (1956) 16–23.

Barrett, C. K. *The Gospel According to St. John: An Introduction with Commentary and Notes on the Greek Text*. 2nd ed. Philadelphia: Westminster, 1978.

Barry, John M. *Roger Williams and the Creation of the American Soul: Church, State, and the Birth of Liberty*. New York: Viking, 2012.

Barth, Karl. *Church Dogmatics* 4/3. Translated by G. W. Bromiley and R. J. Ehrlich. Edinburgh: T. & T. Clark, 1960.

———. *The Epistle to the Romans*. 6th ed. Translated by Edwyn C. Hoskyns. London: Oxford University Press, 1968.

———. *Karl Barth–Rudolf Bultmann Letters*, 1922–1966. Edited by B. Jaspert. Grand Rapids: Eerdmans, 1981.

Barzel, H. "Moses: Tragedy and Sublimity." In *Literary Interpretations of Biblical Narratives*, ed. Kenneth R. R. Gros Louis et al., 120–40. Nashville: Abingdon, 1974.

Bauckham, Richard J. *The Bible and Ecology: Rediscovering the Community of Creation*. Waco: Baylor University Press, 2010.

———. *The Climax of Prophecy: Studies in the Book of Revelation*. Edinburgh: T. & T. Clark, 1993.

———. *God Crucified: Monotheism and Christology in the New Testament*. Grand Rapids: Eerdmans, 1998.

———. *Jesus and the Eyewitnesses: The Gospels as Eyewitness Testimony*. Grand Rapids: Eerdmans, 2006.

———. "Jesus and the Wild Animals (Mark 1:13): A Christological Image for an Ecological Age." In *Jesus of Nazareth: Lord and Christ: Essays on the Historical Jesus and New Testament Christology*, edited by Joel Green and Max Turner, 3–21. Grand Rapids: Eerdmans, 1994.

Bauer, Walter. *Greek-English Lexicon of the New Testament and Other Early Christian Literature*. Edited by Fredrick William Danker. Third edition. Chicago: University of Chicago Press, 2000.

Bauman, Zygmunt. *Modernity and the Holocaust*. New York: Cornell University Press, 2000.

Bayle, Pierre. *Historical and Critical Dictionary: Selections*. Translated by Richard H. Popkin. New York: Bobbs–Merrill, 1965.

Baynes, Leslie. *The Heavenly Book Motif in Judeo-Christian Apocalypses 200 B.C.E.–200 C.E.* Leiden: Brill, 2012.

———. "Horses of Heaven: Equine Imagery in John's Apocalypse." Paper presented to the John's Apocalypse Section, Society of Biblical Literature, Atlanta, 2010.

Beale, G. K. *The Book of Revelation*. New International Greek Testament Commentary. Grand Rapids: Eerdmans, 1999.

Beasley-Murray, George R. *John*. Word Biblical Commentary. Dallas: Word, 2002.

Beck, John A. "Geography as Irony: the Narrative-Geological Shaping of Elijah's Duel with the Prophets of Baal (1 Kings 18)." *SJOT* 17 (2003) 291–302.

Beet, W. Ernest. "Silence in Heaven." *ExpT* 46 (1932) 74–6.

Beker, J. Christiaan. *Paul the Apostle: The Triumph of God in Life and Thought*. Philadelphia: Fortress, 1980.

———. *Paul's Apocalyptic Gospel*. Philadelphia: Fortress, 1982.

Bennett Turner, William. *Figures of Speech: First Amendment Heroes and Villains*. Sausalito, CA: PoliPoint, 2011.

Berdyaev, Nikolai. *Christian Existentialism: A Berdyaev Anthology*. Edited by Donald A. Lowrie. London: Allen & Unwin, 1965.

———. *Dostoevsky*. Translated by Donald Attwater. New York: Meridian, 1957.

Bernard, J. H. *A Critical and Exegetical Commentary on the Gospel according to John*. 2 vols. International Critical Commentary. Edinburgh: T. & T. Clark, 1928. Reprinted 1993.

Best, Ernest. *A Commentary on the First and Second Epistles to the Thessalonians*. Black's New Testament Commentary. London: Adam & Charles Black, 1972.

Betz, Hans Dieter. *Galatians*. Hermeneia; Philadelphia: Fortress, 1979.

Biguzzi, Giancarlo. "John on Patmos and the "Persecution" in the Apocalypse." *EstBib* 56 (1998) 201–20.

Bilde, Per. "2 *Cor*. 4,4: The View of Satan and the Created World in Paul." In *Apocryphon Severin: Presented to Søren Givesen*. edited by Per Bilde et al., 29–41. Aarhus: Aarhus University Press, 1993.

Black, Matthew. "Some Greek Words with 'Hebrew' Meanings in the Epistles and the Apocalypse." In *Biblical Studies: Essays in Honour of William Barclay*, edited by Johnston R. McKay and James F. Miller, 135–46. London: Collins, 1976.

Blake, William. *Illustrations of the Book of Job*. Edited by Malcolm Cormack. Richmond: Virginia Museum of Fine Arts, 1997.

Blenkinsopp, Joseph. *Isaiah 1–39. A New Translation with Introduction and Commentary*. Anchor Bible. New York: Doubleday, 2000.

———. *Isaiah 56–66. A New Translation with Introduction and Commentary*. Anchor Bible. New York: Doubleday, 2003.

Blount, Brian K. *Revelation: A Commentary*. New Testament Library. Louisville: Westminster John Knox, 2009.

Bøe, Sverre. *Gog and Magog: Ezekiel 38-39 as pre-text for Revelation 19,17–21 and 20,7–10*. Wissenschaftliche Untersuchungen zum Neuen Testament 2.Reihe 135. Tübingen: Mohr Siebeck, 2001.

Boehm, Omri. *The Binding of Isaac: A Religious Model of Disobedience*. Library of Hebrew Bible. New York: T. & T. Clark, 2007.

Bonhoeffer, Dietrich. *Creation and Fall: A Theological Interpretation of Genesis 1-3*. Translated by John C. Fletcher. London: SCM, 1959.

———. *Ethics*. Translated by Neville Horton Smith. New York: Touchstone, 1995.

Bonnard, Pierre. *L'Évangile Selon Saint Matthieu*. Neuchatel: Éditions Delachaux & Nestlé, 1963.

Boorer, Suzanne. "The Place of Numbers 13-13 and Numbers 20:2–12 in the Priestly Narrative." *JBL* 131 (2012) 45–63.

Boring, M. Eugene. "Narrative Christology in the Apocalypse." *CBQ* 54 (1992) 702–23.

Bornkamm, Günther. "Die Komposition der apokalyptischen Visionen in der Offenbarung Johannis." *ZNW* 36 (1937) 132–49.

Bost, Hubert. "Le chant sur la chute d'un tyran en Esaïe 14." *ETR* 59 (1984) 5–14.

Bousset, Wilhelm. *Die Offenbarung Johannis*. Göttingen: Vandenhoeck & Ruprecht, 1906.

Bovon, François. *A Commentary on the Gospel of Luke 1:1–9:50*. Translated by Christine M. Thomas. Hermeneia: Minneapolis: Fortress, 2002.

Bowens, Lisa M. "The Role of John the Baptist in Matthew's Gospel." *WW* 30 (2010) 311–18.

Bowlin, John R. "Augustine on Justifying Coercion." *ANCE* 17 (1997) 49–70.

Brant, Jo-Ann. *John*. Paideia. Grand Rapids: Baker Academic, 2011.

Breitbart, Sidney. "The Cain and Abel Narrative: Its Problems and Lessons." *JBQ* 32 (2004) 122–24.

Bright, John. *A History of Israel*. Second edition. Philadelphia: Westminster, 1976.

Brighton, Louis A. *Revelation*. Concordia Commentary. St. Louis: Concordia, 1999.

Brock, S. P. "Origen's aims as a Textual Critic of the Old Testament." In *Studia Patristica*, edited by F. L. Cross, 215-18. Berlin: Akademie-Verlag, 1970.

Brown, Francis, S. R. Driver and Charles Briggs. *A Hebrew and English Lexicon of the Old Testament*. Oxford: Clarendon Press, 1980.

Brown, Peter. *Augustine of Hippo: A Biography*. London: Faber and Faber, 1967.

———. *The World of Late Antiquity*. London: Thames and Hudson, 1971.

Browning, Robert. *St. John in the Desert: An Introduction and Notes to Browning's A Death in the Desert*. Edited by G. U. Pope. London: Henry Frowde, 1897.

Brown, Stephen G. "The Intertextuality of Isaiah 66.17 and 2 Thessalonians 2.7: A Solution for the 'Restrainer' Problem." In *Paul and the Scriptures of Israel*, edited by Craig A. Evans and James A. Sanders, 254–77. Journal for the Study of the New Testament Supplement Series 83. Sheffield: Sheffield Academic, 1993.

Brueggemann, Walter. *Genesis*. Interpretation. Atlanta: John Knox, 1982.

Brumlik, Nicha. "Post-Holocaust Theology: German Theological Responses since 1945." In *Betrayal: German Churches and the Holocaust*, edited by Robert P. Ericksen and Susannah Heschel, 169–88. Minneapolis: Fortress, 1999.

Buber, Martin. *On the Bible: Eighteen Studies*. Edited by Nahum N. Glatzer. New York: Schocken, 1968.

Buber, Martin. *The Prophetic Faith*. Translated by Carlyle Witton-Davies. New York: Harper & Brothers, 1960.

Budd, Phillip J. *Numbers*. Word Biblical Commentary. Dallas: Word, 2002.

Bultmann, Rudolf. *The Gospel of John*. Translated by G. R. Beasley-Murray et al. Philadelphia: Westminster, 1971.

———. *Kerygma and Myth*. Translated by Reginald H. Fuller. New York: Harper & Brothers, 1961.

———. *New Testament & Mythology and Other Basic Writings*. Selected, edited and translated by Schubert M. Ogden. Philadelphia: Fortress, 1984.

Burggraeve, Roger. "'Am I My Brother's Keeper?' On the Meaning and Depth of Responsibility." *ETL* 84 (2008) 341–61.

Burney, C. F. *Notes on the Hebrew Text of the Books of Kings*. Oxford: Clarendon, 1903.

Burridge, Richard. *Four Gospels, One Jesus?* London: SPCK, 1994.

Butterworth, G. W. *Origen on First Principles*. London: SPCK, 1936.

Byron, John. "Cain's Rejected Offering: Interpretive Approaches to a Theological Problem." *JSP* 18 (2008) 3–22.

Cadiou, Rene. *Introduction au système d'Origène*. Paris: Société d'édition "Les Belles Lettres," 1932.

Caird, G. B. *The Revelation of Saint John*. London: A. & C. Black, 1966. 2nd printing, Peabody, MA: Hendrickson, 1999.

———. "The Glory of God in the Fourth Gospel: An Exercise in Biblical Semantics." *NTS* 15 (1969) 265–77.

Calvin, John. *Sermons on Job*. Translated by Leroy Nixon. Grand Rapids: Baker, 1979.

Campbell, Douglas A. "Romans 1:17—A *Crux Interpretum* for the PISTIS CRISTOU Debate." *JBL* 113 (1994) 265–85.

———. "The Faithfulness of Jesus Christ in Romans 3:22." In *The Faith of Jesus Christ: Exegetical, Biblical, and Theological Studies*, edited by Michael F. Bird and Preston M. Sprinkle, 57–71. Peabody, MA: Hendrickson, 2009.

Campi, Emidio. "Genesis 1-3and the Sixteenth Century Reformers." In *Beyond Eden: The Biblical Story of Paradise (Genesis 2-3) and Its Reception History*, edited by Konrad Schmid and Christoph Riedweg, 251–71. Forschungen zum Alten Testament 2. Reihe 34. Tübingen: Mohr Siebeck, 2008.

Camus, Albert. *The Rebel: An Essay on Man in Revolt*. Translated by Anthony Bower. New York: Vintage, 1991.

Carmy, Shalom. "God is Distant, Incomprehensible: A Literary–Theological Approach to Zophar's First Speech." *Tradition* 38 (2004) 49–63.

Carrell, Peter F. *Jesus and the Angels: Angelology and the Christology of the Apocalypse of John*. Society for New Testament Studies Monograph Series 95. Cambridge: Cambridge University Press, 1997.

Cassuto, Umberto. *A Commentary on the Book of Genesis*. Translated by Israel Abrahams. Jerusalem: Magnes, 1961.

Chamberlain, Lesley. *Nietzsche in Turin: An Intimate Biography*. New York: Picador, 1996.

Charles, J. Daryl. "An Apocalyptic Tribute to the Lamb (Rev 5:1–14)." *JETS* 34 (1991) 461–73.

Charles, R. H. *The Revelation of St. John*. 2 vols. International Critical Commentary. Edinburgh: T. & T. Clark, 1920.

Charlesworth, James H., ed. *The Old Testament Pseudepigrapha*. 2 vols. New York: Doubleday, 1983–85.

Childs, Brevard S. *The Book of Exodus*. Old Testament Library. Louisville: Westminster, 1974.

———. "On Reading the Elijah Narratives." *Int* 34 (1980) 128–37.

Chilton, Bruce. "A Comparative Study of Synoptic Development: The Dispute between Cain and Abel in the Palestinian Targums and the Beelzebul Controversy in the Gospel." *JBL* 101 (1982) 553–62.

Christensen, Duane L. *Deuteronomy 1:1–21:9*. Revised ed. Word Biblical Commentary. Dallas: Word, 2001.

Clark, Elizabeth. *The Origenist Controversy*. Princeton: Princeton University Press, 1992.

Clements, R. E. *Isaiah 1-39*. Grand Rapids: Eerdmans, 1980.

Clines, David J. A. "Job's Fifth Friend: An Ethical Critique of the Book of Job." *BI* 12 (2004) 233–50.

———. *Job*. 3 vols. Word Biblical Commentary. Nashville: Thomas Nelson, 2006.

Cogan, Mordechai. *1 Kings: A New Translation with Introduction and Commentary*. Anchor Bible. New York: Doubleday, 2001.

Cohen, Jeffrey M. "Abraham's Hospitality." *JBQ* 34 (2006) 168–72.

Cohn, Robert L. "The Literary Logic of 1 Kings 17–19." *JBL* 101 (1982) 333–50.

Collins, Adela Yarbro. *The Apocalypse*. New Testament Message 22. Dublin: Veritas, 1979.

———. *The Combat Myth in the Book of Revelation*. Missoula, MT: Scholars, 1976. Reprinted Eugene, OR: Wipf and Stock, 2001.

———. *Cosmology and Eschatology in Jewish and Christian Apocalypticism*. Supplements to the Journal for the Study of Judaism 50. Leiden: E. J. Brill, 1996.

———. *Mark: A Commentary*. Hermeneia: Minneapolis: Fortress, 2007.

———. "Psalms, Philippians 2:6-11, and the Origins of Christology." *BI* 11 (2002) 361–72.

Collins, John J. "The Son of Man and the Saints of the Most High in the Book of Daniel." *JBL* (1974) 50–66.

Collins, John J., ed. *Apocalypse: The Morphology of a Genre*. *Semeia* 14. Missoula: Scholars, 1979.

Cope, O. Lamar. "'To the close of the age': the role of apocalyptic thought in the Gospel of Matthew." In *Apocalyptic and the New Testament: Essays in Honor of J. Louis Martyn*, edited by Joel Marcus and Marion L. Soards, 113–24. Journal for the Study of the New Testament Supplement Series 24. Sheffield: Sheffield Academic, 1989.

Craig, Jr., Kenneth M. "Questions outside Eden (Genesis 4:1-16): Yahweh, Cain and Their Rhetorical Interchange." *JSOT* 86 (1999) 107–28.

Craigie, P. C. "Helel, Athtar and Phaeton (Jes 14,12–15)." *ZAW* 85 (1973) 223–25.

Crenshaw, J. L. *Prophetic Conflict: Its Effect upon Israelite Religion*. Beihefte zur *Zeitschrift für die alttestamentliche Wissenschaft* 124. Berlin: Walter de Gruyter, 1971.

Croatto, J. Severino. "Jesus, Prophet Like Elijah, and Prophet-Teacher Like Moses in Luke-Acts." *JBL* 124 (2005) 451–65.

Crocker, Sylvia F. "Sacrifice in Kierkegaard's *Fear and Trembling*." *HTR* 68 (1975), 125–39.

Crouzel, Henri. *Origen*. Translated by A. S. Worrall. Edinburgh: T. & T. Clark, 1989.

Daniélou, J. *The Theology of Jewish Christianity*. Translated by John A. Baker. Chicago: Henry Regnery, 1964.

Davies, W. D. and Dale C. Allison, *The Gospel According to Saint Matthew*, 3 vols. International Critical Commentary. Edinburgh: T& T Clark, 1988.

Davis, Ellen F. "Learning Our Place: The Agrarian Perspective of the Bible." *WW* 29 (2009) 109–20.

Day, John. "The Origin of Armageddon: Revelation 16:16 as an Interpretation of Zechariah 12:11." In *Crossing the Boundaries: Essays in Biblical Interpretation in Honour of Michael D. Goulder*, edited by Stanley E. Porter et al., 315–26. Leiden: E. J. Brill, 1994.

De Villiers, Pieter G. R. "The role of composition in the interpretation of the Rider on the white horse and the seven seals in Revelation." *HTS* 80 (2004) 125–53.

Denaux, Adelbert. "Old Testament Models for the Lukan Travel Narrative." In *The Scriptures in the Gospels*, edited by Christopher M. Tuckett, 271–305. Bibliotheca ephemeridum theologicarum lovaniensum 131. Leuven: Leuven University Press, 1997.

Dever, William. *What Did the Biblical Writers Know, and When Did They Know It? What Archaeology Can Tell Us About the Reality of Ancient Israel*. Grand Rapids: Eerdmans, 2001.

DeVries, Simon J. *1 Kings*. 2nd ed. Word Biblical Commentary. Dallas: Word, 2003.

Dhorme, Édouard. *A Commentary on the Book of Job*. Translated by Harold Knight. New York: Thomas Nelson, 1984.

Dillon, John. *The Middle Platonists: 80 B.C. to A.D. 220*. Revised ed. Ithaca: Cornell University Press, 1996.

Dormandy, Richard. "Jesus' Temptations in Mark's Gospel: Mark 1:12–13." *ExpT* 114 (2003) 183–87.

Dostoevsky, Fyodor. *The Brothers Karamazov*. Translated by Constance Garnett. New York: Barnes & Noble Classics, 2004.

———. *The Brothers Karamazov*. Translated by Richard Pevear and Larissa Volokhonsky. New York: Farrar, Straus and Giroux, 2002.

———. *Complete Letters 1832–1859*. Edited and translated by David Lowe and Ronald Meyer. Ann Arbor: Ardis, 1988.

Doukhan, Jacques. "The Center of the Aqedah: A Study of the Literary Structure of Genesis 22:1-19." *AUSS* 31 (1993) 17–28.

Doyle, Brian. "The Sin of Sodom: yāda', yāda',yāda'? A Reading of the Mamre-Sodom Narrative in Genesis 18-19." *Theology & Sexuality* 9 (1998) 84–100.

Dragga, Sam. "Genesis 2-3: A Story of Liberation." *JSOT* 55 (1992) 3–13.

Drake, H. A. *Constantine and the Bishops: The Politics of Intolerance*. Baltimore: Johns Hopkins University Press, 2000).

Driver, G. R. *Canaanite Myths and Legends*. Edinburgh: T. & T. Clark, 1956.

Drogin, Bob. *Curveball: Spies, Lies, and the Con Man Who Caused a War*. New York: Random, 2007.

Duke, Paul D. *Irony in the Fourth Gospel*. Atlanta: John Knox, 1985.

Durham, John I. *Exodus*. Word Biblical Commentary. Dallas: Word, 2002.

Ehrman, Albert. "What Did Cain Say to Abel?" *JBQ* 53 (1962) 164–67.

Ehrman, Bart D. *God's Problem: How the Bible Fails to Answer Our Most Important Question—Why We Suffer*. San Francisco: HarperOne, 2008.

———. *Misquoting Jesus: The Story Behind Who Changed the Bible and Why*. New York: HarperCollins, 2005.

Eichrodt, Walther. *Theology of the Old Testament*. 2 vols. Translated by John Baker. Old Testament Library. London: SCM, 1961.

Ellul, Jacques. *Apocalypse: The Book of Revelation*. Translated by George W. Schreiner. New York: Seabury, 1977.

Emmrich, Martin. "The Case against Moses Reopened." *JETS* 46 (2003) 53–62.

———. "The Temptation Narrative of Genesis 3:1-6: A Prelude to the Pentateuch and the History of Israel." *EQ* 73 (2001) 3–20.

Enslin, M. S. *Christian Beginnings: The Literature of the Christian Movement*. New York: Harper, 1956.

Epp-Tiessen, Dan. "1 Kings 19: The Renewal of Elijah." *Direction* 35 (2006) 33–43.

Ericksen, Robert P. and Susannah Heschel, eds. *Betrayal: German Churches and the Holocaust*. Minneapolis: Fortress Press, 1999.

Estep, William R. *The Anabaptist Story: An Introduction to Sixteenth-Century Anabaptism*. 3rd ed. Grand Rapids: Eerdmans, 1996.

Eusebius. *The Life of Constantine*. Translated by Ernest Cushing Richardson. Edited by Philip Schaff and Henry Wace. Nicene and Post-Nicene Fathers. Buffalo: Christian Literature, 1890. Reprinted Grand Rapids: Eerdmans, 1952.

Evans, Craig A. and James A. Sanders, eds. *Paul and the Scriptures of Israel*. Journal for the Study of the New Testament Supplement Series 83. Sheffield: JSOT Press, 1993.

Exum, J. Cheryl. *Fragmented Women: Feminist (Sub)versions of Biblical Narratives*. Journal for the Study of the Old Testament Supplement Series 163. Sheffield: JSOT Press, 1993.

———. "'Whose Interests Are Being Served?' An Essay on Feminist Criticism." In *Judges & Method: New Approaches in Biblical Studies*, edited by Gale A. Yee, 65–89. Minneapolis: Fortress, 2007.

Eynikel, Erik. "Judges 19-21, An 'Appendix:' Rape, Murder, War and Abduction." *CV* 47 (2005) 101–15.

Fergusson, David. *Rudolf Bultmann*. London and New York: Continuum, 1992.

Feuillet, A. "L'hymne christologique de l'Épitre aux Philippiens (II, 6–11)." *RB* 72 (1965) 352–80.

Fields, Weston W. "The Motif 'Night as Danger' Associated with Three Biblical Destruction Narratives." In *"Sha'arei Talmon:"Studies in the Bible, Qumran, and the Ancient Near East Presented to Shemaryahu Talmon*, edited by Michael Fishbane and Emmanuel Tov, 17–32. Winona Lake: Eisenbrauns, 1992.

Fiorenza, Elisabeth Schüssler. *The Book of Revelation. Justice and Judgment*. 2nd ed. Minneapolis: Fortress Press, 1998.

———. *Revelation: Vision of a Just World*. Minneapolis: Fortress, 1991.

Fisch, S. *Ezekiel. Hebrew Text & English Translation with an Introduction and Commentary*. Stuttgarter biblische Beiträge. London: Soncino, 1950.

Fischer, Zoltan. "Sacrificing Isaac: A New Interpretation." *JBQ* 35 (2007) 173–78.

Fishbane, Michael. *Sacred Attunement: A Jewish Theology*. Chicago: University of Chicago Press, 2008.

———. "The Well of Living Water: A Biblical Motif and Its Ancient Transformations." In *Sha'arei Talmon: Studies in the Bible, Qumran, and the Ancient Near East Presented to Shemaryahu Talmon*, edited by Michael Fishbane and Emanuel Tov, 3-16. Winona Lake: Eisenbrauns, 1992.

Fishburn, Janet Forsythe. "Søren Kierkegaard, Exegete." *Int* 39 (1985), 229–45.

Fitzmyer, J. A. *The Gospel According to Luke.* 2 volumes. Anchor Bible. Garden City: Doubleday, 1981.

Flowers, H. J. "The Vision of Revelation IV-V." *ATR* 12 (1930), 525–30.

Fohrer, Georg. *Das Buch Hiob.* Kommentar zum Alten Testament. Gütersloh: Gerd Mohn, 1963.

Fokkelman, Jan P. "Structural Remarks on Judges 9 and 19." In *"Sha'arei Talmon:"Studies in the Bible, Qumran, and the Ancient Near East Presented to Shemaryahu Talmon*, edited by Michael Fishbane and Emmanuel Tov, 33–45. Winona Lake: Eisenbrauns, 1992.

Ford, David. *Barth and God's Story: Biblical Narrative and the Theological Method of Karl Barth in the 'Church Dogmatics.'* Frankfurt: Peter Lang, 1981.

Ford, J. Massyngberde. *Revelation: A New Translation with Introduction and Commentary.* Anchor Bible. New York: Doubleday, 1975.

Forestell, J. Terence. *The Word of the Cross: Salvation as Revelation in the Fourth Gospel.* Rome: Biblical Institute Press, 1974.

France, R. T. *The Gospel according to Matthew: An Introduction and Commentary.* New International Commentary on the New Testament. Grand Rapids: Eerdmans, 2007.

Frank, Joseph. *Dostoevsky: A Writer in His Time.* Edited by Mary Petrusewicz. Princeton: Princeton University Press, 2010.

Fredriksen, Paula. *Augustine and the Jews: A Christian Defense of Jews and Judaism.* New Haven: Yale University Press, 2008.

———. *Sin: The Early History of an Idea.* Princeton: Princeton University Press, 2012.

Frend, W. H. C. *The Rise of Christianity.* Philadelphia: Fortress Press, 1984.

Fresch, Cheryl H. "'Cain rose up against Abel': Murder, Mystery and *Paradise Lost.*" *ChrLit* 51 (2002) 191–207.

Friedländer, Saul. *The Years of Persecution: Nazi Germany and the Jews 1933-1939.* London: Phoenix, 1999.

———. *The Years of Extermination: Nazi Germany and the Jews 1939-1945.* London: Phoenix, 2008.

Fyall, Robert S. *Now My Eyes Have Seen You: Images of Creation and Evil in the Book of Job.* New Studies in Biblical Theology. Downers Grove: InterVarsity, 2002.

Garlington, Don B. "The 'Better Righteousness:' Matthew 5:20." *BBR* 20 (2010) 479–502.

Garff, Joakim. *Søren Aabye Kierkegaard: En biografi.* Translated by Knut Johansen. Oslo: Forlaget Press, 2002. English translation *Søren Kierkegaard: A Biography.* Translated by Bruce H. Kirmmse. Princeton: Princeton University Press, 2007.

Garrett, Susan R. "Exodus from Bondage: Luke 9:31 and Acts 12:1-24." *CBQ* 52 (1990) 656–80.

Garrett, Susan R. "Jesus and the Angels." *WW* 29 (2009), 162–69.

Garrett, Susan R. *No Ordinary Angel: Celestial Spirits and Christian Claims about Jesus.* New Haven and London: Yale University Press, 2008.

Garrett, Susan R. *The Temptations of Jesus in Mark's Gospel.* Grand Rapids: Eerdmans, 1998.

Gaventa, Beverly Roberts. "The Cosmic Power of Sin in Paul's Letter to the Romans: Toward a Widescreen Edition." *Int* 58 (2004), 229–40.

———. "Interpreting the Death of Jesus Apocalyptically: Reconsidering Romans 8:32." In *Jesus and Paul Reconnected: Fresh Pathways into an Old Debate*," edited by Todd D. Still, 124–45. Grand Rapids: Eerdmans, 2007.

———. "Neither height nor depth: discerning the cosmology of Romans." *SJT* 64 (2011) 265–78.

Gerhardsson, Birger. *The Testing of God's Son: An Analysis of an Early Christian Midrash.* Lund: C.W.K. Gleerup, 1966.

Gese, Hartmut. "Zur Bedeutung Elias für die biblische Theologie." In *Evangelium, Schriftauslegung, Kirche: Festschrift für Peter Stuhlmacher zum 65. Geburtstag*, edited by Jostein Ådna et al., 126–50. Gõttingen: Vandenhoeck & Ruprecht, 1997.

Geyser, Paul. *Die Sünde Jerobeams.* 1911 reprint. Place of publication not stated.

Gibbs, John G. "The Relation between Creation and Redemption according to Phil. II.5–11." *NovT* 12 (1970) 270–83.

Gibson, Jeffrey B. "Jesus' Wilderness Temptation according to Mark." *JSNT* 53 (1994) 3–34.

Girard, René. *I See Satan Fall Like Lightening.* Translated by James G. Williams. Maryknoll, NY: Orbis, 2011.

Glancy, Jennifer A. "Unveiling Masculinity: The Construction of Gender in Mark 6:14–29." *BI* 2 (1994) 34–50.

Glasson, T. Francis. "Two Notes on the Philippian Hymn [II.6–11]." *NTS* 21 (1974/75), 133–39.

Gollinger, Hildegard. "Das 'grosse Zeichen': Offb. 12—das Zentrale Kapitel der Offenbarung des Johannes." *BK* 39 (1967) 401–16.

———. *Das "grosse Zeichen" von Apocalypse 12.* Stuttgart: Echter Verlag, 1971.

Gordis, Robert. *The Book of Job: Commentary, New Translation, and Special Studies.* New York: Jewish Theological Seminary of America, 1978.

Graham, Gordon. *Evil & Christian Ethics.* New Studies in Christian Ethics 20. Cambridge: Cambridge University Press, 2001.

Greenberg, Irving. "Cloud of Smoke, Pillar of Fire: Judaism, Christianity, and Modernity after the Holocaust." In *Auschwitz: Beginning of a New Era?* Edited by Eva Fleischner, 7–55. New York: KTAV, 1974.

Greenberg, Moshe. *Ezekiel 1–20: A New Translation with Introduction and Commentary.* Anchor Bible. New York: Doubleday, 1983.

———. *Ezekiel 21-37: A New Translation with Introduction and Commentary.* Anchor Bible. New York: Doubleday, 1997.

Greenslade, S. L. *Church and State from Constantine to Theodosius.* London: SCM, 1954.

Greer, Rowan A. "Augustine's Transformation of the Free Will Defence." *FP* 13 (1996) 471–86.

Greggs, Tom. "Exclusivist or Universalist? Origen the 'Wise Steward of the Word.' (*CommRom*.V.1.7) and the Issue of Genre." *IJST*9 (2007) 315–27.

Greidanus, Sidney. "Preaching Christ from the Narrative of the Fall." *BSac* 161 (2004), 259–73.

Grelot, Pierre. "Deux expressions difficiles de Philippiens 2,6-7." *Bib* 53 (1972) 495–507.

———. "Isaïe XIV 12-15 et son arrière-plan mythologique." *RHR* 149 (1956) 18–48.

Grenz, Stanley. "The Flight from God: Kierkegaard's *Fear and Trembling* and Universal Ethical Systems." *PRS* 14 (1987), 147–59.

Griffin David Ray, ed. *God, Power, and Evil: A Process Theodicy.* Philadelphia: Westminster, 1976.

Gross, Walter. "Lying Prophets and Disobedient Man of God in 1 Kings 13: Role Analysis as an Instrument of Theological Interpretation of an OT Narrative Text." *Semeia* 15 (1979) 97–135.

Guelich, Robert A. *Mark 1-8:26.* Word Biblical Commentary. Dallas: Word, 2002.

Gundry, Robert H. "Angelomorphic Christology in the Book of Revelation." *Society of Biblical Literature Seminar Papers* 1994, 662–78. Atlanta: Scholars Press, 1994.

———. *Matthew: A Commentary on His Literary and Theological Art.* Grand Rapids: Eerdmans, 1982.

———. "The New Jerusalem: People as Place, Not Place for People." *NovT* 29 (1987) 254–64.

Gunkel, Hermann. *Genesis.* Translated by Mark E. Biddle. Macon, GA: Mercer University Press, 1997.

———. *Schöpfung und Chaos in Urzeit und Endzeit: eine religionsgeschichtliche Untersuchung über Gen 1 und Ap Joh 12.* Göttingen: Vandenhoeck und Ruprecht, 1895.

Gunn, David M. *Judges.* Blackwell Biblical Commentary. Malden, MA: Blackwell, 2005.

Gutiérrez, Gustavo. *On Job: God-Talk and the Suffering of the Innocent.* Translated by Matthew J. O'Connell. New York: Orbis, 1987.

Gutman, Yisrael. "On the Character of Nazi Antisemitism." In *Antisemitism through the Ages*, edited by Shmuel Almog, 349–80. New York: Pergamon, 1988.

Habel, Norman. *The Book of Job.* Cambridge Bible Commentary. London: Cambridge University Press, 1975.

Hagner, Donald A. "Apocalyptic Motifs in the Gospel of Matthew: Continuity and Discontinuity." *HBT* 7 (1985) 53–82.

———. *Matthew 1-13.* Word Biblical Commentary. Dallas: Word, 2002.

Hahn, Scott W. "Covenant, Oath, and the Aqedah: Διαθήκη in Galatians 3:15-18." *CBQ* 67 (2005) 79–100.

Hall, Amy Laura. "*Self-Deception, Confusion, and Salvation in Fear and Trembling with Works of Love.*" *JRE* 28 (2000) 37–61.

Hanson, Anthony Tyrrell. *The Wrath of the Lamb.* London: SPCK, 1957.

Hanson, R. C. P. "*Origène.*" *ZK* 97 (1986) 276–77.

Harding, Thomas. *Hanns and Rudolf: The German Jew and the Hunt for the Kommandant of Auschwitz.* London: Windmill, 2014.

Harnack, Adolf von. *Der kirchengeschichtliche Ertrag der exegetischen Arbeiten des Origenes.* Leipzig: J. C. Hinrichs'sche Buchhandlung, 1919.

Harris, J. G. *The Qumran Commentary on Habakkuk.* London: A. R. Mowbray, 1966.

Harris, R. Laird, Gleason L. Archer, Jr., Bruce K. Waltke. *Theological Wordbook of the Old Testament.* Chicago: Moody Press, 1980.

Hart, David Bentley. *Atheist Delusions: The Christian Revolution and Its Fashionable Enemies.* New Haven: Yale University Press, 2009.

Haupt, Paul. "The Curse on the Serpent." *JBL* 35 (1918) 155–62.

Hauser, Alan J. and Russell Gregory. *From Carmel to Horeb: Elijah in Crisis.* Journal for the Study of the Old Testament Supplement Series 85. Sheffield: Almond, 1990.

Hays, Richard B. *The Conversion of the Imagination: Paul as Interpreter of Israel's Scripture.* Grand Rapids: Eerdmans, 2005.

———. *Echoes of Scripture in the Letters of Paul.* New Haven: Yale University Press, 1989.

———. *The Faith of Jesus Christ: An Investigation of the Narrative Substructure of Galatians 3:1-4:11.* Society of Biblical Literature Dissertation Series 56. Chico: Scholars, 1983. Reprinted Grand Rapids: Eerdmans, 2002.

———. "Is Paul's Gospel Narratable?" *JSNT* 27 (2004) 217–39.

———. "'The Righteous One' as Eschatological Deliverer: A Case Study in Paul's Apocalyptic Hermeneutics." In *Apocalyptic and the New Testament: Essays in Honor of J. Louis Martyn*, edited by Joel Marcus and Marion L. Soards, 191–215. Journal for the Study of the New Testament Supplement Series 24. Sheffield: Sheffield Academic, 1989.

Hawthorne, Gerald F. *Philippians*. Word Biblical Commentary. Waco: Word Books, 1983.

Hefling, Charles. "Christ and Evils: Assessing an Aspect of Marilyn McCord Adams' Theodicy." *ATR* 83 (2001) 869–82.

Heil, John Paul. "The Fifth Seal (Rev 6,9–11) as a Key to the Book of Revelation." *Bib* 74 (1993) 220–43.

———. *The Transfiguration of Jesus: Narrative Meaning and Function of Mark 9:2–8, Matt 17:1–18 and Luke 9:28–36*. Analecta Biblica 144. Roma: Editrice Ponteficio Istituto Biblico, 2000.

Heim, Knut M. "The (God-)Forsaken King of Psalm 89: A Historical and Intertextual Enquiry." In *King and Messiah in Israel and the Ancient Near East*. Proceedings of the Oxford Old Testament Seminar, edited by John Day, 296–322. Journal for the Study of the Old Testament Supplement Series 270. Sheffield: Sheffield Academic, 1998.

Heinemann, Gustav W. "Gerhard von Rad zum 70. Geburtstag." In *Probleme biblischer Theologie: Gerhard von Rad zum 70. Geburtstag*, edited by Hans Walter Wolff, 11–12. München: Chr. Kaiser Verlag, 1971.

Heliso, Desta. *Pistis and the Righteous One: A Study of Romans 1:17 against the Backgroundof Scripture and Second Temple Jewish Literature*. Wissenschaftliche Untersuchungen zum Neuen Testament 2. Reihe 235. Tübingen: Mohr Siebeck, 2007.

Hendel, Ronald. *The Text of Genesis 1-11*. New York: Oxford University Press, 1998.

Hick, John. "An Irenaean Theodicy." In *Encountering Evil: Live Options in Theodicy*, edited by Stephen T. Davis, 39–52. Edinburgh: T. & T. Clark, 1981.

———. *Philosophy of Religion*. Englewood Cliffs, N.J.: Prentice-Hall, 1963.

Hillesum, Etty. *An Interrupted Life: The Diaries of Etty Hillesum, 1941-43*. Translated by Arnold J. Pomerans. New York: Pantheon, 1989.

———. *An Interrupted Life: The Diaries, 1941-1943 and Letters from Westerbrook*. Translated by Arnold J. Pomerans. New York: Metropolitan, 1996.

Holladay, William L. "Text, Structure, and Irony in the Poem on the Fall of the Tyrant, Isaiah 14." *CBQ* 61 (1999) 633–43.

Hollander, Harm W. "Seeing God 'in a riddle' or 'face to face': An Analysis of 1 Corinthians 13.12." *JSNT* 32 (2010) 395–403.

Hollingdale, R. J. "The Hero as Outsider."In *The Cambridge Companion to Nietzsche*, edited by Bernd Magnus and Kathleen M. Higgins, 79–89. Cambridge: Cambridge University Press, 1996.

———. *Nietzsche: The Man and His Philosophy*. Revised ed. Cambridge: Cambridge University Press, 1999.

Holtz, Traugott. *Die Christologie der Apokalypse des Johannes*. Texte und Untersuchungen 85. Berlin: Akademie-Verlag, 1962.

Hume, David. *Dialogues Concerning Natural Religion*. Oxford World's Classics. Oxford: Oxford University Press, 1992.

Hurst, L. D. "Re-enter the Pre-existent Christ in Philippians 2.5–11?" *NTS* 32 (1986), 449–57.

Jacob, Edmond. *Theology of the Old Testament*. Translated by Arthur W. Heathcote and Philip J. Allcock. London: Hodder and Stoughton, 1958.

Jacobson, Howard. "Genesis IV 8." *VT* 55 (2005), 564–65.

Jauhiainen, Marko. "The OT Background to *Armageddon* [Rev. 16:16] Revisited." *NovT* 47 (2005) 381–93.

Jepsen, Alfred. "Gottesmann und Prophet: Anmerkungen zum Kapitel 1. Könige 13." In *Probleme biblischer Theologie: Gerhard von Rad zum 70. Geburtstag*, edited by Hans Walter Wolff, 171–82. Munich: Chr. Kaiser Verlag, 1971.

Jeremias, Jörg. *Theophanie: Die Geschichte einer alttestamentlichen Gattung*. Neukirchen-Vluyn: Neukirchener Verlag, 1965.

Jewett, Robert. *Romans: A Commentary*. Hermeneia: Minneapolis: Fortress, 2006.

———. *The Thessalonian Correspondence*. Philadelphia: Fortress, 1986.

Johns, Loren L. "The Lamb in the Rhetorical Program of the Apocalypse of John." *Society of Biblical Literature Seminar Papers* 37 (1998) 2:762–84.

Johnsen, Carsten. *The Maligned God*. Mezien: Untold Story Publishers, 1980.

Johnson, Luke Timothy. *The Writings of the New Testament: An Interpretation*. 3rd ed. Minneapolis: Fortress, 2010.

Jonas, Hans. *The Imperative of Responsibility: In Search of an Ethics for the Technological Age*. Chicago: University of Chicago Press, 1984.

Jones-Warsaw, Koala. "Toward a Womanist Hermeneutic: A Reading of Judges 19-21." *JITC* 22 (1994) 18–35.

Kafka, Franz. *The Trial: Definitive Edition* Translated by Willa and Edwin Muir. New York: Schocken, 1984.

Kahn, Pinchas. "Moses at the Waters of Meribah: A Case of Transference." *JBQ* 35 (2007) 85–93.

Kamen, Henry. *The Spanish Inquisition: A Historical Revision*. London: Weidenfeld and Nicholson, 1997.

Kamp, Albert. "With or Without a Cause: Images of God and Man in Job 1-3." In *Job's God*, edited by Ellen van Wolde, 9–17. London; SCM, 2004.

Kamuf, Peggy. "Author of A Crime." In *Feminist Companion to Judges*, edited by Athalya Brenner, 187–207. Sheffield: JSOT Press, 1993.

Kant, Immanuel. *The Conflict of the Faculties*. Translated by Mary J. Gregor. London: University of Nebraska Press, 1979.

———. *On the Old Saw: That May Be Right in Theory But It Won't Work in Practice*. Translated by E. B. Ashton. Philadelphia: University of Pennsylvania Press, 1974.

———. *Practical Philosophy: The Cambridge Edition of the Works of Immanuel Kant*. Edited by Mary J. Gregor. Cambridge: Cambridge University Press, 1996.

———. *Religion within the Limits of Reason Alone*. Translated by Theodore M. Greene and Hoyt H. Hudson. New York: Harper Torchbooks, 1960.

Käsemann, Ernst. "Kritische Analyse von Phil. 2,5-11." *ZTK* 47 (1950) 313–60.

———. *New Testament Questions for Today*. Translated by W. J. Montague. Philadelphia: Fortress, 1969.

Kass, Leon. R. "Farmers, Founders, and Fratricide: The Story of Cain and Abel." *First Things* 62 (1996) 19–26.

Katz, Claire Elisa. "Raising Cain: The Problem of Evil and the Question of Responsibility." *Crosscurrents* (2005) 215–33.

Keener, Craig S. *The Gospel of John: A Commentary*. 2 vols. Peabody, MA: Hendrickson, 2003.

Kerkeslager, Allen. "Apollo, Greco-Roman Prophecy and the Rider on the White Horse in Rev 6:2." *JBL* 112 (1993) 116–21.

Kermode, Frank. *The Genesis of Secrecy: On the Interpretation of Narrative*. Cambridge: Harvard University Press, 1979.

———. *The Sense of An Ending: Studies in the Theory of Fiction with a New Epilogue*. Oxford: Oxford University Press, 2000.

Khiok-Khng, Yeo. "Christ the End of History and the Hope of Suffering: Revelation 5 in the Light of Pannenberg's Christology." *AJT* 8 (1994) 308–34.

Kiddle, Martin. *The Revelation of St. John*. London: Hodder and Stoughton, 1940.

Kierkegaard, Søren. *Concluding Unscientific Postscript*. Translated by David F. Swenson and Walter Lowrie. Princeton: Princeton University Press, 1968.

———. *Fear and Trembling*. Translated by Walter Lowrie. New York: Doubleday, 1954.

———. *Fear and Trembling*. Edited and translated by Howard V. Hong and Edna H. Hong. Princeton: Princeton University Press, 1983.

Kim, Angela Y. "Cain and Abel in the Light of Envy: A Study in the History of the Interpretation of Envy in Genesis 4.1-16." *JSP* 12 (2001) 65–84.

Kjetsaa, Geir. *Dostoevsky and His New Testament*. Oslo: Solum, 1984.

Klemperer, Victor. *I Will Bear Witness 1933-1941: A Diary of the Nazi Years*. Translated by Martin Chalmers. New York: Modern Library, 1999.

Kline, Peter. "Absolute Action: Divine Hiddenness in Kierkegaard's *Fear and Trembling*." *Mod Theol* 28 (2012) 503–25.

Koch, Klaus. *The Rediscovery of Apocalyptic*. Translated by Margaret Kohl. London: SCM, 1972.

Koester, Craig R. "The Death of Jesus and the Human Condition: Exploring the Theology of John's Gospel." In *Life in Abundance: Studies of John's Gospel in Tribute to Raymond E. Brown*, edited by John R. Donahue, 141–57. Collegeville, MN: Liturgical, 2005.

———. *The Word of Life: A Theology of John's Gospel*. Grand Rapids: Eerdmans, 2008.

Kovacs, Judith L. "'Now Shall the Ruler of This World Be Driven out': Jesus' Death as Cosmic Battle in John 12:20-36." *JBL* 114 (1995) 227–47.

Kulka, Otto Dov. *Landscapes of the Metropolis of Death: Reflections on Memory and Imagination*. Translated by Ralph Mandel. New York: Penguin, 2014.

Lambrecht, J. "The Opening of the Seals (Rev 6,1—8,6)." *Bib* 79 (1998) 198–220.

———. "A Structuration of Revelation 4,1-22,5." In *L'Apocalypse johannique et l'Apocalyptique dans le Nouveau Testament*, edited by J. Lambrecht, 77–104. Gembloux: Éditions J, Duculot, 1979.

Lane, William L. *Hebrews 1-8*. Word Biblical Commentary. Dallas: Word, 2002.

LaRondelle, Hans K. "Paul's Prophetic Outline in 2 Thessalonians 2." *AUSS* 21 (1983) 61–9.

Larrimore, Mark, ed. *The Problem of Evil: A Reader*. Malden, MA: Blackwell, 2001.

Laustsen, Carsten Bagge and Rasmus Ugilt. "Eichmann's Kant." *Journal of Speculative Philosophy* 21 (2007) 166–80.

Lee, Pilchan. *The New Jerusalem in the Book of Revelation*. Tübingen: Mohr Siebeck, 2001.

Leibnitz, G. W. *Theodicy: Essays on the Goodness of God, the Freedom of Man and the Origin of Evil*. Translated by E. M. Huggard. Chicago: Open Court, 1988.

Leibowitz, Nehama. *Studies in Bereshit (Genesis) in the Context of Ancient and Modern Jewish Bible Commentary*. 4th ed. Translated by Aryeh Newman. Jerusalem: World Zionist Organization, 1981.

Lemke, Werner E. "The Way of Obedience: 1 Kings 13 and the Structure of the Deuteronomistic History." In *Magnalia Dei, The Mighty Acts of God: Essays on the Bible and Archaeology in Memory of G. Ernest Wright*, edited by Frank Moore Cross et al., 301–26. New York: Doubleday, 1976.

Lenski, R. C. H. *The Interpretation of St. John's Revelation*. Minneapolis: Augsburg, 1963.

Levenson, Jon D. *Creation and the Persistence of Evil.* Princeton: Princeton University Press, 1994.

———. *The Death and Resurrection of the Beloved Son: The Transformation of Child Sacrifice in Judaism and Christianity.* New Haven: Yale University Press, 1993.

Levi, Primo. *Collected Poems.* New Edition. Translated by Ruth Feldman and Brian Swann. New York: Faber and Faber, 1992.

———. *The Drowned and the Saved.* Translated by Raymond Rosenthal. New York: Vintage, 1989.

———. *If This Is A Man.* Translated by Stuart Woolf. New York: Little, Brown, 1991.

———. *Moments of Reprieve: A Memoir of Auschwitz.* Translated by Ruth Feldman. New York: Penguin, 1995.

———. *Survival in Auschwitz.* Translated by Stuart Woolf. New York: Simon & Schuster, 1996.

Levinas, Immanuel. "Useless Suffering." In *The Provocation of Levinas: Rethinking the Other*, edited by Robert Bernasconi and David Wood, 156–67. London: Routledge, 1988.

Lewis, Jack P. "The Offering of Abel (Gen 4:4): A History of Interpretation." *JETS* 37 (1994) 481–96.

Linton, Gregory L. "Reading the Apocalypse as Apocalypse: The Limits of Genre." In *The Reality of Apocalypse: Rhetoric and Politics in the Book of Revelation*, edited by David L. Barr, 9–42. Atlanta: Society of Biblical Literature, 2006.

Lipton, Diana. "Inevitability and Community in the Demise of Moses." *JPJ* 7 (1996) 79–93.

Lockwood, Peter F. "The Elijah Syndrome: What Is Elijah up to at Mt Horeb." *LTJ* 38 (2004) 51–62.

Lohmeyer, Ernst. "Das zwölfte Kapitel der Offenbarung Johannis," *TB* 4 (1925) 285–92.

———. *Die Offenbarung des Johannes.* Handbuch zum Neuen Testament 16. Tübingen: J.C.B. Mohr (Paul Siebeck), 1953.

———. *Kyrios Jesus: Eine Untersuchung zu Phil. 2,5-11.* 2nd ed. Heidelberg: Carl Winter Universitätsverlag, 1961.

Longenecker, Bruce, ed. *Narrative Dynamics in Paul: A Critical Assessment.* Louisville: Westminster John Knox, 2002.

Louw-Nida Greek-English Lexicon of the New Testament Based on Semantic Domains, eds. J. P. Louw and E. A. Nida. 2nd ed. New York: United Bible Societies, 1988.

Luck, Ulrich. *Das Evangelium nach Matthäus.* Zürich: Theologischer Verlag, 1993.

Lust, Johan. "Elijah and the theophany on Mount Horeb." In *La Notion biblique de Dieu: le Dieu de la bible et le Dieu des philosophes*, edited by J. Coppens, 91–100. Bibliotheca ephemeridum theologicarum lovaniensum 41. Gembloux: Duculot, 1976.

Luther, Martin. *The Bondage of the Will. Luther's Works* 33. Translated by Philip S. Watson. Edited by Jaroslav Pelikan et al. Philadelphia: Fortress Press, 1999.

———. *Lectures on Galatians, 1535. Chapters 1-4. Luther's Works* 26. Translated and edited by Jaroslav Pelikan. St. Louis: Concordia, 1999.

———. "On the Jews and Their Lies." *Luther's Works* 47. Translated by Martin H. Bertram. Edited by Franklin Sherman, 135–305. Philadelphia: Fortress, 1971.

———. *Preface to the Complete Edition of Luther's Latin Writings. Luther's Works* 34. Translated by Lewis W. Spitz, Sr. Edited by Lewis W. Spitz and Helmut T. Lehmann, 327–33. Philadelphia: Fortress, 1999.

———. *Prefaces to the New Testament. Luther's Works* 35. Translated by Charles M. Jacobs, 355–410. Philadelphia: Fortress, 1999.

———. "Temporal Authority: To What Extent It Should Be Obeyed." *Luther's Works* 45. Translated by J. J. Schindel. Edited by Walther I. Brandt and Helmut T. Lehmann, 80–128. Philadelphia: Fortress, 1962.

Luz, Ulrich. *Matthew 1-7: A Commentary*. Revised ed. Translated by James E. Crouch. Hermeneia. Minneapolis: Fortress, 2007.

Lytton, Timothy D. "'Shall Not the Judge of the Earth Deal Justly?': Accountability, Compassion, and Judicial Authority in the Biblical Story of Sodom and Gomorrah." *JLR* 18 (2002) 31–55.

MacDonald, Nathan. "Listening to Abraham – Listening to YHWH: Divine Justice and Mercy in Genesis 18:16-33." *CBQ* 66 (2004) 25–43.

Machiavelli, Nicolo. *The Prince*. Translated by W. K. Marriott. El Paso: Norte Press, 2006.

MacMullen, Ramsay. *Christianizing the Roman Empire A.D. 100-400*. New Haven: Yale University Press, 1984.

Mafico, T. J. "The Crucial Question Concerning the Justice of God." *JTSA* 42 (1983) 11–16.

Malesic, Jonathan Jay. "A Secret Both Sinister And Salvific: Secrecy and Normativity in Light of Kierkegaard's *Fear and Trembling*." *JAAR* 74 (2006) 446–68.

Mánek, Jindrich. "The New Exodus in the Books of Luke." *NovT* (1958) 8–23.

Mann, C. S. *Mark*. Anchor Bible. New York: Doubleday, 1986.

Mann, Thomas W. "Theological Reflections on the Denial of Moses." *JBL* 98 (1979) 481–94.

Marchal, Joseph A. "Expecting a Hymn, Encountering An Argument: Introducing the Rhetoric of Philippians and Pauline Interpretation." *Int* 61 (2007) 245–55.

Marcus, Joel. *Mark 1-8: A New Translation with Introduction and Commentary*. Anchor Bible. New York: Doubleday, 1999.

Marshall, I. Howard. *1 and 2 Thessalonians*. New Century Bible Commentary. Grand Rapids: Eerdmans, 1983.

Martin, R. A. "The Earliest Messianic Interpretation of Genesis 3 15." *JBL* 84 (1965) 425–27.

Martin, Ralph P. *Carmen Christi: Philippians ii. 5-11 in Recent Interpretation and in the Setting of Early Christian Worship*. Society for New Testament Studies Monograph Series 4. Cambridge: Cambridge University Press, 1967.

———. *The Epistle of Paul to the Philippians*. Leicester: Inter-Varsity, 1979.

Martyn, J. Louis. "Apocalyptic Antinomies in Paul's Letter to the Galatians." *NTS* 31 (1985) 410–24.

———. "The Apocalyptic Gospel in Galatians." *Int* 54 (2000) 246–66.

———. "Events in Galatia: Modified Covenantal Nomism versus God's Invasion of the Cosmos in the Singular Gospel: A Response to J. D. G. Dunn and B. R. Gaventa. In *Pauline theology 1: Thessalonians, Philippians, Galatians, Philemon*, edited by Jouette M. Bassler, 160–80. Minneapolis: Fortress, 1991.

———. *Galatians: A New Translation with Introduction and Commentary*. Anchor Bible. New York: Doubleday, 1997.

Matheson, David. "Verbal Aspect in the Apocalypse of John: An Analysis of Revelation 5. *NovT* 50 (2008) 58–77.

Matthews, Victor H. "Hospitality and Hostility in Genesis 19 and Judges 19." *BTB* 22 (1992) 3–11.

———. *Judges & Ruth*. New Century Bible Commentary. Cambridge: Cambridge University Press, 2004.

Maynard, Arthur H. "TI EMOI KAI ΣOI." *NTS* 31 (1985) 582–86.

Mazzaferri, Frederick David. "*Martyria Iēsou* Revisited." *BT* 39 (1988) 114–22.

McGrath, Alister. *Christian Theology: An Introduction*. 5th ed. Oxford: Basil Blackwell, 2011.

McKenzie, John L. "The Literary Characteristics of Gen 2-3." *TS* 15 (1954) 541–72.

———. *A Theology of the Old Testament*. London: Geoffrey Chapman, 1974.

McNeill, John T. *The History and Character of Calvinism*. London: Oxford University Press, 1954.

Mead, James K. "Kings and Prophets, Donkeys and Lions: Dramatic Shape and Deuteronomistic Rhetoric in 1 Kings XIII." *VT* 49 (1999) 191–205.

Mealy, J. Webb. *After the Thousand Years: Resurrection and Judgment in Revelation 20*. Journal for the Study of the New Testament Supplement Series 70. Sheffield: JSOT Press, 1992.

Menken, Maarten J. J. *2 Thessalonians*. London: Routledge, 1994.

Michaels, J. Ramsay. "Revelation 1.19 and the Narrative Voices of the Apocalypse." *NTS* 37 (1991) 604–20.

Michelet, Marte. *Den største forbrytelsen: Ofre og gjerningsmenn i det norske Holocaust* (Title in English: *The Greatest Crime: Victims and Perpetrators in the Norwegian Holocaust*). Oslo: Gyldendal, 2014.

Milgram, Stanley. "Behavioral Study of Obedience." *JASP* 67 (1963) 371–78.

———. "The Perils of Obedience." *Harper's Magazine* 247 (1973) 62–77.

Miller, Kevin E. "The Nuptial Eschatology of Revelation 19-22." *CBQ* 60 (1998), 301–18.

Miller, Patrick D. "Divine Command and Beyond: The Ethics of the Commandments." In *The Ten Commandments: The Reciprocity of Faithfulness*, edited by William P. Brown, 12–29. Louisville: Westminster John Knox, 2004.

Minear, Paul S. *I Saw a New Earth*. Washington, DC: Corpus, 1968.

———. "The Wounded Beast." *JBL* 72 (1953) 93–101.

Moberly, R. W. L. *The Bible, Theology, and Faith: A Study of Abraham and Jesus*. Cambridge: Cambridge University Press, 2000.

———. "Did the Serpent Get It Right?" *JTS* 39 (1988) 1–27.

———. *Genesis 12-50*. Old Testament Guides. Sheffield: Sheffield Academic, 1992.

Moessner, David P. "Luke 9:1-50: Luke's Preview of the Journey of the Prophet Like Moses of Deuteronomy." *JBL* 102 (1983) 575–605.

Montgomery, James A. *A Critical and Exegetical Commentary on the Books of Kings*. International Critical Commentary. Edinburgh: T. & T. Clark, 1951.

Morgenstern, Julian. "The Mythological Background of Psalm 82." *HUCA* 14 (1939) 29–126.

Morschauser, Scott. "'Hospitality,' Hostiles and Hostages: On the Legal Background to Genesis 19-1-9." *JSOT* 27 (2003) 461–85.

Mounce, Robert. *The Book of Revelation*. New International Commentary on the New Testament. Grand Rapids: Eerdmans, 1977.

Moxnes, Halvor. "God and His Angel in the Shepherd of Hermas." *ST* 28 (1974) 49–56.

Müller, Ulrich B. "Der Christushymnus Phil 2 6-11." *ZNW* 79 (1988) 17–44.

Murdock, William R. "History and Revelation in Jewish Apocalypticism." *Int* 21 (1967) 167–87.

Murphy-O'Connor, Jerome. *Paul: A Critical Life*. New York: Oxford University Press, 1996.

Neher, André. "Ezechiel, redempteur de Sodome." *RHPR* 59 (1979) 483–90.

Neiman, Susan. *Evil in Modern Thought: An Alternative History of Philosophy*. Princeton: Princeton University Press, 2002.

Nelson, Jr., Neil D. "'This Generation' in Matt 24:34: A Literary Critical Perspective." *JETS* 38 (1996) 369–85.

Nemo, Philippe. *Job and the Excess of Evil.* Translated by Michael Kigel. Pittsburgh: Duquesne University Press, 1998.

Newsom, Carol A. *The Book of Job: A Contest of Moral Imaginations.* New York: Oxford University Press, 2009.

Nicholl, Colin. "Michael, the Restrainer Removed (2 Thess. 2:6-7)." *JTS* 51 (2000) 27–53.

Nietzsche, Friedrich. *The Genealogy of Morals.* Translated by Horace B. Samuel. New York: Boni and Liveright, n.d. [orig. German 1887].

Nolland, John. *Luke 9:21–18:34.* Word Biblical Commentary. Dallas: Word Books, 1993.

Norris, Jr., Richard A. "Two Trees in the Midst of the Garden (Genesis 2:9b): Gregory of Nyssa and the Puzzle of Human Evil." In *In Dominico Eloquio: Essays in Patristic Exegesis in Honor of Robert Louis Wilken*, edited by Paul Blowers, 218–41. Grand Rapids: Eerdmans, 2002.

Nussbaum, Martha C. "Objectification and Internet Misogyny." In *The Offensive Internet: Privacy, Speech and Reputation*, edited by Saul Levmore and Martha C. Nussbaum, 68–90. Cambridge: Harvard University Press, 2010.

O'Brien, Peter T. *The Epistle to the Philippians.* New International Greek Testament Commentary. Grand Rapids: Eerdmans, 1991.

O'Connor, Kathleen M. "Wild, Raging Creativity: Job in the Whirlwind." In *Earth, Wind and Fire: Biblical and Theological Perspectives on Creation*, edited by Carol J. Dempsey and Mary Margaret Pazdan, 48–56. Collegeville, MN: Liturgical, 2004.

O'Day, Gail R. "The Love of God Incarnate: The Life of Jesus in the Gospel of John." In *Life in Abundance: Studies of John's Gospel in Tribute to Raymond E. Brown*, edited by John R. Donahue, 158–67. Collegeville, MN: Liturgical, 2005.

O'Day, Gail R. and Susan E. Hylen. *John.* Louisville: Westminster John Knox, 2006.

Oberweis, Michael. "Erwägungen zur apokalyptischen Ortsbezeichnung 'Harmagedon.'" *Bib* 76 (1995) 305–24.

Origen. *Celsus on the True Doctrine: A Discourse against the Christians.* Translated by R. Joseph Hoffmann. New York: Oxford University Press, 1987.

———. *Commentary on the Epistle to the Romans.* Translated by Thomas P. Scheck. Fathers of the Church 103. Washington, DC: Catholic University of America Press, 2001.

———. *Contra Celsum.* Translated by Henry Chadwick. Cambridge: Cambridge University Press, 1965.

———. *Homélies sur Ézékiel.* Translated by Marcel Borret. Paris: Les Éditions du Cerf, 1989.

Osborn, Eric. "The Apologist Origen and the Fourth Century: From Theodicy to Christology." In *Origeniana Septima*, edited by W. A. Bienert and U. Kühneweg, 51–59. Leuven: Leuven University Press, 1999.

Osiek, Carolyn. *Shepherd of Hermas.* Hermeneia; Minneapolis: Fortress, 1999.

Ovid. *Metamorphoses.* Translated by A. D. Melville. Oxford: Oxford University Press, 1986.

Ozick, Cynthia. "The Impious Impatience of Job." In *Quarrel & Quandary*, 59–73. New York: Alfred A. Knopf, 2000.

Page, Jr., Hugh Rowland. *The Myth of Cosmic Rebellion: A Study of Its Reflexes in Ugaritic and Biblical Literature.* Vetus Testamentum Supplements 65. Leiden: E. J. Brill, 1996.

Pagels, Elaine. "The Politics of Paradise: Augustine's Exegesis of Genesis 1–3 Versus That of John Chrysostom." *HTR* 78 (1985) 67–99.

Pagis, Dan. *The Selected Poetry of Dan Pagis.* Translated by Stephen Mitchell. Berkeley: University of California Press, 1989.

Pangle, Thomas L. *Political Philosophy and the God of Abraham.* Baltimore: Johns Hopkins University Press, 2003.

Pannenberg, Wolfhart, ed., *Revelation as History.* Translated by David Granskou. New York: Macmillan, 1968.

Parker, T. H. L. *John Calvin.* Philadelphia: Westminster Press, 1975.

Pate, C. Marvin *The Writings of John: A Survey of the Gospel, Epistles, and Apocalypse.* Grand Rapids: Zondervan, 2011.

Peake, Arthur S. *The Revelation of John.* London: Joseph Johnson, 1919.

Peels, H. G. L. "The Blood 'from Abel to Zechariah' (Matthew 23,35; Luke 11,50f.) and the Canon of the Old Testament." *ZAW* 113 (2001) 583–601.

Peerbolte, L. J. Lietaert. "The KATÉXON/KATÉΩN OF 2 THESS. 2:6–7." *NovT* 39 (1997) 138–50.

Perechodnik, Calel. *Am I a Murderer: Testament of a Jewish Ghetto Policeman.* Translated by Frank Fox. Boulder, CO: Westview, 1996.

Pérez, Joseph. *The Spanish Inquisition: A History.* Translated by Janet Lloyd. New Haven: Yale University Press, 2005.

Perry, T. A. "Cain's Sin in Gen. 4:1-7: Oracular Ambiguity and How to Avoid It." *Prooftexts* 25 (2005), 258–75.

Plantinga, Alvin. *God, Freedom, and Evil.* New York: Harper & Row, 1974.

———. *The Nature of Necessity.* Oxford: Clarendon Press, 1974.

———. *Warranted Christian Belief.* New York: Oxford University Press, 2000.

Pokorny, Petr. "The Temptation Stories and their intention." *NTS* 20 (1974) 115–27.

Pope, Marvin. *El in the Ugaritic Texts.* Vetus Testamentum Supplements 2. Leiden: E. J. Brill, 1955.

———. *Job: Translated with an Introduction and Notes.* Anchor Bible. New York: Doubleday, 1965.

Powell, Colin. Address to the United Nations Security Council, February 5, 2003.

Prigent, Pierre. *Apocalypse 12: Histoire de l'exégèse.* Tübingen: Mohr-Siebeck, 1959.

Propp, William C. *Exodus 19-40: A New Translation with Introduction and Commentary.* Anchor Bible. New York: Doubleday, 2006.

———. "The Rod of Aaron and the Sin of Moses." *JBL* 107 (1988) 19-26.

Purcell, Nicholas. "The Arts of Government." In *The Roman World*, edited by John Boardman et al., 150–81. Oxford: Oxford University Press, 1986.

Ramsey, George W. "Is Name-Giving an Act of Domination in Genesis 2:23 and Elsewhere?" *CBQ* 50 (1988) 24–35.

Reddish, Mitchell G. *Revelation.* Smyth and Helwys Bible Commentary. Macon, GA: Smyth and Helwys, 2001.

Reim, Günter. *Studien zum alttestamentlichen Hintergrund des Johannesevangeliums.* Society for New Testament Studies Monograph Series 22. Cambridge: Cambridge University Press, 1974.

Reis, Pamela Tamarkin. "The Levite's Concubine: New Light on a Dark Story." *SJOT* 20 (2006) 125–46.

———. "Numbers XI: Seeing Moses Plain," *VT* 55 (2005) 207–31.

———. *Reading the Lines: A Fresh Look at the Hebrew Bible.* Peabody, MA: Hendrickson, 2002.

———. "What Cain Said: A Note on Genesis 4.8." *JSOT* 27 (2002) 107–13.

Rendtorff, Rolf. *The Canonical Hebrew Bible: A Theology of the Old Testament.* Translated by David Orton. Leiden: Deo, 2005.

Resseguie, James L. *Revelation Unsealed: A Narrative Critical Approach to John's Apocalypse.* Leiden: Brill, 1998.

Reston, Jr., James. *Dogs of God: Columbus, the Inquisition, and the Defeat of the Moors.* New York: Anchor, 2006.

Richards, Larry W. "Martin Luther's Legacy on English Translations of Paul: Romans 1:16-17 Revisited." In *Christ, Salvation and the Eschaton: Essays in Honor of Hans K. LaRondelle*, edited by Daniel Heinz et al.,189–204. Berrien Springs, MI: Andrews University Press, 2009.

Ricoeur, Paul. *Interpretation Theory: Discourse and the Surplus of Meaning.* Fort Worth: Texas Christian University Press, 1976.

Rigaux, Beda. *Saint Paul: Les épitres aux Thessaloniciens.* Paris: Librairie Lecoffre, 1956.

Ringe, Sharon H. "Luke 9:28-36: The Beginning of An Exodus." *Semeia* 28 (1983) 83–99.

Rissi, Mathias. "Die Erscheinung Christi nach Off. 19,11–16." *TZ* 21 (1965) 81–95.

———. "The Rider on the White Horse." *Int* 18 (1964) 407–18.

———. *Time and History.* Translated by Gordon C. Winsor. Richmond: John Knox, 1966.

Robinson, Bernard P. "Elijah at Horeb, 1 Kings 19:1–18: A Coherent Narrative?" *RB* 98 (1991) 513–36.

Robinson, J. *The First Book of Kings.* Cambridge: Cambridge University Press, 1972.

Robinson, John A. T. *The Priority of John.* London: SCM, 1985.

Rodin, R. Scott. *Evil and Theodicy in the Theology of Karl Barth.* Issues in Systematic Theology 3. New York: Peter Lang, 1997.

Roloff, Jürgen. *The Revelation of John.* Translated by John E. Alsup. Continental Commentary. Minneapolis: Fortress, 1993.

Roshwald, Mordecai. "A Dialogue between Man and God." *SJT* 42 (1989) 145–65.

Rossing, Barbara. "For the Healing of the World: Reading *Revelation* Ecologically." In *From Every People and Nation: The Book of Revelation in Intercultural Perspective*, edited by David Rhoads, 165–82. Minneapolis: Fortress, 2005.

Rowland Page, Jr., Hugh. *The Myth of Cosmic Rebellion: A Study of Its Reflexes in Ugaritic and Biblical Literature.* Vetus Testamentum Supplements 65. Leiden: E. J. Brill, 1996.

Rowland, Christopher. "Apocalyptic, the Poor, and the Gospel of Matthew." *JTS* 45 (1994) 504–18.

———. "A Man Clothed in Linen: Daniel 10.6ff. and Jewish Angelology." *JSNT* 24 (1985) 99–110.

———. *The Open Heaven: a Study of Apocalyptic in Judaism and early Christianity.* London: SPCK, 1982.

———. "The Vision of the Risen Christ in Rev. i.13 ff.: The Debt of An Early Christology to An Aspect of Jewish Angelology." *JTS* 31 (1980) 1–11.

Runciman, Steven. *The First Crusade.* London: Cambridge University Press, 1980.

Rusak, Tal. "The Clash of Cults on Mount Carmel: Do Archaeological Records and Historical Documents Support the Biblical Episode of Elijah and the Ba'al Priests?" *SJOT* 22 (2008) 29–46.

Russell, David M. *The 'New Heavens and New Earth:' Hope for the Creation in Jewish Apocalyptic and the New Testament.* Studies in Biblical Apocalyptic Literature 1. Philadelphia: Visionary, 1996.

Sabourin, Leopold. "Apocalyptic Traits in Matthew's Gospel." *RSB* 3 (1983) 19–36.

Safire, William. *The First Dissident: The Book of Job in Today's Politics*. New York: Random House, 1992.

Sanday, William and Arthur C. Headlam. *A Critical and Exegetical Commentary on the Epistle to the Romans*. International Critical Commentary. Edinburgh: T. & T. Clark, 1902. Reprinted 1992.

Sanders, E. P. *Paul and Palestinian Judaism: A Study in Patterns of Religion*. Minneapolis: Fortress, 1979.

Sanders, J. A. "Dissenting Deities and Philippians 2,1–11." *JBL* 88 (1969) 279–90.

Santurri, Edmund N. "Kierkegaard's *Fear and Trembling* in Logical Perspective." *JRE* 5 (1977) 225–47.

Sarna, Nahum. *The JPS Torah Commentary on Genesis*. Philadelphia: Jewish Publication Society, 1989.

———. *Understanding Genesis: The Heritage of Biblical Israel*. New York: Schocken, 1966.

Savran, G. "Beastly Speech: Intertextuality, Balaam's Ass and the Garden of Eden." *JSOT* 64 (1994) 33–55.

Schaff, Philip. *History of the Christian Church*, 8 vols. New York: Charles Scribner's Sons, 1910.

Schenk, Wolfgang. *Die Philipperbriefe des Paulus*. Stuttgart: Verlag W. Kohlhammer, 1984.

Schlier, Heinrich. "Vom Antichrist: Zum 13. Kapitel der Offenbarung Johannis." In *Theologische Aufsätze: Karl Barth zum 50. Geburtstag*, edited by Georg von Eichholz et al., 110–23. München: Chr. Kaiser Verlag,1936.

Schmid, Konrad. "Abraham's Sacrifice: Gerhard von Rad's Interpretation of Genesis 22." *Int* 62 (2008) 268–76.

Schneiders, Sandra M. "Touching the Risen Jesus: Mary Magdalene and Thomas the Twin in John 20." In *The Resurrection of Jesus in the Gospel of John*, edited by Craig R. Koester and Reimund Bieringer, 153–76. Tübingen: Mohr Siebeck, 2008.

Schnelle, Udo. *Apostle Paul: His Life and Theology*. Translated by M. Eugene Boring. Grand Rapids: Baker Academic, 2005.

———. "Cross and Resurrection in the Gospel of John." In *The Resurrection of Jesus in the Gospel of John*. Translated by Roy A. Harrisville. Edited by Craig R. Koester and Reimund Bieringer, 127–51. Tübingen: Mohr Siebeck, 2008.

Schulweis, Harold M. "Karl Barth's Job: Morality and Theodicy." *JQR* 65 (1975) 156–67.

Schwarzwäller, K. "Probleme gegenwärtiger Theologie und das Alte Testament." In *Probleme biblischer Theologie: Gerhard von Rad zum 70. Geburtstag*, edited by H. W. Wolff, 479–93. Munich: Kaiser Verlag, 1971.

Schweizer, Eduard. *The Good News according to Matthew*. Translated by David E. Green. Atlanta: John Knox, 1975.

Scotchmer, Paul F. "Lessons from Paradise on Work, Marriage, and Freedom: A Study of Genesis 2:4-3:24." *ERT* 28 (2004) 80–85.

Scott, Mark S. M. "Guarding the Mysteries of Salvation: The Pastoral Pedagogy of Origen's Universalism." *JECS* 18 (2010) 347–68.

Silber, John R. "The Ethical Significance of Kant's *Religion*." In Immanuel Kant, *Religion within the Limits of Reason Alone*, xciv-cxxvii. New York: Harper and Row, 1960.

———. *Kant's Ethics: The Good, Freedom, and the Will*. Berlin: Walter de Gruyter, 2012.

———. "Kant at Auschwitz." In *Proceedings of the Sixth International Kant Congress*, edited by Gerhard Funke and Thomas Seebohm, 177–211. Washington, DC: Center for Advanced Research in Phenomenology and University Press of America, 1991.

Sim, David. *Apocalyptic Eschatology in the Gospel of Matthew*. Society for New Testament Studies Monograph Series 88. Cambridge: Cambridge University Press, 1996.

Simmons, J. Aaron. "What About Isaac? Rereading *Fear and Trembling* and Rethinking Kierkegaardian Ethics." *JRE* 35 (2007) 319–45.

Simon, Uriel. "1 Kings 13: A Prophetic Sign—Denial and Persistence." *HUCA* 47 (1976) 81–117.

Skinner, John *A Critical and Exegetical Commentary on Genesis*. International Critical Commentary. Edinburgh: T. & T. Clark, 1910.

Snow, C. P. "Either-or." *The Progressive* 25 (February, 1961) 24–25.

Solomon, Robert C. "Nietzsche *ad hominem*: Perspectivism, Personality and *Ressentiment*." In *The Cambridge Companion to Nietzsche*, edited by Bernd Magnus and Kathleen M. Higgins, 180–222. Cambridge: Cambridge University Press, 1996.

Solzhenitsyn, Aleksandr I. *A World Split Apart*. Translated by I. A. Ilovayskaya. New York: Harper & Row, 1978.

Speiser, Ephraim A. *Genesis*. Anchor Bible. Garden City, NY: Doubleday, 1964.

Spiegel, Shalom. *The Last Trial: On the Legends and Lore of the Command to Abraham to Offer Isaac as a Sacrifice: The Akedah*. Translated by Judah Goldin. Woodstock, VT: Jewish Lights, 1993.

Stagneth, Bettina. *Eichmann Before Jerusalem: The Unexamined Life of a Mass Murderer*. Translated Ruth Martin. New York: Knopf, 2014.

Stamm, J. J. "Elia am Horeb." In *Studia Biblica et Semitica*, edited by W. C. van Unnik and A. S. van der Woude, 327–34. Wageningen: H. Veenman, 1966.

Stanton, Graham. *The Gospels and Jesus*. Oxford: Oxford University Press, 1989.

———. "Matthew." In *It Is Written: Scripture Citing Scripture. Essays in Honor of Barnabas Lindars*, edited by D. A. Carson and H. G. M. Williamson, 205–19. New York: Cambridge University Press, 1988.

Steenburg, D. "The Case Against the Synonymity of *Morphē* and *Eikōn*." *JSNT* 34 (1988) 77–86.

Stefanovic, Ranko. "The Sealing of the Scroll in Revelation." In *Christ, Salvation and the Eschaton: Essays in Honor of Hans K. LaRondelle*, edited by Daniel Heinz et al., 367–76. Berrien Springs, MI: Andrews University Press, 2009.

Stegner, William R. "The Use of Scripture in Two Narratives of Early Jewish Christianity." In *Early Christian Interpretation of the Scriptures of Israel*, edited by Craig A. Evans and James A. Sanders, 98–105. Journal for the Study of the New Testament Supplement Series 148. Sheffield: Sheffield Academic, 1997.

Stern, Ephraim. *Dor, Ruler of the Seas: Nineteen Years of Excavations at the Israelite-Phoenician Harbor Town on the Carmel Coast*. Jerusalem; Israel Exploration Society, 2000.

Stevens, Marty. "The Obedience of Trust: Recovering the Law as a Gift." In *The Ten Commandments: The Reciprocity of Faithfulness*, edited by William P. Brown, 133–45. Library of Theological Ethics. Louisville: Westminster John Knox, 2004.

Stock, Augustine. *The Method and Message of Matthew*. Collegeville: Liturgical Press, 1994.

Strauss, David Friedrich. *The Life of Jesus Critically Examined*. English translation by George Eliot of 4th German ed. (1846). Edited by Peter C. Hodgson. Ramsay, NJ: Sigler Press, 1994.

Strobel, A. *Untersuchungen zum eschatologischen Verzögerungsproblem*. Leiden: Brill, 1961.

Stump, Eleonore. "Augustine on Free Will." In *The Cambridge Companion to Augustine*, edited by Eleonore Stump and Norman Kretzmann, 134–47. New York: Cambridge University Press, 2001.

Surin, Kenneth. "Theodicy?" *HTR* 76 (1983) 225–47.

Sutherland, Stewart R. *Atheism and the Rejection of God: Contemporary Philosophy and the Brothers Karamazov*. Oxford: Blackwell, 1977.

Sweet, J. P. M. *Revelation*. Philadelphia: Westminster, 1979.

Swenson, Kristin. "Care and Keeping East of Eden: Gen 4:1-16 in Light of Gen 2-3." *Int* 60 (2006) 373–84.

Swete, Henry Barclay. *The Apocalypse of St. John*. 3d ed. London: Macmillan, 1908.

Talbert, Charles H. "The Problem of Pre-existence in Philippians 2,6–11." *JBL* 86 (1967) 141–53.

Tate, Marvin. "Satan in the Old Testament." *RevExp* 89 (1992) 461–74.

Taylor, Vincent. *The Gospel according to St. Mark*. New York: St. Martin's, 1966.

Terrien, Samuel. *The Elusive Presence: Toward A New Biblical Theology*. New York: Harper & Row, 1978. Reprinted Eugene, OR: Wipf and Stock, 2000.

———. *Job: Poet of Existence*. New York: Bobs-Merrill, 1957.

Thompson, Leonard L. *The Book of Revelation: Apocalypse and Empire*. New York: Oxford University Press, 1990.

Thompson, Steven. *The Apocalypse and Semitic Syntax*. Society for New Testament Studies Monograph Series 52. Cambridge: Cambridge University Press, 1985.

Tierney, Brian. *The Crisis of Church and State, 1050-1300*. Englewoood Cliffs, NJ: Prentice-Hall, 1964.

Tonstad, Sigve K. "Appraising the Myth of *Nero Redivivus* in the Interpretation of Revelation." *AUSS* 46 (2008) 175–99.

———. "Blood 'as High as a Horse's Bridle' (Rev 14:20): The Devil Is in the Details." Paper presented at the Society of Biblical Literature Annual Meeting, Washington, DC, 2006.

———. "'The Father of Lies,' the Mother of Lies, and the Death of Jesus." In *The Gospel of John and Christian Theology*, edited by Richard J. Bauckham and Carl Mosser, 193–208. Grand Rapids: Eerdmans, 2008.

———. *The Lost Meaning of the Seventh Day*. Berrien Springs, MI: Andrews University Press, 2009.

———. "*Pistis Christou*: Reading Paul in A New Paradigm." *AUSS* 40 (2002) 37–59.

———. "The Priority of Theology in John (10:37-38)." Paper presented to the Society of Biblical Literature Annual Meeting, San Francisco, 2011.

———. "The Restrainer Removed: A Truly Alarming Thought (2 Thess 2:1–12)." *HBT* 29 (2007) 133–51.

———. *Saving God's Reputation: The Theological Function of Pistis Iesou in the Cosmic Narratives of Revelation*. Library of New Testament Studies 337. London: T. & T. Clark, 2006.

———. "Theodicy and the Theme of Cosmic Conflict in the Early Church." *AUSS* 42 (2004) 169–202.

Torjesen, Karen Jo. *Hermeneutical Procedure and Theological Method in Origen's Exegesis*. Berlin: Walter de Gruyter, 1986.

———. "Influence of Rhetoric on Origen's Old Testament Homilies." In *Origeniana Sexta*, edited by Gilles Dorival and Alain le Boulluec, 13–25. Leuven: Leuven University Press, 1995.

———. "The Rhetoric of the Literal Sense: Changing Strategies of Persuasion from Origen to Jerome." In *Origeniana Septima*, edited by W. A.Biernert and U. Kühneweg, 633–44. Louvain: Bibliotheca Ephemeridum Louvaniensis, 1999.

Torrey, Charles C. "Armageddon." *HTR* 31 (1938) 237–48.

Toussaint, Stanley. "The Significance of the First Sign in John's Gospel." *BSac* 134 (1977) 45–51.

Trible, Phyllis. *God and the Rhetoric of Sexuality*. Overtures to Biblical Theology. Philadelphia: Fortress, 1978.

———. *Texts of Terror: Literary-Feminist Readings of Biblical Narratives*. Philadelphia: Fortress, 1984.

Trigg, Joseph. *Origen*. London: Routledge, 1998.

Trilling, Wolfgang. *Der zweite Brief an die Thessalonicher*. Evangelisch-katholischer Kommentar zum Neuen Testament. Zürich: Benziger Verlag, 1980.

———. *Untersuchungen zum 2. Thessalonicherbrief*. Leipzig: St. Benno-Verlag,1972.

Trites, Allison A. *The New Testament Concept of Witness*. Cambridge: Cambridge University Press, 1977.

Trudinger, Paul. "The 'Our Father' in Matthew as Apocalyptic Eschatology," *DRev* 107 (1989) 49–54.

Tsevat, Matitiahu. "The Meaning of the Book of Job." *HUCA* 37 (1966) 73–106.

Turner, Laurence A. *Genesis*. Sheffield: Sheffield Academic, 2000.

Twain, Mark. *The Adventures of Huckleberry Finn*. In *Works of Mark Twain: Complete and Unabridged*. New York: Gramercy, 1982.

van de Water, Rick. "Reconsidering the Beast from the Sea." *NTS* 46 (2000) 245–61.

van Hecke, Pierre. "'But I, I would converse with the Almighty' (Job 13.3): Job and his Friends on God." In *Job's God*, edited by Ellen van Wolde, 18–26. London: SCM, 2004.

van Unnik, W. C. "A Formula Describing Prophecy." *NTS* 9 (1962-63) 86–94.

van Winkle, D. W. "1 Kings XIII: True and False Prophecy." *VT* 29 (1989) 31–43.

Vancandard, E. *The Inquisition: A Critical and Historical Study of the Coercive Power of the Church*. Translated by Bertrand L. Conway. London: Longmans, Green, 1908.

Voegelin, Eric. *Modernity without Restraint: The Political Religions*. Vol 5 of *The Collected Works of Eric Voegelin*. Edited by Manfred Henningsen. London: University of Missouri Press, 2000.

Vögtle, Anton. "Der Gott der Apocalypse." In *La Notion biblique de Dieu*, edited by J. Coppens, 377–98. Gembloux: Éditions J. Duculot, 1976.

Vollenweider, Samuel. "Der 'Raub' der Gottgleichheit: Ein religionsgeschichtlicher Vorschlag zu Phil 2.6(–11)." *NTS* 45 (1999) 419–21.

von Kellenbach, Katharina. "Am I a Murderer? Judges 19-21 as a Parable of Meaningless Suffering." In *Strange Fire: Reading the Bible after the Holocaust*, edited by Tod Linafelt, 176–91. New York: New York University Press, 2000.

von Nordheim, Eckhard. "Ein Prophet kündigt sein Amt auf (Elia am Horeb)." *Bib* 59 (1978) 153-73.

von Rad, Gerhard. *Genesis*. 2nd ed. Translated by John H. Marks. London: SCM, 1963.

von Wahlde, Urban C. "Archaeology and John's Gospel." In *Jesus and Archaeology*, edited by James H. Charlesworth, 523–86. Grand Rapids: Eerdmans, 2006.

Vonnegut, Jr., Kurt. *Slaughterhouse Five*. New York: Dell Publishing, 1991.

Vos, Louis A. *The Synoptic Traditions in the Apocalypse*. Kampen: J. K. Kok, 1965.

Wallace, Daniel B. *Greek Grammar Beyond the Basics*. Grand Rapids: Zondervan, 1996.

Wallis, Ian G. *The faith of Jesus Christ in early Christian Traditions*. SNTSMS 84. Cambridge: Cambridge University Press, 1995.

Walsh, Jerome. "Genesis 2:4b-3:24: A Synchronic Approach." *JBL* 96 (1977) 161–77.

Wanamaker, Charles A. *The Epistles to the Thessalonians: A Commentary on the Greek Text.* New International Greek Testament Commentary. Grand Rapids: Eerdmans, 1990.

———. "Philippians 2.6-11: Son of God or Adamic Christology?" *NTS* 33 (1987) 179–93.

Wasiolek, Edward, ed. *The Brothers Karamazov and the Critics.* Belmont, CA: Wadsworth, 1967.

Welker, Michael. *Creation and Reality.* Translated by John F. Hoffmeyer. Minneapolis: Fortress, 1999.

Westermann, Claus. *Genesis 1-11.* Translated by John J. Scullion. London: SPCK, 1984.

———. *Genesis 12-36.* Translated by John J. Scullion. Minneapolis: Augsburg, 1985.

Whiteley, D. E. H. *Thessalonians.* Oxford: Oxford University Press, 1969.

———. "The Threat to Faith: An Exegetical and Theological Re-Examination of 2 Thessalonians 2." *JTS* 21 (1970), 168–69 (review).

Wielenga, Bob. ""Mission and the Apocalyptic: a Perspective from Matthew." *IRM* 91 (2002) 111–19.

Wiesel, Elie. "Cain and Abel: He who kills, kills his brother." *Bible Review* 14 (1998), 20–21.

Wiesenthal, Simon. *The Sunflower.* Translated by H. A. Pichler. New York: Schocken, 1976.

Wilcock, Michael. *I Saw Heaven Opened: The Message of Revelation.* Downers Grove: InterVarsity, 1975.

Wildberger, Hans. *Jesaja 13-27.* Biblischer Kommentar Altes Testament. Neukirchen-Vluyn: Neukirchener Verlag, 1978.

Wilder, William N. "Illumination and Investiture: The Royal Significance of the Tree of Wisdom in Genesis 3." *WTJ* 68 (2006) 51–69.

Williams, Roger. *The Bloudy Tenent of Persecution for Cause of Conscience Discussed and Mr. Cotton's Letter Examined and Answered.* Edited by Edward Bean Underhill. London: J. Haddon, 1848 [orig. 1644]. Reprinted Kessinger Publishing's Rare Reprints, n.d.

Williams, Rowan. *Dostoevsky: Language, Faith, and Fiction.* Waco: Baylor University Press, 2008.

Wolff, Uwe. "The Angels' Comeback: A Retrospect at the Turn of the Millennium." In *Angels: The Concept of Celestial Beings—Origins, Development and Reception,* edited by Friedrich V. Reiterer et al., 695–714. Deuterocanonical and Cognate Literature Yearbook. Berlin: Walter de Gruyter, 2007.

Wolterstorff, Nicholas. "Barth on Evil." *FP* 13 (1996) 584–608.

Wong, Ka Leung. "'And Moses raised his hand' in Numbers 20,11." *Bib* 89 (2008) 397–400.

Wood, Ralph C. "Dostoevsky on Evil as a Perversion of Personhood: A Reading of Ivan Karamazov and the Grand Inquisitor." *PRS* 26 (1999) 331–48.

Woodhouse, Patrick. *Etty Hillesum: A Life Transformed.* New York: Continuum, 2009.

Wrede, W. *Die Echtheit des zweiten Thessalonicherbrief.* Leipzig, 1903.

Wright, G. E. *The Old Testament Against its Environment.* London: SCM, 1950.

Wright, N. T. *The New Testament and the People of God.* London: SPCK, 1991.

———. *Paul and the Faithfulness of God,* 2. vols. London: SPCK, 2013.

Würthwein, Ernst. *Die Bücher der Könige.* Göttingen: Vandenhoeck & Ruprecht, 1984.

———. "Elijah at Horeb: Reflections on 1 Kings 19:9-18." In *Proclamation and Presence,* edited by John I. Durham and J. R. Porter, 152–66. London: SCM, 1970.

Yoder, John Howard. *The Politics of Jesus.* 2nd ed. Grand Rapids: Eerdmans, 1994.

Zivotofsky, Ari Z. "The Leadership Qualities of Moses." *Judaism* 43 (1994) 258–69.

Index of Authors

Index of Ancient Documents

Old Testament

Genesis (continued)

Exodus

Leviticus

Numbers

Deuteronomy

Judges

1 Samuel

1 Kings

2 Kings

2 Chronicles

Job

Job (continued)

Psalms

Revelation (continued)

Greco-Roman Writings

Early Christian Writings

Lightning Source UK Ltd.
Milton Keynes UK
UKHW05f1237180518
322763UK00005B/632/P

9 781498 233132